# *Understanding and Managing Cybercrime*

## Samuel C. McQuade, III

*Department of Criminal Justice*
*Rochester Institute of Technology*

PEARSON

Boston • New York • San Francisco
Mexico City • Montreal • Toronto • London • Madrid • Munich • Paris
Hong Kong • Singapore • Tokyo • Cape Town • Sydney

**Series Editor:** *David Repetto*
**Series Editorial Assistant:** *Elizabeth (Liz) DiMenno*
**Senior Marketing Manager:** *Kelly May*
**Composition Buyer:** *Linda Cox*
**Manufacturing Buyer:** *Megan Cochran*
**Editorial-Production Service:** *nSight*
**Composition:** *Laserwords*
**Cover Administrator:** *Joel Gendron*

For related titles and support materials, visit our online catalog at www.ablongman.com.

Between the time website information is gathered and then published, it is not unusual for some sites to have closed. Also, the transcription of URLs can result in typographical errors. The publisher would appreciate notification where these errors occur so that they may be corrected in subsequent editions.

**Library of Congress Cataloging-in-Publication Data**

McQuade, Samuel C.
    Understanding and managing cybercrime / Samuel C. McQuade III.
      p. cm.
    Includes bibliographical references.
    ISBN 0-205-43973-X
      1. Computer crimes. 2. Computer crimes--United States--Prevention. I. Title

HV67773.M396 2006
364.16'8--dc22                                        2005053083

Printed in the United States of America

10  9  8  7  6  5  4         10

## DISCLAIMER

# Contents

**Preface** viii

**Foreword by Charles Wellford** xi

**Acknowledgments** xii

**PART ONE • *Understanding Cybercrime*** 1

**1** *Cybercrime: A New High-Tech Crime Paradigm* 2

*1.0* *Introduction: What Is Cybercrime?* 2

*1.1* *Understanding Human Behavior in Evolving Social and Technological Contexts* 4
1.1.1 Relatively Normal versus Deviant Behavior 4
1.1.2 Normal versus Deviant Use of Information Technology 8
 CYBER TALE 1.1 • *Inappropriate Use of Cell Phones in Public* 8
1.1.3 Normalcy, Deviancy, and Crime in Cyberspace 10

*1.2* *High-Tech Crime Constructs and Terms* 10
1.2.1 White Collar, Financial, and Organized Crime 11
1.2.2 The Emergence of Computer-Related Abuse and Crime 12
 CYBER TALE 1.2 • *Policing without Desktop and Laptop Computers and Other IT Devices* 13
1.2.3 Technology Fusion Brings about Cybercrime 14
 CYBER TALE 1.3 • *Policing with Desktop and Laptop Computers and other IT Devices* 15

*1.3* *The Importance of Defining and Understanding Crime Terms* 16
1.3.1 What Is Cybercrime and Why Should We Care about It? 16
 BOX 1.1 • *Definitional Constructs of High-Tech Crime* 16
1.3.2 Creating, Complying with, and Enforcing Laws and Regulations 18
1.3.3 Research and Justice Systems Improvement 19
 CYBER CASE 1.1 • *Why Definitions of Crime Matter:* State of New York v. Robert Versaggi 19

*1.4* *Principles for Better Understanding Cybercrime and Future Crime Labels* 20
1.4.1 Recognize and Accept that Views of Cybercrime Differ 20
1.4.2 Education and Training Helps Professionals Stay Informed 21
1.4.3 The Inter and Multidisciplinary Nature of Cybercrime and Organization of the Text 22

*Key Terms and Concepts* 26
*Critical Thinking and Discussion Questions* 26
*References and Endnotes* 27

**2** *Information and Other Assets in Need of Assurance* 29

*2.0* *Introduction: What Are We Protecting?* 29

*2.1* *Technology, Information, and Data in Justice and Security Management* 30
2.1.1 Six Primary Characteristics of Information 31
 BOX 2.1 • *Six Primary Characteristics of Data* 32
2.1.2 Data versus Knowledge Management 33
2.1.3 Additional Knowledge and Data Considerations 35

*2.2* *Information Assurance* 38
2.2.1 The Basic Prescription for What Is Needed: CIA 39
2.2.2 Becoming Pragmatic about Information Assurance 42
 CYBER TALE 2.1 • *Who Can You Trust? Credit Card Fraud by "Friends"* 44

*2.3* *Attack Dimensions* 45
2.3.1 Cyber versus Physical Attacks and Security Systems 46
2.3.2 Insider versus Outsider Threats to Assets 47
 CYBER CASE 2.1 • *A Phone Service–Scamming Prison Warden* 48
 CYBER CASE 2.2 • *A Collective of Money-Laundering Professionals* 49
 CYBER CASE 2.3 • *A Double Rip-off Mortgage Scheme* 49
2.3.3 Diagnosing and Responding to Threats and Attacks 50

*2.4*     ***Critical Infrastructure Protection***     **51**
2.4.1    What are Critical Infrastructures and Critical Information Infrastructures?    53
2.4.2    Conceptual and National Differences in Infrastructures    55
2.4.3    Critical Information Infrastructure Protection    55
2.4.4    Can the Net Be Taken Down?    56
*Key Terms and Concepts*    **60**
*Critical Thinking and Discussion Questions*    **60**
*References and Endnotes*    **61**

**3**     *IT-Enabled Abuse, Attacks, and Crimes*     **63**

*3.0*     ***Introduction: How Are Information Technologies Misused?***     **63**

*3.1*     ***Types of Abuse, Attacks, and Crime***     **64**
3.1.1    Writing and Distributing Malicious Code    64
**BOX 3.1** • *Differences between Computer Viruses, Worms, and Trojans*    65
3.1.2    Fraudulent Schemes and Theft    67
**CYBER TALE 3.1** • *How One Student Avoided Being Defrauded Online*    68
**CYBER TALE 3.2** • *A Student Victim of Credit Card Fraud*    70
3.1.3    Interfering with and Disrupting Computer Services    75
**CYBER TALE 3.3** • *How One Student Fought Fraud with Fraud*    75
**CYBER TALE 3.4** • *Suckered as the Result of Porn Curiosity*    76
**CYBER TALE 3.5** • *Denial-of-Service Attacks Hit Gaming Website*    77
3.1.4    Computer Spying and Intrusions    79
**CYBER TALE 3.6** • *Free and Illegal Phone Phreaking*    82
**CYBER TALE 3.7** • *The Infamous Back Orifice Remote Control Tool*    83
3.1.5    Unauthorized and Illegal File Sharing    86
3.1.6    Abuse of Computers and Electronic Devices in Academia    89
**CYBER TALE 3.8** • *Mass-Distributed Illegal File Sharing*    90
3.1.7    Online Harassment and Computer-Enabled Sex Crimes    93
**CYBER CASE 3.1** • *Online Harassment via a Website Soliciting Sex*    94
**CYBER CASE 3.2** • *Cyberstalking Star Trek Voyager's Seven of Nine*    96
*3.2*     ***Evolving Forms of Cybercrimes, Attacks, and Conflict***     **98**
3.2.1    Emerging Crime and Attack Trends    99

3.2.2    Futuristic Forms of Cyber Conflict    102
**CYBER TALE 3.9** • *Installation of Multiple Alien Servers*    103
*Key Terms and Concepts*    **108**
*Critical Thinking and Discussion Questions*    **109**
*References and Endnotes*    **109**

**4**     *Computer Abusers and Cybercriminals*     **113**

*4.0*     ***Introduction: Who Commits Computer Abuse and Cybercrime?***     **113**

*4.1*     ***Behavioral and Social Traits of Abusers, Attackers, and Criminals***     **114**
4.1.1    Social Engineering Tactics    114
**CYBER TALE 4.1** • *Victimized by a Social Engineering Friend*    116
4.1.2    The Adversarial SKRAM Model    117
**CYBER TALE 4.2** • *Three Friends, of Whom Two Were Hackers*    117
**CYBER TALE 4.3** • *Juvenile Geek Paid for Corporate Espionage and Sabotage*    119
4.1.3    What Cybercriminals Fear    122
**CYBER TALE 4.4** • *SKRAM Needed to Create and Use Fake Ids*    122

*4.2*     ***Categorizing Cyber Abusers, Attackers, and Criminals***     **124**
4.2.1    Stereotypical and Other Adversary Profiles    126
4.2.2    Who Are Cybercriminals Really?    129
4.2.3    A More Comprehensive Categorization Schema    131

*Key Terms and Concepts*    **133**
*Critical Thinking and Discussion Questions*    **133**
*References and Endnotes*    **134**

**PART TWO** • *Theoretical and Social Perspectives on Cybercrime*    **137**

**5**     *Theories of Computer-Enabled Abuse and Crime*     **139**

*5.0*     ***Introduction: Why Do People Commit Cyber Abuse and Crime?***     **139**

*5.1*     ***Theories: The Building Blocks of Knowledge and Understanding***     **141**
5.1.1    The Practicality of Good Theories    141
5.1.2    The Process of Knowledge-Building    142
5.1.3    General Criminological Explanations of Cybercrime    142

*5.2*     ***Classical/Choice Theory***     **143**
5.2.1    Rational Choice Theory    144

5.2.2 General Deterrence Theory 144

**CYBER TALE 5.1** • *People Can and Sometimes Do Choose to Change Their Criminal Ways* 144

5.2.3 Routine Activities Theory 147

**5.3 Trait Theory 147**

**BOX 5.1** • *Major Strengths and Limitations of Classical Criminology* 148

5.3.1 Arousal Theory 150

5.3.2 Cognitive Theory 152

5.3.3 Behavioral Theory 153

**5.4 Social Process Theory 155**

**BOX 5.2** • *Major Strengths and Limitations of Trait Theories* 155

5.4.1 Social Control Theories 156

5.4.2 Social Learning Theories 157

5.4.3 Neutralization Theory 159

5.4.4 Labeling Theory 161

5.4.5 Differential Enforcement 162

**BOX 5.3** • *Major Strengths and Limitations of Social Process Theories* 162

**CYBER TALE 5.2** • *Negative Labels as Badges of Honor* 162

**5.5 Social Structure Theory 163**

5.5.1 General Social Structure Theory 164

5.5.2 Social Disorganization Theory 164

5.5.3 Strain Theories 165

5.5.4 Cultural Deviance Theory 166

**5.6 Conflict Theory 166**

**BOX 5.4** • *Major Strengths and Limitations of Social Structure Theories* 167

5.6.1 General Conflict Theory 168

5.6.2 Marxist Criminology 169

**CYBER CASE 5.1** • *The Case of Unabomber Ted Kaczynski* 169

**CYBER CASE 5.2** • *The Presidential Pardoning of Financier Mark Rich* 170

5.6.3 Other Conflict Theories of Crime 171

**CYBER CASE 5.3** • *Making an Example of Martha Stewart?* 171

**5.7 Integrated and Technological Theories 174**

5.7.1 Overview of Integrated Theories 174

**BOX 5.5** • *Major Strengths and Weaknesses of Conflict Theory* 174

**CYBER TALE 5.3** • *Which Theories Help Explain This Criminal Behavior?* 175

5.7.2 Technology-Enabled Crime, Policing, and Security 176

**CYBER CASE 5.4** • *New Crime: Fictitious Characters Socially Engineer Real-World Stabbing* 177

**BOX 5.6** • *Strengths and Limitations of Integrated and Technological Theories* 178

*Key Terms and Concepts* **180**

*Critical Thinking and Discussion Questions* **181**

*References and Endnotes* **182**

**6 The Social and Economic Impacts of Cybercrime 185**

**6.0 Introduction: Who Is Harmed and by How Much Cybercrime? 185**

**6.1 The Human and Financial Costs of Computer Abuse and Cybercrime 186**

6.1.1 Victimization Concepts 187

**CYBER TALE 6.1** • *How Victimization Can Lead to Cybercrime* 189

6.1.2 Harm Experienced by Victims of Cybercrime 190

**CYBER CASE 6.1** • *Cybercrime as Nonviolent Property Crime* 191

**6.2 How Much Cybercrime Is There? 192**

6.2.1 Primary Means of Generating Crime Statistics 193

**CYBER TALE 6.2** • *An Examination of Early Uniform Crime Reports* 194

6.2.2 Overview of Major IT-Enabled Abuse and Crime Studies 197

6.2.3 Research by U.S. Organizations that Track Cybercrime 201

6.2.4 Economic Estimates and Impact Studies of Cybercrime 203

**CYBER TALE 6.3** • *A Worldwide Online Auction Scam* 205

**CYBER TALE 6.4** • *What Are the Economic Impacts of Spam?* 207

**6.3 Why Research the Nature and Extent of Cybercrime? 210**

6.3.1 The General State of Research on Cybercrime 210

6.3.2 Types of Research Needed on Cybercrime 212

*Key Terms and Concepts* **215**

*Critical Thinking and Discussion Questions* **215**

*References and Endnotes* **216**

**7 Emerging and Controversial Cybercrime Issues 219**

**7.0 Introduction: How is IT Creating New Opportunities for Cybercrime? 219**

**7.1 Emerging Potential for IT-Enabled Abuse and Cybercrime 221**

7.1.1 Transformations in Academic Education and Professional Training 221

7.1.2    Online Banking and E-Commerce   222

   **CYBER TALE 7.1** • *Benefits and Risks of Online Auctions*   224

7.1.3    Meeting and Courting Significant Others Online   225

7.1.4    IT-Enabled Democratization   226

   **CYBER TALE 7.2** • *An Obsessive Cyber Spooning Love Affair*   227

**7.2    Controversial Cybercrime-Related Issues   230**

7.2.1    The Computer Hacker Subculture   232

   **CYBER TALE 7.3** • *How the Movie Hackers Inspired One Student to Abuse Computers*   234

7.2.2    The Open Source Community   236

   **BOX 7.1** • *The Death of Cyberpunk*   236

7.2.3    Electronic Gaming Enclaves   238

7.2.4    Online Pornography   242

7.2.5    Information Privacy Protections and Infringement   247

   **BOX 7.2** • *A Discredited Study on the Amount of Internet Pornography*   247

   **BOX 7.3** • *Real-Time Electronic Surveillance, Tracking, and Recording Capabilities Relative to Behavioral, Investigative, and Security Functions*   260

   **BOX 7.4** • *Basic Principles for Safeguarding Information Privacy*   264

*Key Terms and Concepts*   265

*Critical Thinking and Discussion Questions*   266

*References and Endnotes*   267

**PART THREE** • *Managing Cybercrime*   **271**

**8**   *Cyber Laws and Regulations*   **273**

**8.0    Introduction: How Does Society Prohibit Cybercrime?   273**

**8.1    The Rationale and Reach of Cyber Laws and Regulations   275**

8.1.1    Legal Philosophies   276

8.1.2    Concepts of Due Process and Legal Jurisprudence   278

8.1.3    International Agreements for Managing Cybercrime   281

   **BOX 8.1** • *Determining Jurisdiction in Cyber* Suits: Zippo Manufacturing v. Zippo.com   281

   **CYBER CASE 8.1** • *Operation Buccaneer Targets International Warez Groups*   286

**8.2    Bodies of Law Pertaining to IT and Cybercrime Issues   287**

   **CYBER CASE 8.2** • *International Computer Gaming Bust*   287

8.2.1    Constitutional Law and Case Law   288

   **BOX 8.2** • *The U.S. Constitution and its Amendments*   289

   **CYBER CASE 8.3** • ACLU v. Reno: *Striking Down of the Communications Decency Act*   291

8.2.2    Criminal Law   292

8.2.3    Administrative and Regulatory Law   294

   **CYBER CASE 8.4** • *Code Writer Faces Federal Prosecution*   294

8.2.4    Intellectual Property (IP) Law   295

8.2.5    Tort Law   301

   **BOX 8.3** • *Types of Intellectual Property Law Protections*   301

**8.3    How Laws and Regulations Are Created and Administered   303**

8.3.1    Legislative Bills and Executive Approval   305

8.3.2    Implementation and Enforcement of Laws and Regulations   306

8.3.3    Federal Regulatory Agencies with InfoSec Oversight Responsibilities   307

**8.4    Key Federal Cybercrime Laws and Information Security Regulations   311**

8.4.1    Laws Specifying Illegal Use of Computers and Electronic Devices   312

8.4.2    Laws that Facilitate or Limit Cybercrime Investigations   315

8.4.3    Laws Protecting Children from Online Pornography   320

8.4.4    Laws Specifying Information Security Requirements   322

8.4.5    Laws Affording Privacy Protections   323

*Key Terms and Concepts*   327

*Critical Thinking and Discussion Questions*   327

*References and Endnotes*   328

**9**   *Investigating and Prosecuting Cybercrime*   **331**

**9.0    Introduction: What Happens When Cybercrime Laws Are Broken?   331**

**9.1    Collaborative Criminal Justice System Responses to Cybercrime   333**

9.1.1    Roles of Public Law Enforcement and Private Security   335

9.1.2    Dedicated Cybercrime Investigation and Prosecution Units   337

9.1.3    Key Investigative and Technical Assistance Agencies   339

**9.2    Legal Issues Governing Investigative Procedures   341**

9.2.1    Evidentiary Challenges Faced by Investigators and Prosecutors   342

9.2.2    Physical and Cyber Monitoring, Surveillance, and Investigative Operations   350

**BOX 9.1** • Mapp v. Ohio *Results in Nationwide Exclusionary Rule* 353

*9.3*    **Crime Scene Processing and Evidence Management**   **361**

9.3.1    Responding to and Protecting the Crime Scene   361

     **BOX 9.2** • *Typical Crime Scene Processing Equipment*   364

     **CYBER TALE 9.1** • *Searching for Physical and Electronic Evidence of Counterfeiting*   366

9.3.2    Collecting and Preserving Physical and Electronic Evidence   367

     **BOX 9.3** • *Controversy and Evidentiary Challenges of Child Porn Morphing*   371

     **CYBER CASE 9.1** • *The Challenge of Putting a Cybercriminal Behind a Keyboard*   377

9.3.3    Interviewing Victims, Witnesses, and Cybercriminals   380

*9.4*    **Prosecuting Cybercriminals**   **384**

9.4.1    Pretrial Procedures and Hearings   386

9.4.2    Trial Procedures and the Art of Presenting Evidence   390

9.4.3    Trial Verdicts, Sentencing Policies, and Appeals   396

*Key Terms and Concepts*   **401**

*Critical Thinking and Discussion Questions*   **402**

*References and Endnotes*   **403**

**10**    **Preventing Cybercrime with Information Security**   **406**

*10.0*    **Introduction: How Can We Better Protect our Computer Systems and Data?**   **406**

*10.1*    **Personal and Organizational Information Security**   **408**

10.1.1    What Every Person Should Know about Information Security   410

     **CYBER TALE 10.1** • *A Security Lesson about Purchasing Inferior Technology*   413

     **CYBER TALE 10.2** • *A Case of Sloppy Password Administration*   418

     **CYBER TALE 10.3** • *Software Firewall Programs May Not Provide Complete Protection*   421

     **CYBER TALE 10.4** • *The Importance of Patch Management*   422

     **CYBER TALE 10.5** • *Backup Data Only on Trusted Media!*   423

     **CYBER TALE 10.6** • *Broadband Connectivity: Learn to be a Savvy ISP Customer*   429

     **CYBER TALE 10.7** • *Avoid Being Swindled in Online Auction Fraud*   429

     **CYBER TALE 10.8** • *A Security Conscious Traveling Executive*   433

10.1.2    Assuring Protection of Information in Organizations   435

*10.2*    **Advancing the Security Posture of Organizations**   **439**

10.2.1    Security Change Procedures   440

10.2.2    Risk Management   443

     **BOX 10.1** • *Due Care and Diligence*   444

     **CYBER TALE 10.9** • *The Need for Computer Use and Security Policies*   447

*Key Terms and Concepts*   **454**

*Critical Thinking and Discussion Questions*   **455**

*References and Endnotes*   **455**

**11**    **Future Opportunities for Managing Cybercrime**   **457**

*11.0*    **Introduction: Where Can We Go from Here?**   **457**

*11.1*    **What More Can Government Do to Prevent Cybercrime?**   **459**

11.1.1    Preparing to Manage Cybercrime   461

     **BOX 11.1** • *Actions Government Can Take to Prevent and Control Cybercrime, Improve Information Security Capabilities Nationally, and Protect Critical Information Infrastructure*   462

11.1.2    Getting Set and Moving Forward   466

     **CYBER TALE 11.1** • *Information Insecurity at ChoicePoint*   470

*11.2*    **Computer Ethics Education and Intolerance of Cybercrime**   **474**

11.2.1    The Philosophy of Ethics   474

     **BOX 11.2** • *Get Ahead by Joining a Professional Membership Association*   475

     **BOX 11.3** • *Not Everyone Likes Using Computers*   475

11.2.2    Classical Ethics Theories   477

     **CYBER TALE 11.2** • *Unethical Employment Practices: Don't Get Burned!*   480

11.2.3    Computer Ethics   481

     **BOX 11.4** • *Is It Ethical to Use a Work Computer for Personal Reasons?*   484

*Key Terms and Concepts*   **488**

*Critical Thinking and Discussion Questions*   **488**

*References and Endnotes*   **489**

**Appendix: Cyber Stakeholders and Online Resources**     **491**

**Index**     **493**

# *Preface*

Cybercrime is fundamentally a multidisciplinary subject ripe for research and higher education and professional training. Indeed, given the dependence of modernized societies on information systems and critical information infrastructure for myriad societal functions, as well as for physical and information security and political and economic stabilization, there arguably is no subject of greater importance for higher education, professional attention, and public policy formulation. Today the United States of America, along with many other nations throughout the world, face the prospect of perpetually complex crimes that defy rapid understanding and manageability. New forms of information technology (IT)–enabled deviance, crimes, and threats to information systems abound, even as governments throughout the world struggle to pass new crime legislation and propagate regulations to prevent social and economic harm. Additionally government agencies, private sector firms, and not-for-profit organizations necessarily are forming tentative alliances as stakeholders with divergent interests and responsibilities in order to grapple with unprecedented threats to copyright, patent, trademark, and other staples of societies founded on capitalistic free market principles. Hence, the time has arrived for serious professionals, policymakers, educators, students, and citizens of the world as well as netizens of cyberspace to recognize ways in which the high-tech world is being threatened and what can be done about it.

This volume is best regarded as a general introductory textbook on the important subject of what has generally become known as cybercrime. Unlike many useful special interest books that examine specific aspects of this criminological and technological phenomenon, this book takes a broad inter and multidisciplinary approach to the topic. As such, *Understanding and Managing Cybercrime* will be regarded by most instructors as the first general textbook on the most perplexing crime and security topic of the modern age. I have written the book with two primary college student audiences in mind: (1) students who are majoring in computer science, software engineering, or IT administration and especially those who are aspiring to land careers as next-generation IT administrators or information security professionals; and (2) criminology and criminal justice students who will steadily assume positions in government, private, or nonprofit sectors and be required to understand computerized information systems and many types of IT devices that are increasingly being used for managing organizations and for investigating and prosecuting crimes. The book will also appeal to graduate students preparing thesis projects on high-tech crime issues and to other students who may be interested in knowing how their primary field of study relates to evolving forms of deviance and crime enabled with computers, other types of IT devices and information systems including the Internet.

The book has also been written with the needs of college and university professors in mind, as well as professional instructors of information security and high-tech crimes courses. By way of overview, this text ambitiously pulls together myriad topics usually taught in separate courses and even different programs of study to the extent specialty crime or information security courses are available. Instructors will find that this book will aptly support teaching an introductory course in computer/cyber crime or information security, while supporting courses in sociology, law, public administration, public policy or ethics that integrate issues of IT-enabled abuse, crime and threats to computers and information systems. Chapters are logically organized, and they are easy and fun for students to read. Frequently batteries of questions are interjected into the text to make students stop and think.

Chapters are also loaded with current events and real-life examples in the form of student *Cyber Tales* which have the effect of students teaching students about their most interesting, ridiculous, or horrific computer-related experiences. These tales are very instructive, as are the numerous legal cases *(Cyber Cases)* discussed throughout the text. Several chapters also make reference to original computer use, abuse, and ethics research findings carried out in preparation for the writing of this book. In fact a major goal during the development of this book was to make theoretical, behavioral and management sense of computer abuse and cybercrime even as an evolving technological, sociological, and criminological phenomenon. Instructors may be interested to know that several key portions of the text were field tested in the classroom for over a year even while the manuscript was being written in order to receive feedback and input from hundreds of students. Suffice to say the book found favor with students, adjunct and full-time professors, and with law enforcement and information security practitioners.

The book is organized into three parts. Part I addresses technologically evolving social deviance, dimensions of attack versus information and infrastructure security, and computer abuse and IT-enabled crime. Here readers will find conceptually useful models for thinking about risks faced by computing individuals and organizations, and an extremely thorough, accurate and integrated description of ways in which IT can be abused and used to commit crimes. In the classic tradition of criminal justice/ criminology, chapters in Part II are devoted to understanding and categorizing cybercriminals, explaining how their behaviors relate to major criminological theories, and to discussing empirical research pertaining to the social and economic impacts of cybercrimes in its various forms. This section of the book also addresses emerging and controversial IT-enabled crime-related topics. In Part III, emphasis shifts from understanding to managing cybercrime topics including cyber-related laws and regulations, investigation and prosecution of cybercrime, information security practices, and governmental approaches to preventing cybercrime and protecting critical information infrastructures. The final chapter ends with a useful treatise of computer ethics issues. This is followed by an Appendix listing several categories of key organizations involved in managing cybercrime issues. Each chapter includes a list of key terms and concepts and a set of critical thinking and discussion questions that can support homework assignments. A detailed lecture slide show for each chapter is also available to instructors. Please contact your A&B sales rep for details or go online to www.ablongman.com. Please enjoy *Understanding and Managing Cybercrime*—society depends on each of us doing so effectively!

# Foreword by Charles Wellford

In recent years all measures of crime suggest a dramatic decrease in the level and seriousness of crime. For example, the Federal Bureau of Investigation (FBI) reports that index crimes (the seven offenses the FBI has tracked since 1930 as an indicator of the total amount of crime reported to police in the United States) have declined from a high of over 14 million in 1993 to almost 12 million in 2003; a 14 percent decrease in the volume of index offenses (the change in rates was similar). But, and this is a big but, we now know that in any recent year the number of identity thefts alone may approximate 10,000,000; a number comparable to all property index crimes annually reported to police. Furthermore, the vast majority of identity theft crimes are not reported to police. In short, crime is most likely not decreasing at all but experiencing a dramatic shift from crime on the streets to crime by keyboard; from crimes the victim experiences to those the victim does not even know has occurred; from crimes that are routinely reported to police, to crimes, even when known, that are not reported. Crime in the 21st century will be more cybercrime and less (at least proportionately) crime that law enforcement has dealt with during the last two hundred years when government has had primary responsibility for enforcing the criminal law.

Law enforcement, public and private, are facing a new set of crimes, criminals, and techniques for which they are greatly unprepared. *Understanding and Managing Cybercrime* is essential for anyone concerned with crime in this century. There is no other text that provides what most of law enforcement does not have and very much needs—a detailed and original approach to defining, explaining, and controlling cybercrime. Currently education programs addressing these issues are fragmented and frequently nonexistent. Training for law enforcement and information security professionals is even more disorganized. In short, law enforcement and security personnel are entering the age of cybercrime without the education, training, or experience necessary to address the changing nature of crime. Increasingly, training programs and college curricula are introducing courses and even programs of study to address these issues but without a unified text to guide their development.

This is largely due to the fact that the study of cybercrime is multidisciplinary in ways that criminal justice has not previously experienced. Ordinarily when we think of the multi- or interdisciplinary nature of criminal justice we usually mean the use of multiple social and behavioral sciences and the law to understand and control crime. In the case of cybercrime we mean all of that, plus the engineering and hard sciences needed to deal with crime involving information technology. Understanding the behavior of the cyber criminal and the techniques he or she uses is essential to controlling this form of crime. This book explains who abuses computers and other types of electronic devices often to commit cybercrimes, in straightforward ways, inclusive of concepts ranging from social constructions of deviancy and labeling, to motivations of cybercriminals and the techniques they use to commit the crimes. The author accomplishes this by drawing from several disciplines to make sense of cybercrime, cybercriminals, and what can be done by individuals and organizations to address the problem of crime enabled by information technology. By understanding this broad range of disciplines the criminal justice and the information technology specialist will be better able to work together effectively to control cybercrime.

Knowing how theory explains the cybercriminal and how law enforcement can respond to this type of crime is part of the story. Understanding the legal context of cybercrime and how to prevent this type of crime is equally important. In many ways the law of cybercrime is advancing faster than our ability to respond to the crime and the legal changes. For that reason, chapters 8, 9, and 10 alone are worth the price of book. Chapter 8 provides as clear a synopsis of the laws of cybercrime as you can find anywhere. It not only reviews the major laws but does so in a framework that allows the teacher and the student to see how they are related. Chapter 9 on investigating and prosecuting cybercrime is a best practices guide with a strong organizational foundation. At a time when agencies are beginning to understand the importance of cybercrime this gives them a way to assess how well they are organized to respond. Finally, Chapter 10 addresses the critical issue of prevention. Much of current cybercrime can be prevented by relatively simple steps taken by potential victims and the guardians of their information. This chapter lays out in very clear usable ways steps citizens and professionals can take to reduce the likelihood of cybercrime.

One indication of the growing recognition of the need for education and training in cybercrime control is the Federal Cyber Service Scholarship Program. For several years the National Science Foundation has collaborated with the National Security Agency (NSA) to improve course, curriculum, instructional materials, and computer forensics laboratories in order to better educate and train next-generation cyber investigators and information security specialists, and to prepare them for protecting organizations, communities, and the national critical information infrastructure from cyber attacks. Over fifty universities are now certified by NSA as Centers of Academic Excellence providing information security education. The Department of Homeland Security is now also partnering with NSF to support higher education of next-generation information security specialists and investigators. Students enrolled in information security or criminal justice programs will find this book invaluable in addressing the social, behavioral, and technical dimensions of cybercrime.

Increasingly criminals and criminal justice professionals are using information technology to achieve their goals. Unfortunately, the criminals seem to be ahead in this "arms" race. Much like the use of other weapons of crime – firearms – the criminals seem to stay just ahead of law enforcement. Until now law enforcement has not had a comprehensive guide on how to win this race. Now they do! This book offers to beginners and advanced students and professionals the understandings and tools they need to deal with cybercrime and to stay ahead of the criminals who are now utilizing information technology innovatively and will undoubtedly continue to do so in the future. It will do for the study and control of cybercrime what O. W. Wilson did for police administration.

*Dr. Charles F. Wellford is Professor of Criminology and Criminal Justice at the University of Maryland College Park. He also serves as Director of the Office of International and Executive Programs and of the Maryland Justice Analysis Center. He is a past (1995–1996) President of the American Society of Criminology (ASC), in 1996 he was elected a Fellow of the ASC, and in 2001 was selected to be a National Associate of the National Academy of Sciences. He chaired the National Academy of Sciences Committee on Law and Justice from 1998 to 2004 and recently chaired the NAS panels on pathological gambling and a panel on research on firearms. In Maryland he currently serves on the Maryland Sentencing Policy Commission. From 1976–1981 Dr. Wellford served in the Office of the United States Attorney General where he directed the Federal Justice Research Program. The author of numerous publications on criminal justice issues, Dr. Wellford's most recent research has focused on the determinants of sentencing and the correlates of homicide clearance.*

# *Acknowledgments*

This book is dedicated to my past and future students and to college students throughout the United States, who as emerging professionals in numerous fields will bear leadership responsibility for understanding and managing cybercrime within organizations and on behalf of the nation's overall information infrastructure security.

I am indebted to many people who made this book possible. First I wish to thank Jennifer Jacobson, series editor at Allyn & Bacon, for her incredible patience and support while seeing the manuscript through to completion. First-time and experienced authors are well advised to consider this major publishing house through which to release future works. Everyone on the social sciences publishing team is knowledgeable, helpful, and willing to go the extra distance to make a book come together.

Two student research assistants—Nate Fisk and Eric Linden—frequently worked long days and nights on my behalf, traveled to co-present research findings with me at professional conferences, and generally kept me in good cheer. Each of these young men are rising stars and destined for distinguished careers based on their multidisciplinary education in cybercrime, information security, public policy, and technology.

Dr. Tom Castellano, chair, RIT Department of Criminal Justice, was also an enormous source of inspiration and encouragement for my writing. He has been a terrific colleague and also my co–principal investigator for the *RIT Computer Use and Ethics Survey* project, which, as among the largest and most comprehensive studies of its kind, informed the development of key topics discussed in the book.

In addition, my wife Jean Ary served as a research assistant and project supporter. For many months she culled information about breaking cybercrime news for incorporation into the text and fed me and my fellow researchers whenever that was required. She also remained quiet and left me alone for the better part of a year that it took to produce this volume. It was a big sacrifice for both of us, and to which I am indebted to her.

Several other colleagues were also of great assistance. I thank Jennifer Gravitz, Esq., RIT criminal justice and law professor, for her early contributions to research and writing materials for legal and prosecution issues in Chapters 8 and 9. Jennifer, my favorite lawyer (if such a thing is possible!), actively teaches legal research and cyberlaw courses for the RIT Department of Criminal Justice and maintains a private law practice. Detective Joe Hennekey of the Monroe County Sheriff's Department, and a member of the regional U.S. Secret Service Electronic Crimes Task Force, was my "backup"

for thinking and writing about investigating cybercrime. Joe is also acknowledged for his early writing contributions to Chapter 9, and for his outstanding co-teaching role of the cybercrime course that together we offer at RIT. Two other colleagues are similarly recognized for their assistance with information security issues discussed in Chapter 10 and elsewhere throughout the text. Jack Finklea is principle and vice president of security systems for the Telperion Solutions Group, LLC. He is a Certified Novell Administrator (CNA) who has earned numerous other technical certifications. As a Certified Information Systems Security Professional (CISSP) who is also recognized by the Information Systems Audit and Control Association as a Certified Information Systems Auditor (CISA), Jack provides information security and regulatory compliance consulting services to private sector firms and government organizations. Jim Moore, RIT Information Security Officer, has an academic background in mathematics, was a software developer for seven years at IIT Research Institute and a systems administrator for a combination of eight years at Eastman Kodak and Xerox Corporations. As a nationally recognized information security officer who is certified in InfoSec Assessment Methodology and is a Certified Information Systems Security Professional, Jim contributed to IEEE 1387.2 Software Management standards and provided technical review of version 1 of the SANS Step By Step Guide to Incident Handling. I also wish to thank David Bond, the perpetually aspiring cartoonist from the office of grants and contracts at RIT, for contributing the insightful cartoons that grace this text. Next stop, *The New Yorker!* Additional thanks are extended to Kimberley Laris, RIT's former director of business process and audit, and to Chad Wycoff, senior consultant at Ernst & Young, for their input into matters of auditing, information security, and management processes. Thanks are also extended to the reviewers of this manuscript: Susan Brenner, University of Dayton School of Law; Christine Corken, Loras College; and Charles Wellford, University of Maryland.

Several other students deserve mention and thanks, including Sara Berg and other members of the RIT Security Practices and Research Student Association (SPARSA), who helped with field research and provided input into technical and social aspects of computing. Although I am this club's faculty advisor, more often than not they did the advising, even during long weekends at my house when these young men and women manually entered survey data in preparation for the book. I also acknowledge many other students and faculty colleagues at RIT for their support of my research and writing. Thank you, all.

# Part I

# *Understanding Cybercrime*

*Cybercriminal in Action. Cybercriminals are people of any age who use computers, other electronic devices or information systems to violate crime laws.* Photo by Nathan Fisk

In Part I we explore cybercrime as an evolving crime problem rooted in decades of technology development, criminal adoption of computers and other forms of information technology (IT) for illicit purposes, and labels for social constructs of crime involving theft, manipulation, degradation or destruction of data. In Part I you will learn about types of information systems and data that need protection, ranging from personal computers and other types of electronic IT devices to critical information infrastructures upon which computerized nations depend for virtually every aspect of modern living. Part I also provides a comprehensive description of how abuse, attacks, and crimes committed with IT are accomplished. After reading Part I you will understand every known type of cybercrime, which collectively form a new high-tech paradigm that presents unprecedented challenges to criminal justice officials and information security professionals, as well as to organizations of every size and purpose throughout any society that relies on computer data.

# 1

## Cybercrime: A New High-Tech Crime Paradigm

### 1.0 Introduction: What Is Cybercrime?

Do you worry about losing your computer data? Have you or someone you know lost data because of a computer virus or hard drive that crashed or because someone attacked an information system that was not adequately protected or backed up? Do you think the loss could have been avoided with better information security? This book is about how computers and other types of increasingly complex electronic devices are used to commit crime and cause harm. It also addresses how we can better secure computers, other types of electronic information technology (IT) devices, and information systems in order to prevent IT-enabled abuse and crimes, thereby minimizing social and economic harm caused by such behaviors. Hence, as the title suggests, this book is devoted to understanding and managing **cybercrime**—use of computers or other electronic devices via information systems to facilitate illegal behaviors.

To begin to understand cybercrime, let us consider an incident that occurred in 1990. The radio station KIIS-FM in Los Angeles, California, was hosting a "Win a Porsche by Friday" phone-in contest. First prize was a Porsche 944 sports car

valued at $50,000 to be given to the 102nd person who called into the radio station. Kevin Poulsen, a skilled computer hacker, along with several of his friends, used computers innovatively to take control of twenty-five telephone line connections. This enabled them to detect and even block calls from coming into the radio station. In this way Poulsen was able to guarantee that he alone could place the winning 102nd phone call. This was not the only cybercrime Poulsen committed. In 1983, he was arrested for using a computer to hack into what is today the Defense Advanced Research Projects Agency (DARPA), a component of the U.S. Department of Defense. By the time he staged the phone contest fraud he had already established a criminal record, and a year later, on April 11, 1991, was again arrested for computer hacking into Pacific Bell telephone systems.[1]

Kevin Poulsen's story reveals that cybercrimes have been taking place for well over twenty years, that they often involve technological innovation to commit fraud and other types of crime, and that telecommunications systems combined with computers, other types of electronic IT devices and information systems are fundamental to committing these types of crimes. In Chapter 1 we will begin to understand cybercrime as being an increasingly important technological, socioe-conomic, and policy problem made possible, if not inevitable, by **computerization**—widespread use of networked computers and other electronic devices throughout society. As a broad label for technologically evolving forms of crime, cybercrimes continually pose extraordinary new challenges to individuals, organizations, and even entire nations. Modernized societies must continually and increasingly guard against negative impacts resulting from attacks on information systems. This is especially true in nations like the United States that have come to rely on critical information infrastructures for food production, emergency communications, transportation of goods, energy management, commerce and financial services, national defense, and so on.

In the first section of Chapter 1 we will seek to understand human behavior in evolving social

and technological contexts. We will consider socialization and technology transformation processes in modern computerized societies. This is accomplished by focusing on what constitutes relatively normal versus deviant behaviors versus socially abusive and criminal behaviors. Next we will explore the concepts of social sanctions and punishments imposed on individuals who violate social norms and crime laws. In the process you will be introduced to a few other concepts and terms commonly used in the administration of criminal justice. Then we will examine how these concepts, which are traditionally applied to and understood in relation to real-world situations, also pertain to activities in **cyberspace**—that amorphous realm through which the exchange of digitized information takes place.[2]

Next, you will learn how cybercrime evolved from earlier conceptualizations of crime, such as

*People now use computers in combination with other types of IT devices to interact over the Internet, and for research, record-keeping, data analysis and recreation, among other kinds of professional and personal purposes. Oftentimes these activities are accomplished over wireless networks located in Internet cafes, shopping malls, airports, hotels and on college campuses. What possibilities for becoming the victim of cybercrime exist in these environments?* Justin Sullivan/Getty Images, Inc.

white-collar crime, long before computers were commonly used. Here cybercrime is differentiated from *computer abuse, computer crime,* and *computer-related crime* among other terms frequently used when describing crime involving computers. Then we will address the importance of clearly defining and understanding crime terms and why we should care about cybercrime. Reasons include the reality that everyone who uses computers or other types of electronic IT devices are vulnerable to cybercrime attacks on their information systems, that cybercrime has direct and indirect harmful effects on organizations as well as individuals, and that critical infrastructures upon which society depends needs protection from both physical and cyber attacks.

The chapter concludes with a discussion of principles for better understanding cybercrime as it now exists and may exist in the future. These principles have to do with the reality that views of cybercrime differ, that education and training helps professionals stay informed of developments in cybercrime and information security issues, and that to understand and manage cybercrime requires inter-and-multidisciplinary understanding of crime, policing, and security practices. In short, our goal in this first chapter is to understand the new high-tech crime paradigm that we are now struggling to live, work, learn, and play within. The chapter concludes with an overview of the book that hopefully will inspire you to learn more about the role of IT in the commission of crimes, why cybercrimes occur, and what can be done to prevent them or at least mitigate their harmful impacts on individuals, organizations, and society.

## 1.1 Understanding Human Behavior in Evolving Social and Technological Contexts

### 1.1.1 Relatively Normal versus Deviant Behavior

Nearly every day most of us interact with people in private and public places. Our social interactions occur in homes, schools, and places of employment and in other locations such as gasoline stations, retail shopping centers, open spaces and parks, and on public transportation such as buses, subways, and commercial airlines. Interacting with people in a variety of social contexts causes us to become familiar with what are generally considered normal as opposed to abnormal behaviors. This, in turn, results in our learning to recognize and generally accept that behaviors naturally vary according to the rules or social customs of groups, organizations, and communities. Socially acceptable behaviors are shaped over time on the basis of circumstances and other factors, including (1) how people are raised; (2) interpersonal and professional relationships; (3) social class inclusive of socioeconomic status, level of education, and professional accomplishments; and (4) political and religious orientations. With this frame of reference in mind, it is easy to understand that we continually learn and relearn behaviors that are expected of us in various circumstances even as we adapt to social environments that are continually changing. Attend a different school or church, move to a new city or into a dormitory to begin college, join a student club or athletic team, or start a new job, and so on, and you will likely encounter people possessing attitudes, behaviors, and customs different from what you are accustomed to. This is because they probably grew up in different circumstances than you did and have been influenced by innumerable factors such as those listed above. In short, people are, as the old saying goes, a product of their environment, experiences, upbringing, and choices.

**Socialization** is the process of influencing people to behave in certain ways. Each of us, in conscious and unconscious ways, exerts and reinforces our views of appropriate behavior on people with whom we interact. This occurs when we casually or incidentally express approval or disapproval of certain behaviors. Socialization can occur in subtle ways, as when we make passing comments or exhibit certain body language. It also occurs in overt ways, as in our decisions about which activities, social clubs, or organizations to participate in or donate money to; when we formally express our approval or disapproval either orally or in writing; when we obey or enforce societal rules or laws; and so on. It is important to realize that subtle and overt socialization processes occur simultaneously and continuously through our personal and professional interactions and that we both learn and reinforce learning of **social norms** in myriad situations and social contexts. For example, socialization occurs among friends and family members in private and public situations and among professional colleagues while they are in the office, working in the field at job sites, and traveling together to training conferences, and so on. In time, despite widely ranging personalities, preferences, interests, management styles, and organizational affiliations, and despite inevitable disagreements over any number of controversial issues, the majority of individual, group, and societal views about what constitutes "normal," and therefore acceptable, behavior in given situations are established, learned, and reinforced by everyone involved.

As people age, they naturally seek to be rewarded by conforming to social norms as opposed to being punished or sanctioned in some way for misbehaving. Fitting in and abiding by what is expected often leads to increased personal, social, and professional standing and sometimes to greater access, wealth, and influence. As a result, generally accepted standards of behavior are usually quickly understood and widely adopted, practiced, maintained, reinforced, and perpetuated. This process continually occurs throughout society, regardless of differences in social norms among groups of individuals, organizations, or communities. Differing family traditions, organizational cultures, and community standards are all based on this basic set of ideas. In democratic societies formal mechanisms such as rules, laws, and regulations combine with informal means of **social control** to define and help maintain societal order and stability. This occurs even as new standards of socially

acceptable behaviors emerge and eventually become practiced by the majority of people living in a society. Family relationships, schools, churches, and other types of social organizations collectively provide social controls that influence our actions and help establish and reinforce social norms. These principles are important aspects of social process and social control theories of crime that we will explore in Chapter 5 when we consider why people commit cybercrimes.

**Deviant behaviors** are those that differ markedly from established social norms. Deviant behaviors tend to be viewed negatively even though they may not rise to the level of being either abusive or illegal. Conversely, violating crime laws (as explained below) may not be considered deviant if a substantial number of people participate in the illegal activity. The implication is that what is considered deviant is simultaneously determined in nonabsolute terms by criminals *and* law-abiding persons. In addition, political tensions can arise from perceptions of crime-related threats to monetary and other types of assets, and this can lead to declarations of deviancy that inspire government regulation of behaviors.[3] Consider the following.

For several years (in case you had not heard!), sharing of illegally acquired computer software applications and digitized music and movie files has occurred on a large scale throughout society. This is especially true on college campuses, which typically maintain massive computer server memory and processing capabilities, as well as broadband connectivity for thousands of computer-savvy students, faculty, and staff members. Although student sharing of illegally obtained music and movie files is widespread and violates U.S. copyright laws, doing so is usually not considered especially deviant by most students because, as research shows, most of them and their friends do it with regularity. Meanwhile, the Recording Industry Association of America (RIAA) has taken steps to remind students and the general public that such behavior is criminal, and it is increasingly pursuing legal recourse for what it perceives as threats to the monetary interests of its member artists and music production firms.[4] On the contrary, *not* downloading or accepting illicitly obtained software may violate the social norms of a group if the behavior, despite its being illegal, is routinely practiced by many group members.

Behavior can also border on being legal or illegal depending on how crime laws are defined and interpreted. This is not to suggest, however, that illegally downloading music or other types of files is "borderline illegal" or that it should be condoned. Further, *relatively* normal or abnormal and deviant social behaviors, plus behaviors that may be *relatively more or less legal,* should not be confused with what may also be considered *relatively ethical or unethical conduct.* Hence, as shown in Figure 1.1, there are three interrelated and scaleable ways for determining the appropriateness of behaviors:

1. *Relatively normal to abnormal social behaviors,* which may be considered deviant if construed to be sufficiently abnormal
2. *Relatively legal to illegal behaviors,* determined on the basis of crime laws and their interpretation by criminal justice system officials and members of the public
3. *Relatively ethical to unethical behaviors,* judgment about which depends on standards of morality as viewed by individuals and groups in society

As behaviors tend toward being viewed negatively (i.e., relatively abnormal, illegal or unethical), they usually result in negative cognitive and emotional reactions in people observing the behavior. Such reactions range from apathy or mild annoyance, to skepticism and suspicion, to utter disgust and distrust, depending on how offensive the behaviors are and who is involved. Cognitive and emotional reactions to offensive behaviors in turn often bring about varying behavioral responses ranging from ignoring or socially isolating people who are misbehaving, to confronting or even harming individuals who are viewed as being sufficiently out of step with social norms, the law, or standards of ethical conduct. As we all know, when we do things that most people do not approve of, we are likely to be in for it. We in turn are likely to crack down on people who get out of line or annoy us. Everyone in society participates in these social control processes, but people in positions of authority have a special responsibility to help establish, clarify, encourage, model, and enforce standards of acceptable behavior. As the primary sociological mechanism through which civil society is shaped and maintained, these are especially important and worthy goals for parents, managers, professors, or anyone else with influence over children, adolescents, and emerging professionals.

**Social sanctions** are penalties or punishments imposed on individuals who violate social norms, rules or laws, or standards of ethical behavior. Social sanctioning is a process that involves expressing disapproval or imposing sanctions, penalties, or punishments on behavioral offenders. The well-known and widely practiced principle of fitting the sanction, penalty, or punishment to the seriousness of an offense applies to many

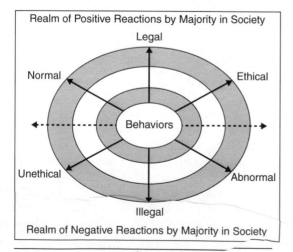

**FIGURE 1.1    *Positive versus Negative Reactions to Behaviors***

ARE WE DOING ANYTHING WE SHOULDN'T BE?

social situations. For example, parents discipline their children, colleges and universities impose penalties on students who are academically dishonest, and in the criminal justice system judges and juries impose punishments on people convicted of crimes. However, challenging or even violating social norms, rules, regulations, and laws may be viewed *positively* despite their having some negative social impacts, as in instances of civil disobedience that participants hope will help bring about needed societal changes. Many college students now consider illegal file sharing ethical because they believe large software firms charge too much for their products and that the recording industry takes unfair advantage of artists and consumers alike.[5]

Individuals or groups who hold views counter to those of the larger society may even consider violating laws to be a social responsibility or duty. For example, although some computer hackers feel they are acting ethically by exposing information security vulnerabilities of systems

they hack into, they are in the context of overall society demonstrating abnormal behavior and are breaking the law. (In Chapter 7 the Hacker Ethic is discussed. There you will learn why this group believes that hacking into systems and releasing security vulnerabilities, among other computer-related behaviors, is acceptable behavior despite violating established social norms of the overall society.

Finally, cycles of social-norming are perpetuated over extended periods of time as new members join groups and find comfort "in the way things are." As this occurs, cultural roots grow deep, resulting in relatively intractable attitudes, belief systems, and behavioral norms. At this stage of societal development, acceptance of individuals into social groups is predicated on prospective members recognizing, understanding, and being willing to conform to behavioral norms—a condition that will remain in place until sufficient circumstances and factors bring about reforms. Then the process is renewed with new or modified norms. In reality, all of this happens simultaneously within and among groups, and it is in this way that "things change with the times" as the old saying goes, or as I like to say, change occurs because of technology over time. Hence, all of the foregoing concepts relate to societal changes occurring as the result of computerization combined with other technological innovations, and therefore to conceptions of what constitutes normal, deviant, abusive, or criminal behaviors involving IT. Simply put, technology inclusive of IT is used in relatively appropriate to inappropriate ways, and judgment about the normality, legality, and morality of such behaviors depends on many circumstances that change over time in and among social groups. Rendering professional judgment about appropriate use of technology (which is not limited to computers or other electronic devices) in various circumstances is a challenge continually faced by information security and law enforcement professionals as they decide what is normal, abnormal, or suspicious versus inappropriate, unethical, and potentially criminal.

## 1.1.2  Normal versus Deviant Use of Information Technology

Social norms and controls often have to do with peoples' ownership, appropriate use, and tolerance of technology. For example, if your cell phone were to ring a tune from www.homestarrunner.com rather than vibrate during class, and then you verbally answered the incoming call rather than sending a text message back to the caller, your disruptive behavior would likely be considered rude and result in disapproving stares from your classmates and the instructor, or worse. To some extent, we are all held socially accountable for using technology in appropriate ways relative to social situations in which we find ourselves. We are especially likely to be held in check in some way for using computers and other gadgets inappropriately or ineptly if our behaviors are considered unusual, disruptive, or offensive. In addition, people

---

**CYBER TALE 1.1**

### Inappropriate Use of Cell Phones in Public

Have you ever been annoyed by someone who told you to call their cell phone number, only to do so and receive a computerized answer that tells you the person you are trying to reach does not have their phone activated? Or how about those people who shout into their cell phones while in public? It never seems to fail that while you're on a bus, subway, or airplane someone is talking into their cell phone far too loudly. Many people say this frequently happens to them in restaurants, theaters, and even in churches, and always seemingly right in the middle of what should be a quiet moment. When it does, the person being called immediately begins grabbing around for their cell phone in a flustered state. Then they speak in hushed tones (and rather sheepishly if they know better) or loudly (either because they are unaware or shameless). Sometimes the ringer is set to its maximum volume or to some cute "song" such as the "William Tell Overture." The last time I witnessed this, the person receiving the call jumped up from his seat in the middle of a business meeting, and as if he were the Lone Ranger on his trusted steed Trigger, galloped out of the room hollering something like "charge" as everyone just sat there, interrupted and in disbelief. Do you think this incident may have affected perceptions of the man's "technological credibility" or managerial discretion? How could the embarrassing and disruptive episode have been avoided? Can you think of other socially inept ways in which people use computers, other electronic devices, or other forms of technology?

are often considered more or less "socially normal" or "abnormal" depending on who is judging their behaviors.

Suppose you purchased a new PDA that allowed you to check email remotely, listen to music files whenever you wish, and multitask with other types of software applications. This could earn you the title of being "cool" and even envied by others. However, buy too many fancy gadgets relative to those owned by your friends, or purchase devices that are considered over the top with respect to their functional capabilities, and you could be labeled a "nerd" or "geek." Yet again, if you did not mind or even desired to be labeled as a nerd or geek because you considered such labels to be a compliment, you could find yourself in *disfavor* for not possessing or knowing all about the latest gadgets to hit the market. Thus, being perceived positively or negatively, in addition to how we use technology, depends on the social context in which we find ourselves and may have either or both positive and negative consequences to some extent.

How behavioral norms are established and reinforced in a sociological, psychological, or criminological sense, as well as how they are maintained and evolve in various cultural and societal situations, can also be affected by the specific technologies involved. Here is a simple example. A college student reported how in high school he used to play "MUD" (Multiple User Dungeon, an old-style computer game). He played online with hundreds of other people even though the game was only text-based and had no graphics. However, by typing in text commands called "emotes," players could express facial expressions for their characters. The student liked to make his game character grumble by typing in the command "/e grumble." Well, one day he was on the phone with a friend who said something annoying. Without realizing what he was doing, he responded aloud by simply saying "grumble" as if he were playing "MUD". This caused his friend to become confused, to which the student responded again, this time in complete sentences to dismiss his "grumble" comment as a joke. Realizing the negative effect the

game was having on his actual interpersonal communications, he quit playing MUD the next day. For this student, the effects of the gaming technology were nontrivial, and it is interesting to note how over time attitudes, behaviors and even language associated with our use of technologies can be affected and thereafter perceived and responded to by others based on their own experiences and relative understanding of devices involved.

As computer and telecommunications technology improve, along with the availability and purchasing of these plus high speed broadband Internet connectivity, text-based communications via computers and other IT devices will be increasingly augmented with visual and audible interaction capabilities on the same or similar types of devices. Some cell phones and telecommunications companies now allow for audible, text and video messaging and real-time interactions. When combined with text, these enhanced communications will more closely resemble interactions in the physical world in which we live. For example, just as we can now see each other when using video cell phones, in the future we will also likely be able to multitask with people on the same or similar types of portable devices. As technology advances, understanding distinct and subtle cultural differences bearing on relatively normal versus abnormal and deviant behaviors in physical and cyber realms and the interplay of these will become increasingly important because it is upon such foundations that democratic societies determine which behaviors should be criminalized. Think of it like this: Once there were horseless carriages which came to be called cars, but initially there were no traffic laws governing how this technology was to be used in society. Consequently, people drove anywhere they could in unregulated ways that were often unsafe and also regarded to be socially inappropriate. By analogy, today's rapidly advancing IT continues to create a technological paradigm in which people throughout the world are negotiating what constitutes safe, secure, and responsible use of computers and other electronic devices. As new forms of IT and technological capabilities emerge, so will associated behaviors of which some will be regulated, sanctioned, or criminally banned.

### 1.1.3 Normalcy, Deviancy, and Crime in Cyberspace

The concepts of normal behaviors, deviant behaviors, and crime logically extend to cyberspace. Just as driving a car or using a cell phone inappropriately can lead to social sanctioning, someone who violates established rules for online interaction may get blamed by others sharing the cyber environment, although this in itself is often considered to be rude and violating online **netiquette** regardless of the original statements made.[6] People who spend a lot of time interacting online generally understand and abide by rules for online activities whether formally specified in forum instructions or informally established and reinforced through chat. Certainly this is true to the extent that a dominant group or majority of participants in a given online environment establish informal rules for posting messages, in much the same way that people driving cars on a highway establish almost unconsciously establish speeds, following distances and signals when changing lanes despite existing traffic laws governing these and other driving behaviors. Similarly, system administrators may also formally set posting standards and policies for using network resources based on commonly understood and practiced standards of professionalism, civility and to a lesser but increasing extent, government regulations regarding legally acceptable computing behaviors. What constitutes normal, deviant, or criminal behaviors, as well as ethical and unethical behaviors, in specific physical and cyber environments vary, but the theoretical principles and processes involved are essentially the same in both physical and cyber realms. Whereas in the physical realm we can determine what is more or less socially normal versus deviant on the basis of speech, body language, amount or style of clothing worn, uses of technology, and participation in various activities, in the cyber realm we must currently rely principally on language expressed through computerized text communications to determine what is or is not acceptable. This can lead to problems like that involving the student who played the computer game MUD. The implication is that what is considered deviant, delinquent, or criminal behavior involving use of technology depends and changes with technology innovations and societal views regarding what constitutes responsible and therefore acceptable behaviors.

## 1.2 High-Tech Crime Constructs and Terms

The **social construction** of reality concerns processes related to viewing society and everything in it as objective or subjective reality (e.g., does the real world really exist?). The subject is embodied in the sociology of knowledge and includes topical issues such as the creation and interpretation of symbols, language, and facts. For our purposes, social construction simply means that over time, and given technological advances and other changes in society, people consider and label certain behaviors as deviant, abusive, or illegal. As technology changes and crimes can be committed, new labels for criminal behaviors are created and applied by society.[7]

For example, the term *wire fraud* came about after criminals started using the telegraph to defraud their victims, and the term *hijacking* was used to label these types of incidents after people flying on airplanes were "kidnapped"—another crime term originally having to do only with stealing children for other illegal purposes. Terms and labels for crime evolve with technologies that make new forms of crime possible. It is important to note that, with regard to social construction, the media, social processes, and legal mechanisms that collectively assign values to particular forms of deviant and criminal behaviors be identified, understood and labeled as such. Richard Hollinger, for example, compared the labeling and social values attendant to modern computer hackers with those of earlier highwaymen and train robbers.[8] Although both groups were initially viewed as folk heroes, eventually society demonized them with labels and descriptions and by offering rewards for their capture.

To better understand the concept of social construction, imagine that you were shipwrecked on a deserted island that had no society, government, or laws. In this situation, nothing you could do would be illegal. You could behave immorally (e.g., by polluting the environment in some way), but this would be a personal matter for which you could not be socially sanctioned or punished. If, however, you were joined on your island by six other castaways, social norms would be established. Eventually, a system of governance and perhaps even laws criminalizing certain behaviors would necessarily be created to help maintain an orderly society. Over time, new forms of deviance, social abuse, and crime would emerge as technologies made these possible, and you and others living on the island would refer to such behaviors by different terms and labels. However, it is likely that the terms and labels would not always be used or understood by everyone in exactly the same way, causing confusion about what precisely was being referred to. Today, we often hear about many types of high-tech crime. If you find yourself confused about the meaning of terms like computer crime, economic crime, financial crime, and organized crime and wonder how the behaviors behind the labels (so to speak) actually differ, you are not alone. For many years, researchers, law enforcement officials, and information security professionals have used these and other terms to label deviant and criminal behaviors even as they struggled to create clear definitions and establish widely shared meanings for new forms of criminality.

In this section you will learn how social, technological, and criminological **constructs** of cybercrime came into mainstream thinking as labels for crimes involving use of computers and other electronic devices. It will become clear how cybercrime differs in important ways from high-tech deviance and computer abuse, as well as forms of crime that also involve computers (e.g., computer crime versus computer-related crime).

## 1.2.1 White-Collar, Financial, and Organized Crime

Cybercrime as a conceptual construct for crime can be traced to the original writings of Edwin H. Sutherland about **white-collar crime**. Sutherland, a sociologist at the University of Chicago during the late 1930s, observed differences between ordinary street crimes such as larceny, robbery, and assault. He noted that although street crimes were usually committed by laboring classes of people, comparably sophisticated crimes involving abuses of power or trust such as theft via embezzlement were most often committed by professionals such as bankers, lawyers, and accountants. Professionals tended to be well educated, have relatively easy access to information and money, and they understood laws and regulations pertaining to banking and particular industries in which they worked. As a result they were able to use their knowledge and positions of trust and power within small firms, large corporations, and government agencies to advance their personal interests in ways that even if not strictly illegal were certainly illicit. Sutherland also observed that criminals of all socioeconomic classes learned and employed simple to complex techniques to commit and get away with their crimes.[9]

During the 1940s and 1950s a growing number of criminologists focused their research efforts on better understanding white-collar crime, which led to another conceptual construct: **financial crime**. This category of crime included theft of money or other financial assets, as well as embezzlement, fraud, and counterfeiting. Drawing from Sutherland's thinking, several researchers observed that financial crimes were often committed by professionally educated or technically skilled individuals, who were often familiar with accounting, banking, and auditing procedures. Hence, most financial crimes were also considered to be white-collar crimes because of the professional knowledge, skill, and abilities usually needed to successfully illegally acquire money or convert financial assets for personal use. Throughout the 1950s some researchers and public officials also recognized the essential role that money played in supporting the activities of **organized crimes** that were carried out in systematic businesslike ways by members of what became known as the Mafia. The result was that organized crimes involving financial crimes were also considered white-collar crimes. This resulted in conceptual confusion about different forms of criminality involving technological means to illegally acquire, transfer, and hide money. Today we know this as money laundering, but this term was not used until the early 1970s in connection with President Nixon's Watergate scandal. Eventually in 1986, a federal law was established to prohibit acquiring, transferring, and hiding of money for purposes of tax evasion or to perpetuate criminal enterprises.[10]

## 1.2.2  The Emergence of Computer-Related Abuse and Crime

During World War II, the United States and her allies used early types of electronic computers to decrypt coded messages intercepted from the Axis powers. After the war computers began to be used in missile guidance systems, and by the late 1950s the banking industry began adopting them to perform simple financial transactions and for account record-keeping. Subsequently, the first recorded **computer abuse** (involving salami slicing[11]) occurred in 1958 by an employee of a Minneapolis bank, and the first federally prosecuted case of

computer crime (involving alteration of bank records) took place in 1966.[12] This prosecution was made possible by existing crime laws that did not in any manner specify what constituted illegal use of computers. This would come later as banks and other types of financial institutions adopted computer technology in support of transferring funds, financial accounting, and customer services (e.g., credit/debit card and ATM services).

Throughout the 1960s, computers were conceived of merely as tools used by insider professionals to commit white-collar financial crimes. During this period the media reported an increasing number of computer abuses and crimes involving corporate or university computer systems. These incidents, combined with social, environmental, and fiscal abuses by corporations, led criminologists to realize that groups of managers and even entire organizations could be criminally culpable. This realization once again inspired new conceptions of crime, including **corporate crime** and **economic crime**—labels that represented further attempts to clarify distinctions in crime in which financial gain continued to be a primary motive for professional-class offenders. Consequently the new constructs of corporate crime and economic crime were also considered to be white-collar crimes that often involved financial crimes committed in or by organizations, inclusive of organized crime organizations.

During the 1960s and 1970s computers were increasingly being used by white-collar professionals in abusive if not illegal ways, although very few researchers payed attention to this. Donn Parker, widely regarded as the founding father of computer crime research and information security practices, was an exception who emerged during this period as a leading thinker and researcher of computer abuse and crime. In his landmark book, *Crime by Computer* (1976), Parker observed that increasing knowledge and use of computers was leading to increasing rates of computer abuse and crime, even though at the time few computer crime laws had been legislated. He also expressed concern that in the process of learning how to use computers, students were being encouraged by their teachers to demonstrate knowledge and skills by committing deviant and even criminal acts (to the extent these were defined by laws) such as hacking into or crashing systems.[13]

In the 1980s researchers continued to try to make sense of technologically evolving forms of crime made possible by increasingly advanced computing and telecommunications technology. The now-established concept of computer crime involved the use of personal computers (PCs) that enabled even nonprofessionals to commit many types of crime that were eventually collectively referred to also as **high-tech crimes**. In the process, criminal justice officials, information

---

**CYBER TALE 1.2**

### Policing without Desktop and Laptop Computers and Other IT Devices

When I began my career in policing in the mid-1970s, no one had a computer on or under their desktop. In those years only mainframe computers existed, and these were hidden behind the walls of records units of rather large public safety and security agencies. State policing agencies, large metropolitan police departments, and progressive private sector security firms utilized computers, but the vast majority of small local policing agencies in the United States, those with 25 or fewer commissioned officers, and numbering over 16,000 at the time, had no computers of their own. Electronic communications among agencies, and by nearly everyone else in society, were accomplished with telephones, fax machines, two-way FM radio systems, and the teletype.

In those days computers were used exclusively to manage police report, criminal history, driver's license, and motor vehicle registration information. Data inputting was done by records clerks, who on a daily basis and sometimes working day and night, would manually type in information contained on police incident, accident, and arrest reports or other hardcopy forms that were used by officers in the field to gather and record information about events and the people with whom they interacted. Personal computers had not been invented, so desktop and laptop computers, to say nothing of PDAs and other types of portable computing devices, were

unimaginable. Most officers felt lucky if they had at their disposal a hand-held radio and a dispatcher who could quickly process transmitted requests for wants-and-warrants checks via the local and long-distance telephone, teletype or radio system.

When I was made a detective in the late 1970s, all of our investigations were still based on hardcopy records. I remember that the original white copy of incident reports went to the records division for data inputting, the pink copy went to the patrol officer who originated the report, and the middle yellow copy went to the detective unit for follow-up investigation. Copying machines were certainly available, but in those days a modernized version of the carbon copy was still in use for many types of forms including those used for recording the towing of vehicles, gathering of property and evidence, contacting or interviewing people on the street, etc. You had to press hard to ensure all the carbon copies were readable. It was not uncommon in a major property or persons crime investigation to have a case file several inches thick, folders loaded with paper containing information that could be linked or correlated for the most part only in one's mind because computerized databases for crime analysis purposes simply were not available. As such, many case details often went unnoticed, mistakes were commonplace, and investigations took a long time, although we didn't realize it—we just used the information technology we had and concentrated on the work at hand.

security professionals (a very small group at the time), members of the public and media, and researchers created various labels for what they viewed as being new types of crime and forms of criminality involving computers. Among other scholars of this period, Jay Albanese sought to explain deviance of business and corporate organizations within the rubric of **corporate criminology**.[14] In 1984, Richard Hollinger, for the first time, defined computer crime as that in which a computer was (1) the *object or target* of crime; (2) the *site of an offense* from which a criminal accessed, altered, destroyed, manipulated, transferred, or sabotaged electronic data; or (3) the *means or instrument* used to commit an offense.[15] During this period state and federal computer crime laws were being legislated. By 1989, the previously established concept of computer abuse, which had already given way to the construct of computer crime, was transformed into yet another new concept called **computer-related crime.**

The concept of computer-related crime took into account rapid changes occurring in computer and telecommunications technology, as well as broader societal implications including myriad technical and legal challenges associated with investigating and prosecuting crimes involving computers. Donn Parker attempted to address these challenges by including in his definition of computer crime any illegal act requiring knowledge of computer technology for its perpetration, investigation, or prosecution.[16] Thus, conceptions of and labels for crime involving the use of computers continued to evolve along with innovative abuses of computer technology. This situation had significant implications for criminal justice officials who were urgently trying to understand, prevent, and control emerging forms of criminality involving computers.

Soon after the conception of computer-related crime began to take hold in the minds of criminologists and law enforcement officials, Nicholson and Cunningham wrote in 1991 about computers also being not simply tools of criminals,

but also symbols for intimidation or deception as in false invoice scams or advertising of nonexistent computer-based services.[17] In 1995, following the creation of the World Wide Web and widespread use of the Internet, David Carter reflected on crimes involving computers that did not fit neatly into existing conceptual categories of crime (e.g., illegal proliferation of sensitive, copyrighted, or proprietary data as in instances of software piracy).[18] The same year, President Clinton, in an address to the United Nations, called attention to the increasingly transnational nature of organized crime made possible in part by computerization.[19]

### 1.2.3  Technology Fusion Brings about Cybercrime

What began sixty years earlier with Sutherland's enduring conceptualization of white-collar crime evolved into a menagerie of constructs, terms, and labels that created utter confusion among practitioners, scholars, and policymakers by the mid-1990s. Debate centered on the unfolding technological nature of computer-enabled crime and how best to conceptualize, categorize, prevent, and control crime. In June 1996 the National White Collar Crime Center (NWCCC), with funding from the Bureau of Justice Assistance (BJA), hosted an academic workshop to explore the confusion surrounding the construct of white-collar crime. At this event several criminology and criminal justice scholars considered how best to think about and label emerging forms of IT-enabled crime.[20]

Meanwhile, Dave Carter and Kathleen Katz,[21] among other scholars and government officials, including the then Attorney General Janet Reno[22] and FBI Director Louis Freeh,[23] acknowledged that computerization was precipitating increasingly complex forms of crime. This general condition was evident in a jumble of new terms being used throughout this time period to label crimes involving the innovative use of computers, such as the following:

**CYBER TALE 1.3**

### *Policing with Desktop and Laptop Computers and other IT Devices*

Beginning in the early 1980s desktop PCs started showing up in police departments in places other than centralized records units. At first the monitors of these machines featured bright green or amber-colored text only, but seemingly overnight there magically appeared "windows" in what people were beginning to refer to as the "desktop." By the mid- 1980s, I found myself using *the single* PC in my department's Patrol Division report-writing area. It was loaded with Windows 3.0 and Microsoft Office's Word and Excel applications that a few of us "hunt-and-peck" typists used to write report narratives and tally and chart the monthly number of crimes and vehicle collisions. Computer mapping programs, as well as crime and intelligence analysis and case management applications had not yet been invented. So we used pin maps to show where crimes were happening (e.g., red pins for rapes and robberies and blue pins for burglaries and other property crimes).

By the time I left active policing in the mid 1990s, computers and other IT innovations had changed everything. Every officer carried a portable radio, and laptop computers were replacing mobile data terminals (MDTs) mounted in patrol cars, although some MDTs were removable. Dispatchers were beginning to use enhanced E-911 and computer-aided dispatching systems, and technicians working in crime laboratories, crime analysis units, and even in the motor pool were using computers to analyze data and solve problems. Looking back, it seems like almost overnight computers entered into and took over policing and our personal lives in ways that we still cannot fully understand or appreciate. Today, field officers use cell phones, portable electronic drug screening devices, and computerized language translation gadgets. When it comes to investigating computer abuse and cybercrimes, investigators now employ computer forensics software tools in conjunction with traditional investigative tools and techniques (a subject addressed in Chapter 9 on investigating and prosecuting cybercrimes). I don't think anyone can fully imagine, much less accurately predict, the ways in which IT will continue to transform criminal justice and security services in modern societies.

- Computer-related crime[24]
- Technological crime[25]
- High-technology crime[26]
- Economic crime and technology-based crime[27]
- New age crime[28]
- Computer and Internet-related crime[29]
- Computer-assisted crime[30]
- High tech crime[31]
- Digital crime[32]
- Electronic crime[33]
- Internet crime[34]

The term *cybercrime* was first coined by Sussman[35] and also by Heuston in 1995.[36] Amidst the many crime labels being introduced through the media and popular literature during this period, cybercrime caught on and took hold with the general public because it sensationalized the reality that networked computers were being used in combination with other electronic devices to commit new variations and forms of crime. Then a 1997 appendix document to the President's Commission on Critical Infrastructure Protection final report reviewed the nature and manageability of so-called cybercrime, as well as prospects for policing cyberspace. The author concluded that (1) widespread computerization was correlated with suspected increasing proportions of crime involving computers and other electronic devices and (2) a crucial but

## BOX 1.1 • *Definitional Constructs of High-Tech Crime*

| | |
|---|---|
| **IT-enabled deviancy** | Behaviors involving use of computerized or telecommunications devices in ways that violate social norms |
| **Computer abuse** | Use of computers in ways that cause harm to individuals, groups, or organizations, that may also violate established policies or procedures, but do not rise to the level of violating existing crime laws |
| **Computer crime** | Behaviors for which one or more computers were required to commit a consummate criminal act (i.e., the overall criminal activity could not have been accomplished without using a computer) |
| **Computer-related crime** | Illegal behaviors in which one or more computers were helpful but not necessary to commit a criminal act |
| **Cybercrime** | Use of computers or other electronic IT devices via information systems such as organizational networks or the Internet to facilitate illegal behaviors |

underemphasized aspect of evolving computer-related crime was metaphysically fused technology—actual use for criminal purposes of computers and other electronic IT devices that shared seamless functionality through direct interconnection or telecommunications systems.[37]

The foregoing history of social constructs for crime involving computers and other electronic devices, combined with the increasing extent and complexity of these crimes, which shall be addressed throughout this book, has led to the need to clearly differentiate various forms of high-tech crimes involving information systems, computers, and other types of electronic devices. Particularly important and useful terms are listed and explained in Box 1.1.

## 1.3 The Importance of Defining and Understanding Crime Terms

Early in the 20th century, crimes in which cars were used as a means of escape became known as "auto banditry," a term that undoubtedly resulted in a good deal of confusion among criminal justice officials. Another form of auto banditry included what is today referred to as "carjacking." In 1971, D.B. Cooper committed the first "hijacking" by threatening to blow up the Northwest passenger jet he was flying on from Portland, Oregon; terrorists in more recent times have also hijacked jetliners for various purposes.[38] Today, we have "computer hacking" and even "computer hijacking," when servers are remotely taken over in order to distribute massive amounts of spam and other malicious types of computer programs.

These are just a few of the many labels that have been used to describe specific types of criminal behaviors throughout history and that have initially confused investigators, policy makers, and the public as to their meaning and resulted in inappropriate responses by government agencies and private sector firms. For example, the Federal Bureau of Investigation (FBI) for several decades focused its enforcement efforts on capturing interstate outlaws rather than mobsters associated with criminal organizations because the FBI did not understand the ill-defined concept of organized crime.[39] In this section, we concentrate on understanding why definitions and constructs of crime are so important for avoiding confusion about evolving forms of cybercrimes.

### 1.3.1 What Is Cybercrime and Why Should We Care about It?

*Cybercrime* is now the term most often used to label activities in which perpetrators use computers or other electronic IT devices via information systems to facilitate illegal behaviors. In essence, cybercrime involves using electronic gadgets to access, control, manipulate, or use data for illegal purposes. IT devices now used to commit crimes include desktop, laptop, and mini computers, as well as cell phones, PDAs, fax machines, digital cameras, voice recorders, scanners, and so on. Such devices are increasingly digital as opposed to analog in their technical design and operations, employ feature-integrated functionality, and are capable of being networked via landline, hot sync, or wireless connections. Cybercrime is defined and explained in this way:

1. Stresses the fundamental fact that computers, often but not necessarily combined with other types of electronic devices, are being used to commit crimes in innovative and increasingly complex ways.
2. Acknowledges that widespread networking made possible by combined computing and telecommunications systems provides innovative opportunities for committing crime on unprecedented scales.
3. Recognizes that crime laws and associated intervention policies are inevitably created by governments in response to criminal adoption of new technologies and that criminal use of IT for abusive if not illicit or illegal purposes occurs in changing social, economic, political, and technological contexts.
4. Can be used as a general yet meaningful label for any type of IT-enabled crime regardless of existing crime constructs and future socio-technological developments affecting the evolution of crime.
5. Is technologically observable, traceable, and measurable and therefore capable of supporting research into the actual nature and extent of evolving crime enabled with IT, and by extension supporting formulation of public policies and practices leading to improved management and prevention of such crimes.

In practice, however, the term *cybercrime* is used and understood in different ways, which causes plenty of problems for researchers, criminal justice officials, information security professionals, public policy officials, technology developers, the media, and members of the public throughout the world. David Wall, a prominent British researcher in this field, wrote in 2001 that "the term cybercrime does not actually do much more than signify the occurrence of a harmful behavior that is somehow related to a computer . . . [and yet] . . . like sticky paper on a shoe, it is a term that cannot be easily shaken off and dismissed as it has quickly become absorbed into popular parlance . . . ."[40] Therefore, the term *cybercrime*, if not specified as indicated above or in another way that accomplishes the advantages listed, may at best be regarded as a general label for many evolving and emerging types of IT-enabled crimes, with the provision that initially, such innovative abusive or harmful activities may not even violate existing crime laws. This concept involves the theory of technology-enabled crime, policing, and security explained in Chapter 5.

Cybercrimes now involve software piracy, illegal file sharing, Web site vandalism, cyberstalking, computer eavesdropping, email spamming, and electronic extortion, among other forms of illegal behaviors. People are also increasingly victims of denial-of-service attacks and spoofing and phishing cons in which, after being duped into believing that an Internet Web site is legitimate, they provide financial and other personal information before being defrauded through illegal use of their credit cards or having their identities stolen. These are just some of the many types of cybercrimes experienced by people, and the organizations in which they work, who suffer harm as the result of stolen or damaged computers, software, and data. All of these and many more forms of cybercrime, computer abuse, and attacks on information systems are discussed in Chapter 3.

As a society we need to be concerned about cybercrime for three fundamental reasons.

First, every person and organization relying on computers have data that are relatively vulnerable to many forms of cybercrime and are thus in need of protection. Second, we all have a societal responsibility to help prevent cybercrimes from occurring and ameliorate harm associated with being victimized. Third, society now extensively depends on vulnerable networked information systems for many life-sustaining functions. These important themes are developed below and elsewhere throughout this text. For example, data in need of being protected, inclusive of critical information infrastructure, are addressed in Chapter 2, the extent of harm caused by cybercrimes is discussed in Chapter 6, and legal issues concerning our responsibilities to help prevent and control cybercrime are covered in Chapter 8.

### 1.3.2  Creating, Complying with, and Enforcing Laws and Regulations

Different conceptions of similar types of crimes occur naturally and are easy to confuse, yet people need to know what constitutes criminal behavior so they can obey the laws society creates. Without clear definitions of crime, people cannot understand how they must conduct themselves or the possible consequences for not doing so. The concept of the **rule of law** underscores the belief that investigation, prosecution, and punishment of illegal behaviors should not be arbitrary. Thus, police officers rely on clearly specified crime laws to investigate only individuals who appear to be acting in a suspicious manner in relation to legally proscribed conduct. Prosecutors, information security professionals, and judges who need to interpret and apply laws and case rulings in ongoing investigations and court proceedings also need clear definitions. As you will learn in Chapter 8, crime laws always include a preliminary section of definitions that specify behaviors that are illegal. Crime laws also include elements of crimes that are specific behaviors that must be

established before someone in the United States can be arrested on suspicion of having violated the law. During prosecution, these same elements need to be proven beyond a reasonable doubt in order for a person to be convicted of having committed the crimes for which they were arrested and formally charged. Hence, the entire criminal justice system and its processes are predicated on clearly defining what society determines is illegal.

As the nature of crimes involving telecommunications and computing technologies have changed, many states and the federal government have created crime laws prohibiting certain types of behavior involving electronic devices. Currently all fifty states and the federal government have at least one crime law that prohibits certain behaviors involving the use of computers and other types of IT devices. Numerous types of cybercrime, if they originated in the United States and involve computer systems of the federal government, are now, under provisions of the USA PATRIOT Act and other federal crime laws, considered felonies or even acts of terrorism. Prior to the terrorist attacks on the World Trade Center and Pentagon on September 11, 2001, however, these same activities may have been considered lesser crimes, or crimes in violation of state laws, if they were considered crimes at all. The USA PATRIOT Act exemplifies how behaviors socially construed as being normal, deviant, or criminal change over time according to events and technologies in use, along with many other societal factors. The implication is that criminal laws evolve with crimes, which evolve with technology. Since technology, and thus the nature of criminal behavior, is constantly changing as criminals adopt new methods and tools, definitions of what is illegal must also change. Consequently, the criminal justice system continually struggles to stay abreast of technology adopted for illicit purposes and to formulate new laws and regulations that prohibit abusive behaviors.

### Why Definitions of Crime Matter:
### State of New York v. Robert Versaggi

On November 10, 1986, hundreds of phone lines at the Kodak Park Complex in Rochester, New York, were shut down or impaired for several hours. Consequently, many employees working under conditions involving the potential for dangerous chemical spills were not able to receive or make telephone calls even to "911" for emergency assistance. On November 11 a second incident occurred, this time interrupting the ability to make phone calls from or to any of Kodak's facilities worldwide. Robert Versaggi, a computer technician employed by Kodak who often worked from home by telephonically accessing the firm's computer systems, was determined to have intentionally caused the incidents.

Versaggi was subsequently prosecuted under New York's relatively new computer crime law.

During the trial his lawyers contended that charges against him should be dismissed because his actions only involved responding to pop-up questions posed to him by Kodak's computer system (e.g., Do you wish to proceed, YES/NO?; Do you wish to kill the program, YES/NO?) but did not constitute tampering with a computer program. In making its decision whether or not to dismiss charges against Versaggi, the court needed to determine whether his conduct was encompassed within the language of the statute and specifically if he had "altered" a program within the meaning of Penal Law § 156.20, which itself did not legally define *alter*. In the end, the court did not dismiss the charge, ruling that Versaggi's actions did make Kodak's computer system "different in some particular characteristic without changing [it] to something else."[41]

### 1.3.3 Research and Justice Systems Improvement

Precise definitions of crime terms also enable researchers to consistently identify and measure the nature and extent of specific types of existing and emerging deviancy, crime, and threats to information systems. Research based on clear definitions in turn facilitates awareness about existing and emerging crime-related problems and helps improve methods of addressing crime-related problems. However, as we have seen, evolving conceptions of crime lead to new terms being used by the media, researchers, and government officials. When this occurs, our ability to understand and address crime and security problems is compromised. Individuals and organizations may alter their use of terms or even use different terms interchangeably to mean the same thing. In his early research during the 1970s Donn Parker referred to "computer abuse" but by 1983 was

using the term *computer crime*, which in 1998 he equated to "cybercrime."[42] Similarly, in 1996 then Attorney General Janet Reno officially referenced "new age crime" but a year later was calling the same phenomena "high tech crime."[43] More recently, in 2004 the National Institute of Justice (NIJ), and the Office of Juvenile Justice and Delinquency (OJJDP), both components of the Office of Justice Programs within the U.S. Department of Justice (and located within the same building in Washington, D.C.), referred in their research program materials to "electronic crime" and "Internet crime," respectively, to describe the same types of crime phenomenon, yet without distinguishing between these or mentioning cybercrime.[44]

In research, the concept of **operationalizing terms** refers to creating precise definitions in order to enable consistent labeling, understanding, and measurement of phenomena. By operationalizing terms, researchers (and practitioners and policy makers) can avoid inappropriately commingling meanings of different types of abuse, deviancy, crime, and security threats. Operationalizing terms helps to prevent confusing research findings that would be of little value for creating crime prevention and information security programs, enacting new crime legislation, or enforcing laws and regulations. Preventing such confusion does generally improve criminal justice and security practices and policies.

Despite the value of precisely defining crime terms and using them in consistent ways, people often refer to overlapping categories of crime with little if any regard to what such terms may mean in the minds of others. Remember that, in the absence of precise terminology and understanding of such issues, individuals may *think they understand* a given situation, presume that others understand it in the same way, and as a result take no or inappropriate action, to the detriment of themselves and others. Individuals who try to understand, explain, and address crime problems cannot be blamed for using various labels, but we should all strive to understand and use terms as precisely as possible. In so doing we are less likely to create or add to confusion about emerging crimes and threats to information security systems.

## 1.4 Principles for Better Understanding Cybercrime and Future Crime Labels

By now you may be wondering what we as individuals can do to influence how the media, government, and society as a whole conceive of and talk about emerging forms of crime and cybercrime in particular. Many books have already been written on how crimes are facilitated with computers, many images and labels for specific types of attacks and cybercrimes have already been established, and we are of course in the inevitable process of socially reconstructing our understanding of all these issues on a grand scale. Three things come to mind: (1) recognize and accept that views of cybercrime differ; (2) education and professional training can help us stay on the cutting edge of thinking and field practices; and (3) understanding and managing cybercrime requires that we recognize the inter- and multidisciplinary nature of cybercrime, regardless of our individual professional specializations and occupations. Let us examine each of these principles in more detail.

### 1.4.1 Recognize and Accept that Views of Cybercrime Differ

People who have experienced loss of data as the result of computer viruses will likely have greater awareness about cybercrime and the potential for various types of attacks to their information systems. They are also likely to have less tolerance for individuals who experiment with writing malicious code and releasing it onto the Internet than someone who has not suffered a similar loss of data. Social and professional experiences, combined with our understanding of how technology can be used for illicit purposes, help shape our views about social deviance, computer abuse, threats to information security, and crime. We would expect people to view cybercrime and the need for information security differently based on their experiences and familiarity with IT. After all, not all investigators think the same or approach problems about crime and security in the same ways, yet investigators who specialize in cybercrimes and computer forensics analysis are all trained to see potential evidence at crime scenes that would go undetected by law enforcement officers without such expertise. In addition, they may use special equipment or investigative methods, a unique vernacular to describe technical aspects of crimes, and special analytical techniques.

Viewing crime problems in different ways also has to do with a person's managerial position or rank within an organization. An information security professional on the front lines of protecting systems may not appreciate fiscal, policy, or political reasons for their organization not being able to immediately purchase needed security items or train personnel as much as a chief information officer might. The perspectives of a chief information officer and other senior managers are likely to be different from the views held by employees of less rank and members of the general public or government policymakers, who are even further removed from the day-to-day challenges of keeping information systems secure at the network systems level. To make matters worse, each of us can only absorb and apply so much information in a given time period. In today's so-called information age, we periodically experience information overload. Consequently, even if we are interested in learning more about a particular cybercrime or information security issue, we may not have the time or mental stamina to take in, much less apply, new information. Add to this the challenge of clearly defining and precisely talking about emerging and evolving forms of crime and attacks, and it is no wonder that many professionals find themselves feeling frustrated, confused, and frazzled.

Sometimes it is easier to stay within the comfort zone of our own limited knowledge and understanding of problems that are on our radar screens on any given day and concentrate on getting the job at hand done rather than worry about other issues. Ignorance is bliss, but only until lack of understanding and inattention to emerging cybercrime problems and the potential for attacks to information systems catch us off guard. A better approach would be to assume that our views and perhaps the views held by others about a given crime or security situation may be important and will naturally differ and range from being somewhat to substantially wrong, especially if new or vague terminology in the context of changing technology is being used to describe it. Thus, it is important to recognize that views of cybercrime differ, as will approaches to preventing and responding to attacks on information systems.

## 1.4.2 Education and Training Helps Professionals Stay Informed

Broad-based education combined with technical training enables us to see and address problems in creative ways. The broader our theoretical frame of reference for understanding crime problems, the smarter we can be about solving crime and security problems. If we also understand research methods and findings that support particular theories of crime, as well as how empirically supported theories have played out in practice, the better positioned we will be on a technical level to weigh in on and respond to particular crime-related challenges. This is just another way of saying that when it comes to defining and managing crime problems, education in addition to technical skills matters a lot. This does not mean you need to become an expert criminologist or technologist to be effective in preventing and controlling cybercrime or otherwise helping improve information security in your organization. Rather, new frames of reference achieved through education and training, indeed the process of becoming better educated and trained, helps enable everyone to reach out intellectually to others for assistance when needed, as well as to help colleagues solve problems in creative, effective, and appropriate ways.

Educated professionals can envision a given situation from many points of view, and this is necessary when addressing the complicated challenges associated with cybercrime. They are also able to think critically and argue and act from positions of informed strength within their political environments—a definite plus for criminal justice and security managers, who are often expected to quickly assess and articulate problems, as well as devise and implement viable solutions to myriad crime and security problems, but with limited resources and lack of understanding by others within organizations. Individuals who, for whatever reason, do not seek enlightenment through education and training are apt to not develop the wisdom needed to effectively deal with emerging crime and security problems. Without the intellectual horsepower to reason and exercise independent professional judgment, they are likely to parrot what others say and take inappropriate actions based on half-truths.

So how big is *your* intellectual toolbox? Be smart about cybercrime and information security. Push yourself as an emerging or established professional to understand crime and security issues in critical ways, with healthy curiosity, suspicion, and even skepticism when called for. Do so also with a genuine spirit of helping develop viable solutions to perplexing problems that you and your colleagues will invariably confront. This is what being an educated, trained, and committed professional is about. Whether you are still in college or already working in criminal justice or the information security profession, remaining educated about and trained in the continually changing nature of technology, cybercrime, and associated issues is among the most important things you can do.

### 1.4.3 The Inter- and Multidisciplinary Nature of Cybercrime and Organization of the Text

Social issues and context, inclusive of the effects of technology innovation, are critical to the ways we need to think about cybercrime. Our understanding of these issues also affects our views over time of the interplay between the administration of justice and security management. As a result, our views of emerging variations of crime and threats to information security, as well as the ways we attempt to manage these, are affected by our understanding of the broader world. Thus, the title of this book, *Understanding and Managing Cybercrime,* reflects the need for inter- and multidisciplinary perspectives to address this unfolding and vexing problem. Indeed, there is today wide recognition and growing acceptance that tackling myriad problems associated with cybercrime and information security requires understanding from many different theoretical and applied perspectives. The position taken throughout this text is that the overall security of information systems throughout society depends on the knowledge, skills, and abilities possessed by cultural anthropologists, sociologists, psychologists, and experts in other academic fields of study being as important as those possessed by computer scientists, IT administrators, and information security professionals. This is because IT permeates all aspects of modern societies, bringing with it the potential for social deviance, abuse, and crime. Political scientists have much to teach us about the role of coercive governments in passing new crime laws in order to deter future crimes on the Internet. Economists can help us understand the risks of unfettered economic self-interest and how this concept relates to the possible need to regulate software development and data aggregation firms in order to force security enhancements in their products and services. Philosophers can instruct us about ethical use of computers and other types of IT devices in a wide variety of circumstances, and criminologists can help us understand why people are deviant, become abusive, and commit crimes.

Recognizing that cybercrime requires inter- and multidisciplinary understanding is critical but not sufficient to societal management of cybercrime. To be truly effective, scholars in various fields of inquiry, along with cybercrime investigators and IT professionals, must incorporate principles of knowledge from different disciplines and approaches to solving physical security, information security, and crime problems. This is not easy, because most of us are educated and trained to approach problems from a particular perspective: IT administrators and software engineers naturally think about network problems in technological ways; to their credit, lawyers in the United States tend to think about unresolved legal issues in terms of Constitutional principles, crime laws, and other types of legislation and regulations; and law enforcement officers, prosecutors, and security professionals naturally focus on the suspicious, illicit, and illegal activities of people they encounter. Certainly, specialized thinking and organizing of our collective efforts is essential because there is so much that goes into preventing crime, ensuring the security of facilities and information systems, and ameliorating the harmful impacts of IT-enabled abuses. After all, no one can possibly be an expert in all these areas. Nonetheless, the imperative is to think about and understand cybercrime in broad theoretical and sophisticated ways and also in logical and practical ways, which is why this book covers the topics it does. On that note, please take a moment to study the table of contents and note the basic theme or scholarly discipline underscoring the book's parts, chapters, and sections.

Part I pertains to understanding cybercrime. Accordingly, Chapter 1 approached cybercrime primarily from the perspective of *sociology*, how society evolves technologically and with respect to understanding and labeling crime constructs. Chapter 2 is concerned with attack methods and the attendant implications for *information systems administration*. Chapter 3 describes types of IT-enabled abuse, attacks, and crimes, and Chapter 4 follows with an explanation of issues regarding computer abusers and cybercriminals. These chapters have to do with *information security* and *criminology*, respectively, and both also relate to the *psychology* of criminal offending.

Part II pertains to theoretical and social perspectives of cybercrime. Chapter 5 presents several *criminological* theories that offer potential for understanding why people abuse information systems, data, computers, or other electronic devices to commit cybercrimes. Chapter 6 describes the harm experienced by cybercrime victims plus the incidence, prevalence, and social and economic impacts of cybercrime. These topics also pertain generally to *criminology*, *sociology*, and *research methods*. In Chapter 7 we explore emerging crime-related issues and controversies that are rooted in concepts of *cultural anthropology*.

In Part III our focus shifts from understanding to managing cybercrime. In Chapter 8 we begin to consider how international treaties, laws, and regulations are formulated, and we discuss an extensive set of cyber-related *laws*. Chapter 9 concentrates on issues of investigating and prosecuting cybercrimes that are integral to *criminal justice*. Chapter 10 describes *facilities and information systems security management*, which draws heavily from these fields, plus *organizational theory, personnel management, and accounting*, which bear on effective *leadership* and transforming agencies and firms. Last, Chapter 11 speaks to how the United States government in collaboration with other nations can better prevent cybercrime, as well as concepts in computer ethics. In so doing, this chapter stresses important concepts in *public policy* and *public administration*, as well as the *philosophy of ethics* as it applies to cyber issues.

I have taken the space here to describe (and italicize) the disciplinary basis of each chapter to stress the importance of inter- and multidisciplinary thinking for effectively understanding and managing cybercrime and to preview what lies ahead. I hope you are already beginning to grasp the interconnections among the topics described above, all of which are vital to understanding and managing computer abuse and threats to information systems and ultimately preventing cybercrime. Can you see why professional managers and administrators working to understand and prevent cybercrime within a government agency, private sector firm, or nonprofit organization would want their employees to know about each of these topics? Conversely, in this age of rapidly evolving cybercrime can you see how criminal justice and information security managers need to know about these issues in multi- and interdisciplinary ways?

Topics covered in this text should be considered basic training for all generalists who desire or must understand, help prevent, and manage cybercrime or help ensure protection of information systems. Much information in this book should be required reading for users of information systems whose negligent actions can contribute to causing as much harm to stand-alone and networked computers as attacks and cybercrimes. The broad educational challenge addressed here is to educate and raise awareness about a very complicated subject—cybercrime. Throughout the book we will consider coherent sets of materials relevant to current and future criminal justice and information security professionals, recognizing that students of these subjects may seldom have an opportunity to take more than one course on cybercrime issues and equally likely may not benefit from a curriculum designed to stress the inter- and multidisciplinary perspectives needed for understanding and managing cybercrime effectively.

A final word of introduction is offered for your consideration. After thoughtful deliberation with many scholars, practitioners, and students it was decided not to title this book *Understanding and Preventing Cybercrime*. This is not to suggest that preventing cybercrime is not extremely important. Indeed, prevention concepts are addressed throughout the text and stressed in Part III. However, as you will learn, it is not possible to entirely prevent any form of crime. In addition, the technologically evolving nature of cybercrime implies that we need to simultaneously manage technology-related processes pertaining to information systems and the security of these in our personal and professional lives, within our organizations, and throughout society. Only by adopting information security as a lifestyle, managing organizations with this concept in mind, and ultimately transforming our overall societal culture to one fully cognizant of IT-enabled abuse and crime and countervailing information security tools and methods, can we prevent cybercrime to any meaningful extent. Thus, cybercrime can only be prevented by better securing information systems and further developing technologies that make this possible and incorporating information security concepts and best practices into criminal justice systems administration, inclusive

of formulating and implementing new crime laws, regulations, policies, and programs. First, however, we need to better understand and manage specific issues related to IT-enabled abuse, attacks on information systems, and crimes.

## 1.5 Summary

Cyberspace is a technology-enabled realm in and through which activities occur, an amorphous computing environment with infinite varieties of information to explore and use. Information we acquire online provides tremendous convenience, enjoyment, and productivity, depending on what we use our computers for; how knowledgeable, skilled, and efficacious we are at using software applications; and the extent to which we can secure our systems and data when working either on- or offline. Getting the most out of online or offline computing also hinges on the attitudes of everyone with whom we interact about responsible use of computers; such as using computers ethically, in ways consistent with social norms and laws that are not abusive of system resources or cause other types of harm. Our attitude toward responsible computing in and out of cyberspace affects the extent to which we tolerate deviant, abusive, or criminal use of computers and other electronic devices.

People interact with each other using computers and electronic gadgets for all sorts of reasons. They form groups and often engage in activities according to their interests and means. As this occurs, philosophies develop, customs are formed, and social norms are established. How people organize themselves, communicate, and interact in cyberspace mirrors what takes place in the physical realm. This comes as no surprise because cyber environments such as chat rooms, discussion forums, and online purchasing centers are usually mere extensions of and therefore equivalent in many respects to physical places of the same type. What constitutes respectful or rude behavior in an online distance-learning environment, for example, is not very different from such behaviors in classrooms with walls and students physically present.

Normal behavior and deviant behavior are interdependent and subjective concepts. Perceptions about what constitutes deviant behavior depend generally on what is regarded as normal behavior. Normal behavior has little meaning unless compared to deviant behavior in given circumstances, and these vary among groups experiencing different situations in different periods of time. Conversely, deviancy has little or no meaning in the absence of social norms. Given that all behaviors range from being relatively normal to deviant, cognitive, emotional, and behavioral reactions to behaviors also range from being relatively normal to deviant according to what is going on in a given time and place. Normal and deviant behaviors are initially experienced, learned, adopted, and affirmed. This process tends to stabilize cultures, although social norms and laws do change and change with environmental circumstances that include technological innovations.

Computing and telecommunications technologies have introduced new standards of behavior for their use and therefore how relatively normal versus deviant technology-related behaviors are perceived, reacted to, and potentially sanctioned in modern societies. What we learn, come to accept, and practice and thereafter reinforce in our own behaviors and in the lives of others with whom we interact in physical environments tends to be mirrored in our online interactions and activities, and vice versa. In other words, principles of social norms versus deviancy and social controls of behavior involving use of technology carry over from the physical realm to the cyber realm of human interaction, and vice versa. Cultural interconnections and similarities between tangible physical environments and intangible cyber environments are not really remarkable, because people live in the real world and most of us in modernized societies routinely use computers for all sorts of things in both on- and offline ways.

Cybercrime represents a new high-tech crime paradigm affecting everyone who uses computers, although some criminal justice and security researchers and practitioners consider cybercrime to be nothing more than traditional crime that came about with developments in computing and telecommunications technology. They are right about this, but because they may not understand the technical nature of many cybercrimes and the associated potential for new and widespread forms of victimization, they may delay or incorrectly organize their crime fighting and information security efforts. At another extreme, cybercrime is often incorrectly seen to consist mostly of spectacular and even unmanageable forms of high-tech crimes that, if left unmanaged, will surely bring chaos to the Internet, threaten national security, ruin any hope for e-commerce, and so on. These viewpoints represent extremes in a range of viewpoints that have much to do with interpreting the implications of technologically evolving forms of abuse, deviancy, and crime.

Constructs of crime are needed for understanding emerging forms of criminality. Reasonably precise and understandable definitions of evolving forms of crime are needed as a basis for accurate communication and understanding of a given crime problem. Clear conceptualizations and definitions of crime enable us to create, obey, and enforce laws and regulations and undertake research to understand crime problems and thereby manage these in effective and economically efficient ways. This is especially true in democratic societies such as the United States that rely extensively on widespread knowledge about and voluntary compliance with existing rules and regulations.

Researchers remain concerned about how conceptions of white-collar crime, well established in the criminological literature beginning in the 1930s, are changing as the result of computerization. Throughout the 1990s, for example, there was considerable debate over what computer crime versus computer-related crime meant.

Unfortunately today, nearly seventy years after Sutherland's conceptualization of white-collar crime and nearly half a century after the first reported instance of computer abuse in 1959, there remains considerable disagreement among criminologists about what constitutes cybercrime versus other forms of crime. Definitions have been provided in this chapter to move the coexisting and inextricable fields of criminology and criminal justice past this conundrum while recognizing that new constructs and labels for crime are tied to technology evolution.

Cybercrime consists of activities in which computers or other electronic IT devices are used to facilitate illegal behaviors via information systems. Cybercrime subsumes but does not contradict or negate the potential importance for further study of earlier conceptualizations of crime enabled by computers (e.g., white-collar crime, computer crime, and computer-related crime). These and other crime constructs established on the basis of research remain important, although a fundamental challenge facing criminologists is to thoroughly understand how networked computers and other IT devices are used to facilitate all forms of criminality. If students are to succeed in future criminal justice, security management, and IT professions they must learn to accept and address the reality of different and inevitably changing perspectives about crime. Through broad-based inter- and multidisciplinary education and professional training, we can remain attuned to technologically evolving crime issues and challenges and thereby help manage naturally occurring tensions that exist among academics, practitioners, and policymakers seeking to better understand and address cybercrime.

## Key Terms and Concepts

Computer abuse, 12
Computer crime, 12
Computerization, 3
Computer-related crime, 14
Constructs, 11
Corporate crime, 12
Corporate criminology, 14
Cybercrime, 1

Cyberspace, 3
Deviant behaviors, 5
Economic crime, 12
Financial crime, 11
High-tech crimes, 13
Information systems, 4
Netiquette, 10
Operationalizing terms, 19

Organized crimes, 12
Rule of law, 18
Social construction, 10
Social control, 5
Social norms, 5
Social sanctions, 6
Socialization, 4
White-collar crime, 11

## Critical Thinking and Discussion Questions

1. Describe two examples of behaviors that would be considered socially "normal" and two examples that would be considered technologically deviant. Explain how one example of each set of behaviors could become reversed (e.g., how a social norm could become deviant and how a deviant behavior could become normal) if circumstances changed).

2. Describe a situation in which you or someone you know behaved in a technologically inept way. What were the circumstances? How, if at all, were informal social sanctions applied?

3. Describe the social circumstances surrounding how you learned to use a computer or other electronic device. Explain acculturation factors that significantly influenced your attitudes about using the technology in certain ways.

4. What do you think society's perception of cybercriminals is? Without revealing specific details of any particular incident, do you think you are a cybercriminal? Why or why not?

5. Is it necessary to create new terms for ordinary crimes committed with more advanced tools? For example, isn't cyberstalking simply the act of stalking someone with a computer via the Internet?

6. Provide three examples of computer-related deviancy. Briefly explain hypothetical circumstances for each example.

7. Provide three examples of computer abuse. Briefly explain hypothetical circumstances for each example.

8. What is the difference between computer crime, computer-related crime, and cybercrime? Provide examples of each.
9. Comment on the usefulness of being able to explain technical aspects of a cybercrime to managers who are not technically adept.
10. Can crime terms ever be permanently defined and completely understood? Why or why not?
11. Suppose you are a manager in a criminal justice agency or other type of organization and you are concerned that other employees might not understand the potential for information security threats to the network. What could you recommend or do to help improve their awareness and security practices?

## *References and Endnotes*

1. Littman, J. (1997). *The Watchman: The Twisted Life and Crimes of Serial Hacker Kevin Poulsen.* New York: Little, Brown & Co.
2. The term cyberspace was first used by William Gibson in his 1984 novel *Neuromancer* to refer to all electronic networks.
3. Wall, D. (2001). Cybercrime and the Internet. In David S. Wall (Ed.), *Crime and the Internet* (pp. 1–17). London: Routledge.
4. Collegiate Presswire Staff Author (2004, November 18). New wave of illegal file sharing lawsuits brought by RIAA. Retrieved July 25, 2005, from http://www.cpwire.com/archive/2004/11/18/1710.asp
5. McQuade, S., & Linden, E. (2005). College Student Computer Use and Ethics: An Empirical Analysis of Self-Reported Unethical Behaviors. Unpublished manuscript, Rochester Institute of Technology, Rochester, NY.
6. Shea, V. (1994). *Netiquette.* San Rafael: Albion.
7. For detailed explanations of social construction see Berger, P. L., & Luckman, T. (1967). *The Social Construction of Reality: A Treatise in the Sociology of Knowledge.* New York: Anchor Books. See also Searle, J. R. (1995). *The Construction of Social Reality.* New York: Free Press.
8. Hollinger, R. C. (1991). Hackers: Computer heroes or electronic highwaymen? *Computers and Society, 21*(1), 6–17.
9. Sutherland, E. H. (1940). White-collar criminality. In Joseph E. Jacoby (Ed.), *Classics of Criminology,* 2nd ed., 1994 edition (pp. 20–25). Prospect Heights, IL: Waveland Press.
10. McQuade, S. (2001). Cops versus crooks: Technological competition and complexity in the co-evolution of information technologies and money laundering. Doctoral Dissertation, George Mason University, Fairfax, VA.
11. Salami slicing involves illegally programming a computer to capture, divert, and accumulate transaction rounding errors to a financial account. For instance, a financial transaction that results in $10.174 could be legitimately rounded down to $10.17, leaving .004 cents to be deposited into a specially created illegal account. Millions of such transactions can accumulate into a significant amount of money.
12. Parker, D. B. (1989). *Computer Crime: Criminal Justice Resource Manual,* 2nd ed. Washington, DC: National Institute of Justice.
13. Parker, D. B. (1976). *Crime by Computer.* New York: Charles Scribner's Sons.
14. Albanese, J. (1984). Corporate criminology: Explaining deviance of business and political organizations. *Journal of Criminal Justice, 12,* 11–19.
15. Hollinger, R. (1984). Computer Deviance: Receptivity to Electronic Rule-Breaking. Paper presented at the annual meeting of the American Society of Criminology, November 7, Cincinnati, OH.
16. Parker, 1989; see note 12.
17. Nicholson, C. K., & Cunningham, R. (1991). Computer crime. *American Law Review, 28*(3), 393–405.
18. Carter, D. L. (1995). Computer crime categories: How techno-criminals operate. *FBI Law Enforcement Bulletin, 64*(7), 21–27.
19. Clinton, W. J. (1995). Address by President Clinton to the United Nations General Assembly. Retrieved October 13, 1997, from http://library.whitehouse.gov/.
20. National White Collar Crime Center and West Virginia University. (1996). Proceedings of the Academic Workshop, Bureau of Justice Assistance Grant No. 96-WC-CX-001. Morgantown, WV: National White Collar Crime Center.
21. Carter, D. L., & Katz, A. J. (1996). Trends and Experiences in Computer-Related Crime: Findings from a National Study. Paper presented at the annual meeting of the Academy of Criminal Justice Sciences, Las Vegas, NV.
22. Reno, J. (1997, April). Computer Crime: The Next Law Enforcement Challenge. *Justice for All.* Washington, DC: U.S. Department of Justice.
23. Freeh, L. (1994, May 1). Violent crime in the U.S.: Restructuring the Federal Bureau of Investigation. FBI Director Speech to the Chicago Executive Club. *In Vital Speeches of the Day* (pp. 418–421). Washington, DC.
24. Carter & Katz, 1996; see note 21.

25. Collier, P. A., & Spaul, B. J. (1992). Forensic science against computer crime in the United Kingdom. *Journal of the Forensic Science Society, 32*(1), 27–34.

26. Arkin, S. S., Bohrer, B. A., Cuneo, D.L., Donohoe, J.P., Kaplan, J.M., Kasanof, R., Levander, A. J., & Sherizen, S. (1989). *Prevention and Prosecution of Computer and High Technology Crime.* New York: Matthew Bender and Company.

27. Gordon, G. R. (1996). *The Impact of Technology-Based Crime on Definitions of White Collar/Economic Crime: Breaking out of the White Collar Crime Paradigm.* Morgantown, WV: National White Collar Crime Center.

28. Reno, 1997; see note 22.

29. Pilant, L. (1997, August). Fighting crime in cyberspace. *Police Chief, 64* (8), 26–43.

30. Gill, M. S. (1997, May). Cybercops take a byte out of computer crime. *Smithsonian,* pp. 114–124.

31. Reno, 1997; see note 22.

32. Power, R. (2000). *Tangled Web: Tales of Digital Crime from the Shadows of Cyberspace.* Indianapolis, IN: Que Corporation.

33. NIJ Technical Working Group for Electronic Crime Scene Investigation. (2001, July). *Electronic Crime Scene Investigation: A Guide for First Responders.* Washington, DC: National Institute of Justice.

34. Office of Juvenile Justice and Delinquency Prevention (2004). Program Announcement: Internet Crimes against Children Task Force Program. Retrieved June 5, 2004, from http://www.ojjdp.ncjrs.org/enews/04juvjust/040203.html.

35. Sussman, V. (1995, January 23). Policing cyberspace. *U.S. News & World Report,* pp. 55–60.

36. Heuston, G. Z. (1995). Investigating the information superhighway: Global views, local perspectives. *Journal of Criminal Justice Education, 6*(2), 311–321.

37. McQuade, S. (1997). *So-Called Cybercrime: Its Nature and Manageability* (Final report of the President's Commission on Critical Information Infrastructure Protection). Appendix report to *Critical Foundations: Protecting America's Infrastructure.* Washington, DC: Government Printing Office.

38. After forcing a landing in Seattle, Washington, Cooper (an alias) collected $200,000 in ransom from police and then forced the crew to depart for Mexico. Shortly after this second takeoff from Seattle, Cooper parachuted, possibly to safety, though this was never officially determined. In 1980, $5,800 of the ransom money was found along the Columbia River.

39. Sifakis, C. (1999). The Mafia Encyclopedia, 2nd ed., p. 195. New York: Checkmark Books.

40. Wall, D. (2001). Cybercrime and the Internet. In Wall, D. S. (Ed.), *Crime and the Internet.* London: Routledge, pp. 1–17.

41. Anonymous (2003).

42. Compare discussions in Chapter 5 of *Crime by Computer* (Parker, 1976) with terms used in *Fighting Computer Crime* (Parker, 1983) and Chapter 1 of *Fighting Computer Crime: A New Framework for Protecting Information* (Parker, 1998).

43. Compare use of terminology in speech titled "Law Enforcement in Cyberspace" given by Attorney General Janet Reno to the Commonwealth Club of California on June 14, 1996, in San Francisco with Reno, J. (1997) Computer crime: The next law enforcement challenge. Washington, DC: U.S. Department of Justice.

44. National Institute of Justice (2004). Electronic Crime Program. Retrieved June 14, 2004, from http://www.ojp.usdoj.gov/nij/sciencetech/text/tecrime.htm.

# 2

## *Information and Other Assets in Need of Assurance*

### 2.0 Introduction: What Are We Protecting?

Everyone has information they consider to be very important and thus valuable and in need of protection. What information do you consider particularly important to safeguard? To whom is it entrusted for safekeeping? Most people consider their personal financial data to be very important and they entrust its safekeeping to a bank, credit union, or some other type of financial institution. Medical and dental records are also very important, especially if you relocate and need to receive follow-up treatment for an illness or injury. Most college students also regard their academic records to be very important and deserving of special protection because they are valuable and private. No one except you, authorized professionals, and information security specialists entrusted for safekeeping information are entitled to see this information. How secure do you think your academic, health care, or employment personnel records are in reality?

In Chapter 1 we explored certain sociological perspectives of deviant, abusive, and criminal human behavior with regard to how these form, are labeled, and lead to formulation of

crime constructs that reflect how technology is used for illicit purposes. In this chapter we begin by considering technology used in criminal justice agencies and security firms, especially as these pertain to capabilities for preventing and controlling crime. Here you will learn about the primary characteristics of information, data versus knowledge management, the concepts of information possession versus information ownership, and why money is a special form of data to consider when deciding how to provide for information systems security.

In the next section we will take up the issue of information assurance, beginning with the concepts of data confidentiality, integrity, and availability (CIA), which many information security professionals have long regarded to be a critically important but insufficient framework for understanding data security in the context of hostile, negligent, and other types of human factors. Explanation of these concepts will establish a foundation for examining the information assurance principles of necessity, human error, and distrust of people and technology. These principles must be employed in order to manage information security systems and safeguard data. In the third section of the chapter you will be introduced to the threat analysis matrix and the threat analysis cube, models that can be used to think about, diagnose, and illustrate possible combinations and methods of attacks against assets.

In the last section of the chapter, we will extend our consideration of these topics to the concepts of critical infrastructure (CI) protection, and protection of critical information infrastructure (CII). Here you will learn about threats to the information systems that communities, states, entire regions, and society depend on and how secure or insecure these may be against physical and cyber attacks from cybercriminals and terrorists. We end the chapter by discussing the potential for portions of the Internet to be taken down, why and how this could occur, and what contingencies are in place to mitigate harmful effects in the event of a temporary large-scale emergency. Once you understand this material you will be ready to delve into the many specific types of information technology (IT)–enabled abuse, attacks, and cybercrimes that threaten information systems and thus all of society.

## 2.1 Technology, Information, and Data in Justice and Security Management

**Technology** consists of combinations of tools and techniques that enable people to do things.[1] Technology is virtually everywhere, an extraordinarily broad concept "linking what is theoretically possible to the products of science, mathematics, and engineering."[2] IT is only one of many functional categories of technology used in criminal justice and security management. Other functional categories (i.e., the purposes for which technologies are used) include apprehension and detention, communications, forensics, protective equipment, records management, surveillance, and transportation. These and other functional categories of technologies are important because they enable protection of facilities and information systems ranging in size from small organizations to expansive networks of organizations and information infrastructure. IT finds its way into many functional categories of technology used in the administration of justice and security management, which underscores that technology is much more than computers or other electronic devices such as PDAs, cell phones, and iPods™. For example, modern modes of transportation rely on computer chips for combinations of electrical, hydraulic, and mechanical interoperability of vehicles including cars, trucks, trains, aircraft, and watercraft. Similarly telecommunications systems, whether landline, cellular, radio, or infrared, are replete with IT components such as switches, crystals, and frequency modulators. Security technologies such as those that employ biometric scanning devices also have IT and databases integrated into their design and operation.

Regardless of what they are designed for, once proven reliable, technologies tend to be adopted and used by increasing numbers of people and organizations for generally good or harmful purposes. Technology can also have unintended positive or negative spin-off effects within organizations and society. In some instances people accidentally discover alternative, constructive, and acceptable ways to use technologies. Information security professionals for example, may learn how to do things differently and better by experimenting with IT. In other instances, technologies can lead to unintended social or economic harm and unfortunately are also deliberately experimented with for deviant, abusive, or criminal purposes. This is why new variations, if not new forms, of technology-enabled deviance, social abuse, and crime occur.[3]

**Technology diffusion**, the widespread adoption of tools and techniques throughout society, depends substantially on users' preferences for certain product features along with their perceptions about what is needed to accomplish certain tasks. How much a technology costs, how it is likely to be perceived and used by employees or other users, and its compatibility with technological systems already being used within organizational settings, as well as market and social forces, also affect the extent and rate of technology diffusion. Preferences also have to do with a given user's knowledge, skill, and ability to use particular devices. These general conditions and principles have throughout history held true for all kinds of technology in varying geographic, social, economic, political and cultural environments.[4]

Criminal justice and security are closely associated in their core missions and use of technologies. Professionals in both fields, for example, are concerned with protecting facilities, persons, and property, inclusive of both physical and cyber assets. Members of criminal justice agencies and security firms, as well as security professionals and risk managers in other types of public agencies and private sector organizations, conduct investigations using a variety of similar technologies. They also apprehend, detain, and question perpetrators suspected of misconduct. Originally the fields of criminal justice and security were ad hoc in their organization and unspecialized in their operations. Officers in both fields tended to be generalists who accomplished any and all tasks expected of their agency, firm, or organization. For this reason, law enforcement and security specialists were able to do their jobs using relatively simple and general-purpose tools and techniques. Unlike early criminal justice agencies and security firms, modern organizations increasingly rely on several categories of very specialized and comparatively complex technologies and technological systems. In most instances these have been specifically designed to facilitate accomplishment of specific tasks required of personnel who specialize in using certain tools on the basis of technical professional training. Computer forensics experts and information security officers employed in either public or private sector organizations, for example, are specialists who use particular software tools to analyze data indicative of crime or breaches in information systems security.[5]

Complex technologies in the administration of criminal justice and security management are often depicted in popular television shows.

Additionally, "cop shows" increasingly feature crimes involving elements of cybercrime that are investigated and solved through computer and crime scene and laboratory forensics analysis, combined with traditional investigative methods such as surveillance and interviewing. Television and popular culture contribute to common beliefs that expert use of sophisticated and readily available technology enables quick detection and successful investigation of crime if not outright prevention of crime. Unfortunately, although the good guys have certain technological advantages over criminals, when it comes to cybercrimes, IT tools and techniques used by criminals often exceed the capabilities of criminal justice and security professionals.

Consequently, law enforcement and security professionals must continually play catch up, and they must learn to expect and watch out for new variations of IT-enabled crime and threats to information systems. This is important in the larger context of worldwide computerization because **technological complexity** hinders our ability to completely understand and manage environmental, economic, political, social, and other factors affecting the development, adoption, and widespread use of criminal justice and security technologies, as well as innovative use of technologies for illicit purposes by cybercriminals. To fully understand cybercrime and threats to information security systems at levels inclusive of individual computers, computer networks, and information infrastructures, we must grasp the nuances of information (i.e., what we are trying to protect) in fundamental ways.

### 2.1.1 Six Primary Characteristics of Information

Good information security begins with understanding what information we are trying to keep secure, which has to do with understanding which information is most valuable and why. This in turn involves understanding where and how data are used and the reality that all data regardless of the nature of the content have several primary characteristics. As explained by Donn Parker, they include information kind and type, representation, form, and medium, plus numerous secondary characteristics.[6] Here we add residence and transport status, plus perception of value as primary characteristics that also matter greatly for deciding which information needs to be protected and how. Hence, if you wish to adequately protect information, you need to know its kind and type, symbolic representation, form of structure and format, save-out and storage medium, residence and transport status, and perception of value.

These six primary characteristics of data are fairly self-explanatory, but it is important to also understand their interrelationships. For example, *kind,* as defined in the Box 2.1, pertains to content contained on Web pages, in word processing documents, on paper, and so on. This is important for information security purposes because different kinds of perpetrators or information system attackers are drawn to different kinds of information. Similarly, how information is represented may affect how vulnerable it is to particular cybercriminals. Many people would

not recognize one form of computer programming code from another. Consequently, in the absence of other intelligence about a particular set of codes, they would have no way of knowing how it is used or whether it is worth stealing. However, if the data were in a different form, they might recognize it for what it is and depending on their objectives, either destroy, manipulate, degrade, copy, and/or steal it. Therefore, the type and level of information security required pertains to the characteristics of given data relative to threat capabilities of potential attackers. Many similar explanations are possible for understanding the relative importance and interplay of all six primary characteristics of information. However, it is absolutely essential that information security professionals have a clear understanding of which information is regarded as most valuable and on what basis this determination has been made. Knowing this will often dictate which specific information with respect to its primary characteristics receives the most resources for its protection.

Now let us specifically consider how data is saved. Your school work may be recorded on

## BOX 2.1 • *Six Primary Characteristics of Data*

| | | |
|---|---|---|
| 1. | **Kind** | Information that is "descriptive, instructive, expository, factual, fictional, monetary, artistic," etc.[7] |
| 2. | **Representation** | Information in graphical, coded or symbolic form (e.g., alphabetic, numeric, or written in a computer programming language) |
| 3. | **Form** | A reference to the structure or format of information (e.g., written in prose, listed in tables, visually summarized in tables, etc.) |
| 4. | **Medium** | How information is stored or saved (e.g., written on paper or saved onto a CD-ROM or other type of portable disk, a thumb or key drive, or onto the hard drive of computer or iPod, etc.) |
| 5. | **Residence and transport status** | Pertains to combinations of physical and cyber locations, as well as types of media on which data can be stored and relocated. |
| 6. | **Perception of value** | What potential attackers think data may be worth, independent of how valuable it really is. |

paper and/or saved in electronic form in one or more locations requiring use of one or more simple to complex tools and techniques to secure it adequately. As indicated in Box 2.1, residence and transport status includes many types of electronic storage media such as thumb or key drives (which I try to keep with me just in case I need to save something from a computer or other device). If I were a cyber criminal, this commonly used and therefore unsuspicious device would enable me to easily copy information and transport it undetected if I could access an unprotected computer or other device with a USB port. Of course my willingness to take such a risk would depend on my perception of the value of the information as well as my technical skill for acquiring it. Thus, the six primary characteristics of all information relate specifically to opportunities for cybercrime and therefore also to the need for sound information security practices that take data characteristics into consideration.

### 2.1.2 Data versus Knowledge Management

What is information? What is data? What is knowledge? What is meant by data and knowledge management, and what have these concepts to do with preventing cybercrimes and securing information systems? To answer these questions let us briefly consider the following concepts, which criminal justice students may not already know and that I promise will be the most technical topics described in the entire textbook.

***Bits, Bytes, Code, and Data.*** A **bit** is the "1" or "0" digit used in machine language to tell a computer "either this or that" and that no other choices are possible. A **byte** is a sequence of eight bits (e.g., 10011010 or 11010001 or 11110001). A **programming word** is a sequence of eight bytes. Programming words are combined into **programming sentences,** and these

are further combined into **programming paragraphs** that comprise instructions called **code** that tell computers what to do. A computer programmer is a person who specializes in writing codes that instructs a computer what to do. **Software** is any type of programming **application** for doing something with a computer. Microsoft Office® is a set of several software applications including Word®, Excel®, Access®, PowerPoint®, and Outlook® that many people use to accomplish business-related, academic and personal tasks with computers. Other brand-name sets of software applications designed for use on various computer operating systems inclusive of Windows®, MAC®, and Linux®, etc., are used for general office and many specialized purposes.

Software programming, or simply code, is a type of intellectual property because it represents a unique creation by its developers. Complex software that enables a computer to serve myriad purposes is normally created by several if not dozens or even hundreds of people who combine their expertise to produce commercial or open source programming solutions. Some cybercriminals, depending on their interests, motivations, and technical skills, among other factors, act alone or in groups to write malicious computer codes such as viruses, worms, Trojans, and adware/spyware, or combinations of these harmful programs. Collectively, malevolent computer code is called **malware** (as in malicious software). Bits, bytes, words, and all greater assemblages of code comprise **data**. Data also consists of computer input and output, which as you know pertains to information put into and then executed and generated by a computer. Hence, the expression "garbage in, garbage out," or **GIGO,** means that information produced by computers can only be as good as the data inputted. As such, a cybercriminal need only access and manipulate input data or code used to process it to affect the quality and value of outputted information. Again this has implications for securing facilities as well as information systems in order to prevent cybercrimes.

*Information, Intelligence, and Knowledge.* We are in the process of creating a hierarchy of increasingly larger concepts, which taken together comprise a range of assets that need to be protected. As indicated above, bits combine to make bytes, which form code that produces data that may also be considered **information** which we will define as content that is understood. Many people make a distinction between data and information, but we will use the terms interchangeably because both data and information may: (1) be qualitative or quantitative in its structure and meaning, (2) exist in either or both electronic and hardcopy forms, and (3) be inputted into, processed by, and outputted from computers. In addition, both data and information can be understood correctly or misinterpreted, as well as degraded, misused, abused, and stolen. Given generally accessible and affordable IT devices, each may also be easily transformed into different types of media and transferred between locations in one or more forms. Again, as you can readily deduce, this has important implications for information security. To illustrate this concept consider the following 2001 case of international credit card fraud, which illustrates interconnections between hardcopy and electronic forms of information and data and the importance of controlling physical copies of credit card purchase receipts.

Once a year a couple vacationed in beautiful Puerto Vallarta, Mexico, known for its tropical forested mountains, mineral-rich volcanic slopes, and sunny ocean beaches—a potentially great spring break getaway location. Several months after returning to the United States from their lovely vacation one year the couple received a credit card statement that reflected a recent charge from a hotel in Puerto Vallarta, although not the one they had stayed at. The man contacted the financial institution that issued the credit card, which supplied him with a photocopy of the charge slip. On it was a signature that was neither his nor his wife's. Since their credit cards had not been lost or misplaced, it was obvious that someone had acquired the account number

by accessing paper copies or receipts at the hotel they did stay at and that verification of authority to use the card by signature and photo ID had not taken place. Clearly several security protocols were not being followed by merchants in Puerto Vallarta. Fortunately under federal law, U.S. residents are only responsible for the first $50.00 in unauthorized charges, so the couple was able to have their credit card numbers canceled and reissued without incurring a substantial loss. Note how this story exemplifies how information and data amount to the same thing, can be electronic or hardcopy, and can exist in various locations at which they are vulnerable to being illicitly acquired, misused, changed, or destroyed. Hence, the implications for information security are considerable.

To continue with our hierarchy, allow me, as a former security and police officer, to suggest that **intelligence** may be defined as information used for probabilistic reasoning and decision making. More intelligence is generally better than less intelligence, but the quality of intelligence is crucial, and this depends on its credibility (does it seem plausible?), validity (does it check out?), and reliability (does it come from trusted sources?). Intelligence is evaluated information about something previously unknown, and this too is very important to law enforcement investigators and security professionals. Conclusions about terrorist threats being credible and specific are made on the basis of intelligence analysis, which essentially involves determining the likelihood that a known threat can and will be carried out. This concept is very useful for information security professionals, who must continually scan the environment for possible, credible, and specific threats to facilities, information systems, and ultimately CI and CII (discussed later in the chapter).

After people have analyzed and determined the strength of intelligence, they are prepared to make informed decisions on the basis of what they can be reasonably sure they know. Possessing **knowledge** implies the importance of also knowing how you know something and being satisfied with this as a basis for deciding a course of action. **Epistemology** is the study of knowledge and generally pertains to how we know what we think we know. Periodically I will challenge students to explain how they know something they wrote in their term papers or said during a class discussion. You should do this often in your mind and when solving problems having to do with information security and cybercrime. For example, ask yourself, "How do I know that I know my computer data is safe?" If you are hesitant or are not sure, you have at least one and potentially several problems. The same goes for organizational environments that rely on networked computing resources. Professionally engage your colleagues to determine how it is that specific information is known, what assumptions have been made, and equally important, what is not known. By employing such logical inquiry you will be able to understand the root causes and potential best solutions to a given security threat or related problem.

Knowing how you know things is the key to managing data systems security. By extension, managing knowledge requires understanding (in reverse order) intelligence, information, data, coding, and so on. If you understand what data is, how it is generated, and how it relates to formulating intelligence and knowledge about security and investigative decisions that must be made, you are on your way to becoming wise by not taking what you know or others tell you for granted. Check your facts. Check your assumptions. Check your facts and assumptions over and over again. Strive to continually discern, on the basis of careful analysis and reassessment of facts and assumptions, that which is correct, incorrect, unknown, and suspicious.

### 2.1.3 Additional Knowledge and Data Considerations

Upto this point we have considered at a general level the nature of information that needs to be secure in dynamic operational contexts. In reality, huge amounts of data of every imaginable kind, representation, form, and medium exist within computerized information systems and transport media, and its relative value is constantly being perceived by authorized users, by potential abusers within organizational settings, and by attackers throughout society. This is just another way of saying that ideally everyone has access to data they need and are authorized to possess and use, and that unauthorized persons also prowl in and around information systems seeking data for malevolent purposes. It is also true that periodically nearly everyone has access to data they are not authorized to possess or use. Put differently, data can change from being legitimately to being illegitimately accessed, possessed, and used. Sometimes this happens through deliberate abuse, and at other times it may be the result of a policy change or negligence. The driver's license, student ID, or bankcard in your wallet, for example, contains personal information about you and of value to you, but these items can be lost, stolen, or damaged, putting you at potential risk and causing you to worry and be inconvenienced until they are located or replaced. Can you see how theft as well as accidental loss of a medium and data can occur without your always being able to determine with certainty why a loss occurred even though you know it did? Understanding why data was lost can be just as important as understanding what was lost.

***Possession versus Ownership.*** This brings us to two fundamental data concepts: **information possession** and **information ownership**. Possession of information pertains to data that you have in your mind, on your person, or within your immediate control. Papers in your backpack, music files saved on the hard drive of an iPod that's in your pocket, and other types of electronic files on a computer you are using qualify as being in your possession. Suppose, however, that you loan your iPod to a friend so she can listen to music while shopping and running errands. At that point, she would possess the music files and you would not (if they were not backed up on another system under your control), although you would still retain ownership of data as well as the iPod, even though they are not in your possession.

Now let's say your friend betrays your trust and claims the iPod and/or the music files as her own. Your rightful ownership is now questionable and your future ability to repossess the property is also at risk because you relinquished absolute possession and control of the device and data it contains. To get the iPod and music files back you may need to report the items stolen and produce documents or witnesses who can attest to your rightful ownership of the device and song data. Ownership pertains to a person's legitimate claim to property inclusive of information. Further, a person can be the sole owner of information even on shared computer systems such as those maintained by a college or university, or they may share ownership of information stored on either stand-alone or networked computer systems. To carry this idea to completion, information may be (pay attention—this can get confusing) possessed and owned, owned but not possessed, possessed but not owned, or neither possessed nor owned by one or more persons simultaneously in myriad locations depending on the IT and storage media involved. Once again, this has significant implications for understanding and managing cybercrime and security of information systems.

Distinguishing between rightful and authorized possession and ownership of data has tremendous implications for information security, investigation and prosecution of cybercrimes, and for civil action in cases of alleged copyright, trademark, patent and trade secret infringement. Further, the six primary characteristics of all information discussed earlier (see Box 2.1) may also have specific implications for establishing rightful ownership, especially in cases involving multiple simultaneous data possession and potential joint ownership. As a former police officer, I can tell you that the old adage of "possession is nine-tenths of the law" has a certain amount of merit, because most people who possess property have not stolen it and because most people protect their property from being stolen, or at least we believe they should. So, on a practical level, if you lose control of your data or IT device on which it is stored, you may expect to have your ownership of it questioned, and if you cannot somehow prove that you are the rightful owner, you may lose legal entitlement to use or profit by it. Who do you trust with what information? What steps do you take to control possession and ownership of your IT devices and data?

***Money as a Special Form of Data.***    When you think of money, what comes to your mind? Perhaps you think about cash, say $10 or $20 bills in your wallet or purse. I've been married for a long time, so I feel fortunate if I have a few coins in my pocket for an occasional cup of coffee! Both bills and coins are forms of money because they represent and store value while also providing a medium of exchange. In addition to currency and coinage, what other forms of money can you think of (i.e., ways in which you can exchange data representing value for goods or services)? Travelers' checks, money orders, promissory notes and cashiers' checks are hardcopy equivalents of money because they are tangible and can be used to purchase items or pay bills. They can also be exchanged for currency, as well as converted into or recorded as electronic data representing money, as when you return from summer vacation with a few leftover travelers' checks and deposit them into your checking account and then perhaps pay bills electronically via online banking.

Money is just another form of data that can be either hardcopy or electronic in form, which means funds associated with a given individual or financial account can simultaneously exist in either form, in various places, and in various combinations of instruments (e.g., cash, money orders, bond and stock certificates). Electronic forms of money include wire transfers (which happen to be a primary means of **money laundering**) and data transferred between financial accounts with credit, debit, or smart cards. In

1997, Joseph DeMaria allegedly used his car dealership to facilitate the exchange of $250,000 cash derived from illicit drug sales for checks issued to an associate as brokered by a third individual for a laundering fee of $5,000. As such, one financial institution (the car dealership) in one state used a rather simple funds transfer and conversion method to launder money in various locations.[8]

Money, as everyone recognizes, is a primary target of thieves. If money exists as a form of electronic data, such data is a natural target of cybercriminals. Money is also a near universal means of establishing and perpetuating power and exerting influence in a myriad of political situations, which has implications for corruption carried out by organized crime. In Chapter 3 you will learn about how organized crime and terrorist organizations engage in illegal enterprises and electronically launder money to perpetuate these activities. This means cybercrimes involving the movement and transformation of monetary data is central to domestic and transnational criminal organizations. The trick to keeping money data secure is to be mindful of its six primary characteristics while also tracking and managing its lawful possession and ownership in dynamic transformational environments. Therefore, remember that **money** is essentially: (1) a *medium of exchange,* (2) a means for *storing value,* and (3) a *unit of account.* Also understand that money in any electronic form is essentially data of special importance because:

- First, it is inherently valuable after being acquired. Unlike consumable items or durable property such as appliances or computers (which must be stolen and then fenced, often through a broker, in order to get cash), transference of electronic money requires relatively little if any physical involvement or interaction by cybercriminals. This reduces their risk of being detected and caught and increases potential profit by not having to pay a middleman a brokerage fee.

- Second, it can take many different forms and be easily transformed into different and multiple mediums of value storage. By transforming a large portion of an illicit sum of cash into money orders, credit cards, travelers' checks, and so on, as well as secretly shifting it to clandestine foreign bank accounts in countries with strong bank secrecy (i.e., privacy protection) laws, criminals make their spending habits and investment structures harder for investigators to identify. In other words, the transcendency of data representing money makes it harder to determine which activities and persons involved are illicit.

- Third, financial data transformations can be made easily and quickly as a result of online banking and mobile computing combined with a continuing desire by banks and other types of financial institutions as well as merchants to compete for your business (and money) by making exchange services available (e.g., buy groceries with a debit card and get $40 cash back). To a large extent, flexible financial data exchange allows individuals with nominal computing skills to become their own banker, accountant or stock broker and thereby move and transform money from the privacy of their home or office, while traveling, and so on. These factors combine to make money the most valuable and necessary type of data to protect.

- Fourth, acquiring money illegally is a primary goal of criminals, especially in large amounts by organized crime and terrorist groups who need money to finance operations and perpetuate illegal enterprises throughout geographic regions. However, criminal organizations also invest in, create, and operate legitimate businesses as a way of acquiring even more operating capital for both illicit and legitimate businesses. In so doing, they also reduce the suspicions of investigators as well as the overall financial and legal exposure of their operations. By divesting their sources of income and capital investments, organized criminals can use computers to hide money and the full extent of their enterprises. This is particularly important in criminal cases involving civil asset forfeiture in addition to criminal prosecution, as is typically pursued by prosecutors in drug smuggling cases. The implication of all this is that distinguishing between legitimate and illegitimate businesses, and therefore also between clean and dirty money, can be very difficult, and this underscores the reality that finance-related cybercrimes and financial data interplay is inherently complex yet important to understand for information security purposes.

• Fifth, money can be transferred between financial accounts located in several nations, all

*Electronic Money Transfer/Transaction. ATMs (automated teller machines) are commonly used day and night to make cash withdrawals or deposits and to transfer and effectively convert funds from one form of data or tangible asset into another. What opportunities for criminals does this form of technology create?* Photo by Nathan Fisk

having relatively strong bank secrecy laws affording considerable privacy to account holders and thus protecting against the prying eyes of foreign intelligence and federal law enforcement officers. Additionally, because funds can be moved into foreign bank accounts and used to acquire assets or otherwise support criminal operations abroad, criminals can take advantage of inconsistent and inadequate international laws, treaties, and regulatory conventions governing investigative and prosecution methods.

• Sixth, since acquiring money is a primary goal of criminals specializing in fraud and other types of financial crimes, people with money and individuals who do not understand the nuances of IT, such as many elderly people throughout the world, are especially vulnerable to being victimized through physical and/or cyber attacks, an important concept that we will address in some detail in Section 2.3.

## 2.2 Information Assurance

**Information assurance (IA)** is a relatively new term for information security, but with the implication that in addition to protecting data, we must also be concerned with assuring its confidentiality, integrity, and availability (CIA). IA came into vogue in connection with the President's Commission on Critical Information Infrastructure Protection (PCCIP), which was established in 1996 by Presidential Decision Directive 63 (PDD 63). For over a year the PCCIP explored America's vulnerable critical infrastructures (CI) and critical information infrastructure (CII) to physical and/or cyber attacks from criminals and terrorists. In 1997 the commission released its final report, *Critical Foundations: Protecting America's Infrastructures*, which made several recommendations for improving physical and information systems security at national, regional, and state levels, and within both the public and private sectors. Computer systems identified as needing greater protection were those that facilitate food production, manufacturing, transportation, communications, financial services, energy consumption, and national defense, among systems in other sectors vital to the national security and well-being. More will be said about CII in the last section of the chapter. For now however, you should understand that: (1) IA is the most widely used term for information security practices; (2) the goal of IA is to assure the CIA of data on systems; and (3) IA concepts and principles apply to personal, organizational, state, regional, and national computer systems.

Types of information in need of assurance include financial accounts and credit history; medical records and school and personnel employment data; intellectual property, proprietary product development, and manufacturing processes; marketing, customer, and sales information; criminal histories; and data pertaining to physical and information security systems. This list is far from complete, but it should provide you with a sense of what is at stake if information systems and the data they contain are not adequately protected. Can you name other types of information that need to be protected? How about classified government information pertaining to weapons development or impending military interventions overseas? Would you not also agree that ongoing criminal investigations of cybercrimes require special assurances, even perhaps to the exclusion of some investigators who do not have a need to know facts and circumstances of particular cases being investigated and who are also unlikely to be in a position to contribute any useful information?

The important points here are that many different types of information and data require differing levels of assurance inclusive of CIA and that providing information assurance is a responsibility as distributed as the information itself. Institutions and professionals who manage information on your behalf need to be cognizant of IA and protect your data for authorized use. Banking officials, for example, must be able to access your financial accounts in order to effect and log transactions. Similarly, doctors must be able to monitor your health and prescribe new treatments based on your medical history records and keep all such information confidential. Professors need access to your grades and related school information in order to adequately provide you with academic advice and other assistance you may need as a student. IA is a two-way street: professionals who access and use your personal data share responsibility with you for assuring its protection.

On some level, each of us is a de facto IA officer—a guardian of data and systems that others have entrusted to us or that we use. In other words, we are all responsible for IA, although depending on the type of information at stake, some people may be legally and ethically more responsible than other individuals for protecting it. On a personal level, you must to the extent possible ensure the IA of your personal data, files, and systems or risk losing them. If you personally do not adequately provide for IA, your data and that of others who use a shared or networked computer system are susceptible to being manipulated, destroyed, denied, or stolen. If you have ever been unable to submit a term paper or homework on time because your system was compromised, then you know what I am talking about.

### 2.2.1 The Basic Prescription for What is Needed: CIA

**Confidentiality**, **integrity**, and **availability** of information systems and data contained on systems—what information security professionals refer to simply as **CIA**—are the three fundamental concepts for ensuring IA. You can think of CIA as the means to put IA into practice. Thus, a primary goal of information security professionals is to ensure CIA of the systems and data for which they are responsible. However, just as each of us must aid in IA, so must we also assume personal responsibility for assuring the

CIA of our privately owned, possessed, or controlled data and systems. CIA is so important for implementing overall IA that further explanation of all three component concepts is in order.

***Data Confidentiality.***  Confidentiality pertains to privacy of data and therefore to technological capabilities and human willingness to keep information from prying eyes. People and organizations need to keep all data entrusted to them private unless it is intended or needed to be publicly available. Privacy expectations come about as a result of people trusting individuals with whom they exchange information and on the basis of informal agreements or formal contracts that their data will remain confidential. CIA has specific technology, legal, and interpersonal relationship implications.

First, privacy expectations are independent of the primary data characteristics discussed above and thus also of technology used for its protection. This means, on the one hand, that data can be expected to remain private regardless of its characteristics and the technology used to facilitate its generation, use, exchange, and storage. On the other hand, data may remain confidential through the use of a variety of tools and techniques, but the effectiveness of such technologies varies and depends on innumerable factors including, for instance, what an attacker might use to gain access to a system containing data being sought. You are right to hope that your data will remain confidential, but only within the limits of technology expertly used for its security. The implication is that if you wish to ensure the confidentiality of your information, you must acquaint yourself with the relative potential of the technologies used to secure it, along with the good will and technical abilities of individuals who will be using them to protect your data.

Second, expectations of privacy are legally determined on the basis of administrative and ultimately judicial interpretations of the Fourth Amendment of the U.S. Constitution. Legal issues

pertaining to lawful searches of computer systems and electronic devices, as well as seizure of information by authorities in connection with criminal and civil investigations, are discussed later in the text. Here, you should note that in general you have limited legal expectations of privacy regarding data about you that is maintained on government and nongovernmental computer systems that you do not own or control. Unfortunately none of us can completely control how confidential data about us will be accessed and used. Courts, for example, have ruled that no expectation of privacy exists regarding personal information saved on computers owned and maintained by a person's school or employer. This does not imply, however, that system administrators who can legally access your personal information actually do or would even want to. Ultimately we must do the best we can to ensure the confidentiality of our data and of that which is entrusted to us. We can start by adopting the practice of not sharing data that we do not want somebody to know and by assuring others who entrust data to us that we have the technological capability, professional responsibility, and personal willingness to keep it confidential within legal limits.

Third, as just indicated, data confidentiality has interpersonal social and professional relationship implications. Data privacy requires trusting people to use technology responsibly and with respect for you, your computer and electronic devices, and your personal information. However, people make mistakes and accidents happen and this may result in confidential information being released without the data owner's permission or knowledge. In other instances, data is damaged, lost, stolen, or publicly exposed as a result of attacks on information systems or cybercrimes of another sort. Regardless of the cause, when information is compromised, there is a natural tendency to blame people who are responsible. In instances of professional negligence finding fault is completely appropriate and may lead to data recovery and positive changes for ensuring data confidentiality in the future. However, to the extent private information is expected to remain confidential but does not, social and professional relationships will be damaged perhaps irreparably if it is determined that people entrusted with safekeeping data were negligent. Therefore, be careful with whom you entrust your data and be careful when accepting data from people whom you like and respect. Ensure that you are capable of protecting its confidentiality within the bounds of social, professional, and legal expectations of privacy or you may find yourself on the receiving end of personal animosity, professional ridicule, and a lawsuit.

*Data Integrity.*    **Data integrity** refers to information being kept in its original or intended form and not being intentionally or unintentionally tampered with. Data integrity means that when you open up an electronic file, it is in exactly the same condition as when you saved it. Not only does the data appear to be the same, but the underlying programming code that you cannot see is also exactly the same as when you were last working with a document. Computer code in the form of adware and spyware often has adverse affects on a computer system and may also be malicious in its programmed intent, yet these programs can remain undetected for long periods of time and affect the integrity of data files, software applications, and the overall operating system that you rely on.

Adequate information assurance requires data integrity with respect to all six primary characteristics previously discussed. This means data must be protected in ways that preserve its kind, form, representation, and medium in all states of use, storage, or cyber transmission and physical transportation so that its value and perceived value remain intact. The implication is that data integrity can be compromised in a variety of ways that have negative consequences even if files are not actually altered but are believed to have changed nonetheless. In other words, data integrity can be as

much about perceptions of data not being tampered with, as with its actually not being tampered with. This means data integrity has substantially to do with perceptions of human and technological integrity (i.e., can they be trusted to keep data safe?).

*Data Availability.*    **Data availability** pertains to data being reasonably accessible to authorized users. This is a primary goal of system administrators whose job it is to ensure data confidentiality and integrity and that it can actually be accessed and then used. After all, what good is privacy and integrity of data if it cannot be accessed and used? However, data accessibility also makes it proportionately vulnerable to being attacked. Store data in an encrypted form, behind a firewall, on a secure system not connected to the Internet, and with the access terminal located in a single room kept locked, within a facility that is also locked and guarded in numerous ways, and you can rest assured that, barring a natural disaster or bombing, your data will be secure. Obviously it will not be easily accessible, and therein lies the age-old conundrum of how to balance the availability of data with its confidentiality and integrity.

This shows that CIA constitutes opposing goals and thus inevitable tradeoffs. Generally speaking, to maximize data availability is to risk its integrity and confidentiality. Conversely, if data confidentiality and integrity are emphasized, availability of data may suffer. However, this is not strictly true because technology (combinations of tools and techniques) can be used to mitigate negative tradeoff effects.

Professionals trained in IT systems administration and information security practices have long recognized inherent tradeoffs in attempting to maximize CIA. Professional judgment in deciding the best design and management strategy for a given information system and set of circumstances will vary. CIA appropriate for secret data maintained by an intelligence agency within the federal government, or very confidential data like that managed by a private sector financial institution, may be very different than what is required in a college or university computing environment where nearly unrestricted access to information and relatively few confidentiality requirements are the norm.

## 2.2.2 Becoming Pragmatic about Information Assurance

Since simultaneously maximizing all three components of CIA is not possible, we need to become pragmatic in our thinking and delivery of IA. We must also recognize that although CIA is necessary for IA, it is insufficient as an overall framework for providing IA because it does not adequately address human factors involved in information systems security or intentional misuse, abuse, and commission of cybercrimes.[9] Put differently, IA is all about people using technology appropriately while recognizing that many (perhaps most) people will not always use technology in fully responsible ways. The fundamental assumptions underlying the need for IA are that

- IA is absolutely necessary for everyone because of our increasing reliance on information systems for vital societal functions as well as organizational and personal undertakings.
- IA is premised on understanding the characteristics of data plus inevitable neglect combined with potential abuse and misuse of information systems.
- Most people understand data at a general level, but few know how to safeguard it adequately; thus both people and technology must be distrusted to some extent, even as they are also trusted.

In this section of the chapter we address these assumptions respectively as IA principles pertaining to (1) the necessity of providing IA given limited resources and inevitable security investment tradeoffs, (2) the reality that IA is primarily about people and thus about human factors,

and (3) the need to distrust both people and technology because they can only be trusted alone or in combination to some extent.

***The Principle of Necessity.*** *We do what we must and more of what we can with available resources given inevitable tradeoffs.*

This principle of IA reflects the reality that people and organizations must do certain things to protect their information systems, but they have limited resources and must therefore prioritize, make choices, and settle for solutions that may not be optimal or preferred. We are all familiar with the need to make choices, but how do you go about deciding what to do when you cannot do everything? The short answer is that you begin by doing what you must. Deciding what you must do involves the difficult task of determining the likely consequences of not doing everything and then prioritizing what you will do on the basis of anticipating least likely and relatively less consequential harms. For example, given the choice to upgrade your personal firewall or pay the rent in a given month, you are probably better off paying the rent, especially if an alternative means of temporarily protecting your online computer activity can be arranged (e.g., not connecting to the Internet from home until you do have a personal firewall).

This is very straightforward, but information security tradeoffs at the organizational level are often much more complicated. This is because most organizations must assure CIA of enormous amounts of data with all six primary characteristics described above, in dynamic environments involving dozens if not hundreds or even thousands of system users. Organizations must also comply with laws and government regulations pertaining to their production or service operations, working conditions, and provisions for information assurance. Business owners and corporate executives know that ignoring or skirting laws and regulations is borrowing trouble, so they must be complied with, as must core business practices that produce income. Unless information assurance investments are required by law or directly relate to a firm's core mission, they must often unfortunately be put on an organization's wish list.

With this in mind, information security professionals must do more of what they can with available funds, expertise, and management support after or in furtherance of complying with laws and regulations in ways consistent with core business operations. For example, training personnel may be less expensive than new IA technology investments but help people become more productive while also meeting certain IA standards required by laws or regulations. Decisions about what to invest in for IA also depend on which specific information assets are most valued. This implies the need to be constantly aware of the state of your organization's assets, mission, and growth strategy in order to develop and implement appropriate IA investments and tactics. This subject will be revisited in Chapter 10 in the context of how to effect organizational changes for enhanced information assurance.

### The Principle of Human Factors. *Information assurance is first and foremost about people, not technology.*

People generate, use, and save information, and people use technology to accomplish these things. When things go wrong, it is people who are responsible and must also be held accountable, not machines such as computers, which merely carry out the instructions of human beings. We see this clearly when cybercrimes are committed by people and when people fail to adequately protect their computer systems. People are fallible. We all err in judgment and make mistakes; we cause accidents and inadvertently cause pain and suffering. If we do so intentionally or through our own negligence or recklessness, we may well have violated the law and are then subject to investigation, prosecution, and punishment. If our illegal actions involved the use of a computer or other IT device via an information system a cybercrime will have been committed. Human factors involving tangible objects are inextricable aspects of all cybercrimes; thus IA is first and foremost about people, not technology.

There is, however, a natural tendency for IT oriented people to view possible solutions to data related problems only in technical ways rather than in terms of human behaviors and non-technological organizational systems. Students majoring in computer science, software engineering, and IT administration, for example, often think about information security problems only in terms of better hardware or software. The old expression, "To a carpenter everything looks like a nail," succinctly conveys this idea. However, a computer outfitted with the best hardware firewall on the planet along with continually updated patch and antivirus protections will not overcome a user who writes his or her password down on a sticky note and leaves it on a computer screen in an insecure office or cubicle. It is also worth noting that social engineering, which is discussed in detail in Chapters 3 and 4, is fundamentally about cybercriminals tricking victims into granting system access or otherwise giving up confidential data. Defrauding people is at the heart of many types of IT-enabled crimes. This in turn implies that sound information security necessitates an element of distrust.

### The Principle of Distrust. Do you believe computer systems are fallible? Do you believe everyone can be corrupted for a price? Law enforcement and security management is premised on the reality that neither technology nor people can be trusted unconditionally. Good security policies, procedures, and practices take into account the reality that everyone periodically makes mistakes, experiences personal difficulties, and may under extraordinary circumstances be tempted to commit crimes. If you believe otherwise, you are naïve. In 1998, Jerome R. Sullivan was an FBI supervisory special agent charged with embezzling funds seized during execution of criminal search warrants. Thereafter he created a false paper trail and lied to FBI investigators to

steer them away from the truth. Court records revealed that Sullivan was involved in an ongoing pattern of criminal activity over a five-year period including embezzlement of $422,434.[10]

Benjamin Franklin reportedly once said, "Distrust and caution are the parents of security."[11] Indeed, human fallibility is why intelligence and law enforcement agencies conduct extensive background checks on prospective employees, inclusive of credit checks, driving records, criminal history, school transcripts, drug and substance abuse examinations, and so on. A candidate who abuses drugs or is experiencing financial difficulty is correctly considered to be of higher risk for employment in a sensitive position. The same principle holds true for existing employees—those experiencing personal difficulties may be correctly reassigned to less sensitive positions in order to relieve their responsibility and stress and to help reduce the risk of their being compromised in some way. The point is that people cannot be trusted unconditionally, which implies everyone is to be *distrusted* to some extent.

The same principle applies to technology. Even though computers and other electronic devices function as machines with minimal or no errors, they do make errors as the result of defective programming, broken parts, and so on. Therefore, information systems must also be distrusted to some extent. The problem of course is that as managers we must rely on and therefore trust both people and machines while also being wary of both and their interplay. For example, users who are computer savvy may be trusted to update software patches and virus protections while also using strong passwords and keeping them

---

**CYBER TALE 2.1**

### Who Can You Trust? Credit Card Fraud by "Friends"

After high school I moved to another city with some friends in order to begin college. I did not realize it then, but my roommate and our boyfriends had an expensive drug habit. My friend and her boyfriend would always take money out of ATMs with my bankcard. At first the amounts taken were little, so it took a while for me to realize that theft was occurring. Later, as the situation progressed, I changed my account access codes, but having lost trust in my friend, I slept with all my important information and belongings in my pockets. However, a couple of months later when I went to buy gas, my card was denied for insufficient funds even though I had deposited over four hundred dollars two days earlier.

It turned out that my "friends" had cleaned out my account and then disappeared. I did not see them again for months, and the police would not do anything about the money. During the months they were gone I thought everything was fine and just went about my business. Whenever I received credit card bills I never actually looked at them. Instead I'd just pay the amount due and forget about it. What a mistake! For four months my old "friends" had been using my credit card information to order stuff offline and then sell it to pawn shops for money to support their drug habits. I found this interesting because I was still in possession of all my credit cards.

On reflection, I realized that I never secured my statement information or shredded documents containing such personal information. So even after changing my account information and access codes, my *former* friends simply copied information from account documents, but they never took the cards so that I would not realize that I was being victimized until it was too late. They ended up charging over $3,500 on my credit card accounts. The police told me I was stupid and that there wasn't much they could do. In the end my former friends had to pay off the accounts, but they always made the payments late if they made payments at all, which screwed up my credit rating.

*Anonymous Student*

confidential. However, they may also abuse network resources by downloading illegal copies of music files or data-intensive files containing photographs for nonbusiness purposes. A user who is less savvy may compromise the overall security of a network by introducing malware without even knowing it, but would never pirate music even if he or she knew how. Hence, information security professionals must continually exercise good judgment about whom to trust relative to their capability to abuse technology intentionally or misuse it through negligence, while also continually assessing potential problems attributable to technology independent of people who use information systems.

## 2.3 Attack Dimensions

In committing cybercrimes, perpetrators use a variety of IT to facilitate scanning, stealing, analyzing, manipulating, storing, sharing, and/or destroying information. We also know information sought for any of these purposes by cybercriminals varies considerably, although in the beginning of the chapter we considered personal financial, health, and academic information as being of particular value to most college students. In what ways might such information be vulnerable to attack, or otherwise have its CIA compromised as a result of particular tools and methods being used by cybercriminals? Suppose we consider school notes, assignments, and other materials you need for an important class you are taking. Where do you keep the information, and in what form? Are some of the course materials in hardcopy, perhaps in the form of books or a notebook, while other materials are saved on a computer? On what other media do you keep valuable information, and where is the medium kept when not being used? How secure are those locations? Where else is your information kept, and who else knows about this? For example, do you have a file folder or file cabinet in which to save larger amounts of school materials and information

so you will not have to lug them around but can still locate them easily when needed? Do you back up electronic information originally generated and saved to a laptop, to a desktop computer at home, or perhaps to server space allotted you by your college or university? Do you sometimes convert hardcopy to electronic data by scanning it so it can be stored on a disk rather than on paper only?

As time passes we all tend to accumulate lots of information. Perhaps you save materials for all the classes you take, and presumably you also save banking, health, and other types of personal records. In time you will likely begin to save additional versions of some information on different media and perhaps store them in several places. Unless you follow very strict backup, overwrite, and filing system procedures, some of the information you save is bound to be more dated and different in form and thus less or more accurate and valuable to you and would-be cybercriminals who want it for some reason. Have you ever created two or more copies of the same file, knowing they are not actually the same and later wondered how important the *older* version of a file is? If you use two or more electronic devices to store information, you know exactly what I am talking about.

We also need to be concerned with the number of locations in which information is stored, regardless of the medium involved. What are the relative advantages and disadvantages of backing up and then securing information in hardcopy versus electronic ways? How many copies of information should be made? The answer to these questions of course depends on many factors including available technology, the true value of the data, how confidential and available the data needs to be, how and for what purposes it will be used, and so on. Sometimes data management procedures can result in creating more backup copies than necessary, along with more places and devices that consequently need to be secured and maintained. If only one copy of vital information gets in the wrong hands, it may be disastrous to you or your organization. Further, because you may have saved or stored data in multiple locations and potentially in more than one form depending on technology used, it may not be directly transferable or secured as easily as if it were kept in only one place and medium. Does this mean that keeping fewer copies is always better for security? Not at all! Depending on the situation, more copies may provide better security, at least with respect to backups. Another strategy is to maintain a master copy, inventoried copies, and control logs that track which materials and in what form(s) are in the possession of other people.

Depending on where electronic or manual records management devices are kept (e.g., in your computers or other IT devices, file cabinets, in boxes or storage rooms) they will be more or less accessible and secure. A folder containing papers in a locked file cabinet located within a locked office in a secure building is obviously more secure than papers lying visible on a desk in a common area shared by many people. Similarly, a computer system in a locked office and also locked down with strong access password protection (i.e., at least eight randomly chosen alpha-numeric characters that do not spell a word or name) is obviously more secure than a computer left turned on in an accessible area. Hence, information saved in either hardcopy or electronic form may be relatively more or less secure depending on several factors, including security technology combined with the number and relative security of physical and cyber locations in which information is stored. It is also useful to realize that, although rarely recommended, information can be very safe in nonobvious places and essentially insecure places. A scrap of paper listing all your valuable passwords that you keep hidden in a book on a shelf may be more secure than the same data saved on an electronic file, encrypted and stored on a secure computer system that other people manage—it just depends. In short, data characteristics (review Textbox 2.1) combined with the number of copies, amount of

access, and number of locations in which data is stored, plus relative security afforded to them vary and matter a great deal to the overall security of information and therefore to preventing cybercrimes. In this section we explore these issues in considerably more detail, with emphasis on dimensions of attacks. In Chapter 3 we will closely examine many specific types of attacks and cybercrimes.

### 2.3.1  Cyber versus Physical Attacks and Security Systems

The foregoing examples reveal that attacks on information systems can be either physical or cyber in nature, be directed against physical and/or cyber assets, and occur in one or more locations. This implies that computers are tools that can be used offensively and defensively while also being the objects of cyber or physical attacks. For example, a computer can be used to hack into another computer in order to steal data, in which case the incident would in the technological sense be a cyber attack against cyber assets. A computer could also be used to launch a cyber attack against physical assets, such as national CI that are controlled by computer systems. However, we can also imagine instances in which a physical attack caused physical damage to physical assets including computers but had no impact on the data contained on the computers (e.g., burglary and vandalism). Then again, if someone broke into an office, they could also inflict harm to cyber assets if they attacked computers and destroyed hard drives that alone contained the affected data.

Figure 2.1 illustrates that attacks launched against organizations range from being relatively less to more physical in nature and can involve theft, damage, or destruction to combinations of physical and cyber assets. However, it is important to note that all forms of attacks on information systems and cybercrimes involve physical as well as cyber dimensions (i.e., real-world physical actions by human beings using tangible tools

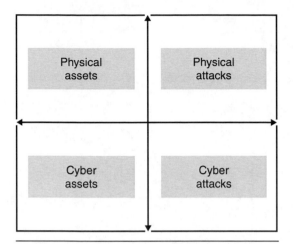

| Physical assets | Physical attacks |
| Cyber assets | Cyber attacks |

**FIGURE 2.1** *Threat Analysis Matrix*

and observable methods). Even so-called automated crimes, in which computers can allegedly employ artificial intelligence programming to carry out criminal acts, involve (1) tangible devices that were originally programmed by real a person in a physical location, (2) electronic interactions via physical telecommunications facilities and other types of physical infrastructure, and (3) theft, damage, disruption, denial, or destruction of information, leading to tangible losses for crime victims who are also real human beings. Never forget that physical aspects and therefore human factors are involved in all forms of computer abuse and cybercrimes. Given human nature, these abuses will inevitably be committed, even by authorized users of information systems, to the extent that adequate safeguards are not in place and carefully managed.

Regardless of the tools, techniques, and type of assets targeted in an attack, it is the physical nature of computers and information systems that underlie human aspects of cybercrimes, not the amorphous dimensions of cyberspace or those who occupy it in a virtual sense. In other words, cybercrimes are not committed by intangible bogeymen who are out there somewhere. Rather, cybercrimes, like any other form of crime,

are committed by people who live in the real world and who physically use tangible computers or other electronic devices as tools to benefit themselves at the expense of others. In short, computers do not commit crimes; people do, using tools, which is just another way of saying that all cybercrimes involve humans and technology, and hence are to be more or less distrusted as previously discussed.

It is important to remember when designing policies and procedures to prevent harm to information systems and data, and also when investigating and prosecuting cybercrimes, that people are physical beings who must attend to their bodily needs even though we all rely on information systems for our physical needs and enjoy using computers for many aspects of modern living. As social beings, people are naturally inclined to interact with each other for personal and professional reasons. As pointed out in Chapter 1, most of us live in family units of one kind or another; we work, play, are educated, and socialize in small to large groups, and over time through social norming processes we learn to function more or less successfully in organizations, institutions, and cultures. The human condition bears directly on the need for and design of data environments and on incidents involving theft or harm to information systems and data. As such, cybercriminals will always leave cyber or tangible clues that can be discovered and necessarily considered in an overall social and organizational systems context. This reality will be revisited in Chapter 9 which is devoted to investigating cybercrimes and prosecuting cybercriminals.

### 2.3.2 Insider versus Outsider Threats to Assets

All sorts of organizations secure a variety of a data. Online commerce firms, for example, need to secure customers' credit card and other personal information. With respect to providing security from external attacks, this can be accomplished with firewalls, confidential usernames and passwords,

I'M AS HIGH TECH AS THE NEXT GUY, VIRGIL, BUT A DIGITAL VIDEO
SURVEILLANCE SYSTEM NEVER TOOK A CHOMP OUT OF NOBODY'S ASS.

and even encryption of customer data once it is entered into databases. What about securing data against internal abuse and misuse? Contrary to common misperceptions about cybercrimes, the vast majority are not externally derived cyber attacks targeting cyber assets (e.g., computer hacking and theft, degradation or destruction of data in electronic form). Instead, most cybercrimes are committed by employees or others who have access if not also authority to use particular information systems and data. It follows that much insider cybercrime is committed by individuals who possess some level of technical computing skills, along with professional accounting, financial management, and/or legal training (i.e., white-collar criminals who have motive, opportunity,

CYBER CASE 2.1

---

### A Phone Service–Scamming Prison Warden

In 1995, Robert Fauver, the Warden of the Bradford County Prison in Pennsylvania, was charged with mail fraud and money laundering for misappropriating funds paid in connection with an inmate "call home" program. According to court records, Business Telecommunications Systems, Inc. (BTSI) was contracted to install and supply phone services for this purpose. BTSI charged a monthly fee to the county for inmates' use of phones, less a monthly fee charged by the prison, which, under Fauver's administration, served as phone service licensor. The call home program lasted only six months, but the monthly check arrangement from the county to the prison for administering the phone service continued for over two years, during which time Fauver converted the funds for personal use.[12] In this case, Warden Fauver had insider authority and control of monetary data without close accounting oversight.

and means to commit financial crimes, intellectual property theft, corporate espionage, or similar crimes using computers or other electronic devices). Cyber cases 2.1, 2.2, and 2.3 provide examples of how insiders abusing computerized information systems have committed embezzlement, fraud, and other types of financial crimes, sometimes in furtherance of drug smuggling or other street crimes.

Many firms outsource their Web storefront and billing application development needs. In the course of maintaining these systems, employees of both retail firms and companies contracted for Web development likely have ongoing access to

CYBER CASE 2.2

### A Collective of Money-Laundering Professionals

From December 1994 through March 1995 Angela Nolan-Cooper, a licensed attorney, brokered the sale of 50 kg of cocaine to Michael Taylor through an undercover federal Internal Revenue Service (IRS) special agent for $17,000 per kilogram. Nolan-Cooper and Taylor conspired with four others including a public accountant, a car salesman, and others in positions of trust. This enabled them to falsify financial records and move large amounts of cash in order to launder funds stemming from the sale of illicit drugs. Their methodology included creating a front company, LAR Productions, Inc., for the sole purpose of legitimizing illicit money through cash deposits into company bank accounts.

They used attorney-controlled escrow accounts to introduce, layer, hide, and then integrate dirty money into legitimate business affairs. For example, they intentionally rented out legitimate business office space to a sham company controlled by narcotics traffickers and purchased and leased cars in which they created hidden compartments in order to hide and smuggle drugs and cash. They also wire-transferred cash ($85,000 on one occasion) to a financial account located in the Cayman Islands. The total amount of funds laundered during four months of criminal activity was approximately $226,000.[13] Can you see the ways in which this crime spree involved physical and cyber dimensions?

CYBER CASE 2.3

### A Double Rip-Off Mortgage Scheme

Joseph A. Alegria was a corporate officer in Banker's Finance Mortgage Corporation (BFMC), a Puerto Rican lending institution that held first-position mortgages on numerous properties. For several months in 1994 Alegria sold dozens of mortgages to Citibank North America by purporting to cancel its first-position claim and transfer entitlement. Cancellation and transfers of mortgages by BFMC to Citibank did not take place in forty-eight instances, resulting in losses exceeding $5,000,000. Furthermore, Alegria arranged fraudulent papers inducing BFMC customers to pay Citibank but then arranged foreclosure on delinquent mortgage

payments still legally owed to BMFC. He also converted checks paid to BFMC to himself, which he was able to do as an insider employee with oversight responsibilities for such transactions. In the course of their investigation, authorities discovered Alegria had defrauded three additional lending institutions and numerous individual customers using the same basic scheme.[14] Given computer-based banking and insurance and mortgage services that existed in 1994, can you imagine what types of data, information systems, and other technologies Alegria accessed and used to commit these crimes?

databases containing customer information. To what extent should all employees of both firms be entrusted with access to such data? Using a program such as Cold Fusion or a similar powerful program commonly used for legitimate database connectivity and dynamic Web development, an unscrupulous employee could rather easily conduct queries, assemble and distribute, or even sell the credit card and other personal data of hundreds or even thousands of customers. Similarly, school, college, and university computer networks may be especially vulnerable to internal attacks from naturally curious and technically savvy students, who have unprecedented access to computers, little or no formal computing ethics training, and learn to use computers in environments often supervised by school administrators who may be unaware of information and network security issues.

Many computer science students have recounted incidents in which their junior or senior high school students' computer systems had been compromised. One student related that with no intention of causing harm, he simply began double-clicking icons on his school's library web site and found himself having root-level access to the main server of the school district. Further clicking presented an icon of his school's logo in Microsoft's Paintbrush application, so in the daydreaming manner of a bored seventh grader, he cyber-doodled on the icon. Several days later when he received a notice from the library about an overdue book, he noticed that the school's logo in the upper corner of the letter contained his doodling. In this case the student reportedly was able to fix the image, apparently without anyone else ever noticing the problem, but he still wonders about the extent of damage he could have caused if he had intended to. Historically most of these types of crimes have gone undetected, under-reported, or unreported.[15] Only to the extent that school and other types of organizational officials and IT administrators comprehend the potential for such abuse from authorized and unauthorized system users can prevention efforts be implemented.

### 2.3.3 Diagnosing and Responding to Threats and Attacks

The variety of ways in which cybercrimes can occur suggests the need for a way to diagnose incidents in order to formulate strategies for quickly responding to threats and attacks to information systems. To this point we have considered possibilities for combinations of physical and cyber attacks launched against physical and cyber assets committed by insider employees (or other trusted system users), or by outsiders without authorized access to information systems. Hence, the possible number, variety, and impacts of attacks faced by individuals, organizations, and government agencies are limitless. Figure 2.2 illustrates possible ways in which cybercrimes can occur with respect to asset, attack, and attacker status dimensions represented respectively by $X$, $Y$, and $Z$ axes, where: $X1$ = cyber assets, $X2$ = physical assets, $Y1$ = cyber attacks, $Y2$ = physical attacks, $Z1$ = insider attackers and $Z2$ = outsider attackers.

Conceptually, all cybercrimes can be located somewhere within the threat analysis cube. For example, an incident involving an outside hacker who uses a computer to break into a firm's system and then steals electronic data files would be located at an imaginary point contained within

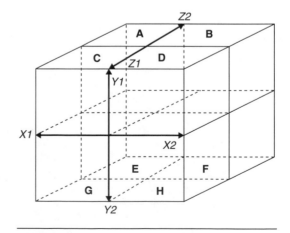

**FIGURE 2.2    *Threat Analysis Cube***

the smaller cube defined by $X1$, $Y1$, and $Z2$. Can you see how this point is located within subcube A toward the upper left rear corner of the threat analysis cube? Similarly, an incident involving an insider accountant who uses pen and paper to manipulate financial data on hardcopy records in order to embezzle funds from her firm would be located at a point corresponding to $X2$ (physical asset in the form of paper), $Y2$ (physical attack using a pen), and $Z1$ (insider employee). In this case, the point $X2$, $Y2$, $Z1$ positions the incident within the subcube H in the lower right front corner of the threat analysis cube. These realistic attack scenarios are easily understood because they represent simplistic actions by single individuals. In reality, attacks often involve multiple perpetrators who launch attacks from within and/or outside the organization and who employ a range of physical to cyber methods against combinations of physical to cyber assets. In other words, cybercriminals may work in groups and use various means in order to accomplish a range of objectives against multiple targets, located in different places, in different forms, on various media. Furthermore, all of this can occur during a single incident or in a series of cybercrimes spanning days, weeks, months, or longer.

Making multiple incident point plots within the threat analysis cube to represent various activities of one or more perpetrators associated with a single event or series of events is also possible, and this may be helpful for understanding the dynamics of abusive and illegal behaviors involved in certain incidents. In any situation, the idea behind conceptualizing abuses, attacks, or crimes along the XYZ axes of the threat analysis cube is to quickly assess at a general level the type of incident that needs investigating and managing and then match these dynamics to individuals who are capable of the behavior. In Chapter 4 we will explore the adversary assessment model known as SKRAM, originally described by Donn Parker, which can be used to further diagnose incidents with respect to offender skill, knowledge, resources, systems access authority, and motivations.[16]

Before you begin reading the next section, note that the threat analysis cube can represent many types and levels of information systems. For example, it could represent either your desktop or laptop computer or the combination of them. Alternatively a threat diagnostic cube could represent one or more servers on a network maintained by an organization. By extension, one or more cubes could represent networks of information systems, as in the case of interconnected critical information infrastructures, a major topic considered in the next section. Whether and how investigators or information security professionals use the threat analysis cube is of course up to them, as long as they never forget the range of possible ways in which system abuses and cybercrimes can occur.

## 2.4  Critical Infrastructure Protection

In August of 2003, the United States experienced the largest power outage in its history not caused by a natural disaster. What began with the failure of a single nuclear power plant in Ohio was quickly followed by the failure of two additional Ohio electric power-generating plants that were unable to provide sufficient reserve power to meet customer demand. Within hours there were serious electrical outages across the state, and Ohio sought supplemental electricity from other generating plants throughout the U.S. power grid. Power plants diverting electricity to meet Ohio's request for more power began automatically shutting down to avoid burning out or otherwise disconnected from the affected grid area in order to avoid a nation-wide catastrophe. It was too late, however, for many northeast cities. New York City lost power for several hours, Detroit's power was not restored for 30 hours, and Cleveland took 31 hours to get its electricity back on. It was 72 hours before power was restored everywhere, which means some people did not have lights, could not use air conditioners, could not pump gasoline, and so on, for three straight days.[17]

*Telecommunications and computing capabilities depend on electricity. Electrical power supply plants and switching stations such as this one located on Three Mile Island on the Susquehanna River in Middletown, Pennsylvania, form the backbone of America's critical information infrastructure capabilities. As such, they are considered to be prime targets for physical and cyber acts of terrorism, and require the highest possible levels of national security as well as other public health and safety precautions.* Phil Degginger/Getty Images, Inc.

How many times have you experienced a power outage? What were you not able to do? In retrospect, did the absence of electricity merely inconvenience you or were you completely prevented from accomplishing things you had planned to do? How long did the outage last? What would you have done if the power outage had lasted several days or even a few weeks? Electricity, as you know, is the power source of computers and therefore the basis for committing many types of cybercrimes as well as carrying out many aspects of information security. Without electricity, many things simply cannot be done, at least not in the way we are used to accomplishing them or expect them to occur. This means that abuse and crimes involving information can still occur when the power goes out, and this is especially true to the extent that facilities, security depends on electricity. The implication here is that with or without electricity, computers, information systems, and data still need to be protected. Now let us expand our consideration of the importance of electricity and its implications for security.

The interdependent critical infrastructures and critical information infrastructures explained in this section enable modernized societies to function. If you research something on the Internet, communicate using any form of computing or telecommunications device, or ride in any form of public transport, it is because computers powered by electricity enable you to do so. Weather forecasts aired on television, environmental control settings in buildings, and cars equipped with fuel injection or onboard GPS/GIS navigation systems among myriad other technological systems are the result of computerization ultimately made possible by electrical energy. The same is true of the amount and quality of items harvested or mined, produced by agricultural centers and industrial manufacturing firms, shipped by warehouse and transport operations, or inventoried, advertised, and sold by retail outlets.

Banking and other financial services also depend on electrically powered computer systems. Without power and problem-free computer systems, depositing or withdrawing funds, shopping online or in person, and the making payroll becomes impossible. On June 4, 2004, the Royal Bank of Canada reported that a computer programming problem resulted in more than 10,000 provincial government employees not receiving paychecks totaling $11.4 million. More than 3,000 additional city government and power utility workers were also affected. The programming error, although not indicated to be the result of a cybercrime, took several days to fix, during which time hundreds of cash-strapped people were undoubtedly without funds to pay their bills and purchase groceries, fuel, and other needed items.[18]

Computers are everywhere and are integral to all modern technological systems. IT is now engineered into virtually all the machines and technological systems that enable modernized societies to function. The concept of **interdependency** pertains to inextricably interconnected parts of an overall socioeconomic and technological system. As the Internet has come to represent and support visions of an information superhighway, the backbone of a **U.S. National Information Infrastructure (NII)**, society itself may be regarded as an IT-enabled system consisting of smaller interdependent systems all connected to support justice administration, security and crises management, health care, environmental monitoring, transportation, education, research and development, entertainment, recreation, manufacturing, banking, national defense, and so on.[19]

The concept of **globalization** (a result of computerization) pertains to a world consisting of interdependent nations, each comprised of and reliant on interconnected technological systems. While offering many benefits, we also know that since at least the early 1990s, these systems have provided an attractive means to commit cybercrimes via the World Wide Web and are now also targets for physical and cyber attacks, especially during times of war between nations.[20] In 1996, the United States became the first country to officially address national vulnerabilities associated with interdependent technological systems. According to the PCCIP, **infrastructure** consists of

"the framework of interdependent networks and systems comprising identifiable industries, institutions (including people and procedures), and distribution capabilities that provide a reliable flow of products and services essential to the defense and economic security of the United States, the smooth functioning of governments at all levels, and society as a whole."[21]

Essentially, a nation's infrastructure consists of all technological systems and facilities that enable its society to function. Buildings, airports, and other public transportation facilities and seaports are all examples of infrastructure—so are roadways and railways inclusive of bridges, tunnels, and traffic monitoring and signaling control systems. Mining and manufacturing facilities, electric power and water utility plants, natural gas and petroleum refineries and pipelines, as well as wired and wireless telecommunications systems all exemplify the concept of infrastructure. No wonder that during times of war between nations, infrastructure is often targeted for destruction or disruption. Terrorists also periodically attack components of infrastructure upon which many people depend in order to maximize the attention given to a violent incident such as a bombing. In Chapter 3, we will consider how cyberterrorism and network-centric warfare constitute forms of IT-enabled cyber conflict.

## 2.4.1 What are Critical Infrastructures and Critical Information Infrastructures?

**Critical infrastructures** (CIs), as defined by the PCCIP, are combinations of systems and facilities "which are so vital that their incapacitation or destruction would have a debilitating impact on [a nation's] defense or economic security."[22] Thus, critical infrastructures are the essential technological components required for a nation's survival. **Critical information infrastructures** (CIIs) are subcomponents of CI that are also required for a nation's survival, but these consist of interdependent electrical energy, communications, and computing systems. In other words, CIIs are electronic technological components of the CI that enable nations to exchange data needed to produce essential goods and services that people rely on in their everyday lives. **Networks and services integral to CII** include[23] (1) electrical power grids, the Internet, and online services; (2) public switched telephone, public safety, and defense and national security data networks; (3) cellular, commercial satellite, radio, broadcast and cable television networks, and direct broadcast satellite TV; and (4) education, financial, health, publishing and entertainment information services, and so on. Specific **components of CII** consist of data input, processing and output hardware and software; electronic devices such as keyboards, monitors, telephones and cell phones, fax machines, scanners, printers, digital cameras and video devices, and PDAs; data storage medium including drives, disks and data, and video and audio tapes ranging in physical sizes and memory capacities; copper and fiber-optic cable, wire, and microwave nets; and of course, human beings who use, abuse, and misuse them.

When CII malfunctions for any reason, things cannot be done. In December of 2004, a combination of weather conditions and computer problems forced Comair, a subsidiary of Delta Airlines, to cancel 1,100 flights, stranding thousands of holiday travelers throughout the nation. The computer system used to schedule flights crashed after being overwhelmed as the result of passenger cancellations and delays caused by snowstorms throughout middle America. The severe weather also caused major power outages throughout the Southeast and Midwest, further resulting in widespread inability to turn on lights, effectively heat homes and businesses, and pump gasoline and other sources of liquid fuel for heat and transportation.[24] Obviously CII may also malfunction as a result of attacks or cybercrimes, such as those involving hacking, denial of service, and/or release of malware onto the Net, affecting any combination of components, networks, or services. Between 1993 and 1995, unidentified intruders reportedly attacked service control and signal-transfer points; network

elements and network element managers; and systems that supported billing, provisioning, loop maintenance, document support, digital cross connections, and R&D. Since that time similar incidents have occurred with increasing regularity in the United States and other computer-reliant countries.[25]

Three specific large computer networks that the United States relies on for the exchange of data, and that effectively constitute the bloodlines of America's CII, are the Internet, Mil Net, and Internet II. These systems were developed during the last fifty years beginning with R&D undertaken at the Massachusetts Institute of Technology (MIT) in the late 1950s. In 1983, the original ARPANET, developed by MIT in collaboration with several other universities and the Department of Defense, split into Mil Net and the Internet, which thereafter were respectively used for military versus civilian and commercial purposes. Internet II was also created to support communications associated with R&D activities of federally funded research and development centers inclusive of federal labs, colleges, universities, and certain other academic institutions that house supercomputers or receive research funds from the federal government. Essentially, Internet II provided a replacement for the original ARPANET. Each of these mega networks consists of wired and wireless electronic systems, employs different protocols for communications switching (to send and receive messages between locations) and information security standards and has different data and server exchange capacities.

The basis for message traffic routing over the Internet is the Generic Top Level **Domain Name System (DNS)**, which provides for universal resource locator (URL) addresses (e.g., those ending with the familiar .com, .org, .gov, and .edu) and maps numerical machine identifiers to geographic locations. This system was developed in 1998 by the U.S. Department of Commerce's National Telecommunication and Information Administration with support from a California-based corporation, the Internet Corporation for

Assigned Names and Numbers, in cooperation with foreign governments and entities including the World Intellectual Property Organization. The Generic Top Level Domain Memorandum of Understanding is the formal document that provides an international framework for ongoing administration and enhancement of the DNS. Policies contained in this document were developed in cooperation with the Internet Assigned Numbers Authority (IANA), which manages the DNS to promote Internet stability and robustness for all types of communications purposes. IANA works with the advice and oversight of the Internet Policy Oversight Committee, whose members represent an international body of key government, industry, academic, and not-for-profit organizations.[26]

### 2.4.2 Conceptual and National Differences in Infrastructures

International policies for administration and enhancement of the DNS include no definitions or protocols pertaining specifically to CI or CII. Because resources of the world, both natural and manmade, are inherently limited, nations have defined critical infrastructure and survival in relation to the existence of CI and CII differently.[27] In other words, governments and people throughout the world think about CI and CII in different ways. For example, the government of Canada defines national critical infrastructures (NCI) as "physical and information technology facilities, networks and assets, which if disrupted or destroyed would have a serious impact on the health, safety, security or economic well-being of Canadians or the effective functioning of governments in Canada."[28] Note the subtle but important differences and implications between the U.S. PCCIP concepts of CI and CII (previously defined) and Canada's NCI.

In addition to various and evolving conceptions, labels, and definitions of core technological systems upon which nations depend, there has been a gradual evolution of protection strategies pertaining to CI and CII throughout the world.

Originally, critical infrastructures were considered to be those whose prolonged disruptions could cause significant military and economic dislocation. Today however, CI may include national monuments (e.g., the Washington Monument), where an attack might cause a large loss of life or adversely affect a nation's morale.[29] Austria, Australia, Canada, Finland, France, Germany, Italy, the Netherlands, New Zealand, Norway, Sweden, Switzerland, the United Kingdom, and the United States now differ with respect to their specification of critical sectors, policy initiatives, organizational structures, and approaches for providing early warning of threats to CI and CII.[30]

Definitions of CI vary according to fundamental questions such as, "Critical for whom, under what circumstances, and for how long?" The issue here rests on the reality that "critical" and "survival" depend on a given nation's perceptions of priorities and upon who makes decisions about the allocation of limited resources in emergency situations. Critics of broad interpretations of CI claim, for example, that sources of information such as television and AM/FM radio broadcasting, even though used to make public announcements in emergencies, are less important than having adequate clothing, shelter (e.g., heat), and food to eat. Advocates of broad interpretations of CI, however, argue that noncritical systems are integrally engineered into critical systems and that without subsystems, major systems will not function. Differing interpretations are important because they may affect the types and levels of national resources devoted to protect systems from widespread harmful affects caused by a range of natural disasters and cyber conflicts (e.g., cybercrimes, cyberterrorism, and network-centric warfare). Do you think in the aftermath of Hurricane Katrina, which struck several Gulf coast states in August of 2005, that it was more important to re-establish electrical and communications systems, or to provide medical assistance, food, water, and shelter to the tens of thousands of people living in New Orleans and many other places that were directly impacted by the winds and flooding of the storm? Can you see how distribution of services and supplies needed for human survival especially during times of crises depend on CII?

## 2.4.3 Critical Information Infrastructure Protection

**Critical information infrastructure protection (CIIP)** is now considered a vital aspect of national security policy planning. The **U.S. Department of Homeland Security (DHS)** was created following the terrorist attacks on September 11, 2001, as authorized by Congress in The Homeland Security Act of 2002. This law gave DHS lead responsibility for protecting CII within the United States. The act also resulted in reassigning numerous existing federal law enforcement agencies, security, and emergency services as DHS components. Agencies that now help make up DHS include the Federal Emergency Management Agency (FEMA), the U.S. Coast Guard, the U.S. Secret Service (USSS), the Bureau of Immigration and Customs Service inclusive of the U.S. Border Patrol, and the National Infrastructure Protection Center (NIPC), formally of the Federal Bureau of Investigation. The act precluded also transferring the FBI's Computer Investigations and Operations Section (CIOS), thereby retaining authority of the Bureau to investigate cybercrimes along with the Secret Service and myriad other federal, state, and local law enforcement agencies.[31] Another law, the National Security Intelligence Reform Act, enacted in December of 2004, contains provisions for restructuring numerous federal intelligence agencies, many of which are concerned with preventing and interdicting cybercrimes committed by transnational organized crime and terrorist groups.

DHS now consists of the following five major directorates:[32]

- *Border and Transportation Security (BTS)* is the largest of the DHS directorates. It is responsible for maintaining border security and transportation systems. BTS consists of the Transportation Security Administration, the former U.S. Customs Service, the U.S. Border Patrol and other border security functions of the former Immigration and Naturalization Service, the Animal & Plant Health Inspection Service, and the Federal Law Enforcement Training Center (FLETC) located in Glynco, Georgia.
- *Emergency Preparedness and Response (EPR)* works to ensure that the United States is prepared for, and able to recover from, terrorist attacks and natural disasters.
- *Science and Technology (S & T),* coordinates DHS efforts in research and development of security and counterterrorism technologies, including those needed for preparing for and responding to terrorist threats involving weapons of mass destruction.
- *Information Analysis and Infrastructure Protection (IAIP)* identifies and assesses a broad range of intelligence information concerning homeland security threats.
- *Management* is the directorate responsible for budgeting, personnel matters, and other DHS administrative issues.

Other important subdirectorate components of DHS are the[33]

- *Office of State and Local Government Coordination:* supports and helps coordinate homeland security and emergency response services provided by local, state, and federal governments.
- *Office of Private Sector Liaison:* provides businesses, trade associations, and other nongovernmental organizations with a means to offer assistance and register concerns pertaining to the protection of critical infrastructures, among other issues.
- *Office of Inspector General:* serves as an independent and objective inspection, audit, and investigative body to promote efficacious and legal DHS operations and administration.

Additionally, the National Infrastructure Advisory Council (NIAC) "provides the President through the Secretary of Homeland Security with advice on the security of information systems for critical infrastructure supporting economic sectors

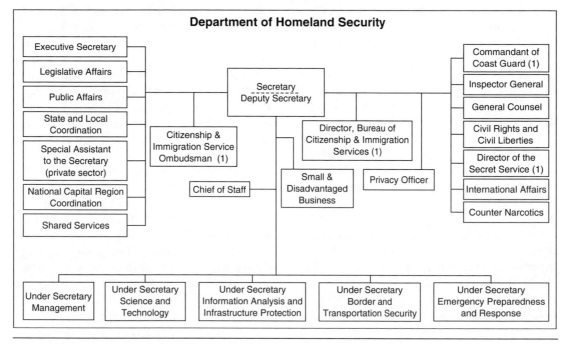

**FIGURE 2.3**  *Organizational Chart of the U.S. Department of Homeland Security*

*Source:*  U.S. Department of Homeland Security Web site.

such as banking and finance, transportation, energy, manufacturing, and emergency government services."[34]

### 2.4.4  Can the Internet Be Taken Down?

There is nothing new about protecting CII, which has been occurring in the United States since World War II, but in earlier historical periods nations did not rely on electronic systems for commerce, provision of utility services, transportation, education, and a myriad of government and private sector services to the extent that modern societies now do.[35] Given the extent to which societies now depend on electricity to operate the telecommunications and computing systems upon which nations increasingly rely, physical protection of CI and cyber security of CII as defined by the PCCIP is paramount to the national military and economic security of the United States and allied nations. According to the computer security

intelligence firm Mig2 in January of 2003, the United States, United Kingdom, and Germany are the nations whose government agencies were most frequently attacked via the Internet.[36] Studies undertaken by the U.S. Department of Defense suggest that organized crime, terrorist organizations, or other nations may have already launched computer viruses and worms of a limited nature against U.S. targets including the Pentagon in order to test the security of U.S. critical infrastructure. Such attacks, if real, would certainly constitute threats to national security.

On November 2, 1988, Robert T. Morris, Jr., a graduate student at Cornell University and son of a chief scientist at a division of the National Security Agency (NSA), launched a self-replicating worm on the government's ARPANET to test its effect on UNIX computer systems. Within a very short period the worm spread and jammed up over 6,000 government and university system computers. During this incident, a substantial portion of the Internet throughout the northeast United States became inoperable. This incident alone demonstrated that the Internet is vulnerable to being taken down, at least on a limited scale and for the time needed to launch additional multifaceted, staged attacks.

Could a more complex worm or other form of cyber attack take down the Internet today on a larger scale and for a longer period of time? If so, to what extent could inoperable portions of the Internet compromise critical national military and economic capabilities, and what other consequences could occur? Experts in infrastructure protection disagree about the answers to these and other questions pertaining to the defense capabilities for assurance of the nation's CI and CII. Some experts have warned that a massive, well-planned attack on U.S. CCI could result in substantial portions of the Internet being taken down for operationally useful periods of time.[37] This implies that cyber attacks on CII could be combined with physical attacks on CI facilities and could be staged to occur at different times in different locations and involve combinations of complex methods, all in connection with criminal, terrorist, or nation-state attack scenarios. (These possibilities will be taken up in more detail in Chapter 3.)

While governments throughout the world are likely to be the targets of foreign nations or terrorist organizations, possible motives of organized crime groups for launching massive cyber attacks against a nation's CII are far less clear, perhaps even illogical. On the one hand, organized crime thrives on the stability of government-protected economies to sustain its *legal* business enterprises. More legal goods and services can be provided for profit during peacetime when people are gainfully employed and generally have more disposable income and security restrictions are relaxed. On the other hand, organized crime also profits via black markets, money laundering and tax evasion, which are potentially most lucrative in relatively poorly regulated geographic, political, and economic environments. Even so, adolescent hackers with no specific foreign agenda have already demonstrated their ability to compromise secure systems of the

U.S. government. In 1998, authorities detected intrusions into Department of Defense computer systems that appeared to be coming from the Middle East. Owing to the timing and the ongoing Iraqi weapons inspections at the time, it was assumed that these attacks were originating from Iraq. A subsequent investigation called Solar Sunrise, however, found the perpetrators to be two teenagers from California and another from Israel. The teens were later prosecuted but not found guilty of any international conspiracy or any connection to organized crime or terrorist groups.[38]

Cyber attacks today are much more complex and potentially destructive than Morris's worm. Information security systems are also much stronger than they were twenty years ago. On balance, is the Internet more or less secure today than it was in 1988? Although no one can answer this question for all CII sectors, nearly all security experts agree that the open nature of U.S. society makes CI relatively vulnerable to physical attacks, and therefore CIIs are also vulnerable to the effects of physical attacks as well as cyber attacks such as those involving complex denial-of-services attacks and malware.

## 2.5 Chapter Summary

Technology is needed to carry out, investigate, and prevent virtually all forms of crime. Thus, technology is fundamental to the capabilities *and* vulnerabilities of criminals and to those of police, other types of criminal justice agencies, and the managed security industry. Functional categories of technologies pertain to the purposes for which technologies are used. IT is primarily used for computing and telecommunications, and therefore it is fundamental to the administration of justice and information security. Cybercriminals also use computers and other electronic devices in illicit ways to gain and then exploit technological advantage over others for their own selfish purposes.

Protecting information requires fundamental understanding of data, the information systems on which it exists, and the physical environment surrounding and supporting the functioning of these systems. Bits, bytes, words, sentences, and paragraphs combine to form programming codes, a specific type of data comprising intellectual property in its own right. Information is composed of data sets that when combined and validated to form intelligence provide the basis for making informed decisions relating to information security and law enforcement investigations, among other issues. At a general level and for basic security purposes, data and information may be regarded as the same thing.

All information has six primary characteristics: kind, representation, form, medium, residence and transport status, and perception of value. All information and data are not equal in value. That which is regarded as more valuable requires relatively greater protection than less valuable information and data. Electronic forms of money are a special type of data that, like tangible currency, financial notes, and so on, requires the highest possible security. Everybody who uses IT may lay claim to owning or possessing information, two interrelated concepts that should affect how we go about protecting data we consider valuable and/or that we are responsible for.

*Information assurance* (IA) is a relatively new term for information security that encompasses the classic framework of data confidentiality, integrity, and availability (CIA); possibilities of multifaceted attacks and assets; and the role of human factors in protecting information systems. IA is a robust concept, but information security professionals must be savvy about human nature as they attempt to implement it in the design of information systems security. The principles of necessity, human factors, and distrust offer starkly realistic perspectives that must be considered on a daily basis as information security professionals interact with and manage people, data, and information systems.

Information assets are contained on information systems located within and among physical facilities. Preventing cybercrimes involves protection of *both* physical facilities and information

systems against *both* physical and cyber-based attacks that may involve perpetrators working alone or in combination, from inside or outside of an information systems environment, and using a wide variety of tools, techniques, and tactics. Put differently, cybercrimes almost always involve aspects of traditional "physical crime." Conversely, many types of traditional crime also depend on perpetrators using information and IT to plan and carry out their attacks.

The threat analysis matrix and the threat analysis cube can help professionals conceptualize the nature of a given threat, abuse, attack, or crime. However, it is generally believed that most cyber abuse, attacks, and crimes are committed by trusted individuals or small groups of insiders who already have access to data on information systems. All of us are potential cybercrime victims. In unwitting ways we can all contribute to the overall vulnerability of a physical facility and information systems through our own negligent use of security-related information and IT. For example, if we are sloppy in protecting our personal computer by not updating antimalware definition patches, we will invariably expose all computers on a given network to online viruses, Trojans, worms, and other malicious forms of programming such as spyware.

Critical infrastructure (CI) and critical information infrastructure (CII) comprise the technological systems that nations rely on for essential products and services. CI and CII are defined by nations somewhat differently, and these concepts continue to evolve with greater understanding about potential technological threats and ways to safeguard physical facilities and information systems. In the United States, the Department of Homeland Security has primary authority and responsibility for protecting CI facilities and CII systems. A key strategic question pertains to possibilities for taking down the Internet for what has been termed operationally useful periods of time. The implication is that large-scale, multiphase, and multidimensional attacks on CII and CI by criminals or terrorists present unprecedented concerns for U.S. national security because of our society's reliance on these systems.

In this period of evolving high-tech crime, it is essential that criminal justice and security professionals understand the potential for and inextricability of attacks on CI and CII. Professionals must also understand how technology is or could be used in crimes generally and for security and investigative purposes. Accordingly, they must also understand the principles, processes, conditions, factors, and potential impacts of the use of technologies to commit crimes, as well as of preventing, controlling, and managing the impacts of crimes ranging from physical to cyber in their modes of operation. With such understanding, security professionals will be better able to recognize causes and correlates of illicit behaviors and anticipate the potential for such behaviors. They will also be able to prevent and control future crimes involving attacks on information systems while managing security issues within their organizations and communities. After all, managing crime and cybercrimes and the effects of these involves understanding and using technology wisely.

## Key Terms and Concepts

Application, 33
Availability, 39
Bit, 33
Byte, 33
CIA, 39
Code, 33
Components of CII, 54
Confidentiality, 39
Critical information infrastructure protection (CIIP), 55
Critical information infrastructures (CII), 53
Critical infrastructure (CI), 53
Data, 33
Data availability, 41
Data integrity, 41

Domain Name System (DNS), 54
Epistemology, 35
GIGO, 33
Globalization, 53
Information, 34
Information assurance (IA), 38
Information ownership, 35
Information possession, 35
Infrastructure, 53
Integrity, 39
Intelligence, 34
Interdependency, 53
Knowledge, 34
Malware, 33
Money laundering, 36

Money, 37
Networks and services integral to CII, 54
Programming paragraphs, 33
Programming sentences, 33
Programming word, 33
Software, 33
Technological complexity, 31
Technology, 30
Technology diffusion, 30
U.S. Department of Homeland Security (DHS), 56
U.S. National Information Infrastructure (NII), 53

## Critical Thinking and Discussion Questions

1. Explain why physical security and cyber/virtual security of assets are equally important. Name three ways of providing or enhancing both security and cyber/virtual security. For each tool or technique listed, provide an example of the type of asset to be protected.
2. Think about a particular source of data. Explain who currently owns and possesses it and explain the legal basis in general terms. Then provide an example of what could happen to alter the ownership or possession status of data. Be specific about the IT involved.
3. Describe an event in your life involving three different forms of money, in which you lost some portion of the funds. What contributed to your losing some of your money? What could you have done differently to prevent this from happening?
4. In your own words, define data (1) confidentiality, (2) integrity, and (3) availability. Then briefly explain why these concepts are essential but insufficient aspects of IA.
5. Describe a hypothetical example of the principle of necessity at work in a physical and/or information security situation. Be specific about what actions were required and why.
6. Describe a hypothetical example of the principle of human factors at work in a physical and/or information

security situation. Be specific about which actions taken by people resulted in compromising facilities or systems and what might have been done to prevent this situation from occurring.

7. Describe a hypothetical example of the principle of distrust at work in a physical and/or information security situation. Be specific about why individuals and technologies cannot be completely trusted in the situation.

8. Use the Internet or another source of information to locate an example of cybercrime. Briefly describe the incident with respect to the tools and techniques used to perpetrate the incident. Then further analyze and describe the incident with respect to the XYZ dimensions of the threat analysis cube described in subsection 2.3.3.

9. Explain the fundamental difference between CI and CII. Provide an example of a hypothetical attack on each and possible damage or harm that could result. Also describe possible interfacility and systems effects or consequences (i.e., how an attack on either CI or CII could affect the other).

10. Describe a situation in which you lost electrical power. What caused the power outage? When and where did this happen, and for how long were you without electricity? What were you not able to do? What did you do instead? What could you do to avoid the hardships you experienced?

## References and Endnotes

1. McQuade, S. (2001). *Cops versus Crooks: Technological Competition and Complexity in the Co-Evolution of Information Technologies and Money Laundering.* Fairfax, VA: George Mason University.

2. National Academy of Engineering, & National Research Council (1991). *People and Technology in the Workplace* (p. 4). Washington, DC: National Academy Press.

3. McQuade, 2001; see note 1.

4. Cowan, R. S. (1997). *A Social History of American Technology.* New York: Oxford University Press.

5. McQuade, 2001; see note 1.

6. Parker, D. B. (1998). *Fighting Computer Crime: A New Framework for Protecting Information.* New York: Wiley Computer Publishing.

7. Parker, 1998; see note 6.

8. United States of America v. Joseph DeMaria. U.S. District Court for the Southern District of Florida (Indictment/Case no. 95-855-CR-MOORE); and/or 919 F. Sup. 429 via 1996 U.S. Dist. LEXIS 3007, 1997.

9. Parker, 1998; see note 6.

10. United States of America v. Jerome R. Sullivan. U.S. District Court for the Southern District of Florida (Indictment/Case no. 97-CR-490-Gold); and/or 28 F. Supp. 2d 1365 via 1998 U.S. Dist. LEXIS 19277, 1998.

11. Franklin, B. (1733). *Poor Richard's Almanac.* Retrieved March 7, 2005, from http://en.wikiquote.org/wiki/Benjamin_Franklin.

12. United States of America v. Robert Fauver 1995 #469.

13. United States of America v. Carl D. Ellis 1997 #475.

14. United States of America v. Jose E. Alegria 1998 #479.

15. Willis, R. (1988). White-collar crime: the threat from within. In John J. Sullivan and Joseph L. Victor (Eds.), *Criminal Justice 88/89* (pp. 44–49). Guilford, CT: Dushkin Publishing Group.

16. Parker, 1998; see note 6.

17. Discovery Channel (2003). *The American Power Outage of 2003.* New York: NBC News Productions.

18. Staff Author (2004, June 4). Bank Glitch Leaves 10 Million Canadians without Paycheque. Retrieved November 4, 2004, from http://www.canadaeast.com/apps/pbcs.dll/article?AID=/20040604/TTEBRIEF/306040085/-1/FRONTPAGE. Times & Transcript.

19. Moteff, J. (1998). *Critical Infrastructures: A Primer.* Washington, DC: Congressional Research Service.

20. National Research Council (1991). *Computers at Risk: Safe Computing in the Information Age.* Washington, DC: National Academy Press.

21. President's Commission on Critical Infrastructure Protection (1997, October). *Critical Foundations: Protecting America's Infrastructures,* p. B-2. Final report of the President's Commission on Critical Infrastructure Protection. Washington, DC: Government Printing Office.

22. President's Commission on Critical Infrastructure Protection, 1997, p. B-1; see note 17.

23. Science Applications International Corporation (SAIC). (1995). *Information Warfare: Legal Regulatory, Policy, and Organizational Considerations for Assurance.* Report for the Chief, Information Warfare Division (J6K) Command, Control, Communications, and Computer Systems Directorate. Washington, DC: Joint Staff, The Pentagon.

24. Staff and Wire Reports (2004, December 27). Travelers shake off 'worst Christmas.' *USA Today.* Retrieved December 27, 2004, from http://www.usatoday.com/travel/news/2004-12-26-airport-aggravation_x.htm.

25. SAIC, 1995; p. 2–7; see note 23.

26. gTLD-MoU Policy Oversight Committee (1998). Generic Top Level Domain Memorandum of Understanding. Retrieved December 25, 2004, from http://www.gtld-mou.org/.

27. Asia Pacific Network Information Centre (2004). Critical Infrastructure FAQ. Retrieved June 5, 2004, from http://www.apnic.net/info/faq/critical-infrastructure-faq.html#2.

28. National Critical Infrastructure Program (NCIAP) (2003, July). *An Assessment of Canada's National Critical Infrastructure Sectors.* Retrieved June 3, 2004, from http://www.ocipep.gc.ca/critical/nciap/nci_sector1_e.asp. Ottawa: Public Safety and Emergency Preparedness Canada.

29. Moteff, J., Copeland, C., & Fischer, J. (2003, January 29). *Critical Infrastructures: What Makes an Infrastructure Critical?* Washington DC: Congressional Research Service.

30. Dunn, M., & Wigert, I. (2004). *International CIIP Handbook: An Inventory and Analysis of Protection Policies in Fourteen Countries,* 2nd ed. Andreas Wenger and Jan Metzger (Eds.). Zurich, Switzerland: Swiss Federal Institute of Technology.

31. U.S. Department of Homeland Security (2002). *Department of Homeland Security Reorganization Plan.* Retrieved November 2, 2004, from http://www.dhs.gov/interweb/assetlibrary/reorganization_plan.pdf.

32. U.S. Department of Homeland Security (2004). DHS Organization: Department Components. Retrieved November 2, 2004, from http://www.dhs.gov/dhspublic/ interapp/editorial/editorial_0086.xml.

33. U.S. Department of Homeland Security, 2004; see note 32.

34. U.S. Department of Homeland Security (2004). DHS Organization: National Infrastructure Advisory Council. Retrieved November 2, 2004, from http://www.dhs.gov/dhspublic/display?theme=9& content=3445.

35. Cordesman, A. H., & Cordesman, J. G. (2002). *Cyber-Threats, Information Warfare, and Critical Infrastructure Protection.* Westport, CT: Praeger.

36. Greenspan, R., & Gaudin, S. (2003). 2003: Year of the Worm? Retrieved March 14, 2004, from, http://www.clickz.com/stats/big_picture/applications/article.php /1301_1577811.

37. Frontline (2003). *Cyberwar.* Public Broadcasting Service.

38. Vatis, M. A. (2000). Statement to the Senate Judiciary Committee, Criminal Justice Oversight Subcommittee and House Judiciary Committee, Crime Subcommittee, Washington, DC. Retrieved March 12, 2004, from http://www.usdoj.gov/criminal/cybercrime/.

# 3

## IT-Enabled Abuse, Attacks, and Crimes

### 3.0 Introduction: How Are Information Technologies Misused?

When people abuse information technology (IT), they use computers, other types of electronic IT-devices, or information systems to deceive, assail, or cause various kinds of harm to individuals, groups, or organizations. In how many different ways can this occur? We have all heard of computer hacking, spamming, and illegal file sharing among other steadily growing forms of computer-enabled crime and abuse. What is involved in these and other types of IT-enabled abuse, attacks, and crimes? What is the difference between a computer virus, a Trojan horse, and a worm, and how do these malicious forms of code affect our computers? How does credit card fraud differ from identity theft fraud since both involve illegal acquisition and use of financial accounts? How are spyware and adware designed to function and why should we care? In what other ways are computers, PDAs, cellular phones, and other gadgets used alone or together to cause harm? In what ways are people harassed, threatened, and stalked online? Could cyberterrorism actually impact the critical information

infrastructures (CIIs) upon which the nation depends?

In this chapter we will review all the major ways in which computers and electronic devices are currently misused to commit social abuse, attacks, and crimes that harm other members of society. We will begin Section 3.1 by examining the writing and distribution of malicious computer programs including viruses, Trojans, and worms. Then we will consider various fraudulent schemes and theft, interference with and disruption of computer services, as well as computer spying and intrusions. This will be followed by descriptions of illegal file sharing, academic dishonesty, online threats and harassment, and computer-enabled stalking and sex crimes.

In Section 3.2 we will examine emerging forms of cybercrime and threats to information systems, problems associated with the increasing complexities of cybercrimes, and futuristic forms of cyber conflict such as transnational organized crime enabled by IT and information systems. We will also discuss cyberterrorism involving threats to national CIIs and the information- and network-centric warfare now challenging the government agencies that seek to establish secure, safe, and stable economies, security, and justice systems throughout the world. And you will learn about the cyber conflict continuum, a conceptual model for understanding the full range of IT-enabled abuse, attacks, and crimes in relation to the responsibilities and technological capabilities of civilian law enforcement versus those of military agencies for managing these problems.

## 3.1  Types of Abuse, Attacks, and Crime

The bulk of this chapter is devoted to explaining the many ways in which computers and other types of electronic IT devices and information systems can be abused, attacked, or used to commit crimes. You will learn about every major type of cybercrime with the help of interesting, and perhaps even astonishing, examples. As you read, keep in mind that each of the types of cybercrimes described may be committed in combinations of ways, ranging from being relatively simple to complex and often involving social engineering (i.e., manipulating people to do things) in one or more ways. These important issues will be elaborated on in Chapter 4.

### 3.1.1  Writing and Distributing Malicious Code

The nature and effects of malicious code have frequently been compared with biological viruses that infect living organisms. Since the late 1970s innumerable computer viruses and other types of malicious software programs, now commonly referred to as **malware,** have been created and distributed onto computer networks throughout the world. Specific types of malware include **viruses**, **Trojans**, **worms,** and **adware** or **spyware**. These programs interfere with the operating system or otherwise harm files and data on computers and other devices on which they become installed. Malware can be created

on personal computers at home, work, or school; become implanted on systems via downloading files, visiting Web pages, or using infected media;[1] and can be distributed via either public domain, illegally obtained, newly manufactured, or newly purchased but returned and resold software.[2] Computers and other electronic devices that are not running fully patched software, and that are not protected with current anti-virus and anti-spyware programs, are susceptible to becoming infected with new forms of malware that are continually being written and released onto the Internet or distributed in other ways.

In Chapter 10 we will discuss patches, malware prevention software, and malicious coding definitions in more detail. For now you should know that all three of these preventive measures are needed to specifically guard computers and increasingly other IT devices such as PDAs and cell phones against new forms of malware.

When computer users become aware that certain computer and device operating problems are the result of malware, they usually say their system has become infected with a virus or programming **bug**. This metaphor is somewhat apt for relatively inexperienced computer users who may not understand that infections amount to computer programs contaminating one or more computer files and/or other subprograms within a host or connected computers. However, a programming bug is more accurately thought of as unintended computer program flaws not discovered during software design and beta testing by authorized manufacturers or by customers who deliberately seek out problems so they can be fixed before widespread commercial distribution. Coding errors are also discovered by programmers and consumers following product releases, and these need to be fixed with after-market programming patches made available online by the software developers or skilled members of the open source community. This section is primarily concerned with viruses, Trojans, and worms. Later we will separately address adware and spyware, distinguishable on the basis of what they are designed to do (i.e., to advertise versus spy on computer users). For now you should know that similarities between different types of malware including adware and spyware have created considerable confusion about what these programs are and how they infect and negatively affect computer systems.

New strains of malware, especially if they infect the computers of large numbers of Internet users, are often said by nontechnical users and the media to be "computer viruses" rather than distinguished as viruses, Trojans, or worms. This has led to unnecessary public confusion about relatively simple but important differences in malware. Many users believe, for example, that a virus is a particular type of Trojan capable of automatically spreading to other programs and perhaps turning them into Trojans too. Other people claim that only computer programs that cause damage (other than merely self-replicating and consuming system memory) are viruses. Still other people use the term *Trojan* to refer only to non-self-replicating software as a way of distinguishing Trojans from viruses, while making no mention of worms. In fact, malware can be defined and categorized in a variety of ways, depending on the different ways in which they attack and spread from computer to computer. Unfortunately there has been and remains considerable confusion about these definitions among both technical and non-technical users. Efforts are currently being made by software industry and information security professionals to further clarify and standardize definitions for various types of malware. Box 3.1 lists the most widely accepted definitions of viruses, Trojans, and worms that differentiate them according to how they work and their intended effects. Depending on the types of coding involved, malware can infect computers throughout a network, causing damage to applications, files, and operating systems. Whether the damage is merely annoying or massively destructive depends on several factors such as the author's imagination and technical programming skills, the available bandwidth and capabilities of the computers or other electronic devices involved, and the amount and effectiveness of prevention, containment, and cleaning measures employed by users.

## BOX 3.1 • *Differences among Computer Viruses, Worms, and Trojans*

- A **virus** is a program analogous to a biological virus that infects our bodies. It reproduces itself without a user's knowledge or permission by searching out and embedding itself into executable programs. Viruses propagate only with the assistance of users (i.e., when the host program is shared, often through email or downloading files off the Internet, and is then executed). Viruses may carry destructive payloads that can damage computer operating systems, applications, or files but are not necessarily harmful except to the extent that they consume system resources.
- A **worm** is a self-contained program (or set of programs) capable of spreading complete copies or segments of itself to other computers without intervention by a user. Unlike a virus, they do not need to be clicked on and executed to carry out any number of functions ranging from annoying to destructive as they worm their way through an invaded computer operating system.
- A **Trojan** (or Trojan horse), as its name implies, is a disguised computer program that appears to be doing one task but is actually doing another as intended by its designer. As with worms and viruses, Trojans range from being innocuous to very disruptive and harmful in their effects. This implies that Trojans, at least in theory, may also be beneficial, although most computer users would object to the unauthorized code being on their systems if they knew it was there.

As with the definitional issues mentioned in Chapter 1 and elsewhere in the text, it is important that we use terms as accurately and consistently as possible to promote understanding for purposes of everyday communication and improved systems design; for investigation, prosecution, and security enhancement; to research the nature and extent of IT-enabled threats; and to evaluate prevention, detection, and control measures for addressing malicious computer programming and its effects. In so doing we increase the potential effectiveness of all these activities. We also help in the creation of uniform laws, regulations, and interpretations of them by courts reviewing computer abuse and cybercrime cases. Fortunately, procedures for preventing software infections in the first place, for ridding computers of malware, and for restoring system functions afterwards are fairly universal although not always completely successful. In any event, the best thing we can do initially is understand what these forms of system abuse and attacks are

and learn to recognize their effects when they occur.

Writing malicious code is a passion or a hobby for some people throughout the world, and results in increasingly complex forms of software capable of causing a full range of harmful effects (e.g., from being a mere nuisance to a single user or computer system to causing massive data destruction or denial of computer services to millions of Internet users). What matters for the creator of malware also varies, but goals may include displaying technical abilities through creative programming, monetary gain, dissemination of political messages, extortion, disruption of computer services, and trafficking of illegal pornography and software, among other abusive and/or criminal goals. Writing code with unprecedented capabilities on the basis of one's computer knowledge and technical programming skill, even if it has harmful effects, can be thrilling for some people. Malware that tricks people into downloading and activating a virus, then instructs a computer to

DEAR, DO YOU REMEMBER THAT STRANGE EMAIL I TOLD YOU ABOUT?

infect itself and potentially millions of other computers located around the world in a matter of moments are forms of art that some technically skilled programmers thrive on. Disguise a Trojan to appear like a sexy picture of a popular star so people will be tempted to click on the file attachment and BANG—absent updated operating system and application patches, plus updated malware definitions—the computer and other systems to which it is connected become infected.

Authors of malware have created plug-and-play applications that facilitate writing malware by less technically competent programmers. Want to write a destructive virus, worm, or Trojan? No problem: instructional Web sites and programs are easily found on the Internet and are available free of charge, although you may not always be able to discern whether the application itself contains spyware or some other type of malware just like the one you want to create.[3] Creating, advertising, and accessing harmful code are currently protected in the United States as forms of expression guaranteed by the First Amendment of the U.S. Constitution. Only the act of posting it online or otherwise distributing harmful code is currently illegal. So, although writing a virus is not illegal in the United States, releasing it onto the Internet is. However, programmers should not be naïve about writing malware or searching for or accessing information on how to create malicious code, because these activities are increasingly viewed with suspicion by law enforcement and intelligence agencies as indicators of criminal intention or association and potentially as threats to CIIs and therefore national security.

Merely researching how to create malware is like researching how to make a bomb; it is not illegal, but in this age of worldwide terrorism, doing so raises red flags for investigators monitoring threats to infrastructures and national security. Programming enthusiasts often find such monitoring practices by government agency analysts and investigators to be offensive. However, legislative provisions providing increased authority and investigative flexibility to law enforcement officers and intelligence agents has come about because of largely heretofore unchecked activities of malicious computer hackers and programmers who have attacked key information systems vital to the economic and military well-being of the United States and other nations. So if you are a computer science or software engineering student who likes to experiment with malicious programming, by all means pursue your education or hobby in a safe way but don't be surprised if authorities begin monitoring your online systems activities and one day ask you pointed questions about what you are doing and why. It is also worth noting that the same skills needed to create malware are also needed to help defend national security and CII. Controversial topics related to this issue will be taken up in Chapter 7 in the context of the computer hacker subculture and elsewhere in connection with recruitment, background checks, and hiring policies of federal law enforcement and intelligence agencies and private sector information security firms.

### 3.1.2 Fraudulent Schemes and Theft

Fraudulent schemes involving accounting, market systems, and IT in some form have existed for centuries. In the 1830s, networks of semaphore signaling towers resembling windmills, often atop hills located several miles apart, were used by soldiers in the French army of General Napoleon Bonaparte to quickly send messages regarding troop movements across great distances. This same system of communication was reportedly used to convey fraudulent crop prices. After conspiring with crop purchasers in major cities, signalmen in the towers would send messages to rural villages alleging deflated market prices. In response, farmers would sell their harvested crops for less than they were worth, thereby allowing the city-based fraudsters to resell loads of wheat, barley, corn, and other foodstuffs for the higher market price with an inflated profit margin.[4]

Today's high-tech fraud schemes employ the same general concept: use of tools and techniques to defraud people out of their money or property. In short, **fraud** involves acquiring anything of value by deceit. Fraud committed using stand-alone or networked computers or other types of electronic IT devices can be accomplished in several ways that are particularly deceptive because the techniques involved often require technical understanding of how IT and computers can be abused. In this subsection we consider credit card fraud, identity theft, and other types of market and online fraud schemes.

**3.1.2.1  Credit Card Fraud.**  Credit card fraud can be committed in several ways, all of which involve making purchases after establishing a fraudulent account with false identification, pretending to be a legitimate account holder while making purchases, or simply making charges against legitimate accounts without authorization. In May of 2000, five Russian hackers were arrested for the theft of over 5,400 credit card numbers from online retailers. The perpetrators of this scam allegedly stole over $630,000 before they were apprehended.[5] Credit card fraud can also be committed on smaller scales by individual perpetrators using simple schemes to defraud consumers, merchants, and lending institutions. One student reported how a teenage friend was able to commit credit card fraud online using an underground search engine to locate tools for generating fake as well as valid credit card numbers—a technique known as "carding." These account numbers are then used to purchase items online and have merchandise delivered to locations the fraudster knows to be safe, such as the house of a family on vacation. After arranging for delivery of the merchandise, it is a simple matter to watch the location intermittently, pick up the package after it is dropped off, and make off with the stolen goods. This example reveals a somewhat older although still-practiced method of high-tech credit card fraud. Members of the HoneyNet project, which purposely leaves computers vulnerable

---

**CYBER TALE 3.1**

### How One Student Avoided Being Defrauded Online

Over several months a girl and I developed a rather close relationship by sending email and photographs to each other. One day the girl, who said she lived in Boston, announced that she would be coming to New York and would like to meet me in person. Naturally I was thrilled and began making preparations for her visit. During this period I happened to learn how to determine the approximate physical location of a computer based on the IP address indicated on email messages. This is how I noticed that the IP address on emails sent from my new girlfriend were from Indonesia. "That's right, the babe is sending email from the South Pacific—bet on it!" was the response I got from my friends who were also aware of the universal IP addressing index system.

I asked my girlfriend online about the seeming inconsistency, to which she wrote back saying her dad worked in Indonesia and that is where the ISP account had been opened. As the day of her visit approached she sent another email saying that she unexpectedly needed to visit her grandmother in Hawaii and could not come to New York after all. Already suspicious, I checked and learned that the phone number the girl provided for the hotel in Hawaii was invalid. I concluded she must be a phony and might not even be a girl. I figure this person was probably just trying to socially engineer me into giving up personal or financial information in order to commit a fraud of some sort. For all I know, I may have been one of dozens of people being set up for a con.

*Anonymous Student*

to attackers in order to study computer intrusion techniques, have found networks of automated credit card bots operating through Internet Relay Chat (IRC). (See page 99 for a definition of the term bot.) Through specific commands, these bots can be commanded to release harvested credit card numbers, check numbers for validity, and even list online stores that the cards have been verified to work at.[6]

Larger reputable online merchandising firms prevent this form of fraud by building in database purchasing rules that match the credit card numbers used to purchase goods with other account information such as the cardholder's name, address, and account password. This information is often used along with the card's three- or four-digit security code to help assure that a credit card being used for an online purchase is actually in the possession of a person authorized to make the charge. To overcome fraud prevention checks, attackers often seek and acquire additional information about accounts and authorized cardholders. Fraudsters usually also take care not to place an order by telephone or online in way that can be traced to them.

Another method of credit card fraud involves offering popular items for sale on online auction sites at very low prices, allowing bidders to run up the price, receiving payment for the merchandise, and then never shipping the items. Sometimes teams of fraudsters will collude in order to raise the price with of course no desire to actually purchase the item, which in fact may not even exist. In any illicit online auction sale, as winning bidders provide personal and credit card account numbers, this information will sometimes be used to commit additional fraud by purchasing items on online or via telephone. Information about how to commit online fraud is abundant on the Internet, as are Web sites that specialize in illegally selling credit card account information for fraudulent purposes.

In the early 1990s, AOHell, a now obsolete software program, could be downloaded for free off the Internet. This program enabled cybercriminals to perform various abusive or illegal functions via an early version of America Online. One function allowed fraudsters to send, with a single click, a phishing message to everyone in a given chat room. The fake message, purportedly from an AOL technical representative, convinced many naïve users to update their AOL account information, which of course resulted in unaware users responding with personal and financial information that could be used to commit crimes in their names. Fortunately, AOL has taken steps to stop AOHell and help prevent similar programs and schemes from being used to manipulate customers or interfere with the firm's services.

### 3.1.2.2 Identity Theft Fraud.

**Identity theft** involves acquiring and then unlawfully using personal and financial account information to acquire goods and services in someone else's name. Essentially, identity theft is credit card fraud and other forms of fraud gone wild. Identity thieves typically pretend to be someone else and use their victim's personal, employment, and financial account information to acquire credit and/or illegally make purchases. Identity thieves also fraudulently sign leases on rental property, pay rent and utility bills, and even purchase cars, luxury items, and houses in the names of their victims. Identity theft can occur over an extended period of time to the extent that victims are unaware it is happening. This can occur when consumers do not pay attention to their monthly credit card checking, and savings account statements to detect unauthorized purchases. As long as fraudulent purchases are not extraordinary relative to past purchases on a given account, security screening procedures designed to detect and validate the legitimacy of impending or recent purchases, such as courtesy telephone calls to consumers that are now conducted by most credit and financial account providers, will not be triggered.

Identity theft is a form of cybercrime that encompasses fraud involving any type of monetary or credit instrument along with personal identification documents. Thus, every time you make a

---

**CYBER TALE 3.2**

## A Student Victim of Credit Card Fraud

A student described how he became the victim of credit card fraud but initially did not realize what was occurring. He used his American Express® credit card to make an online purchase, after which he promptly received the correct items. Two months later he was contacted by the merchandiser, who advised him that during the time of the transaction their e-commerce subcontractor experienced a server security breach resulting in the student's credit card number and other personal information becoming known to persons unknown. The student examined his billing records and noticed no problems, so he did not at the time request American Express cancel and reauthorize the credit card account.

Several more weeks passed and then the student began receiving odd email receipts from e-commerce sites that he had never visited. In one case, he received a receipt for a watch that had apparently been sent to another party in a different state who had a different email address. Again, however, his American Express billing records showed nothing unusual. Then one day a new billing record showed a $400 charge for Yahoo! Domain services that he had not ordered. The student quickly contacted American Express officials, who canceled the charges against his card and issued him a new credit card account number. Since that time the student has received a box full of novelty software that was ordered by an unknown person who used a third party's name and credit card information. He has also received a telephone call from a jewelry store attempting to confirm a $6,000 order, this time involving his name and telephone number as the person placing the order but using someone else's valid credit card account number. Can you see how even some personal information about you can lead to a string of crimes being committed in your name?

---

transaction that involves revealing your name, address, phone number, date of birth, driver's license number, and/or social security number, you are increasing the risk that someone will use your information to perpetrate identity theft. This is true of online, phone, and traditional in-person purchases that produce records of transactions listing sales information that any unscrupulous employee can simply copy and use for fraudulent purposes. What distinguishes identity theft from ordinary credit card and other forms of fraud, however, is criminal assumption of someone else's identity (or more likely, multiple identities simultaneously). This often results in nearly complete ruin of the victims' credit, often before they even become aware that fraud is being perpetrated in their name. As credit card account limits reach the maximum amounts authorized, victims are unable to make credit purchases, make mounting minimum monthly payments, or secure additional credit or loans until the matter is investigated and their damaged credit rating is restored. This may take several weeks or even months. In the interim, victims of identify theft may experience repeat victimization as the result of being denied an apartment or job opportunity because they are considered a poor credit risk. People applying for positions in financial institutions, security firms, law enforcement or other types of government agencies which oversee or process financial or intelligence data in particular may be denied jobs for this reason.

Secondary identity theft victimization can also occur as the result of fraudsters impersonating victims in nonpurchasing situations, as, for example, after being stopped by police for a traffic violation. A survey report commissioned by the Federal Trade Commission revealed that more than one million victims of identity theft from 1998 to 2003 had their personal ID fraudulently used by someone else during a police investigation of a traffic violation or criminal offense.[7] You may think police officers should not make such errors. However, street policing and detective work has many situational demands. Unless an officer (who is often rushed and may be working at night, in poor lighting, in busy traffic conditions and inclement weather, etc.) is paying attention to identification details and other information provided by every individual he or she encounters, it is perfectly understandable that an imposter will not initially be detected especially since the credibility of false IDs is continually improving along with high-definition scanning and printing capabilities of IT. Frequently, the truth about an imposter is later discovered with assistance from a fraud victim whose identification was fraudulently used to deceive police.

### 3.1.2.3 Web and Email Spoofing and IM Spimming.

**Web and email spoofing** involves creating Web sites, Web-based traffic, or email messages that appear legitimate but are in fact fakes designed to obtain consumer information that can be used to commit fraud. Usually Web and email spoofing are used in conjunction, as when an attacker sends an email with a link to a spoofed Web site. Periodically people receive email that *appears* to be from a legitimate source such as a bank, retail firm, utility company, or other business. Phishing emails usually are purportedly from technical service representatives or managers, and they usually contain instructions pertaining to the false need to update purchasing account information. To do so, users need only click on the link provided in the email and then fill out a data entry form provided on the Web site they are linked to. In this type of Web/email spoofing attack, the Web site appears to be official but is actually located on the attackers' server. The only way users can know this is by observing odd syntax appearing in the URL address box of their Web browser and deducing

that it is probably not legitimate. The problem of course is that many of these scams now employ very credible URL syntax along with letterheads, company logos, official and reasonable sounding instructions, as well as confirmation contact information such as a mailing address, email, or phone number that customers can contact if they have questions, all designed to maintain the appearance of legitimacy. If you were to use these contacts, you may or may not receive a response. There are several variations to this basic scam, which is why most firms conducting business online periodically warn customers that they will never initiate this type of correspondence and that customers will never be asked to validate or change account information online or over the phone. However, fraudsters who employ Web and email spoofing are getting more sophisticated all the time, and many people who do not heed such warnings are conned and victimized again and again as their names and other confidential information such as their home or business addresses, telephone numbers, financial account numbers, and other information needed to fraudulently purchase things online is distributed all over the Internet.

MessageLabs, a leading provider of managed email security services to businesses worldwide, reportedly detects 80–100 new phishing Web sites each day, which shows how ubiquitous this form of cybercrime has become. In October of 2004 the firm detected a phishing scam designed to capture online banking details without requiring users to respond or click on a Web site link. Instead, users only had to open an email, which activated a computer program that attempted to rewrite certain files on their computers. When they subsequently accessed their online banking accounts, their Web browsers were redirected automatically to a fraudulent Web site from which their personal and account details were stolen.[8] Reportedly, computer users could prevent this from happening by disabling their Windows Scripting Host. Additionally, according to Alex Shipp, a senior antivirus technologist at MessageLabs, "most banks have advised their customers to be wary of any email asking for personal banking details." In this type of attack merely opening an innocent-appearing email could result in users automatically revealing their online banking account information.[9]

Phishers are also reportedly recruiting money launderers by sending email spam (discussed in more detail later) to unwary computer users who they hope will help them funnel and disguise illicit income. Think about it: phishers need to electronically siphon money from the accounts of fraud victims into their own financial accounts in a way that is not easily detected. Another way of doing this is to entice an accomplice into opening a legitimate bank account. Then after acquiring personal account information from and/or about victims, the phisher can transfer funds illegally accessed within the same banking system into the new account. Accomplices recruited to establish such accounts use false identification of course and are typically paid a flat fee or a percentage of the overall amount of funds stolen, much as are unscrupulous bankers, accountants, and lawyers who are periodically recruited and paid by organized crime to launder money.

Not all phishing is criminal, although it may be regarded as socially abusive because its purpose is to deceive people into believing things that are not true or doing things based on false information. During the fall of 2004 Alek Komarnitsky of Lafayette, Colorado, decorated his home with more than 17,000 lights to celebrate Halloween, Thanksgiving, and then Christmas. He also created a Web site that featured photos and Web cam video of his house. His home lighting system drew the attention of the Denver-based TV station KMGH, which flew a helicopter over the house to broadcast footage of the sensation to area viewers. Kormarnitsky himself was aboard the flight, claiming that visitors to his Web site could remotely control his home's computerized light show online. However, unbeknownst to TV viewers, and over four million visitors to his Web page, his wife was actually inside the house manually turning sets of lights on and off. When asked later about the deceit, Kormarnitsky claimed the hoax was just his way of promoting holiday cheer.[10]

Fortunately, Komarnitsky's hoax did not apparently result in any specific or substantial indirect harm. No one, for example, is known to have done something on the basis of the prank that resulted in negative consequences for themselves or anyone else, although TV station personnel wasted time and money. The incident reveals how gullible people can be, especially when trusted media sources, which have also been duped, widely report fraudulent facts and contrived circumstances as being true. Avoiding fraudulent schemes, such as those involving Web site and email spoofing, require us to always maintain a level of distrust about the people and technology we are interacting with. Seeing is not always a solid basis for believing, much less for doing something about a situation.

All of the forgoing concepts also apply to fraud involving instant messaging. Thus, the instant messaging form of spam, commonly referred to as **IM spim**, can be used to facilitate cybercrime. Hence, illicit **spimming** involves instant messages that attempt to deceive people into revealing personal or financial information or entice them to participate in a scheme of some sort. Spim can also contain links or otherwise direct victims to spoofed Web sites or have fraudulent or trigger-attack documents of various kinds attached so that when users open them their computer systems become infected. As previously indicated, we must never forget that these and other forms of cyber attacks often occur in combination, over periods of time, and in very clever ways. Therefore, just as you must be on your guard against various types of crimes if you go out alone at night in a strange area, you must also be on your guard every time you interact with people, documents, and Web locations online. Often they are not what they appear to be, and just because you detect and avoid one type or level of fraud does not mean another associated with the first is not just around the cyber corner.

*3.1.2.4 High-Tech Disaster Fraud, Online Hoaxes, and Other Fraud Schemes.* Financial aid following tragedies caused by humans and natural disasters is often essential to provide food, clothing, temporary shelter, medical supplies, infrastructure cleanup, and sanitation for disease control. Relief agencies such as the American Red Cross usually request monetary donations because it offers flexibility for purchasing needed goods and services while minimizing shipping costs and delays in providing assistance to victims. Following the infamous aircraft terrorist events of September 11, 2001, and the earthquake and tsunami disaster that struck several Pacific island nations on December 26, 2004, people from around the world provided monetary donations and volunteered to help victims of these disasters. Governments from around the world pledged and provided financial assistance plus other types of support in each of these instances, as they have following many other disasters. Unfortunately, tragedies present opportunities for disaster fraud in which people are duped into providing charity that lines the pockets of fraudsters rather than helping victims in need.

High-tech disaster and other types of cyber fraud can take different forms, including (1) **telemarketing fraud** methods that play on donor sympathies to fraudulently solicit funds for fictitious human service agencies; (2) **false advertising schemes,** as when, for example, a portion of funds spent on products are pocketed instead of being forwarded to disaster victims as promised; (3) **service provider fraud,** as when repair or cleanup contractors make off with funds without performing work promised; (4) submitting **false damage claims** to insurance firms or government agencies such as the Federal Emergency Management Agency (FEMA) of the U.S. Department of Homeland Security; (5) **insider trading** such as "pump-n-dump" schemes in which stock market brokers spread false rumors that a company's stock is about to take a sharp price increase, thereby inducing people to buy, and then suddenly pull out their own stock investments

after the increased purchases falsely inflate the price; (6) **cybersmear campaigns** (the opposite of pump-n-dump schemes), in which individuals or firms are defamed for actions that did not occur and this ends up costing them money; and (7) **ad hoc frauds** that adopt one or more of these or other methods of conning people out of their money, possessions, or information.

In 2001 following the terrorist attacks on the World Trade Center and Pentagon, the National Fraud Information Center reported:[11]

• An incident in which a man received an email requesting financial support for a group of computer experts attempting to locate Osama bin Laden and specified a bank account in Estonia to which funds should be sent
• False Web site accusations that Snapple®, a popular beverage firm owned by Cadbury-Schwepps, maintained an association with Osama bin Laden
• A telemarketing scheme in which voice mail was used to solicit assistance funds for 9-11 terrorist victims but that was not authorized by any known or registered not-for-profit relief agency.

Another form of high tech fraud is a **hoax** delivered via email or an IM message that describes one or more security vulnerabilities and what should be done to fix the problem(s). Often the message appears to be from a legitimate source and provides professional instructions such as deleting particular files that are allegedly malware programs but are in fact files integral to a computer operating system. Unsuspecting victims locate and delete these files only to discover their computer will no longer operate properly. To avoid these scams, users must never take such messages at face value, even if they are received from a friend or other known source. Instead, they should confirm with their operating system manufacturer and/or malware service provider (e.g., Norton, McAfee, etc.) that the problem and recommended fix are legitimate. Often software problems, descriptions of hoaxes, and repair instructions are listed by these firms to help users avoid unnecessary problems.

Hoaxes and scams can also involve sympathy or get-rich-quick schemes. Have you ever received an email describing a rare and urgent opportunity to invest in something online, get out of debt quick, or assist someone from another country with a vexing financial, medical, or some other type of personal problem? I frequently receive these scam messages, although thankfully my email spam software automatically filters most of them out of my inbox and places them directly into an email trash bucket. Often the messages appear with a subject title such as "Congratulations," "Please respond," "Dear Sir," "Read this," or "Urgent request"and may even be tailored to include a user's first and/or last name as in "Dear Sam." The message then describes some outrageous situation involving desperate people who need help and how with minimal assistance from you, a large sum of money can be moved between international financial accounts in order to provide relief to those who are suffering. All that is needed is for you to provide a telephone or fax number, business address, or valid banking account number that the funds can be temporarily moved into, and for your trouble you will receive a reward, fee, or commission. Beware! These messages compel compassion, exploit greed, or play to the egos of users who receive them.

Most of these messages are fairly unsophisticated, and many are poorly written in broken English (perhaps to appear more legitimate). Often they do not initially request financial assistance or bank account details; rather, they urge people to indicate their interest and willingness to help. However, depending on the amount and quality of intelligence gathered on potential victims by fraudsters, scam messages seeking assistance can be tailored in ways that enhance their credibility, as when appearing to be from a friend in need of assistance. These types of scenarios are discussed later in relation to spamming attacks.

Once the fraudsters know they have a potential victim paying attention to their message, they will send a series of additional messages to size up their mark for a customized fraud. In the process, more details about the sad situation or money-making opportunity are provided in order to trick naïve victims into giving away information about themselves (especially financial account information), investing in something for quick and large profits, or doing something else that seems innocent and helpful but is actually part of a much larger crime scheme.

What many Internet users do not realize is that the authors of these email messages are located in countries that provide little law enforcement or regulatory oversight of their tactics. Consequently, the Internet service providers (ISPs) used by these cybercriminals do not routinely screen for fraudulent messages, nor are they compelled to provide government investigators with suspicious customer email traffic data even if officials were inclined and technically competent to investigate such crimes. So people all over the world are routinely bombarded and propositioned with email scam offers, and unfortunately some people who wish to help or are in need of fast money respond, only to be defrauded.

Fraud as the result of people using computers and the Internet has become so prevalent that some users have begun to fight back. For example, at 419eater.com, you can read dozens of stories of people who responded to fraudulent emails by pretending to be willing participants and then reverse engineer the scam, directing it at the scam artists. Some of these vigilante fraud-fighters have even been known to send packages COD to the scammers with the intention of sticking them with substantial shipping and international importation fees. However, merely opening spam sent as part of a fraudulent scheme may result in an individual being marked and tracked as a potential victim who is worth sending more scam offers to.[12] In addition, you should know that by participating in reverse engineering vigilantism you may also be committing a crime. My advice is to simply delete rather than open or respond to any potentially fraudulent messages (e.g., those sent from sources you do not recognize). In this way you will not waste your time processing foolish messages nor signal to fraudsters that you are a potential mark. In the event a real friend needs your help, they will likely let you know in person, via the telephone, or in some other way that enables you to verify the situation.

### 3.1.3 Interfering with and Disrupting Computer Services

Everyone knows that cable TV theft is illegal and that acquiring or modifying that little black box to convert a scrambled signal into viewable content is not very difficult to do. Cable theft is so common that television and radio public service announcements are broadcast in many locations to warn people of stiff penalties for this type of cybercrime. In a variation of basic cable theft, Tony R. Wingman of Minerva, Ohio, was sentenced by a federal court judge in April of 2004 to a year and a day imprisonment, plus three years of supervised probation, for illegally modifying and distributing fifty-one DSS Satellite (direct TV) access cards and for knowingly and with the intent to defraud, making, acquiring, or possessing "analog, digital or electronic images of $50.00, $20.00, $10.00 and $5.00 U.S. Federal Reserve Notes, in violation of Title 18, United States Code, Section 474."[13] Other forms of computer-enabled abuse and cybercrimes that involve interference with or disruption of computerized

---

**CYBER TALE 3.3**

### How One Student Fought Fraud with Fraud

It is rare that an Internet or email user has not experienced some form of fraudulent activity online. One student reported his experience of being duped into participating in a **pyramid scheme** available through a popular online selling outlet. The scheme promised participants the ability to acquire a brand new in-the-box version of Playstation 2 (PS2) for the ridiculously low price of $20. According to the instructions, this could be done by paying the $20 up front and then getting twenty additional people to participate in the same process. Being inexperienced with this form of fraud, the student paid his $20 and began recruiting additional participants to do the same thing. Then he realized he was being ripped off, that in fact he had paid $20 to strangers who would never actually send him a PS2. But he did not realize that by using a telecommunications system to raise money in connection with the fraud he had become an unwittingly accomplice in a felony crime.

In his ignorance, and in order to exact revenge, the student began selling access to the pyramid scheme Web site for $20 via an HMTL link placed on a pay-for-access Web site of his own creation. His site also included a disclaimer in very small print that people were only purchasing the right to use the link to the original Web site that would explain how to actually purchase PS2 for $20. In this way he thought he could avoid criminal responsibility. Sure enough, several gullible and greedy people soon paid him more than $1,000. Then he began receiving emails from irate customers who realized they had been double-scammed: once by the student and again by operators of the original PS2 pyramid scheme. Many defrauded customers were reimbursed following a Federal Commerce Commission (FCC) investigation that also reportedly resulted in the pyramid scheme organizers being fined $150,000 for maintaining a fraudulent purchasing environment. The student narrowly escaped federal prosecution.

### Suckered as the Result of Porn Curiosity

I was curious about, but inexperienced in, viewing online pornography. In order to get a temporary membership to view a little porn online I provided my credit card number to a site to verify I was over 18 years of age. Having secured a "free temporary membership" along with a "trial viewing password," I entered a second Web site that provided a few enticing photographs and short video streamers of sexually explicit material. There were also links to several different categories and much larger volumes of pornography. Had I exited the site at that point, I probably would have been OK. However, I decided to enter the next layer of porn pages without carefully reading a disclaimer and billing statement at the bottom of an entrance page that specified that initial and per-minute access fees would be automatically charged to my credit card if I viewed additional layers of content. I spent about ten minutes in seven porn content areas. Several days later a credit card bill showed up in excess of $350 for approximately 70 minutes of total viewing. Unfortunately, I learned there was nothing illegal about the tricky advertising method or online sales, so I had to pay the charge.

*Anonymous Student*

or telecommunications services that negatively impact large numbers of users include denial-of-service (DoS) attacks, email spamming, sending unsolicited adware, and cracking passwords. Let us consider each of them.

### 3.1.3.1 Denial-of-Service (DoS) and Distributed DoS Attacks.

A **denial of service (DoS) attack** accomplishes exactly what its name implies: computers or services being attacked are prevented from being used by authorized users. DoS attacks can be accomplished in three general ways. The first, and easiest, is by simply disrupting the physical components of a computer or network. For example, if I cut the power cord to your computer, that would deny your access until the cord is replaced. In theory, a large-scale DoS attack of this kind could result from a physical or cyber attack on electric system infrastructure, thus preventing computer and telecommunications from operating. A second DoS attack method is to disrupt software and thereby prevent a computer or networking equipment from being fully used for particular tasks. DoS attacks can also be accomplished by overwhelming system resources, such as bandwidth capacity or hard drive space. By arranging for thousands or millions of messages to bombard a specific computer server, cybercriminals can overload a system, causing it to slow down or crash, thereby denying some level of service capacity, if not complete service, to users.

Reportedly, students acting as computer lab assistants were able to access and crash at will their high school's primary server. They frequently did so during a seventh-period computer and software engineering class in order to avoid having to do assignments in class and to get out of school early. Whenever the students got bored in class, they used a computer on the network to run an exploit that affected certain software and effectively crashed the server. Without the server, there was no way to complete computer programming assignments, and since it was near the end of the school day, students were usually dismissed to go home. The teacher reportedly never discovered why the server was so apt to crash during his seventh-period class. Eventually, a new system administrator got wind of what was occurring and stopped the nonsense.

**CYBER TALE 3.5**

### Denial-of-Service Attacks Hit Gaming Website

It started off as relatively innocuous, at least from the site user's point of view. I wasn't more than mildly annoyed the first time the site failed to load. Highly trafficked online game help sites run by fans go down from time to time with simple server problems, and I assumed this was more of the same. A little while later, the site was back up and everything seemed normal. Then late that night before I went to bed, the gaming forum started getting really laggy, timing me out a few times before I gave up for the night.

When I checked the news section of the forum the next morning, there was a note about denial-of-service (DoS) attacks that had struck the game site the previous day. The attacks continued, and you could tell from additional messages from the site owners that they were becoming really angry. The Web site being attacked was one of the larger and more popular help sites for the game in question, and complaints were beginning to show up on it as well as on official game manufacturer site forums. On the third day of the DoS attacks the forums were restructured so that a limited number of people could be active at the same time. This relieved bandwidth pressure, but it was frustrating having to reload everyone's posts in order to stay fully abreast of conversations that were taking place.

Meanwhile news posts were announcing that servers were becoming increasingly jammed by ping-flooding. One site had to switch URLs to stop the pinging. Eventually, the forums returned to normal, and I found it interesting to learn after all of this, my firewall log showed indications of pinging from the game site that had experienced the DoS attacks. It is quite possible that whoever was attacking the game site was using zombie computers that automatically attempted to get access to my computer too. Thank goodness for my personal firewall.

*Anonymous Student*

*3.1.3.2 Spamming.* Do you periodically receive unexpected and unwanted email or IM from sources that advertise a product, make an announcement, or convey a message about which you could not care less? I do, and find it disruptive and annoying. **Spam**, which was originally named for a Monty Python sketch featuring the delicious canned meat product of the same name, is the term most often used to refer to any type of unsolicited electronic message. However, not everyone agrees with this broad general definition. Increasingly for state and federal regulation purposes, spam is differentiated as being "unsolicited commercial email (UCE), which excludes unsolicited political messages and possibly outright fraudulent ones; unsolicited bulk email (UBE); unsolicited commercial bulk email (UCBE); and unsolicited electronic mail solicitations (UEMS), which would include even single unsolicited emails."[14]

**Spamming** involves sending hundreds, thousands, or even more unsolicited electronic messages within a short period of time. Spamming can also occur intermittently for weeks or months or continue indefinitely until filtering software is installed to help fix the problem. Spam is usually sent out by mass marketing firms that are often contracted to generate millions of messages per day for nearly every imaginable product. Some of these advertisements are appreciated by some users who respond with inquiries or make online purchases. Other consumers, in addition to being annoyed by spam, are also offended by the topics or content of the messages, which frequently have to do with stimulating or enhancing a person's sexuality. Mass marketing with spam is often triggered on the basis of the Web sites visited. For example, if you frequent porn sites, you may subsequently receive electronic messages from firms offering to sell you sex-enhancing drugs or devices or pornography-viewing membership services. Through the use of tracking cookies and images, spam may be designed so that by merely opening up the message, your computer is identified as belonging to a potential customer, thus resulting in more spam being sent to you.

Some cybercriminals now use spam coupled with spyware and phishing scamming techniques as a way of technologically mining computer nodes and personal information that can be used to carry out particular types of attacks (e.g., a botnet DoS attack in which a person's computer is remotely taken over to become a server through which millions of messages can be sent without the user's knowledge to overwhelm a targeted server or network). In October of 2004 a series of spam messages were sent to email users around the world. These messages contained an opt-out link purporting to remove users from an email distribution list and prevent future mailings, as is now required by U.S. federal law. However, when this link was clicked, users were directed to a web page that exploited an unpatched JavaScript vulnerability within a popular web browser, immediately downloading software that would turn the victim's computer into a spam server without the user's knowledge or consent. This type of complex attack using fraudulent email and malicious web programming only becomes more popular as the number of publicly known vulnerabilities within web browsers increases. Reading spam can also expose users' systems to malware attached to the spam message and to being targeted for online frauds such as the case above which involves Web and email spoofing. A new form of spam involves sending text messages over cellular phone networks in a way that results in those receiving the calls being charged for them.[15]

### 3.1.3.3 Adware.

Like spam, adware has become an increasing problem for both personal and commercial users of email or instant messaging software. **Adware** is a type of computer program that enables unsolicited advertising banners to pop up onto computer screen desktops or be integrated into communication software such as AOL Instant Messenger (see the banner above the buddy list?). Adware can be used for legitimate advertising, and banners' continued appearances on many types of legitimate software along with stationary advertisements is evidence of financial payoffs being realized through this form of legal marketing. However, many users consider adware to be malicious because it is typically installed on computers without permission and through unscrupulous methods. Once installed, adware will remain and consume system resources until it is detected and removed with special software designed for this purpose (discussed in Chapter 10). Adware can also be inadvertently installed when (1) a user downloads software that has the adware bundled with it, (2) when the user is tricked into installing the software through deceiving online pop-up ads, or (3) upon visiting a Web site that automatically exploits a security flaw in Web browser software.

Once on a system, adware will often appear to be part of a computer's operating system. Many adware programs are capable of producing manufacturer pop-up ads, changing the contents of a start-up menu, or changing the designated Web browser home page set by a user to a Web site advertising particular products or services. This type of adware is notoriously difficult to remove from a computer system, although many software applications have been designed specifically to aid in the removal of known adware programs. Note that as mentioned elsewhere, adware and spyware programs are very much alike, and many people consider them to be essentially the same thing because they are often designed, distributed, and used in conjunction (e.g., a single program that tracks where you go online in order to determine what types of products or services you may be interested in purchasing and then automatically arranges for you to receive spam or pop-up ads targeting your consumer interests).

### 3.1.4 Computer Spying and Intrusions

Spyware is often used to surreptitiously determine what Web sites you visit and thereby determine consumer interests and preferences that can be used to target adware advertising or otherwise socially engineer naïve users into becoming a victim of a fraudulent scheme. In this subsection we explore several deliberate ways in which computer spying and intrusions occur. Note, however, that several of these methods are used by system administrators and other IT professionals for legitimate purposes, which serves as a reminder that computers, other types of electronic devices, and technology in general can be used for good or to cause harm.

#### 3.1.4.1 Packet Sniffing, Port Scanning, and Password Cracking. 
Packet sniffing, port scanning, and password guessing are common techniques employed as integral aspects of the complex multifaceted attacks discussed later in the chapter. They are also techniques legitimately used by system administrators and information security professionals to ensure the health of networks. For now, let us briefly consider what is involved when each of these techniques is used for abusive or criminal purposes. **Packet sniffing** is the act of capturing and interpreting network traffic, which sounds more complex than it really is. Have you ever eavesdropped on a telephone conversation in your home by picking up another telephone? Packet sniffing is similar, except that instead of listening to two people talk, you use a computer (usually a laptop) to detect and monitor two (or more) computers communicating. This is done in order to understand network traffic patterns and to intercept unencrypted data. When you consider that email and Web traffic by default is not encrypted and that shared network drives also transfer data unencrypted, also by default, dangers associated with packet sniffing become very clear. Essentially, if you can read something, so can a cybercriminal who is sniffing your data in transit. An analogy would be when a person monitors a house from across the street using binoculars, a radio scanner to pickup cordless telephone conversations, or laser devices aimed at window glass to detect and record sound vibrations and conversations going on inside a building or vehicle.

Packet sniffing is accomplished simply by installing special applications designed to passively monitor network traffic and display the results of a "sniff" in an understandable format on the monitoring system. Packet sniffing programs can be either commercial or open source products specifically designed for use by system administrators who need to detect bottlenecks in data traffic flow, or they may be programs developed by individual or groups of cybercriminals with the explicit intention of detecting, monitoring, and capturing valuable data transmissions. As such, packet sniffing applications are used in corporate espionage, among other types of cybercrimes.

Packet sniffing over wired networks can be either a simple or complex task, depending on the configuration requirements. Packet sniffers are typically limited to the network segment they are located on. For less technically inclined readers, just imagine a telephone line in a house you happen to be in and that you want to listen in on what was being said. You go to another telephone somewhere in the house, quietly pick up the receiver, and cover the microphone so that just like in the movies people talking cannot hear you breathe. Although you can clearly hear this conversation, you cannot hear other telephone conversations taking place at the same time on different telephone lines. This is exactly like packet sniffing over a wired network. You can only monitor the data moving between the computers to which you are connected. However, sniffing over a wireless network is completely different. Imagine instead a large number of people shouting conversations back and forth in a large room. All you need to do to hear any given conversation is pay attention to particular people talking. Sniffing over a wireless network is similar. Every computer on a given wireless network is on the same segment, so all traffic going to all of the computers can be intercepted by a cybercriminal using a sniffer. Remember this the next time you are sitting in a coffee shop, airport, or other location and decide to jump onto a wireless network. In so doing, you are essentially allowing anyone with a laptop and packet sniffing application to monitor and intercept everything you are doing as well as communications and files sent to you by other people over the Internet. We will revisit this issue in Chapter 10 when considering WiFi network security.

**Port Scanning** is simply scanning a computer via a network connection to determine what types of services a given computer has available to access either through legitimate or illegitimate means. When a computer provides a network service, such as hosting a Web site or an email relay, the computer assigns a port number to the software application running the service. When traffic is sent to the computer with a port number specified, the computer knows which application to send the traffic to, after which the receiving computer typically sends an acknowledgement back. Thus, by sending brief transmissions to all open ports and waiting for a reply, an attacker can potentially obtain a list of all applications and running services on any given computer and thereby deduce how to launch an attack. However, just because a cybercriminal can port scan any device that has an operating network interface does not make the device vulnerable to attack. To expand on the packet sniffing analogy, many Internet-enabled devices simply do not have windows or doors to peer into, so lurking around and banging on the walls of a building does not mean valuables inside will or even can be damaged or stolen.

**Operating system profiling** and **application fingerprinting** refer to profiling system vulnerabilities through port scanning in a way that detects how a given computer is configured and can be effectively attacked. By knowing, for example, that a targeted computer is running a particular operating system, cybercriminals would know what exploits are likely to be most effective and/or they could design customized exploits to carry out a cyber attack against a system known or believed to contain valuable information. This type of scenario is within the realm of corporate espionage and organized crime attacks. Special firewalls are now available that in addition to blocking hacking attempts also provide disinformation about an operating system or application fingerprint in order to confuse cybercriminals using this method of attack. However, if a cybercriminal can determine when communication ports are open, they can plan attacks in phases.

To expand on the earlier analogy, imagine now that the person who has been watching and lurking around a house begins looking for alarm system signs and decals, examining the types of door and window locks, and essentially scoping out the technology he will need to overcome when the break-in takes place. Port scanning, like packet sniffing, requires software applications that are available either commercially or via open source, and both varieties can be used for legitimate or illegal purposes. System administers can employ port scanning software to check the effectiveness of their operating system and application patch-up installation procedures. Cybercriminals use port scanning software to carry out attacks on computers and other electronic devices that have network interfaces. In 2003, Cisco became the first company to widely deploy voice over Internet protocol (VoIP) network telephones (not to be confused with cellular phones). These useful devices are examples of network-resident appliances capable of being port scanned simply because they have an IP address.

**War driving** is typically accomplished by a person using a laptop computer outfitted with a wireless connection card who drives or walks around a residential or commercial area in search of wireless networks. This activity typically leads to acquiring free Internet access sometimes in order to capture sensitive data in transit or even gain access to corporate servers containing trade secrets. Sometimes people also do this to obscure their identity in order to receive or transmit data involved with criminal activities. On November 22, 2003, police in Toronto, Canada, stopped a man driving the wrong way on a residential street. After noticing the driver was naked from the waist down, the investigating officer determined the man had been downloading child pornography by illegally connecting to the wireless network of an in-home computer system located nearby. Subsequent investigation and search of the man's home resulted in seizure of ten computers and hundreds of CDs and floppy disks containing thousands of illegal child pornography images.[16] Depending on signal strength, unprotected wireless systems can be detected and connected to from distances ranging from 30 to as far as 300 yards away.

**Password Cracking** is a means of computer intrusion that involves figuring out a password needed to access a computer, other electronic device, or information system for legitimate or criminal purposes. Have you ever lost or forgotten a password? System administrators are frequently asked to recover someone's forgotten password or to access password-protected computer files left behind by a departed employee. Similarly, computer forensics investigators are periodically required to get into systems to investigate suspected crimes. Cybercriminals attempt to guess passwords in order to gain improper or illegal access to computers, other devices, or information systems in order to manipulate, damage, destroy, or steal data.

The easiest, although not necessarily the most effective, way of cracking a password is to guess it. This may not be that difficult if the password is a person's name, a common word, or label of something of known importance. One cybercrime investigator explained that he can often quickly deduce an uncooperative subject's system password by carefully studying items such as greeting cards, photographs, or other memorabilia in the suspect's desk or work area. In one case, the person whose system was suspected of harboring evidence of crimes was a devout fan

of the Dallas Cowboys football team. All sorts of Cowboys trivia adorned the person's work area, so within two minutes the investigator had cracked the computer password, "Cowboy#1."

In addition to guessing passwords, software cracking/recovery tools are available for purchase and as open source applications off the Internet. They work on a wide variety of devices, operating systems, and applications that may all have different levels and specific passwords. Some of these tools are very powerful, capable of generating millions upon millions of passwords in very short periods of time in what amounts to automated guessing that is also known as brute force attacks. Such powerful cracking tools combined with more powerful computers available to cybercriminals underscore why passwords need to be changed often and consist of at least eight randomly selected upper and lower case alphanumerical characters that do not form a proper name or word or in anyway represent something that people know or could find out about you. A password such as gu7$Pdz2 is an example of a strong password that would at least inhibit if not prevent someone from gaining illegal or unauthorized access to a system.

### 3.1.4.2 Phone Phreaking.    Phone phreaking involves illegally accessing telecommunications systems for exploration of fraudulent purposes in ways that avoid connection charges. Increasingly, improvements to telephone security systems have prevented this form of cybercrime from taking place. However, some phreakers still attempt to use their knowledge of telephone system technology and homebrew electronic tools known as "boxes" to illegally access phone networks and make illegal calls at no charge to themselves.

Notice how a combination of tools and techniques can be employed to carry out cybercrime (i.e., varying types of electronic equipment combined with deceiving telephone operators into facilitating wire fraud in violation of federal law). Can you see how phreaking can be an aspect of more complex and ambitious attacks, such as in the incident described at the beginning of

## CYBER TALE 3.6

### *Free and Illegal Phone Phreaking*

Phone phreaking used to be rather easily accomplished using a tone dialer and other inexpensive items commonly available at electronics stores. A "red box" mimics the tones of pay phones, which can be played after depositing coins in some pay phones as if to make a local or long distance call. By playing back these tones into the microphone of the telephone receiver, it is sometimes possible to make phone calls without depositing any additional money. Using this method, I was able to make over $150 worth of telephone calls throughout a two-week period at no charge. After tiring

of making domestic calls, I attempted to make international calls the same way. Although more difficult, I was still often able to socially engineer telephone company operators into placing the call on my behalf after claiming that for some unknown reason a connection could not seem to be made. Later I shared my successes with friends, who over a period of several weeks created a map showing the locations of telephones that had varying potential for a phone phreaking. That was back in high school when I was really stupid and not worried about being able to get a decent job.

*Anonymous Student*

---

Chapter 1 involving Kevin Poulsen, who took control of a telephone company's computerized call switching system in order to win a Porsche offered in a radio station's phone-in contest? The point is that different types of IT-enabled attacks and crime are often carried out in combination. This implies the need for users to be aware of current and potential attack tools and methods in order to prevent harm from occurring to their computer systems, data, finances, and lives. It also implies that law enforcement investigators, information security professionals, and computer forensics examiners must stay abreast of existing and potential forms of attack if they are to remain able to combat evolving forms of cybercrime.

### *3.1.4.3 Spyware and Key Loggers.*

Spyware is very similar to adware, and as previously indicated, a single program can simultaneously function as both spyware and adware. The major difference is that **spyware** is typically designed to actively monitor, track, and record the computing activities of a user, such as their Web browser history or keystrokes. Adware, however, is designed to send advertising to consumers based on their Web activity and purchasing information. **Keystroke logger programs** are a form of spyware that track every keystroke and

word typed by a user inclusive of passwords, financial account numbers, and other information. Key logging software can be programmed to periodically send recorded data via an intranet or the Internet to a collection server. As with adware, spyware and key logger programs can be used legally for, respectively, commercial marketing by vendors and by employers to monitor the keystrokes and other computer activities of employees. These types of programs can also be used by unscrupulous advertising firms to data mine for personal information on individuals in order to sell it to mass marketing firms and by cybercriminals for any number of illegal purposes.

Spyware and key logging programs are widely available for purchase and accessible free of charge on the Internet. As with the other network administration software tools described above (e.g., packet sniffing, port scanning, and password cracking programs), "plug and play" spyware and key loggers are also unfortunately easy to use by cybercriminals. Even cybercriminals with minimal technical programming skills can surreptitiously install these programs on the computers of individuals being targeted for a cyber attack. Such programs can be secretly embedded within file attachments to email and IM messages that are designed to socially engineer naïve users into clicking on them, thereby launching an undetectable installation procedure. Once installed, the program goes to work monitoring and recording the user's computer activities and may automatically send reports back to the culprits who sent out the original message. Another way to acquire spyware is by visiting Web sites maintained by operators with specific marketing interests, who will then use information obtained via spyware in their programming and use of adware.

Spyware and keystroke loggers typically run whenever a computer is on, silently recording all keystrokes, program activities, and Web sites visited. By design, the program will make this information available to its creator either by sending a message with a log report or by giving the creator access to the system on which it resides to see exactly what the user being spied on is seeing and therefore also doing with their computer. Spyware is notorious for making computers run slowly, and it is not uncommon for naïve users to have several undetected spyware (and adware) applications running simultaneously on their systems. Chances are that if your system suffers from pop-up adds or seems to run

slowly, it is because it has been infected with adware and/or spyware programs. As will be discussed in Chapter 10, detecting these programs and cleaning your system can normally be accomplished by acquiring, installing, and frequently using commercially available or open source anti-malware programs.

*3.1.4.4 Computer Hacking and System Trespassing.* In a generic and classical sense, hacking involves manipulating technology to do things better or for purposes for which the technology is not intended.[17] Technology manipulation, whether of a model railroad, a household appliance, or a major telecommunications network, is what provides many hackers with the "kick," or thrill, they seek.[18] This relates to the curiosity, exploration, technical knowledge, and skill that are fundamental to the hacker subculture and hacker ethic, which will be addressed in Chapter 7. For our purposes, hacking primarily pertains to illegally gaining access to one or more computer systems after exploiting security vulnerabilities or defeating security barriers such as passwords or firewalls and then either exploring

**CYBER TALE 3.7**

### The Infamous Back Orifice Remote Control Tool

In 1998, when file sharing was just becoming popular, various new forms of malware and backdoor programs were being released onto the Internet. One student recalled how most people in his dorm actively engaged in file sharing, but because antivirus protection programs were not very robust or extensively used, computers quickly became infected. During this time the infamous Back Orifice remote administration tool was developed and released onto the Internet. This was a particularly nasty program that created a trap door in an infected operating system, allowing cybercriminals to remotely control computers. For example, the

program enabled hackers to see what students were typing on their keyboard, view images and text on desktops, listen to music being played on an infected computer, and even control use of a WebCam to watch someone work on a computer. By virtue of key logging, attackers were also able to acquire usernames and passwords to other computer networks to which a user had access and to read correspondence to and from the user and other people. Fortunately, although strains of the Back Orfice remote control tool still exist in the wild (Internet), virus detection, definition, and system restoration applications can now help users to protect their computers against such malware.

data, stealing data, and/or introducing a foreign programming function (e.g., malware) to a computer system or network.

Hacking computer systems typically involves committing a series of various computer abuses or cybercrimes such as Web and email spoofing, illegitimate packet sniffing, port scanning, and running spyware. Doing any of these things illicitly along with other cybercrimes and socially engineering people into giving up confidential information such as passwords are common aspects of contemporary malevolent computer hacking. In other words, hacks are typically not a single event. Rather, serious computer hacking is a process that, like other forms of criminality, often consists of one or more actions: being inspired to action, becoming curious, exploring and researching, conducting cyber and/or physical surveillance and planning, designing attacks, and specifically programming exploits (which may include any combination of the methods described in this chapter). Hackers also confer with trusted experts, test programming and security barriers, gain access to systems, and create backdoors in programs that can be used for future access. They persist in monitoring the activities of users on a system, harvesting data of interest or value, and manipulating one or more aspects of a system or Web site, and may use all that they have learned, built, and implemented to create a platform from which to launch other attacks. Depending on the amount of dedication, time, and other resources applied, hacking ranges in nature from being a part-time hobby of relative amateurs to a full-time programming and attack enterprise committed by individuals or crews of cybercriminals who possess any number of technical skills and motivations and who may instances be hired or compensated in other ways to carry out their attacks. By extension, system trespassing refers to accessing information systems without permission, as in instances of externally derived hacking attacks, but may also be accomplished by insiders who exceed their authority and system permissions

to explore parts of a network for any number of reasons. Thus, insider employees who exceed their authority to improperly access parts of computer systems may be charged with computer trespassing under state and possibly federal computer crime laws. Obviously, insider attackers who exceed their authorized permissions and trespass within networks can also perform other hacking-related activities (i.e., any of the attack methods described in this chapter) just as if they were outsiders. However, insiders typically already have the advantage of being able to access physical and cyber spaces, as well as access to people with whom they will socially engineer or have already established trusting relationships. Insiders may also attempt to make an attack appear as if it were launched from the outside, if they do not in fact collude with outsiders to perpetrate a particular or series of cybercrimes.

Computer hacking and system trespassing ranges from innocuous exploration of computer systems—for example to see if a system can be cracked and what data it contains—to somewhat harmful attacks involving malicious pranks such as drawing a mustache on the Web site photo of a public official (which actually happened to former U.S. Attorney General Janet Reno) to exceedingly damaging attacks involving significant manipulation, destruction, or theft of classified government or proprietary private sector data, as in instances of corporate espionage. The following real cases exemplify types of exploits and the potential range of harm caused by hacking into systems of academic institutions:

• Students in a private high school once developed the ability to log into the school's network using a fake username and password. These were completely indistinguishable from those of legitimate user accounts. With such access, the students were able to pull off pranks such as using a hex editor to change pull-down directory menus into various insults about a student who was not liked. One of the malicious "labbies" who created this capability also electronically plagiarized the disliked student's computer coding homework script. Eventually the student who did this was discovered and expelled.

- In January of 2005 hackers illegally gained access to and downloaded personal information of more than 30,000 students, faculty, and staff of George Mason University in Fairfax, Virginia. The university established a hot line to inform victims that personal information including their social security numbers had been stolen and what steps they could take to try to prevent it from being used in cybercrimes such as identity theft. The university had been in the process of replacing students' social security numbers with a unique student identification number when the hacking occurred.[19]

### 3.1.4.5 Distributing Programming Vulnerabilities.
Dozens of new software flaws are discovered every day. Invariably, many of these flaws are security vulnerabilities that when exposed are then exploited by computer hackers who are intent on exploring, gaining some level of control of, causing damage to, or stealing from a given system. People who discover security and other types of programming flaws, whether employed as developers or other users of computer programs, provide a valuable service in the software community. However, when a security programming vulnerability is released with working exploit code, malevolent users will most certainly use it for illicit or illegal purposes until the program developers engineer a patch to fix the problem. Effective patches can take considerable money and time to develop and even more effort, time, and other resources before becoming known and widely adopted by users throughout cyber society. This is especially true when vast numbers of common users are not in the habit of routinely updating their operating systems, software applications, and virus definitions.

Meanwhile, malevolent users create new variations of exploits in order to take advantage of vulnerabilities distributed on the Internet and to overcome patches that they know are in the works. As this happens, software developers must respond by monitoring innovative strains of malware so that their product patches fix discovered vulnerabilities and guard against anticipated exploits. Ideally they are able to create a final patch, if not a new version of the software, in order to correct all previously discovered vulnerabilities and prevent future attacks. Obviously the sooner a robust patch or new version of an application or operating system can be developed, the more likely it will thwart development of malicious code specifically designed to take advantage of programming flaws. This general condition underscores principles of the theory of technology-enabled crime, policing, and security that will be discussed in Chapter 5. However, it does nothing to resolve the longstanding debate about the appropriateness of employing known hackers to help solve computer programming and security problems, or to address electronic spying by government agencies, corporations, and other types of firms and organizations competing for technological, intelligence, and/or market advantages.

### 3.1.4.6 Corporate and Government Espionage.
Technologies used to legitimately monitor IT systems are also used for electronic monitoring, surveillance, and spying by corporate and government entities. Whereas **monitoring** involves systematic, continual, legitimate, and either active or passive observation of persons, places, things, or processes, **surveillance** involves the observation of suspicious persons or activities by police, security, or government agents for specific evidence of crimes or other wrongdoing. Surveillance can also be undertaken by agents and contractors of corporations or firms, who often face stiff market competition and need to understand what their competitors are up to. Surveillance by private sector firms including security companies or by law enforcement or intelligence officials is usually covert and carried out with legal authority. Surveillance for illegal purposes is universally publicly condemned as being unethical,

even though it is widely practiced by individuals, groups, unscrupulous firms and organizations linked to domestic or international criminal or terrorist networks.

The term **spying** refers to illegal government or corporate espionage, which is also widely condemned although practiced in the interest of preserving national security or unfairly achieving a competitive market advantage. Espionage, if exposed, may have negative legal, political, or financial repercussions. In March of 2002, the Commission for the Review of FBI Security Programs revealed the shocking details of how for over 22 years, Supervisory Special Agent Robert Hanssen routinely exploited vulnerabilities in the bureau's human and information security systems to spy on behalf of the Soviet Union and later Russia to provide these nations with "vast quantities of documents and computer diskettes filled with national security information of incalculable value."[20] Hanssen's treason was particularly disturbing because his trusted insider status afforded him access to classified materials vital to the security of the United States, because his activities went undetected within the FBI for over two decades, revealing security and auditing system weaknesses within the nation's presumably most capable law enforcement agency, and because his betrayal led to the executions of foreign intelligence operatives employed by the United States.

Surveillance and spying focus on individuals, activities, buildings, open-space properties, or vehicles of interest, and are carried out in ways that involve (1) stationary, mobile, or cyber operations that require various types of technologies to enhance visual, hearing, and/or data traffic analysis capabilities of operatives and analysts; (2) recording of events, locations, days and times, and patterns of behaviors or activities; (3) monitoring of radio, telephonic, or in-person conversations, as well as electronic correspondence such as email or instant messaging; and/or (4) systematic monitoring, retrieval, and analysis of public, open source, and discarded unshredded hardcopy records pertaining to travel, personal, and professional associations, financial purchases, and so on. Discarded trash is a favorite source of legally collected evidence of crimes, as well as indications of ongoing or impending government or corporate activities. Note the combined physical and cyber technological dimensions implied by these data gathering and analysis possibilities. Always remember that virtually all computer and other forms of IT-enabled abuse and crime involve some element of physical activity by human beings that can potentially be anticipated, observed, or otherwise detected and thus prevented, interdicted, or investigated using traditional means after the fact. This reality will be reemphasized and explained in more detail in Chapter 9, which focuses on investigating and prosecuting cybercriminals.

Espionage by corporate and other types of private sector firms principally targets trade secrets and other proprietary information deemed valuable by competing entities. Such information may include the chemical composition of products or particular processes used in manufacturing. It may also include pricing, cost, and client and personnel data such as salary figures that could, if known, be used to lure clients or employees to a competing firm or to undercut market rates. Even information pertaining to executives' travel and vacation schedules may provide useful intelligence on what is occurring within a competing firm. Richard Power, in his book, *Tangled Web: Tales of Digital Crime from the Shadows of Cyberspace*, describes several real-world examples of corporate espionage that involve a myriad of technologies, targeted items, victims, investigative methods, and subsequent criminal charges, some under provisions of the Economic Espionage Act of 1996.[21]

### 3.1.5 Unauthorized and Illegal File Sharing

Most readers of this text are aware of the controversies surrounding unauthorized and illegal file sharing. Indeed, there is considerable variance in estimates of the harm caused by illegal file sharing (which will be discussed in Chapter 6), as well as ethical issues surrounding various business practices of the recording industry. Here we consider what this form of cybercrime is, how it came about, how it is accomplished, and to some extent where society now stands on the issue.

### 3.1.5.1 Applications Software Piracy.

The earliest form of widespread computer-enabled copyright violations involved software programs being copied and exchanged on floppy disks among family members, friends, and colleagues. During the early 1980s, as today's college students were being born into societies with increasing numbers of affordable desktop computers and other electronic devices, many users did not realize that sharing software without authorization, what came to be known as "piracy," constituted criminal and/or civil violations of U.S. federal and/or state copyright laws. Copying or distributing software without authorization was then as now also illegal in numerous other nations, and also prohibited by international treaties among nations with long histories of mutual interest in respecting and protecting copyrighted materials. Throughout this period, various computing technologies, such as file transfer protocol (FTP), USENET newsgroups, bulletin board systems (BBS), and Internet relay chat (IRC) were also increasingly used in various ways and in combination to facilitate piracy of software. When these were coupled with Microsoft Windows® and later the rising popularity of the Internet in the early 1990s, software piracy expanded internationally as never before because these later technologies enabled increasing and vast numbers of ordinary computer users to exchange data, files, and software applications online. Indeed, throughout computing history, illegally copied software has simply been transferred more or less effectively with legitimate tools adopted by pirates for illicit sharing. From USENET newsgroups, electronic bulletin board systems and FTP sites all the way to contemporary peer-to-peer (p2p) and swarming software—all have been used to transfer illegally copied copyrighted materials.

### 3.1.5.2 Illegal Downloading of Music and Movie Files.

In 1999, a teenager named Shawn Fanning developed the **Napster** software that first enabled users to share music files through a central server. Users simply needed to type in the name of a desired song, its author, or an album/CD, and Napster would search through the computers of Internet users who were also using the software to share folders of songs, then match the sought-after song information and return the results as song files to the requester. Napster could be downloaded for free off the Internet, and because it was so easy to use, almost overnight became the preferred tool for downloading music files. Eventually, enthusiasm for Napster resulted in its becoming a firm that, according to the Recording Industry Association of America (RIAA), was profiting by illegally distributing copyrighted music through a central computer server. The RIAA brought civil action to halt downloading of music made possible by Napster's client–server network, and in 2001, U.S. District Court Chief Judge Marilyn Hall Patel ordered Napster to stop distributing copyrighted material through its network. Thereafter, Napster began offering sound tracks and CDs via direct sales and music downloading services for fees from which copyright royalties are paid. Several other companies now also provide music downloading services for a fee, some of which are being purchased and experimented with by colleges and universities throughout the United States in efforts to prevent illegal downloading via campus computer networks. However, millions of people, college students in particular, continue to use legally available and legitimate open source software such as Kazaa Lite, WinMX, DC++, LimeWire, eDonkey, Direct Connect, IMesh, Gnutella, and BearShare to illegally download copyrighted music, full-length movies, and software applications.

In 2004 the Ninth U.S. Circuit Court of Appeals, in a lawsuit filed by Metro-Goldwyn-Mayer (MGM) Studios Inc., found Grokster Ltd and StreamCast Networks Inc., creators of the popular Grokster and Morpheus p2p downloading software, not liable for piracy committed by users of their applications.[22] The federal court's ruling was based substantially on the landmark 1984 Supreme Court "Betamax" decision (Sony v. Universal Studios), which proclaimed, among other things, that under principles of the fair use doctrine established by the Copyright Act of 1976, consumers could duplicate copyrighted materials for personal use and technology developers could profit from tools designed to facilitate legal copying of copyrighted materials.[23] In addition, the high court ruled that technology developers had no duty to monitor illegal activities of law violators who used their tools. Thus, from a legal perspective, the so-called "vicarious copyright infringement theory" was struck down. However, at issue in the recent case of MGM Studios Inc. et al v. Grokster Ltd. et al, was whether technology developers should profit from tools which are known to facilitate illegal copying if not specifically developed for such purposes, even though the basic technology (e.g., p2p file sharing) also has, and is used, for legitimate purposes. Thus, on June 27, 2005, the U.S. Supreme Court unanimously ruled that evidence of unlawful intent by both Grokster Ltd and StreamCast Networks, Inc., to induce and facilitate illegal sharing of copyrighted materials existed. Accordingly, "One who distributes a device with the object of promoting its use to infringe copyright, as shown by clear expression or other affirmative steps taken to foster infringement, going beyond mere distribution with knowledge of third-party action, is liable for the resulting acts of infringement by third parties using the device, regardless of the device's lawful uses."[24] Note that although the case was remanded for civil trial by a lower court, careful interpretation of the Supreme Court ruling does not outlaw development or use of p2p file sharing technology for legal purposes.

Today the most common way of pirating music, movies, and software is still through pure **peer-to-peer (p2p) networks,** which, unlike the original Napster software that relied on a central server for indexing and search purposes, allow for direct searching and exchange of data between users' computers. By eliminating a central server in which large numbers of data-intensive files can become bottlenecked, p2p networks diffuse requested traffic across many computers simultaneously, enabling people to exchange data in a manner more technologically efficient than traditional client–server networks, depending on available bandwidth and the combined capabilities of the computers involved. As previously indicated, connecting to a p2p network and illegally downloading songs, movies, or applications is easily accomplished with software packages still legally available on the Web for free, although U.S. based software developers are now specifically prohibited from intentionally creating, selling or profiting from tools that enable copying and sharing of copyrighted materials if they know they will be used for such illegal purposes and go beyond merely making them available.

Illegal and legal p2p networking has combined to bring about the **direct access revolution,** in which consumers can initiate communications with and even purchase music directly from artists. Artists who do not have recording contracts with recording firms and consumers who may have particular tastes in music not offered by mainstream recording labels or who prefer to pay somewhat smaller amounts for unconventional music, often of very good recording quality, find this situation to be mutually beneficial. In effect, such artists and consumers have created a nontraditional market for music that operates without formal advertising, contracts, regulation, or taxation. This evolving market condition has some recording industry and government officials worried. However, there is nothing inherently illegal about these selling or purchasing practices or the technology that makes this possible, so long as applicable taxes are paid, court rulings are abided by, and other regulatory conditions are met.

P2p networks have existed for a long time and they are also used extensively to exchange legal copies of copyrighted works in addition to augmenting needed bandwidth in certain locations. However, the gaming, music, and movie industries have been infiltrated by pirates who often acquire and distribute copies of entertainment files on the Internet before they are officially released for purchase by the general public. Illegal copies are normally initially acquired by[25] (1) unscrupulous insider employees of production or marketing firms who acquire and donate nearly final versions to the illegal open source underground for mass distribution via so-called **top sites**, (2) hackers who accomplish the same thing by penetrating the information security systems of these firms, (3) "dumpster diving" at manufacturing (rip) plants that typically discard as defective ten to fifteen percent of CDs and DVDs produced, or (4) secret video taping of movies by people in studios or theaters who then release these files of varying sound and picture quality onto the Internet. Recent examples of entertainment files illegally acquired and prematurely released onto the Internet include the computer game *Half Life 2* and the movie *Hulk*.[26]

Cybercriminals who reportedly operate clandestine top sites initially "seed" the Internet with a certain limited number of illegal copies of movies and song tracks. Top site operators employ several methods to avoid detection and infiltration by authorities into their underground scene. They include establishing a hierarchy of roles with corresponding levels of account access and content distribution authority, frequently changing authorized usernames and passwords, **bouncing** between servers to prevent identification of IP addresses, and **encryption** of files and messages exchanged. After movies or song tracks are initially distributed by a top site to first-level p2p networks, they are reproduced until millions of computer users throughout the world are able to illegally download them off the Internet in a manner that is difficult if not impossible for investigators to backtrack to the original top site distributors. This situation is now exacerbated by a data exchange technique known as **swarming**, employed by specially designed software applications that enable unethical computer users who seek pirated content to exchange only portions of data files, which for technical reasons, and in accordance with the recent U.S. Supreme Court ruling in MGM Studios Inc. et al v. Grokster, Ltd et al may not be illegal. Suffice it to say that exchange of copyrighted materials via p2p networks remains an evolving area of law, which is closely related to controversy surrounding software development activities of the open source community discussed later in Chapter 7.

### 3.1.6 Abuse of Computers and Electronic Devices in Academia

Are you an honest student? Do you try your best to do well on assignments and exams, without cheating, or have you on occasion used a computer or other electronic device to plagiarize works or buy papers? Do you know people who have cheated, on assignments or exams? In this subsection we address abuse of computers and electronic devices in academia by students as well as professors, who in rare instances fake research results. We show how much cheating occurs, explain the implications of this for students and the overall integrity of academia, and describe alternative high- and low-tech ways of cheating. Before doing so, however, it is useful to compare abuse of IT in academia with other forms of cybercrimes discussed throughout this chapter.

Compare, for instance, academic cheating with computer hacking. Both often involve planning and use of IT for deceptive purposes in various ways that take place over a period of time, by one or more people in order to defraud. Whereas academic cheating is not illegal per se, cheating on a licensing exam by an individual who is qualified to take it on the basis of having earned a college degree violates most state crime or administrative licensing laws. Cheating

**CYBER TALE 3.8**

## Mass-Distributed Illegal File Sharing

Internet relay chat (IRC) allows people from all over the world to connect to different networks in order to chat and send files. Some people engaged in IRC join underground not defined groups that establish chat rooms and instant messaging networks in order to exchange illegal copies of music, movie, or software application files. One day after joining a Warez "rip" group, I was asked by fellow group members to become a "dump" in order to store and help facilitate illegal file sharing. This was primarily because the university's server space combined with its broadband connection afforded the group a large "pond and pipeline" through which to exchange large music and movie files quickly. At first I did not realize the technological implications of what I had agreed to do. However, within a few days I became aware that compressed versions of new movie and music releases were being exchanged via my computer on the university network by persons from all over the world.

Previously I had only occasionally downloaded or exchanged music or movie files with acquaintances, but now my computer had become a "bot" through which unlimited file sharing took place by people I did not even know. Frequently my computer bogged down or maxed out because

of the amount of illegal copyrighted material moving through it. Originally I thought it was cool that within minutes of games, music, movies, and software files being posted on an FTP Web site by a Warez rip group, they would magically appear on my computer. I was emboldened by online messages from fellow chatters to "keep up the good work" and "continue providing the newest releases."

Eventually my computer was configured to scan fellow chatter's IPs for fast .edu (academic) connections. I was no longer merely a "dump" through which files could be exchanged or a courier to distribute FTP files illegally once they were acquired. My computer and I had risen to "scanner" status in order to recruit new members and thereby perpetuate illegal file sharing. I was no longer naïve about what was going on or my role in making it possible. I had become a willing member of a criminal enterprise that rationalized its actions on the basis of a philosophy that information and entertainment files should not be restricted and that the $12–20 cost of CDs and DVDs was too high. It was then that I swore off this insanity. Now I rarely buy music, but I no longer pirate at all.

*Anonymous Student*

---

in college may result in expulsion. In effect, using IT to cheat involves computer abuse that causes harm by degrading the reputation of colleges and universities, plus the integrity of academia, as the result of unqualified students passing classes and receiving degrees they have not earned. Students who cheat also harm themselves, other students, future employers, and society as a whole. Consider that students who cheat on assignments or exams may pass their classes and graduate but will likely under-perform in their future jobs because of lack of knowledge or technical skills, thereby ripping off employers. This in turn, if not addressed, will

harm the reputations of their academic institutions and eventually result in decreased placement opportunities for other graduates and enrollment declines. Cheating on tests or assignments in situations involving proportioned (i.e., curved) scores also results in direct victimization, as when cheaters receive "A" grades and raise the curve, causing some lower scoring but honest students to receive lower grades than they deserve or even fail an assignment, exam, or course.

Academic dishonesty therefore is like other forms of fraud in its intent, methods, and effects. Because computers and other electronic

IT devices are so often used to cheat, it is treated here as a form of computer abuse that may rise to the level of being criminal in instances of cheating on qualifying license exams, faking funded research findings, and so on. Let us now briefly examine three forms of academic dishonesty as the computer abuses or cybercrimes they really are—plagiarism, cheating on exams or assignments, and faking research.

### 3.1.6.1 Plagiarism.

Plagiarism involves claiming, as your own, research or writing that is not of your own thinking or effort, or referring to passages in written works as if they were the product of your own thinking without giving adequate attribution to their authors. Vast amounts of readily accessible Internet content, combined with browser search and copy-and-paste application features, ease the ability to plagiarize.[27] Many student-run Web service sites and for-profit companies offer term papers on an exchange basis or for sale (e.g., $5–10 per page for term papers, plus additional fees for hardcopy shipping or express processing via email, etc.). "In most states, it is illegal to sell papers that will be turned in as student work," although this does not stop term paper mills that maintain Web sites from receiving thousands of hits per day.[28] Additionally, a seeming decline in the amount and/or quality of secondary and higher education pertaining to proper academic citation methods (as well as computer ethics) may contribute to high-tech plagiarism, although low-tech plagiarism such as copying information out of books without citing sources also still regularly occurs.[29]

Studies indicate that if plagiarism is viewed to occur widely on a given campus, students will be more inclined to plagiarize. These conclusions coincide with research indicating that plagiarism also increases with peer approval, and support for this such as often exists among members of fraternities and sororities.[30] Sometimes these groups also organize note taking and cram sessions based on archived copies of exams accumulated over several semesters and from innumerable courses taken by current and former members of the fraternity or sorority.[31] In effect, such organizations perpetuate cheating through data gathering, acculturation of new members, and reinforcement of deviancy that may involve various types of computing and other technologies.

### 3.1.6.2 Cheating on Exams and Assignments.

Studies reveal that women cheat less than men and that students of both genders attending small liberal arts colleges cheat less than students attending large universities.[32] Low-tech forms of cheating on exams have long included copying answers from other students or using crib notes written on hands and even planted in the examination room prior to the test. Acquiring copies of exams in advance of taking a test is another method of cheating, as is listening to recordings of likely materials to be on a test with a Walkman, iPod, or other miniaturized listening device during an exam. Baseball caps hide wandering eyes from unaware exam proctors who allow hats to be worn during tests, just as calculators and other devices can store math formulas and other vital information if it has not already been written down by a student on a tennis shoe or the inside flap of a purse or backpack left open within view on the floor. Exchanging text messages and/or visiting Web sites during exams in order to get correct answers are two other high-tech methods of cheating in exams. Accessing restricted files in order to copy computer code on a computer science or software engineering homework assignment also constitutes academic dishonesty.

Many other simple to complex methods of individual and group cheating are possible. For instance, simple whispering among friends, or small groups developing complex hand signals that correspond to locations on desktops to indicate A, B, C, or D answers are known to occur.[33] Students have posted lecture notes onto their own Web sites to access with electronic devices during exams and have engaged in high-tech team cheating, as when a few students divvy up questions to research and post up or otherwise distribute answers to questions using electronic devices during exams. (In case you are wondering, most professors know about these methods—we are not stupid.) Another method of cheating is to prematurely electronically access test answer keys often made available by professors after exams. In 2004, twelve students at the University of Maryland at College Park were discovered to have cheated on an exam after they used electronic devices to access a Web page created *by professors* prior to the exam that purposely contained an incorrect answer key—an academic sting.[34]

### 3.1.6.3 Scientific Misconduct.

Students are not the only ones who cheat. In rare instances teaching faculty and research scientists fake their methods, data, or findings. This form of cheating is mentioned here because it is fraudulent, socially abusive, and usually involves computers or other electronic devices or systems. Incidents of scientific misconduct can also involve enormous stakes for society and huge amounts of money stemming from funded research grants, new or improved products, innovative manufacturing processes, and so on. Hence, genuine *and* faked research has implications for trade secrets and economic espionage, and both have much to do with trusting people and technology. In academia, notoriety attendant on scientific discoveries as well as tenure and promotions within university systems are also at stake for many professors. All this means that scientific misconduct is another form of cybercrime to be considered in the menagerie of technology-enabled abuses and concepts relating to information assurance discussed throughout this book.

With over 10,000 employees in sixteen countries, Bell Labs is widely considered to be the world's preeminent inventor and innovator of communications technologies. Since its founding in 1925, research at Bell Labs has resulted in more than 28,000 patents pertaining to pivotal discoveries relating to "transistors, digital networking and signal processing, lasers and fiber-optic

communications systems, communications satellites, cellular telephony, electronic switching of calls, touch-tone dialing, and modems. Bell Labs scientists have received six Nobel Prizes in Physics, nine U.S. Medals of Science and eight U.S. Medals of Technology." From 1998 to 2001, a physicist named J. Hendrik Schön, working with other researchers at Bell Labs, conducted experiments in superconductivity, molecular crystals, and molecular electronics. He reported major discoveries that were subsequently used as a basis for publishing several academic journal articles. However, an internal investigation determined that the data had been fabricated by Schön, the first incident of scientific misconduct ever to arise from research conducted at Bell Labs.[35]

In another case, scientists at Lawrence Berkeley National Laboratory withdrew the original claims of Victor Ninov as having discovered element 118 in the course of analyzing data used in cyclotron experiments by using customized software that at the time he alone understood how to operate. Only months later, after initial experiments could not be replicated, did a colleague of Ninov familiarize himself with the software, only to discover that Ninov's claims could not be supported by the original research data.[36] "Analysis of a computer log file gave evidence that data had been cut and pasted and numeric values had been changed."[37] Ninov insisted he was innocent and that others who had access to the computer on which the data was archived could have been responsible for faking it. However, independent research teams, even after spending considerable time trying to reproduce Ninov's findings, were unable to do so.[38]

To counter possibilities of scientific misconduct, academic journal referees and editors review articles before they are published to ensure that proper methods of data collection and analysis were followed. However, even the researchers may not always understand on a technical level what is taking place in particular aspects or phases of a study because the work being done is not within their area of expertise. Consequently, they trust each other to get their data collection and analysis right. Frequently it is only after a reported breakthrough and careful reanalysis by scientists who were not part of the original research team that flawed research methods, data analysis, or findings are discovered. This is the whole basis for oversight and approval agencies such as the federal government's Food and Drug Administration (FDA) taking months and even years to approve new foodstuffs or prescription drugs for market release.

### 3.1.7 Online Harassment and Computer-Enabled Sex Crimes

Using computers and other electronic devices to harass or threaten people or commit sex-related crimes are common forms of cybercrimes that often have disturbing specific impacts on victims and broader negative implications for society. Harassment may be a form of threat. Conversely, threats comprise a form of harassment when several are made in a given period of time. In addition, harassment or threats may relate to sexual relationships or motivations of offenders, although this is not always the case. Here we consider cyber harassment and threats, cyber stalking, pedophilia, and the creation, distribution, and possession of illegal pornography facilitated with computers or other electronic devices.

***3.1.7.1 Cyber Harassment and Threats.*** In January of 2005, Christopher Pierson, 40, of Ruskington, Lincolnshire, in the United Kingdom pled guilty to emailing "grossly offensive content" with "the purpose of causing distress and anxiety." His communications, which purported to be from the "Foreign Office Bureau" in Thailand, falsely reported that recipients' family members missing in the December 2004 tsunami that struck islands and coastlines throughout the Indian Ocean region were confirmed dead. Pierson, who reportedly sent the messages using the email account "ukgovfoffice@aol.com," had no official government role or

authority and simply made up the harassing messages.[39] You can imagine that the people who received these messages were shocked, distraught, and deeply offended, but do you regard the messages as a form of harassment or threat? Whereas **harassment** generally means "to annoy, torment repeatedly and persistently," a **threat** is an "expression of an intention to inflict something harmful."[40] Both types of behaviors, although defined differently by different states' crime laws, are illegal regardless of the technology used by offenders.

Direct harassment via the Internet can take the form of threatening or massive amounts of emails or instant messages, electronic sabotage, or distributing malware to targeted individuals. Indirect harassment may include impersonating people online, sending spam in their names, subscribing them to unwanted mailing lists, or posting false and/or unauthorized information about them on the Web, and doing so in a way that further leads to their being sent harassing messages online by other parties.[41] IT-enabled threats and harassment also occur in chat forums, and as the result of online purchasing agreements gone awry. Perpetrators of online harassment and threats may also route unwanted messages through anonymous **remailer systems** in attempts to protect their own identity or be conveyed through cell phone and other electronic devices capable of transmitting text messages. In 2003 Scottish police cited mobile phone text messaging for a 70 percent increase in the number of reported incidents involving threats and extortion, from 514 to 875 crimes, of which 450 allegedly involved "phone texting."[42]

Harassing messages may be purely insulting, include private information as a form of harassment, or contain threats to harm individuals or their property. Groups are also threatened and harassed for political reasons. In 1998, Richard Machado was the first person convicted in the United States of sending hate email, the result of his having sent Asian students at the University of California derogatory email in which he threatened to kill them.[43] Similarly, Kingman

## *Online Harassment via a Web site Soliciting Sex*

In December 1998, Darren S. Kochanowski was arrested for aggravated harassment in Pough-keepsie, New York, for conspiring with a comput-er- savvy coworker to create a Web site featuring his former girlfriend in sexually suggestive pho-tographs and her offering to meet with strangers for sex. The Web site included the victim's home address and both her residential and work tele-phone numbers. Posting of this information re-sulted in her receiving phone calls at work from men who desired her company. Only then did the victim learn about the Web site. Frightened and angry, she called investigators with the New York State Police, who, using computer forensics tech-niques, traced the creation of the Web site to Kochanowski.[47]

Quon was convicted in 1999 and sentenced to two years imprisonment for emailing death threats to Hispanic professors and students throughout the United States.[44]

IT-enabled harassment is not limited to college and university environments. So-called "cyberbullying" by children and adolescents aged 9–14 now reportedly occurs with alarming frequency and may have devastating impacts on young people targeted by their friends or ene-mies in primary and secondary schools. Thou-sands of children surveyed in 2004/2005, or through independent reporting by them or their guardians to organizations that specialize in on-line safety issues, indicate cyberbullying occurs throughout the United States and has led some school officials to hold awareness assemblies, modify school policies, or extend disciplinary ac-tions to off-campus online activities in cases in-volving students within a school system. This form of harassment often entails several kids picking on a victim through mass email, instant messaging, or Web postings. Content may include sensitive per-sonal information, unflattering pictures, or false al-legations. Young people can be emotionally and psychologically traumatized when subjected to this form of harassment, while those inflicting the harm are able to do so without having to engage the victim in person.[45]

It is also possible to orchestrate harassment of individuals by third parties. On January 28, 2005, Bess Carney of Burlington, Vermont, was charged in connection with allegedly opening an email account in a coworker's name, then sending herself threatening emails in that person's name. The person was subsequently scorned by other coworkers and family members because they be-lieved she had been threatening Carney. The ha-rassment continued until investigators determined it was actually Carney who had sent the threaten-ing emails to herself.[46] The Carney case exem-plifies the weird ways in which computers can be used to deceive, threaten, and harass. These types of cybercrimes are particularly discon-certing because many victims of online harass-ment and threats experience feelings and other harm similar to those experienced by victims of violent crimes. In fact, online harassment and threats may occur in connection with other crimes involving physical, emotional, or psycho-logical harm.

Have you ever been harassed or threatened? Did this occur online? If you were the victim of ha-rassment or threats, how did you feel and what did you do? Do you think there are a lot of computer-enabled harassment or threats on your campus or in your community? There is very little research data about the nature and extent of crimes involv-ing online threats or harassment. However, a sur-vey conducted at the Rochester Institute of Technology in 2004 revealed that within the pre-ceding year:

- Seventeen percent of the 873 undergraduate students surveyed at random reported that someone had used a computer to harass or embarrass them, and forty-one percent of these victims reported they experienced two or more incidents.
- Eight percent of students reported having been threatened online at least once, with thirty-two percent of these victims indicating they had been threatened two or more times.
- Thirteen percent of students indicated that they know their friends have made threats online, three percent admitted to harassing other people, and about one percent admitted making threats online.

This study also revealed that most online threats were committed by males against other males and pertained to relationships between significant others, flaming in the context of Internet chat, and/or male bravado (i.e., guys just being macho).[48]

### 3.1.7.2 Online Stalking and Pedophilia.

Stalking is repeated harassment and threatening actions such as following people and watching their movements, appearing at their homes or places of business, making annoying or intimidating phone calls, leaving messages or objects where they can be found by the victim, or vandalizing a person's property. In April of 2004 Trish Barteck of Woodridge, New Jersey, was stalked by Jonathan Gilberti, also of Woodridge, who watched Barteck from his vehicle as she trimmed bushes in her front yard. Barteck eventually spotted Gilberti watching her, so she called the police. Investigators learned that Gilberti had been led to believe from an Internet chat forum that Barteck wanted to be raped. The false impression had been created by a spiteful relative who pretended to be Barteck online. Messages describing Barteck, where she lived, and other details had previously resulted in another unknown man approaching her for sex, but it was not until the stalking event that everything was pieced together. It turned out that this was not the first time Gilberti had responded

to these types of fraudulent invitations. He subsequently received a ten-year prison term for three counts of attempted rape, and in January of 2005 New Jersey passed a new law making it illegal to use a computer or other electronic device to incite a crime.[49]

**Cyberstalking** involves using a computer or other electronic IT devices to monitor the activities and movements of people without their knowledge for purposes of intimidation, sexual gratification or domination, or other illicit motives. Jurisdictions differ in how they define this form of criminal behavior. Some states require a person to actually threaten a person or a person's family member with violence. Other states only require that a person be intimidated in the course of being followed or receiving messages.[50] The federal government codifies illegal interstate stalking by any technological means as behavior that places a person in reasonable fear of death or bodily injury.[51] Regardless of statutory provisions specifying what constitutes stalking, people who experience cyberstalking can be just as frightened, if not more frightened, than victims of traditional in-person stalking. Once again note that as with other forms of cybercrime, cyberstalking may involve both online and physical activities.[52]

Cyberstalking frequently involves the perpetrator acquiring information about their victim over time from online and/or other sources. This information is then used for illicit purposes not limited to monitoring, threatening, or harassing victims. For example, just as in cases involving harassment or threats, online stalking can involve posting true or untrue information and photographs (or links to them) in chat forums or on Web sites in a manner leading to third parties contacting one or more victims. Such postings may include true personal or professional contact data along with derogatory or embarrassing personal information about which others want to know more. Alternatively, postings may falsely indicate a victim's sexual preferences or desires for companionship, as in the Bartek case described

## Cyberstalking Star Trek: Voyager's Seven of Nine

In 1999, Jeri Lynn Ryan, famous for her role as Seven of Nine on the television series *Star Trek: Voyager*, became one of the first known victims of cyberstalking. A deranged fan named Marlon Pagtakhan began harassing Ryan by sending sexually suggestive notes to her at a Hollywood movie studio. Initially the notes were handwritten, but then were replaced with hundreds of emails that included threats to Ryan's husband. After police ordered Pagtakhan to cease his communications to Ryan, he sent more email indicating he would cease communicating if she donated $30,000 to a charity. Next he posted a video of himself on his Web site to explain why his actions did not constitute threatening behavior. Police arrested Pagtakhan in November of 2000 and charged him with stalking and extortion under provisions of California state crime laws. In May 2001 computerized evidence including the emails and video mentioned above were used to convict him of the charges. He was sentenced to five years probation, required to seek mental health treatment, and prohibited from using computers for the full term of his probation.[53]

above. Cynthia Armistead of Atlanta, Georgia, received harassing telephone calls and emails. Her harasser also reportedly posted messages to a USENET discussion forum falsely advertising Armistead's availability as a prostitute, which resulted in her receiving numerous additional unwanted emails and phone calls.[54]

Cyberstalking may also be in furtherance of **pedophilia** (i.e., stalking of children for sexual purposes) and can lead to children being sexually assaulted, kidnapped, or even murdered. Children whose online activities are not closely supervised by parents or other responsible adults are especially vulnerable to being cyberstalked and socially engineered into giving up personal information about themselves (e.g., likes and dislikes, hobbies and habits, where they go to school, and with whom they live). This information can then be used by **pedophiles** to plan how to best go about arranging to meet the child in person or kidnap the child. These dangerous crimes receive considerable attention from state and local cybercrime investigators, who periodically pose online as children in order to identify and arrest individuals predisposed to this type of criminal behavior.

Cyberstalking involves many other methods and purposes, and may occur between intimates or strangers. In general, stalkers seek to establish control over their victims, which implies that cyberstalking can target people who live or work within relatively close proximity to the offender. Remember, this form of cybercrime may involve combinations of physical and cyber activities, although electronic communications may reduce offender inhibitions and increase the relative number of threats conveyed. Online forums make it possible for individuals to stage threatening or stalking situations, as when they play the parts of both offender and victim in order to elicit rescuing email from others privy to the exchange. At an opposite extreme, clandestine, murderous stalkers are like cats; they secretly prey upon, playfully terrorize, and stage various online or offline encounters with their victims before killing them. Cyberstalkers are also like cats even if their stalking does not result in murder, because as indicated above, they may physically follow, watch, and send messages to their victims, as well as psychologically terrorize them by leaving surveillance photographs, symbolic objects, or other items in conspicuous locations where they will be found by victims. If you ever suspect someone is watching you in person or online, make sure you document all the circumstances and immediately inform authorities.

*Online cyberstalking and pedophilia occur frequently and may potentially be committed simultaneously against more than one victim. Online pedophilia often involves cybersex instant messaging inclusive of photos purportedly of people involved, although individuals who carry out such crimes often pretend to be someone other than themselves and may even take on multiple online identities in order to entice, deceive, or otherwise socially engineer their victims into doing things.* Photo by Nathan Fisk

*3.1.7.3 Illegal Pornography.* As declared by the U.S. Federal Communications Commission, which regulates public broadcasting and electronic communications over the Internet, "obscene speech is not protected by the First Amendment and cannot be broadcast at any time." To be considered obscene, content must meet the following three conditions: first, average people applying community standards must find that it appeals to obsessive interest in sex. Second, the content must depict or describe explicit sexual conduct in patently offensive ways. Third, and as established by the U.S. Supreme Court, the content taken as a whole must lack serious literary, artistic,

political, or scientific value.[55] The bottom line is that pornography depicting adults in sexually explicit acts is generally not illegal, although what constitutes illegal pornography varies among local jurisdictions throughout the United States. Creating, distributing, and possessing child pornography, however, is banned in all U.S. states, territories such as Puerto Rico, and districts such as the District of Columbia. The same is true in most other nations. In addition, content depicting *bestiality* (humans having sex with animals), *necrophilia* (sexual contact with dead persons), or *sadomasochism* (infliction of pain or torture in combination with sexual acts), among other types of sex-related behaviors, and pornography are banned in most U.S. jurisdictions and in many but not all other nations. Consequently, content that may be legal in one nation but illegal in another exists online in abundance. Although responsible adult entertainment content providers do not intentionally portray child and other forms of illegal pornography, illegal content is sometimes mistakenly interspersed with legal content.

Makeup, lighting, and camera angles can all be combined to make female and male models appear older than they are. Sadly, underage persons are sometimes lured into pornography productions, if not also manipulated, sold, or forced into managed sex exhibition, cybersex, and/or prostitution.[56] Kidnapping and international smuggling of young girls and boys for these purposes is now a transnational crime phenomenon taking place throughout the world, especially in impoverished nations where victims face dire economic circumstances.[57] Sex slavery resulting in online sex and pornography that features child and adolescent models can be problematic for law enforcement officers investigating online sex crimes, who must make determinations about a victim's identity, whereabouts, and true age at the time of filming. Investigators must also determine whether depicted content is of real persons or merely holographic images made to look like underage persons (which although not currently illegal in the United States, remains an exceedingly controversial issue).

Content depicting minors can also cause legal problems for perpetrators who intentionally produce, download, or possess pornographic images and for consumers who inadvertently download or possess such content, despite Web site proclamations that all models portrayed are consenting adults. In other words, people who download images of minors who appear and are reported to be over eighteen years of age may in some jurisdictions still be held criminally liable. Other aspects of illegal pornography is addressed further in several other chapters and sections of the text.

## 3.2 Evolving Forms of Cybercrimes, Attacks, and Conflict

There is plenty of evidence that several types of cybercrimes, especially those involving creation and distribution of malware, are becoming more complex in their technical design, diffusion capability, and destructive effects. Although the examples described here are far from conclusive, they do support the general belief of numerous scholars, information security professionals, and officials positioned in government agencies throughout the computerized world that the number, sophistication, and costs of cybercrimes and malware in particular are increasing. Reasons for these trends include the combination of rapidly expanding telecommunications and high speed Internet connectivity, increased computing power, user friendliness and technological interoperability of software systems and electronic devices, increased opportunities to commit IT-enabled abuse and crime as the number of computer networks and adept computer users rise, the difficulty of detecting and responding to cyber abuses and crimes, potential for lucrative payoffs, information security technology limitations, and generally inadequate criminal justice investigation and prosecution awareness, expertise, and resolve to go after the full variety of cybercrimes now being committed.

In this section we will examine emerging crime and attack trends and consider what may lie ahead for information security professionals, criminal justice officials, and IT users everywhere who are vulnerable to being harmed as the result of IT-enabled abuse, attacks and cybercrimes. We will also address futuristic forms of cyber conflict, specifically interconnections and prospects for cybercriminal technology adoption by traditional and emergent transnational organized crime and terrorist organizations. The chapter ends with a discussion of how IT has revolutionized warfare strategies and tactics, which are now also being used by the military to combat organized crime and terrorist operations throughout the world.

### 3.2.1 Emerging Crime and Attack Trends

The complexity of cybercrime derives from combinations of methods used in single or multiple attacks and from the ability of these to be carried out simultaneously or staged over time by numerous individuals or groups across multiple geopolitical jurisdictions that have different computer crime laws. Additionally, cyber attacks differ significantly with respect to the number of targeted computer nodes, systems, and victims, as well as potential direct and indirect harm and costs. Many spammers, for example, are no longer content to limit their activities to disseminating spam; some appear to also use spyware and adware designed to defeat software filters in combination with spamming. In the same way that Web proxies may be configured to permit legitimate use by interested parties, spammers and scammers take advantage of poorly configured email relays that allow them to send anonymous unsolicited bulk email via third parties at someone else's expense and blame.[58] Recent evidence now indicates that spammers are able to infect a user's computer with programming that routes spam back through the user's ISP, making such messages appear more legitimate and difficult for ISP technicians to identify on the basis of known spammers who have been blacklisted.[59]

Markus Jakobsson, codirector of the Center for Applied Cybersecurity Research at Indiana University, reports that sophisticated tricks that make fake messages look more plausible could result in increased cybercrime victimization. New forms of attacks may also exploit online social networks or auto-adapt messages to an individual's known circumstances as determined through cyber intelligence gathering and analysis. Clever phishing messages now routinely refer people to Web sites that look exactly the same as legitimate e-commerce firms determined to have been used by victims targeted for these attacks. Coding tricks can hide the true identity and purposes of these fake Web sites, resulting in many victims unwittingly handing over confidential information such as login names, passwords, and financial account information.

Phishing scams of this nature are not new, but automating remote distribution of such messages via botnets is. **A bot** is a remote control computer program designed for a single purpose, such as spamming or DoS attacks, or even for multiple purposes. In November of 2004 phisher attacks reportedly resulted in a **botnet** being created through unprotected home PCs that had been taken over in ways not obvious to the owners. One recent attack overlaid the browsing bar on Microsoft's Internet Explorer® browser with a fully functioning fake one in order to hide the true origins of the Web site users were looking at. This resulted in fictitious email messages directing unsuspecting victims to fraudulent Web sites in order to update personal financial or security information. Additionally, there is increasing evidence that standardized instructional toolkits allow relatively untalented programmers to carryout these types of sophisticated attacks and that increasing varieties of such attacks are launched from within the United States and abroad and are now capable of self-mutating in various ways depending on defensive countermeasures encountered even after being initially released (i.e., they are polymorphic).[60]

Future attacks will likely be even more complex and deceptive. Phishing gangs might fake network problems, and other types of cybercriminals are already known to launch DoS and distributed DoS attacks on targeted servers as diversions for more insidious cybercrimes. Future phishing attacks could be "context aware" according to Markus Jakobsson and take advantage of what attackers can find out about potential victims. An example might involve emails sent to people who bid for items at online auctions. The email could falsely claim that a person had won the item and ask for personal details to complete the sale. Later, an attacking bot could mine social networks, such as Orkut, to find out personal information of potential victims to use in additional cybercrimes (e.g., to create false electronic messages appearing to come from a friend, coworker, or relative of the targeted victim). Another type of attack could fake a problem with a user's Internet access and then send an email posing as a service firm capable of fixing the problem.[61]

Given the pace of malware innovations, some researchers have speculated that the future will bring about even nastier forms of malicious code. For example, **cryptoviruses** could potentially attack a computer and encrypt all stored data, requiring the victim to pay a ransom to get it back if it were not backed up and protected.[62] Cyber extortion is not new, but writing and releasing code to extort multiple victims in this way represents another potential future form of cybercrime.

Clearly, malware is becoming increasingly complex in its technical design and impact capabilities (i.e., for denial, disruption, destruction, or theft of data).[63] Consider the Chernobyl virus that in April 1999 was spread via users executing an infected file often attached to an email message. It was designed simply to erase the entire hard drive and overwrite the system BIOS of a victim's computer.[64] More recently, in the spring of 2004, a variant of the Mimail.A worm created a very legitimate appearing fake pop-up screen on computers of PayPal customers. The message claimed that the online e-commerce firm had lost the customer's purchasing account information and requested the customer to resupply his or her credit card or banking details.[65] If the customer did, the information was sent to the author of the code. Another mass-mailing worm, called Bugbear.B, discovered in June 2003, was programmed to spread through networks of banks and guess financial account passwords. It also possessed keystroke logging, backdoor, antivirus and defeating firewall capabilities.[66]

Speed of malware diffusion is also an important indicator of increasing complexity, unmanageability, and potential harm of emerging malware attacks. Within the first nine hours after its release in July 2001, the Red Code virus had infected 250,000 computers, prompting fears by government officials that it could slow the Internet when it re-emerged on August 1. "The worm was originally designed to die out late in the month, but began spreading again in August as a result of infected computers with incorrect time or date settings. Code Red II, which arrived on August 4, spread faster and installed a 'back door' on infected computers that left the machine vulnerable to future hacking."[67] At one point the Sobig.F worm released in the summer of 2003 stole addresses from victims' computers and spread so rapidly that nearly six percent of all Internet email traffic contained the worm.

Security experts estimated in January of 2004 that nearly 20 percent of all email traffic on the Net carried the Mydoom virus that reprogrammed infected computers to attack the Web site of a particular software firm hated by many members of the open source software community. Similarly, Slammer was designed to attack Microsoft's SQL Server—an online database application used extensively by government agencies and large commercial firms. It "flooded the Internet with 55 million blasts of data per second and in only 10 minutes colonized almost all vulnerable machines."[68] Sasser, released in early May of 2004, spread worldwide so fast that on the second day after its release it constituted forty percent of all malware traffic on the Net, affecting e-commerce firms such as Delta Airlines, American Express, and the Associated Press among many other companies.[69] So-called **Warhol worms** like Slammer and Sasser spread faster than humans can react, posing threats that even world-class antivirus service firms and government-supported computer emergency response teams have extraordinary difficulty contending with.

The Computer Emergency Response Team (CERT) Coordination Center at Carnegie Mellon University in Pittsburgh, Pennsylvania, has been observing Internet activity since 1988. Recent trends observed in information security attacks and cybercrime include an increase in the level of automation of information attack tools. They typically include a capability to scan for potential victims, compromise vulnerable computer systems, propagate attacks, and coordinate management of attacks. Attackers are now using more advanced techniques to disguise malware, thereby negating the effectiveness of antivirus software and intrusion detection systems. For example, **root kits** replace basic file and process management capabilities on a computer. As such, these clandestine software packages, which are now available on the Net, enable technically savvy cybercriminals to mask the particular nature of malware embedded onto operating systems as if there were two sets of auditing books: one showing how the computer ought to be working and another showing how the cybercriminal has reprogrammed the computer to actually function. In addition to obfuscating the nature of attacks, **automated attack tools** now enable programmers to create self-morphing modes of attack that change even as they spread throughout network environments and encounter varying security protections.

So-called **metamorphic worms**—"ones that can shift their shapes so radically that antivirus companies cannot recognize they're a piece of malware"—could become a reality in the not-too-distant future, along with viruses designed to infect digital cell phones in such a way as to stick an unsuspecting victim with a huge phone bill.[70] Some attack tools are even capable of upgrading or replacing detected or defeated aspects of their coding, such that they are in effect **self-evolving polymorphic tools** capable of being executed on different operating system platforms. In recent years the number of newly discovered programming vulnerabilities reported to CERT has more than doubled, indicating the increasing difficulty for system administrators to consistently update operating systems and applications. Intruders are often able to discover system vulnerabilities before consumers are aware of them and vendors are able to correct them, and although people rely on firewalls for protection from intruders, "some protocols marketed as

being 'firewall friendly' are, in reality, designed to bypass typical firewall configurations."[71] The interdependent nature of the Internet enables attacks from multiple sources to be launched against single or multiple victims, increasing the potential for asymmetric attacks, distributed DoS attacks, and self-propagating worms containing destructive payloads. Attacks on the Internet domain name system (DNS) or attacks that use routers or are designed to compromise routers are considered to be particularly threatening to critical information infrastructures (CIIs).

The complex technologies used to commit crimes tend to prevent investigators from understanding the conditions affecting the evolution and potential impacts of social deviance, computer abuse, and cybercrime. IT used for both communications and transportation, for example, is changing the nature and extent of many types of crime and security threats to both cyber and physical infrastructures in ways not easily recognized, understood, or managed.[72] In addition, technological advancements not limited to IT have enabled the emergence of new forms of transnational organized crimes involving drug smuggling, trafficking in weapons and controlled substances, and money laundering.[73] Who among Americans will ever forget September 11, 2001, when members of the Al Qaida terrorist network hijacked commercial airlines in order to launch attacks on the World Trade Center and the Pentagon? Their actions involved imaginative and daring homicidal techniques combined with relatively complex to simple tools—computers to gather intelligence and communicate their plans and plastic box cutters to take over the aircraft and presumably take out the pilots. Since that fateful day, there have been numerous other significant terrorist attacks attributable to Al Qaida or affiliated terrorist organizations throughout the world, many involving dozens of deaths and even hundreds of people wounded.[74] However, the extent to which information systems, computers and other electronic devices were used to plan and execute these crimes is not fully understood, though surely interrelated computing and telecommunications technologies are facilitating the ability of terrorists to wreak havoc throughout the world in unprecedented ways.

The strategic cybercrime-management challenge is related to software development firms' reliance on employees to anticipate and discover vulnerabilities prior to product releases or during beta testing, and for high-tech crime investigators to anticipate the potential for abusive and illegal use of IT in all its forms. Seeking technological advantage in order to avoid detection and prosecution for personally distributing attacks on the Internet, however, some authors of malware simply post their malicious code to Web sites for someone else to find and distribute. Hence script kiddies lacking sufficient skill to author their own malicious code, and in order to gain recognition from their peers, are prone to finding and using malware programs created by more talented code writers. In addition, skilled and unskilled code writers alike have been known to scan the Internet, including Web sites maintained by antivirus protection firms, to discover vulnerabilities and get ideas for innovative malware. According to Clive Thompson, a respected technology reporter, this modern virus epidemic results from a "symbiotic relationship between the people smart enough to write a virus and the people dumb enough—or malicious enough—to spread it."[75]

In any case, the net result (pun intended) is that, like a destructive genie released from its bottle, technological forces promoting a revolution in computer abuse and cybercrime are being released via computerization in ways that cannot be fully anticipated, prevented, or controlled. As if having a mind of their own, destructive malware such as Warhol worms initially cause extensive havoc that is substantially unpreventable by antivirus programs or other technological measures. Even after protection measures are developed, the original code and its variants linger in cyberspace waiting for unwary users to access it with their unprotected computer systems. The implication is that each generation of

computer user and technology must be vaccinated against known threats that have previously plagued the Internet. However, unlike some deadly naturally biological viruses such as smallpox that are believed to have been all but eliminated through systematic vaccination of human populations, destructive code is prone to being invented and innovated by humans—the cyber equivalent of committing genocide or crimes against humanity.

### 3.2.2  Futuristic Forms of Cyber Conflict

Fast-evolving computer and telecommunications technology has in the past decade sparked a good deal of angst among military, intelligence, and police authorities throughout the world. While each group acknowledges the benefits IT provides their own operations and nations as a whole, they also worry that IT could be used to cause catastrophic damage and harm to CIIs. For several years these fears and related matters have been described in literature pertaining to cyberterrorism, information warfare, and network-centric warfare. Akin to the social constructs of crime discussed in Chapter 1 (e.g., white-collar crime and computer-related crime), these forms of cyber conflict are not mutually exclusive. Each relies on using combinations of relatively simple to complex cyber and/or physical tools and techniques to achieve dominance over perceived enemies. Although these forms of IT-enabled conflict are not within the realm of mainstream criminal justice and information security issues, it is important to understand them in the context of emerging technological complexity associated with emerging forms of cybercrimes.

***3.2.2.1 Cyberterrorism.***    **Terrorism** can be defined as the systematic use of violence, terror, or intimidation to achieve an end.[76] Often the ends or desired goals of terrorism are political or religious in nature, as in efforts to overthrow a system

**CYBER TALE 3.9**

## *Installation of Multiple Alien Servers*

A college student studying IT administration was contacted by someone via instant messaging who claimed to be a prospective student who simply wanted information about the college. Subsequent chat over several days developed into an online friendship, but the student who had been contacted had no idea that he was being conned into giving up information about himself and the computer system he was using. In time he noticed an unusual directory inside his computer's antivirus directory. It was at that point that he realized he had been hacked and, with the help of even more technically skilled friends, he was further able to determine that his new instant messaging buddy had been able to convert his computer into a server for malicious purposes.

After deleting the server functions, the student told his IM buddy about the discovery, but, never imagining that he would be hacked again, did not bother to install a personal firewall. Unimpressed and undeterred, the IM buddy hacked the student's computer again and this time destroyed over 40 gigs of data. Only then did the student install a personal firewall and begin monitoring logs of denied attempted accesses to his system. In the days that followed he noticed that many probes originated from within his own college network, an indication that fellow students, including perhaps his own friends, were not to be trusted. However, five addresses were from outside the college network. With the personal firewall installed, the outside-network attackers eventually discontinued their penetration efforts, as a steady barrage of attempted attacks emanating from within the college network environment bounced harmlessly off his protected system. Naturally the student assumed that this was the end of his problem.

One day while bored and watching a virus scan of his hard drive, the student noticed a strange file path located inside his computer's recycling bin. At first he could not locate the precise location of the path and associated files. Then by accident he discovered the source directory for the strange files—another server was on his computer, its installation dating to the time when the first hack was discovered. It turned out that not one, but *two* alien servers had originally been placed on his computer by the IM buddy. Fortunately the second alien server had been inactive since the installation of the personal firewall program. Today the student employs a router and multiple firewalls on his home computer system, and whenever he experiences quirky system behavior he performs a complete diagnostic check to help guard against the possibility that his computer has been attacked yet again. In general, if you ever discover one foreign program inside your computer, you should assume two, three, or even more exist and you should take steps with assistance from technical experts as needed to eradicate them from your system.

---

of government or eradicate, people of a particular race, ethnicity, or faith. Ends may also be less philosophical and more criminal in nature, as when mobsters or gang members, organized on the basis of race or ethnicity, combined with preferred types of illegal business enterprises in particular geographic regions, engage in systematic extortion of community residents or business people by threatening to cause personal injury or destruction of property if protection money is not paid. Even cyberstalking by definition may be regarded as a limited form of terrorism because individual or groups of victims may be harassed, threatened, and intimidated and experience harm from violence.

**Cyberterrorism** by extension may be defined relatively broadly or narrowly depending on the motivations of the offenders, the scale of technology used, the number of offenders or jurisdictions involved, the type and number of victims targeted, the amount of harm caused, and so on. Here we will consider cyberterrorism primarily with respect to using IT to carry out large-scale attacks on CIIs and thereby intimidate, terrorize, inconvenience, or otherwise harm large numbers of people for political, economic, or religious ends. As discussed in Chapter 2, CIIs include computerized systems that control communications, power supplies, government, transportation, food production and distribution, finance and banking, and manufacturing and retail functions of society in metropolitan or regional areas.

Organized criminals and terrorists have much in common.[77] In the first place, organized criminals terrorize individual and groups of crime victims. Second, terrorists are in many instances structured into hierarchical and/or networked organizations. Third, both groups use computing and telecommunications technologies to accomplish their objectives (e.g., to obtain financing, launder money, plan operations, maintain communications, and recruit new members). Web sites, encrypted communications, chat rooms, computer viruses, and e-commerce are now all suspected of being used by organized groups of criminals and terrorists to accomplish their goals or advance their radical agendas. In November of 2004 officials at the FBI publicly expressed concern that organized criminals including terrorists were capable of orchestrating large-scale computer hacking and identity theft schemes in order to profit or cripple CII on a large scale.[78] Fourth, organized crime groups and terrorist cells prefer to operate in areas with little government control, weak law enforcement, and open borders—regions that afford few restrictions on cross-border smuggling or internal movement of personnel, money, supplies, and contraband.[79] This is why the mountainous regions of Afghanistan were so attractive to terrorists seeking to avoid apprehension by U.S.-led coalition forces following removal of the Taliban government in that nation in November, 2001. However, Islamic radical fundamentalists reportedly also

took sanctuary in countries with rough terrain, highly developed information infrastructures, and pro-Islam dispositions such as Malaysia, from which to conduct world-wide operations.[80] Hence, the operational capabilities of criminals and terrorists, enhanced by modern computing, telecommunications, and transportation technologies, have blurred distinctions between these groups such that officials seeking to manage either form of conflict must now consider both.

There has never been a confirmed or acknowledged incident of cyberterrorism, although there have been suggestions that the Code Red DoS attack directed at the White House, which infected 300,000 computers, and the Nimda virus, with an estimated cleanup cost of $3 billion, both launched in 2001, were tests of CII defenses by terrorist groups. In another case, named Moonlight Maze, investigators established that attacks on Department of Defense systems increased as cyber defenses were raised. It was also determined that attackers, traced back to a mainframe computer in the former Soviet Union, were monitoring U.S. military troop movements. In connection with these attacks, it was further determined that several suspected Al Qaida operatives have technical backgrounds, some have experience in infrastructure control systems, and they have used computers outside the United States to conduct reconnaissance on national critical infrastructure defense capabilities.[81]

Despite the foregoing evidence, cyberterrorism is still considered only a theoretical possibility by many experienced national defense and security officials. However, the view that a cyberterrorist attack could cause significant damage for operationally useful periods of time is steadily gaining credence among forward-thinking law enforcement, intelligence, and military leaders.[82] Dick Clark, the former national security advisor to three U.S. presidents, and an open critic of the Bush administration's approach to the U.S. worldwide war on terrorism, reported that militaries of the world's most powerful nations now use the Internet to spy on their enemies and prepare for cyber attacks.[83] Presumably this includes the United States, which has unmatched cyber intelligence capabilities. Knowledgeable individuals like Clark, and many other government officials and private sector executives involved in protecting critical infrastructures throughout the world, would rather err on the side of caution by being prepared for and possibly preventing a major cyber attack than retrospectively respond to repair damage to information systems and physical infrastructures after a catastrophic event has occurred.

### 3.2.2.2 Information and Network-Centric Warfare.
War boils down to delivery of information and energy, which implies the central role of IT in warfare.[84] Waging war in the information age involves launching cyber attacks along with physical attacks against targets deemed to have military significance. **Information warfare (IW)** represents one aspect of modern warfare, in which enemies are conceived of as information-reliant systems.[85] IW doctrine also recognizes that competitive advantage lies in achieving dominance over the IT realm of the battle space rather than only over the physical realm with troops, ordinance, and other means of conventional warfare.[86]

**Information dominance** refers to having overall control of an enemy's entire electronic spectrum and thereby all of their cyber *and* physical operational capabilities.[87] If an opponent can control its enemy's systems and data, it can also control what its enemy can see, communicate, and do; this is the logic behind achieving information dominance. Cripple the information systems and infrastructure of your enemy, destroy their command and control (C2) systems, isolate and disable hostile forces before defensive reactions or effective counterattacks are possible, and you will win the war.[88] Thus, victory in theory can be achieved by quickly, systematically, and thoroughly denying, degrading, manipulating, and/or destroying an enemy's IT capabilities, information systems, and data.

The concept of IW was first popularized in 1994 by Winn Schwartau, who wrote a book titled

*Information Warfare: Chaos on the Electronic Superhighway.*[89] In 1995, with IW already being widely addressed in military journals and magazines, Martin Libicki, a respected military scholar, identified seven conceivable types of IW tactics including (1) command and control warfare (C2W), (2) intelligence-based warfare, (3) electronic warfare (EW), (4) psychological warfare, (5) hacker warfare, (6) economic information warfare, and (7) cyber warfare. Libicki theorized that each of these (and perhaps other) forms of IW could be used separately or in combination to defeat one or more enemies on large or small scales.[90]

The ability of a nation to carry out cyber and physical attacks while also defending its own cyber and physical assets in a modern battle sphere, as well as defending critical information and other infrastructures within a conflicted region, is an extremely complex, even daunting, challenge. Nonetheless, for many years the U.S. military has had the ability to accomplish battlefield tactics and objectives by using a vast array of sophisticated, solid state, interoperable computing and telecommunications technologies to simultaneously defend and attack command, control, communications, computer, and intelligence (C4I) systems from land-, air-, and sea-based vehicles and platforms.[91] During the Persian Gulf War in 1992, for example, the United States used networked intelligence gathering and communications to devastatingly deploy **smart weapons** to knock out Iraq's C2 centers, which effectively blinded and incapacitated their ability to strike back at coalition forces. Accordingly, many military commentators think the Gulf War was the first actual limited example of IW. Given today's interdependent critical information-based infrastructures, it is possible for cyber attacks to disrupt power grids,[92] undermine economies electronically,[93] or influence mass social psychologies of an enemy populace through media and propaganda[94] while simultaneously launching unmanned aerial reconnaissance vehicles in preparation for delivering smart bombs using stealth bombers incapable of being detected by enemy radar. Doing so with modern IT provides commanders on the battlefield with the capability to decide more quickly and act more decisively than ever before and thus achieve information dominance and win battles as never before.

In the summer of 2002, President Bush enacted National Security Presidential Directive 16 to initiate national defense planning and policy development for launching cyber attacks against enemies. Then in February 2005, during a hearing convened by the U.S. Senate Armed Services Committee, military leaders from the U.S. Strategic Command disclosed that an elite computer attack network (CAN) unit called the Joint Functional Component Command for Network Warfare (JFCCNW) had been created for such purposes. Dubbed as the most world's most "formidable hacker posse," JFCCNW may be capable of penetrating, manipulating, and destroying enemy computer systems through releasing destructive worms on computer networks, releasing fake intelligence information, or taking down Web sites operated by enemy nations or terrorist organizations, among other classified tactics.[95]

Battlefield tactics and capabilities that integrate IT and other forms of technology are referred to as **network-centric warfare (NCW)**, a concept encompassing traditional and futuristic forms of attacks, defense capabilities, and warfare. (Note: *network-centric warfare* [NCW] is the term most often used by proponents of the concept within the U.S. Navy. However, the term *rapid decisive operations* [RDO] is preferred within the Army, and *effects-based operations* [EBO] is used by Air Force officials. Each of these concepts is primarily concerned with establishing technological and informational dominance in modern battle spaces.[96]) The overall concept of NCW centers on physical, informational, and cognitive domains.[97] Together, these domains address C4I, surveillance, and reconnaissance information needed to win military conflicts. Hence, IT-enabled warfare today involves a much wider range and combination of information and energy delivery strategies than previously conceptualized as

IW.[98] Managing modern battle spheres, as well as potential cyberterrorism, is complicated because it necessitates understanding[99] (1) the meaning of information itself (i.e., information can be conceived of as a target, weapon, resource, or realm); (2) the level of effect (i.e., tactical, operational, or strategic effects); (3) the conflict objective (e.g., limited C2W battlefield dominance or an act of terrorism versus systematic and perhaps clandestine infrastructure disruption or destruction); (4) the phase of conflict (i.e., a state of war, impending attack crisis, or some lesser degree of conflict such as terrorism or crime); (5) the actors involved (i.e., nations, terrorists, or criminals); (6) the types of systems affected (e.g., military only or broader telecommunications, transportation, or energy systems); and (7) the fundamental orientation of the attacker and warranted responses (i.e., offensive and/or defensive modes of operation).

Figure 3.1 depicts these factors in the context of **information age conflict** consisting of interplay between cybercrime, terrorism, and warfare and the management requirements of components of military, private sector security, and public sector policing. Collectively, these components must collaborate within a **cyber conflict continuum** (i.e., a zone of shared responsibility) to ensure relative peace over chaos, especially in war-torn regions of the world. Remember that these forms of conflict overlap to some extent: crimes and acts of terrorism with and without IT occur during wars and even amidst battles. And each form of conflict can vary in its scope and scale and also combine at the operational level and with respect to the social, economic, and political impacts involved.

What matters for prevention and mitigation of harmful impacts on a war-torn society rests not merely in recognizing new technological realities surrounding these forms of conflict, but in determining which components of modernized societies are best suited to effectively manage the range and varieties of computer-enabled abuse, crime, terrorism, and attacks now faced

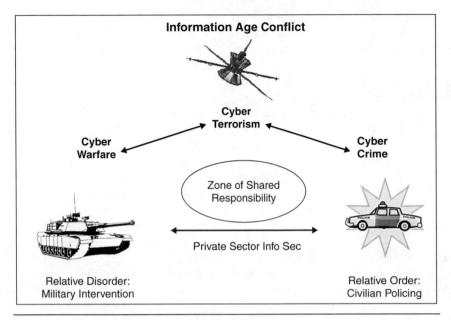

**FIGURE 3.1** *Information Age Conflict*

also by nations not at war. As should be clear by now, no conceptual construct or label can uniquely and adequately capture all aspects of IT-enabled conflict: all constructs and labels for crime and warfare are somewhat ambiguous. Experts will never completely agree on what constitutes an act of cyber warfare versus an act of cyberterrorism, nor of cyberterrorism versus a large-scale deadly crime enabled with computers and other types of electronic devices. What matters is that IT underpins all these forms of conflict and associated harm.

The consequence of not understanding who is in charge of managing the myriad cyber conflict contingencies is that the duties and functions of the military, intelligence, and civilian law enforcement agencies, as well as those of the private sector security industry, are becoming increasingly blurred.[100] In 2004 Iraqi civilian sector security firms specializing in facilities and dignitary protection were under contract with the U.S. government, even as military forces carried out peacekeeping operations, and law enforcement specialists from coalition nations were involved

in training Iraqi police. The initial creation and ongoing reorganization of the Department of Homeland Security in 2002 revealed the desire in the United States to make sense out of differing forms of information age conflict by reestablishing the roles, authority, and responsibilities of government agencies created during an earlier and very different period of technological threat.

Policies for protecting America from foreign as opposed to domestic threats to national security, as a result of new potentialities created by IT, were perceived to merit priority from 1940 through the 1960s. During this period confusion surrounding the roles of the FBI and other civilian and federal law enforcement agencies, versus military and intelligence agencies, abounded. Specific advancements in IT during the Cold War (e.g., IT-enabled missile and satellite spying technology) exacerbated fears of communist insurgency and eclipsed national policy concerns about domestic crime. Hence, organizational interplay and even confusion regarding legal responsibilities in relation to technological capabilities of federal government components is nothing new.

Today interpretations of attacker associations, intentions, capabilities, warnings, rules of engagement, and acceptable mitigation strategies are changing as the nature of IT-enabled crime, national security measures, international peacekeeping, and nation-building efforts throughout the world evolve and arise anew. As the nature of society and threats to it change, so too must our technologies, legal authorities, organizational structures, and policies affecting mechanisms within the government that provide security, order, and protection.

## 3.3 Summary

Never before has society produced, stored, and communicated the volume of information that it does today. That society does so globally and with minimal effort is taken for granted and is due largely to readily available, affordable, and interoperable computing and telecommunications devices. Today's computers, scanners, fax machines, and satellite-linked cellular phones, among many other types of electronic devices, are used pervasively to generate, store, and transmit information for myriad abusive and criminal purposes. These activities include many variations and combinations of writing and distributing malicious codes, fraudulent schemes and theft, interfering with and disrupting computer services, computer spying and intrusions, unauthorized and illegal file sharing, abuse of computers and electronic devices in academia, and online harassment and computer-enabled sex crimes.

The paradigm of transnational crime has co-evolved significantly in the past decade with developments in computing, telecommunications, transportation, and other forms of technology. Distinctions between organized crime and terrorism are increasingly difficult to make, obfuscated in particular by the transitional and transnational nature of IT-enabled abuse, attacks, and crime. As cybercrimes have become increasingly complex, police, information security, intelligence, military and other government policymaking officials, along with scholars and investigative journalists throughout the world, generally agree that computerization, globalization, and the apparition of cyberspace are factors underlying changes in the nature of crime, terrorism, and warfare.[101] Officials worry that combinations of physical and cyber attacks against critical infrastructures and CIIs could be launched by technically skilled, military-minded terrorists.[102] While technologically powerful nations such as the United States increasingly rely on IT for all facets of national defense, less technologically developed nations and terrorist organizations may resort to combining traditional and information warfare tactics to achieve their goals. Shared concern about these issues has for several years played out in a growing body of literature that describes these emerging crime-related threats as new conceptions of social conflict under the rubric of cyberterrorism, information warfare, and (increasingly) network-centric warfare that combine to challenge traditional separation of military, intelligence community, and civilian law enforcement and information security duties and functions.

### Key Terms and Concepts _____

| | | |
|---|---|---|
| Ad hoc frauds, 73 | Cryptoviruses, 100 | False advertising schemes, 73 |
| Adware, 64 | Cyber conflict continuum, 106 | False damage claims, 73 |
| Application fingerprinting, 80 | Cybersmear campaigns, 73 | File transfer protocol (FTP), 87 |
| Automated attack tools, 101 | Cyberstalking, 95 | Fraud, 68 |
| Bot, 99 | Cyberterrorism, 103 | Harassment, 93 |
| Botnet, 99 | Denial of service (DoS) attack, 76 | Hoax, 73 |
| Bouncing, 89 | Direct access revolution, 88 | Identity theft, 69 |
| Bug, 64 | Encryption, 89 | IM spim, 72 |

Information age conflict, 106
Information dominance, 105
Information warfare (IW), 105
Insider trading, 73
Internet relay chat (IRC), 69
Keystroke logger programs, 82
Malicious coding definitions, 64
Malware, 64
Metamorphic worms, 101
Monitoring, 85
Napster, 87
Network-centric warfare (NCW), 106
Operating system profiling, 80
Packet sniffing, 79
Password cracking, 81
Patches, 64
Pedophiles, 96
Pedophilia, 96
Peer-to-peer (p2p) networks, 88
Piracy, 87
Port scanning, 80
Remailer systems, 93
Root kits, 101
Self-evolving polymorphic tools, 101
Service provider fraud, 73
Smart weapons, 105
Spam, 77
Spamming, 77
Spimming, 72
Spying, 86
Spyware, 64
Surveillance, 85
Swarming, 84
Telemarketing fraud, 73
Terrorism, 102
Threat, 93
Top sites, 89
Trojans, 64
Viruses, 64
War driving and walking,
Web and email spoofing, 71
Warhol worms, 100
Worms, 64

## Critical Thinking and Discussion Questions

1. In recent years there has been a dramatic increase in the number of worms, viruses, and Trojans released on the Internet. Why do you think this has occurred? Explain.
2. Credit card fraud and identity theft have benefited from the Internet and have become an important topic for credit card companies to address. What precautionary methods do you believe can be taken to prevent these types of crimes?
3. Remembering our discussion in Chapter 1 about the social construct of crime labels, does the term *cybercriminal* or other labels for high-tech crime offenders such as *hacker, phreaker, fraudster,* or *script kiddy* have any real significance?
4. What are the ethical implications (if any) of writing and distributing adware and spyware? Would you take a job where you had to write adware or spyware? Why or why not?
5. Is it necessary to create new terms for ordinary crimes committed with more advanced tools? For example, isn't cyberstalking simply the act of stalking someone with a computer via the Internet?
6. How, if at all, is using a telephone to stalk or harass someone any different from using a computer since both technologies are electronic devices that facilitate communication?
7. The Electronic Crime Needs Assessment places an emphasis on encryption as a problem faced by state and local law enforcement cybercrime investigators, mentioning that it will become increasingly present in electronic crimes. Do you agree with this? Why or why not?
8. Find an article discussing an actual or potential incident of cyberterrorism. In an essay, discuss how the attack was or could be accomplished and discuss how the incident may have been or could be avoided.
9. Explain commonalities between organized criminals and terrorists. Comment on how these relate to ideas of social constructs, constructs of crime, and definitional dilemmas discussed in previous chapters.
10. How and on what legal basis should the state's coercive power be organized to prevent, detect, and respond to threats against national security and civil order in a society increasingly reliant on, and therefore exposed to electronic attacks on, information infrastructures?
11. Describe hypothetical attacks conforming to each of the seven primary types of information warfare originally identified by Martin Libicki. How difficult would it be for a nation to defend against these types of attacks? Explain your answer.

## References and Endnotes

1. Forcht, K. (1992). Bolstering your computer's immune system. *Security Management, 36*(9), 134–135.
2. Lee, M. J. (1991). Computer viruses, computer hackers: security threats of the 1990's. Unpublished manuscript.

3. Thompson, C. (2004, February). The virus underground. *New York Times*. Retrieved November 10, 2004, from http://www.nytimes.com/2004/02/08/magazine/08WORMS.html?ex=1100235600&en=e27d746ecc37cfcb&ei=5070&oref=login.

4. Standage, T. (1998). *The Victorian Internet*. Markham, Canada: Thomas Allen & Sons.

5. Staff Author (2000). Credit card hackers busted in Moscow. *St. Petersburg Times*. Retrieved March 24, 2004, from http://www.ihwc.spb.ru.

6. Honeynet Research Alliance (2003, June 6). Know your enemy–A profile. Retrieved July 22, 2005 from http://www.honeynet.org/papers/profiles/cc-fraud.pdf

7. Synovate. NOTE–The author is a firm commissioned by the FTC for this report. (2003). *FTC Identity Theft Survey Report*. Washington, DC: Federal Trade Commission.

8. MessageLabs (2004). New phishing emails automatically steal bank log in details: new technique sidesteps the need for user intervention. Retrieved December 29, 2004, from http://www.messagelabs.com/news/detail/default.asp?contentItemId =1229&region.

9. MessageLabs, 2004; see note 8.

10. Forelle, C., & Holt, N. (2004). High-tech holiday light display draws everyone but the skeptics. Retrieved December 29, 2004, from http://online.wsj.com/public/article/0,,SB110417399327110132,00.html.

11. National Fraud Information Center (2001) Disaster-related frauds continue. Retrieved January 3, 2005, from http://www.fraud.org/news/news.htm.

12. Wall, D. (2004). Son of Spam: Crime Convergence in the Information Age. Presented at the Annual Conference of the American Society of Criminology, February 18, Nashville, TN.

13. Office of the U.S. Attorney, Northern District of Ohio (2004). Ohio man convicted on charges of producing counterfeit U.S. currency and illegally modifying or "hacking" Direct TV access cards. Retrieved November 23, 2004, from http://www.cybercrime.gov/winigmanSent.htm.

14. Sullivan, B. (2004). Now, two-thirds of all e-mail is spam: and in the U.S., spam tops 80 percent mark. Retrieved December 30, 2004, from http://www.msnbc.msn.com/id/5032714/.

15. Roberts, P. (2004). Virus worms its way into cell phones: Russian firm reports first computer worm that spreads via phone networks. Retrieved November 22, 2004, from http://www.pcworld.com/news/article/0,aid,116508,00.asp.

16. Staff Author (2003, November). Half-naked driver faces Net charge. *London Free Press*. Retrieved February 19, 2005, from http://www.canoe.ca/NewsStand/LondonFreePress/News/2003/11/22/264890.html.

17. R. Utrecht, as cited by Taylor, P. A. (1999). *Hackers: Crime in the Digital Sublime*. London: Routledge.

18. Staff Author (2004, November). Movie swappers put on notice. Retrieved November 31, 2004, from http://www.usatoday.com/money/media/2004-11-05-glickman_x.htm.

19. Potter, D. (2005, January 11). Hackers capture info from George Mason U. *USA Today*. Retrieved January 11, 2005, from http://www.usatoday.com/tech/news/computersecurity/hacking/2005-01-11-gmu-hack_x.htm?csp=34.

20. Commission for the Review of FBI Security Programs (2002). *A Review of FBI Security Programs* (p. 7). Washington, DC: U.S. Department of Justice.

21. See Chapter 10 in Power, R. (2000). *Tangled Web: Tales of Digital Crime from the Shadows of Cyberspace*. Indianapolis, IN: Que Corporation.

22. Staff Author (2005). MGM v. Grokster brief. Retrieved July 24, 2005, from http://www.extempprep.org/grokster.html

23. see 464 U.S. 417

24. U.S. Supreme Court (2005). Metro-Goldwyn-Mayer Studios Inc. et al v. Grokster, Ltd., et al.: Certiorari to the United States Court of Appeals for the Ninth Circuit. No. 04-480. Argued March 29, 2005, decided June 27. Retrieved July 24, 2005, from http://www.eff.org/IP/P2P/MGM_v_Grokster/04480.pdf

25. Howe, J. (2005). The shadow Internet. Retrieved January 15, 2005, from http://www.wired.com/wired/archive/13.01/topsite.html.

26. Howe, 2005; see note 25.

27. Scanlon, P. M. (2003). Student online plagiarism: how do we respond? *College Teaching, 51*(4), 161–165.

28. Groark, M., Oblinger, D., & Choa, M. (2001). Term paper mills, anti-plagiarism tools and academic integrity. *EDUCAUSE Review*, September/October edition, no number available 40–48.

29. Scanlon, P. M., & Neumann, D. R. (2002). Internet Plagiarism among College Students. Unpublished manuscript, Rochester Institute of Technology, New York.

30. Storch, E. A., & Storch, J. B. (2002). Fraternities, sororities and academic dishonesty. *College Student Journal, 36* (2), 247–253.

31. Collison, M. (1990). Survey at Rutgers suggests that cheating may be on the rise at large universities. *Chronicle of Higher Education, 37*(8), A31.

32. See for example, Davis, S. F., Grover, C. A., Becker, A. H., & McGregor, L. N. (1992). Academic dishonesty: prevalence, determinants, techniques, and punishments. *Teaching of Psychology, 19*(1), 16–20.

33. Davis et al., 1992; see note 32.

34. Read, B. (2004, July). Wired for cheating: some professors go beyond honor codes to stop misuse of electronic devices. *Chronicle of Higher Education*.

Retrieved November 22, 2004, from http://chronicle.com/free/v50/i45/45a02701.htm.

35. Lucent Technologies (2002). Bell Labs announces results of inquiry into research misconduct: independent committee concludes that one scientist published falsified and fabricated data; all other co-authors cleared of misconduct. Retrieved January 2, 2005, from http://www.lucent.com/press/0902/020925.bla.html.

36. Johnson, G. (2002, October 15). At Lawrence Berkeley, physicists say a colleague took them for a ride. *New York Times*, p. F1.

37. Moore, J. W. (2002). Scientific misconduct. *Journal of Chemical Education, 79*(12), 1391.

38. Moore, 2002; see note 37.

39. Tsunami hoax e-mailer jailed (2005). Retrieved February 19, 2005, from http://www.crime-research.org/news/25.01.2005/920/.

40. Webster's II. (1995). *New College Dictionary.* Boston: Houghton Mifflin.

41. Ellison, L. (2001). Cyberstalking: tackling harassment on the Internet. In David S. Wall (Ed.), *Crime and the Internet* (pp. 141–151). London: Routledge.

42. BBC Staff Author (2003). Texting blamed for crime rise. Retrieved December 8, 2004, from http://news.bbc.co.uk/2/hi/uk_news/scotland/2954045.stm.

43. Ellison, L. 2001; see note 40.

44. Ellison, L. 2001; see note 40.

45. Swartz, J. (2005, March 20). Cyberbullies: intimidation lurks online in form of a young, faceless force. (Article originally published by *USA Today.*) Rochester, NY: *Democrat and Chronicle*.

46. Joyce, B. (2005). Woman accused in unusual computer crime. Computer Crime Research Center. Retrieved February 19, 2005, from http://www.crime-research.org/news/28.01.2005/927/.

47. Loundy, D. J. (2003). Computer crime, information warfare and economic espionage (pp. 310–312). Durham, North Carolina: Carolina Academic Press.

48. McQuade, S., & Schreck, C. (2005). Correlates of Cybercrime Victimization. Manuscript in progress.

49. Hopkins, K. (2002). 'Cyber-rape' outlawed: N.J. cracks down on computer-aided crime. Retrieved February 17, 2005, from http://www.crime-research.org/news/01.19.2005/910/.

50. Office of the Attorney General (1999). *Cyberstalking: A new challenge for enforcement and industry.* Washington, DC: U.S. Department of Justice.

51. 18 U.S.C 2261A. This is a law; title 18 U.S. (criminal) Code, Subsection 2261A.

52. McGuire, M. (2004). Killing Me Softly: Homicide, Suicide and Genocide in Cyberspace. Paper presented at the Annual Conference of the American Society of Criminology, November 17, Nashville, TN.

53. Farache, E (2001, May 3). "Star Trek" stalker sentenced. Retrieved November 13, 2004 from http://www.eonline.com/News/Items/0,1,8209,00.html.

54. Ellison, L. 2001; see note 40.

55. Federal Communications Commission (2004). Obscenity, indecency, & profanity. Retrieved June 5, 2004, from http://www.fcc.gov/parents/content.html.

56. Staff Author (2001). Sex slavery: the growing trade. Retrieved January 15, 2005, from http://archives.cnn.com/2001/WORLD/europe/03/08/women.trafficking/.

57. Chinov, M. (2000). Aid workers decry growing child sex trade in Cambodia. Retrieved January 15, 2005, from http://archives.cnn.com/2000/ASIANOW/southeast/09/18/cambodia.pedophile/index.html.

58. AusCERT (2004). Home page of the Australian Computer Emergency Response Team. Retrieved November 10, 2004, from http://www.auscert.org.au/.

59. Ilett, D. (2005). It's official: spammers are hijacking ISPs. Retrieved March 4, 2005, from http://news.zdnet.co.uk/internet/security/0,39020375,39190123,00.htm.

60. Leyden, J. (2004). Phishers tapping botnets to automate attacks. Retrieved November 26, 2004, from http://www.theregister.co.uk/2004/11/26/anti-phishing_report/.

61. BBC Staff Author (2004, October, 10). Users face new phishing threats. British Broadcasting Company, World Edition, London. Retrieved November 11, 2004, from: http://news.bbc.co.uk/2/hi/technology/3759808.stm.

62. Symantec (2004). w32.Crypto security response. Retrieved November 11, 2004, from http://securityresponse.symantec.com/avcenter/venc/data/w32.crypto.html.

63. CERT Coordination Center (2004). *Overview of Attack Trends.* Pittsburgh, PA: Carnegie Mellon University.

64. CERT Coordination Center (2003). Incident note IN-99-03: CIH/Chernobyl virus. Retrieved November 11, 2004, from http://www.cert.org/incident_notes/IN-99-03.html.

65. Thompson, 2004; see note 3.

66. Symantec (2003). W32.Bugbear.B@mm security response. Retrieved November 11, 2004, from http://securityresponse.symantec.com/avcenter/venc/data/w32.bugbear.b@mm.html.

67. Reuters Staff Author (2001, August). Virus costs skyrocket: coping with computer attacks tops $10 billion. CNN America, Inc. Retrieved November 11, 2004, from http://www.cs.nmt.edu/~cs491_02/IA/viruscost.htm.

68. Thompson, 2004; see note 3.

69. Keizer, G. (2004, May 7). Sassser worm impacted businesses around the world. United Business Media. Retrieved November 11, 2004, from http://www.techweb.com/wire/26804909.

70. Thompson, 2004; see note 3.

71. AusCERT, 2004; see note 54.

72. President's Commission on Critical Infrastructure Protection (PCCIP) (1997). *Critical Foundations: Protecting America's Infrastructures*. Washington, DC: Government Printing Office.

73. National Research Council (1999). *Transnational Organized Crime*. A summary workshop report by the Committee on Law and Justice, Commission on Behavioral and Social Sciences and Education. Washington, DC: National Academy Press.

74. U.S. Department of State, Bureau of Public Affairs, Office of the Historian (2004). Significant terrorist attacks 1961–2003: A brief chronology. Retrieved July 24, 2005, from http://www.state.gov/r/pa/ho/pubs/fs/5902.htm.

75. Thompson, 2004; see note 3.

76. Webster's II (1995). *New College Dictionary*. Boston: Houghton Mifflin.

77. Shelly, L. (2002). The nexus of international criminals and terrorism. *International Annals of Criminology, 20*(1/2), 85–92.

78. Christie, M. (2004, November 10). Cyber crime tools could serve terrorists – FBI. Reuters, Miami. Retrieved November 13, 2004, from http://www.reuters.com/newsArticle.jhtml;?storyID=6777533.

79. Shelly, L., 2002; see note 77.

80. iDEFENSE (2003). Will Malaysia Emerge as a Pro-al Qaeda Cyber Terrorist Haven? Security Advisory 10.16.03. Retrieved March 18, 2004, from, http://www.idefense.com.

81. *Frontline* (2003). Cyberwar. Public Broadcasting Service.

82. *Frontline*, 2003; see note 81.

83. Warner, B. (2004, November). Nations use net to spy, plot attacks ex-Bush aid. Reuters. Retrieved November 13, 2004, from http://www.reuters.com/newsArticle.jhtml;?storyID=6729139.

84. Singer, A., & Rowell S. (1996). Information warfare: an old operational concept with new implications. *Strategic Forum* (December edition, p. 2). Washington, DC: National Defense University.

85. Warden, C. A. (1995). The enemy as system. *Airpower Journal*, Issue .fs.g, pp. 41–55.

86. Arquilla, J. (1994). The strategic implications of information dominance. *Strategic Review*, Summer edition 24–30.

87. Cooper, J. R. (1996). Another view of information warfare: conflict in the information age (p. 12). In J.D. Schwartzstein (Ed.), *The Information Revolution and National Security: Dimensions and Directions*.

Washington, DC: Center for Strategic & International Studies.

88. Jensen, O. E. (1994). Information warfare: principles of third-wave war. *Airpower Journal*, Winter edition 35–43.

89. Schwartau, W. (1994). *Information Warfare: Chaos on the Electronic Superhighway*. New York: Thunder's Mouth Press.

90. Libicki, M. C. (1995). *What is Information Warfare?* Washington, DC: Center for Advanced Concepts and Technology, Institute for National Strategic Studies, National Defense University.

91. Haeni, R. (1996). Information warfare: an introduction. *Soldier-Scholar: A Journal of Contemporary Military Thought, III*, 3–10.

92. Science Applications International Corporation (SAIC) (1995). *Information Warfare: Legal Regulatory, Policy, and Organizational Considerations for Assurance*. Washington, DC: Joint Staff, The Pentagon.

93. PCCIP, 1997; see note 72.

94. Stein, G. J. (1995). Information warfare. *Airpower Journal*, Spring edition 31–39.

95. Lasker, J. (2005). U.S. military's elite hacker crew. Retrieved April 19, 2005, from http://www.wired.com/news/privacy/0,1848,67223,00.html?tw=rss.TOP.

96. Hennekey, J. (2004). Network Centric Warfare: What Ever Happened to Effects Based Operations and Rapid Decisive Operations? Submitted in partial fulfillment of a Masters Degree, U.S. Army War College, Carlisle Barracks, Pennsylvania.

97. Alberts, D. S., Garstka, J. J., Hayes, R. E., & Signori, D.A. (2001). *Understanding Information Age Warfare*. U.S. Department of Defense: CCRP Publication Series.

98. Stein, for example, conceives of information warfare as the use of information to achieve national objectives. See Stein, G. J. (1995). Information warfare. *Airpower Journal, Spring*, 31–39.

99. See, e.g., Cooper, J. R., 1996 (note 87) and note that the author was only describing factors associated with IW, but as an analog to IC, his analysis has been expanded here to include all scales of cyber conflict.

100. Singer & Rowell, 1996; see note 84.

101. See e.g., Schwartau, W. (1994). *Information Warfare*. New York: Thunder's Mouth Press; and Campen, A. D., Dearth, D. H., & Goodden, R. T. (Eds.) (1996). *Cyberwar: Security, Strategy, and Conflict in the Information Age*. Fairfax, VA: AFCEA International Press; and Schwartzstein, S.J. (1996). *The Information Revolution and National Security*. Washington, DC: Center for Strategic & International Studies.

102. Christie, (2004); see note 78.

# 4

## Computer Abusers and Cybercriminals

### 4.0 Introduction: Who Commits Computer Abuse and Cybercrime?

Have you ever caused some type of harm or crime with a computer or other type of electronic IT device? If you have, you are typical of most computer users. When surveyed, the majority of college students admit they periodically abuse computers or other electronic devices in some way, and many individuals admit they periodically also commit crimes using IT.[1] Examples include illegally downloading music or movie files without paying for the right to do so or installing pirated software without a copyright license. If you have not committed a crime, perhaps you have abused a computer by guessing passwords with cracking software, viewing data you were not privileged to see, or using an electronic device to cheat on an exam or assignment. Perhaps you have abused your employer's computer system by downloading for personal use large amounts of data-intensive files, thereby slowing the performance of the organization's network that others depend on to do their jobs efficiently.

Criminology is the study of crime. Key challenges in this field are to understand who in society is deviant or abusive and why some people commit crimes while others do not. A fundamental assumption (or hope) is that criminals are somehow different from *us*, that we are among the good people in society who avoid causing harm by obeying rules, laws, and regulations. By asserting this assumption we are able to live with ourselves while necessarily condemning the behaviors of others, or at least the worst behaviors of violators who are caught. We can also develop and implement policies, programs, and procedures intended to prevent abuse and crime. Thus, naturally, when it comes to IT-enabled deviance, abuse, and crime, criminologists are very concerned with learning who is involved and why. However, as you are about to learn, the variety of ways in which computers, other electronic devices, and information systems may be abused and used to commit crimes means that many if not most of us are the very people we label as deviants, abusers, or criminals. In this chapter we will continue our discussion of types of computer abuse and cybercrimes by concentrating on the human factors involved, and we will push forward to better understand how this takes place and by whom. Then in Chapter 5 we will explore the theoretical reasons people commit computer abuse and cybercrimes.

In the first section we will explore behavioral aspects of computer-enabled abuse, attacks, and crimes, beginning with a slight variation of Donn Parker's SKRAM model, which can be adopted to assess combinations of individual and group adversary knowledge, skills, resources, access to valued physical and information system environments, and motivations to commit computer abuse and IT-enabled crimes.[2] This is followed by discussion of numerous ways in which perpetrators manipulate potential victims into doing things, collectively referred to as social engineering tactics. Then we will consider what cybercriminals generally fear and why understanding this can be advantageous to information security professionals, law enforcement investigators, and prosecutors as they work to understand and manage cybercrimes.

In the second section of this chapter we will explore why it is necessary, although problematic, to categorize cyber abusers, attackers, and criminals. We will discuss why stereotyping is often convenient but tends to mask the true nature of abusive and criminal activities with respect to attack goals, methods, criminal motives, and mental states, all of which need to be determined in the course of investigations and later substantiated during prosecution of cybercriminals. You will also learn why and how perpetrators of crimes committed with the aid cf computers have historically been categorized, and you will be presented with an updated set of twelve types of offenders corresponding to current major classifications of computer-related neglect, abuse, attacks, and crimes.

## 4.1 Behavioral and Social Traits of Abusers, Attackers, and Criminals

Cyber-related abuse, attacks, and crimes are committed by people with malevolent intentions who use computers, other electronic IT devices, or information systems to cause harm to individuals, groups, organizations, infrastructures, or society as a whole. Perpetrators who do these things make it their business to identify, target, and exploit victims. In the process they use their knowledge, skills, abilities, and resources in varying technological and social circumstances. However, they do not rely exclusively on IT to accomplish their goals. Instead, they carry out their attacks employing social awareness, charisma, and other personal attributes in order to gain advantages while interacting with other people in person and online. In this section we will consider these behavioral and social factors of IT-enabled social abuse and crime. First we will consider methods through which manipulation of potential victims is accomplished. This is called social engineering: influencing people to unwittingly behave in certain ways, provide information, or otherwise enable and even help commit cybercrimes. Then we will consider the adversarial SKRAM model for understanding the skills, knowledge, resources, system accessibility, and motives of offenders. The section ends with a discussion about fears shared by most cybercriminals and how understanding these can be useful to information security professionals and law enforcement investigators.

### 4.1.1 Social Engineering Tactics

Social engineering is a critical aspect of many forms of cybercrime that typically involves getting victims, such as employees of a firm or agency, to reveal confidential personal, financial, or security information or otherwise grant an attacker authority to access a computer system or physical environment in which valuable information may be stored. When access to an online or physical environment is achieved, attackers can then proceed to the next phase of their cybercrime. Social engineering may occur in person, online (e.g., email, instant messaging, chat forums), via hardcopy correspondence, by telephone or cell phone, or by any other means of communication.

Additionally, social engineering may involve using suggestive body language or creating other environmental circumstances to induce particular thoughts, attitudes, or beliefs. According to Donn Parker, specific social engineering tactics include at least:[3]

- *Baiting* someone with appropriate jargon and sufficient facts into doing something.
- *Name-dropping* in order to imply familiarity or relationships with those in positions of authority as well as tacit approval for accessing secure information.
- *Bulletin-board reading* as a means of gathering intelligence on individuals, firms, government agencies, and so on.
- *Reading initial log-on screens* to acquire basic contact information such as help desk telephone numbers and system availability hours.
- *Mixing fact and fiction* to achieve a perception of plausibility among those evaluating an attacker's request for information or access.
- *Exaggerating and lying* about the criticality of a situation or, conversely, about why the security or other information being sought "is not a big deal."
- *Asserting authority (pulling rank) or impersonating real or fictitious individuals* to con an individual into revealing information, providing online or physical access, or merely to establish psychological dominance that can be played upon as needed in the future.
- *Intimidating, threatening, or shocking* individuals into spontaneously giving up otherwise secure information or access.
- *Scorning, browbeating, belittling, aggravating, or exhausting* individuals into complying with an attacker's demands for information or access to a system or environment.
- *Praising, sympathizing with, flattering, or aggrandizing* the individual targeted to put him or her off guard via positive messages rather than negative messages.
- *Persistently calling false alarms* in order to engineer a victim into disabling certain security safeguards because they are too burdensome to maintain.

Other means of social engineering described by Parker include two or more suspects engaging in a good guy/bad guy con or other conspiracy in order to win over cooperation from the victim; displaying artifacts, credentials, or other paperwork that apparently authorizes an attacker to access information, an information system, or physical environment; falsely enticing individuals with payments of some kind or by falsely conveying sexual attraction; and eliciting loyalty on the basis of either personal friendship or professional collegiality.

Among computer hackers and other types of cybercriminals, Kevin Mitnick is a legend. Over several years he mastered social engineering methods in order to manipulate technology and people and thereby deceive, violate privacy, and steal information. His co-authored book, *The Art of Deception* (2002), details how he carried out several cybercrimes, often by manipulating people without using computers or other types of IT devices.[4] Mitnik, who was arrested and prosecuted for his crimes, has expressed remorse and pledged to help people understand how they can protect themselves from being socially engineered and why they should not do what he did. He asserts from his experiences what information security professionals have long understood about securing facilities, computers, and information systems: humans are the weakest link and most vulnerable component of information assurance. Through use of one or more of the social engineering tactics described above or similar methods, people can usually be manipulated into helping a determined cybercriminal accomplish his or her objectives.

Regardless of how social engineering is employed, the goal is to get people to do the bidding of the attackers, who often masquerade as someone in authority, someone in need, or someone with a rightful claim to specific information in order to accomplish a worthy task. Because most of us are socialized to be helpful, if not also especially trusting of persons in authority, we are vulnerable to being psychologically, emotionally, and socially manipulated in ways that may result in our voluntarily (albeit unwittingly) giving up security access or information to an attacker. After all, most of us wish to be helpful and responsible in carrying out our responsibilities, so why not be responsive to the requests or suggestions of people who are trusted, need help, or are in positions of authority? Ironically, our desire to be helpful, coupled with years of being socialized and acculturated to be friendly, courteous, and kind makes us vulnerable to being socially engineered, especially by organizational insiders, acquaintances, and even friends with whom we have already established rapport and trust.

A student's friend once employed social engineering on computer bulletin boards that tricked participants into giving up their usernames, passwords, and even credit card numbers. For example, he used a phishing program to facilitate posting a message like "Due to telephone line noise, your password has been lost. If you wish to stay connected to the service, please enter your username and password . . . ." New participants to the bulletin board (who were often computing novices) often responded with their login information, only to have it immediately recorded by the phishing program, which would then automatically attempt to login and, if successful, record for future reference the account information of every duped victim. By adding subaccounts to the user's authorized account, the social engineer could gain free Internet access and carry out credit card fraud or other cybercrimes in the unsuspecting victims' names.

Just as computer abuse and cybercrimes may occur in various ways, in different places,

---

**CYBER TALE 4.1**

### Victimized by a Social Engineering Friend

On the evening of my birthday, while out eating dinner with friends, I used my Sidekick pager to remotely access the instant messaging program on the computer back in my dorm. After exchanging some messages with friends to tell them they should be out enjoying dinner with me, I signed off and proceeded to have a good meal. Later when I returned to the dorm I discovered that the instant messenger on my computer had also been signed off, which could not have happened as the result of my using the Sidekick pager earlier in the evening. I reasoned that it must be the result of routine maintenance and then attempted to sign back in using the computer. However, I received an error message indicating that my password was invalid. Again I tried to sign on but it was no use. No matter how carefully I typed my password, the program would not let me in.

I began to worry, and as an IT student, thoughts of system compromise raced through my mind. How could a competent IT major like me get hacked? Then I remembered that my friend, a fellow IT major, had given me programs to try out, one of which required me to provide my instant messaging username and password. Naturally I confronted my friend, who admitted that he had manipulated me into using his program, which had provided him with the login information. I was really angry, but all I could do was change my password and clean my computer of all strange programs, including the one called "Annoyeurizer" that my friend had given me to try out. Eventually we stopped talking to each other. I guess that's what being manipulated and becoming the victim of a computer crime will do to a friendship.

*Anonymous Student*

and over extended periods of time, social engineering is usually not isolated to a particular event. Rather, it is often a carefully planned and executed series of behaviors involving[5] (1) targeting people, facilities, or information systems, for abuse, attacks, and crimes; (2) conducting research and developing intelligence on security vulnerabilities; (3) developing rapport with individuals who control access to facilities and/or information systems; (4) violating trust established with such persons; and (5) using the intelligence gathered to commit one or more abuses, attacks, or crimes. Figure 4.1 shows these steps and indicates that the process of social engineering may continue indefinitely, extending to multiple victims as cybercriminals expand their curiosity or greed, activities, and criminal enterprise. Who can you trust, with what, to what extent, and under what circumstances?

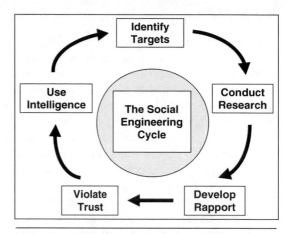

**FIGURE 4.1** *The Social Engineering Cycle*
Diagram by Author. Inspired by Mitnick, K.D., & Simon, W.A. (2002). *The Art of Deception: Controlling the Human Element in Security.* Indianapolis, IN: Wiley Publishing.

---

**CYBER TALE 4.2**

### *Three Friends, of Whom Two Were Hackers*

Three teenage friends used computers for school work and recreation and periodically found themselves with extra time to maliciously experiment with computers. One day Fred and Jack decided to play a practical joke on Pete. They located a Trojan called Net Bust on the Internet that enabled taking over unprotected computers and then figured out a way to deploy it on Pete's computer using AOL AIM. In order for the scheme to work, it was necessary for Fred and Jack to learn Pete's Internet protocol (IP) address, so Fred and Jack convinced Pete that something was wrong with *their* computers and that in order to fix the problem, Pete needed to go to a specific Web site (which displayed *his* IP address) and read some particular numbers off to them. In other words, Fred and Jack socially engineered Pete into giving up his IP address.

    After attaining Pete's IP address they used Net Bust to open up his computer's CD ROM drives and monitored what Pete was looking at on his computer. They were also able to instruct Pete's Internet browser to pornographic and other types of Web sites, shut down his operating system, and delete various files. Net Bust also allowed Fred and Jack to log into and take command of Pete's system at will in order to conduct other types of abuse. Ironically, when Pete's parents realized what was taking place, they asked Fred, who they knew was skilled with computers, to fix their son's machine. Fred responded but neglected to tell Jack about it, so as Fred was fixing Pete's machine, Jack accessed it using the Net Bust software, which resulted in Fred exposing Jack as the attacker, but only after receiving a $25 gift certificate from Pete's parents for helping to diagnose the problem, identify the culprit, and thereafter fix problems with Pete's computer. In the end, Jack confessed to Pete's dad (who was a state trooper!) but never revealed that Fred had also been involved in the scheme from the beginning.

*Anonymous Student*

## 4.1.2 The Adversarial SKRAM Model

We frequently hear about the need for investigators and prosecutors to determine the motive, opportunity, and means for a person to commit a crime. By establishing these factors, a person of interest can be considered a suspect and become the focus of more intensive investigation, possibly leading to his or her arrest, formal charges, and conviction. This classic framework for thinking about the potential for particular individuals to have committed cybercrimes is valuable but of comparatively limited use for understanding the specific technical skills needed to carry out particular types of IT-enabled abuse, attacks, or crimes.

Donn Parker is credited with developing an attacker assessment model that subsumes the classic motive, opportunity, and means framework for establishing suspects in an investigation. Known as **SKRAM**, his model is adapted here to refer to the **skills**, **knowledge**, **resources**, and technical **authority** to access and manipulate physical and cyber locations and data, and intensity of **motives** for committing cybercrimes.[6] Law enforcement investigators and information security professionals can use these five key elements to profile those capable of committing cybercrimes before, during, or after an attack on information systems. For example, the elements may be used to differentiate individuals who are technically skilled in programming and knowledgeable of computers, miniature electronic devices, and/or networking, from individuals who are not. Let us now consider each of these elements in more detail and then consider how they can be used to categorize cybercriminals.

### 4.1.2.1 Skills.
Skill pertains to differing levels of aptitude, expertise, or competency. Naturally people differ in their skills proficiency, but in general they tend to like doing things they are good at and to be good at things they like to do. This principle is not always true, however, as in instances in which people are good at things they hate to do because they are unchallenging or unpleasant. What is important to understand is that cybercriminals possess skills that have

been developed over time, and they have technological preferences for committing certain types of cybercrimes in certain ways. This is known as an offender's modus operandi (or simply M.O.). Skills can be acquired through formal education or training, experiences and through informal practice. Sufficient practice with particular tools may result in an individual developing tacit knowledge about technologies, systems, and processes. Tacit knowledge is akin to being able to do something without really thinking about it. When a person senses that a tool such as a keyboard feels right, or when he or she instantly remembers how to accomplish a particular computing or other type of task because the memory of how to do it is stored in both mind and muscles (e.g., which keys to stroke without really thinking about it), that person's skill level is consistent with a higher level of expertise not shared by people less experienced using a particular tool, technique, or system. This simply means that cybercriminals can become experts at using particular tools like computers and certain types of software in certain ways and for certain purposes.

When cybercriminals achieve substantial success in accomplishing their crimes as the result of acquired expertise, experience shows they are unlikely to vary their M.O. If they do vary their routine they are likely to make mistakes and risk getting caught. Keep in mind that social engineering tactics are integral to the full range of abuses, attacks, and cybercrimes described in the previous chapter. Thus, cybercriminals who possess both excellent interpersonal and information processing skills are well positioned to use computers and other types of electronic IT devices to deceive people and carry out attacks successfully. Kevin Mitnik was notorious for his ability to socially engineer people into providing him with all sorts of information and access to facilities and systems. Cybercriminals must learn how to do what they do, and it may take years for an individual to become very good at hacking, phishing, stealing identities, and so on. The implication is that cybercriminals, like other types of offenders, possess a wide range of skills, knowledge, resources, access to systems, and motives. As illustrated in Cyber Tale 4.3, skills not possessed may be elicited or purchased, including from technically capable juveniles who will not likely face the prospect of adult criminal prosecution if they are caught by authorities. Donn Parker also reminds us that even people with learning disabilities, or those who are otherwise dysfunctional in some way, can learn to use computers effectively for malicious purposes and thus should not be overlooked as possible cybercriminals in cases involving high skill levels.[7]

***4.1.2.2 Knowledge.*** Knowledge pertains to familiarity with facts in subject areas, such as knowledge of operating systems, electronic communication devices, or the design of facilities and physical or information security systems used by a particular firm. Law enforcement investigators, information security professionals, IT managers and administrators, and prosecutors all require knowledge of human nature in order to be successful. Cybercriminals require knowledge about how to write computer code to create malware or launch denial of service attacks or who within a criminal organization or underground network has skills needed to complement their own in order to carry out an attack. The implication here is that skills and knowledge,

---

**CYBER TALE 4.3**

### *Juvenile Geek Paid for Corporate Espionage and Sabotage*

As someone who became fascinated by computers and especially the Internet at the age of twelve, the chance to work on computers was a dream. My first job, at the ripe age of fourteen, was working for a local Internet service provider (ISP). By then I already knew how to create Web sites and do several other things with computers, but I had no idea how valuable my skills were. I was just happy to be making a whopping $5.50 per hour, cash of course, since I was too young to be officially employed. In those days new ISPs seemed to start up every day. One day the CEO of our company was frantic. We were losing customers right and left because the quality of our service had declined for reasons no one quite understood. The CEO suspected that a smaller start-up company was sabotaging our server location, and eventually evidence of this was acquired. In the interim the CEO wanted the problem stopped and he wanted revenge. Knowing that I was very capable, he told me to "Fix em, good boy." He also said he did not want to know anything about it.

At this time, there were basic viruses, but they were easily defeated. I needed something simple, but system critical. With a little investigating, I determined that the enemy firm used four standard abuse email addresses to reply to customer complaints with automated messages like "Thank you for bringing this problem to our attention . . . ." All of these addresses were on NT 3.51 machines, with IIS. This means that every reply email included the entire message sent in the original message. It only took about 2 hours to send 10,000 messages to two of those addresses, each message containing a file attachment. With the reply-to address set as another one of the auto responders, the unique messages kept bouncing back and forth until the servers crashed. Even after the servers went down, the mail protocol indicated the firm's administrative server would continue trying to deliver the message for five days. This effectively wiped out the ability of the firm to provide Internet services for several days.

Looking back on it, I realize what I did was very illegal and I am ashamed of what happened. At the time I was blinded by the fun of the job. As for the CEO, I found out years after leaving that summer job that he was arrested for money laundering and tax evasion.

*Anonymous Student*

though different, are in practice closely related concepts that must be considered when evaluating someone's capability to successfully attack or commit crimes or defend against them.

Acquiring knowledge requires learning, and this in turn requires an investment in time, effort, and probably money. I suppose as a college student you already know this. You may also know that when people are interested in a subject, they will tend to learn about it more easily and quickly than someone who does not share their interest, all other factors being equal. Since cybercriminals require specific and general knowledge to commit crimes, it is often useful to investigate what suspected individuals are believed to know and how they acquired their knowledge in relation to what would have been required to carry out the cybercrimes being investigated. The knowledge needed to carry out a crime can be acquired in several different ways (e.g., taking a class, reading books or articles, gleaning information off the Net either from Web sites or Internet relay chat [IRC] forums). People also learn from their parents, friends, and professional associates. Prisoners convicted of using computers to commit white-collar crimes often share how they successfully committed crimes, as well as the mistakes that led to their incarceration.

### 4.1.2.3 Resources.

Cybercriminals require resources to misuse, abuse, destroy, degrade, deny, or steal information. Time, money, hardware, software, and non-computing tools such as cars and many other types of technologies are all resources that may be needed in various amounts and combinations to carry out particular attacks or crimes. Resources may be purchased or acquired, either through borrowing, stealing, or eliciting others to help. It may also be possible in some instances to make do with available technology by creating alternative ways to commit cybercrimes. The existence of interoperable devices and systems means that cybercrimes can be increasingly accomplished through alternative means and with readily available and affordable hardware and software tools. Cybercriminals may, in general, be more intelligent, educated, and technologically inventive than common thieves or street criminals because their activities by definition require using IT. Therefore, it is useful when designing security systems to consider what types of resources would be needed to defeat physical and cyber defensive capabilities and the likelihood of this occurring. By extension, it is also important when investigating cybercrimes to determine the type and extent of resources that were available, used, and/or not used by cybercriminals.

### 4.1.2.4 Authority.

Authority refers to policy and technical permissions required to access facilities or information systems. With respect to information systems, this is synonymous with what system administrators often refer to as rights or privileges to access certain data. As discussed in Chapter 3, people may commit computer trespassing merely by exceeding their permissions, rights, or privileges to access particular areas of a network they are not authorized to explore. Hackers acquire technical authority to access networks by learning the usernames and passwords of those who have authority. In addition to allowing access to certain data, technical access permissions may be configured to allow or deny users to open, read, write, control, append, and/or delete files and programs, as well as control who can do these things. An individual is said to have **root control** if he or she has power over all the permissions of all system users. Hence, a primary goal of many cybercriminals is to acquire root control in order to access all parts of a given network. With that level of authority, they can also install applications such as spyware and key logger programs, create false usernames and passwords, set and modify users' controls, and create backdoors that afford unfettered future access to information systems.

### 4.1.2.5 Motives.

Motives for committing cybercrimes include the desire to explore, manipulate, damage, destroy, or steal data for personal use or profit, as in cases of corporate espionage. Motives may also include revenge, as in cases of disgruntled or terminated employees who wish to get back at their former firm, managers, or coworkers. Cybercriminals may have one or several motives, all of which may pertain to different past events as well as particular aspects of attacks and crimes. In other words, how crimes are carried out, who or what they are directed against, and the nature and extent of harm inflicted may all be inspired by different motives.

For law enforcement investigators, information security professionals, or prosecutors, it is important to differentiate between motives for committing crimes in the legal sense and operational goals and objectives associated with carrying out attacks and crimes, either of which may have many facets or change over time. It is also important to understand that the *intensity of motives* harbored by cybercriminals can be just as important as the motive itself. Obviously there are extreme differences in the levels of determination of terrorists who carry out suicide attacks versus other types of criminals who are not willing to die committing a crime. The same principle applies to the full range of cybercriminals, regardless of the particular attacks or crimes undertaken and the technology used. People who are desperate are more determined to achieve needed skills, acquire needed knowledge and resources, and employ daring, cunning, and technological imagination to commit crimes.

In theory the combination of skills, knowledge, resources, authority, and intensity of motive can be calculated intuitively, if not actually, to the extent that these factors can be quantified in some way. If the combinations of these factors are divided by the level of information assurance in place, a measurement of the overall threat capability of a given cybercriminal in particular circumstances can be determined. This possibility is represented by the formula $(S * K * R * A * M) / IA$, where $S$ = skill, $K$ = knowledge, $R$ = resources, $A$ = authority, $M$ = intensity of motives, and $IA$ = countervailing information assurance capabilities. In addition the SKRAM of two or more individual attackers could be combined to determine the overall threat capability of a cybercrime crew over time relative to the overall information assurance capabilities in place. Information assurance capabilities would logically consist of technological and human factors associated with physical and cyber infrastructure protection combined. Collectively, the offensive and defensive factors comprise an adversarial SKRAM model, in which the theoretical possibility of calculating the overall threat potential posed by a crew of cybercriminals is depicted in Figure 4.2.

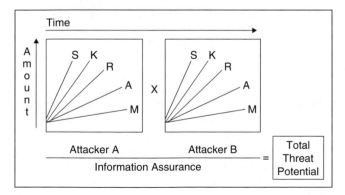

**FIGURE 4.2** *Threat Potential of Cybercrime Crew*

## CYBER TALE 4.4

### SKRAM Needed to Create and Use Fake IDs

It was the summer after senior year—the jobs were good, kids had too much time on their hands, empty shore houses were plentiful, and every weekend there was at least one house party going on. Nearly everyone drank and partied each weekend, but since they had just graduated from high school, everyone was only 18 or 19. Two of my friends wanted to find ways to broaden their options for illegally purchasing and consuming alcohol. Sure, they could continue paying certain classmates, older friends, or even strangers to pick them up something from the liquor store, but those methods were all too dangerous or difficult or suspicious for them. The solution was rather simple: they could manufacture their own driver's licenses with different information and then purchase the alcohol or frequent bars themselves. After all there were numerous ways of obtaining a counterfeit license or identification cards: inner-city copy centers using real license templates and materials that required little or no proof of identification, several online services offering real templates or actual prefabricated licenses, or even falsely assuming an identity by illegally producing required documents at DMV centers for a renewal ID. None of these methods really suited the creative and frugal sides of my friends, so they agreed to make their own false IDs.

The process was ridiculously easy, well established, and even published by numerous sources. The real challenge was pulling it off perfectly. The templates, or image files, of driver's licenses and ID cards for every state in the nation are readily available on the Internet, through peer-to-peer networks, and in underground chat rooms. The templates are either taken from hacked DMV networks or ID creation services or scanned in manually, all resulting in high-quality replications. The security devices of the desired ID scheme are usually detailed on DMV and ID service Web sites or they can be determined by closely examining a real ID. The "Anarchist's Cookbook"—the infamous compilation of lewd and dangerous ideas widely circulated on the Internet—is another source of instructions. Suffice to say, my friends had no difficulty researching how to create a realistic driver's license, and they quickly settled on a state that did not use a bar-coding system and only a simple hologram design.

The road to alcoholism that summer next required only a trip to Office Max, the art supply store, and a print job. Armed with their instructions, some glossy photo paper, laminate material, a special color-changing paint, and a new razor blade, the boys quickly took some digital photos of themselves, stuck these on the driver's license template (with a pirated drawing program), used the appropriate font to fill in their personal information, followed the algorithm listed for the licensing number scheme, and then printed the false IDs out on some shiny paper. They produced a template of the hologram logo and applied the special paint to the laminate. Once dried, the image was cut and laminated and immediately toted to a local liquor store. Since that summer my friends have used their fake IDs successfully at local liquor stores and several bars, as well as out-of-state locations. They both decided it was wise to charge a few bucks for making fake IDs for their closest friends in order to make back the money they spent on supplies. They will probably continue to use their "adult IDs" until they are arrested, or their twenty-first birthdays, whichever comes first.

*Anonymous Student*

### 4.1.3  What Cybercriminals Fear

To this point we have explored social engineering methods used by cybercriminals and the adversarial SKRAM model for understanding human factors and capabilities involved in committing computer abuse, attacks, and cybercrimes. This positions us to consider what cybercriminals fear and why this is important and potentially useful for understanding adversaries, designing security systems, and investigating cybercrimes. Let us first consider fear itself. Just as we all possess a certain amount of and varieties of skills, knowledge, and resources that we can draw upon to accomplish daily activities, solve unexpected problems, and respond to emergencies, most of us also periodically experience varying levels of fear that which we perceive threatening and/or do not understand.

A **phobia** is a "persistent, illogical or abnormal fear of a specific thing or situation [or] a strong dislike or aversion" for something.[8] Social phobia and specific phobia, as described by the American Psychiatric Association, are classifications of anxiety disorders. Whereas social phobia is abnormal shyness that may contribute to alcoholism or eating disorders as ways of coping with anxiety, a specific phobia is triggered by clearly identifiable objects or situations resulting in anxiety responses.[9] Acrophobia (fear of heights), claustrophobia (fear of closed-in spaces), and arachnophobia (my childhood fear of spiders) are examples of specific phobias. Many people have some level of fear about other things that may not rise to the level of a phobia, for instance, going to the dentist or using a form of technology (e.g., flying, driving). People express and manage fear in various ways. Some individuals avoid particular objects or situations or they suppress their fears. Other people, as indicated above, overeat or resort to drug abuse. Brave individuals confront fear in constructive ways and may learn to overcome things that frighten them.

What has all of this to do with cybercrime? Lots! Consider that social engineering by cybercriminals is often designed to instill, enhance, and then exploit the fear of potential victims. Many elderly people unfamiliar with computer technology are easily duped by fraudsters because they do not understand computing and are fearful of being defrauded. Cybercriminals also have many fears of their own, such as the fear of being discovered, arrested, prosecuted, and convicted for their crimes. This relates to other fears such as being publicly shamed, ridiculed, embarrassed, or misunderstood. Cybercriminals may also fear loss of their jobs, professional status or license, possessions, or interpersonal relationships as the result of their illicit activities. While they are committing crimes, they may also fear malfunctioning technology, unpredictable or changing circumstances related to human factors or technology (e.g., procedural changes or defensive or intrusion detection technology upgrades), not anticipating contingencies related to these changes, and other aspects of criminal operations. They may also fear attacks from other cybercriminals or organizations, being ratted out by confederates, or becoming the target of counter-surveillance and manipulation by investigating law enforcement officers.

Fear results in varying levels of psychological and emotional distress brought on by reactions to perceptions of real or imagined phenomena, and it is experienced differently by different people. Thus, opportunities exist to play on the fears of cybercriminals and induce fear through the design of security systems, via investigative and prosecution methods, and by threatening to impose severe punishments on offenders who are caught. These strategies relate specifically to theories related to crime prevention discussed in Chapter 5. If law enforcement investigators and information security professionals can deduce cybercriminals' general and specific motivations and fears, they can design investigative strategies and potentially even technological systems to their advantage. As expressed by Donn Parker, "hackers and malicious hackers, who typically perpetuate a different type of crime, for different reasons . . . require different safeguards to keep them away from your valuable information."[10] In general, this has to do with understanding human nature relative to ways in which technology can be used to establish psychological, operational, and technical advantage in order to deter and prevent attacks and crimes. Said differently, by understanding and anticipating cybercriminals' motivations and fears, law enforcement and information security professionals can employ tools and techniques to make security appear as formidable and threatening as possible. With sufficient intelligence about individual and groups of offenders, these professionals can also potentially counter social engineer cybercriminals into deviating from their M.O.s and making mistakes.

## 4.2 Categorizing Cyber Abusers, Attackers, and Criminals

A major goal of criminologists is to explain ways in which criminals differ from law abiding people. Researchers who seek to understand criminals are also interested in determining how they differ from each other. To this end, research is periodically undertaken to differentiate criminals, create categories of offending behaviors and offenders, and validate these typologies. By doing so, researchers can create prevention, interdiction, and offender treatment programs that focus on particular types of crime and offenders.

Associated with each form of abuse, attack, or crime described in Chapter 3 are cyber offenders who possess personal attributes (i.e., SKRAM) that affect their inclination and ability to cause harm with computers and other electronic IT devices. The range of abusive and criminal behaviors previously described suggests important differences between individual and groups of cybercriminals. By categorizing cybercriminals into discrete groups, we can improve our understanding of specific types of IT-enabled abuse, attacks, and crimes, as well as our understanding of the offenders themselves. For example, by creating two categories, for example, computer abusers versus cybercriminals, we can potentially understand the SKRAM of each in relation to their age, gender, and ethnicity; technical computing skill and general knowledge of IT systems; employment and professional status; and interpersonal relationships and lifestyles. Understanding different types of computer abusers versus cybercriminals in these and other fundamental ways enables researchers to carry out comparative research and studies that replicate and thereby substantiate findings of previous research. As well, formulation of crime laws, associated government regulations, policies, and programs; development of investigation, prosecution, and information security best practices; and setting of industry standards of due care and diligence are made possible.

Criminologists have long sought to meaningfully distinguish between different types of computer abusers and cybercriminals, but often their efforts have resulted in classification schemas of relatively limited and fleeting value, if not also being contradictory in some respects.[11] Historically, typology development of offenders in the area of computer-enabled abuse and crime has been intellectually scattered, based primarily on inductive reasoning derived from limited sets of personal interviews or media representations of offenders, and not formulated or tested empirically. How then are we to think about categorizing cybercriminals?[12] To begin with, and on a fundamental level, we must determine who deserves to be labeled as an abuser and/or a criminal. This is not straightforward. For example, does it matter whether a person commits one crime or several crimes in order to be considered or labeled a criminal? How does time affect labeling? If a person committed a crime years ago, perhaps as a juvenile, is it fair to still regard him or her as a criminal or as an adult who committed a crime once upon a time? In the United States juvenile arrest records are sealed so that young offenders are not saddled with criminal records when they achieve legal status as an adult. Perhaps a person needs to be actively abusing computers or to have been convicted of one or more crimes or be on active probation or parole in order to be appropriately labeled a criminal. Do you agree that there are important distinctions that the criminal justice system should make between the illegal actions of first or few-time offenders versus career criminals who engage in criminal lifestyles? Who shall we regard and label as criminals?

Logically we could group individual offenders on the basis of the types of abuses, attacks, or crimes they commit. We could also

I COULD DO THIS ALL OVER THE INTERNET, BUT I'M A "HI-TOUCH" CRIMINAL.

create categories according to their socio-demographic characteristics (e.g., age, gender, race, ethnicity, professional status, income, level of education, technical computing skills). This is frequently done. As for cybercriminals, it may make sense to differentiate offenders on the basis of motivations or intensity of motives (i.e., drive to carry out their plans), types of technologies used, types and amounts of harm caused, professional associations or interpersonal relationships, and so on. Obviously there are many ways to categorize offenders, each with relative advantages and disadvantages. This suggests that different criteria are appropriate for different purposes according to the needs of researchers, criminal justice officials, and information security professionals. Yet, all categorization schemas are bound to overlap or be conceptually incomplete by virtue of the definitional distinctions made. In short, categorization criteria are needed, they require labeling offending behaviors and offenders,

and they should promote understanding of real-world crime problems.

The inherently changing nature of technology and crime has led some scholars to argue that labeling crimes, forms of attack, and perpetrators is of little practical value.[13] L. E. Coutourie argued that, because cybercriminals are an eclectic group, meaningful profiling may not be possible.[14] Scholars who take this view believe that defenders of information systems and investigators of cybercrimes are better off simply reacting to technologically evolving crime threats rather than dwelling on inevitably changing conceptualizations and definitions of crime. Most scholars believe, however, that cybercrimes involve "sufficiently different occupations of perpetrators, environments, modi operandi, forms of assets lost, time scales, and geography from traditional crimes to identify the subject as a unique type of crime that warrants explicit capabilities and action."[15] On balance, therefore, categorization of cybercrimes and cybercriminals appears to be appropriate and necessary for purposes of general communication, research, investigative specialization, and security technology R&D, as well as development of crime laws, criminal justice policies, and best practices for preventing, interdicting, investigating, and prosecuting IT-enabled abuses and crimes while also ameliorating different types of harms experienced by victims.

In the remainder of this section we will explore the stereotypical adversary profile and other more specialized cybercriminal classification schemas that scholars have developed since the early 1990s. We will also consider who cybercriminals really are, irrespective of these schemas, and think about alternative ways of categorizing them. Then we will consider a new categorization schema that for the time being is comprehensive and takes into account behavioral and other factors, including evolving technologies being used to carry out increasingly complex forms of computer-related abuse, attacks, and crimes.

### 4.2.1  Stereotypical and Other Adversary Profiles

Since the early days of known computer abuses, individuals who abuse and misuse computers have been stereotyped as being predominately young, educated, white males who are curious about computing and telecommunications technology, possess technical computer and programming skills, and have little if any criminal history.[16] Additional classic descriptions of computer abusers and cybercriminals have included being (1) personally motivated and professionally ambitious; (2) overqualified for certain jobs and often employed as insiders in positions of trust; (3) bored in school; (4) loners and socially inept, more interested in machines than interpersonal relationships (e.g., a preference for computer gaming over participating in traditional team sports or physical activities); (5) insatiably curious about and in need of exploring computer systems; (6) disrespectful of established rules of

conduct and bureaucratic procedures; and (7) antagonistic toward authority figures inclusive of organizational administrators and corporate and government officials and power structures. Many of these characteristics are consistent with media reports about the computer hacker subculture, which we will explore in Chapter 7.

On January 31, 2005, Jeffrey Parson was sentenced to eighteen months in federal prison for releasing Variant B of the Blaster Worm in August of 2003. This computer virus infected nearly 50,000 computers, caused millions of dollars in damage, and shook confidence in the trustworthiness of the Internet. At sentencing, Federal Judge Marsh Pechman noted that Parson, a white male, was computer savvy and only 18 years of age at the time of his crimes and that he had been a loner who spent long periods of time holed up in his house using his computer, with virtually no human interaction, much less parental supervision. Prior to his sentencing, Parson cooperated with the Seattle Public Schools in Washington State in producing an educational video to warn teenagers of the dangers of excessive computing and the harm caused by writing and releasing malicious code onto the Internet.[17] Many characteristics exhibited by Parson prior to his arrest were consistent with stereotypical computer hacking, which often appeals to young, bright, socially reclusive, and technologically curious males.

Donn Parker argued as early as 1976 that the most dangerous computer abusers were individuals who knew as much about the design of systems as their creators and that, although most offenders fit the profile above, few professional criminals had the requisite computing knowledge and skills to constitute a serious threat to information systems or society. Parker had studied the jobs held by known computer abusers and criminals, including executives, managers, bank tellers and cashiers, accountants, bookkeepers, and auditors and systems analysts, to conclude that "the best way to identify the potential population of perpetrators is on the basis of the unique skills, knowledge, and access possessed by people engaged in computer technology."[18] It was undoubtedly Parker's early research of correlations between offender behaviors and knowledge and skills needed to hold jobs that led to his creation of the SKRAM model for assessing threat capabilities posed by cybercriminals.[19] He predicted that with computerization, additional professionals and white-collar criminals would adopt computers for illegal purposes. How right he was. Since that time several other researchers have taken up the cause of categorizing cybercriminals.

- In 1991 M. L. Lee identified (1) *hackers*, who gain unauthorized access to computer systems, (2) *crackers*, specializing in defeating computer security systems, (3) *phreakers,* who defraud telephone companies, and (4) *pirates*, who illegally copy and distribute copyrighted software.[20]
- In 1995 Young argued there were principally (1) *utopians,* who desire to contribute to society by exposing security vulnerabilities; (2) *cyberpunks,* who are fundamentally malicious and cause harm to Web site and other forms of cyber assets that offend them; (3) *cyber spies,* who engage in surveillance of the computing activities of individuals, firms, or government agencies; and (4) *cyber terrorists,* who are capable of and willing to disrupt critical information infrastructures and cause associated harm throughout society in order to advance their political agendas.[21]
- In 1998 Donn Parker correctly observed that the following fuzzy categories of cybercriminals overlap one another: (1) *pranksters,* who perpetuate tricks; (2) *hackers,* who idealize the original hacker ethic in terms of curiosity, competition, using computers to learn, and espousal of social justice; (3) *malicious hackers,* who are intent on causing harm; (4) *personal problem solvers,* who often resort to crime when their efforts to resolve matters through legitimate means fail; (5) *career criminals*, who support themselves via cybercrimes; (6) extreme advocates, also known as terrorists, who

advocate social, political, or religious views through criminal actions; and (7) *malcontents, addicts, and irrational and incompetent persons*, a catchall category for all other types of cybercriminals.[22]

- In 1999 Dorothy Denning categorized (1) cyber *activists*, those who legally use the Internet to protest and advocate for social and governmental reforms, (2) *hactivists,* who illegally trespass into computer systems and commit other forms of cybercrimes for personal or organizational reasons including profit, and (3) *cyber terrorists* (meeting Young's description above).[23]
- In 2001 David Wall specified four categories of cybercrime consisting of (1) *cyber trespassing* undertaken by offenders inclusive of Young's four-part schema above but differentiated into principled hacking and unprincipled cracking activities; (2) *cyber deception and theft,* meaning "acquisition harm that can take place within cyberspace" inclusive of credit card fraud, theft via online banking, and "cyberpiracy" such as new forms of digitized intellectual property theft; (3) *cyber pornography and obscenity* inclusive of trading of sexually explicit content on the Internet; and (4) *cyber violence,* referring to online stalking and harassment.[24]
- In 2004 the author and fellow researcher Tom Castellano, using statistical factor analysis, identified five discrete types of cybercriminals among college students at the Rochester Institute of Technology, including: (1) *hackers,* who disrupt or deny computer services, publicly disclose security flaws, and write/distribute malware; (2) *harassers,* who use computers to harass, threaten, and give out passwords without permission; (3) *pirates,* who steal music, movies, or software; (4) *academic cheats,* who use computers or other electronic devices to plagiarize or cheat on assignments or exams; and (5) *data snoops,* who guess passwords or illegally gain access to information systems solely to look at data and files.[25]

The author and fellow researchers found that although these five groups are quite distinct, individual cybercriminals within any group might offend in other ways. For example, many students identified as pirates on the basis of illegally downloading music or movies also acknowledged that they periodically cheat on assignments or exams. Similarly, some academic cheats admitted that they have committed credit card fraud. Hence, students who misuse computers and other electronic IT devices often do so in more than one way.

There are no universally agreed upon definitions or categorizations for cybercriminals. This makes it difficult to compare research findings about the nature and extent of abuse and crimes enabled by computers and other types of electronic devices and information systems. The absence of agreed-upon characterizations, definitions, and categorizations raises the specter of who, in technologically oriented and computerized societies, may *not* be a computer abuser or cybercriminal. Moreover, as people necessarily become more technologically adept in computer-driven societies, an increasing number of crooks who are capable and willing to innovatively use computers and other IT devices continue to emerge, irrespective of what researchers, criminal justice officials, and information security professionals decide to call them or their activities.

People are increasingly using and carrying electronic devices on their person, in their vehicles, in their homes and offices, and during recreational and other types of activities. This has the effect of equipping people who are unscrupulous and capable of committing IT-related abuses and crimes, while simultaneously allaying suspicions

*Millions of people are increasingly using and carrying IT devices on their person, in their vehicles, while traveling, within homes and offices, and to recreational events, etc. This societal condition has the effect of equipping unscrupulous people with opportunistic and planned means of committing IT-enabled abuse and crimes in virtually any location while simultaneously allying suspicions about why they are carrying such devices. Who among these IT users might therefore not be a cybercriminal?* Landon Nordeman/Getty Images, Inc.

about why they are carrying such devices. Several factors contribute to the difficulty of categorizing cybercriminals, including:

- Relatively few trained and interested researchers in cybercrime issues
- Little financial support for behavioral research and other social science aspects of cybercrime
- Overlapping offender qualities or behaviors requiring subjective cut points for determining category groupings
- Difficulty in identifying cybercriminals and gaining entry into their social groups in order to observe their lifestyles, organizational structures, and financial operations
- Socio-technological changes that continually alter opportunities for crime and associated behavioral patterns.
- Ubiquitous and rapidly evolving IT that enables people to commit so many different types of abuse and crime in virtually any circumstance.

Despite these difficulties, concepts, labels, definitions, and categorizations of high tech crime and criminals are necessary for differentiating types of threats to information systems and infrastructure. It is important to remember that a fundamental assumption in the study of deviance and crime is that people who behave abnormally or in illegal ways are somehow different from *us*. However, self-report studies consistently reveal that nearly everyone has at some time in their lives committed at least minor crimes, although only a minority of people are caught and prosecuted for relatively nonserious, incidentally committed crimes. This truism combined with the variety of ways in which computers and other IT devices can be used for abusive and/or criminal purposes implies that many if not most users may be considered cybercriminals, depending on how that term is understood and applied.

Are *you* a computer abuser or cybercriminal? What types of cyber abuse or crimes, and over what period of time, should result in someone being labeled a cybercriminal? If you have ever used a computer or other type of electronic IT device that caused harm in some way, on what basis should you *not* be considered a cybercriminal or at least a computer abuser? The point is that, with rare exceptions, users periodically misuse or abuse computers and other electronic devices in ways that cause harm and are sometimes criminal. In addition, just as while driving we inevitably commit minor traffic violations that we may not even realize and thereby collectively contribute to unsafe driving environments, even infrequent abuse and misuse of IT devices contribute to inefficient, insecure, and unsafe computing environments. An information system is only as secure and safe as its weakest node or user.

### 4.2.2 *Who Are Cybercriminals Really?*

Negligent misuse, deliberate abuse, and crimes are periodically committed by users of computers and other electronic IT devices, yet it remains important to differentiate to the extent possible specific aspects of offending behaviors and traits of cybercriminals. Who are cybercriminals *really*? The problem of course is that cybercrime is a term representing a broad conceptual framework inclusive of white-collar crime, financial crime, economic and corporate crime, and IT-enabled socially abusive behaviors that may not be universally illegal. The concept also encompasses negligent behaviors and misuse of computers or other electronic devices that threaten information systems or compromise the legitimacy of societal institutions or social processes (e.g., using electronic devices to cheat in academia). Identifying traits of cybercriminals is further confounded, as explained in Chapter 6, by the fact the no federal statistics are systematically generated or maintained on criminological classifications of important crime constructs such as white-collar crime or computer crimes, per se. What we know from research comes primarily from a very limited number of self-report offender or victimization studies  conducted sporadically since the early 1990s. Recognizing this serious limitation, here is what may be reasonably inferred about the age, gender, race, ethnicity, education, technical skill, computer knowledge, employment and professional status, and social and criminal relationships of cybercriminals.

***4.2.2.1 Age, Gender, Race, and Ethnicity.***
According to the U.S. Department of Justice, at
the end of 2003, 2,085,620 people were incarcerated in federal or state prisons or local jails. This
number reflects a 2.6 percent increase over the
2002 year-end level and a somewhat smaller average annual growth rate of 3.5 percent since
1995. Approximately 482 people per 100,000
U.S. residents are incarcerated. The number of
women under the jurisdiction of state or federal
prison authorities exceeds 100,000, and the number of men exceeds 1.3 million.[26]

The majority of convicted criminals in the
United States are white males less than twenty-
five years of age, but persons of color (especially black males) are disproportionately arrested,
prosecuted, and incarcerated for drug-related and
violent crimes. The vast majority of offenders
convicted of white-collar and computer-related
crimes are white males. This presumably is also
true of individuals convicted of computer hacking or trespassing, as well as computer-related
harassment, online threats, cyberstalking, computer-enabled pedophilia, and possession of illegal pornography. This is not to suggest that
nonwhites and females are not also cybercriminals, as many members of these groups also
commit computer abuse and crimes enabled
with computers or other other IT devices.

Studies of computer ethics have generally
found males to be less ethical than females, and
delinquency studies have long indicated that males
report higher levels of involvement in deviant and
criminal behaviors than do females. It is commonly believed, and with good reason, that the majority of computer hacking is committed by males
under twenty-five years of age and that most illegal
music, movie, and software piracy is also committed by males in their late teens or early
twenties. Richard Hollinger found this to be true
of male college students self-reporting their software piracy and hacking activities and noted that
gender differences increase in disfavor of males
when higher levels of incident frequencies are examined. In his study of 1,776 students at a southern

university in 1991, he found that three males for
every one female student participated in software
piracy, but that males were only 2.5 times as likely
to admit that they had gained unauthorized access
to a computer account.[27] Arrest, prosecution, and
civil suit court records also support this general
perception. Most white-collar criminals are educated males with professional status employed in
positions of relative power and trust. As greater
numbers of college-educated women continue to
enter the workforce and assume managerial, technical, and executive positions, the number and proportion of certain types of female cybercriminals
are likely to increase.

***4.2.2.2 Education, Technical Skill, and Com-
puter Knowledge.***   Cybercrimes are predicated
on varying levels of knowledge, skill, ability and
willingness to use computers or other types of
electronic IT devices for illicit purposes.[28] We may
reasonably assume, therefore, that cybercriminals
develop the attributes necessary for committing
computer abuse and cybercrimes via formal education and professional training, combined with informal learning from friends and associates, and as
the result of their own curiosity, drive, and access
to devices and systems with which to practice. It
may also be reasonable to assume that the majority of cybercriminals acquired their knowledge and
skill of using computers and other IT devices as
the result of being raised in relatively affluent families and attending schools that offer access to such
technology. Poor people who cannot afford computers, and who must often attend under-funded or
technologically deplete public schools, are less
likely to acquire the knowledge and skills needed
to accomplish many sophisticated types of cybercrimes. However, some types of cybercrimes are
committed with cellular phones and other relatively affordable IT devices that nearly all members of
society may acquire and use.

***4.2.2.3 Employment and Professional Status.***
Computerization has afforded nearly everyone in
modern societies with access to IT gadgets. This

fact, combined with the multitude and combinations of ways in which computer abuse and cybercrimes may be committed, implies that cybercriminals are employed in all sectors— government, private, and nonprofit—and in all types of agencies, firms, and organizations. Gone are the days when white-collar crime offenders alone commit offenses with computers. Certainly individuals of professional status commit a substantial number of cybercrimes, but so do unemployed teenagers and college students, as well as so-called blue-collar workers who never or rarely use computers on the job but nonetheless possess computers or other electronic devices of their own. However, authorized access to information systems owned and maintained by organizations that employ professionals afford unscrupulous employees substantial opportunities to commit computer abuse and cybercrimes to the extent that information security policies, procedures and supervised practices are not instituted.

### 4.2.2.4 Interpersonal Relationships and Lifestyles.

Another fundamental concept relating to who cybercriminals really are has to do with interpersonal, professional, and criminal relationships. Cybercriminals have family, friends, and coworkers. They also enjoy a range of activities, not all of which involve IT-enabled abuse or crimes, although in some instances they join groups of like-minded individuals who share their passion for computing. The Ready Rangers Liberation Front is one among many dedicated software-writing groups whose members associate via cyberspace for creative inspiration, technical assistance, and social support.[29] Another is 29A, a group of elite programmers known to write malicious code and expose security vulnerabilities as a way of enhancing information security.[30] Many similar groups publish programming inventions of their members as a way of achieving notoriety. Association among programming cybercriminals is also promoted through online chat, in-person parties, urban and regional business meetings, and even international conferences such as DEFCON.

Purported to be the world's largest underground hacking event, DEFCON is held annually in Las Vegas and attended by thousands of self-proclaimed hackers eager to meet new associates, demonstrate their technical abilities, or learn new skills.[31] Hackers also develop interpersonal relationships and learn new ways of exploiting systems via IRC networks, and, arguably to a lesser extent, through *2600 Magazine* and other publications available in bookstores or online. University campuses that offer programs in computer science, software engineering, and IT and network administration also provide rich opportunities for social learning from peers.

Cybercriminals learn to commit offenses in a variety of ways. Some stumble into relationships and lifestyles that involve illegal activity, such as illegally sharing music, movies, and software. Other people have friendships that revolve around computing activities that may in time gravitate towards mischievous, malicious, or criminal behaviors. People who would otherwise never think of committing certain types of computer abuse or crime, when afforded powerful computers or other electronic communications devices, end doing so because it is so easy (e.g., to locate and download illegal pornography or copyrighted materials, cheat on assignments or exams, anonymously spy or post- fictitious information about others at a distance, locate and abuse malware available on the Internet, or make fake IDs and drivers licenses).

### 4.2.3 A More Comprehensive Categorization Schema

Given that nearly all users of information systems may be considered at least periodic abusers of IT and information systems and also periodically commit cybercrimes, how should we categorize cybercriminals? One potentially useful approach is to identify major types of known cybercrimes and then profile individuals known to commit those specific types of offenses. From the general categories of cybercrimes discussed in Chapter 3, twelve categories of IT abusers and cybercriminals emerge, including:

1. **Negligent users**, who violate security policies or do not practice sound information security practices and thereby expose their data or that residing on a network to harm
2. **Traditional criminals** who use computers or other types of electronic devices for communications and/or record keeping in support of their illegal activities
3. **Fraudsters and thieves** including those who phish, spoof, spim, or otherwise deceive people for financial gain
4. **Hackers, computer trespassers, and password crackers** (also known as white or gray hat hackers), who, in the tradition of the original hacker ethic, use computers to illegally explore, learn about, and take control of systems in order to pull mischievous pranks and who may also find, exploit, or expose security vulnerabilities
5. **Malicious code writers and distributors** who create, copy, or release disruptive or destructive viruses, Trojans, worms, or adware and spyware programs
6. **Music, movie, and software pirates**, who use IT to violate copyright laws by illegally copying, distributing, downloading, selling, or possessing software applications, data files, or code
7. **Harassers and extortionists**, who use technologies to threaten, annoy, or coerce
8. **Stalkers, pedophiles, and other cyber sex offenders,** who use online and/or in-person methods, when needed, to acquire illegal sexual pleasure from or power over people
9. **Academic cheats**, who use a variety of tools and techniques to plagiarize or cheat on assignments or exams or who fake research methods or findings for profit or fame
10. **Organized criminals** including ethnic gangs that use computers or other IT devices in the course of their legal and illegal business enterprises
11. **Corporate, government, and freelance spies**, who use simple to complex tools and methods of espionage including spyware and key logger applications to snoop for personal or professional purposes
12. **Cyber terrorists,** who seek to advance their social, religious, or political goals by instilling widespread fear or by damaging either critical infrastructure or critical information infrastructure.

Activities of and harm caused by individual or groups of offenders are not mutually exclusive and as previously discussed can also involve widely ranging combinations of motives and attitudes, employment status, access to facilities and information systems, and use of IT, plus knowledge, skills, and resources that if not immediately possessed can be acquired, given sufficient time, money, and interpersonal connections. Therefore, abusers of IT and cybercriminals who specialize in committing particular forms of cybercrime may periodically or routinely practice more than one form of abuse, attack, or crime.

## 4.3 Summary

Behavioral and social factors are important aspects of IT-enabled abuse, attacks, and crime. Perpetrators employ a broad set of social engineering methods along with IT and other technologies to accomplish their goals. These include, but are not limited to, baiting, name dropping, exaggerating or lying to people to get them to provide information or security clearances; reading bulletin boards and log-on screens to gain intelligence on potential victims; and asserting authority, bullying, or threatening people, in order to penetrate a facility or information system. The social engineering methods an offender uses may relate to his or her overall SKRAM (i.e., skills, knowledge, resources, authority, and motives). Taken together, these attributes enable investigators to develop profiles of individual or groups of cybercriminals. In the process they may also discover particular fears of cybercriminals, and how to take advantage of these fears in the course of their investigations and prosecutions, as well as in the design and management of information security systems.

A major challenge is to logically categorize abusers, attackers, and criminals. Historically, perpetrators have been classified on the basis of inconsistent criteria of fleeting value, and this has contributed to the belief that categorizing cybercriminals is of little value. However, categorizing cybercriminals is needed to differentiate between demographic factors of perpetrators, technologies employed, environments in which cybercrimes occur, forms of assets lost, timescales involved, geopolitical jurisdictions affected and so on. Although several alternative categorization schemas have been suggested since the early 1990s, there is no universally accepted typology of cybercriminals. In addition, it must be recognized that all categorizations are inherently limited by several factors, suggesting the importance of situational

and flexible criteria with which to classify cybercriminals. Based in part on empirical research findings and consideration of literature inclusive of prior categorizations of computer crime offenders, the author has advanced a set of twelve offender types corresponding to all major types of IT-enabled abuse, attacks, and crimes. These are negligent users; traditional criminals; fraudsters and thieves; hackers, computer trespassers, and password crackers; malicious code writers and distributors; music, movie, and software pirates; harassers and extortionists; stalkers, pedophiles, and other cyber sex offenders; academic cheats; organized criminals; corporate, government, and freelance spies; and cyber terrorists. In reality, cybercriminals carry out different types and combinations of illicit actions in the course of committing abuse, attacks and/or crimes, thus underscoring the difficulty and limitations of categorizing offenders.

## Key Terms and Concepts

Academic cheats, 132
Authority, 118
Corporate, government, and free-lance spies, 132
Cyber terrorists, 132
Fraudsters and thieves, 132
Hackers, computer trespassers, and password crackers, 132
Harassers and extortionists, 132
Knowledge, 118

M.O., 118
Malicious code writers and dis-tributors, 132
Modus operandi, 118
Motives, 118
Music, movie, and software pirates, 132
Negligent users, 132
Organized criminals, 132
Phobia, 123

Resources, 118
Root control, 120
Skills, 118
SKRAM, 118
Spies, 132
Stalkers, pedophiles, and other cyber sex offenders, 132
Tacit knowledge, 118
Traditional criminals, 132

## Critical Thinking and Discussion Questions

1. What do you think society's perception of cybercriminals is? Without revealing specific details of any particular incident, do you think you are a cybercriminal? Why or why not?
2. Describe a time when you were socially engineered into doing something you did not wish to do. What happened? When did you realize you were being conned? How could you have put a stop to the manipulation?

3. What would you recommend criminal justice agency managers, information security professionals, and IT administrators do within their organizations to prevent social engineering that could otherwise result in security breaches?
4. Go online and find an example of cybercrime. Analyze what occurred and speculate about the combination of skills, knowledge, resources, systems access, and motivations the perpetrators would have

needed to commit the cybercrime without getting caught.

5. When, if ever, do you think it is appropriate to stereotype offenders? Explain your answer with respect to both understanding and managing and preventing cybercrime.

6. Do you think the media stereotypes all or certain types of cybercriminals? Explain your answer and provide an example to support your claim.

7. Find an example of cybercrime in the news. Based on what took place, categorize the offenders into one of the twelve categories listed and described in Section 4.2.3. Then briefly explain the actions of the offenders and why you chose to categorize them in the way that you did.

8. List several things that must be considered when devising a classification schema for computer abusers and cybercriminals.

9. What do you think terrorists might fear the most? Do you think the fears of cyber terrorists differ from terrorists who do not use computers or other electronic IT devices via information systems to carry out attacks? Why or why not?

10. What is the relationship between an offender's fear and his or her overall SKRAM? For example, do you consider an offender's ability to reduce his or her fear by acquiring greater knowledge about a security system to be a priority? What might this depend on? Use the same type of reasoning to explain the relationship between an offender's fear and one other component of the SKRAM model.

## *References and Endnotes*

1. McQuade, S., & Linden, E. (2005). College Student Computer Use and Ethics: An Empirical Analysis of Self-Reported Unethical Behaviors. Unpublished manuscript: Rochester Institute of Technology, New York.

2. Parker, D. B. (1998). *Fighting Computer Crime: A New Framework for Protecting Information.* New York: Wiley Computer Publishing.

3. Parker, 1998, pp. 148–154; see note 2.

4. Mitnick, K. D., & Simon, W. A. (2002). *The Art of Deception: Controlling the Human Element in Security.* Indianapolis, IN: Wiley Publishing.

5. Mitnick & Simon, 2002; see note 4.

6. Parker, 1998, pp. 136–138; see note 2.

7. Parker, 1998, p. 136; see note 2.

8. Houghton, B. (2004). A Brief Timeline in the History of Computers. Retrieved October 23, 2004, from http://www.ceap.wcu.edu/Houghton/EDELCompEduc/Ch1/historykeylist.html.

9. American Psychiatric Association (1994) *Diagnostic and Statistical Manual of Mental Disorders,* 4th ed. Washington, DC: American Psychiatric Association.

10. Parker, 1998, p. 135; see note 2.

11. Consequently, criminological theories that explain the onset of cybercrimes and particular aspects of cybercriminal behaviors are underdeveloped, and relatively few empirical studies of the nature and extent of cybercrimes have been undertaken. These topics are taken up in detail in Chapters 5 and 6, respectively.

12. McQuade, S., & Castellano, T. (2004). Cyber-Offending Patterns among a College Student Population: Development of an Empirical Typology. Paper presented the Annual Conference of the Academy of Criminal Justice Sciences.

13. See National White Collar Crime Center, & West Virginia University (1996). *Proceedings of the Academic Workshop*, Bureau of Justice Assistance Grant No. 96-WC-CX-001. Morgantown, WV: National White Collar Crime Center.

14. Coutourie, L. E. (1989). Computer criminal: an investigative assessment. *FBI Law Enforcement Bulletin, 58* (9), 18–22.

15. Parker, D. B. (1989). *Computer Crime: Criminal Justice Resource Manual,* 2nd ed., p. 1. Washington, DC: National Institute of Justice.

16. Parker, D. B. (1976). *Crime by Computer.* New York: Charles Scribner's Sons.

17. Shukovsky, P. (2005). Blaster worm attacker gets 18 months. MSNBC. Retrieved January 31, 2005, from http://msnbc.msn.com/id/6883312/.

18. Parker, 1976, p. 45; see note 16.

19. Parker, 1998; see note 2.

20. Lee, M. J. (1991). Computer Viruses, Computer Hackers: Security Threats of the 1990's. Unpublished manuscript.

21. See chapter by Wall, in Wall, D.S. (Ed.) (2000). *Cybercrime and the Internet.* London: Routledge.

22. Parker, 1998, pp. 145–147; see note 2.

23. Denning, D. (1999). Activism, Hactivism and Cyberterrorism: The Internet as a Tool for Influencing Foreign Policy. Paper sponsored by the Nautilus Institute and presented at the December 1999 Workshop on Internet and International Systems: Information Technology and American Foreign Policy Decision

Making. Retrieved October 19, 2004, from http://69.44.62.160/archives/info-policy/workshop/papers/denning.html.

24. Wall, 2001; see note 21.

25. McQuade, S., & Castellano, T. (2004). Computer-Related Crime Theories Tested: Self-Report Survey Findings. Paper presented at the Annual Conference of the American Society of Criminology in Nashville, TN, November 17.

26. Bureau of Justice Statistics (2005). Prison Statistics. Retrieved February 1, 2005, from http://www.ojp.usdoj.gov/bjs/prisons.htm.

27. Hollinger, R. C. (1993). Crime by computer: Correlates of software piracy and unauthorized account access. *Security Journal, 4* (1), 2–12.

28. Parker, 1989; see note 15.

29. Ready Rangers Liberation Front. Internet home page. Retrieved November 10, 2004, from http://rrlf.host.sk/.

30. Thompson, Clive (2004). The virus underground. *New York Times*. Retrieved November 10, 2004, from http://www.nytimes.com/2004/02/08/magazine/08WORMS.html?ex=1100235600&en=e27d746ec c37cfcb&ei=5070&oref=login.

31. DEFCON (2004). Internet home page. Retrieved November 11, 2004, from http://www.defcon.org/.

# Part II

# *Theoretical and Social Perspectives on Cybercrime*

*People of all ages use computers for school, work, and recreation, among other purposes, and this is just the beginning of what computer technology holds for the future. Here we see a group of computer users having a great time. Unfortunately some individuals and groups use computers and other types of IT devices in ways that are controversial, abusive or that violate crime laws. Why is this?* Photo by Nathan Fisk

In Part II, in order to further understand cybercrime, we will build on what we have learned about social deviance, technology, and methods of attacking facilities, information systems, and infrastructures and about computer abusers and cybercriminals. In Chapter 5 our goal will be to understand theoretical explanations for why people use computers and

IT to cause harm. In Chapter 6 we will explore victimization, social and economic harm caused by cybercriminals, and how much cybercrime there is. Chapter 7 will present a very interesting set of discussions about emerging and controversial cybercrime issues. You will read about how IT-enabled abuse and cybercrimes relate to technological changes in society. Discussions will address the computer hacker subculture, the open source community, electronic gaming enclaves, legal pornography, and information privacy protections and infringement.

# 5

# *Theories of IT-Enabled Abuse and Crime*

## 5.0 Introduction: Why Do People Commit Cyber Abuse and Crime?

Have you ever wondered *why* some people abuse, misuse, and even commit crimes using computers, other types of electronic IT devices, and information systems but other people do not? Is it simply because offenders choose to disobey rules or crime laws, or do other factors, having to do with their attitudes, the way they think, and with whom they associate, also affect their choices and behaviors? Perhaps people become deviant and abusive and commit crimes because of how and where they were raised and educated. Maybe it is because of inequalities in life that prevent people from achieving success such as meaningful and supportive relationships with other people, safe and affordable housing, a college education, satisfactory employment, or professional status. Could crime also be committed as the result of biological or psychological traits or because of these traits combined with any of the previously mentioned factors?

What do we really know about why people are deviant, abusive, or criminal in their behaviors using computers or other types of IT devices? Why do people commit cybercrimes?

Research reveals that crime occurs as the result of people choosing to behave in particular ways as influenced by social and other factors that may be beyond their direct control. Understanding these potential causes, their interplay, and their relative effects on deviancy, social abuse, and crime can be vexing for criminologists, public officials, and members of the public, who must ultimately pay taxes to support the criminal justice system and make other personal expenditures to help prevent crimes. Understanding why crime occurs is especially challenging for victims of abusive behavior and for criminal justice officials and security professionals who dedicate themselves to preventing crime and ameliorating its impacts. Criminal justice officials and security professionals are also concerned with understanding patterns of crimes with respect to what happened, when, where, and how. Once baseline information of this sort is known, the goal is to investigate additional facts and circumstances as quickly and thoroughly as possible in order to determine who committed the offense.

On a more fundamental level, it is important, for the protection of society, to understand why social deviance, abuse, and crime occur because in so doing we are potentially better able to prevent cybercrimes. Understanding theoretical explanations of cybercrime can also enable professionals to better gather and analyze crime and intelligence information, investigate and prosecute offenders, and design enforcement programs that target particular offending by individuals or groups. Unfortunately, criminologists have historically paid scant attention to theoretical explanations of high-tech crime or to the role of technology in the commission, prevention, or control of crime.

Writings of the classical school of criminology on rational choice and deterrence theories, for example, examined 18th century legal structures and criticized punishments arbitrarily imposed without regard for human rights, justice, or fairness.[1] These writings did not, however, consider in any depth the role or importance of technology used to commit crime, nor did they address the social, physical, and psychological implications of technologies used to punish offenders.[2] Similarly, 19th century positive school theories that began to consider biological and psychological traits of individuals in relation to their propensity to commit crime ignored the role of technology even when using scientific methods, making assumptions of pathology, classifying types of criminals, attempting to predict crime, and treating criminals as patients deemed to be suffering from illness.[3] Even in the 20th century, following the emergence of the field of criminology from sociology beginning in the 1930s, scholars did not undertake research into the role of technology in crime, although academics have generally recognized that technologies are needed to accomplish an increasing variety of criminal acts.

Given the relative inattention that researchers have historically paid to the theoretical role of technology in the administration of justice and security management, it is a small wonder that many public officials, criminal justice practitioners, and information security professionals often know or care relatively little about crime theories which seek to explain why people behave in ways that are harmful to others. After all, their professional responsibilities tend to revolve around understanding how tools and methods were actually used to commit crimes and practical ways in which technology can be used to prevent or investigate crimes and protect information systems. In short, practitioners generally care more about stopping crimes before they occur and solving crimes after they take place than understanding why crime occurs or the ways in which technology contributes to law breaking. This is completely understandable, but unfortunate because as explained in Chapter 1, our knowledge of and ability to apply theories in practical situations has a great deal to do with how well we are ultimately able to prevent IT-Enabled abuse, attacks, and crimes, and ameliorate their harmful effects.

This chapter discusses these issues as it describes several prominent crime theories and their potential application to cybercrime. I begin by explaining what a theory is, reiterating the importance of understanding substantiated theories of crime causation, and describing how the process of knowledge-building through scientific inquiry is accomplished. Then I introduce six general categories of criminological theories, which are discussed in separate sections. Numerous principles, concepts, and specific theories of crime within the six general categories of crime theories pertaining to choice, human traits, social factors, and the integration of these factors are made relevant to computer abuse, threats to information systems, and cybercrimes. A primary goal of this chapter is to convey in simple terms theoretical explanations for why people commit abuse and crime using computers, other types of electronic IT devices, and information systems. Essentially, the chapter applies a broad set of well-established criminological theories to cybercrime issues, situations, and examples.

Students majoring in criminal justice or criminology will find this information interesting because it will build upon theories of crime causation they may have already studied or make crime theories they already know about explicitly relevant to cybercrime and information security issues. Given the relative inattention criminologists have paid to applying established crime theories to computer abuse and cybercrime issues, this review may be needed by many students of criminal justice and criminology and also appreciated by their instructors. Students majoring in other subjects such as computer science, software engineering, or IT administration, who may not have previously taken a course in criminal justice, much less, theories of crime, or who may take only one course on cybercrime issues while in college, will also find this chapter interesting and useful for understanding why people abuse technology, cause harm, and commit crimes using computers and other IT devices. This chapter has been written especially with the needs of these students in mind. The material here is introductory (some criminologists might say superficial) and necessarily speculative in places. This is because there has been extremely little empirical testing of established theories to explain in explicit terms why cybercrimes occur. Nonetheless, the information presented here is fundamental to understanding and ultimately preventing computer abuse and cybercrimes on small or large scales. It is also intended to stimulate the thinking of criminologists by suggesting the types of questions that need to be answered through research.

## 5.1 Theories: The Building Blocks of Knowledge and Understanding

### 5.1.1 The Practicality of Good Theories

A **theory** is simply an interrelated and testable set of propositions that explain a phenomenon. Professionals in all fields use theories to help transform confusing issues into understandable and manageable issues. This is certainly true of criminal justice and information security professionals who must understand and manage cybercrime. However, some practitioners and students who have never studied theories, or did so in uninspiring ways, balk at their importance. Let me assure you that theories of crime are immensely interesting, fun to learn and debate and potentially very useful in the real world of crime fighting and protecting information systems. I know, because I spent most of my professional

life chasing criminals and protecting people and property from harm, without a full appreciation of the power of theories to make sense of the world and help solve problems logically and constructively. Theories provide us with images of what something is, and what is happening all around us. Kurt Lewin, widely regarded as the founder of modern social psychology, is credited with saying that there is nothing more practical than a good theory. A good theory will provide answers to questions about a challenging phenomenon such as cybercrime. Theories also help us name something as being this, but not that, while also providing mental frameworks for thinking about states of change in dynamic environments (i.e., what is occurring, why, and why in certain locations and by certain technological means but not others). Theories can also provide us with insights for developing effective and just crime prevention and enforcement policies and programs, as well as security guidelines for protecting information systems and infrastructure.

People who do not appreciate the value of sound theories are fond of saying things like, "In the real world theories have very little to do with practice." Unfortunately, this statement is partially true because in practical situations there may be little time to reflect on and apply theories, even though research may have substantiated that a new way of interpreting a situation or doing things is better than previously established ways. In policing and security operations, field commanders in the midst of a crisis cannot call "time-out" in order to theorize about what to do next. Either they know and can appropriately apply the latest research findings or they cannot, in which case they must act only according to their judgment, experience, and training, even though these qualifications may be considerable. This is unfortunately also true in circumstances in which they have wrong information, only part of the correct information, or some combination. In other words, practitioners must do the best they can with the information at hand, but theories—even good ones—may in practice get overlooked or improperly applied, especially when seasoned practitioners are accustomed to relying on their experience and training without regard to perspectives grounded in sound research findings.

Few criminal justice and security officials have studied crime-related theories sufficiently to employ them in detail on a regular basis, much less in times of crisis. Fewer still are able to evaluate the relative importance of theories that could be employed in a given situation. After all, and in fairness, they are not researchers. They have not been trained to think as researchers. Consequently they have limited knowledge from which to respond creatively and effectively on the basis of theoretical principles to unusual problems such as those posed by cybercrime. This is not to suggest that criminal justice and security professionals are not learned, capable, dedicated, and effective in their positions. Rather, in many situations taking practical action on the basis of in-depth theoretical understanding is not always possible. Nonetheless, as stressed in Chapter 1, we should strive to remain educated, trained, and cognizant of inter- and multidisciplinary perspectives when solving problems related to information security and cybercrime.

A good theory is also one that is grounded in solid research findings, that can be applied in many practical situations, and that will withstand close scrutiny through hypotheses testing over time. Practitioners as well as scholars can benefit from theories and from each other's knowledge and experiences. Just as theories can and should inform practice, real-world experiences drive the need for new theories to explain emergent aspects of IT-enabled abuse, threats, and crime. The National Institute of Justice (NIJ) of the U.S. Department of Justice is known for including both researchers and criminal justice practitioners in its developmental meetings to explore and help formulate national policies regarding emerging crime issues. In my experience the best criminal justice and security researchers and practitioners understand and genuinely value each other's perspectives, they embrace their respective roles and interdependent

relationships, and their professional and personal lives benefit by them doing so.

### 5.1.2  The Process of Knowledge-Building

It is no accident that theories emerge in their time according to what is going on in the world, and they tend to come about when things need to be explained. In 1994, shortly after the creation and widespread use of the World Wide Web, news media featured reports on "data rape" "cyberstalking" and "New Age crime" among other sensational terms and labels for emerging cybercrime. These reports alarmed the public and raised awareness about crime enabled by computers and the Internet but did little to shed light on why these crimes were occurring, the full nature and extent of associated problems, or what could be done about it. The reports did, however, help raise public awareness about IT-Enabled crimes and the need for enhanced information security, which prior to widespread use of personal computers and creation of the Web, few people cared about. Consequently the time was right for researching cybercrime and threats to information systems. New crime phenomena had inspired creation of new terms, indeed the new construct of cybercrime, which in turn inspired new ideas and the need for new definitions and exploratory research to determine what was taking place. Eventually such exploratory research resulted in better potential explanations of cybercrimes as it was evolving in and across computerized nations. Research also began and is continuing to provide important new perspectives for solving information security problems. The time has now come to understand and better manage the problem of cybercrime in society on the basis of well-established theories of crime.

### 5.1.3  General Criminological Explanations of Cybercrime

As described by several authors of criminology textbooks, there are essentially six general categories of theories for explaining criminal behavior:[4] (1) classical/choice, (2) trait (i.e., biological and psychological positivism), (3) social process, (4) social structure, (5) social conflict, and (6) integrated theories. These theoretical categories were developed over several decades of insightful writing and research dating to the mid-1700s. Each consists of main points and interrelated principles, as well as concepts and/or specific theories that help explain why some people commit crimes. However, no single category or specific theory within a category adequately explains why crime occurs in all instances. Additionally, each general category of crime theory has relative strengths and weaknesses (which are explained at the end of each of the following sections). This is why the integrated theories mentioned in Section 5.7, and particularly the theory of technology-enabled crime, policing, and security, which specifically addresses the role of technology in crime, are increasingly important within the field of criminology for understanding how to formulate successful public policies for preventing cybercrimes. Let us now consider each of these theoretical categories, along with specific principles, theories, and examples of how they relate to cybercrime.

## 5.2 Classical/Choice Theories

**Classical criminology**, also generally known as **choice theory**, is derived from the underlying assumption that people commit crime because they choose to. This basic way of thinking about crime causation began with the pioneering writings of Italian social thinker Cesare Beccaria. In 1744 Beccaria wrote a famous article, "On Crimes and Punishment," in which he argued that people sacrifice a portion of their freedom to the state in order that public safety for the common good of society can be achieved. Beccaria recognized that laws set conditions under which otherwise independent and isolated people can unite to form societies. Laws, he insisted, must

reflect consensus rule or else they could not endure, and **punishment** exceeding that necessary to deter offenders and preserve public security is unjust by nature. Beccaria believed, for example, that **torture**, commonly practiced throughout the Middle Ages and still periodically used in some countries to punish criminals or extract information from suspected terrorists, always penalizes the person who experiences it but may on balance benefit the majority of criminals who would otherwise not be deterred from committing horrendous crimes. The **death penalty**, he argued, was patently unjust except when a criminal exerted influence from within prison that resulted in threats to a nation's security.[5]

Beccaria also believed that the **certainty, swiftness, and severity of punishment** combined to deter people from committing crime (Figure 5.1). Have you ever been deterred from breaking a rule or committing a crime because you feared being caught and swiftly and harshly punished? This basic idea is as powerful today as it was in earlier times when it effectively underpinned the logic of utilitarian philosophers like Beccaria who first articulated the usefulness of creating fair laws and imposing certain and swift punishment with discretion in order to maximize obedience to the state, all in the interest of promoting public security and well-being. This basic principle also underlies the need of individuals to give up certain liberties for the greater security of society, as in nations struggling to combat

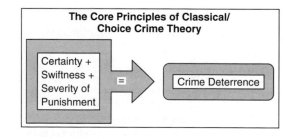

**FIGURE 5.1** *The core Principles of Classical Choice Crime Theory*

terrorism while preserving privacy rights that are potentially jeopardized by powerful computer-aided intelligence gathering and analysis tools. Hence, classical criminology recognizes that the justice system (1) can influence decision-making of potential offenders who may choose to obey or violate crime laws, and (2) attains its legitimacy from people who exchange a portion of their personal freedom for crime control and personal security provided by the government.

## 5.2.1  Rational Choice Theory

**Rational Choice Theory** holds that people are rational and weigh the potential costs and benefits of committing crime. Goals or benefits of committing crime may include acquiring money or other goods and services, exacting revenge, gaining recognition, becoming thrilled, and so on. Certainly people who commit cybercrimes do so for many reasons. Donn Parker, among other notable computer crime researchers, has indicated that thrill-seeking is a common motive of hackers.[6] Can you see how the concept of weighing potential benefits against potential costs is fundamental to making choices, and how rational choice theory can also be applied to changing circumstances in people's lives? A key to using this theory to understand attackers is realizing that what seems irrational to you may to the offender be very rationale and even necessary.

Rational choice theory goes to the heart of crime prevention and information security programs that seek to promote compliance with existing crime laws, regulations, organizational policies, and procedural rules for using and securing system resources. Through education and training, people can better understand the rationale behind these rules, internalize potential harms and sanctions for noncompliance, and choose to abide by organizational and societal standards of behavior on the basis of logic and reason for the common good of everyone. System administrators and other IT professionals seeking to reduce security vulnerabilities associated with human factors should seek to incorporate the principles of rational choice theory into their policies, program planning, and management activities.

## 5.2.2  General Deterrence Theory

**General deterrence theory** essentially combines choice theory with rational choice theory because people can be deterred from choosing to commit crime on the basis of the severity, swiftness, and certainty of punishment. According to this theory, stiff fines, long jail terms, and extremely harsh penalties such as corporal or capital punishment deter people from committing crime in the first place or encourage them to commit lesser crimes or, if they cannot be completely

---

**CYBER TALE 5.1**

### People Can and Sometimes Do Choose to Change Their Criminal Ways

After being in college for over four years I've shed my small town naïvety and made a concerted effort to stop pirating music and software. The benefits of pirating do not outweigh the possible repercussions. I am currently a professional in the IT field and I hope to continue as a professional in this field. I do not need any criminal record looming over my head. I can honestly say I now legally own every mp3 file in my collection. The same can be said for all of my software. The deterrent for me is the negative image a criminal record would show my current employer and that it could potentially prevent me from getting a different job in the future.

*Anonymous Student*

deterred, to at least cause less harm to persons or property. A key aspect of deterrence is making potential and actual punishments widely known. In an effort to deter cyber copyright infringement, the Computer Crime and Intellectual Property Section of the U.S. Department of Justice maintains a Web site listing adjudicated and ongoing software piracy cases, among other types of cybercrimes.[7] For example, on August 17, 2004, Alex Rodriguez was arrested in New York City and charged with one count of criminal copyright infringement for selling more than ten copyrighted software applications having a total retail value in excess of $5,000. If convicted, he could be sentenced to 10 years in federal prison and fined twice the gross gain or loss from the offense up to $250,000.[8]

The Rodriguez case focused on illegal selling of software applications such as Macromedia Flash MX (a program related to Web site development that normally retails for approximately $499) to an undercover FBI agent for $30. As previously discussed in Chapter 3, copyright infringement also pertains to illegal downloading and distribution of music and movie files, among other protected forms of content, without authorization. Some college students, within the framework of classical criminology and deterrence theory, believe they will not be investigated or prosecuted for illegally downloading only a small number of songs as compared to other people who have downloaded hundreds or even thousands of songs. Certainly the government does not have sufficient resources to prosecute everyone who pirates music, movies and software, and often only the worst offenders are targeted for investigation by law enforcement. This situation is analogous to numerous other types of crime and law enforcement efforts, such as control of drug markets by focusing arrests on pushers and people who illegally consume large amounts of controlled substances; or reducing illegal speeding on highways by ticketing drivers who exceed the posted limit by a certain minimum amount (e.g., 15 mph). However, thousands of small-time drug users and speeders also find themselves under investigation by police, and many of these offenders end

up receiving stiff fines and other penalties for their illegal actions. Are you willing to risk incarceration, steep fines, and your professional future over a small or even large number of songs, or some other type of cybercrime violation?

Imposing and thereafter making known penalties received by law violators is the fundamental concept underlying general deterrence theory. However, informal sanctions can also deter people from committing IT-enabled abuse and cybercrimes. For example, if you think people who you know and respect will disrespect you for using computers or other electronic IT devices in socially unacceptable, abusive, or criminal ways, you may be less likely to behave in those ways. In the computer use and ethics study undertaken by the author at the Rochester Institute of Technology (RIT) in 2004, over 800 randomly selected college students were asked how likely it was that they would be caught and severely punished for several different categories of IT-enabled abuse or crime, including: (1) sending spam email; (2) guessing passwords, giving out passwords, or gaining unauthorized access in order to look at or change data or files; (3) disclosing security vulnerabilities or flaws; (4) illegally downloading or sharing music, movies, or software; (5) committing plagiarism or cheating on assignments or exams; (6) disrupting computer services or spreading malicious code; (7) possessing or using someone's credit card number without permission; and (8) using a computer or other device to harass or threaten someone. Student survey responses are listed in Table 5.1.

As you can see from Table 5.1, students who responded to this survey believe there is relatively little chance they will be caught or severely punished for these types of IT-enabled abuse or crimes. Further analysis reveals an average estimate of 1.72 on the 0–4 scale regarding students' estimates about the likelihood of being caught. Analysis also resulted in a mean perception of 2.44 for the severity of punishment likely to be imposed if students were caught for any of the cybercrimes or IT-enabled abuses listed. Hence, the students surveyed generally believed they were not that likely to be caught, and even if

**TABLE 5.1**  *College Student Report about the Likelihood of Being Caught and Punished for Specific Types of IT-Enabled Abuse and Crime*

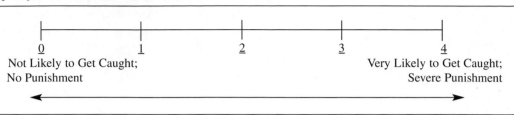

|  | Mean Scores | |
| --- | --- | --- |
| *IT-Enabled Abusive or Criminal Behavior* | *Getting Caught* | *Punishment* |
| 1.  Send spam email | 1.28 | 1.44 |
| 2.  Guess or give out passwords or gain unauthorized access to a computer system in order to look at or change data or files | 1.24 | 2.22 |
| 3.  Disclose security vulnerabilities or flaws | 1.48 | 1.84 |
| 4.  Illegally download or share music, movies, or software | 1.37 | 1.59 |
| 5.  Commit plagiarism or cheat on assignments or exams in school | 1.90 | 2.58 |
| 6.  Disrupt computer services or spread malicious code | 2.37 | 3.55 |
| 7.  Possess or use someone's credit card number without permission | 2.13 | 3.30 |
| 8.  Use a computer or other device to harass or threaten someone | 1.97 | 2.87 |

they were caught, the punishment imposed would in general not be very severe.[9] Further analysis of the data in Table 5.1 reveals that the difference between severity of punishment and likelihood of being caught for any particular offense ranges from a low score of 0.14 for sending spam email, to nearly equally high scores of 1.18 for disrupting computer services or distributing malicious code, and 1.17 for possessing or using credit card numbers without authorization. Thus, students are on average more afraid of being caught and punished for the latter forms of cybercrime than for spamming, which is also against the law.

What do you think about these research findings? Are they consistent with your own views about cybercrimes and punishment? At a general level, what do the data indicate about deterrent effects against committing cyber-crimes such as sending out spam, launching denial-of-service (DoS) attacks, distributing malware, or committing credit card fraud? How do students' perceptions of the likelihood of being caught and punished correspond to your own views of the seriousness of these different types of cybercrime? Should society strive to increase perceptions of the possibility of being caught and more harshly punished? If you were an advocate of public policies based on the rational choice and general deterrence theories, you would of course say "yes" because, taken together, these theories posit that people act on available information to make informed choices as to whether the potential benefits of committing specific crimes are worth the risk of getting caught, plus the certainty, swiftness, and severity of punishment likely to be meted out by the criminal justice system.

Recall, however, that a person may also be deterred from committing IT-enabled abuse or crime on the basis of informal sanctions such as those imposed by employers, schools officials, or others whom they respect, especially if these involve personal embarrassment, shame, or public humiliation after violations are discovered. The RIT survey also revealed that, in general, students were generally more concerned about respected adults and employers learning of their IT-enabled abuses or crimes than they were about family members or friends finding out they had committed any form of cybercrime. Why do you suppose this is the case? Can you think of ways in which public shaming could be used to help prevent certain types of computer abuse or cybercrimes at your school, place of employment, or elsewhere in society?

### 5.2.3  Routine Activities Theory

Within the framework of classical/choice theory, perceptions of opportunities to commit crime are very important. **Routine activities theory** builds on this foundation by claiming that crimes are more likely to be committed by motivated offenders who have suitable targets in the absence of capable guardians. According to Cohen and Felson, the founders of this theory,

*. . . illegal activities must feed upon other activities, the spatial and temporal structure of routine legal activities should play an important role in determining the location, type and quantity of illegal acts occurring in a given community or society. Moreover, one can analyze how the structure of a community organization as well as the level of technology in a society provide the circumstances under which crime can thrive. For example, technology and organization affect the capacity of persons with criminal inclinations to overcome their targets, as well as affecting the ability of guardians to contend with potential offenders by using whatever protective tools, weapons and skill they have at their disposal. Many technological advances designed for legitimate purposes—including the automobile, small power tools, hunting weapons, highways, telephones, etc.—may enable offenders to carry out their own work more effectively or may assist people in protecting their own or someone else's person or property.[10]*

Routine activities of perpetrators, as well as those of potential victims and other actors, thus result in opportunities for committing and preventing cybercrimes with technology. As such, routine activities theory has important implications for understanding crimes committed with or prevented with computers, other electronic IT devices, or information systems. Routine activities theory is described here in the context of classical criminology because it closely relates to choices made by criminals when deciding which targets to strike and regarding possibilities for being investigated, prosecuted, and punished. Can you think of examples of computer abuses or cybercrimes that have occurred as the result of the routine activities of perpetrators? Conversely, can you think of instances of computer abuse or cybercrimes that may have been prevented because of target hardening of information systems or infrastructure by potential victims or because of technology-related actions of information security professionals, criminal justice officials, or other so-called capable guardians in society?

### 5.3  Trait Theories

**Trait theories** of crime posit that people commit offenses because of biological characteristics and/or psychological disorders. Human traits that contribute to the intentional or unintentional commission of crimes are an individual's responses to discrete or interrelated genetic, biochemical, or psychological factors. Taken together, such factors may create a condition that the perpetrator cannot resist, or may not even know about, much less be responsible for. Trait theories provide a theoretical framework that is also sometimes referred to as biological and psychological **positivism**, a term derived from approximately the mid 19th century, when scientists in a number of emerging fields of study began to conduct formal theory testing in positively deterministic ways (i.e., using deductive reasoning, and data collection, measurement, and analysis) otherwise known as hypothesis testing.

## BOX 5.1 • *Major Strengths and Limitations of Classical Criminology*

The major strength of classic criminology/choice theories is that they help explain why any type of computer abuse or cybercrime is committed regardless of a perpetrator's gender, race, ethnicity, social class, religion, or SKRAM (discussed in Chapter 4). The concept of choice is fundamental in crime studies based on rational choice theory. Choice also pertains to the elements of certainty, severity, and swiftness of punishment imposed on crime law violators as described by general deterrence theory. It is easy to understand why people with relatively much to lose (e.g., money, property, and professional status) may be more easily deterred than those who have little or nothing to lose by committing a given cybercrime. The major strength of routine activities theory is that at a general level it addresses the important role of technology in committing and preventing cybercrime. It also provides a useful framework for understanding and predicting criminal targeting behaviors at a general level and for conceptualizing in general ways how people, facilities, and information systems targeted by cybercriminals can be better protected.

A major limitation of classical criminology is that it does not posit underlying reasons for why people commit crime or take into account that some people apparently cannot be deterred from committing crime. General deterrence theory does not take into account crimes of passion in which a perpetrator in the heat of the moment may not fully consider the potential penalty. Prisons in the United States currently house thousands of murderers who knew in advance that, if arrested and convicted, they would likely receive a very long prison sentence, perhaps even life without possibility of parole, or that they could be executed if capital punishment was legal and practiced by the state in which they committed their crime. Critics of general deterrence theory also point out that some terrorists, in order to advance their cause, are willing to commit suicide in the course of committing their crimes.

Similarly, rational choice theory cannot be universally applied because very young or immature persons, and those suffering from certain types of mental disorders, as well as people whose judgment is physiologically impaired by drugs, intoxicating beverages, or other substances, may not be capable of making rational decisions before or during the commission of crime. In addition, what is rational for one individual or group of offenders may be completely irrational to other people. Some people, for example, regard dealing drugs as a perfectly rational way of escaping poverty. Similarly, terrorists who blow themselves up may rationalize that their rewards in the hereafter are worth the harm caused to themselves and others in violation of crime laws. In addition, routine activities theory does not explain technological innovations or shifts in the nature of crime, policing, or security methods or the implications of these for preventing crimes including those enabled by IT. The theory also fails to address technology-related attributes of individual or groups of offenders beyond the concept of motivation.

Charles Darwin was an early positivist who became famous in the field of biology for his studies of animal and plant species and for publishing his 1859 *Origin of Species,* in which he described the concepts of common descent, natural selection, and a general theory of evolution. Similarly, early attempts to understand causes of crime involved measuring physical characteristics of convicted or executed prisoners, soldiers, and medical patients and then comparing the results with similar measurements of people known to be aggressive, violent, or criminal. Cesare Lombroso was an Italian physician who became famous in the 1880s for this early variety of biological determinism. Eventually this line of research resulted in **somatotyping**, a method of classifying criminals on the basis of their physical characteristics.[11] Although contemporary **biosocial theory** seeks to explain crime on the basis of physical and mental traits, combined with social and environmental factors, early biological trait research including somatotyping studies have been discredited on both theoretical and methodological grounds and are today widely regarded as being inherently racist. After all, cybercriminals (as will be explained in Chapter 6) are people of all races whose crimes have nothing to do with their physique.

Nonetheless, it is possible that biochemical factors and processes within the body, including those that are genetically predetermined or that result from ingesting (or not ingesting) needed food, drugs, or other substances, may affect intelligence and decision making and thereby indirectly contribute to crimes committed by affected individuals. Defendants using the so-called "Twinkie defense" at trial have claimed that their need for a sugar fix contributed to their behaving violently and/or with diminished capacity to formulate premeditated intent.[12] Similarly, severe cramps, nausea, and mood disorders associated with premenstrual syndrome (PMS) may cause some women to act irrationally and commit crime. Ninety percent of women of reproductive age suffer from some PMS symptoms, and a small subset of them may actually experience psychotic symptoms.[13] Exposure to dangerous amounts of naturally occurring substances or contaminants found in the environment, and especially in water supplies (such as lead, mercury, or copper), may also contribute to hostile, impulsive, or criminal behavior. Research also suggests that radiation from certain types of light sources may influence antisocial behavior.[14] Is it possible that long-term exposure to bright computer screens may contribute to the onset of irrational or abusive human behaviors in ways not currently understood?

Many people suffer from mental disorders that can affect their decision-making and behavior. Bipolar disorder occurs in people with extreme mood swings that alternate between wild elation and deep depression. Schizophrenia is a particularly serious disorder in which people hear nonexistent voices or hallucinate.[15] Can you think of how any of these or other types of mental disorders could help to explain IT-enabled

abuse or crime? Brain dysfunction brought on by malignant tumors or other types of neuropsychological conditions may also contribute to crime, as evidenced by research that reveals murderers exhibit brain impairment at a rate 3 times greater than the general population. Research also shows that males with higher levels of androgens (male sex hormones) such as testosterone, are more inclined to become violent.[16] Males are generally regarded to be more aggressive than females and are responsible for committing the vast majority of violent crimes.[17] In the computer use and ethics study conducted at the RIT in 2004 (Table 5.1), male college students were much more likely than female students to commit acts of computer abuse or cybercrimes and they generally reported less ethical attitudes regarding use of computers and other types of IT devices.[18]

Disorders of impulse control such as kleptomania (an uncontrollable urge to steal), pyromania (the urge to start fires), and pathological gambling (uncontrollable impulses to bet) may relate to criminal behavior among some afflicted individuals. Disorders of these types may present a condition aggravated in ways not readily discernable in certain individuals, which contributes to their committing crime in ways also not readily understood. For our purposes, a key element is technology and its potential influence on human decision-making and abusive or criminal behaviors. Consider, for example, this question: the possible effects of computerized gambling technology on pathological gamblers? In 1999 the National Research Council, following a year-long review of research on gambling, concluded in part that by changing the subjective experience of gamblers, computerized gaming has the potential to alter how often, how long, and how much people gamble: "The characteristics of game technologies, such as the number of gambles offered per time period, the physical and informational environment of games, game rules, speed of play, probabilistic structure, cost per play, and jackpot size, appear to affect gambling preferences and habits."[19]

Obviously rational decision-making can also be compromised by intoxicating beverages and/or illegal drugs. How do you think computer and console games or computers used for online gambling from homes or other locations compare in their effects on human self control to the effects of computerized slot machines in gambling casinos? If computer design, functionality, or content can be conclusively linked to human judgment and behaviors, what are the implications for information security, computer abuse, and cybercrime? These are the types of research question traits theorists could explore within the context of arousal theory, cognitive theory, and behavioral theory.

## 5.3.1 Arousal Theory

Stimuli provided by computer-enabled gaming machines, especially those located in noisy, busy environments with many conflicting sources of stimuli, may lead to cognitive overload, negating peoples' awareness of their surroundings and ability to make rational decisions.[20] Have you ever known someone to become mesmerized and zone out while playing computer games? South Korea is a very connected nation, with more than half of its population of approximately 50 million people having access to the Internet. More than 10 million Koreans now have high-speed connections to the Internet. Many of the nation's 25,000 Internet cafes, also known as "PC rooms" or "PC bangs," are open all 24 hours. On October 9, 2002, South Korean police responded to an Internet cafe call to investigate the death of Kim Kyung-jae, a 24 year-old man who witnesses said had been playing computer games almost nonstop for 84 hours with no decent sleep or food.[21] Evidently Kyung-jae had become transfixed on gaming to the point that he neglected his bodily needs, which lead to his death.

People can become aroused through many kinds of activities. Unusual, pleasurable, risk-taking, and thrill-seeking behaviors can provide temporary relief from otherwise mundane situations and lifestyles. For some people, the greater the risk or danger, the more rewarding the experience, assuming they survive and at minimal costs. Some computer hackers are believed to break into systems for the thrill of doing so.[22] Perhaps such individuals become more aroused as the difficulty and risks of breaking into computer systems increase. **Arousal theory** is a trait theory that posits that people prefer a level of arousal which if not maintained leads to their committing crime, even though people vary in how they process environmental stimulation. Is it possible that otherwise bored computing sensation seekers need their "gaming fix" or that people need more and more variations of online pornography in order to satisfy their need for sexual arousal? Is it possible that individuals, cyber stalkers for example, may become aroused with feelings of power or control by using computer technology to harass, threaten, or abuse? Do some people find release for their otherwise violent or sex-related thrill-seeking by using computers?

In what other ways can people use computers or other IT devices for arousal, and what are the implications of this for computer abuse, cybercrime, and information security? Consider the following hypothetical examples:

- A person seeking arousal at work abuses his computer to game, gamble, view pornography, or track impending sales on an online auction site. In addition to wasting time and potentially causing distractions, these activities consume system resources and unnecessarily expose the employer's network to malware.
- An unchallenged computer programmer working for a large corporation writes a script to hack into the company's computer system for sheer entertainment. The sensation or thrill sought by the programmer may be emotionally and/or physiologically gratifying, similar to satisfaction other people receive from playing a computer game (whether of violent or nonviolent content).
- A gifted high school student bored with his computer programming class sees other students

as computing idiots and the teacher's assignments as a joke, so he begins to wonder about the inner workings of the software other than that being used in class. More than merely interested, he becomes excited to figure out where the operating code in a computer game is located and what it consists of. As his skill increases, greater challenges are needed to satisfy his need for arousal, so he begins to illegally explore vulnerabilities of government computer systems.

Research has substantiated that humans can maintain states of arousal for extended periods of time by using electronic devices. Again consider the world of casino gambling, in which firms increasingly use theme-based slot machines equipped with blinking lights and musical tones to entice betting for extended periods of time. If you have ever experienced the unmistakable "ching-ching-ching" sound of casino tokens steadily clanging into the metal tray of a slot machine, then you know what I am talking about. Did it ever occur to you that the blinking lights, noisy alarms, and steady but not too rapid discharge of just so many tokens are specifically designed to stimulate your physiology and affect your judgment while also drawing envious looks from surrounding gamblers, all of which combine to heighten your sensation of winning and keep you gambling while enticing others to gamble as well? This is evidence of the potential alluring effects of electronic devices in creating and maintaining states of arousal. Obviously becoming aroused is not limited to computing activities, nor does all computing activity that causes people to become excited have negative implications (i.e., for computer abuse, cybercrime, or information security). Still, criminologists, cybercrime investigators, and information security professionals need to be aware of these issues so that their expertise remains yoked to breaking research findings as they become available.

Research pertaining to the potentially addictive effects of computing is in its infancy, yet there is plenty of anecdotal evidence that extensive periods of computing can cause real physiological, psychological, emotional, social, and economic harm. One very bright student who was not able to concentrate in class and who showed signs of being tired, but exhibited no indications of alcohol or drug abuse, revealed that his fascination with a computer game caused him to forgo his studies and stay up very late for several nights in a row. When asked whether or not he thought he was making the right choices, the student acknowledged that the computer game was problematic but that he intended to get back on track as soon as he won. Evidently he did not realize that many computer games are designed so that players never actually win, or they allow a player to advance in levels of playing difficulty only by investing extraordinary time and/or developing exceptional skill. Hence time, money, and effort spent on computer gaming presents opportunity costs (i.e., the other things you could do with your time, money, and abilities). Another student reported how he had become obsessed with computer gaming, chatting, and online auctions but eventually ceased his unhealthy behaviors after realizing that his use of computers for these purposes was indeed excessive and having negative impacts on other areas of his life.

**Internet addiction disorder,** the term first coined by Dr. Ivan Goldberg on a Web site in 1997 as a parody of problematic computing behaviors, is not currently among the mental disorders officially listed in the American Psychiatric Association's *Diagnostic and Statistical Manual of Mental Disorders.*[23] However, symptoms of so-called "computer addiction" or "Internet addiction" should not be taken lightly. Just as the effects of excessive drinking or substance abuse or a mental or personality disorder may combine or directly cloud a person's judgment and cause him or her to behave irrationally, obsessive use of computers *for any purpose* can contribute to poor health and jeopardize success in many areas of life. Online and traditional counseling services, including those now offered by many colleges and universities, are available to help people suffering from any condition that may be aggravated as a result of excessive computer use. If you know someone who may be in danger of "becoming lost in cyberspace" realize that this may be symptomatic of any number of very serious medical conditions. Consider encouraging the person to seek professional assistance, or confer with a registered or licensed health care professional about what you can do to help.

### 5.3.2  Cognitive Theory

**Cognitive theory** pertains to how people perceive and relate to the world around them; how they go about making decisions, solving problems, and resolving conflicts; and what influences their moral development. Cognitive theorists try to understand how people process information in order to make what we hope are correct and moral decisions. People who are given to interpreting information about their surroundings incorrectly may be further inclined to make inappropriate decisions, act abusively, and even commit crimes as a result. What do you think? Can real environments combined with virtual environments created with software, affect a person's ability to process information correctly? Are you more comfortable working, playing, or interacting in one type of physical or virtual environment as opposed to others? Would you rather be alone with and into your computer, hanging out chatting and gaming with people online, or do you prefer to socialize in person? Do you think your preferred social and physical environment, however enabled with technology, helps or hinders your ability to process information effectively and make correct as well as moral decisions?

As previously indicated, biochemical imbalances caused by diet, drugs, or other substances, plus gender, psychological, genetic, and personality disorders can cause some individuals to become inattentive, nervous, impulsive, depressed, hyperactive, paranoid, aggressive, antisocial, and so on. If not controlled, these and other factors, according to cognitive theory, may contribute to affected individuals committing crime. Therefore, criminologists and public officials who accept trait theory explanations for crime often take the position that offenders are sick and need to be treated rather than punished. People may also suffer from personality disorders that destabilize acceptable behavior patterns. Personality traits that may be linked to crime include impulsivity, hostility, and aggression. Conduct and anxiety disorders, as well as hyperactivity, attention deficit disorder, and depression may also contribute to crime-related behaviors. For example, individuals who respond to frustrating events with exceedingly strong negative emotions or who feel very stressed and/or harassed by such events, may suffer from antisocial personality disorder, which has been linked to violent and criminal behavior. How, if at all, might such disorders explain computer abuse or cybercrime?

On Thanksgiving Day in 2002, Shawn Woolley, of Hudson, Wisconsin, used a handgun to commit suicide while sitting in his apartment at his computer.[24] When his mother found his body, she noted the monitor still had Everquest on the screen, the computer game Shawn was known to play for 12 hours per day. Having been diagnosed "with depression and schizoid personality disorder, symptoms of which include a lack of desire for social relationships, little or no sex drive and a limited range of emotions in social settings," Shawn reportedly had quit his job, ignored family members, and escaped into the fantasy world of Everquest. Then, according to Shawn's mother, something involving the characters in the computer game drove him to commit suicide.[25] Although this tragic story on the surface seems to indicate that incessant computer gaming may have contributed to Shawn's death, research has not substantiated how, if at all, computers may cloud judgment and result in self-destructive or other harmful behaviors to oneself or others. However, since the human brain functions on the basis of biochemical electrical impulses, it may be possible that under the right circumstances computers affect judgment and contribute to harmful behaviors of certain people in ways not currently understood.

### 5.3.3 Behavioral Theory

Do you feel comfortable using *your* keyboard? Do the keys "just feel right" to you compared to those on someone else's keyboard? What you are experiencing is **tacit knowledge**: memory about tools and techniques stored in our minds and muscles that allows us to go on autopilot using particular technologies to accomplish specific tasks. Some people find incredible pleasure in using specific tools with which they feel comfortable, but incredible discomfort if required to use technology with which they are unfamiliar. Although research has not yet made explicit connections between tacit knowledge and criminal modi operandi (i.e., technological ways in which criminals prefer to commit crimes), could it be that preferences for using specific tools and techniques influence how people choose to go about committing cybercrimes? Do you think it is possible that individual cybercriminals may prefer specific hardware or software products because of their look and feel? In what ways do the appearance, feel, and overall functioning of technology affect human behavior?

New research has revealed that preferences for interacting with computers rather than with persons are associated with certain types of IT-Enabled abuse and crime. In the 2004 study at RIT, the author found that of 873 students who took the survey, 4.4 percent would rather chat online than in person; 9.0 percent indicated that computers helped them feel in control; 13.3 percent reported that they enjoy experimenting with other people using computers; 15.7 percent indicated that they enjoy using computers to explore with other people; and 23.8 percent revealed that they enjoy using computers to compete with other people. Collectively these five attitudinal and behavior dimensions were labeled **computer efficacy** because the students who agreed or strongly agreed with all five sentiments expressed their relative affinity for these types of computer-enabled activities. For these students, using computers to communicate interpersonally, acquire control, experiment, explore, and compete was more efficient and/or effective than trying to accomplish these things in person.

Table 5.2 lists data regarding how several types of computing activities by these individuals (labeled in the chart as true geeks) compare with computer-enabled activities of other students (labeled nongeeks). Note that true geeks reported spending fourteen times as many hours playing computer games as nongeeks. These students also spend comparatively more time shopping and

**TABLE 5.2  *College Student Computer Activity***

| | Median Times per Week | | Median Hours per Week | |
|---|---|---|---|---|
| *Computer Activity* | *True Geeks* | *Nongeeks* | *True Geeks* | *Nongeeks* |
| School/academics | 5.0 | 7.0 | 7.9 | 10.0 |
| Work/employment | 0 | 0 | 0 | 1.0 |
| Computer gaming | 5.5 | 1.0 | 14.0 | 1.0 |
| Online gambling | 0 | 0 | 0 | 0 |
| Online shopping | 1.0 | 0 | 1.0 | 0 |
| Financial management | 0 | 0 | 0 | 0 |
| Looking at pornography | 2.0 | 0 | 1.0 | 0 |
| Managing mail | 5.0 | 7.0 | 1.0 | 2.0 |
| Chatting online | 7.0 | 7.0 | 5.0 | 5.0 |

looking at pornography online and less time on academics and managing email. The amount of other computer-enabled activities including employment tasks, online gambling, managing finances, and chatting were essentially the same for both groups of students.

These findings are interesting to a point, but what is striking and theoretically relevant for understanding cybercriminals is that statistically significant correlations were found in the computer efficacy of:

- 4.3 percent of students who prefer to *chat* online rather than in person, have used a credit card or number without authorization, used a computer or other electronic device to cheat on exams, disrupted computer services, given out someone's password without their knowledge or permission, or made online threats.
- 9.0 percent of students who felt computers help them feel *in control* and their having used a credit card or number without authorization, purchased papers to use as their own on school assignments or used a computer or other electronic device to cheat on exams, written and released computer viruses, or given out someone's password without that person's knowledge or permission.
- 13.3 percent of students who enjoy *experimenting* with computers and their having illegally downloaded music, movies, and software; used a credit card or number without authorization; purchased papers to use as their own on school assignments or used a computer or other electronic device to cheat on exams; spammed using email; written and released computer viruses; publicly released security vulnerabilities; given out passwords; or made threats online.
- 15.4 percent of students who enjoy *exploring* with computers and their having illegally downloaded music, movies, and software; used a credit card or number without authorization; purchased papers to use as their own on school assignments or used a computer or

other electronic device to cheat on exams; spammed using email; disrupted computer services; written and released computer viruses; and given out passwords or made threats online.
- 23.8 percent of students who enjoy *competing* with computers and their having illegally downloaded music, movies, and software; used computers or electronic devices to plagiarize, buy papers, copy code, and cheat on assignments and exams; spammed using email; disrupted computer services; written and released computer viruses; given out passwords; hacked into systems; or made threats online.

Eleven students surveyed (1.3 percent of the study sample) claimed all five of these sentiments by scoring the maximum possible on questions pertaining to their IT-related feelings. As a group, their combined sentiments were positively correlated to their having committed several types of computer abuse or cybercrimes. Specifically, individuals with maximum computer efficacy reportedly copied computer code to use as their own on assignments, used a computer or other electronic device to cheat on one or more exams, and disrupted computer services and hacked into systems in order to look at data and files. All these research findings were statistically significant meaning that it is extremely unlikely they were the result of mere chance. The basic point here is that the more prone students are to using computers the more likely they are to commit IT-enabled abuse and crime.

This small group also reported spending considerably more time online in what arguably are unproductive ways (e.g., gaming and viewing porn) and less time on academics when compared with the computing activities of other students. Table 5.2 reveals that, as a group, the amount of time students with maximum computer efficacy reportedly spent each week on gaming alone was fourteen times as much as other students. They also reported that when communicating online they preferred chatting via instant messenger or Internet relay chat (IRC) than via email. For these individuals (labeled true geeks in Table 5.2) there exists a statistically significant positive correlation between their affinity for computing, inclusive of computer gaming, and specific offending behaviors, namely academic dishonesty, denying or interrupting computer services, and accessing computer systems without authorization solely to look at data or files. It is important to note that although this data links the amount of time spent computing in certain ways with a combination of personal computer-related preferences and with several types of offending behaviors, this does not mean computers, computer gaming, or other types of computer-enabled activities cause a person to abuse computers or other types of IT devices. Mere association between factors, even when statistically significant and therefore beyond the likelihood of chance alone, does not equate to causation.

## 5.4 Social Process Theories

**Social process theories of crime** are predicated on the idea that people do or do not commit crime as an indirect consequence of how they were raised, educated, and acculturated in society. According to this perspective, the nature and extent of a person's familial and other social bonds (e.g., having caring and nurturing parents and supporting relationships with friends and being involved in school clubs, religious groups, or other types of guiding organizations) determine whether people behave in socially acceptable and responsible ways or become abusive or criminal. As a major category of criminological explanations for crime, social process theories, including the ones described in this chapter, are among those best supported with empirical research findings. As a result, most criminologists have high regard for social process theories and their potential importance for developing public policies and programs aimed at preventing crime. In other words, according to the social process perspective, effective reduction of crime can be achieved with policies and programs that promote responsible parenting, development of moral responsibility, concern for community wellness, and so on. However, as you will read, little research explicitly connecting this category of crime theories to the onset of

**BOX 5.2 • *Major Strengths and Limitations of Trait Theories***

A major strength of trait theories is that they attempt to explain why some people commit crimes for seemingly irrational reasons or cannot be deterred from committing crimes because of biological and/or psychological factors beyond their control. Biological and psychological causes of crime may be interrelated and are often used along with other major theoretical perspectives such as classical/choice criminology to explain crime committed by individuals. Arousal, cognitive, and behavioral theories offer key insights into why people may abuse computers or other electronic IT devices even to the detriment of themselves or in order to inflict harms on others by committing cybercrimes.

The general criticism of trait theories is that although some people suffer from physical or mental disorders, they can usually be treated to an extent that restores their ability to make rational decisions, to behave in socially acceptable ways, and to be deterred from committing crime. Moreover, most people diagnosed with mild disorders do not commit crimes, even though they are capable of doing so and are not being treated for their condition. The concept of computer or Internet addiction disorder is not currently officially recognized by the American Psychiatric Association as a disorder of impulse control. The implication is that the criminogenic role of technology generally, and of IT in particular, on decision-making is unclear. However, chemical, environmental, and technological factors have been shown to affect human minds and bodies in ways that may contribute to while not directly causing abusive, harmful, and criminal behaviors.

cybercrimes has been undertaken, so as in other sections of this chapter, you are provided with examples of potential applications of specific social process theories and asked to think about how these might explain abuse and crime committed with computers, other types of electronic IT devices, and information systems.

### 5.4.1  Social Control Theories

**Social control theories** form a subcategory of social process theories that examine the effects of social bonds on law-abiding behavior. This means social process theories attempt to explain why people *obey* rather than violate rules, regulations, and crime laws.[26] Social control is usually studied with regard to ways in which positive social or environmental processes affect individuals' choices and behaviors. In this theoretical perspective, interpersonal and institutional factors matter a great deal (e.g., how parents, schools, or churches influence decisions *not* to commit crimes). By understanding and promoting these institutional mechanisms of social control, criminologists believe positive changes can be made within homes, organizations, and the broader society to increase law-abiding behavior. Thus, with respect to preventing cybercrimes, the aim of social control theories is to discern what can be done to promote responsible use of computers and other types of IT devices among different individuals and groups of people in myriad social and professional circumstances. What is it about people who use computers responsibly rather than to cause harm? Were they raised by nurturing parents who encouraged responsible use of computers from a very young age? Were most law-abiding IT users while growing up influenced in positive ways regarding their use of computers and other communications devices? Specific social control theories that may offer some insights into the answer of this question include containment theory, social bond theory, self-derogation theory, and control balance theory. Here are brief descriptions of each.

**5.4.1.1  Containment Theory.**  **Containment theory** was first espoused by Walter C. Reckless in the 1950s. This theory claims that people are influenced to not commit crime by external environmental factors combined with internal factors. According to this view, a person can be pushed toward deviance involving inappropriate use of IT but also contained by organizational and social factors governing ethical and legal use of IT, along with a personal drive to abide by established social norms for using computers and other electronic IT devices.[27] In what ways do you feel "contained" from committing cybercrimes?

**5.4.1.2  Social Bond Theory.**  **Social bond theory** was initially developed in the late 1960s by Travis Hirschi, who popularized the belief that social bonds between individuals and groups based on attachment, commitment, involvement, and shared values prevent delinquency and crime.[28] Are you now involved with a student club, athletic team, or other social group that would disapprove of your abusing computers or other types of IT devices? Can you see how a person's attachment, commitment, involvement, and shared values with people in these or other types of groups could influence their decisions not to commit crimes involving IT? How do you think college and university officials, faculty, or IT administrators could capitalize on this powerful theory to encourage responsible use of computers by students? If your college or university has a student club that focuses on computer science, software engineering, or IT administration, how if at all does it promote socially responsible use of computers, other electronic devices, and information systems?

**5.4.1.3  Self-Derogation Theory.**  **Self-derogation theory** came about through the research of Howard B. Kaplan, who in the 1970s asserted that ridiculed juveniles lose self-esteem, fail to comply with social norms, and resort to deviant or criminal behaviors.[29] Studies have supported this claim but also the possibility that self-esteem can be regained through criminal activities.[30] Do you think a person who suffers from low self-esteem as the result of being socially rejected could regain a sense of self-worth by using computers for abusive or criminal purposes? Do you think this theory supports the stereotype of computer hackers being loners who furiously program for hours at a time and earn social recognition through development of clever malware, discovery and exposure of security vulnerabilities, or audacious stunts involving illegal use of computers?

### 5.4.1.4 Control-Balance Theory.

**Control-balance theory** was conceived by Charles R. Tittle in 1995 and recognizes the importance of both containment and social bonds but insists that the ratio between these concepts must be balanced in order to optimize compliance with existing rules, laws, and regulations.[31] In other words, external and internal restraints on behaviors combined with social attachments, commitments, involvement, and shared values are all needed to induce a person to not commit crime, but they are needed in just the right amounts, which will vary among individuals and situations. How in practical ways could IT professionals or criminal justice and security professionals employ this somewhat complicated concept to encourage compliance with computer-use polices, government regulations, and crime laws? As with other social control theories, control-balance theory has yet to be tested as a plausible way to encourage people to use IT in nonabusive and legal ways.

## 5.4.2 Social Learning Theories

Can you recall a situation in which over a period of time you developed a relationship with someone you admired, sought to learn from, and as time passed desired to impress with new-found knowledge and capabilities that person helped you to acquire? As social beings, we are all naturally drawn to seek acceptance and approval from others who we admire and respect and to learn from them to the extent possible. Parents, teachers, coaches, other respected adults and professional colleagues can all influence our attitudes, behaviors, and overall success in life. Conversely, it is rare that people who were law-abiding, successful, or model citizens did not receive considerable support along their way in life. Even as adults, people benefit from loving and capable people who are willing to help them learn how to solve problems and overcome adversities.

**Social learning theories** based on this general idea constitute a second subcategory of social process theories. Essentially, social learning theories posit that cybercriminals abuse and commit crimes using computers and other forms of IT because they learn how to do so from other people. As a theoretical construct, social learning is organized around four major concepts, the first two of which are subtheories. As depicted in Figure 5.2, these are (1) differential association theory, (2) differential reinforcement/punishment theory, (3) definitions, and (4) imitation. To understand the full implications of social learning theory, let us now consider these subtheories and concepts and how they interrelate.

### 5.4.2.1 Differential Association Theory.

**Differential association theory** describes a process in which individuals learn acceptable and unacceptable behaviors in different social contexts. Friends and family members, as well as school, church, and other social settings all provide different contexts for associating with other people. Different environments provide people with various ways in which to learn and behave in ways that range from being considered acceptable to unacceptable by members of the dominant group the person is associating with. By associating with a group of criminals, an individual will, according to this theory, learn its **normative definitions**—attitudes and behaviors deemed acceptable by the group but viewed as being unacceptable by society as a whole.[32] If you live in a dorm that socially promotes music piracy, you may have witnessed

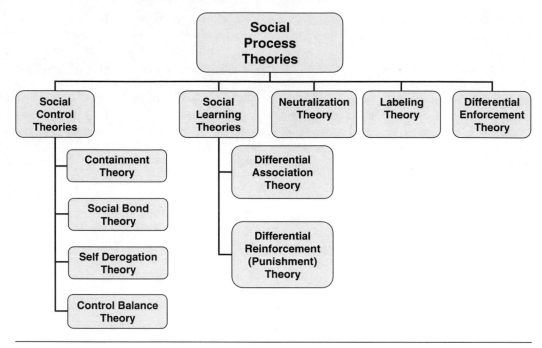

**FIGURE 5.2**    *Overview of Social Process Theories*

this theory in action (e.g., a relatively small and fairly homogenous group of students that illegally downloads music and adopts the view that "this is what we do"). The social environment is such that newcomers become accustomed to the pirating attitudes and practices of the group and, barring other factors, quickly learn how to pirate and thereby fit in with the group.

The effects of differential association theory are complete when, as the result of associating with and sharing the normative definitions of fellow pirates or other types of computer abusers or cybercriminals versus those of law-abiding students, the newcomers come to believe their abusive or illegal behaviors are actually OK, and perhaps even the right thing to do. Following his 1989 study of 1,766 college students at a southern university, Richard Hollinger reported that the more a student's friends were involved in computer hacking or software pirating, the more likely that student would be involved in the same activity.[33] Similarly, William Skinner and A. M. Fream

found, as the result of a 1991 study, that college students are very susceptible to learning about computer crime because their friends can be quite influential, a source for learning how to bypass security systems and restore functionality following virus attacks, and they also often provide each other with pirated software.[34] When it comes to your own knowledge and use of computers, who, if anyone, do you look up to? Do they exemplify responsible use of computers? To what extent do you think your own attitudes about using computers are influenced by this person?

### 5.4.2.2 Differential Reinforcement/Punishment Theory.

**Differential reinforcement theory** (also known as **punishment theory**) pertains to anticipated and actual consequences of behaving in ways consistent with either **positive definitions** or **negative definitions** (i.e., appropriate or inappropriate behaviors, respectively). Put differently, this theory holds that acceptable behaviors are the result of positive reinforcement combined with punishment, whereas unacceptable behaviors are the consequence of reinforcement without punishment. Positive and negative definitions—the preferential attitudes and behaviors of the group in which learning takes place—can be created and reinforced in a variety of formal or casual manners. Computer crime laws, for example, provide a formal source of negative definitions for how members of societies should not use computers. However, as indicated in the previous example of piracy in a dorm, a group of student users could informally establish their own positive and negative definitions, which may not be consistent with the computer use policies of a college or the social norms of the larger student body. In this situation, although incoming students may still learn to pirate from residents of the dorm, they do so in a context of formal and informal positive (do this) and negative (don't do that) definitions combined with potential punishment if they are caught for behaving in ways regarded by their college or university to be improper. In this environment positive acceptable behaviors are rewarded by people acting as **reinforcers**, and negative and unacceptable behaviors are punished or sanctioned in some manner by **punishers**. It is notable that establishment of positive and negative definitions, as well as corresponding rewards and punishment, may occur through a combination of in-person and on-line exchanges. Ideally the level or degree of a reward or sanction will in the view of the larger society be proportionate to the rule abiding or offending behavior and thereby promote the perception of fairness and future voluntary compliance with positive definitions. Differential reinforcement/punishment theory predicts that criminal behavior will diminish when punishment and rewards are consistently and fairly administered.

The third component of social learning theory is **imitation**, which refers to modeling the behaviors of others. Respected people in positions of authority are especially able to wield significant influence over an individual eager to learn and please. Adolescents frequently try to earn recognition and respect from their parents, teachers, coaches, or other individuals who they look up to by behaving in ways they believe will bring acknowledgement and approval. This is closely related to the concept of peer pressure, which has more precisely to do with conforming (perhaps involuntarily) to given group norms. Criminologists generally believe that imitation is more important during the initial stages of learning deviant behaviors, because that is when a person is most impressionable regarding exciting new ways of doing things.[35] Young people enticed by computers will naturally look to technologically adept peers to imitate, impress, and receive approval from, especially in the absence of parents or other respected adults who may be unable to teach them about IT or unwilling to extend praise for computing accomplishments. When you think back to your early computing experiences, from whom did you learn the most? Can you see how learning to abuse computers and other electronic IT devices may result from falling in with the wrong crowd?

### 5.4.3 Neutralization Theory

All states and the federal government now have computer crime laws, and most people understand that software piracy, unauthorized downloading of copyrighted songs and movies, email spamming, and hacking into computer systems, among other types of computing activities, are illegal. Even so, students who arrive at college with a weak sense of computer ethics and moral standards regarding usage of computers and other IT devices may be significantly influenced by new friends, roommates, older students, and social groups to use such devices in ways that are unethical, abusive, and/or criminal. When this occurs, **neutralizing definitions** have often been created to rationalize the illicit behavior. This process is integral to **neutralization theory**, which posits that people rationalize their illegal behaviors and/or the harmful effects of committing crimes. For example, they may say or think things like, "Everybody is doing it" or "Heck, the item is overpriced, and besides, only large corporations and not individuals are affected." As

one student recently put it, "We all know at least one person who has an illegal copy of Windows XP or burns audio CDs from illegally downloaded MP3s because they donot want to waste money on the album, or they cracked a game in order to finish that last level since it was good, but just not worth the $19.99 sales price." Thus, neutralization is all about rationalizing and justifying abusive and illegal behavior.

Neutralization theory offers a sound explanation for certain types of cybercrime such as pirating music, movies, or software because offenders need not personally confront their victims and because there is often nothing tangible other than a keyboard and storage media that they can or must touch. Since they cannot see the Internet or the people who create content, victims, if they are contemplated at all, become faceless entities, computer systems, or perhaps corporations rather than real people whose livelihoods and well-being are compromised as the result of copyright infringement. The same holds true for other types of IT-Enabled crimes such as Web vandalism, distributing malware, launching DoS attacks, and so on. Similarly, a person who uses a computer to commit fraud or identity theft or steal money

from another person's bank account sees nothing more than their own computer and content on a screen, not the results of harm inflicted on either the account holder, banking personnel, investors in the banking institution, or taxpayers, who must ultimately foot the bill under Federal Deposit Insurance Corporation (FDIC) rules.

Cybercrimes of this sort may be committed from the comfort and privacy of a residence or other location that effectively detaches the offender from society—no messy social interactions to manage or physical harm to reconcile. Such can be the dehumanizing nature of computers and the Internet and the reason neutralization theory is of special importance to understanding why some cybercriminals use computers, other types of IT devices, and information systems to disassociate themselves from the immediate harmful affects of their crimes. After all, even their accomplice the computer, in a manner of speaking, which consists only of wires, metal, plastic, silicon, and glass, cannot object to or judge their actions. What an insidious technological means through which to neutralize the effects of crime, akin to push-button warfare, in which soldiers in sterile technological environments are able to launch attacks without confronting their enemies face-to-face. The dehumanizing effects of computers may have significant implications for crime prevention or offender community restoration programs that are based on promoting if not compelling interaction between offenders, victims, and other members of a community in which crimes were committed.

### 5.4.4 Labeling Theory

The development, level, and maintenance of a person's self-esteem are important aspects of social process theories, because a person's self-esteem has much to do with the effectiveness that rewards and sanctions have on behaviors. **Labeling theory** pertains to the effects that being negatively labeled by respected persons or institutions has on behavior. According to this theory, if respected adults or individuals in authority such as parents, teachers, security professionals, or criminal justice officials refer to a young offender in negative terms (i.e., name-calling and use of other demeaning language), self-esteem will be lowered and undesirable behavior will continue and may even become worse. As negative labeling and lowering of self-esteem continues, undesirable behavior is effectively perpetuated. In other words, as offenders adapt and mold themselves to the negative way others see and refer to them, they may continue or even increase the variety and amount of their deviant, abusive, or criminal computing behaviors. Stigmatized juveniles may adopt and achieve a self-fulfilling prophesy of failure and resign themselves to committing deviant, delinquent, or criminal behavior. According to labeling theory, the cycle of misbehavior, followed by labeling and recurrence of misbehavior, occurs because juvenile offenders naturally respond to negative messages received from the people who they admire, respect, and even love.

It is important to understand that labeling in the criminological sense is much more than teasing someone or giving them a derogatory nickname. Rather, labeling involves a long-term process that perpetuates low self-esteem and offending

behavior. However, people respond to labels differently, even if the labels are intended to encourage or discourage certain behaviors. For some people, a negative label is insulting and they will continue to misbehave as a form of rebellion. For other people what is intended to be a negative label may actually be regarded as a compliment or badge of honor and result in misconduct nonetheless. Young computer users in elementary, junior high, and even high school are quite impressionable and likely, by virtue of their relative immaturity and developing self-confidence, to be especially vulnerable to the effects of positive and negative labeling. Further, the effects of labeling can change with fluctuations in self-confidence, self-esteem, and attendant social circumstances. As people age, mature, and become more self-confident, labels have less meaning, although few of us outgrow our natural desire for a kind word or compliment.

Success and corresponding positive labeling in one aspect of a person's life may have positive spin-off benefits in other areas of life. The opposite is also true, mostly for developing juveniles, although broader negative labeling within a community may be detrimental to the development and maintenance of a positive self-image for relatively young and older people alike. Perhaps when the media portrays computer savvy individuals as hackers, crackers, or software pirates, it sets the stage for labeling to occur throughout society, adding to the mystique of criminal subcultures and enticing certain individuals to become involved. Many aspects of labeling theory have potential applications to computer abuse and cybercrime behavioral issues.

Have you ever been positively or negatively labeled? Did the labels pertain to your use of technology in some way? How did the label make you feel? Do you think your self-esteem, attitudes, or behaviors were affected by labeling? At some point did you outgrow the label and perhaps even change your self-image as well as the way others viewed you? How do you think being called a "geek" or "nerd" makes some people feel? What are the implications of this theory for preventing computer abuse and cybercrime?

**CYBER TALE 5.2**

### *Negative Labels as Badges of Honor*

Sometimes what may seem like a negative label can actually be a badge of honor. While growing up I became very skilled with computers and I became associated with a warez (piracy) group. My friends and family often called me a hacker, which enthralled and inspired me to continue illegally downloading and distributing music. I was not actually a hacker, although that is what people called me, and it was a positive label in my mind even though it had negative connotations for the public at large. Consequently I began putting my Internet handle (nickname) on all the software I distributed, which only served to increase my fame and pride. Eventually the importance of being recognized within the warez community wore off as other things in my life became more important.

*Anonymous Student*

### 5.4.5  *Differential Enforcement*

An important extended aspect of labeling theory involves the concept of **differential enforcement**, the idea that the law is enforced differently on groups of individuals who have been negatively stereotyped. Have you ever been negatively labeled or perhaps singled out for investigation or violating rules or laws because of your age, attitude, or association with a group? Perhaps while

## BOX 5.3 • *Major Strengths and Limitations of Social Process Theories*

The major strength of social process theories is that they go beyond the mind and body of individual offenders to consider societal factors that contribute to the moral development of people and their learning how to commit abusive acts or crimes. If these effects are not countered, such individuals may ultimately adopt a lifestyle of deviancy, abuse, and crime. According to this theoretical perspective, cybercriminals learn to abuse computers or other types of electronic IT devices in the course of social processes occurring within institutional environments. Homes, schools, churches, neighborhoods, and places of employment all combine to create relatively healthy or unhealthy environments for learning how to succeed in society and use technology responsibly. As opportunities for learning how to use IT responsibly increase and are reinforced, crime enabled by IT will diminish. Conversely, if irresponsible use of computers and other types of electronic devices is learned and reinforced, IT-enabled abuse and cybercrimes can be expected to increase.

The major weakness of social process theories is that although several of these integrate aspects of classical/choice theories (i.e., rational decision making and deterrence), they negate other major factors that may contribute to crime, including how society itself is organized, managed, and maintained, as well as differing biological or psychological traits among individual offenders. Social process theories as traditionally researched and applied have not considered in much depth the role of technology in learning and acculturation processes related to crime committed by individuals or groups of offenders in society. Criminologists do not have in-depth understanding, for example, of how human preferences for using different technologies to commit crimes are established, maintained, and changed although it is widely understood that over time criminals learn from each other and develop technological preferences for committing their crimes generally referred to as modus operandi, or simply "MO". Social learning theory therefore, appears to have special importance for explaining how people come to adopt tools and techniques and then employ them to commit computer abuse and cybercrime.

you were growing up, local police officers were reputed to pick on teenagers in your community. Do you recall your friends being stopped by police apparently just because they were young, hanging out together, or dressed in a certain way? If this sort of thing ever happened to you, how did it make you or your friends feel? Do you think differential law enforcement by police or unequal enforcement of rules by others with authority to impose punishment may actually induce some people enraged at being singled out to commit computer abuse or cybercrimes? Can you imagine a situation in which a group of hackers launch retaliatory DoS attacks against school, government, or personal computer systems because they believe they have been wrongly labeled, accused, and/or punished on the basis of their appearance or associations?

## 5.5  *Social Structure Theories*

In the social structure perspective of criminology, unequal opportunities and distribution of wealth are fundamental to explaining why crime is committed by certain individuals and manifests as it does throughout society (Figure 5.3). Social structure theories take into account all the elements of the preceding categories of theories (i.e., classical/choice, trait, and social process theories) but also emphasize larger societal factors such as safe and affordable housing, receiving a good education, earning a good living, having access to quality health care, and being treated fairly by the criminal justice system. Social structure theorists argue that some people may be driven to commit crime if they cannot access, achieve, or maintain sufficient levels of these things. Thus, people who are in need of necessities, or who desire more money, status, or the prestige derived from acquiring expensive items may illegally use computer systems to get what they think they need or deserve. Within the context of social structure theories, general living conditions, education and employment opportunities and status, accumulation of property, along with other social accomplishments, combined with access to exclusive clubs or entitlements on the basis of class or wealth, are all important issues to be considered in explaining why some people commit crime. This section explains four social structure theories: general social structure theory, social disorganization theory, strain theories, and cultural deviance theory.

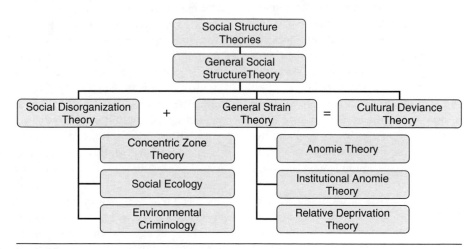

**FIGURE 5.3**  *Overview of Social Structure Theories*

### 5.5.1 General Social Structure Theory

**General social structure theory** is the view that socioeconomic class is the primary cause of crime. This theory points out that a considerable amount of crime, and most violent crime, is committed by individuals who are relatively poor or are members of youth gangs and who are frequently unemployed and financially constrained to live in urban ghettos. Additionally this theory holds that people of all ages, but especially children and seniors who live in poverty, are especially vulnerable to the effects of substandard education, unemployment, and crime. A systematic inability to accumulate wealth means that most poor people are destined to live their lives disenfranchised of opportunities to better themselves. As such, their stake in society and willingness to comply with its rules, regulations, and crime laws are reduced.

You can imagine that many poor individuals are among the "computer have-nots," so presumably their ability to commit many types of cybercrimes is relatively limited. Do you agree with this premise? Can you think of exceptions? What about drug dealers who never use a desktop or laptop computer but who do use cell phones or PDAs to organize contact and sales data and to send and receive messages to and from suppliers, customers, or confederates? Are the "computer haves" rather than the "have-nots" more likely to commit cybercrimes? With respect to cybercrimes and information security, who in technological terms comprises these supposed differing groups of individuals? Moreover, if while growing up a person's social class and quality of education allow considerable access to computers, how might the combination of these factors contribute to that person committing cybercrimes in his or her formative years or later in life? Do you think that coming from a relatively wealthy family and having routine access to computers and other types of electronic devices could actually contribute to one's ability and propensity to commit cybercrimes? Would this view help explain the classical stereotype of hackers being generally young, of middle to higher socioeconomic class standing, technically inclined, and without a criminal record?

### 5.5.2 Social Disorganization Theory

**Social disorganization theory** focuses on the systematic breakdown of societal institutions such as family units, educational systems, employment opportunities, and physical infrastructure, particularly in urban areas. As these otherwise stabilizing factors break down, society itself becomes disorganized, forcing people to increasingly look out only for themselves rather than their community. Neighborhoods occupied by immigrants may become isolated as a result of language barriers, different cultural norms, and prejudicial attitudes that negatively affect employment opportunities and may also engender hostile feelings that lead to crimes being committed against them. Shifting residential status as people relocate to take new jobs or change school districts also contribute to social disorganization. According to social disorganization theory, real-world neighborhoods affected by social isolation and disorganization typically become poorly maintained, graffiti appears, trash accumulates, and properties are abandoned. How, if at all, do you think computing relates to these concepts?

Social disorganization theory is often associated with the work and writings of sociologists Robert Park and Ernest Burgess, two early Chicago School researchers who in the 1920s pioneered the concept of **social ecology** that pertains to connections between the structure and organization of human activity. The concept of **concentric zones**, the idea that urban decay and crime decrease the further one travels out from a central urban core, was pioneered by Clifford R. Shaw and Henry McKay, also of the Chicago School, during the same time period.[36] **Environmental criminology**, also known as criminology of place, is a relatively new concept that emphasizes physical locations and geographic factors in crime causation, along with principles of social ecology and routine activities theory. This paradigm presumes that some people are criminally motivated and that effective crime prevention requires systematic retrospective analysis of crime patterns, offender and victim populations, and where these groups live, work, go to school, shop, and spend their free time, etc.[37] **Crime prevention through environmental design** is a set of principles applicable to designing exterior environments that include landscaping, lighting, the ability to monitor secluded areas, and ease of access.[38]

Do you think these issues are analogous to cyberspace and to the commission of cybercrimes in either virtual or tangible realms? Can Web site URLs and patterns of criminal activities in cyberspace be compared with crime "hot spots" in the physical realm in which we live? Has computerization resulted in people becoming more physically isolated and therefore less committed to maintaining the appearance of and social interactions within the tangible neighborhoods in which they live? Perhaps social isolation precipitated by an affinity for computing can contribute to certain people committing computer abuse or cybercrimes. Recall that in the 2004 study of computer use and ethics by college students at RIT, some students expressed preferences for interacting through computers or being alone online rather than socializing with other people in person, unaided by electronic communications devices. Self-reported offending behaviors of these individuals were positively correlated with their computer efficacy (i.e., their preference to interact with other people with and through computers rather than in person).

In criminology, the concept of community efficacy generally pertains to peoples' willingness to look out for the well being of people living in their neighborhood. However, is virtual anonymity and posing as someone other than your true self made possible with computers and the Internet akin to strangers passing through places with disregard for each other and therefore contributing to a form of cyber **anomie**? Do you think cyberspace is relatively organized or disorganized, caring or uncaring, and could socio-structural shifts in the virtual realm akin to physical and population transitions within neighborhoods and commercial areas create conditions ripe for cybercrime? Given the often interconnective ways in which computers and other IT devices are used online to support social interactions and business dealings even as people interact with each other in person, there is perhaps no bright line to distinguish where for criminological purposes the physical realm ends and the virtual one begins. In other words, it may be possible that increasing Internet connectivity is enabling traditional forms of crime to shift towards cyber versions of these, a situation exacerbated by lack of in-person social interactions and community efficacy. To put it another way, do you think it possible for people to care for and protect a cyber community as much the neighborhood in which they really live, work or play? Increasingly these are the types of questions that need to be asked in the field of criminology and the issues that researchers should explore if we are to understand why cybercrimes occur as they do via combinations of real-world places and virtual spaces.

### 5.5.3 Strain Theories

Strain theories comprise a subcategory of social structure theory that has generally to do with frustration incurred as the result of unrealized expectations. Robert K. Merton championed this line of thinking in the 1930s. It is essentially the belief that if people are unable to achieve personal or professional goals, they experience strain that may result in their committing crime in order to achieve their goals through illegal means. This powerful concept involves three potentially interrelated subtheories: (1) **anomie theory,** the notion that social breakdowns occur because wealth and power are stratified by social and professional class and/or status; (2) **institutional anomie theory,** the idea that anomie pervades U.S. culture in particular because the desire to achieve the American Dream undermines social and community values other than accumulating wealth and consumerism; and (3) **relative deprivation theory,** which refers to mistrust and resentment brought about as the result of economic and social inequality (i.e., the relative deprivation people experience causes them to commit crime).[39] Is it possible that cybercrimes are committed because of the resentment individuals or groups harbor toward others with greater wealth or social status or the technological opportunities to achieve. Wealth and states? Do you suppose some "computer have-nots" in society may resent "computer haves" to an extent that drives them to commit traditional crimes or cybercrimes?

**General strain theory** posits that multiple sources of stress such as not being able to achieve desired personal or professional goals, removing positive stimuli, introducing negative stimuli, or generally creating strain in peoples' lives causes them to commit crimes. How would you feel if after graduating from college you worked very hard to earn a promotion at your new job, only to realize several years later that your employer had no intention of ever significantly rewarding your performance or your contributions or loyalty to the firm? Would you become sufficiently resentful to seek revenge and cause damage to the company's computer system? Conversely, suppose you were demoted and could no longer afford some of the things you and your family had become accustomed to. Could this drive you to commit crime, not because you sought revenge, but because you wished to attain the things that you strongly desired in order to maintain, if not improve, your social and professional status?

Can you imagine financial strain becoming sufficient for you to use your knowledge of computers and accounting data to embezzle funds or attempt to sell trade secrets or some other type of valuable proprietary data? Can you think of other instances in which computers or other types of IT devices could be used innovatively to carry out crimes committed because of strain? Do you suppose most white-collar crimes are caused by strain—an inability to realize one's goals or perceived needs? Could it also be that strain associated with the need to do well in college induces some students to cheat on papers or exams using computers or other electronic devices? Fear of not succeeding may exacerbate preexisting strain individuals feel and cause them to commit crimes. What other types of computer abuse and cybercrimes could result from strain?

### 5.5.4  Cultural Deviance Theory

**Cultural deviance theory** posits that factors associated with both social disorganization and strain theories combine to create a unique underclass that possesses values in conflict with conventional social norms. According to this theoretical paradigm, subcultures can form within a dominant underclass of people consisting of members for whom committing crime may actually be in compliance with a unique set of values. In other words, for people in the subculture, behaving illegally is not wrong and may even be proper. This process involves learning to accept positive and negative definitions for behaviors that are contrary to those of society at large. So this is like social learning theory occurring in a unique cultural setting that actively promotes law breaking behavior. The central tenet is that people become socially isolated and begin to behave in ways that are acceptable within their subculture but that are regarded as deviant, abusive, and even criminal by the larger society. Do you know of subcultures in which behaving in certain ways regarded as improper by the vast majority of society is endorsed and perhaps encouraged?

Do you think crime such as hacking into computer systems in order to expose security vulnerabilities can be explained by cultural deviance theory? After all, the hacker subculture (which you will learn about in Chapter 7) espouses cyber exploration plus unlimited access to and sharing of information. Thus, detecting and revealing security vulnerabilities, while consistent with values held by hackers, challenges values generally held by the majority of computer users. Perhaps this logic is better applied to people who specialize in creating and distributing malware (i.e., malicious viruses, Trojans, and worms) rather than hacking into systems. In this programming underworld members compete with each other to create and make available destructive code loathed by computer users throughout the world. Can the behavior of people who write and illegally distribute malware be explained by cultural deviance theory? Given that IT spans international borders and is inclusive of innumerable cultures throughout

**BOX 5.4 • *Major Strengths and Limitations of Social Structure Theories***

The major strength of social structure theories is that traditionally they have recognized the social and physical context in which crimes occur and the reality that although people are able to adapt to, cope with, and even accept a wide variety of undesirable, unequal, and unfair living conditions, the conditions themselves may cause people with greater needs or aspirations and/or less tolerance or opportunity to resort to crime in order to just get by or further ahead in life. Hence, social structure theory explains crime committed by people of all social classes. Rich and poor people alike periodically experience strain in their lives, sometimes the result of unfulfilled expectations.

The major limitation of social structure theories is that not everyone living in poor neighborhoods, nor those who are poorly educated, unemployed, or under-employed, resorts to crime in order to achieve their goals. Nor do individuals who have relatively little computer training or access to IT. Nor, obviously, do all people who are relatively well off commit crime. In fact, in the author's law enforcement experience, most people, regardless of their personal and professional circumstances, are law-abiding, responsible, moral, and contributing members of society (at least most of the time). Conversely, relatively disadvantaged and advantaged people commit crimes for reasons other than their living conditions, social or professional opportunities and status, and periodic strain experienced in the normal course of life. Nonetheless, several social structure theories offer powerful insights into and explanations for why some people commit crimes. A major challenge and potential opportunity for researchers is to meaningfully apply concepts of social structure theories, traditionally applied only to physical environments, to online social interactions and crimes that occur in cyberspace.

the world, researchers may in the future actively consider this theory to help explain why cybercrimes are committed in certain ways and among certain people who share unique values.

## 5.6 Conflict Theories

Can you think of individuals or groups in society who harbor resentment toward the government, corporations, or those who wield political or economic power? Do you know people who are concerned about the potential for technology abuse by the government, corporations, or those who are extraordinarily wealthy? Are there individuals or groups who use IT to promote their political views, and who could potentially use their positions of influence to carry out cybercrimes to achieve even more power or control over the means of production in society, and in the process enrich themselves with even more wealth? Do you think that because information allows development of knowledge and therefore may be considered a form of power, control of IT systems

through which the creation and sharing of information occurs could be abused in ways that, if not criminal, could lead to conflict between those who have access to computers and those who do not?

In this section we will explore how several theories within the branch of **conflict criminology** may pertain to cybercrime. Before doing so, however, it is important to distinguish between conflict, consensus, and pluralist views of social organization and political power. First, note that each of these three basic ways in which people tend to think about society are based on the assumption that the rule of law provides a critical foundation needed for social order in civil societies. This simply means that laws are the rules we live by and they are necessary to ensure orderly, predictable, and relatively safe and secure environments in which to live. However, views of social organization differ with regard to how political forces, processes, and associations in society affect formulation, implementation, and enforcement of laws, regulations, and public policies governing social issues and technology and therefore affect the means of production and perpetuation of power and wealth.

According to the **consensus view of social organization,** the majority of people living in a given society agree about what is right and wrong and therefore what should be regarded as deviant, abusive, or criminal. This notion was originally addressed in Chapter 1 to explain the concept of technology-enabled deviance, as well as social abuse and crimes committed with computers, other types of electronic IT devices, and information systems. The consensus view of social organization is reinforced by schools, churches, government agencies, businesses, and many types of social organizations that work together to promote the common good. Additionally, according to this view, laws are created via democratic processes that represent the majority of people in society and they are consistently and fairly enforced without regard to social class, employment status, race, religion, ethnicity, and so on. In short, the consensus view holds that the justice system sees and treats everyone equally under the law. IT therefore is an essential means to administering social and criminal justice fairly, and societal conflicts are resolved through consensus and majority-based rule-making.

The **pluralist view of social organization** in contrast recognizes that society consists of many groups of stakeholders who possess differing interests and concerns, as well as differing bases of wealth and power with which to advance their agendas in order to make society a better place to live. Many concerns of pluralist groups pertain to the purposes for which IT is used by different segments of society. For example, a considerable amount of controversy surrounds use of IT by criminal justice and security organizations in ways that affect personal privacy albeit for crime prevention and detection purposes (e.g., surveillance of open public spaces, developing and securing integrated justice information systems to amalgamate disparate databases without regard to personal privacy, and use of data mining tools by intelligence and law enforcement agencies to discern evidence of terrorist associations or impending terrorist attacks). Consequently, the pluralist view of social organization asserts that political conflict stemming from use of technology and other factors is inevitable. It must be managed in a civil way by the collective actions of a plurality of groups working together, and sometimes in opposition, for the betterment of society. "Hence, from a pluralist perspective, the law, rather than reflecting common values [as in the consensus view], exists as a peacekeeping tool that allows officials and agencies within the government to settle disputes effectively between individuals and groups."[40]

The **conflict view of social organization** asserts that rich and powerful people orchestrate power relationships in society to protect their own interests at the expense of those who are less wealthy and influential. According to the conflict view of crime, this causes conflict between social classes, relative depravity within lower classes, and crime committed by lower class persons who are disenfranchised, resentful of those who are affluent, and may be indifferent toward other poor members of society who compete with them in a desperate struggle to get by or ahead in life. In this view power may derive from a person's social class, wealth, gender, or general means to control how society produces goods and provides services. By extension, how technology is used in society, indeed technological advancement perceived as detrimental to society, may also factor into criminal motivations. This was certainly true for Unabomber Ted Kaczynski, which is why even as a Harvard-educated professor he rejected many of the entrapments of capitalist society, chose to live in relative poverty, and then targeted professionals who he believed unduly influenced aspects of society's technological means of production and therefore were responsible for pollution and other negative spin-offs that threatened social well-being and world peace (see Cyber Case 5.1).

### 5.6.1 *General Conflict Theory*

**General conflict theory** is alternatively known as conflict criminology or Marxist criminology. Tenets of this theory are that: (1) society consists of disparate groups that possess many different views about what is right or wrong; (2) political

## The Case of Unabomber Ted Kaczynski

In April of 1995 social recluse Theodore Kaczynski, who lived alone in a very small rustic cabin outside of Lincoln, Montana, was arrested as the infamous Unabomber. For approximately eighteen years Kaczynski sent explosive letters to researchers and corporate officials who he believed were key proponents of technologies that would ultimately bring an end to life on earth. For several years FBI Special Agent Bill Tofoya, and many other law enforcement officers, attempted to determine who the Unabomber was by employing high-tech means including the posting of a composite sketch and certain case details online—reportedly the first time the Bureau had done so in a criminal case.

The Unabomber arrest followed a tip provided by Kaczynski's brother, who recognized expressions used in an extensive manifesto titled *Industrial Society and Its Future* that was published by large U.S. newspapers including the *New York Times* and the *Washington Post*. In the manifesto Kaczynski explained how technology controlled by intertwined corporate and government management sectors perpetuated capitalism within the United States and would ultimately bring ruin to society. This was his rational for sending the explosive letters that killed three people and wounded twenty-three others in sixteen separate mail bombing incidents.[41] On balance, do you think computing as a form of technology and computerization now occurring throughout the world is beneficial or harmful? Given cybercrime and threats to critical information infrastructures, will society's reliance on computers and networking become its undoing?

conflict between groups is inevitable, resulting in competition in the accumulation and exercise of power; and (3) laws and mechanisms to enforce them (e.g., the police) are tools used by the rich and powerful to retain ultimate control of society, upon which they depend for their wealthy lifestyles. Conflict criminology is fundamentally about tension between society's haves and have-nots and how this tension may contribute to crime.

Do you think class envy, which has much to do with perceptions of technology-enabled wealth and power, may cause some people to commit crime? Can you also see how conflict criminology factors into controversial issues in society having to do with inequitable distribution of political power and technological means of acquiring wealth? Consider, for example, profit-seeking startup firms or open source community advocates (discussed in Chapter 7) who must battle giant hardware and software manufacturing corporations for product recognition and service contracts. Also consider people who view the copyright protections afforded to music and movie producers to be unfair and technologically antiquated. Can you see why, given their views, these people may be

tempted to illegally download the music of artists under contract with major recording studios but opt instead to purchase music of artists who are not in league with or perceived to be taken advantage of by major labels? Can you also see why conflicting views of fairness in society, including the belief that information needed to learn about topics of interest should not be owned, could inspire malevolent hackers to attack government or corporate Web sites in defiance of "the system"?

### 5.6.2 Marxist Criminology

The belief that power is in the hands of those who control the technological means of production within a society was first substantially expressed by Karl Marx in the late 1800s amidst the Industrial Revolution then sweeping much of the world. The writings of Marx and his contemporaries contributed a great deal to the Bolshevik Revolution in Russia in 1917, which eventually transformed that nation into a communist society that became the Union of the Soviet Socialist Republics (USSR).[42] The USSR was America's archenemy throughout the Cold War, which was precipitated and carried out by computer-enabled missile, satellite, and other technology used for espionage. Although Marx himself never wrote explicitly about crime, he did make clear his belief that rich and powerful people in society control the technological means of production at the expense of working class people who need to sell their labor in order to survive. Hence, the general belief that ruling and working classes compete over naturally limited resources and wealth in society is at the heart of Marxist criminology. This view of crime causation asserts that the more economically stratified a society becomes, the more necessary it is for the ruling class to decide what should be illegal and then create and enforce new laws in order to keep working class people in their place. Meanwhile the ruling class will often escape investigation and prosecution for violating laws of their own creation.[43]

#### 5.6.2.1 Instrumental Marxism.   **Instrumental Marxism** is the theory that laws and those who enforce them are tools or instruments used by the rich and powerful to retain their status.[44] Theorists who hold this view often note that the vast majority of police officers seem to concentrate on preventing or investigating street criminals rather than offenses committed by relatively well-educated, wealthy, and powerful white-collar crime offenders. Further, according to this view, even though individual officers may not be malevolent in their service to the ruling class (after all, they are working class people too), the overall criminal justice system in a capitalist society is structured to oppress working class people while protecting the interests of the rich and powerful. Therefore, the only real solution to lessening crime and its harmful effects, and promoting equality in the administration of justice, is creation of a socialist society.[48]

CYBER CASE 5.2

### *The Presidential Pardoning of Financier Mark Rich*

Just before leaving office in January of 2001, President Bill Clinton exercised his constitutional power and issued pardons to several people convicted of committing federal crimes. Among those pardoned was a very wealthy financier named Marc Rich, who in 1983 was indicted by a federal grand jury for not paying approximately $48 million in taxes owed in connection with 51 instances of alleged tax fraud and with illegally conducting oil deals with Iran during the 1979 oil embargo.[45] If the tax evasion and oil embargo crimes did occur as alleged by federal prosecutors, they must have been carried out with computers and information systems maintained by financial institutions in the United States and in other nations. Rather than face federal charges against him, however, Rich fled to Switzerland, where he still lives.

Presidential pardons are ordinarily granted for compelling reasons and in the interest of justice. However, there were irregularities in how the Rich case was administered within the Department of Justice and the White House just hours before Clinton left office. This resulted in bipartisan Congressional investigations into the possibility that large donations made by Rich's former socialite wife, Denise, to the Democratic Party and to help fund a presidential library in Clinton's honor, was actually a bribe to secure a pardon from the president. When testifying before Congress afterwards, Denise Rich refused to answer certain questions in order to avoid self-incrimination, which is a legal right established by the Fifth Amendment of the U.S. Constitution.[46]

As recently as March of 2005, Rich was still being investigated by Congress, this time in connection with the oil for food scandal allegedly involving former Iraq dictator Saddam Hussein and highly placed officials at the United Nations.[47] Regardless of the facts of these incidents, which have yet to be fully determined by Congressional investigators, can you see why people possessing relatively little power and wealth would think that criminal justice is unfairly administered, and that the system itself may be a tool of the rich and the powerful in society?

## Making an Example of Martha Stewart?

On December 27, 2001, Martha Stewart received an illegal stock tip from Douglas Faneuil, a former assistant brokerage agent at Merrill Lynch, who sent her an email indicating that Sam Waksal, a personal friend and CEO of ImClone Systems, a firm in which Stewart had invested, was bailing out of his own stock. Faneuil would later claim that he was ordered to convey the tip to Stewart by Peter Bacanovic, his superior at Merrill Lynch. Acting on the tip, Stewart sold $230,000 of ImClone Systems stock and saved $50,000 in losses she would have incurred had she not sold the securities.[49] Then on January 31, 2002, Ann Armstrong, a professional assistant to Stewart, altered the contents of the tip-off email previously sent from Faneuil.[50]

After an extensive government investigation, Martha Stewart was charged with securities fraud and lesser crimes and was eventually found guilty in federal court on several counts of lying to government investigators, obstruction of justice, and conspiracy.[51] She was not convicted of the most serious charge, securities fraud, and consequently was sentenced to five months incarceration in a federal prison, plus five months of house arrest (wearing an electronic monitor on her ankle), and she received a $30,000 fine.[52] Throughout the investigation, her trial, and after being released from prison Stewart never admitted any wrongdoing. Some people believe she was just being made an example of for comparatively minor offenses. What do you think? What role did her immense wealth and celebrity status have on the administration of justice in her case? And what role did IT have with regard to her being able to commit the crime, and subsequently to her being successfully prosecuted?

---

**5.6.2.2 Structural Marxism.** Structural Marxism takes instrumental Marxism a step further. According to this theory, capitalism is the root cause of crimes that lower class people are bound to commit. Deemed unproductive trouble makers, lower class people can be legitimately arrested or otherwise controlled by middle class law enforcers who, having been seduced into serving the establishment, effectively live off crime committed by the poor and unwittingly perpetuate the ability of the rich and powerful to control society. According to structural Marxist theory, therefore, it is important to maintain a critical mass of middle class laborers with a reasonably rewarding lifestyle so they will not rebel. Meanwhile, it is the responsibility of the affluent to manage society and not toil at laboring or become entangled in crimes such as those committed by the poor. Indeed, when the rich do commit crimes, they tend to be fraud and other forms of white-collar crime and IT-Enabled abuse of banking regulations or accounting procedures. Finally, according to structural Marxism theory, members of the power elite must ensure that people within

their own class obey laws and are generally held accountable, lest they undermine their own power-control system.

Given this theory, can you see how vast amounts of information and potential political power enabled by IT and the Internet could be threatening to existing groups empowered with society's rule-making authority? Can you see why politically active hackers, called "hactivists," frequently attack and deface government and corporate Web sites? Can you also see why in this view of criminology it is important for the rich and powerful to periodically make an example out of one of their own?

### 5.6.3 Other Conflict Theories of Crime[53]

Several emerging conflict theories of crime build on and attempt to relate concepts of general conflict theory and Marxist criminology to the problems of modern and relatively high-tech societies. They are briefly discussed here with respect to their specific prospective implications for cybercrime and information security.

**Left realism,** also sometimes referred to as realist criminology, critical realism, or radical realism, is the perspective that in the final analysis, crime causes real problems for real crime victims and that the idea of little guys being oppressed by capitalist society elitists is largely a myth.[54] Left realism criticizes the romanticizing of street criminals as folk heroes fighting for social justice or political freedom. Hence, the idea of hackers fighting for free and unfettered access to information systems, or that members of this subculture (discussed in Chapter 7) should be extolled for attacking government and corporate computer systems, is counter to the views of left realists. As a group, left realists are actually right-leaning conservatives who recognize the pros and cons of capitalism and do not believe that law enforcement or justice system are tools of the rich and powerful. Left realists also believe that needed reforms in criminal justice systems can only result from acknowledging the behaviors of criminals and the impacts they have on crime victims and from being realistic about the political power and processes required to effect meaningful social change.[55]

**Feminist criminology** is concerned with the unequal and generally less powerful wealth and status of women as compared with men in most societies. According to this branch of criminological theory, women living in male-dominated societies are often disproportionately poor, uneducated, and powerless within institutional structures and thus vulnerable to being systematically abused and victimized by men. Criminologists holding this general view further argue that gender is just as much a social construct as a biological fact and that unequal distribution of power, wealth, and status between the sexes create conditions leading to crime being committed by some women.[56] Females who endure sexual, emotional, psychological, professional, social, or economic domination by males are seen as victims of an unjust patriarchal society, who periodically commit crimes in desperation to escape their situation or who seek revenge for the abuses they have suffered.

Since the inception of modern computing in the late 1950s, men have been drawn much more than women to enroll in colleges to study computer science, software engineering, and IT administration. Why is this? Are men more technologically inclined than women? Do you think a larger proportion of boys or girls, like computer gaming and playing around with electronic gadgets? How, if at all, do you think online interactions made possible by computers and other electronic IT devices neutralize the potential for gender-based domination in either virtual or real environments? If men are in general more comfortable and confident using IT, than women, what are the implications for even greater domination of women in high-tech societies and the potential for gender-based computer abuse and cybercrimes? Based on the 2004 RIT computer use and ethics study, researchers found that men disproportionately commit computer abuse and cybercrimes. Men also commit proportionately more cybercrimes against women than women do against men.[57] Does this surprise or alarm you? Can you see how these findings could support the feminist criminology perspective?

Feminist criminology consists of radical, liberal and socialist views each depicting men in somewhat different ways. Radical feminism sees men as violent, aggressive brutes who dominate women sexually. Liberal feminists observe that although men dominate women, they do so because culture inappropriately perpetuates gender-specific roles and responsibilities. Socialist feminists allege that oppression of women is the result of the economic structure of capitalist societies. How do you think these ideas relate to the reality that most crimes, including cybercrimes, are committed by males? What is it about IT that disproportionately attracts male students to study computer science, software engineering, and network administration? Do you think IT exacerbates criminal tendencies in males already responsible for committing disproportionate amounts of crime including cybercrimes? And in what ways do males use computers and other types of electronic IT devices and information

*Computer science, software engineering, and IT administration courses tend to be dominated by male students. Why is this, and what are the implications for developing next-generation information security professionals, as well as for understanding and managing computer abuse and cybercrimes that are disproportionately committed by males in society?* Photo by Nathan Fisk

systems to victimize women systematically in society?

To round out this discussion of conflict theories, it is important to mention postmodern criminology and peacemaking criminology. Whereas **postmodern criminology** is the label used for a collection of emerging ideas that call into question the veracity of other general approaches to explain why crime occurs, **peacemaking criminology** essentially claims that crime can only be prevented as the result of increasing social justice. The concept of **restorative justice**, also known as community justice, has as its goal to make right the harmful effects caused by criminals to the extent possible and thereby restore community and interpersonal bonds (i.e., respect, tolerance, forgiveness, cooperation, etc.) between offenders and their victims.[58] These perspectives have been emerging within the field of criminology for several years, and research has demonstrated that restorative justice policies and practices have considerable promise for healing ill-will within communities in which crimes have been committed by individuals and groups. Perhaps online communities could benefit from practicing restorative justice principles, although currently the potential of these and other conflict perspectives to prevent cybercrimes or to ameliorate their harmful impacts is unclear.

**BOX 5.5 • *Major Strengths and Weaknesses of Conflict Theory***

Do you think people who abuse computers, other types of electronic IT devices and information systems are mainly looking out for their own interests or are somehow engaged in a battle against the power elite in society? For some people, one of the most appealing things about conflict theories of crime, and Marxist criminology in particular, is that these perspectives are tantamount to righting wrongs and doing honorable things for the betterment of society. Donn Parker, famous for his early computer crime research and writing on information security practices, attributes the actions of some criminals to a variation of the Robin Hood Syndrome—the notion that offenders "steal from the rich and keep the booty" rather than giving it to the poor, although their actions may be rationalized on the basis of serving a higher cause (e.g., financially supporting their families, exposing security vulnerabilities created by large and greedy software corporations, or espousing the hacker ethic as it relates to free access to information held on government databases).[59] In this regard conflict theories provide useful insights into certain types of computer abuse and cybercrimes. Feminist criminology may also be of special importance for understanding computer abuse and cybercrime with regard to male-dominated professions and programs of study that stress computer science, software engineering, and IT administration knowledge, skills, and abilities.

As appealing as conflict ideals may be for some people, most cybercrimes, it can be argued, are committed for purely selfish reasons rather than to correct social or economic wrongs. In addition, who is to say that crimes committed with computers by the rich and powerful are more reprehensible than crimes committed with IT by people who are relatively poor or have little influence? Moreover, if conflict theorists are correct in their views about unequal distribution of wealth and power being a core reason for crime, we would expect to see lower levels of crime in socialist nations compared with capitalist nations such as the United States. However, when it comes to cybercrimes, research has not substantiated this thesis. In addition, there is no denying that legal checks and balances built into the workings of government, prosecution of elite members of society, and vast amounts of available information about governments and corporations available on the Web reflect consensus and pluralist views of social organization as much if not more than the conflict view of social and political organization.

## 5.7 Integrated and Technological Theories

At this point you may be thinking that the foregoing categories of theories and the concepts and theories within each category interrelate and if combined would offer compelling explanations for why cybercrimes are committed. This is exactly what integrated theories of crime do. Technological theories, however, concern issues of technology invention, innovation, adoption, implementation, routine and emergency use, maintenance, evaluation, and diffusion. Historically, technology theories have not been integrated with crime theories, which may seem odd since computer abuse and cybercrimes are predicated on IT that can be adopted for illicit purposes,

as well as crime prevention, investigation, analysis, management purposes, and so on. This section provides a brief explanation of integrated crime theories, followed by a short description of the theory of technology-enabled crime, policing, and security developed by the author in the course of researching the evolution of IT-Enabled crime.

### 5.7.1 Overview of Integrated Theories

When integrated theories of crime were originally conceived of in the mid 1970s, they were referred to as multifactor theories because they attempted to combine aspects of theories within or across classical/choice, trait, social process, social structure, and/or conflict perspectives of criminology.[60] Consider the following example: a person can learn alternative normative definitions by associating with a group of criminally prone individuals, then, wanting to fit in, choose to commit cybercrimes he or she learned how to carry out and rationalize his or her own illegal behaviors as well as the collective illegal behaviors of the group. We discussed this type of hypothetical situation occurring in a college dormitory in which incoming first-year students learn from their peers how to illegally download music or movies. If these now interrelated theories are coupled with the concepts of social class and upbringing and the possibility of biochemical influences on decision-making, we have effectively integrated the choice, social structure, social process, and trait perspectives of crime in order to better explain why some people may abuse computers, other electronic IT devices, and information systems in order to violate crime laws.

Many other combinations of crime theories are plausible, which is essentially what integrated theories are—combinations of concepts and theories stitched together to explain more variation in the commission of crimes. Several authors of criminology textbooks have identified and explained several integrated theories of crime that

---

**CYBER TALE 5.3**

## Which Theories Help Explain This Criminal Behavior?

Back in my sophomore year of high school I had a very diverse group of friends, and everyone had different interests. My best friend happened to be involved heavily with computers. He built them, played games, downloaded music and software, etc. He also happened to have broadband, so he always had the latest games and top music. I was jealous and wanted to be just like my friend (**imitation** and **social learning theory**). I could have asked my friend to burn CDs for me, but I couldn't ask him all the time, and besides, back in 1998 CD burners were only around 2x4x, so it was a slow process and the sound quality was not always great.

After my parents subscribed to broadband, however, I started illegally downloading my own music (**choice theory**). At this time, my friend and I had to be two of the only people in school who had broadband and CD burners. On a plus note, Napster was in its glory days, which made getting music especially easy. We were profit motivated. We burned albums for people usually a week before they were available publicly. We sold them for $5 a CD, which was pretty good profit because CD-R discs cost roughly only a dollar at the time. We sold about fifty CDs a month, which translated into about $100 monthly income for each of us—pretty good spending money (**rational choice theory**). Sales were small at first, but soon our immediate friends told their friends and we began to take orders for music.

Did the teachers care? No. The teachers bought as many CDs as the students at reduced costs or none at all, of course (**differential reinforcement theory**). Even my parents seemed to encourage my small "business" since it helped pay for our broadband Internet service. At the time, everyone we associated with thought it was no big deal (**differential association theory**), and even the RIAA (Recording Industry Association of America) was not paying attention in those days. Eventually inexpensive CD burners became popular, so our sales declined, but not before we also got into bootlegging movies and games, selling them for around $10 per game and $7 per movie. Although I don't do it anymore because the rewards are not there and the RIAA is cracking down (**general deterrence theory**) at that time all this made me feel like some kind of big-time drug pusher. We made a lot of money, and people knew who we were, but all I really cared about was their money so I could get the things I wanted (**strain theory**).

*Anonymous Student*

researchers have developed, including so-called latent trait theories and developmental theories.[61] These theories tend to be rather complex, so explaining them even briefly would exceed space limitations in this text. Students wishing to understand these and other criminology theories in more detail are encouraged to review any of several very good textbooks on theories of crime, such as *Criminology* by Larry Siegel, and *Criminology Today* by Frank Schmalleger, both of which inspired development of this chapter and are extensively used in college courses. The remainder of this chapter is devoted to explaining a very important theory that integrates several of the crime theories you have just learned about, along with technology theories, to explain the role of technology in co-evolving crime, policing, and security management.

## 5.7.2  Technology-Enabled Crime, Policing, and Security

The theory of technology-enabled crime, policing, and security (TCPS) is a new integrated theory of crime that incorporates many ideas expressed in earlier writings about the causes of crime combined with principles of technology invention, innovation, adoption, implementation, training, use, personnel supervision, maintenance, evaluation, and diffusion. This theory builds upon the writings of Edwin Sutherland, who first considered how criminals learn simple to complex techniques from each other.[62] It also considers the work of L. E. Cohen and Marcus Felson, who identified routine activities of crime victims and perpetrators inclusive of their use of technologies to, respectively, guard against and carry out attacks.[63] The theory is also based on elements of classical criminology (i.e., choice and deterrence theories), as well as components of various social process, social structure, and conflict theories. It also takes into account aspects of trait theories, especially arousal, cognitive, and behavioral trait theories.

Many aspects of TCPS are well-known concepts, widely accepted and even take for granted by law enforcement officers and security professionals. However, articulated as a new integrated theory of crime, TCPS explains how and why tools and techniques are adopted by criminals, as well as by law enforcement and security professionals, albeit for countervailing purposes. The theory also accounts for: (1) the technological evolution and relative complexity of new forms of crimes; (2) the technological and economic factors that perpetuate innovative forms of social abuse and crimes; and (3) technological shifts in criminal, policing, and security management capabilities. The following list conveys the essence of what may be the most important broad theoretical explanation for understanding and managing the rapidly changing nature of computer abuse and and IT-enabled cybercrimes:[64]

- Technologies are combinations of tools and techniques ranging from simple to complex in their design, materials, construction and manufacturing processes, adoption, social implementation, technical and systems integration, and applications. Criminals, police, and security professionals employ a full range of technologies that are available for similar and countervailing purposes.
- New forms of deviance, social abuse, or crime, that is, *new forms of crimes*, are committed through innovative use of technology. Initially new forms of crime are not well understood and therefore relatively complex, because investigative experts tend not to be able to explain to other investigative experts how criminals are using technologies.
- Faced with relatively complex crimes and attendant management problems, police, security professionals, and prosecutors innovate with countervailing technologies to overcome and if possible stay ahead of the technological gains made by criminals. With increased understanding and law enforcement interdiction, *new crimes* transform into better-understood *adaptive crimes*, and laws making criminally adaptive behaviors explicitly illegal begin to be enacted.

- The process of formulating and enacting new crime laws and regulations raises public awareness of crime problems threatening to society. Combined with media attention about these issues, attitudinal and behavioral changes emerge in ways that precipitate arrest and prevention of adaptive crimes.
- Eventually, adaptations of laws are widely adopted and diffused as a form of legal and social technology that leads to increased investigation and prosecution. When this happens, once new, and then adaptive crime transforms into *ordinary crime* that is much better understood, routinely recognized and responded to,

and may be systematically targeted for prevention.
- Enhanced enforcement, combined with continual technological advances, compels smart criminals intent on getting away with ordinary crime to adopt new technologies. This begins anew the cycle of technological competition between criminals versus police and security professionals (i.e., the emergence of deviance and social abuse, new crime, adaptive crime, and ordinary crime).
- Criminals who do not adopt new technologies are at greater risk of being caught unless and until their technological capabilities exceed

## CYBER CASE 5.4

### *New Crime: Fictitious Characters Socially Engineer Real-World Stabbing*

On June 29, 2003, a fourteen-year-old boy named John, of Manchester, England, used his home computer to socially engineer a sixteen-year-old friend named Mark to kill him. John nearly died from stab wounds inflicted by Mark, who became caught up in a bizarre online maze of characters, activities, and interactions that included Web cam-enabled and in-person sex acts. The homosexual relationship of these boys culminated with Mark attempting to kill John on orders from a fictitious British secret agent named Janet, who had been created and role-played online by John in an Internet chat forum.[65]

Police solved the case by analyzing 58,000 lines of chat text, examining CCTV tapes of the alleyway in which the stabbing occurred, and interviewing the boys, their family members, teachers, and other people familiar with their activities and relationships. During an extensive background investigation, it was learned that John had been psychologically troubled for several years, apparently in connection with not having a father or other male adult role model or mentor in his life. After receiving a laptop computer from his mother in order to improve his schoolwork, he learned to achieve power by creating an online world of characters he could control, even to the extent of using

them to manipulate a gullible teen in the real world into committing murder. Prior to the stabbing, John's classroom attention and social interactions declined, he began refusing meals, and he went for extended periods without sleep in order to compulsively create, recreate, and live vicariously through the fantasy world of his online characters (one of which was himself playing himself).[66]

Mark, who was also a middle class boy from Greater Manchester, was charged with attempted murder and sentenced to two years of supervised probation after already spending several months in confinement during the investigation. For his part, John became the first person ever charged in England with inciting his own murder. He subsequently received intensive psychiatric treatment. He also received three years supervised probation, was banned from contacting Mark, and prohibited from accessing the Internet without close adult supervision.[67] The fact that John committed this crime as a troubled youth and in the process victimized both himself and Mark using a computer, fictitious characters, and combinations of online and in-person encounters, demonstrates how IT can facilitate deceitful, manipulative, and destructive behaviors. Which crime theories do you think best explain the bizarre behavior of John and Mark?

those of law enforcement and security professionals. Similarly, law enforcement and security professionals must consistently develop, adopt, and diffuse new technologies or risk falling behind in their crime-fighting capabilities. Over time, recurring criminal and police/security innovation cycles have a ratcheting-up effect akin to an arms race.

• Crime, policing and security management become increasingly complex as a function of increasingly complex tools and/or techniques employed by criminals, police, or security professionals. The result is perpetually complex, technology-enabled crime, policing, and security management—a never-ending competition

in which police and security professionals will, in general, react to criminological innovation.

• Tools and techniques, once developed, adopted, and understood, tend to remain in use by criminals, police, and security professionals because of their continuing functionality and/or constraints to technology development or adoption. The result is a full range of relatively simple (ordinary) to relatively complex (new) forms of crimes and countervailing investigation and protective methods.

• Criminals, police, and security professionals are always wondering about their adversaries' activities, and each group may not fully understand

---

## BOX 5.6 • *Strengths and Limitations of Integrated and Technological Theories*

The major advantage of integrated theories is their ability to explain complex issues in ways that make sense at general levels. Most people know that many factors can contribute to a person's decision to commit crime, including biological and psychological traits, how they were raised and acculturated, their neighborhood environment and quality of schools, and potentially, societal level issues having to do with views of power, wealth, privilege, and so on. As such, integrated theories appeal to people intuitively to the extent that particular aspects and interplay of lesser included theories can be clearly stated by researchers, instructors, and practitioners attempting to use them in practical ways. In reality, of course, we do not know precisely why crime occurs at the societal level; there are just too many factors that must be weighed on a case-by-case basis. For this reason, in-depth consideration of the role of technology in the commission of crimes can shed light on how and why crime occurs. This represents a fundamentally different approach to understanding crime but may be immensely important for considering how to interdict specific crime problems, as well as strategically manage evolutionary factors of crime not limited to particular places in time.

The major disadvantage of integrated theories is that they are nonspecific and predicated on existing support for lesser included theories. Because they are broadly conceived, their applicability to general populations consisting of unique individuals with their own sets of circumstances and potential crime-precipitating factors often makes them inapplicable, especially in narrow interdiction and prevention programming situations. One theory does not explain all crimes, nor will any given integrated theory explain the actions of all criminals or groups of criminals, especially in varying geographic, cultural, economic, and political circumstances. This is problematic on a fundamental level because a primary goal of criminological research is to explain variability in populations of offenders, as well as variability among people who do not violate crime laws. In other words, lesser theories that offer specific insights about crimes committed by certain classifications of individuals may be more valuable than integrated theories that only explain things in general ways. In reality, effective crime policies and practices are based on a combination of sound lesser and more general integrated theories. They are also need to be applied circumstantially with regard to differences in communities and use of technology inclusive of computers, other types of electronic IT devices, and information systems.

the consequences of their own operations (i.e., use of technology). This can result in unintended positive and negative spin-off effects. Over time, technology employed in crime, policing, and security management is better understood and thus relatively less complex. In the case of crime, it is (we hope) more manageable, except to the extent that criminal innovations disrupt relatively stable technological competitions between law-abiding and-violating forces of society.

## 5.8 Summary

Theories consist of interrelated and testable sets of propositions that, when combined with systematic data gathering and analysis, enable us to understand, explain, and effectively respond to challenging crime-related problems. The process of knowledge-building occurs over extended periods of time and necessarily involves active collaboration of practitioners and trained researchers to understand the true nature and extent of problems. Formulation of theories dates to ancient times and has improved with respect to the knowledge and technologies that make discovery of new theories and testing of extant theories possible. Little theories explain relatively simple issues; big or general theories are often combined to explain more complicated issues. Dozens of pluasible theories exist in every academic field, each supported by a history of less to more empirical research of varying quality.

Solving complex real-world problems typically requires drawing from more than one field of study. Understanding and managing cybercrime is an enormous challenge requiring application of knowledge from several fields of study. This is why cybercrime is often described as an inter and multidisciplinary problem. As first indicated in Chapter 1, fields of study bearing on understanding and managing cybercrime include at least history, sociology, criminology, psychology, economics, security management, computer science, software engineering, IT administration, accounting, business management inclusive of leadership and organizational change issues, criminal justice, public administration, public policy, political science, and the philosophy of ethics. Researchers, policy makers, and practitioners specializing in all these fields have important contributions to make toward better understanding, managing, and ultimately preventing computer abuse and cybercrimes on small to large scales, and in varying cultural, technological, economic and political environments.

To advance our understanding of why computer abuse and cybercrime occurs as it does, this chapter considered a traditional theoretical framework consisting of six categories:

- Classical/choice theories generally have to do with rational decision-making and deterrence given perceived certainty, severity, and swiftness of punishment inclusive of formal and informal sanctions.
- Trait theories pertain to biological and/or psychological disorders or conditions that may have interactive effects on decision-making, leading to a person committing crime.
- Social process theories explain why people do not or do commit crime in relation to how they were raised, educated, and generally acculturated within families, groups, and societal institutions such as schools, churches, and other types of organizations.
- Social structure theories build on each of the above-mentioned categories of theories to include consideration of social and economic class as precipitating conditions of crime.
- Conflict theories have to do with differing consensus, pluralistic, and conflict views of social organization and political processes in relation to the formulation and enforcement of crime laws based on wealth and other forms of power.
- Integrated theories combine aspects of theories from one or more of the above categories to address the complexities associated with why people use computers, other electronic IT devices, or information systems to cause harm and commit crime.

Each of the categories of crime theories can and should be applied to understanding and managing cybercrime. However, few scientific studies of the nature and extent of computer abuse and cybercrimes have been conducted. (This issue is addressed in considerable detail in the next chapter). In addition, criminologists have traditionally not considered in much depth the theoretical role and attendant issues of technology in committing, managing, or preventing crimes. This is problematic because cybercrime as we have defined it pertains to computer abuse and violations of crime laws using computers and other IT devices that are usually networked via information systems. In other words, understanding the problem of cybercrime in society and doing something constructive about it requires much better inter and multidisciplinary understanding of the role of technology and particularly of IT in the commission of crime.

The implication is that just as technologies enabling crime are continually being invented and innovated, theories to explain why crimes are committed by individuals and groups of people are also necessarily developed, tested, and modified to make society safer, more secure, and fair in its administration of justice. The theory of TCPS is an integrated theory that combines long-held conventional wisdom about technological competition in crime fighting and aspects of established theories from criminology and several other academic disciplines to explain the onset, evolution, and diffusion of crime. On balance, TCPS, as a general theory of crime that emphasizes technology factors and their interplay with other categories of crime theories listed above, offers an important framework for understanding the rapidly changing nature of computer abuse and cybercrimes.

Other important theories that researchers should consider applying as a basis for better understanding why people abuse computers, other electronic IT devices, or information systems to commit cybercrimes include (1) arousal, cognitive, and behavioral trait theories and (2) learning, differential association, and differential reinforcement social process theories—plus and in combination with rational choice and general deterrence theories. Undertaking credible research of the kind needed to understand why computer abuse and cybercrime occurs is critically important, but it is not easy and it requires enormous amounts of curiosity, will, collaboration, time, and money. In the next chapter we will examine the results of rather limited research on the social and economic impacts of cybercrime and continue this discussion about research needed in the field of crime studies.

## Key Terms and Concepts

Anomie, 165

Anomie theory, 165

Arousal theory, 150

Biosocial theory, 148

Certainty, swiftness, and severity of punishment, 143

Choice theory, 143

Classical criminology, 143

Cognitive theory, 152

Computer efficacy, 153

Concentric zones, 164

Conflict theory/criminology, 167

Conflict view of social organization, 168

Consensus view of social organization, 167

Containment theory, 156

Control-balance theory, 157

Crime prevention through environmental design, 165

Cultural deviance theory, 166

Death penalty, 143

Differential association theory, 157

Differential enforcement, 162

Differential Reinforcement Theory, 158

Environmental criminology, 164

Feminist criminology, 172

General conflict theory, 168

General deterrence theory, 144

General social structure theory, 164

General strain theory, 165

Imitation, 159

Institutional anomie theory, 165

Instrumental Marxism, 170
Internet addiction disorder, 151
Labeling theory, 161
Left realism, 172
Negative definitions, 158
Neutralization theory, 159
Neutralizing definitions, 159
Normative definitions, 157
Peacemaking criminology, 173
Pluralist view of social
    organization, 168
Positive definitions, 158
Positivism, 147
Postmodern criminology, 173

Punishers, 159
Punishment, 143
Punishment theory, 158
Rational choice theory, 144
Reinforcers, 159
Relative deprivation theory, 165
Restorative justice, 173
Routine activities theory, 147
Self-derogation theory, 156
Social bond theory, 156
Social control theories, 156
Social disorganization
    theory, 164
Social ecology, 164

Social learning theory, 157
Social process theories, 155
Social structure theories, 165
Somatotyping, 148
Structural Marxism, 170
Tacit knowledge, 153
Theory or technology-enabled
    crime, policing,
    and security, 176
Theory, 141
Torture, 143
Trait theories, 147

## *Critical Thinking and Discussion Questions* _____

1. How is technology used in the routine activities of cybercriminals to commit computer abuse, attacks, or crime? How is technology not being effectively used by victims or the guardians of society to help prevent these actions or minimize damage and harm caused?

2. Suppose a college student who has relatively little disposable income illegally downloads 20–30 copies of different songs and/or movie files per week. When asked why she does this she replies, "Look, I know it's illegal, but I can't afford the CDs. Besides, all my friends are doing it, and no one ever gets caught, so why shouldn't I get a little free entertainment too?" Which general category of criminological theory best explains the student's behavior? Which specific theory within that general category of crime theory best explains her behavior?

3. The Recording Industry Association of America (RIAA) has sued thousands of individuals for illegally downloading songs in violation of U.S. copyright laws, and courts have imposed civil penalties, often in excess of $5,000. Do you think the amount is sufficient to deter most people from committing this form of cybercrime? Why or why not? Comment on how severe and certain the punishment for piracy would need to be in order to deter most of your friends from pirating music.

4. Visit the Web pages sponsored by the Computer Crime and Intellectual Property Section of the U.S. Department of Justice showing adjudicated and ongoing cyber cases being prosecuted (see Appendix A). Of the cases that have been tried and punishments

imposed, which do you agree with? Why? Conversely, for which cases do you think the punishments did not fit the crimes committed? Why not?

5. Provide a hypothetical example of illegal computer behavior(s) that is consistent with each of the general categories of crime theories listed below. Provide sufficient details of the crime you have in mind and then explain how these circumstances fit the theoretical category. To the extent possible, name specific theories.

   a. Choice/classical criminology (e.g., general deterrence theory)
   b. Trait (e.g., arousal, cognitive, or behavioral)
   c. Social structure (e.g., general strain theory)
   d. Social process (e.g., learning theory or differential reinforcement theory)
   e. Conflict theory (e.g., structural Marxism)

6. For each of the examples in question 2, suggest a theory-based practical approach to reduce threats posed by similarly inclined people. In other words, what prevention strategy would you recommend to prevent people from committing similar crimes or attacks?

7. Go online and find an example of a real incident of computer abuse or cybercrime. Analyze the article and then explain the criminal actions on the basis of one or more theories discussed in this chapter.

8. Write a short essay that briefly describes a real incident of computer abuse or cybercrime with which you are familiar. Analyze the incident with respect to crime theories discussed in this chapter and explain why you think the theory best explains why the people

involved did what they did. (Note: DO NOT reveal any crimes you personally committed. Write in the third person, e.g., "I once knew a guy who . . . ."

9. Reflect on when you were first introduced to computers. Describe this period in your life with respect to differential association theory and/or differential reinforcement (punishment theory). Who did you learn from, what influence did they have on your using computers responsibly or irresponsibly, and how did rewards or punishments for using computers in certain ways affect your attitudes and behaviors?

10 Comment on your nickname or that of someone you know. How, if at all, does the nickname relate to their behaviors? Do you or this other person like the nickname? Explain why or why not.

11 Think of a person you know who was labeled by authority figures (see labeling theory). Explain what precipitated the labeling, the different ways in which labeling took place, and the effect it had on the person's attitudes or behaviors.

12 What sort of strain would be required for people you know to use a computer to (1) plagiarize, (2) cheat on an assignment, and (3) cheat on an exam? Explain how various levels of strain differ with respect to your perception about the seriousness of each of these types of academic cheating.

13. Use the crime theories discussed in this chapter to analyze Cyber Case 5.4 pertaining to using fictitious characters to socially engineer a real-world stabbing. Review the case description carefully, and attribute at least three criminological theories to explain various motivations and actions by John and/or Mark.

## References and Endnotes

1. Williams, F. P., & McShane, M. D. (1993). *Criminology Theory,* 3rd ed. Upper Saddle River, NJ: Prentice Hall.

2. Bentham, J. (1789). An introduction to the principles of morals and legislation. In Joseph E. Jacoby (Ed.), *Classics of Criminology,* 2nd ed, 1994 edition (pp. 80–83). Prospect Heights, IL: Waveland Press.

3. Williams, F. P., & McShane, M. D., 1993, p. 5; see note 1.

4. See for example the categorization of crime theories by Siegel, L. J. (2000). *Criminology,* 7th ed. Belmont, CA: Wadsworth Publishing.

5. Beccaria, C. (1764). On crimes and punishments. In Joseph E. Jacoby (Ed.), *Classics of Criminology,* 2nd, 1994 edition (pp. 277–285). Prospect Heights, IL: Waveland Press.

6. Parker, D. B. (1998). *Fighting Computer Crime: A New Framework for Protecting Information.* New York: Wiley Computer Publishing.

7. U.S. Department of Justice (2004). Listing of intellectual property crimes cases. Retrieved October 31, 2004, from http://www.usdoj.gov/criminal/cybercrime/ipcases.htm.

8. Office of the U.S. Attorney, Southern District of New York (2004). Manhattan man arrested on federal charge of selling pirated computer software. Retrieved July 31, 2004, from http://www.usdoj.gov/criminal/cybercrime/rodriguezArrest.htm.

9. When behavior-specific mean scores of the likelihood of getting caught were compared with the severity of punishment likely to be imposed, it was further learned that differences in every category of behavior were statistically significant, indicating that there is virtually no possibility that differences reported by students were the result of chance.

10. Cohen, L. E., & Felson, M. (1979). Social change and crime: a routine activity approach. In Joseph E. Jacoby (Ed.), *Classics of Criminology,* 2nd ed., 1994 edition (pp. 66–74). Prospect Heights, IL: Waveland Press.

11. Sheldon, W. (1949). *Varieties of Delinquent Youth.* New York: Harper Brothers.

12. Staff Author (1978). Twinkies made him do it? Oh No News. Retrieved February 12, 2005, from http://www.ohnonews.com/twinkie.html.

13. Downs, L. L. (2002). PMS, psychosis and culpability: sound or misguided defense? *Journal of Forensic Science, 47* (5).

14. See the discussion on biochemical conditions and crime by Siegel, 2000, pp 152–154; see note 4.

15. American Psychiatric Association (1994). *Diagnostic and Statistical Manual of Mental Disorders,* 4th ed. Washington, DC: American Psychiatric Association.

16. Booth, A., & Osgood, D. W. (1993). The influence of testosterone on deviance in adulthood. *Criminology, 31,* 93–118.

17. Bureau of Justice Statistics (2005). Prison statistics. Retrieved February 1, 2005, from http://www.ojp.usdoj.gov/bjs/prisons.htm.

18. McQuade, S., & Castellano, T. (2004). Computer-Related Crime Theories Tested: Self-Report Survey Findings. Presented at the Annual Conference of the

American Society of Criminology in Nashville, TN, November 17.

19. National Research Council (1999). *Pathological Gambling: A Critical Review*. Washington, DC: National Academy Press.

20. Gopher, D., & Donchin, E. (1986). Workload: an examination of the concept. In K. R. Boff, L. Kaufman, and J.P. Thomas (Eds.), *Handbook of Perception and Human Performance* (pp. 41–48). New York: John Wiley.

21. Gluck, C. (2002). South Korea's gaming addicts. London: BBC News. Retrieved November 13, 2004, from http://news.bbc.co.uk/1/hi/world/asia-pacific/2499957.stm; and Staff Author (2004). Just click no. Article originally published by *New Yorker Magazine* on January 13, 1997. Retrieved November 13, 2004, from http://www.psycom.net/iasg.html.

22. Parker, D. B., 1998; see note 6.

23. American Psychiatic Association (1994). Diagnostic and statistical manual of mental disorders (4th ed.). Washington, DC: American Psychiatric Association.

24. Staff Author (2002). Addicted: suicide over Everquest? CBSNEWS.com. Retrieved February 13, 2005, from http://www.cbsnews.com/stories/2002/10/17/48hours/main525965.shtml.

25. Miller, S. A. I. (2002, March 30). Death of a game addict. *Journal Sentinel*. Retrieved February 13, 2005, from http://www.jsonline.com/news/state/mar02/31536.asp.

26. Siegel, L. J., 2000, p. 234; see note 4.

27. Reckless, W. C. (1967). *The Crime Problem*. New York: Appleton-Century-Crofts.

28. Hirschi, T. (1972). A control theory of delinquency. In Joseph E. Jacoby (Ed.), *Classics of Criminology*, 2nd ed., 1994 edition (pp. 251–258). Prospect Heights, IL: Waveland Press.

29. Kaplan, H. B. (1980). *Deviant Behavior in Defense of Self*. New York: Academic Press.

30. Schmalleger, F. (2004). *Criminology Today: An Integrative Introduction*. Upper Saddle River, NJ: Pearson-Prentice Hall.

31. Tittle, C. R. (1995). *Control Balance: Toward a General Theory of Deviance*, p. 234. Boulder, CO: Westview Press.

32. Akers, R. L. (1998). *Social Learning and Social Structure: A General Theory of Crime and Deviance*. Boston: Northeastern University Press.

33. Hollinger, R. C. (1993). Crime by computer: correlates of software piracy and unauthorized account access. *Security Journal, 4*(1), 2–12.

34. Skinner, W. F., & Fream, A. M. (1997). A social learning theory analysis of computer crime among college students. *The Journal of Research in Crime and Delinquency, 34*(4), 495–519.

35. Akers, R. L., 1998; see note 32.

36. Siegel, L. J., 2000, pp. 185–197; see note 4.

37. Adler, F., Mueller, G. O. W., & Laufer, W. S. (1998). *Criminology*, 3rd ed., p. 169. Boston: McGraw Hill.

38. Feins, J. D., Epstein, J. C., & Widom, R. (1997). *Solving Crime Problems in Residential Neighborhoods: Comprehensive Changes in Design, Management and Use*. Washington, DC: National Institute of Justice.

39. Siegel, L. J., 2000, pp. 189–202; see note 4.

40. Schmalleger, F., 2004, p. 245; see note 30.

41. Schmalleger, F., 2004, p. 252–253; see note 30.

42. Schmalleger, F., 2004, pp. 266–267; see note 30.

43. Schmalleger, F., pp. 269–270; see note 30.

44. Schmalleger, F., p. 271; see note 30.

45. Reaves, J., 2001; see note 42.

46. Reaves, J., 2001; see note 42.

47. Staff Author, 2005; note 44.

48. Schmalleger, F., pp. 270–271; see note 30.

49. Ackman, D. (2004). Martha, Dennis and corporate scandals. Retrieved online March 4, 2005, from http://www.forbes.com/management/2004/03/08/cx_da_0308topnews.html.

50. Associated Press Staff Author (2004, February 20). Fast facts: case against Martha Stewart. Fox News Channel. Retrieved March 5, 2005, from http://www.foxnews.com/story/0,2933,112077,00.html.

51. Ackman, D., 2004; see note 49.

52. Farrell, G. (2004, July 16). Stewart sentenced to five months in prison. USA Today. Retrieved March 5, 2005, from http://www.usatoday.com/money/media/2004-07-15-stewart-usat_x.htm.

53. Schmalleger, F., 2004, pp. 270–282; see note 30.

54. Schmalleger, F., p. 273; see note 30.

55. Schmalleger, F., p. 273; see note 30.

56. Schmalleger, F., p. 274; see note 30.

57. McQuade, S., & Schreck, C. (2005). Correlates of Cybercrime Victimization. Manuscript in progress. Rochester Institute of Technology.

58. Karp, D. R., & Clear, T. R. (2000). Community justice: a conceptual framework. In *Criminal Justice 2000*. Vol. 2. *Boundary Changes in Criminal Justice Organizations*. Washington, DC: National Institute of Justice.

59. Parker, D. B., 1998, p. 142; see note 6.

60. Siegel, L. J., 2000, p. 287; see note 4.

61. See Chapter 10 in Siegel, L. J., 2000; see note 4.

62. Sutherland, E. H. (1940). White-collar criminality. In Joseph E. Jacoby (Ed.), *Classics of Criminology*, 2nd ed., 1994 edition, (pp. 20–25). Prospect Heights, IL: Waveland Press.

63. Cohen, L. E., & Felson, M., 1979; see note 10.
64. McQuade, S. (1998). Towards a Theory of Technology Enabled Crime. Unpublished manuscript, Institute of Public Policy, George Mason University.
65. Carter, H. (2004, May 24). Bizarre tale of boy who used Internet to plot his own death. The Guardian UK News. Retrieved February 5, 2005, from http://www.guardian.co.uk/uk_news/story/0,3604,1227318,00.html.
66. Bachrach, J. (2005). Bizarre tale of boy who used Internet to plot his own murder. Vanity Fair, February, 86–101.
67. Carter, H., 2004; see note 65.

# 6

## *The Social and Economic Impact of Cybercrime*

### *6.0 Introduction: Who Is Harmed and by How Much Cybercrime?*

Have you ever been the victim of a cybercrime that resulted in data loss or other types of harm? Do you know a regular computer user who has *not* been victimized in a manner involving computers or other types of IT devices? How much cybercrime is there, what types of organizations are most afflicted, and what are the human and financial costs? Do you think it is important to report cybercrime when it occurs? Can you imagine why some victims would not wish to report a cybercrime to authorities? Who tracks emerging cybercrime threats and the amount of cybercrime in society? Why, if at all, do you think this information might be important?

Cybercrime is frequently in the news. Television, radio, newspaper, magazine, and online news sources commonly feature stories about new computer viruses being released onto the Internet, computer hackers defeating government computer security systems, and counterfeiting schemes in which real money was illegally scanned and printed out with home computers before being illegally spent on merchandise. Media reports also frequently describe computer piracy of software programs, digital MP3 music files, and DVD-formatted movies, as well as unauthorized removal, distortion, or destruction of confidential information stored on information systems. Many news reports include descriptions of Web site vandalism, cyberstalking, computer eavesdropping, and even electronic bank heists. Identities are stolen; some people lose their life savings in fraudulent virtual gambling casinos. Illegal child pornography is easily accessible and widely available online, as are digital images of children performing lewd sex acts. These are only some examples of cybercrimes that capture public imagination and worry policy makers, criminal justice officials, and information security professionals.

Cybercrimes are reportedly occurring throughout the computerized world in record numbers. As discussed in Chapter 3, these crimes are being committed in more imaginative, daring, and complex ways. They are also apparently having more harmful social and economic impact on individuals, organizations, and society than ever before. Cybercrimes create fear about lost, damaged, or stolen data among computer users everywhere, as well as fear of experiencing damaged property or being physically harmed in some cases. In addition, the nature and extent of cybercrimes is raising concerns about information security throughout society, among individuals, families, and communities—right up to the largest corporations and highest levels of government. Although cybercrimes and their impact on people and organizations is very real, sensational reports by the media can either cast doubt or falsely increase concerns about the seriousness of specific aspects of the problem. However, the number and variety of reported incidents from reputable sources underscores a very real crime threat that calls for far greater understanding about its extent and harmful impact. The primary purpose of this chapter is to discuss research on the known extent and harmful effects of illegal activities involving computers or other electronic IT devices used via information systems.

The chapter begins with a discussion of the human and financial costs of computer abuse and cybercrime. You will learn about **crime victimization** concepts and the types of harm experienced by victims of cybercrime. The second section focuses on the importance of conducting research into the nature of cybercrimes (e.g., types of attacks, types of offenders and why they do what they do), and the extent of cybercrimes (e.g., how much cybercrime occurs, where and how much harm it causes). In the third section, we will review three sets of research that primarily concern the extent of cybercrimes. These include major empirical crime studies, research by organizations that track cybercrime, and economic impact studies undertaken primarily by organizations concerned about large-scale copyright infringement such as those involving illegal copying, downloading, possession or use of music, movies, or software. The chapter ends with an assessment: what we know and do not know on the basis of research. In this section you will also learn reasons for the lack of research on cybercrime, policy implications of not knowing more about cybercrime, and types of research needed to improve our understanding, management, and prevention of cybercrime.

The major goals of this chapter are to (1) provide insights into what victims of cybercrime experience and must endure after they, their computer systems, or their organizations are attacked; (2) explain the importance of research for understanding and managing cybercrime-related issues and attendant problems; and (3) emphasize that in the real world, policymaking and development of sound investigation and security practices cannot wait for additional research into the nature and extent of cybercrime: professionals must do what they can with existing knowledge to develop needed information assurance technologies, protect information systems from attacks, investigate and prosecute cybercrimes, and ameliorate harm caused by computer abuse and illegal use of computers, other IT devices and information systems.

# 6.1  The Human and Financial Costs of Computer Abuse and Cybercrime

Each year millions of people suffer harm from cybercrimes, including loss of data, money, and time. Many people do not understand how their computer systems have been compromised, much less what they can do to avert impending harm and restore optimum functionality. Other people are harassed, threatened, and even stalked online and/or in person by someone using a computer. Victims of cybercrime whose identities are stolen suffer emotionally and experience financial hardship as bills for purchases they believe they are responsible for mount and are mistakenly paid while legal obligations to pay legitimate bills are not met, even as they seek to stop ongoing fraud in their name and resolve credit discrepancies. Other victims lose their life savings because of other kinds of online fraud including pyramid schemes, con games and stock market securities fraud, and as the result of online gambling in virtual casinos that may or may not be regulated or even legal depending on the state or nation in which the gaming services or establishment are located. Still other victims of cybercrimes lose their jobs because the firms they worked for lost crucial information but had no business recovery plan or data restoration capability. These are some of the many issues we address in this section.

## 6.1.1 Victimization Concepts

For every cybercrime, there is a cybercrime victim. Therefore, logically, victims of cybercrime could be classified according to any corresponding categorization of cybercrimes. The criminal justice system often distinguishes between **victims** of violent crime versus property crimes. Criminal justice officials and security professionals also recognize widely ranging kinds of **harm** and loss that victims of crime experience. These are important realizations, because they remind us to remain sensitive to the needs of crime victims and other people affected by crimes who need professional services. Even people who are under investigation for cybercrimes and presumed innocent until proven guilty in a court of law are entitled to have their rights, computer systems and devices, data, other property and persons protected by criminal justice and security officials as required by legal safeguards. For these reasons, it is useful to conceive of crime victims and potential victimization broadly and in ways other than those corresponding to types of crime or harm. Let us now consider concepts of direct, indirect, and tertiary victimization, as well as the concept of victimless crimes, and how these concepts relate to harm experienced by victims of cybercrimes.

### 6.1.1.1 Primary, Secondary, and Tertiary Victimization. **Primary victimization** refers to individuals, groups of people, and organizations who suffer direct harm to their data, information systems, other property, or person as the result of computer abuse or cybercrime. Primary victimization is up close and personal. It

costs victims time, money, and credit ratings. Victims directly affected by cybercrime often need to recover their data or replace and/or upgrade their computers or other devices in consultation with knowledgeable IT professionals and technology vendors. Primary victims of cybercrime are entitled and encouraged to report the incident to the police. As a result of reporting the crime to police, they may need to interact with investigators and prosecutors on several occasions, thereby spending time away from their jobs, schools, or other obligations. Victims directly affected by cybercrimes often experience fear, especially in cases involving harassment, threats, or cyberstalking. Victims of other types of computer abuse, attacks, and cybercrimes, may not even realize that their data, information systems, lines of credit, or other assets are being affected until significant damage has occurred. Managers of organizations victimized by cybercriminals may need to spend additional time, money, and effort interacting with certified information security professionals in order to improve the protection of enterprise-wide systems, including training of personnel in systems and facilities protection procedures.

On January 29, 2004, organized crime gangs were reported to be shaking down Internet gambling sites on the eve of the Super Bowl by threatening to launch denial-of-service attacks against online casino gambling and sports-betting firms. In some instances, targeted firms located in the United Kingdom and other European nations, and extending to the Caribbean, reported receiving threats to pay up or be shut down beginning a September of 2003. One firm reportedly received a demand that $30,000 be wired via Western Union to an offshore bank account or they would risk being attacked. Another threatening email sent to several firms demanded they pay $15,000 for six months of "protection." As a small number of firms opted to pay the extortionists, private security professionals and police indicated that the cybercriminals, who were professional, technically competent, and serious about profiting, were possibly based in Eastern Europe and Russia.[1]

Similarly, in 2004, Daniel I. Videtto, the president of MicroPatent, a patent and trademark services firm, received threatening email messages from an unknown extortionist who threatened to expose proprietary and customer data unless he was paid $17 million. With assistance from a private investigation firm, a former Central Intelligence Agency (CIA) psychological profiler and police investigators, the cyber perpetrator was eventually traced to Hyattsville, Maryland, where he was arrested while preparing additional threatening messages to send online.[2]

**Secondary victimization** refers to individuals, groups of people, and organizations whose information systems or personal well-being have been negatively affected as the result of a cybercrime even though they were not directly targeted by computer abusers or cybercriminals. Secondary victimization is often experienced by family members, friends, and professional associates of primary victims as a result of indirect harm attributable to computer abuse or cybercrimes. For every form of direct computer abuse or cybercrime, there may exist one or more forms and types of secondary victims as well as primary victims. For example, when a woman is being cyberstalked, she may naturally (and wisely) become more wary when in strange places and more suspicious of people she does not know. As a primary cybercrime victim, her fear may result in irritability, loss of sleep, and other unusual behaviors that negatively affect her concentration, work performance, and ability to be intimate with family and friends. These individuals, including the woman's coworkers and employer, are secondary victims because they too are negatively affected by the effects of the cyberstalking. Consider further that, although an individual, business, or other entity such as a nonprofit organization or government agency may be directly victimized by a cyber perpetrator resulting in direct and secondary impact, it is important to understand that society as a whole is also harmed by

illegal behavior. In the realm of computer abuse, consider mass illegal downloading of music, movies, or other graphics-intensive files by a single individual. Such piracy directly or indirectly costs software developers and artists real money. In addition however, other users of a system abused for pirating data intensive music, movies, and other content suffer as the result of compromised computing capability of their affected network. Some colleges and universities with excessive illegal file sharing experience network slowdowns to such an extent that legitimate exchanges of email and other file sharing is cumbersome if not impossible to accomplish. The same holds true for abused networks of other types of organizations, whose owners and employees may experience real secondary victimization as a result.

**Tertiary victimization** refers to broader societal impacts of crime, which individual victims may not even know about but nonetheless are negatively affected by. Malware that ends up infecting thousands of computers and results in millions of dollars in cleanup, data recovery, and system restoration costs incurred by government agencies and private organizations may result in higher taxes or prices charged for goods and services to consumers as a means of paying for these losses and for technology upgrades to prevent future attacks. Similar to tertiary costs of conventional shoplifting, pirating of music, movies, and software costs honest consumers throughout society more money for these items, if they are priced higher than would otherwise be necessary in order to compensate for the online theft.

Cybercrime against a single individual may simultaneously have primary, secondary, and tertiary victimization effects. Recall from Chapter 4 that spam is now sometimes being sent to a user, then back-routed to that person's Internet service provider (ISP), and redistributed to numerous subscribers of the ISP, including the person who received the original message (who in effect receives the same spam twice). This means the individual was victimized initially by having his or her system negatively affected by the original message and bot programming that sent it to the ISP. The individual, the ISP, and other subscribers then became secondary victims when the spam was redistributed. In addition, the original victim, the ISP, and all subscribers, along with everyone else in society, bear the cost of the unwanted traffic in the form of slower system functioning, annoyance and distraction, and higher prices charged for Internet connectivity.

### 6.1.1.2 Victimless Crimes.

The concept of societal harm caused by the illegal behavior of individuals willingly participating in crime underscores the legal authority of the state to prosecute violators of so-called **victimless crimes** such as prostitution and illegal drug use. Illegal online gambling also harms society and individuals who voluntarily participate in these crimes. Consider members of society who must bear the criminal justice costs of enforcing these laws, prosecuting those accused of committing such crimes, and punishing offenders. A person who illegally gambles online and loses substantial amounts of money also negatively affects the financial well-being of his or her family, who are secondary victims who will suffer indirect harm. Software piracy is often mistakenly thought of as a victimless cybercrime because many offenders believe that only large corporations experience financial losses when software is not legally purchased. However, as indicated above, smaller software developers and retail merchants, as well as employees and stockholders of small firms and large corporations, are indirectly harmed by piracy when, for example, they lose customers, contracts, and even their jobs

---

**CYBER TALE 6.1**

### How Victimization Can Lead to Cybercrime

Sometimes a person can be victimized and even resort to criminal activity as an indirect consequence of someone else's illegal actions. A student once informed me how her roommate set his computer to automatically (and illegally) download music files all night long. Of course while the computer was downloading songs it was also vulnerable to uploading files because security measures to guard against this had not been taken. It turned out that in addition to maintaining a large collection of illegally acquired music files, the roommate also possessed a very large collection of legal pornography, which other students on campus knew about. While the computer was auto-downloading music, "other greedy file sharers" were uploading the roommate's porn while he slept.

Meanwhile the female student was up late attempting to use her own computer to download graphics-intensive course materials that she needed to study for an exam the next day. However, her downloading attempts via the same broadband cable connection in their shared apartment were repeatedly denied by their Internet service provider (ISP). In effect, the student was competing with her roommate's computer for bandwidth. Eventually she discovered what was going on, but by the time she turned off her roommate's computer, their ISP had temporarily suspended the service for excessive downloading in violation of the firm's policy against this. By then it was 2 a.m. Desperate for the examination materials, but unable to download them via her own ISP connection, she resorted to hacking into a neighbor's unencrypted wireless router, through which she then accessed the university system to get what she needed. Can you see how becoming a cybercrime victim may contribute to a person's decision to abuse or illegally use computer resources? Do you think this student was justified in committing the crime of hacking because someone else's abuse negatively affected her ability to get the data she needed to study for an exam?

as a result of declining sales. Even offenders may become victims of their own illegal activities as when, in the process of downloading illegally acquired copies of software containing malicious code (e.g., viruses, Trojans, and worms), they end up infecting and possibly damaging their own systems which other people may also use and rely on. An adolescent who unintentionally introduces malware onto their family's computer while engaged in peer-to-peer file sharing for illegal purposes is just one example of how this can happen.

## 6.1.2  Harm Experienced by Victims of Cybercrime

### 6.1.2.1  Data, Property, and Financial Losses.
Cybercrime victimization most often involves infected software, damaged hardware systems, and destruction, denial, degradation, or theft of data. This includes information pertaining to personal and professional contacts, schedules and travel plans, online purchases and financial accounts data, health and medical history records, academic grades and transcripts, and so on. These and many other types of data need protection because you and others with whom you share or entrust data depend on its being accurate, complete, and accessible for legitimate uses. Unfortunately, many people inadequately protect their information systems because they do not know how, cannot afford to in all the ways they wish, are outfoxed by cybercriminals, or are simply negligent. Markus Jakobsson, codirector of the Center for Applied Cybersecurity Research at Indiana University, has estimated that sophisticated attacks against information systems equipped with standard security devices and default software settings can penetrate computer defenses fifty percent of the time. Research data from the center also indicate that as many as three percent of people who receive phishing email attacks end up being defrauded.[3]

### 6.1.2.2  Emotional and Psychological Harm.
Anyone who has ever been the victim of a crime can appreciate the annoyance, anger, despair, and suffering that comes from personal injury, property damage, and, as is often the case with cybercrime, loss of data, time, and money. Cybercrime victims are always inconvenienced, and many become frustrated with officials of criminal justice agencies, IT technicians, information security professionals, and financial institution personnel who may be insensitive to their needs, losses, and lack ability to help solve their problems. Conversely, law enforcement investigators and information security professionals may not fully understand or properly respond to some cybercrimes, thereby adding to the grief experienced by victims, many of whom also experience fear and substantial emotional or psychological harm. Online pedophilia and child pornography can cause serious **emotional and psychological harm** to unsuspecting children and adolescents who are easily enticed into dangerous online communications, Web-based sexual activities, or in-person encounters with adults who would abuse them for sexual gratification or profit. Online stalking, harassment, and threats can also be frightening to juveniles and adults alike and cause emotional distress that contributes to the onset of psychological disorders.

Cybercrimes may also indirectly result in **physical harm** to a person's property and potential injuries or even death to one or more individuals. As discussed in Chapter 2, the prospect of this occurring on massive scales, in the context of network-centered warfare or cyber terrorist attacks on critical infrastructures, is a theoretical possibility. For this reason cybercrimes may, depending on the circumstances, be considered either nonviolent (property) crimes or violent crimes against people. However, most crimes involving computers are nonviolent property crimes that also would qualify as financial crimes if a primary goal of the perpetrators is to illegally acquire money or financially gain in some way. Theft, embezzlement, credit card and securities fraud, identify theft, corporate espionage, and money laundering are types of financial crime that frequently involve illegal use of computers.

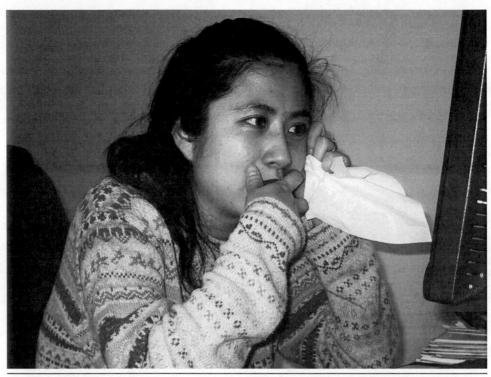

*Victims of cybercrimes experience many types of harm, including those which are emotional and psychological in nature. Have you ever been the victim of crime? What kinds of harm were caused and how did you feel at the time and afterwards?* Photo by Nathan Fisk

CYBER CASE **6.1**

### *Cybercrime as Nonviolent Property Crime*

In March and April of 2000, Vitek Boden conducted a series of 46 electronic attacks on the Maroochy Shire (Australia) sewage control system after a job application he had submitted was rejected. The computer hacking incident caused millions of liters of raw sewage to spill out into local parks, rivers, and even onto the grounds of a Hyatt Regency hotel. "Marine life died, the creek water turned black and the stench was unbearable for residents," according to Janelle Bryant of the Australian Environmental Protection Agency.

Boden was discovered to be the perpetrator of this cybercrime after police, who pulled him over for a traffic violation, discovered radio and computer equipment in his car. A subsequent computer forensics investigation revealed that Boden's laptop had been used at the time of the attacks and that his computer's hard drive contained software for accessing and controlling the sewage management system. Boden was sentenced to two years in prison for his crime.[4]

#### 6.1.2.3 Social, Professional, and Organizational Harm.

Victims of cybercrime may also experience **social**, **professional**, **and organizational harm**. Social harm includes such things as being ridiculed, labeled, or ostracized as the result of becoming a victim of cybercrime. You can imagine this sort of **victim blaming** in instances involving technologically inept persons who had not taken adequate information security precautions. Similar and potentially more damaging professional related harm can also occur, as in instances involving insecure facilities, IT, or information systems. On June 7, 2004, *Newsweek* magazine reported that a laptop computer containing information on as many as 100 Drug Enforcement Administration (DEA) investigations, many involving confidential informants, was missing. Originally the laptop was reported stolen from the car of an inspector general auditor assigned to review payouts made by DEA agents to informants. However, an investigation revealed that the auditor had actually destroyed and discarded the laptop to cover up the fact that he had accidentally damaged it.

This incident distressed agents, who feared that if the computer fell into the wrong hands, drug traffickers would discover the identities of confidential informants and potential agents involved in undercover operations. Two years earlier the DEA and FBI were both found by the Office of the Inspector General of the U.S. Department of Justice to have inadequate security controls over sensitive information and items including laptop computers.[5] These incidents resulted in stress and other negative professional consequences for agents involved, as well as organizational harm including embarrassment for the DEA as units scrambled to improve security. Other kinds of harm commonly experienced by organizations as a result of computer abuse, negligence, and cybercrimes include loss of proprietary and other valuable data, employee effectiveness or morale, systems capabilities, and credibility among stockholders and potential investors. Loss of computerized services, data, and revenue generation capability can also render a firm insolvent in very short order. It is widely estimated that 60 percent of companies that lose their data in the course of a major cybercrime or other disaster will go out of business within six months.[6]

## 6.2 How Much Cybercrime Is There?

In this section we focus on understanding sources of crime statistics and learning about how much cybercrime and associated harm may exist. Odds are that if you have not already been the victim of a cybercrime by the time you entered college, you will have been victimized at least once by the time you finish your two- or four-year degree. In the study of 873 randomly selected students from the Rochester Institute of Technology (RIT) in 2004, one out of three students surveyed reported having been the victim of at least one cybercrime during the previous twelve months. However, approximately one-fourth of survey respondents reported having been victimized two *or more* times in that period of time. Table 6.1 summarizes the study findings pertaining to the type and extent of computer-related victimization reported by students.[7]

The survey instrument used in this study also contained numerous questions about offending behavior. In effect, it was a study that explored the nature and extent of both IT-enabled crime victimization and offending, inclusive of crimes committed against and by the same people. This is somewhat unusual. Most crime statistics are generated through police reporting methods, victimization surveys, or criminal offender studies. Rarely does a single research project employ more than one of these approaches to examine the nature, extent, and harmful effects of crime within a given population, time, and place. Let us now consider what each of these three primary methods of generating estimates of the extent of and harm resulting from crime and the comparative advantages and disadvantages of each.

**TABLE 6.1**   *Computer-Related Victimization among College Students in Preceding 12 Months*

| *Type of Computer-Related Victimization* | *Number of Student Victims* | *Percent* |
| --- | --- | --- |
| Virus/malware infection | 435 | 48 |
| Denial-of-service attack | 115 | 14 |
| Hacking | 99 | 12 |
| Identity theft | 55 | 6 |
| Other online fraud | 27 | 3 |
| Online harassment | 149 | 17 |
| Online threats | 68 | 8 |
| Cyberstalking | 52 | 6 |
| Stolen IT equipment | 23 | 3 |
| Other cybercrime | 20 | 2 |

*Source:* 2004 RIT Computer Use and Ethics Survey

## 6.2.1 Primary Means of Generating Crime Statistics

The amount of crime among and associated harm done to a population are typically estimated either through police reporting of crimes reported to them, crime victimization surveys, or self-reported offender studies. Each of these methods is useful but limited. Estimates of crime made on the basis of **police crime reporting** can be advantageous because they are records of crimes responded to, investigated, and thus confirmed by public officials to have occurred. In addition, law enforcement agencies exist in all localities and states, and these agencies generally provide for systematic and convenient means of reporting crime by virtually anyone regardless of whether or not they personally were victimized. This means police reports collected from several agencies will contain information about the full range of crimes within a given time period and geographic area inclusive of facts about victims and offenders, types and amounts of harm caused, and other details pertinent to understanding ongoing crime trends and how to prevent or interdict crime.

The disadvantage of estimating crime on the basis of police reports is that at least half of the crimes committed in society are never reported to police. Criminologists know this from victimization surveys in which people acknowledge not reporting crimes to police. Victims often say they

did not report a crime because they thought it was no big deal, not worth their time or that of the police, and they did not wish to become involved in a protracted investigation and subsequent court procedings requiring their appearance on numerous occasions. Victims also explain nonreporting on the basis of fearing retaliation, feelings of personal shame or embarrassment (as is frequently the case in sex crimes), and distrust of the police or lack of confidence that the criminal justice system can or will actually prosecute and adequately punish offenders and make them pay for property damage and other costs associated with harm caused. In addition, victims of cybercrimes may not report these to authorities because they may not even realize that crimes against them have taken place. We have already discussed how this can happen in instances of computer hacking, identity theft, and various other types of fraud. Have you ever been the victim of a crime and decided not to report the incident to the police? Have you been the victim of a cybercrime and not realized it until after a period of time had elapsed? Did this delay affect your decision to not report the incident to authorities?

Banks and other financial institutions are often reluctant to report theft of money because in so doing they must reveal inadequate security capabilities and risk losing customer and investor confidence. In addition, although police classification and reporting of crimes in the United States is standardized by state government reporting procedures and the FBI's **Uniform Crime Report (UCR) system,** police agencies voluntarily participate in the UCR system and do not always strictly adhere to the crime categorization schemas when providing summary reports to higher levels of government. In rare instances, police officials may intentionally reclassify or not include certain crimes in their summary reports in order to maintain the appearance of crime rates being lower than they actually are. The combination of all these reasons means that police reports by themselves, even those assembled from throughout the nation by the U.S. Department of Justice, are unfortunately inaccurate estimates of crime rates.

The second way in which the amount of crime is estimated is with **victimization surveys**. In this type of research individuals are surveyed in-person or by phone, mail, or online about crimes they have experienced. The National Crime Victimization Survey (NCVS), conducted on an ongoing basis by the Bureau of Justice Statistics in collaboration with the U.S. Census Bureau, involves telephone contact with individuals and members of families in ways that retain victim anonymity and the confidentiality of their responses to a large battery of questions pertaining to the type and number of crimes experienced, harm experienced, and other issues such as whether or not they reported the crime to police. The obvious advantage of victimization surveys is that they reveal crimes not reported to police while also confirming or refuting general patterns of crime made known via police reporting systems such as the UCR. As a result, more accurate estimates of the extent of

---

**CYBER TALE 6.2**

### An Examination of Early Uniform Crime Reports

In the mid 1990s while employed as a social science program manager at the National Institute of Justice (NIJ) of the U.S. Department of Justice, I had occasion to visit the small Office of Justice Programs research library located in our building. I was curious about crime statistics, particularly data pertaining to computer-related crime as it was then conceptualized. It did not take me long to realize that the federal government did not systematically collect, much less analyze and publish this kind of statistical information. However, a few scattered reports having to do with crime enabled by computers, and many reports pertaining to other specific types of crime and related facts were reported in abundance, especially by the Bureau of Justice Statistics (BJS) and the FBI through the Uniform Crime Report (UCR). It was a slow afternoon in the federal bureaucracy, so I proceeded to browse through the official crime records of the United States. This led me to examining the very first UCR summary produced by the FBI in the early 1930s. It was about five pages long, and for the first time reported the number of Part I and Part II crimes that had occurred in the nation during the previous year. At the bottom of the report was the approval signature of J. Edgar Hoover, FBI Director.

As a criminal justice history buff, I found this report fascinating, but what was initially amazing to me was the ridiculously low number of crimes listed. Then I discovered that only a handful of law enforcement agencies had voluntarily participated in the UCR process in that first year. Of course increasing numbers of agencies contributed crime statistics to the annual UCR in following years, but it dawned on me that for several decades the crime statistics in the United States (and most certainly in other nations) were grossly inaccurate, generated manually with pencil/pen and paper, and then added up without the benefit of electronic devices. How inaccurate, incomplete, and nonrepresentative do you think those early reports of crime were? Do you think computers have significantly increased the accuracy of crime reporting in the United States, as well as making reporting easier? Or do you think public policies and programs to address crime problems are still being developed on the basis of distorted information?

crime in a given jurisdiction can be ascertained by examining both UCR and NCVS data for specific time periods. Victimization surveys, such as the NCVS, also enable researchers and criminal justice officials to explore details of crimes and the experiences of victims not captured by standardized police forms and summary reports. For example, in 1999–2000 the National Center for Missing and Exploited Children sponsored the Youth Internet Safety Survey, consisting of telephone interviews conducted over a seven-month period with 1,501 youths ages 10 to 17. The survey found that:

Approximately one in five had received an unwanted sexual solicitation online within the previous year; one in four youths solicited experienced distress; one in seven solicitations also involved attempted contact with the youth in person, over the phone or via postal mail; and 48 percent of the solicitors were themselves juveniles.[8] Detailed information like this about the experiences and routine or precipitating activities of crime victims, such as what if any crime prevention or security precautions were employed before and after crimes were committed, can greatly add to our understanding of why and how specific types of cybercrimes take place, and thereby help us to develop effective crime prevention practices, programs, and policies.

Several problems are, however, associated with victimization surveys. First, unless the study includes a somewhat large random selection of the population within a given geographic area, research results are not likely to be representative of all crime incidents and the associated experiences of all crime victims. Second, depending on how victimization surveys are administered, they will systematically exclude certain types of people who may have been victimized. For example, a snail mail survey sent to residents and business owners will systematically exclude homeless persons, who usually have no regular means of receiving such correspondence. Similar limitations apply to other technological means of administering surveys. In addition, many crime victims are reluctant to talk about their experiences, especially to strangers

conducting impersonal research. All people, including crime victims, periodically have difficulty remembering the details of incidents, especially if they happened in the distant past, thus potentially compromising the accuracy of responses to survey questions. Have you ever participated in a crime victimization survey, and if you have, were you completely forthcoming? How accurate do you think you were able to be in your responses to questions even if you voluntarily participated in a study that guaranteed your answers would be confidential and not be attributed to you personally?

The third basic way in which the amount of crime can be estimated is with **self-report offender studies**. This type of research can also provide information about crimes unreported by victims while providing insights into why and how they were committed. These types of studies tend to be rare and generally consist of small, nonrepresentative samples of offenders, many of whom are either reluctant to go into the details of their crimes, embellish upon them, or lie about what occurred. In studies involving in-custody offenders (which for several reasons are even more rare), the information reported about crimes is further suspect because inmates may minimize or distort their actual involvement in order to manipulate researchers or correctional officials, or otherwise positively influence their legal case situation. Offenders, like crime victims, may also have difficulty remembering the details of particular incidents, especially if they occurred years, months, or even weeks earlier. Nonetheless, information provided by offenders can be revealing of crime in ways that other research methods cannot achieve. For example, in the 2004 RIT computer use and ethics survey mentioned earlier, students who admitted using IT for abusive and illegal activities could be generally classified into one of five specific offending categories. This type of information would be impossible to ascertain or deduce from campus or public police reports or victimization survey data.

Each of the three primary ways of determining the extent of crimes committed has advantages and disadvantages. This implies the need for conducting crime research in more than one way to achieve an accurate sense of particular types of abuse or crimes taking place within a given place and time period. The further implication is that we need to be cautious about all estimations of crime, as well as cost estimates of the harm associated with crimes. By extension, we must also regard all estimates of information systems attack trends, and other reports of potential security threats to physical facilities and information systems, with a large grain of salt. This is not to imply that all research on any particular type or source of computer abuse, attack trends, or estimations of the extent of crime and associated harm are intended to mislead. Rather, the aim here is to point out that all research is inherently limited and potentially flawed in the design of its methodology, the technological means by which it was undertaken, the size and location of subjects studied, its data collection and analysis procedures, and ultimately with respect to the competencies and interpretive judgments of researchers performing the work.

Recall from Chapter 2 that information assurance necessarily involves distrusting human factors and technology to some extent, and that assessing the quality of intelligence information about crime and security threats requires professional judgment regarding the source of data collected and analytical methods employed to make sense of it. So the next time you come across or are presented with crime or security-related statistics, ask yourself and perhaps other people, "How can we be confident that the information is reasonably accurate, complete, and representative of reality?" Consider reports that assert that most computer hacking is committed by dishonest or disgruntled employees who have authorized access to information systems rather than by hackers or nonemployees operating from outside an organization. Should we believe such reports on face value, or inquire as to how the source reporting the information knows that *they* know this before we take any security actions to guard against

particular computer hacking threats? Here is another example: Some experts believe that sensational cybercrimes, such as online extortion, cyberstalking, and virus planting in sensitive government systems, are a small percentage of crime that occurs via the Internet. Other experts believe that most cybercrimes consist of theft of trade secrets and intellectual property and cellular phone fraud. Which sets of "facts" are we to believe, given our own limited basis of experience and naturally occurring bias? Can both sets of facts be true in the same period of time, or perhaps regarding different locations or among differing types of cybercrime victims? Is another set of crime "facts" also possible? What information about the source of information and method used to generate data, conduct analyses, and formulate conclusions would you as a criminal justice, information security, or IT administration professional want to know before deciding on a course of action pertaining to these crime issues?

For several reasons discussed later in the chapter, very few empirical research studies have been conducted of computer abuse, computer crime, or computer-related crime. Numerous studies have been conducted on computer ethics, most of which have asked convenient samples of college students to respond to hypothetical scenarios and choose from alternative possible courses of action. As of this writing, there has never been a large-scale, comprehensive general population study of cybercrime per se, substantially owing to confusion about what cybercrime is and how it can be systematically observed or asked about. In addition, police reports and crime-related databases typically do not contain specific or uniform information about technologies used to commit crimes.

In addition, computer crimes, computer-related crimes, and cybercrimes are not classified as specific violations of laws in the national UCR system, so they are not reported under these names even if distinctions between these social constructs of crime (as discussed in Chapter 1) were made at the operational level of reporting.

Moreover, computer abuse may or may not violate crime laws, consequently such lesser levels of illicit conduct have not been systematically incorporated into police reporting, much less systematically studied at the societal level in any depth. Consequently, what we do know about IT-enabled abuse and crime (i.e., "computer crime" in a conventional sense) is based on a relatively small set of empirical studies, some research by organizations that track attack and crime trends, and some economic impact studies usually done in connection with music, movie, or software piracy. Let us now consider several specific studies and sources of research-based information.

### 6.2.2 Overview of Major IT-Enabled Abuse and Crime Studies

As indicated above, our understanding of cybercrime as it occurs and continues to evolve throughout the world is based on a rather limited set of empirical studies, along with periodic reports generated by government, academic, or nongovernmental organizations (NGOs). In this subsection, findings from several of the most important available research studies conducted to date are briefly summarized. The goal here is to give you a sense of how and what is generally understood about computer abuse and computer crime came to be known through research beginning about 40 years ago, and how over time and especially since the late 1990s the number of studies have increased and collectively expanded in scope to document the nature and extent of crimes enabled by computers, other electronic IT devices, and the Internet. Note that the following set of studies, while among the most important ever conducted, should not be considered exhaustive because other studies involving relatively small numbers of respondents, nonscientific sampling procedures, and in consistent or otherwise unremarkable findings have also been conducted.

- In the mid-1960s, Donn Parker began following reports of computer abuse reported by the media, reported to law enforcement agencies, or that otherwise became known through informal means such as professionals reporting incidents at conferences on computing. As of 1976, he was able to report a mere 174 verified cases of computer abuse, plus another 200 instances that could not be verified. His analysis indicated an exponentially increasing trend in the number of reported or known instances of computer abuse, and he offered a dire warning of what was to come.[9]

- In 1984, the American Bar Association (ABA) completed the first national survey of computer abuse and crime. The organization surveyed approximately 1,000 private and public sector organizations (including *Fortune* magazine's list of the 500 largest U.S. corporations, numerous banking, accounting, financial services, and computer/electronics firms, all major federal government departments and agencies, all state attorneys general, and a sample of district attorneys) and concluded, among other findings, that (1) 48 percent of respondents (136) experienced known and verifiable incidents of computer crime in the preceding twelve months; (2) total losses reported by all 283 respondents ranged from $145 million to $730 million; (3) 39 percent of respondents (110) indicated that they had not been able to identify perpetrators of known computer crime incidents, while 78 percent of respondents (221) indicated that perpetrators were individuals within their organization; and (4) approximately one-third of respondents who experienced computer crime indicated that none of the known incidents were reported to law enforcement authorities.

- In 1984, the American Institute of Certified Public Accountants (AICPA) surveyed 5,127 banks and 1,232 insurance companies. Two percent of the banks (105) and the three percent of the responding insurance companies (40) reported experiencing at least one case of fraud related to electronic data processing in the previous 12 months. Sixteen percent of the frauds were reported to involve more than $10, and more than 80 percent of the frauds involved amounts under $100,000.[10]

- In 1985, President Reagan's Council on Integrity and Efficiency, having surveyed federal agencies, found 172 relevant cases of computer fraud or abuse ranging in costs from zero to $177,383, with the highest proportion in the $10,000 to $100,000 range.[11]

- In 1986, a survey of Forbes 500 corporations related to fraud and electronic transfer of funds estimated that banks nationwide lost $70 million to $100 million annually from automatic teller fraud. The study completed by O'Donoghue et al. of Mercy College, found that 12 banks reported 139 wire transfer fraud incidents within the preceding 5 years, with an average net loss (after recovery efforts) of $18,861 per incident. However, researchers concluded that the potential loss per wire transfer incident averaged nearly $1 million.[12] Further, 56 percent of respondents experienced losses by computer in 1984–1985, of which 85 percent were suspected of having been committed by insider employees. Average financial losses experienced by corporate victims were reportedly $118,932, and more than half the firms victimized did not report the incident to law enforcement.[13]

- In 1987, the American Bar Association, in a study of 300 corporations and government agencies surveyed, found that 24 percent reported having been the victim of computer-related crime in the preceding year, with losses ranging from $145 to $730 million.[14]

- In 1989, a study commissioned by the Florida Department of Law Enforcement surveyed 382 law enforcement agencies, 20 state attorney's offices, and 898 other public and private sector organizations, and reported that 25 percent of respondents (175) had been victimized by computer crime in the proceeding 12 months, and that monetary losses experienced by some organizations exceeded $1 million.[15]

- On the basis of another study conducted in 1989, this one of 1,766 undergraduate students at a Southern University that focused on academic dishonesty, and included questions about students software pirating and unauthorized accessing of computer account activities, Richard Hollinger found (and later reported in 1993) that a significant number of students admitted participating in computer-related deviant acts. Specifically, during a 15-week semester preceding the survey, 10 percent of respondents reported they had pirated software (4.1 percent only once and 1.5 percent 9 or more times); 3.3 percent of students surveyed had violated another person's account/files/privacy (50 percent of respondents who indicated affirmatively said they did it only once during the semester); and 11.1 percent reported they had committed one of these two offenses at least once, while only 2.1 percent were involved in both activities within the preceding 15-week semester. Hollinger also found that males were three times as likely as females to pirate software, and 2.5 times as likely as females to gain unauthorized access to a computer account; that older students more often engaged in software piracy, owing probably (in those days) to courses requiring their use of computers; and that married students, despite their ages, reported the lowest levels of illegal activity. Extrapolating from the survey data, Hollinger estimated that at the university surveyed there would be 3,500 instances of felony piracy and over 1,000 instances of illegal intrusions per semester.[16]

- In 1991, 3,000 virtual address extension sites located in North America and Europe were surveyed, resulting in 72 percent of respondents indicating a breach of information security during the preceding 12 months, of which 43 percent were criminal in nature.[17]

- In 1993, William Skinner and Anne Fream built on Hollingers's previous study to survey 581 students, again at a Southern U.S. university, this time with the intention of testing elements of social learning theory (discussed in Chapter 5). As such, this research represented the second self-report computer crime offending survey of college students, and the first time that a study was designed specifically to determine whether a particular criminological theory could explain the onset of computer-enabled offending behavior. Students were asked about their lifetime, past year, and past month offending behaviors in the following five areas: (1) software piracy, (2) guessing passwords, (3) gaining unauthorized access solely to browse, (4) gaining unauthorized access to change info, and (5) writing/using virus-like programs. Hypotheses analyses pertained to (a) differential reinforcement/punishment, (b) taking on definitions of (i.e., rationalizing) computer criminality, and (c) imitation—three of four key aspects of social learning theory (see Chapter 5). Data analysis revealed that 49.7 percent of respondents had committed one (or more) of the five behaviors listed above, causing researchers to conclude that social learning theory provided a strong conceptual framework for understanding the onset of computer crime committed by college students.[18]

- In 1996, David Carter and Andra Katz of Michigan State University conducted a national survey of 600 corporate security directors who were members of the American Society of Industrial Security (ASIS). More than 98 percent of respondents, as indicated in 151 returned and useable surveys, had been the victims of computer-related crime, and 43 percent were victimized more than 25 times, and most crimes were committed by insider employees. These researchers also found that intellectual capital (i.e., confidential business, customer and trade secrets, and new product plans) was the number one target of theft.[19]

- In 1999, Congress funded the National Center for Missing and Exploited Children to commission a National Youth Internet Safety Study. This study was completed by David Finkelhor, Kimberly Mitchell, and Janis Wolak of the Crimes against Children Research Center located at the University of New Hampshire. The research involved telephone interviews with 1,501

randomly selected youths ages 10 to 17 and their parents. These researchers found that 20 percent of youths surveyed were sexually solicited over the Internet within the preceding year, and 3 percent were either asked to meet the solicitor in person, received a telephone call, or were sent regular mail, money, or gifts. One in 4 youths were exposed to pictures of people who were either naked or having sex, and 1 in 17 was threatened or harassed online. One-fourth of youths victimized in these ways reported feeling distressed by the incidents, however less than 10 percent of sexual solicitations and 3 percent of unwanted exposure episodes were reported to the police, an Internet service provider, or a hotline service. About 25 percent of youths who were solicited for sex online, and 40 percent of those exposed to sexual material, told their parents. In addition, only 17 percent of youths and about 10 percent of parents could name a specific authority to report such incidents to, while one-third of parents in households with Internet access employed filtering or blocking software to protect their children from exposure to unwanted content.[20]

- In 1999–2000, following the National Youth Internet Safety Survey, Ilene and Michael Berson of the University of South Florida conducted an online survey targeting girls 12 to 18 years of age. The survey, hosted on the Web page of *Seventeen Magazine,* asked a series of questions pertaining to online behaviors and crime victimization. The *Seventeen Magazine* survey was later replicated on a New Zealand web site also popular among girls of the same age group, thus providing a comparison of 10,800 responses presumably from girls living in the United States with 347 responses presumably from girls living in New Zealand. Findings revealed that 30 percent of respondents from both nations spend at least 3 to 5 hours per week online, that 15 percent spend 12 or more hours per week online, and that with some differences, girls living in both nations spend approximately the same amount of time online. Researchers also found that 58 percent of girls spend most of their online computer time communicating via instant messaging or email, and that 16 percent primarily spend online time in chat rooms. Fifty nine percent of survey respondents to the U.S. *Seventeen* Magazine survey versus 34 percent of respondents to the New Zealand survey reported they had revealed personal information such as their name, address, date of birth, and school to people they had met online; 25 percent of girls in each survey reported having sent a picture of themselves to a stranger online; and 12 percent of United States versus 24 percent of New Zealand girls had agreed to meet a stranger they had met online in person or had actually done so. The study also revealed that although girls who had spoken with their parents about Internet safety were less likely to engage in risky behavior, girls older than 16 actually chatted and met with online with strangers in person much more often than did younger girls.[21]

- From July 2000 through June of 2001, the University of New Hampshire researchers mentioned above conducted another study of 630 police investigation reports of Internet crimes against persons under 18 years of age involving an arrest. During this year-long period, law enforcement agencies made an estimated 2,577 arrests for: (1) online-related sexual assaults and other sex crimes including production of child pornography (39 percent of arrests), (2) soliciting sex from undercover officers posing as minors (25 percent of arrests), and (3) possession, distribution, or trading of child pornography (36 percent of arrests). Researchers also found that 67 percent of offenders possessed child pornography, of which 83 percent were of children 6 to 12 years of age, and 80 percent depicted sexual penetration of minors. In addition, the majority of offenders were found to be white males, and 3 percent of offenders arrested were 17 years of age or younger. Of cases studied, 79 percent involved more than one investigating agency, state and local law enforcement agencies were involved 85 percent of the time, and federal agencies were involved 45 percent of the time.[22]

- In 2001 the Bureau of Justice Statistics, in collaboration with the U.S. Census Bureau, conducted a pilot study test for what may become an ongoing national survey of cybercrime against business. Results of the study revealed that of the 42 percent of 500 companies sampled (198 firms), 74 percent had been the victim of some type of cybercrime during the previous year. Specific cybercrimes specified in the study and identified by varying percentages of respondents as having been committed against their businesses included computer viruses infecting systems (64.1 percent), denial-of-service attacks (25.3 percent), and vandalism to a Web site or sabotage to internal systems data (18.7 percent). Responding representatives of many firms also reported being victims of embezzlement (4 percent), fraud (8.6 percent), and theft of proprietary information (6.1 percent).[23]

- In 2002, the Cyberspace Research Unit located at the University of Central Lancashire in Preston, England, completed a survey of 1,369 students ages 9 to 16. Questionnaires were administered to students at 10 schools in the Lancashire region of that country, and focused on computer supervision, use of Internet safety devices and adherence to safety guidelines, use of chat rooms, and exposure to sexual content and harassment via online chat. The study revealed that 68 percent of students regarded their school as their primary source of Internet safety instruction, that most had Internet access from their home computers, 28 percent of which were equipped with software content filters. However, 30 percent of respondents indicated they were able to disable the software filter, and many students reported engaging in unsafe chat with strangers online, often involving harassment or communications in which they had pretended to be several years *older* than they actually were at the time of the exchange.[24]

- In 2003, the Federal Trade Commission released a report of a major study on identity theft fraud indicating that 27.3 million Americans had been the victims of identity theft in the preceding 5 years, including nearly 10 million people within just the preceding 12 months. Reportedly these crimes cost businesses and financial institutions $48 billion and consumer victims over $5 billion in direct out-of-pocket expenses.[25]

- Beginning in April of 2004, the author and colleagues at the Rochester Institute of Technology and SUNY Brockport universities located in New York State conducted a series of four college student computer use and ethics surveys. This series of studies is notable because they all involved large sets of randomly sampled students, and asked large batteries of theory-driven questions pertaining to computer ethics along with offending and victimization-related behaviors. Several specific findings from the first of these studies involving 873 RIT students are reported throughout this book, and analysis of data collected in the other surveys is in progress.

## 6.2.3 Research by U.S. Organizations that Track Cybercrime

Several different U.S. government agencies and nongovernmental organizations now conduct research on the nature, extent, and impacts of cybercrime, as well as threats to information security systems. Notable organizations include the San Francisco regional office of the FBI in partnership with the Computer Security Institute (CSI), FBI headquarters in Washington, DC, in partnership with the National White Collar Crime Center (NWCCC) with funding from the Bureau of Justice Assistance (BJA), and the Computer Emergency Response Team (CERT) at Carnegie Mellon University in Pittsburgh. Similar organizations in other nations also conduct this type of research. In recent years there has been international cooperation to develop survey instruments and conduct analyses in order to provide comparable findings

about the extent of computer-enabled crimes in relatively high-tech nations. For example, the Australian Computer Emergency Response Team (AusCERT) conducts an annual survey modeled after the joint FBI/CSI survey conducted annually in the United States. Here is an overview of research activities conducted by key organizations based in the United States, along with contemporary findings about the extent of crimes and information security breaches committed with computers and/or via the Internet:

### 6.2.3.1 The CSI/FBI Computer Crime and Security Survey.
For several years the CSI, in partnership with the San Francisco regional office of the FBI, has conducted a survey of IT managers and information security specialists employed in government agencies, nongovernmental organizations, and private sector firms. The purpose of this annual survey is to raise awareness of information security issues and help measure the nature and extent of information security breaches experienced by organizations, and also shed light on the amount of computer-enabled crime occurring generally throughout the United States. In 2004 (the ninth study conducted by CSI/FBI) representatives of 494 such organizations responded to the survey to indicate, among other findings, that (1) computer hacking and trespassing appears to be declining, as are total losses resulting from breaches of information systems, and (2) organizational reporting of cybercrime declined, owing to concerns about the potential effects of negative publicity.[26]

The overall value of the annual CSI/FBI report is that it provides an overview of national cybercrime and information security trends from people who are in the business of fighting cybercrime and know what they are seeing and talking about. In previous years' studies, respondents have indicated that their combined fears of espionage committed by U.S. competitors, foreign competitors, and foreign governments are greater than their fears of independent hackers (e.g., external cyber attackers) or disgruntled employees (i.e., internal attackers of cyber and physical data). Of course such statistics belie conventional wisdom that stolen proprietary information is in most instances taken by insider employees with access to IT systems, plus the reality that cybercrimes, as explained in Chapter 2, may involve combinations of physical and cyber attacks launched from outside and/or inside an organization by more than one person, over periods of time, and against various locations housing hardcopy records or systems containing digitized records.

The annual CSI/FBI report is inherently limited because it does not seek a representative sample of cybercrime victims from the general population of computer and other IT device users. Instead, it provides a good overview of a somewhat broad although incomplete spectrum of cybercrimes and information security issues being experienced by organizations from the point of view of experts working within particular types of organizations to the exclusion of others (e.g., large firms, academic institutions, and health services and government agencies but not small businesses and nonprofit organizations). From a scientific research point of view, this is problematic because the respondents may be biased in their responses to questions asked, and they do not necessarily provide information about the full range and combinations of cybercrimes that are perpetrated against individuals not connected with the organization asked to respond to the survey. In short, the CSI/FBI report may best be regarded as a trend and consensus report about the kinds of cybercrime and information security issues that policymakers, executives and managers of organizations, and law enforcement and information security professionals should consider paying attention to.

### 6.2.3.2 The NWCCC/FBI Computer Crime Survey.
In 2004, the NWCCC, in partnership with the FBI, published its fourth annual Internet Fraud Crime Report, which is based on complaints received by the Internet Crime Complaint Center (IC3) of the NWCCC. The report revealed that complaints regarding fraud and

other types of financial crimes and cybercrimes had increased nearly 70 percent over 2003 numbers. Other general findings were that (1) fraud via the Internet was the type of cybercrime most frequently reported to the IC3 (71 percent of all complaints), with 15.8 percent of them stemming from nondelivery of merchandise and 5.4 percent the result of credit/debit card fraud; (2) check, phishing, and confidence game frauds accounted for the highest median dollar losses incurred by individual victims; (3) nearly 75 percent of known perpetrators were male; (4) most victims of cybercrime, as well as people who lost the most money and who reported cybercrimes to authorities, were male (for every $1.00 lost by a woman, a male victim lost $1.97); and (5) email and fraudulent Web pages were the two most common technological means of fraud.[27]

The annual IC3 report is very useful for tracking the extent of fraud committed via the Internet, gauging the extent of financial impact on victims of cybercrimes, and collecting certain information about both victims and perpetrators of some types of cybercrime. By examining proportions of the types of cybercrime complaints received, this annual report can also help determine priorities for cybercrime prevention policies, public awareness campaigns, educational or training programs, and so on. The report traditionally also provides information about the geographic locations and jurisdictions from which cybercrimes are perpetrated. For example, about 79 percent of all cybercrimes against U.S. victims in 2004 were perpetrated by offenders also located within the United States. Other countries of cybercrime origin mentioned in the 2004 study (in approximate figures) were Canada (3 percent), Nigeria (3 percent), Italy and the United Kingdom (2 percent each), plus Greece, Romania, France, Spain, and China (at 1 percent or less, and listed in declining order).[28]

The limitation of the IC3 report is that it relies on victims who are willing to report cybercrimes against them and who know about the NWCCC and the ways they can make a report to the IC3. Additionally, the report concentrates on financial crimes committed online, regardless of whether or how computers versus other types of IT devices were known to be used. The report does not include the many other types of computer abuse and cybercrimes known to exist, nor does it provide insights into the full range of known cybercriminals and the corresponding types of cybercrime victims. As such, the IC3 report is limited in ways similar to those of police report methods discussed earlier (i.e., it relies on voluntary reporting, arbitrary classification of crimes, nonrepresentative sampling, etc.).

### 6.2.3.3 *Carnegie Mellon University CERT Attack Tracking.* For several years the **Computer Emergency Response Team (CERT)** Coordination Center of Carnegie Mellon University has tracked and made available computer security vulnerabilities and fixes, data concerning types of attacks and intruder trends, and other useful information generally related to preventing cybercrime and improving information security. Each year, in addition to providing many other services, the Coordination Center publishes an annual report detailing its activities and providing an overview of the types of attacks and cybercrime threats relative to the overall state of information security capabilities in the United States. *The CERT Summary*, released on a quarterly basis, also disseminates information about Internet security issues. Many information security professionals wisely make it a point to stay abreast of the latest information, analytical findings, and security recommendations provided in this publication.[29]

As you have probably already deduced, ongoing analysis of attack and information security trends, as reported in periodic and annual reports by CERT Coordination Centers worldwide, provide insightful information that is potentially useful for preventing cybercrimes. CERT can also analyze types of attacks and their associated complexities and thereby make inferences about cybercriminals, including geographic regions throughout the world from which attacks are launched. However, the very purpose of the CERT centers, to routinely provide tactical and emergency information to security and investigation services, precludes their ongoing research and reports from advancing our strategic knowledge and understanding of cybercrimes, cybercriminals, or victims of cybercrimes in any comprehensive way. Currently, there exists no single government, academic, private sector, or nongovernmental organization with the capability and mission to provide such information. Consequently, understanding and managing continually evolving cybercrime requires periodic review of research reports produced by several different sources, including independent university researchers.

### 6.2.4 *Economic Estimates and Impact Studies of Cybercrime*

The purpose of **social and economic impact studies** is to determine the nature and extent of harm caused by illegal activity or other types of potentially harmful behaviors, actions, events, conditions, and so on. Economists employ several research methods and analytical techniques, often referred to as "modeling," to produce estimates of harm and to formulate conclusions for improving public policies, programs, and field practices. Typically this type of research involves (1) adopting a suitable theoretical framework to guide thinking about how to analyze a given situation, (2) making reasonable assumptions about the problem being studied, (3) collecting or generating data on several aspects of the issue, (4) quantifying certain key data in monetary terms, (5) conducting analysis using computers and special software to generate estimates of the economic impact on a given activity (e.g., crime or intervening enforcement strategy) would have on the situation, and (6) formulating conclusions and recommendations about what should be done to improve society overall especially with regard to economic efficiency.

Unfortunately, economic impact studies of crime, and therefore also cybercrimes, are notoriously difficult to conduct. In the case of cybercrimes and other broad constructs of crimes enabled with IT, this measurement difficulty is substantially due to definitional problems about what does or does not fit into a particular set of crime categories or type of violation needing to be measured. This fundamental problem has plagued the United States and international computer-enabled crime researchers for many years. Another major difficulty of determining precise or even reasonable estimates of harm involves acquiring reliable data about a given category or type of crime. Independent of definitional problems as we discussed in Chapter 1, crime data either already exists or it needs to be generated through original research of some kind. We have already discussed the limitations of police reporting, victimization, and offender studies. Yet another major hurdle is placement of crimes within times and places and with respect to reported costs of harm caused.

In June of 1990, Craig Neidorf, in connection with *Operation Sundevil*, was accused of publishing trade secrets and breaching confidentiality by publishing a document stolen by a hacker from the BellSouth telephone company. The document in question was transported across state lines, so federal prosecutors in this case attempted to prove that Neidorf had violated the interstate transportation clause of the U.S. Constitution. In order to do so, they needed to demonstrate the document was worth at least $5,000 and that it was "property" as defined by the Interstate Transportation of Stolen Property Statute. An expert witness from BellSouth testified that the document was worth nearly $80,000. However, upon cross examination, it was shown that the same document was available to the public for only $13 through a toll-free number operated by BellSouth itself. Subsequently, the criminal charges against Neidorf were dropped, to the embarrassment of BellSouth officials and federal government prosecutors.[30]

Can you see why a researcher considering whether or not to include the Neirdorf case in an economic impact study of intellectual and proprietary data theft could become perplexed? What value would the researcher assign to the property? For which geographic jurisdictions could the data be applied? Since the case was eventually dismissed, should it also be excluded from a study about the economic impacts of crime? How exactly should the researcher define "intellectual and/or proprietary data theft" for purposes of deciding which cases to include and how to differentiate findings pertaining to these concepts? In this subsection, we will consider economic estimate and impact studies regarding three categories of cybercrimes (i.e., white-collar crime, malware and piracy). Then, in Section 6.3, we will consider why research into the nature, extent, and harm caused by cybercrime is increasingly important despite recent improvements in the number and quality of studies undertaken.

### 6.2.4.1 White-Collar Crime.

In Chapter 1, we briefly considered how in the 1930s Edwin Sutherland conceived of white-collar crime. Throughout the decades that followed, numerous criminologists conducted studies of this crime construct and its costs to society. And for many years the NWCCC has been a leading advocate of policy and research on many aspects of white-collar crime. However, the fundamental challenge that researchers have always faced is how to precisely define this form of criminality and then locate and/or generate data to analyze, in order to produce findings regarding its specific costs, and related social and economic impact. Remember from Chapter 1 that the construct of white-collar crime encompasses many types of financial, organized, and computer-enabled crimes.

For this reason, researchers often focus their studies on a narrow aspect of white-collar crime, such as a type of financial crime, and then concentrate on one or more specific types of financial crime such as embezzlement, money laundering, or fraud. Similarly, researchers may examine a sub-category crime such as identity theft and narrow it down even further to examine specific types of fraud such as credit/debit card, check, disaster, medical services, or insurance fraud. As you can see from these examples, the focus may be on either an *industrial sector* such as insurance or medical services fraud, on an *environmental condition* such as disaster fraud or intentional illegal environmental pollution by companies and corporations, or on a *technological means* such as credit/debit card, check, or Internet-based fraud—all of which may involve use of computers or other types of electronic IT devices via the Internet, thereby constituting cybercrimes. Hence, the analytical challenge of measuring, or more likely estimating, the economic costs of white-collar crime as well as cybercrime is one of disentangling constructs and labels and data pertaining to these or other crime constructs of interest.

Despite analytical challenges, a number of studies have indicated that the economic impact of white-collar crime (a corollary to and indicator of cybercrime) during the 1990s varied from $40 billion to over $200 billion annually, while costs of computer-aided attacks on government and corporate networks ranged from $500 million to $8 billion annually.[31] In

---

**CYBER TALE 6.3**

## *A Worldwide Online Auction Scam*

A fraudulent email appearing to come from the online auction company eBay, informed account holders that they needed to resend their customer account information. The message looked authentic, contained a very formal legalistic header, and described how the auction firm needed to update its customer database. The email directed respondents to a Web site that featured the firm's famous logo. Information sought included the customer's name, address, credit card number, social security number, date of birth, mother's maiden name, and bank account information. The message was actually a clever way to systematically gather personal and financial information from millions of eBay customers.

A student serving in a co-op position remarked how the Chief Financial Officer (CFO) of the company fell for the scam and sent in the organization's account that had previously been used to make online auction purchases. Fortunately the student suspected the message was a scam and on his own initiative sent out an email warning everyone who worked in the company including the CFO. Within minutes of sending out the warning the CFO appeared in the doorway of the student's office "as white as ghost" exclaiming that he had made a terrible mistake!

Together they called the bank to cancel the credit card and other banking account information the CFO had provided to the fictitious look-alike auction site and thereby managed to prevent what otherwise would surely have resulted in credit card fraud.

The incident led to a formal thanks to the student, who was also sworn to secrecy so that all the other employees in the firm would not know what a "dunce" the CFO had been. However, this exact type of email periodically resurfaces on the Internet, distributed to current, former and non-eBay customers alike. NEVER provide this type of personal or account information without first validating that the party making the request is legitimate. Reputable firms that sponsor online purchasing programs usually maintain explicit policies and procedures against contacting their customers in the manner described above. If however, you receive a message like the one sent to the CFO, you can normally easily verify that an actual problem related to your account exists before providing information by contacting the firm in a manner other than that requested in the email message received. What do you suppose the worldwide social and economic costs of online auction fraud such as occurred in this incident may amount to? What factors would you include in a study of this type of cybercrime?

1997 it was reported that while conventional bank heists totaled approximately $60 million annually (an average of $7,500 per incident) and have a conviction rate of over 80 percent, total losses from bank-related thefts enabled by computers can range from $500 million to $10 billion annually, net an average of $250,000 per incident, and result in less than 2 percent of offenders getting caught.[32] Additional statistics on specific types of white-collar crime, including but not limited to credit card fraud, disaster fraud, health care fraud, identity theft, insurance fraud, money laundering, organized crime, and telemarketing fraud, may be found on the home page of the NWCCC (listed in Appendix A).[33]

***6.2.4.2 Malware.*** The economic impact of malware, particularly damage resulting from release of viruses and worms onto the Internet, may be overcoming the costs associated with other types of cybercrime such as credit card fraud and copyright infringement. Damage caused by computer viruses and worms may be exacerbated by the ubiquity and relatively homogenous design of today's computer networks, operating systems, and software applications that allow the malware to spread quickly until control measures are developed and implemented.[34] In January 2003, cyber attacks from worms and viruses numbering almost 20,000 cost a record $8 billion in damages throughout the world.[35] One security firm estimated that worldwide combined costs of the Slammer, Blaster, and Sobig malware programs unleashed during 2003 were $82 billion.[36] According to officials at Computer Economics in Carlsbad, California, costs associated with cleanup and lost productivity brought on by other high profile computer viruses and worms include:[37]

- Explorer (released in December 1998): $1 billion
- Melissa (released in March 1999): $1.2 billion
- Love Bug (released in May 2000): 50 variants hit more than 40 million computers and cost in excess of $8.7 billion

- Code Red (released in July 2001): infected more than 1 million computers and cost $1.1 billion in clean-up costs and $1.5 billion in lost productivity
- SirCam (released in July 2001): infected more than 2.3 million computers and cost $1.035 billion.

The world cost of responding to computer viruses and worms may quickly be approaching the total cost of all other cybercrime combined. Responding to the "I Love You" virus, allegedly written by a student in the Philippines, cost somewhere between $1 and $10 billion worldwide. Although identified, the student was not prosecuted because he did not break any laws in that country. Thus, failure to create and enforce relatively standardized computer crime laws negates potential deterrent effects of apprehending and punishing those who write and release malicious code onto the Internet. Rapid widespread damage to computer systems as the result of malware released on the Internet is aggravated further by the homogenous nature of today's computer networks, combined with insufficient protection policies, procedures, and practices within a majority of firms and agencies, as well as the desire by many creators of malware to realize profits in addition to wreaking havoc.[38]

***6.2.4.3 Traditional Piracy and Illegal File Sharing.*** Early cost estimates of software piracy and component theft increasingly occurring via the Internet ranged, as reported in 1995, from $7 billion to $24 billion worldwide annually.[39] In 1995, Dorothy Denning reported that "the Software Publisher's Association identified 1,600 bulletin boards carrying bootleg software and estimated that $7.4 billion worth of software was lost to piracy in 1993; by some industry estimates, $2 billion of that was stolen over the Internet."[40] With the increase in attention being paid to illegal peer-to-peer file-sharing since the debut of Napster in late 1999, one would imagine that plenty of research has been performed on

**CYBER TALE 6.4**

### *What is the Economic Impact of Spam?*

Spam is very annoying for some people and may be considered a form of harassment if steps required by law are not taken to prevent someone from receiving unwanted messages. As the result of the CAN-SPAM Act of 2003, consumers living or conducting business within the United States must now be afforded the ability to opt out of receiving spam by any U.S. firm that sends it. Nonetheless, spam continues to be a huge problem for many individuals, some businesses, academic and other nonprofit organizations, government agencies, and ISPs whose computer network and service capacities are often excessively affected by massive amounts of unsolicited email sent through their systems. According to MessageLabs, Inc, which specializes in tracking spam and helping companies prevent and eliminate spam-related systems problems, two-thirds of all electronic messages sent to their 8,500 client firms in April of 2004 was unsolicited commercial email.

Another firm, Postini Inc., which also monitors email in connection with the Internet and computer-related services it provides to its customers, often tracks over 200 million messages in a single business day. Postini Inc. officials reported in a Congressional hearing in May 2004 that 83 percent of emails it filtered for mostly U.S. clients was spam, an increase of 5 percent since January 2004, when the CAN-SPAM Act went into effect. According to the Anti Spam Research Group, spam costs every individual computer user between $30 and $50 per year. Firms however, lose an estimated $730 in productivity for every worker who uses unfiltered email.[41]

Yet depending on the capabilities of particular filtering applications in use, computer users may still be required to mentally process at least the name of the sender and subject title of the email before deciding whether or not it is really spam, or an important message the filter mistakenly interpreted as spam. To what extent is your work affected by spam? Do you use spam filtering software? Do you think estimates of the costs associated with spam are correct? Do you think the economic impact of spam on firms varies according to the type of organization and technological aspects of information systems used, among other factors? Which other factors do you think would need to be considered in a comprehensive economic impact study of spamming?

---

the economic impact of p2p file-sharing.[42] In fact, several studies of the economic impact of traditional pirating and more contemporary illegal file sharing have been undertaken. On the basis of these studies, many key players in the entertainment and software development industries who are rightfully concerned about copyright protections have claimed that piracy, broadly defined, is responsible for billions of dollars in damages worldwide. The Motion Picture Association of America (MPAA) claims losses totaling $3.4 billion in 2004, with expected losses of $5.4 billion in 2005.[43] Similarly, the Business Software Alliance (BSA) claimed that global losses in software sales totaled $13.08 billion in

2002,[44] and the International Intellectual Property Alliance (IIPA) claimed that $2.5 billion was lost in music sales worldwide during 2004, not including the United States.[45]

Unfortunately, studies of the economic impact of software pirating and illegal file sharing either lump electronic or so-called **digital piracy** together with **traditional piracy** or, as with the MPAA figure above, fail to consider digital piracy at all.[46] This is problematic because although traditional piracy and digital piracy are often thought about together and referred to as being one-and-the-same thing, they are qualitatively different activities. Both traditional piracy and contemporary digital piracy violate copyright laws in some way.

However, traditional piracy, stemming from its origins in pre-Internet computing years (look back at section 3.1.5), typically involves illegal acquisition and selling of a copyrighted work via a tangible medium such as a computer disk. Electronic or digital piracy is different, because it normally occurs over the Internet and does not involve a simultaneous exchange of money for a tangible item containing copyrighted materials. Hence, we have the concept of illegal "file sharing," in which massive amounts of copyright-protected materials are being simultaneously exchanged nearly free among millions of computer users located throughout the world versus a comparatively smaller number of traditional pirates who are physically limited in their ability to exchange data on disks in-person in particular places.

An important analytical challenge, which has important implications for cybercrime prevention and enforcement efforts, is to distinguish between data on these two basic forms of piracy and also measure their economic impact when it may be impossible to accurately determine how much theft is occurring via either technological means. To address this issue, researchers investigating traditional and digital piracy of songs or movies have, on the one hand, often assumed in designing their studies that every song track or movie exchanged on the Internet represents a lost CD or DVD sale in a retail outlet. However, this assumption does not control for potentially the vast majority of file sharers, who would not pay to listen to the music or to see the movie. (In studies conducted by the author at RIT during the 2004–2005 academic year, it was found that approximately 40 percent of students surveyed would not pay a cent for any song or movie if they were able to illegally download it for free off the Internet.) On the other hand, researchers who do not make this assumption cannot establish a precise positive or even negative correlation between illegal file sharing of copyrighted works and declining retail sales. It may be possible, for example, that illegal file sharing has undetermined advertising benefits that are not considered in economic modeling studies of the issue.

To support this possibility, file sharing enthusiasts periodically point out that Hollywood is realizing unprecedented profits on new movie releases,[47] even though the majority of profits from many movies derive from post-release sales of DVDs and VHS tapes, not from movie theater showings. Music files may be different. Some people who acquire illegal copies of music files do so in order to screen the songs or artists and then buy a given song or CD if they like what they hear. Given human nature, and the fact that most file sharers are young people, often in college and who have limited financial resources,[48] would you agree that these somewhat honorable individuals are probably few and far between? Most observers of this important crime-related problem agree that illegal file sharing probably accounts for a good deal of lost music and software sales revenue, especially in the case of traditional or digital software piracy in which users typically install an application and forget about the disk or file until their system crashes and they need to reinstall the program. Here again, from an analytical standpoint, it is very important when designing economic impact research studies to differentiate technological means for traditional versus digital piracy and relate these to differing market commodities and consumer preferences. Observing a decline in music sales following the onset of illegal p2p is not the same as verifying that the drop in sales was fully caused by this form of cybercrime, as enabled with *legal* p2p technology. Other still largely unexplored combinations of technological, social, and economic factors could be contributing to various forms of piracy occurring throughout the world in ways not currently understood.

Consequently, researchers have come to very different conclusions about these issues. For example, researchers in one study who observed real-time downloading behavior concluded that p2p music piracy actually had no significant net impact on the music industry.[49] In contrast, researchers in another study (without any measurement of actual downloading behavior) claimed that p2p music piracy explained the entire drop in recent music sales.[50] The majority of economic impact studies, however, indicate that illegal p2p file sharing has some impact on the affected software and entertainment industries, the result of a combination of various economic and social factors.[51] On balance, the economic impact of illegal p2p file-sharing of music, movies, and software appears to be of several kinds, but the relative effects of specific contributing factors have not been clearly and comprehensively determined. Thus, pirating as a form of cybercrime appears to have important negative social and economic consequences for society—although at this stage of investigation researchers disagree on fundamental issues of definition, methodology, and analysis all of which can affect specific findings and conclusions about the nature, extent, and economic impact of traditional and/or digital piracy.

Although many college students and others benefit personally from not paying for music acquired by illegal p2p file sharing, allow me to ask, How would you like to be the person who loses his or her job in a music store because of declining sales revenue? Would it matter to you whether or not the real loss in revenue could be scientifically attributed to digital piracy, traditional piracy, or any other type of criminal activity? The truth is that any type of music, movie, or software piracy, as with all crimes, tends to benefit those who violate the law while causing either direct, indirect, or tertiary harm to law-abiding individuals, groups, and organizations. The larger and in some ways more fundamental question that social and economic impact studies attempt to answer is, Who is harmed, how, and how much? In the area of illegal p2p file sharing of any type of copyrighted materials, as well as several other types of cybercrimes, substantially more research is needed in order to answer such questions accurately.

THIS IS OUR METHOD FOR IDENTIFYING ILLEGAL FILE SHARERS: THE DARTBOARD ALGORITHM

## 6.3  Why Research the Nature and Extent of Cybercrime?

Since the nature of crime continually evolves with technology, and we cannot on a permanent basis articulate what "it" is in precise terms for legal, public policy, and crime prevention and control purposes, why bother trying to research its existing nature, extent, and harmful impact on society? Does it really matter how much computer abuse or cybercrime occurs, to say nothing of incremental or even radical technological changes in its nature? Does it also really matter what the various types of harm and associated costs of cybercrime are? After all, cybercrimes are bound to continue to occur and evolve, and we have already indicated major problems associated with reliably estimating amounts of primary, secondary, and tertiary harm attributable to crime. Is it not more important to concentrate on protecting information systems and investigating and prosecuting cybercrimes regardless of how they are defined, how much occurs, and what the estimates of harm are? Moreover, given the enormity of cybercrime issues, how can we comprehend what is known with certainty about variations of crime enabled with computers, other electronic IT devices, and via information systems occurring in a given time and place?

Vexing questions such as these are not easy to answer, and they indicate why some researchers and most practitioners since the first computer abuse in 1958 have advocated not getting hung up on labels.[52] Instead, many scholars and criminal justice and security professionals argue for doing the best research possible with available resources while getting on with the important business of fighting crime regardless of why it occurs or what it is called. Given the technologically evolving nature of cybercrime, this is a perfectly understandable attitude and a respectable position to take if you are willing to ignore, accept, and perhaps even help perpetuate confusion surrounding the dynamic technological aspects of IT-enabled crime and its effects throughout society. This section summarizes the general state of research on cybercrime and suggests several specific types of research that could improve our understanding of IT-enabled crime and help us to manage and potentially prevent more of it.

### 6.3.1  The General State of Research on Cybercrime

How much cybercrime is there, and what is its social and economic impact on society? All research indicates there is plenty to go around. Since the early 1940s innumerable studies have sought to measure aspects of emergent interrelated crime constructs, including white-collar crime, financial crime, organized crime, computer crime, economic crime, computer-related crime, and corporate crime. More recently we have seen efforts to qualify and quantify measures for so-called digital crime, electronic crime, Internet crime, and of course cybercrime. As discussed in this chapter and elsewhere throughout the text, social constructs, terms, and labels for crimes involving the same or similar behaviors and technology confound efforts to uniquely and systematically provide estimates of the extent and impact of illegal activities. Today, notwithstanding many important contributions of qualified researchers and the ongoing efforts of several reputable government agencies and nongovernmental organizations, there remains relatively little scientific research on new incidences, overall prevalence, rates within varying populations, causes, and correlates of crimes involving computers and information systems or on individuals who choose to commit crimes with computers and/or other types of IT devices. In short, the state of empirical research and general body of literature pertaining to these issues are extremely limited.

Research testing specific criminological theories to determine causes and correlates of illicit, unethical, abusive, and/or criminal use of computers is very rare and tends to involve convenient samples of college students. As indicated above, the first known study of this type was undertaken by Hollinger, who in 1989 surveyed

1,766 undergraduate students about their giving or receiving pirated software and accessing another person's account or files without the owner's knowledge or permission.[53] This was followed in 1993 by an expanded study conducted by Skinner and Fream, who also found that a substantial amount of computer abuse and crime occurred on college campuses and that key aspects of social learning theory provided a reasonable general explanation for computer crimes inclusive of software piracy.[54] In 2004, McQuade and Castellano built on these studies with the first in a series of surveys conducted at RIT, the first of which is often referred to in this book (see for example, Table 6.1 pertaining to computer-related victimization experiences of college students). However, virtually no studies of a general population have yet been published that take into account the theoretically complex phenomenon of cybercrime, operationalized as activities in which computers or other electronic IT devices are used to facilitate illegal or socially abusive behaviors via the Internet.

Generating reliable statistics of cybercrimes is hindered by inconsistent conceptualizations and flawed research methodologies.[55] Indeed, "estimates of financial losses due to technology abuse vary widely, depending on what forms of abuse are considered, and how much underreporting by corporations (and other types of victims) is assumed."[56] It has also long been known that most companies are reluctant to report cybercrimes to law enforcement for fear of losing public confidence or exposing weaknesses in their information security.[57] Other major reasons for the lack of data and research on crimes committed with computers or other types of IT devices include: (1) the priority given to violent crimes by public officials and victim advocacy organizations; (2) relatively indifferent attitudes of many police and prosecutors to nonviolent crime; (3) the technical and intimidating nature of crimes committed with computers and other IT devices; (4) easy treatment of cybercriminals by courts even when prosecuted; (5) the inadequacy of training for police officers and security professionals to recognize

and respond to, and adequately investigate cybercrimes; and (6) the ever-changing capabilities of computers and those who abuse them.[58]

It is especially difficult to measure the prevalence of cybercrime in nations that do not have laws explicitly prohibiting such behaviors or that lack officially sanctioned reporting methods such as the UCR system and NCVS used in the United States. Even countries that do employ such methods for tracking crime do not adequately update them to include underlying technological changes in the nature and extent of crime, changes which may pose significant threats to organizational, community, state, or even national security. It is generally believed, for example, that a substantial portion of transnational financial crime constituting economic and security threats to many regions throughout the world originates in former Soviet Bloc countries such as Ukraine, Russia, and the Baltic States. Such crimes can be attributed to a number of factors: (1) organized crime groups looking for ways to broaden their sphere of influence, (2) the lack of a mature model for policing such crimes and the resources to support it, (3) the resulting lack of fear of apprehension and retribution, (4) the vast pool of potential victims, and (5) the ease with which financial resources can be transported around the globe.[59] As supported by a growing body of research being undertaken by independent scholars, and sometimes supported by government, non-government, and private sector organizations, there is every reason to believe that losses associated with computer abuse and cybercrime are significant and increasing. Yet research mechanisms for routinely and systematically measuring these losses are virtually nonexistent.

Research in social science issues, including studies of crime, seeks to answer questions about the nature, extent, and impact of problems faced by society. Through research and better understanding of crime combined with IT-related issues, we are better informed to enact cybercrime laws and regulations, formulate public policies, and initiate programs that make sense for cybercrime prevention and control and to develop better technologies for protecting information systems. However, in the absence of good science, we are destined to muddle through trying to prevent cybercrime and deter and arrest cybercriminals even as political tensions increasingly influence definitions and regulation of perceived crime-related threats, and as groups seek to exert control over Internet usage for their own purposes. Given the conceptual confusion about the offending behaviors of cybercriminals (as discussed in Chapter 4), as well as victims of cybercrime and the extent of harm incurred as the result of cybercrime, what ought criminologists to do?

### 6.3.2 Types of Research Needed on Cybercrime

Future research on cybercrime issues needs to be informed by what David Wall has referred to as **"new criminologies"** that would further and explicitly combine criminology with other fields of study such as sociology, geography, and psychology.[60] As stressed throughout this book, cybercrime requires understanding crime, technology, victimization and myriad attendant issues from the perspectives of accounting, biology, business management, computer sciences (inclusive of software engineering and IT and database administration), criminal justice, criminology, cultural anthropology, economics, ethics, security facilities and risk management, history, human services and social work, information security, legal studies, political science, psychiatry, psychology, public administration, public policy, research methods, sociology and statistics. This suggests by the way, possibilities for college students to major or minor in any of these subject areas and focus their independent research on cybercrime-related issues.

As a point of departure, it may be useful for officials to convene a national forum leading to widespread adoption of a definition of cybercrime such as the one used throughout this book: crime committed with computers or other electronic IT devices via information systems (which includes

intranets and the Internet). In the process, officials could perhaps settle on using a single overall container label such as *cybercrime* to the exclusion of other terms (e.g., digital crime, electronic crime, or Internet crime) on the basis of less rigorous theoretical underpinnings. The 2001 Computer Security Survey undertaken by BJS which specifically examined cybercrime against businesses, is a very useful step forward, but in the long run only to the extent that other crime labels and terms are used consistently, especially by other federal agencies involved in conducting or sponsoring criminological research.[61] Why is BJS conducting a national survey program on "cybercrime" while its sister agency, the National Institute of Justice (NIJ) is managing a research program on "electronic crime" while yet another sister agency, the Office of Juvenile Justice and Delinquency Prevention (OJJDP), is funding child exploitation research via the Internet? Each of these federal government agencies are components of the Office of Justice Programs (OJP), and headquartered in the same building in Washington, D.C. They are sponsoring needed research, but inaccurate conceptualization or inconsistent terminology used by leading federal criminal justice research agencies is confusing to researchers, criminal justice and security practitioners, and to the media and public.

Realistically, it may not be possible to settle on one label and a single definition for cybercrime because, as we have discussed, many terms for IT-enabled crimes have already been adopted and are now used interchangeably by several invested individuals, groups, government agencies, and other types of organizations. This is a conundrum that dates to Donn Parker's early research during the 1960s on computer abuse. On the one hand, labels and terms must be definitively operationalized in research. On the other hand, crime evolves technologically, implying that labels and definitions need to be flexible and are inherently limited by categorization issues such as those discussed in Chapter 4. Recall that fitting crime, offenders, or victims into one category versus another is, in the final analysis, subjective. Numerous respected scholars have called attention to these challenges.

Beyond conceptualization, definitional, and labeling challenges, society needs far greater understanding of the causes and correlates of crimes committed with computers and other types of IT devices, whether networked or not. This need extends to greater understanding of the direct, indirect, and tertiary impact and harm experienced by individual, groups, and organizational victims of cybercriminals. Given the specter of transnational crime enabled with IT and transportation technologies, and the potential threat of cyberterrorism, both of which pose threats to national security, sponsors of research are compelled to expand conventional notions of crime in order to explore and understand potential causes, correlates, and harmful impact of increasingly complex and integrated forms of criminality. Research methods for determining the *nature of cybercrime* and the harm it does would include attack analyses, historical analyses, survey and interview-based research, ethnographies (e.g., of the hacker subculture), and secondary data analysis to determine on a comprehensive basis what is already known, and the underlying strength of the science through which it was determined. Methods for measuring the *extent and amount* of harm caused by cybercriminals would include victimization studies, police reporting system studies, self-reports by perpetrators of computer abuses and cybercrimes, and economic impact studies following close examination of the types of harm and associated policy-related variables required for incorporation into analyses of the problem. Increasingly, and to the extent that crime poses national security threats, it may also be appropriate to consider merging research capabilities of criminologists with those in analytical components of federal law enforcement, intelligence, and defense agencies. After all, and as discussed in Chapter 3 with respect to information age conflict (see Figure 3.1), the nature of cyber threats to society spans legal authorities and responsibilities of local, state, and federal government agencies.

Society also needs much better understanding of why IT-enabled crimes occur as they do and why individuals are drawn to use certain technological devices and methods to violate the law. Criminals have always learned to use available technologies by adopting simple to complex tools and techniques to their needs. But we actually know very little, about how cybercriminals select technologies and the potential criminogenic effects of computers and other relatively high-tech gadgets. Is it possible that electromagnetic emissions produced by high-tech gadgets affect human decision-making in adverse ways that contribute to criminal behaviors? Does hiding behind a computer rather than confronting a victim in person embolden cybercriminals? If so, what specific personality and psychological traits do these individuals possess and how could our knowledge of these be used to increase crime deterrence? What technological factors contribute to the adoption of tools and techniques by criminals? If such factors could be identified, what are the potential implications for cybercrime investigations, crime prevention education, healthcare intervention, professional ethics training, and information security management? These and many other questions, too numerous to list here, go to the heart of better understanding and managing cybercrime through research. Much work remains. Indeed, we have hardly begun to truly understand IT-enabled crime, those who abuse IT, or the social and economic impact that cybercrime has on society.

## 6.4 Summary

Each year millions upon millions of individuals become victims of cybercriminals; millions of businesses, not-for-profit organizations, and government agencies also experience attacks on their computer systems and other crimes involving computers. Often such cases involve employees or other trusted insiders who have access to the organization's computer system, or outsiders who hack into systems or defraud people using computers online. Incidents range from unauthorized and relatively innocuous "data snooping" to theft of trade secrets resulting in myriad social and economic costs throughout society.

Computer abuse and cybercrime such as these, and many other types of crime involving computers, other types of electronic IT devices and information systems result in primary, secondary, and tertiary victimization and associated harm. Whereas primary victimization involves direct harm to individuals, groups, or organizations, secondary and tertiary victims experience indirect harm as the result of incidents in which they were not targeted. So-called victimless crimes, such as using illegal drugs or illegally sharing movie or music files, indirectly harm, everyone in society who must in some way bear the costs associated with market prices for technology upgrades, government regulation, and law enforcement. Harm may be caused to data and other types of property, and range in financial value. Harm may also be emotional or psychological in nature and have negative social or professional impact. Physical harm may be the indirect result of cybercrimes, as in instances of cyberterrorist attacks on critical information infrastructures that result in systems and facilities damage and injury to people.

Guesstimates about the amounts and impact of specific types of white-collar crime and cybercrime are legion. In truth, no one knows how much cybercrime exists or what the full range and costs of negative impact is. Moreover, research methods for establishing the full social and economic impact of cybercrime are not well developed and largely unproven. Generally speaking, there is a scarcity of reliable research throughout the world pertaining to the nature, extent, and impact of cybercrime and threats to information systems. For example, it is currently impossible to determine or even accurately estimate the amount of malware created and released onto the Internet or the extent to which its intended effects actually take place. Mechanisms to provide this type of tracking and analysis simply do not yet exist. The relatively weak state of empirical research on cybercrime is due in part to cybercrime being an international phenomenon as opposed to just a domestic crime problem. Its influences can be felt to varying degrees around the world in relatively more or less computerized nations.

Given the perpetually enabled technological dynamics inherent to the invention and innovation of cybercrime, combined with varying worldwide stakeholder interests, reliable methods and mechanisms for undertaking research on cybercrime will be difficult if not impossible to develop, implement, and administer in consistent ways. Nonetheless, all nations have infrastructures in need of protection, and increasingly these are of the critical information infrastructure variety that are susceptible to malware attacks, and so on. In recent years our understanding of cybercrime and threats to information systems has begun to improve through the efforts of independent researchers and those employed by organizations such as CERT, the FBI, CSI, and the NWCCC. Often working collaboratively, these and other organizations have added specific types of information to a handful of scientific studies that currently comprises a very thin body of empirical research on IT-enabled crime issues.

To adequately understand cybercrime as it exists today *and will exist in the future,* much more needs to be understood about its underlying technological characteristics combined with human factors involved in its commission. To understand the interplay of technology and human factors in evolving high-tech crime is to truly understand what cybercrime is, versus what it is *not.* In the absence of such an understanding, people are apt to accept mere rhetoric and sensationalism as an accurate portrayal of new forms of crime. This, combined with a lack of understanding of history, will compromise our ability to understand what society can and should do to address computer abuse, cybercrime, and threats to information security.

## Key Terms and Concepts

Computer Emergency Response Center (CERT), 203
Crime victimization, 186
Data, property, and financial losses, 190
Digital piracy, 207
Emotional and psychological harm, 190
Harm, 187
Carnegie Mellon University CERT Attack Tracking, 203
CSI/FBI Computer Crime and Security Survey, 201

NWCCC/FBI Computer Crime Survey, 202
New criminologies, 212
Physical harms, 190
Police crime reporting, 193
Primary victimization, 187
Secondary victimization, 188
Self-report offender studies, 195
Social and economic impact studies, 203
Social, professional, and organizational harm, 192
Tertiary victimization, 188

Traditional piracy, 207
Uniform Crime Report (UCR) system, 193
Victim, 187
Victim blaming, 192
Victimization surveys, 194
Victimless crimes, 189

## Critical Thinking and Discussion Questions

1. Find an online news article detailing a cybercrime and the financial losses incurred as a result. Write a short summary of what happened and explain what impact it had on the victim(s) of the crime.

2. Write a short essay about a cybercrime incident you know about. Explain what happened and the types of primary, secondary, or tertiary harm experienced by the victim(s). Comment on whether you think the victims were well served by criminal justice officials or information security professionals with whom they interacted during or after the incident.

3. List, explain, and provide examples of the three major ways that crime is measured in the United States.

4. Describe major challenges and potential pitfalls associated with conducting research into the nature of a crime phenomenon (e.g., the types of abuses involved, who the offenders are, and why they violate the law).

5. Describe major challenges and potential pitfalls associated with measuring the extent of crime (e.g., how much of it exists, in what forms, and where).

6. Explain the basic differences between studies that examine the nature, extent, and economic impact of crime.

7. Locate and read a research report on the nature, extent, or economic impact of computer abuse, computer crime, or computer-related cybercrime. Describe the basic methodology used to generate findings. Then comment on what the report does not address, and how reliable and valid you think the findings and conclusions of the study are. Finally, discuss whether you would consider making policy or program changes in a criminal justice agency or security firm on the basis of the research.

8. Do you believe current methods for tracking and reporting cybercrime are accurate? Why or why not? What if anything do you believe could be done to make tracking and reporting of cybercrimes more accurate? Explain your answer in terms of specific things the government, academia, and private or nonprofit sectors can do.

9. Locate IT-enabled crime statistics for your city or state (many local and state police agencies provide these online in the form of annual reports). Describe what you found. Explain the implications of your findings.

10. Visit the Bureau of Justice Statistics Web page at www.ojp.gov (search for the Bureau of Justice Statistics in the OJP pull-down directory window). Locate and summarize available statistics on IT-enabled crime. What do you conclude? What are the implications for criminal justice and security managers and policymakers?

## References and Endnotes

1. Warner, B. (2004, January 29). Net crime gangs hit gambling sites. London: Reuters. Retrieved November 5, 2004. from http://seclists.org/lists/isn/2004/Jan/0091.html.

2. O'Brien, Timothy L. (2005, August 7). The rise of the digital thugs. *New York Times*. Retrieved August 11, 2005 from http://www.nytimes.com/2005/08/07/business/yourmoney/07stalk.html?pagewanted=1&ei=5088&en=ae9a5df12bf889d9&ex=1281067200&partner=rssnyt&emc=rss

3. BBC Staff Author (2004) Users face new phishing threats. London: British Broadcasting Company, World Edition. Retrieved November 11, 2004, from: http://news.bbc.co.uk/2/hi/technology/3759808.stm.

4. Smith, T. (2001). Hacker jailed for revenge sewage attacks. Register.com. Retrieved June 11, 2004, from http://www.theregister.co.uk/2001/10/31/hacker_jailed_for_revenge_sewage/.

5. Isikoff, M. (2004). Missing: a laptop of DEA informants. *Newsweek*. Retrieved November 5, 2004, from http://www.msnbc.msn.com/id/5092991/site/newsweek/.

6. National Archives and Records Administration. (2004). Facts on demand. Retrieved March 1, 2004, via http://www.archives.gov/index.html.

7. McQuade, S., & Schreck, C. (2005). Correlates of Cybercrime Victimization. Manuscript in progress. Rochester Institute of Technology.

8. Finkelhor (2000).

9. Parker, D. B. (1976). *Crime by Computer.* New York: Charles Scribner's Sons.

10. U.S. Congress (1987). Defending Secrets, Sharing Data: New Locks and Keys for Electronic Information. NTIS No. PB88-143185). Washington, DC: Office of Technology Assessment.

11. U.S. Congress, 1987; see note 9.

12. U.S. Congress, 1987; see note 9.

13. Cited by Hollinger, R. C. (1993). Crime by computer: correlates of software piracy and unauthorized account access. *Security Journal, 4*(1), 2–12.

14. United Nations Commission on Crime and Justice. (1997). *Manual on the Prevention and Control of Computer-Related Crime.* New York: United Nations.

15. Herig, J. A. (1989). *Computer Crime in Florida 1989.* Tallahassee: Florida Department of Law Enforcement.

16. Hollinger, R. C. (1993). Crime by computer: Correlates of software piracy and unauthorized account access. *Security Journal*, Vol 1, No. 4, pp. 2-12.

17. United Nations Commission on Crime and Justice, 1997; see note 13.

18. Skinner, W. F & Fream, A. M. (1997). A social learning theory analysis of computer crime among college students. *The Journal of Research in Crime and Delinquency, Vol 34,* No. 4, pp. 495-519.

19. Carter, D. L., & Katz, A. J. (1996). Trends and Experiences in Computer-Related Crime: Findings From a National Study. Paper presented at the annual meeting of the Academy of Criminal Justice Sciences, Las Vegas, NV.

20. Finkelhor, David;Wolak, Janis;Mitchell, Kimberly (2000, June). *Online victimization: A report of the nation's youth.* Washington, D.C.: National Center for Missing and Exploited Children.

21. Berson, I. R. and Berson, M. J. (2005, Spring). Challenging online behaviors of youth: Findings from a comparative analysis of young people in the United States and New Zealand. *Social Science Computer Review, Vol 23,* No. 1, pp. 29-38.

22. Wolak, J.; Mitchell, K.; Finkelhor, D. (2003, November). *Internet sex crimes against minors: The response of law enforcement.* Washington, DC: National Center for Missing and Exploited Children.

23. Bureau of Justice Statistics (2004). *Cybercrime Against Business: Pilot Test Results, 2001 Computer Security Study.* Washington, DC: U.S. Department of Justice.

24. Cyberspace Research Unit (2002). *Young people's use of chat rooms: Implications for policy strategies and programs of education.* Report to Subgroup F, Home Office Internet Task Force. Preston, England: University of Central Lancashire.

25. Synovate (2003). *FTC Identity Theft Survey Report.* Washington, DC: Federal Trade Commission.

26. Computer Crime Research Center (2004). *Computer Crime and Security Survey.* San Francisco: Computer Security Institute/FBI.

27. Internet Crime Complaint Center (2004). *IC3 2004 Internet Fraud: Crime Report.* Washington, DC: National White Collar Crime Center/FBI.

28. Internet Crime Complaint Center, 2004; see note 20.

29. CERT Coordination Center (2005). CERT home page. Retrieved March 5, 2003, from http://www.cert.org/.

30. Godwin, M. (2004). When copying isn't theft: how the government stumbled in a "hacker" case. Retrieved July 18, 2004, from http://www.eff.org/IP/phrack_riggs_neidorf_godwin.article.

31. Gill, M. S. (1997). Cybercops take a byte out of computer crime. *Smithsonian, May,* 114–124.
    Libicki, M. C. (1996). Protecting the United States in cyberspace. In Alan Campen, Douglas Dearth,

and Thomas Goodden (Eds.). *Cyberwar: Security, Strategy and Conflict in the Information Age.* Fairfax, VA: AFCEA International Press. Charney, S. (1992). Justice Department responds to the growing threat of computer crime. *Computer Security Journal, 8*(2), 1–12; and Cook, W. J. (1989). Thefts of computer software. *FBI Law Enforcement Bulletin, 58*(12), 1–4.

32. Borchgrave, A. D. (1997). Electronic bank robbers flourish. *The Washington Times*, April 21

33. National White Collar Crime Center. (2005). NW3C home page. Retrieved March 27, 2005, from http://www.nw3c.org/.

34. Bace, R., Geer, D., Metzger, P., Pfleeger, C. P., Quarterman, J. S., and Schneier, B., et al. (2003). CyberInsecurity: the cost of monopoly. Retrieved March 12, 2004, from http://www.ccianet.org/index.php3.

35. Mi2g Ltd. in Greenspan, R., & Gaudin, S. (2003). 2003: year of the worm? Retrieved March 14, 2004, from, http://www.clickz.com/stats/big_picture/applications/article.php /1301_1577811.

36. Thompson, C. (2004). The virus underground. *New York Times*. Retrieved November 10, 2004, from http://www.nytimes.com/2004/02/08/magazine/08WORMS.html?ex=1100235600&en=e27d746ecc37cfcb&ei=5070&oref=login.

37. Reuters Staff Author (2001, August 31). Virus costs skyrocket: coping with computer attacks tops $10 billion. CNN America, Inc. Retrieved November 11, 2004, from http://www.cs.nmt.edu/~cs491_02/IA/viruscost.htm.

38. Bace, R., et al., 2003; see note 27.

39. Sussman, V. (1995). Policing cyberspace. *U.S. News & World Report*, January 23.

40. Denning, D. E. (1995). Crime and crypto on the information superhighway. *Journal of Criminal Justice Education, 6*(2), 323–336.

41. Sullivan (2004) #72785.

42. U.S. Congress (2004). Peer-to-peer piracy on university campuses. An update hearing before the Subcommittee on Courts, the Internet, and Intellectual Property of the Committee on the Judiciary. House of Representatives 108th Cong. Retrieved from http://judiciary.house.gov/media/pdfs/printers/108th/96286.PDF.

43. Motion Picture Association of America (2004). MPAA studios take action against major p2p server operators to stem global movie piracy. Retrieved February 24, 2005, from http://www.mpaa.org/CurrentReleases/2004 12 14 WwdeP2Actions.pdf.

44. Business Software Alliance (2003). Eighth annual BSA global software piracy study. Retrieved February 8, 2005, from http://www.bsa.org/globalstudy/2003 GSPS.pdf.

45. International Intellectual Property Alliance (2005). IIPA 2003-2004 estimated trade losses due to copyright piracy. Retrieved March 7, 2005, from http://www.iipa.com/pdf/2005 Feb10 LOSSESAMERICAS.pdf.

46. Motion Picture Association of America, 2004; see note 37.

47. Motion Picture Association of America (2002). Valenti reports record-breaking box office results, continued decrease in production costs and praises movie industry war efforts in ShoWest address. Retrieved March 9, 2005, from http://www.mpaa.org/MPAAPress/2002/2002_03_05a.htm.

48. Jones, S., & Lenhart, A. (2004). Music downloading and listening: findings from the Pew Internet and American life Project. *Popular Music and Society, 27*(2), 185–189.

49. Oberholzer, F., & Strumpf, K. (2004). The Effect of File Sharing on Record Sales: An Empirical Analysis. Unpublished Manuscript, Harvard Business School, Cambridge, MA.

50. Liebowitz, S. J. (2003). Will MP3 downloads annihilate the record industry? The evidence so far. University of Texas at Dallas, Department of Finance & Managerial Economics. Retrieved March 10, 2005, from http://papers.ssrn.com/sol3/papers.cfm?abstract_id=414162.

51. Boorstin, E. (2004). Music Sales in the Age of File Sharing. Unpublished senior thesis. Princeton University.

Hui, K., & Png, I. P. L. (2002). *Piracy and the Legitimate Demand for Recorded Music*. National University of Singapore, School of Computing. Retrieved March 10, 2005, from http://ssrn.com/abstract=262651; Peitz, M., & Waelbroeck, P. (2004). The Effect of Internet Piracy on CD Sales: Cross-Section Evidence. *CESifo Working Paper Series No. 1122*. Retrieved March 10, 2005, from http://ssrn.com/abstract=511763; Rob, R., & Waldfogel, J. (2004). Piracy on the High C's: Music Downloading, Sales Displacement, and Social Welfare in a Sample of College Students. NBER Working Paper No. W10874. Retrieved March 10, 2004, from http://ssrn.com/abstract=612076.

52. Parker, D. B. (1976). *Crime by Computer.* New York: Charles Scribner's Sons.

53. Hollinger, R. C., 1993; see note 17.

54. Skinner, W. F., & Fream, A. M., 1997; see note 19.

55. Wall, D. (2001). Cybercrime and the Internet. Chapter 1 in David S. Wall (Ed.), *Crime and the Internet* (pp. 7–8). London: Routledge.

56. Sivin, J. P., & Bialo, E. R. (1992). *Ethical Use of Information Technologies in Education: Important Issues for America's Schools.* Washington, DC: National Institute of Justice.

57. National Research Council (1991). *Computers at Risk: Safe Computing in the Information Age.* Washington, DC: National Academy Press.

58. See Collier, P. A., & Spaul, B. J. (1992). Forensic science against computer crime in the United Kingdom. *Journal of the Forensic Science Society, 32*(1), 27–34; Carter, D. L., & Katz, A. J., 1996; see note 16.

59. Goodman, S. E., & Sofaer, A. D. (2000). The transnational dimension of cyber crime and terrorism. Retrieved February 8, 2004, from http://www-hoover.stanford.edu.

60. Wall, D., 2001; see note 47.

61. Bureau of Justice Statistics (2004). *Cybercrime against Business: Pilot Test Results, 2001 Computer Security Study.* Washington, DC: U.S. Department of Justice.

# 7

# *Emerging and Controversial Cybercrime Issues*

## *7.0 Introduction: How is IT Creating New Opportunities for Cybercrime?*

In what ways and to what extent do computer systems affect the lives of your family, friends, coworkers, and other members of society? Do you personally rely on computers for academics, online chat or entertainment, or to manage your financial affairs? How about your friends? Do they generally use computers about as much and for the same types of things that you do, or do they use computers differently? Do you or your friends prefer using Macs, while others insist on using PCs? Would you consider yourself a relatively casual user of computers, or are you more of a "power user" who multitasks, using a number of software applications simultaneously for different purposes? What about at your place of employment? Who uses computers, for what purposes, and how proficient in their use of applications and ability to help protect your organization's computer network are they? Take a minute right now to think about the preceding set of questions. Then read the next paragraph which poses several additional questions for your consideration.

Do you spend a good proportion, perhaps too many hours each day, using computers to browse and connect with others in cyberspace? Do you know an Internet junkie who seems to prefer working alone or with others via computers rather than interacting with them offline? When you connect, what sort of information do you seek? Are you concerned about too much information about you or others you know being available on the Internet and the potential for violations of privacy? What if any are the types of computing activities do you regard as being unethical? Regardless of the amount of time you spend using computers off and online and your personal sense of computer ethics, do you think of yourself simply as someone who uses computers, or do you consider yourself a "netizen" of the cyber realm with certain rights and responsibilities while interacting in and/or out of cyberspace? Do you advocate for or protest against controversial computer-related issues? If you do, can you sense yourself being pitted against other stakeholders possessing interests different from your own? How do you feel about people who engage in computing activities or hold attitudes toward computing that are different than your own?

These questions represent several important issues underscoring the essential goal of this chapter, which is to establish a broader social and political context for understanding computer ethics, IT-enabled deviance and abuse, and cybercrime. This information is provided as a foundation for thinking about the formulation of laws and regulations and managing and preventing cybercrime that begins in Chapter 8 and continues through Chapter 10. How and why we use computers and other electronic IT devices, conceive of cyberspace, spend time and interact with others in the cyber realm, and our sense of computer ethics has much to do with the overall type of computer users we are and whether we comply with computer-related social norms and laws, as well as our expectations of others in these regards. These issues also affect whether we consider cyberspace to be either (1) a civil place through which interactions and transactions of all sorts can occur securely and for the mutual benefit of everyone involved or (2) a "wild" space in which information residing on systems or being exchanged is up for grabs by anyone who is technically capable and motivated to deny, manipulate, steal, or destroy it.

In this chapter, we will initially focus on computerization as the force and means through which civil society is steadily being transformed into cyber society and how this transformation is providing new motivations and opportunities for cybercrime. **Cyber society** consists of everyone who uses computers or other types of electronic devices to connect to the Internet for any purpose. This includes people of all races, ethnicities, and creeds who are young or old, healthy or unhealthy, rich or poor, and powerful or disempowered; individuals with all levels of education; people who work in low-, medium-, or high-tech jobs; plus people who, regardless of being connected at a particular moment, also use computers offline and occupy tangible spaces to engage in required living activities such as eating, sleeping, and other physical activities. Thus, although cyber society has primarily to do with technological interconnectivity rather than tangible places, it mirrors and is inseparable from people and their activities in the real world. Increasingly the opposite is also true: all of our lives are affected by computers, and this in turn makes each of us relatively more or less exposed to being victimized by cybercriminals who also operate on and offline depending on the nature of their planned or ongoing attacks on information systems and other criminal activities. Remember, as discussed in earlier chapters, cybercrimes are often carried out over long periods of time by insiders and/or outsiders with varying levels of SKRAM, against tangible and/or cyber assets, via physical and computerized means. (Take a quick look back at the threat analysis cube depicted in Figure 2.2, and the combined potential of cybercrime crew members as depicted in Figure 4.2).

To understand the worldwide cyber society, we will first consider the emerging potential for computer abuse and cybercrime in several contexts, specifically in academic research and education, online banking and e-commerce, meeting and courting significant others online, issues pertaining to IT–enabled democratization, and other social interactions and tracking of people. Next we will discuss controversial cybercrime-related issues and stakeholders with respect to the hacker subculture, the open source community, electronic gaming enclaves, and the online legal pornography movement. Here again emphasis is given to explaining these issues in relation to opportunities for cybercrime and therefore to potential cyber environments through which we may become victimized unless adequate safeguards are in place. In the process, we will explore the differing interests, concerns, and activities of various stakeholders including government agencies, industrial sector and professional membership associations, and nongovernmental organizations (NGOs). This discussion is supported by a list of key cyber stakeholders in Appendix A. Through such organizations, people like you and me help define social norms, establish legal rights, and through civic interactions, help enforce, reinforce, or challenge laws and regulations related to computing activities on and offline. This introduction will provide the foundation for thinking about how to manage and prevent cybercrimes and threats to computers, other IT devices, and information systems discussed in Part III of the book.

## 7.1 Emerging Potential for IT-Enabled Abuse and Cybercrime

Computers have changed "how we work and play, how we get information, how we interact with our neighbors (even how we define our neighborhood), and how we organize our family lives."[1] Clearly computerization has resulted in many new opportunities for cybercrime. When there were only a few computers, there could only be a few computer criminals, and relatively few victims of cybercrime. When computers were relatively more technologically simple, computer-enabled crimes were also comparatively simple. Computerization, however, has introduced technological and social system complexities that present new, increasing, and more challenging types of threats to the computer systems on which modern societies rely. In this section, we will explore several emerging cyber-social activities and trends that have particular implications for new variations of older forms of IT-enabled deviance, abuse, and crime.

### 7.1.1 Transformations in Academic Education and Professional Training

Today's college students are among the **N-generation**, the first to have grown up with computers being an integral aspect of their lives.[2] Many college students in their early twenties report that at the age of seven or even younger they were the primary users of their household computers.[3] For this generation, computers were also typically used in their primary and secondary schools often by students as well as teachers. As recalled by one undergraduate student, when he was a ninth grader in high school he reported every morning to a computer-based homeroom for daily announcements. Today at the Rochester Institute

of Technology the author teaches Web-enhanced classes in so-called smart rooms that have multimedia technology permanently installed and support either wired or wireless Internet connectivity.

Professional training and certification courses also use IT to full advantage, as when computer-enabled "shoot–do not shoot" simulation technology is used to train police and security officers in appropriate instances of applying deadly force in tactical situations. Additionally, as the result of technology R&D throughout society, we are creating a generation of technologically savvy workers capable of assuming innumerable positions in government, private, and not-for-profit sectors that increasingly require basic computing skills. As knowledge begets new knowledge with IT, so too are newer forms of IT invented and innovated in what once again is evidence of perpetual innovation of technology inspired by competition. The effect is seemingly unstoppable growth in the creation of new information, as well as unprecedented access to it—all the result of interconnected databases, faster and more affordable computing technology, easier to use software applications, and larger memory storage capacities, as well as increasingly easier access to high bandwidth Internet connections for data transmissions between more and more capable users, and so on.

The positive effects of computerization in academia have been nothing short of phenomenal. I cannot imagine writing this book, conducting research, teaching courses, or communicating effectively with my students and colleagues throughout the world without my laptop computer.

However, we should not allow ourselves to be carried away by the obvious benefits of computers to education, research, and training. Remember our fundamental rules about technology: In addition to being continually developed, it can be used for either good or evil and has positive as well as negative unintended consequences. In other words, technology helps us solve problems but also creates new problems that need solving. In academia, for instance, I have observed among students an increasing tendency to

"Google" exclusively when conducting research for papers and other assignments rather than also read traditional and oftentimes more reputable hardcopy resources not available online.

Many students also seem never to have learned how to compose in non-chat/email speak, as evidenced by term papers written in cyber vernacular. The convenience of IT has also created in new opportunities for students to cheat on examinations and assignments in rather clever ways and for unscrupulous tenure-track professors under pressure to "publish or perish" to plagiarize or fake research if left unchecked. Faculty also benefit from Google™, among other search engines, which now offers a scholar's version that filters out nonacademic search results. Broadband Internet connections available through university computer servers also enable, for instance, illegal downloading of music, movie, and application files by unethical faculty and staff as well as students. The main point is that academic transformations enabled by IT have provided new opportunities for cyber-related deviancy, abuse, and crime, several which we discussed in Chapter 3.

### 7.1.2  Online Banking and E-Commerce

Many computer users shop online for virtually every kind of commodity including expensive items such as computer equipment and even automobiles. I purchased my current home as the result of first seeing photographs of it on the Internet. At the time (in 2001), video tapings downloadable off the Web were also being used by realtors to show the inside and outside of homes and businesses. Perhaps, however, you know people who are reluctant to buy goods online, even from established and reputable catalog or auction companies such as Amazon.com, Cabellas, or eBay, or from popular retail outlets such as Old Navy, Target, or Nike? Do you also know people who may periodically shop online but are fearful of online banking or of managing

their credit cards online, or with computers at all, preferring instead to keep track of their finances with a paper checkbook? As we have already learned, people have preferences for using technology, and this is of considerable importance when trying to understand the likelihood of someone committing or being vulnerable to a particular form of cybercrime or information system attack.

When it comes to online banking and e-commerce, people have a right to be suspicious, if not also fearful, about the security of their credit cards and other personal information. After all, IT has been used for decades, and long before there were computers, to defraud, cheat, and steal. Today cybercrimes involving compromised financial records occur with regularity and are reported by the media, often in sensational ways. This situation can be considered in different ways. On the one hand, such media reporting raises awareness and may increase prevention of cybercrimes involving financial account data. On the other hand, fears about online shopping and banking may be overblown, given today's increasingly standardized security precautions, combined with public awareness of precautions that need to be taken. Even popular Internet service providers (ISPs), as well as retailers, banks, and other types of firms now advertise security services they provide for their online customers, even as hardware and software developers continually improve upon and standardize technical solutions for information security.

Did you know, for example, that if your Internet browser uses standard encryption (and it probably does), any information you send to a secure Web site is encrypted? This means the chances of your data being intercepted and read by someone are fairly slight. Your data could be intercepted and unencrypted with considerable time and effort, but few cyber criminals have this capability and even fewer would go to the trouble of singling out your message to attack among billions of messages sent over the Internet each day. Further, who would go to all the effort to steal one credit card number when some e-commerce companies make the mistake of storing all their customer financial information unencrypted in their databases? Moreover, as you have already learned, most cybercrimes are believed to be committed by insider employees or other individuals who have physical access to computers and cyber access to information systems housing valuable data.

If this is true, why are so many people fearful of banking or buying things online? Well, as indicated above, everyone's financial information always has been and always will be vulnerable to misuse by unscrupulous employees of banks, other types of financial institutions, and retail firms who have access to the computer systems on which it is stored. Data is also vulnerable to attacks from outsiders who have the capability of hacking into computer systems. Unfortunately a number of e-commerce companies exacerbate this situation by irresponsibly using otherwise reputable database software, as when their system administrators install applications but do not bother to change default passwords and other default settings for which security exploits have been developed. Consequently, the contents of some consumer information databases are susceptible to being stolen, manipulated, or otherwise compromised by anyone who can access the data and is familiar with the default password settings used by software development firms.

Thus, many people remain afraid of shopping online because they fear having their credit card number and/or other personal information stolen. Do you think their fears are valid? Did you know that, periodically, ATM machines located in obscure locations are altered with card reading devices? These gadgets appear to be an integral part of the ATM but in fact are external battery-powered attachments fitted to the swipe mechanism in order to double-read and record your card's data. In addition, a video camera records you punching in your PIN. Then crooks who may have been watching you the entire time retrieve the device

immediately (or within a day or two) in order to extract your credit/debit card information and use your PIN to commit credit card fraud and/or clean out your bank accounts using the same ATM that you successfully withdrew money from earlier.[4]

Some people who have no objection to buying things with credit cards in person, over the telephone, or via "snail mail" simply do not trust the Internet, even though, as you will recall from Chapter 2, the wires and routing terminals that make the transaction connections possible are exactly the same and components of the nation's critical information infrastructure. Credit card receipts are frequently stolen from retail establishments or fished out of trash dumpsters. Any devious manager, clerk, waiter, or other employee can simply jot down a customer's name and credit card information from a transaction receipt that is either kept for record-keeping purposes or discarded (rather than being shredded). Earlier in Chapter 2 we read about just such a case involving a couple who, after vacationing in Puerto Vallarta, Mexico, returned home to receive a credit card statement showing false purchases evidently committed on the basis of their account information becoming known via hardcopy records of their hotel stay. Employees who are dishonest and technologically savvy can accomplish the same thing by using a card swiping device that stores data for later retrieval or they can create fictitious identification or purchasing cards, although this is somewhat more difficult (review Cyber Tale 4.4, SKRAM needed to create and use fake IDs).

Clearly shopping and banking online involve some hazards, but they are probably just as safe as conducting financial transactions in other ways, provided consumers take adequate precautions (discussed in Chapter 10) and ensure that the firms they deal with do also. Under federal law, consumers are only liable for the first $50 of a fraudulent transaction involving a credit card, regardless of the purchasing transaction method (i.e., via online, telephone, mail, or in-person purchasing). Hence, there are actually good security reasons to make certain purchases with a credit card whether online or in person, and some fears about participating in online banking and e-commerce on the basis of information security may be misplaced. Consumers ought to be just as concerned about receiving quality goods purchased online as they are about the security of their personal and financial account information during or after an online or in-person transaction.

The transnational and cyber nature of the financial services industry places all of us at some risk; a pound of healthy awareness combined with a cup of suspicion and a dash of fear is always in order when money is involved. After all, the safety of the distributed operating platforms used by multinational financial institutions is often difficult to ensure even by the IT professionals responsible for maintaining such systems.

## CYBER TALE 7.1

### Benefits and Risks of Online Auctions

In the summer of 2003 a college student really wanted a particular cell phone and he found it for sale on a popular online auction site. He set his maximum bid at $225, knowing that it retailed for over $400. Because the auction allows other people to see, on the basis of an email link, who is bidding when and how much, it is possible to contact other bidders directly. In this case the student was contacted by a third party who offered to sell him an identical phone for $185, claiming that it was a wholesale surplus item he acquired through a "going out of business sale." The student expressed interest and doubts, and he insisted that if such a sale were to take place it would need to occur through the auction site and that the seller would need to provide a receipt.

Evidently the seller, sensing he had a live one to con, empathized with the student and then offered to sell him three phones at a group discount of $360 (i.e., $120 per phone) but only if a direct sales agreement were settled on because the seller did not have the time or patience to fool around with online auctions. This was too tempting an offer. The student reasoned that he could buy three phones for $360, keep one for himself, and sell two for approximately $400 each, thereby profiting over $440 minus shipping expenses. The student was not about to be taken, so he agreed to send a money order for $128 (the price of one phone plus $8 shipping) in order to inspect the product, after which, if everything worked

satisfactorily, he would pay the balance and the seller would send the remaining two phones.

Twenty days, $128, and thirty emails later the student realized he had been conned, so he became a cyber sleuth and found a phone number he believed to be that of the seller, who apparently lived in another state. The phone number turned out to be for a woman who lived in the same building as the seller, and she told the student that she had been receiving lots of calls from people complaining that they had not received their cell phones and other merchandise. The student called the police in the city where the seller and the woman lived and filed a complaint. The local detective took down all the information and asked the student to provide a copy of the original online sales agreement and emails exchanged with the seller.

Weeks later the detective informed the student that thanks to his complaint an investigation uncovered a cyber fraud ring so big that it was turned over to an FBI computer crimes task force. The detective gave the student contact information for the lead investigating FBI agent, who he tried to call several times to determine the status of the case and request that restitution be ordered by the court in the event of a conviction. Unfortunately the FBI agent reportedly never returned the phone calls or emails made by the student, who then felt victimized by both the seller and the criminal justice system despite his own greed and lack of judgment.

This, coupled with increased mobility of individuals' assets, increases opportunities for financial crimes to be committed at the systems level. That means inadequate technological safeguards and cyber laws may reduce the viability of and competitiveness in global banking and e-commerce markets because investors and consumers alike will be reluctant to accept heightened risks of doing business under such circumstances.[5]

### 7.1.3 Meeting and Courting Significant Others Online

Most people have or at least desire a special someone to share their lives with at least for a time, if not permanently as in marriage or civil union. For most of us the desire for a significant other begins in early dating years and depending on circumstances may last for many years or begin anew following the death of a spouse or loved one, divorce, and so on. Unfortunately for millions of people, professional or personal circumstances interfere with meeting and beginning a long-term relationship with someone compatible. Fortunately for many of these people, computers and computer-based dating services can now be used to encounter interesting people and establish relationships online that may lead to long-term in-person friendships or more. Many people who are now in long-term relationships report how they initially met online and then eventually met in-person, fell in love, and created new lives together. However, meeting and courting online is not without risks, and many people have become crime victims as the result of socializing online.

People who go online in search of companionship may be vulnerable for several reasons including a strong desire for a new relationship, the natural tendency to want to be appealing to others, and the need to share personal information with relative strangers in the course of establishing a new relationship. They may also be inexperienced using computers and thus unaware of the threats posed by interacting online. However, even people not seeking new friends and associates online may find themselves being harassed, threatened, or even cyberstalked for any number of reasons (review descriptions of these forms of cybercrime in Chapter 3). Just as when making online purchases, when developing relationships online, certain precautions are in order. Here are three stories about college students that illustrate what can go wrong when striking up online relationships.

A female student and her girlfriend were bored during summer break, so they decided to cruise online for a couple of "hotties." Through a dating service they found two guys who were also college students in upstate New York. Eventually, after sending the obligatory photos and so on, the couples decided to meet. After driving a long distance, the two girls ended up meeting with "a couple of old fat farts who were smelly and missing teeth." This story raises the need to ensure that if you use an online dating service, you understand the firm's privacy policies and information security practices, as well as personality profiling analyses often advertised for no or a low introductory fee. Reputable dating service firms will to the extent possible validate in several ways the actual existence and truthfulness of individual customers' profiles before referring customers to each other, or allowing customers to participate in online communications through sponsored chat rooms even if offered through secure Web sites. In addition, reputable dating services will at a minimum take affirmative steps to safeguard personal information provided by customers about themselves for relationship matching purposes, as well as customer financial account information and transactional data such as that involving credit card purchases for personal profiling or relationship matching services. However, online dating services are generally not regulated by government agencies, do not consistently subscribe to professionally established standards for information security, and generally have detailed disclaimers of liability regarding unauthorized access of personal or financial data provided by customers, as well as harm experienced as the result of interpersonal interactions stemming from communications brokered by the dating service.

Considerable numbers of online relationships are established, however, without the assistance of online dating services, as in our second example, in which two malicious female students decided to go online and pretend to be gay men. Eventually their pretense resulted in arranging for a gay man to show up at an uninvolved girl's house for a date with her unsuspecting dad. In this case, the girls were very disrespectful of the other girl and her father, not to mention the gay individuals they interacted with online before pulling off the prank. Some online relationships end neither humorously nor without consequences. Often this has to do with the greater potential for deceit inherent in online as opposed to in-person interpersonal relationships. In February 2005, a Jordanian man and his wife, who had separated and began separately to search for new romance on the Internet each found someone intriguing whom they eventually decided to meet with in preparation for getting married. When they actually did meet after three months of courting online, they discovered their new lovers were each other! Immediately the man accused the woman of cheating, and she called him a liar. The episode sealed their divorce.[6]

In our third example, a very attractive female student, who was an accomplished violinist, found herself chatting online with other musicians about instruments they played, favorite songs, groups they played in, and so on. Unbeknownst to the student, one of the chatterers began socially engineering her into describing in more detail what she thought her particular talents were and where she thought she could improve. Typical of these kinds of scams, the chatter conveniently turned out to be a violin instructor who just happened to live in the same area as the student and would give her some pointers if she came to his studio. To make the offer more attractive, he said he would even have his wife prepare a little brunch and would invite an orchestra conductor

he knew to listen to her audition for an upcoming musical. Such a fortuitous opportunity was too good to pass up. When the student got to the man's house, located three hours away, his wife was not there and his friend the conductor had called to indicate that he was running an hour late. So the student began playing her violin for the man to get some pointers. Naturally there came a point where he had to hold her a little from behind in order to demonstrate what she could do differently, and it turned out that the pointers she needed were how to escape from being accosted! She was so rattled by the experience she never reported the incident to the police and has never again chatted online.

In my view this student was lucky not to have been raped or seriously injured. What could she have done differently to avoid placing herself in this situation? Do you think you could be socially engineered into doing something similar, especially if enough intelligence about you and aspects of your life were developed overtime in indiscernible ways? Remember that the urge to establish relationships, and the need to get things done with and through other people, periodically results in all of us being in positions in which we need to simultaneously trust and distrust people as well as the technology we use to interact with them.

## 7.1.4 IT-Enabled Democratization

Millions of people without access to computers are not able to fully participate in cyber society and therefore are also limited in their ability to either commit cybercrimes or become cybercrime victims. However, IT is increasingly enabling people to learn about and participate in democratic processes in tangible civil and cyber societies in unprecedented ways. In this subsection, I will briefly describe the emerging phenomena of Internet blogging, smart mobs, and electronic voting as evidence of IT-enabled democratization, while explaining how these new forms of communicating online and civic participation may be creating new opportunities for cybercrime.

**CYBER TALE 7.2**

### An Obsessive Cyber Spooning Love Affair

Most online relationships tend to wither and fade after a month or so because of the amount of effort needed to maintain interest, often in the absence of an initial in-person interaction. However, in this instance a student called "Gabriel" was able to enjoy an online relationship for several months because he invested an inordinate amount of time online chatting with his new-found love. Early mornings, late nights, skipped meals and classes, neglected showers . . . anything and everything was given lower priority so he could spend extra time "cyber spooning" with his darling. This was good for him and her, but not for his friends, who had to put up with his negligence, odd behavior, and poor hygiene.

One day several months later "Luke" was in the common area of a college dorm complaining to another friend "Lance" about Gabriel's progressively worsening obsession with his cyber love. Since Lance was Gabriel's roommate, he knew all about the cyber love affair and was both concerned about and irritated by Gabriel's behavior, which included making everyone late to class or other appointments on more than one occasion because of his obsessive online chatting. As Luke and Lance continued to complain and wonder when and how it might all turn out they spotted Gabriel's laptop on a nearby table. Guessing the password for Gabriel's computer took only minutes since it was predictably merely a modification of his girlfriend's name.

What began with relocating Gabriel's desktop application shortcuts to obscure directories on his computer escalated to several more severe forms of tampering and harassment including (1) creating a screen-shot of the desktop devoid of shortcuts to give the impression that the desktop had ceased to function, (2) changing the AOL instant messenger password so Gabriel could not chat with his girlfriend, and (3) configuring browser bookmarks to erroneously point to pornographic Web sites while also signing Gabriel up to receive electronic and hardcopy newsletters from various sex-oriented groups. The latter led to rumors about Gabriel's sexual preferences, and this resulted in new and more insidious forms of harassment from a number of other students as well as online spam and suggestive emails from strangers.

As you may have guessed, I am "Lance" and I eventually came clean with Gabriel after he broke up with his girlfriend and got really mad at me. What we both learned from this experience has to do with respecting others in relationships involving computers, realizing that compulsive behavior involving computers can take many harmful forms, and that online relationships can affect those in the physical realm and vise versa. Additionally, no one can be completely trusted to not violate computer privacy and therefore use of strong passwords is absolutely essential if you wish to be secure in your computing.

*Anonymous Student*

### 7.1.4.1 Blogging for Crime and Justice.
**Blogging** is a form of unedited, online, real-time journalism carried out by one or more people as they observe and/or participate in real-world newsworthy activities and events. For example, a person may "blog" a baseball game or convention by getting online, typically with a laptop computer or other portable electronic device such as a PDA with a keyboard, to report that she or he is "in the middle of things and here is what is happening." Reporting by one person may inspire reporting by other bloggers, who ordinarily have little or no interaction with each other, even though they are covering the same event. In many ways bloggers are like mainstream media reporters, except that their product combines the benefits of text reporting with live broadcasts.

The result is a written record of news events produced in real time, but that can be added to by readers who may be getting other news about the same or related events through different media. Imagine a situation in which you are reading a blog online about an unfolding sporting, political, or terrorist event while watching a CNN television report about the same event. Then you have your own thought about what is happening, or about circumstances reported by CNN but not thus far reported in the blog, so you decide to update the blog with your own thoughts and other information. The logic behind this new form of reporting is the collective analysis of raw unfiltered news provided by as many people as possible. The potential risk lies in not having established rules pertaining to confirming news stories before airing or printing them for public consumption.

When coupled with links to other Web sites, digital photos and video recordings of events, the effect can be striking for individuals who prefer to get their news online and unedited rather than through conventional edited newspaper, radio, or television reporting. In addition, since blogging reports can be cataloged and responded to in real time by recipients, online streams of consciousness can emerge in ways that produce real-time analysis and public reactions to the news events being reported. In other words, when people get their news from blogging reports, they can also respond with reactions, make requests, and offer interpretations of their own, thus becoming part of a breaking news story. Hence, we have a new form of real-time collective journalism in which participating members of the cyber society help in the production process and may also inspire rapid reactions and responses not limited to people who are online for the original reporting.

Special software tools and service providers now support blogging for a variety of personal and commercial purposes by telecommunications, public relations, and financial management firms. Blogging services also now exist to aid in the exchange of criminal justice information between investigators of law enforcement agencies. The Western States Information Network (WSIN), for example, provides blogging forums used by West Coast local, state, and federal law enforcement agencies to post onto the Web unrestricted or sensitive information in real time about ongoing investigations. WSIN was founded in 1981, and until recently communications between investigators were restricted to email and a secure intranet, both of which had certain technology disadvantages for field officers (e.g., having to wait for a Web master to post all incoming messages). Blogging software now enables officers to post messages and file attachments (e.g., mug photos) directly to a searchable, confidential and secure forum in real time and also provide analysis and remarks, thereby collectively assisting in a variety of different types of investigations including but not limited to those of cybercrimes.[7]

Any subject, event, or person is subject to being blogged about, and every type of digitized data can be posted (legally or illegally) onto a blog, including Powerpoint® presentations, text messages from cell phones, and audible recordings of speeches or private conversations. With over nine million blogs currently on the Internet and 40,000 new ones emerging each day,[8] the amount of information posted in blogs presents unprecedented opportunities for law enforcement to legally data mine this type of open source information for leads in unsolved crime cases, as well as for intelligence gathering in order to monitor the activities of suspected criminal groups. Can you think of other ways in which blogging or blogs could be useful to law enforcement or security professionals?

Blogging related to broader criminal justice concerns occurs through a variety of Web site forums. Throughout 2005 an organization called Crim Law maintained a Web site (crimlaw.blogspot.com) consisting of a variety of interesting blogging commentary about legal and criminal justice issues developing throughout the United States. Much of the information was not covered in traditional media outlets, which are naturally limited by available reporting and production staff, print space, and/or airtime. In addition, a few blogging forums are now maintained and contributed to by criminal justice and law students from particular colleges or universities and beyond. For example, law students at Duke University now routinely blog about controversial criminal and social justice issues such as homeland security implications for civil rights, gay marriage, and abortion.

Here it is interesting to note that social norms and laws governing privacy, copyright, advertising, fairness, and libel as these pertain to blogs and blogging are just beginning to develop within the cyber society, thus paving the way for unfettered deviance, abuse, and crime.[9] Indeed, blogging can conceivably be used for illicit purposes, as when corrupt corporate or securities exchange officials orchestrate online reporting and reactions by others about impending changes in stock values, new products or services, changes in organizational leadership, or other developments affecting perceptions of an organization's value. Similarly, individuals may be able to create false online identities or deliberately post erroneous news about events in order to induce others to behave in certain ways. Hence blogging used for criminal or other illicit purposes could conceivably take the form of mass social engineering, propaganda designed to influence deviant, abusive, or even criminal actions by others. Further, anything posted online is potentially easily retrievable by unsuspecting individuals using Google, Yahoo, or other popular search engines. This is especially true to the extent a deceptive blog gains participation and/or is associated with well known public events, such as natural disasters or terrorist attacks—events already established (in Chapter 3) as ripe circumstances for committing cyber fraud. How popular do you think blogging is as a means for acquiring news? Do you comment in or read blog reports? How many individuals do you think it would take to create a blog leading to false investments or other forms of fraud? Could twenty, ten, five, two, or even one person assuming multiple online identities orchestrate a fictitious blog, or otherwise dominate the discussion occurring via a legitimate blog in order to steer the news and reactions

of people in a certain way? Please do not try this from home or school, but just imagine how blogging as a form of technology can be used to create new forms of old crime.

### 7.1.4.2 Smart Mobs, Political Activism, and Crime.
**Smart mobs** are mobs of people who simultaneously and collectively use computing and telecommunications technology to network, act quickly en masse, and augment or possibly circumvent traditional media to achieve their political or social objectives. Coordinated efforts undertaken in this way amplify and focus the power that a conventional mob has. This concept was first articulated by Howard Rheingold in his book *Smart Mobs: The Next Social Revolution* (2003), where he cited numerous incidents around the world involving coordinated social processes and simultaneous real-time effects resulting from mobile communications and computing being used by large numbers of people.[10] For example, Rheingold reported how government protestors organized to send tens of thousands of text messages via mobile phones during a four-day period in January of 2001 that led to the removal of President Joseph Estrada of the Philippines. During the 2004 U.S. presidential race, smart mobbing involving as many as 750,000 people occurred via the moveon.org Web site, which used instant messaging and mobile communications to organize protests against the war in Iraq.[11]

In addition to being used as a means of civic participation, a small-scale form of smart mobbing has also been used for criminal purposes. So-called **swarm crimes** in Rio de Janeiro, Brazil, have reportedly involved an adult criminal recruiting a teenager to recruit several eight- to ten-year-old kids and supplying all the juveniles with disposable cell phones. At a designated time, all the youngsters converge around and pickpocket a small group of targeted tourists. Afterwards, they run off and use their inexpensive cell phones to call the teenager to arrange to turn in their loot for small amounts of cash. The teenager in turn exchanges the booty for a larger sum of cash provided by the adult criminal who then fences the stolen property for profit. The beauty of this form of crime is that it can be organized to occur rapidly, and if any of the kids or the teenager is caught by authorities, they can only provide a disposable cell phone number and a description of the higher up wholesaler. Additionally the crime can be repeated in several locations using the same gadgets unless or until suspicions develop, in which case the crime method is easily replicated with a new set of disposable cell phones and willing participants who are often desperate for money.[12] Cell phone text messaging is also being used to harass and threaten. In 2005, Scottish police attributed a 70 percent increase in crime to "phone texting" involving threats and extortion.[13]

### 7.1.4.3 Electronic Voting and Potential Voting Fraud.

The extremely close and controversial results of the 2000 U.S. presidential election between Al Gore and George Bush highlighted problems associated with mechanical voting machines. These devices are designed to literally punch holes in paper ballots in order to enable machine reading of votes. However, unlike programming punch card devices that were new and integral to second generation computer data input during the late 1960s and early 1970s, aging voting machines that use this same basic technology often leave hanging chads on ballots that cause counting inaccuracy, disqualification of legally cast votes, and claims of election fraud, especially in instances of other types of voting irregularities.

To overcome such problems, in 2001–2005 Nevada installed and successfully tested touch-screen voting machines for use in county- and state level-elections, thus paving the way for other states and political jurisdictions to adopt similar computerized voting devices. However, concerns about assuring the confidentiality, integrity, and authenticity of votes cast electronically remain in many polling jurisdictions throughout the nation. Officials worry that hackers may be able to break into insufficiently protected information systems and manipulate or destroy electronically cast votes,

thereby calling into question overall election results. *Votergate,* a documentary produced in 2004, showed how easily the software used by voting machines could be manipulated to alter votes after they were cast, while preserving the appearance of complete information security. Another concern has to do with the periodic need for recounts, so all computerized voting machines, such as those used in Nevada, must be capable of producing a tangible record of every vote cast.

Punch card style voting machines are still used in a majority of polling jurisdictions in the United States, and it will be expensive and time consuming to completely change the voting technology throughout the nation. Is the technological changeover worth the cost and effort? Since vote-counting in America and other nations is still successfully conducted with paper ballots, and since paper receipts must still be produced in instances requiring recounts, should older technology, even if repaired or remade, be used in the United States instead of modern, fully computerized voting machines? Which form of voting technology do you think provides the least opportunity for election fraud?

## 7.2  Controversial Cybercrime-Related Issues

To this point, we have discussed the transformation of civil society into an information society organized around networked computers. Computerization is also affecting ways in which crimes are committed, as well as civil and criminal justice processes. Essentially, everyone whose life is touched by computers is potentially affected by cybercrime or its conceptual analog, IT-enabled infosec and criminal justice. Consequently, computer users everywhere share an interest in helping assure a safe, secure, and just cyber society. As discussed in Chapter 5, we also know that perceptions of social, economic, and political tension in society as potential contributing factors in crime causation tend to fall into either the consensus,

*The United States is progressively replacing old-style manual lever-action punch-card voting machines with touch screen voting machines that automatically tabulate votes via computer networks. The newer machines are typically capable of printing a record of votes cast and supporting election result recounts if necessary. Do you think the newer technology helps prevent or better enables election fraud?* AP Wide World Photos

pluralist, or conflict views of social organization and political processes. In each of these views, individuals and groups struggle to be heard politically and influence power relationships and the distribution of wealth in society. Increasingly, wielding of political power involves using IT in conventional and deliberately innovative ways (e.g., blogging and smart mobbing).

A **stakeholder** is an individual, group, or entity with a vested interest in the formulation and outcomes of laws, policies, regulations, products, programs, processes, procedures, and so on. Stakeholder groups concerned about issues related to cybercrime include privacy and advocacy organizations; federal, state, and local law enforcement officers and prosecutors; the private security industry; training and technical assistance enterprises;

research institutions and professional membership organizations; IT, computer, and software development and manufacturing firms; regulatory agencies; a variety of policy-making committees, boards, commissions, and task forces; and computer users everywhere. Appendix A lists several categories of stakeholders and specific prominent IT-oriented entities along with their particular areas of interest, concern, and expertise. Take a moment to scan this list. As you do, think about how as stakeholders in cyber society they differ in their views about IT-related issues and how their influence affects construction of laws, regulations, and public policies, as well as research and development of technologies pertaining to cybercrime. For example, following the terrorist attacks on September 11, 2001, intelligence agencies within the Department of Defense announced plans for a Total Information Awareness Program (TIAP) for analyzing disparate databases for clues about the identity of terrorists or impending terrorist attacks. However, several other stakeholders, including the American Civil Liberties Union (ACLU), that were concerned about **privacy** and potential overreaching by federal intelligence and law enforcement agencies, raised concerns in congressional hearings about the proposed program. Actions taken by the ACLU and other privacy advocates effectively stalled plans to develop and implement a TIAP pending further study of its cost and provisions for safeguarding privacy.

Stakeholders, whether they are individuals, groups, or organizations politically aligned in a given cause, involve themselves in government decision- and rule-making processes in order to help shape public policies for responsible and ethical use of computers. In reality, these processes involve the interactive and collective efforts of government agencies, commercial firms, industrial sectors, and not-for-profit organizations. In Chapter 8, we will review how laws and regulations are formulated, and revisit the role and importance of stakeholder groups in helping to shape perceptions of social norms, fairness, deviancy, abuse, and crime in cyber society. Here, in this chapter, we will explore controversial issues with respect to particular stakeholder groups and potentialities for cybercrime along with the implications of these for information security. Specifically, we will consider the computer hacker subculture, the Open Source Community, gaming enclaves, and the legal pornography movement, all of which involve large populations of computer users with differing and sometimes overlapping interests (e.g., to assure legal protections for their online activities while avoiding unnecessary government scrutiny via law enforcement and regulation). Our consideration of these issues does not mean that everyone or even the majority of people involved in the aforementioned groups or activities behave abusively, unethically, or illegally. Rather, the goal in exploring these four major issues in some detail is to acknowledge their importance and more fully

consider the social, economic, and political contexts in which cybercrimes occur. Put differently, computer abuse and cybercrime does occur in connection with each of these activities, though only a small proportion of participants violate state or federal computer crime laws.

### 7.2.1  The Computer Hacker Subculture

The computer **hacker subculture** began in the late 1950s with electrical engineering students at the Massachusetts Institute of Technology (MIT) who possessed curiosity and passion for understanding first generation mainframe computers. In those early years of computer technology there were of course no formal programs of study in computer science, much less computer design software engineering, or IT administration students. These academic specializations and students enrolled in such programs of study would come about as computers evolved as challenges associated with computerization became more complex and required greater understanding of the technology. Early computer technology challenges inspired tireless puzzle solving among early electronic students at MIT, who banded together to work on, play with, and program computers. These students, and many others like them at colleges and universities across the country, came to be known as **computer hackers**, a term derived from electrical engineering students hacking away for many hours at a time to solve programming challenges when not otherwise occupied fixing electric signaling problems on the MIT Tech Model Railroad Club train layout.[14] Since that time, hackers have been variously defined as individuals possessing extraordinary curiosity about, enthusiasm for, and expertise in computer programming. In addition, hacking ideology has undergone significant changes corresponding to the shifts in computing technology that have enabled commission of many types of computer abuse and cybercrime. In this subsection, we focus on contemporary issues and debate surrounding computer hacking as an activity and major ideology of cyber society and what may lie ahead for divergent members of the subculture.

Let us begin by briefly describing the concepts of culture and subculture. **Culture** may be defined as behaviors and beliefs characteristic of a particular social, ethnic, or age group and may reflect states of human development and associated values. A society may consist of several different cultures within a given period of history and geographic boundaries. No particular culture is inherently better or worse than any other culture, regardless of technology used by its members, although as we discussed in Chapter 1, dominant cultural values exert more influence in the formulation and enforcement of societal norms and laws than do less dominant ones, and technology factors heavily into the formation, stabilization, and transformation of cultures. A **subculture** is a group that has social, economic, ethnic, or other traits distinctive enough to distinguish it from others within the same culture or society. Traits indicative of subculture may include shared values, behavioral patterns, unique vernacular, lifestyles or styles of dress, and distinctive use of technology. There are many types of subcultures, and the word itself should not connote anything inherently negative or derogatory, although people who are not involved with or who do not understand a subculture may view its members with suspicion because they are different. Police officers comprise a subculture because they generally share common values, wear the same clothing and gear (e.g., uniforms), communicate with a unique vernacular, and behave in ways distinctive from others in society.

When the hacker subculture formed in the late 1950s, mainframe computer systems were so expensive that only government agencies, large corporations, and universities had them. In order to truly learn about the computers, students had to use them, but access was severely restricted and limited typically to a certain number of programming or processing hours per week. As curiosity and the complexities of computational problems increased, so did competition for authorized access. Students, however, were often not given much priority, so breaking into computer labs and tricking system administrators into allowing unauthorized or extra computing time on university mainframe computers was common. Such behaviors carried over into general attitudes regarding how and why computers should be used, access to and authority over computer systems, and ownership of information. The students developed intense curiosity and pleasurable obsessions with computer programming and problem solving, unique terms, and behavioral patterns such as working late into the night to solve computer-related problems. In the process they also developed mistrust of authority figures, especially those who controlled access to coveted computers of which only one or two might exist on a given campus.[15] Eventually a guiding set of principles emerged for using computers. Known as the **hacker ethic**, these principles are essentially that[16]

- Access to computers should be unlimited and total.
- Always yield to the hands-on imperative.
- All information should be free.
- Mistrust authority—promote decentralization.
- Hackers should be judged by their programming and hacking talent, rather than on the basis of academic degrees, money, property, or professional status.
- People can create art and beauty with computers.
- Computers can change lives and society for the better.

Hackers generally hate bureaucracy, boredom, and wasted time. However, exploration, creativity, results, and efficiency in computer programming and expert use of IT are highly valued. Respect among hackers is earned by creating elegant programming code or doing things with computers in original ways even if this means breaking rules, policies, regulations, or laws. Thus principles of the hacker ethic are interpreted and circumstantially applied in ways suiting individual and groups of hackers.

In the mid-1980s scholars began to observe that cybercrimes and cybercriminals were not necessarily strictly harmful to society and that some hacking and hackers were wrongly perceived and judged. In 1990, Dorothy Denning wrote: "Hackers are learners and explorers who want to help rather than cause damage, and who often have very high standards of behavior."[17] In *Hackers: Heroes of the Computer Revolution* (1984), Steven Levy, in addition to describing the hacker ethic bulleted above, explained three generations of hackers up to that time: (1) *true original hackers* of the 1950s–1960s, (2) *hardware hackers* inclusive of phone phreakers and other computing innovators in the 1970s, and (3) *gaming hackers,* who pioneered many computer games in the 1980s but who were not especially interested in cracking systems to explore information.[18] Many scholars have suggested that by uncovering design flaws and security deficiencies, hackers are helpful to security professionals. As early as 1989 information systems

managers were exploring ways to approach hackers in order to turn them into colleagues for security purposes.[19] Even so, Donn Parker in that year concluded that some computer crime perpetrators exhibited a "Robin Hood Syndrome" because they differentiated strongly between harming people, as individuals versus organizations regarded, as highly immoral by their standards.[20] As technology changed and hacking ideals were practiced via the Internet and its millions of under-protected information systems, hackers committed an increasing number of crimes and were at once sensationalized and stereotyped by the media as educated, curious, mischievous, and technically oriented young white males with no criminal record. The image of Broderick, who starred in the 1983 movie *WarGames*, and most of the starring characters in the 1995 movie *Hackers,* fit the hacker stereotype.

---

## CYBER TALE 7.3

### How the Movie **Hackers** *Inspired One Student to Abuse Computers*

I had been reading about hackers off and on for two years or so, but had not yet truly learned enough to really understand the implications of the hacker scene and ethic. So, in 1995, when the movie *Hackers* came out, I thought that all of my questions would be answered. In hindsight, it was not exactly the cinematic masterpiece I initially hoped it might be. However, it certainly made an impact on my life and transformed a passing interest in hacking into an obsession of sorts. I wanted to have immense amounts of power and to visit hidden places just like the characters in the movie. Later, I realized life, even for real hackers, wasn't really how the movie portrayed it. However, the movie did inspire me to learn about computers, and probably did not dissuade me from cheering a little

when my friends took over my high school's network.

The movie also introduced me to electronic music, which nobody in my town had ever heard of at the time. It also inspired me to try to use a mini-cassette recorder to make free phone calls on a pay phone. The technique is actually known as "red boxing." In phreaking terms, each color of box (think electronics boxes) performs a different function. The red box simply recorded (or generated) the tones made after coins were deposited into a pay phone, then played them back. On some phones, this technique worked immediately. On others, it was necessary to dial the operator and social engineer him/her into dialing the number for me. "Hi, the 6 button is broken on this phone, could you dial…" Incidentally, this illegal trick still works today, and my father still wonders why I spent $20 on a mini-cassette recorder all those years ago!

*Anonymous Student*

Given the history of computer hacking, combined with profiles of individuals who have been arrested for trespassing into information systems under state or federal computer crime laws, the stereotype is not without factual basis. However, competent people of any age, gender, race, or ethnicity can commit hacking and other forms of cybercrime. Note that the original cohort of student hackers at MIT are now all at least in their seventies. Part of the problem facing less criminally prone hackers, is that, unlike other forms of criminality involving IT, which as discussed in Chapter 1 underwent social construction and labeling processes, the concept of *hacking* and term *hacker* never changed, despite generational changes in the nature of this group's overall intentions and behaviors, enabled with improved computing and telecommunications technologies. During the 1990s, as groups of hackers reinterpreted and/or reapplied the original hacking ideology in their commission of more and increasing varieties of computer crimes, ideological splits in the subculture emerged. This caused some criminologists to question whether there is or ever was a hacker subculture or if there is more than one subculture, based on the extent to which criminal versus noncriminal activities are encouraged and carried out by group members. Although this debate continues, there is general agreement that what began as mischievous behavior limited to college campuses has evolved into increasingly malevolent and criminalized behaviors throughout the world as a function of hackers using available technology once used only to legally explore, create, and learn.

Today, hackers constitute an important group of stakeholders in the cyber society. Hackers who are true to the original hacker ethic essentially believe that information and information systems should be freely accessible so that people can learn about and improve the world and that computers are intended for self-satisfaction if not self-actualization via exploration, discovery, problem-solving, and creativity. They also believe that power in society should be decentralized, that

authority figures cannot be trusted, and that personal recognition should be based on technical talent rather than wealth, class, professional position, education, and so on.[21] True original hackers were not primarily abusing or criminal in their intentions, and many of them who are still living long for the days when mischievous computer exploration was not formally and significantly sanctioned by society. Newer generations of hackers are less idealistic, and there is general consensus among observers of the subculture that hackers as a group have steadily become increasingly malevolent in their intentions and more capable of causing harm as the result of the power of the technology being used and worldwide dependence on computerized systems. Thus, it is important to recognize ranges in ideology that drive computer hacking behaviors.

For several years hackers have held an annual international conference in Las Vegas, Nevada, called **DEFCON**, which is attended by thousands of members of the subculture. They make presentations, socialize, and learn new computing skills. Some hackers are recruited at DEFCON by federal intelligence and law enforcement agencies to become programmers, system analysts, or information security professionals. Hackers have also formed regional and even local groups that hold workshops and social events of their own. Some of today's hackers are qualitatively very different in their intentions, behaviors, and the harm they cause than the original hackers, who acted primarily on the basis of curiosity and exploration through computers rather than using computers maliciously for greed. Hackers with good and bad intentions continue to help promote computer innovations, computerization, and advances in information security. People should recognize these important contributions while also keeping in mind that hacking as defined in crime laws can result in manipulation, denial, theft, or destruction of data for all sorts of reasons, as well as damage to information systems and attendant harm to individuals, groups, and organizations that depend on these for myriad purposes.

## BOX 7.1 • *The Death of Cyberpunk*

Cyber society is a dynamic, constantly fluctuating space. Cultures, subcultures, communities, enclaves, and movements in cyberspace arise and diminish over time just as in the real world. An example of one component of cyber society that appears to have faded out in recent years is the so-called cyberpunk movement that originated as a subgenre of 1980s science-fiction novels and movies. Filled with premonitions of a dark, gritty technological underworld, many computer hackers immediately related to these novels. Thereafter cyberpunk evolved into an encompassing descriptor of anyone involved in the computer underground.

The term *cyberpunk* was originally coined by Bruce Bethke in 1980 but has been applied to literary works as early as George Orwell's sci-fi novel *Nineteen Eighty-Four* in part because of the novel's dark feel and emphasis on technology. Other influential authors of the cyberpunk genre include Bruce Sterling, Rudy Rucker, and Neal Stephenson. One could argue that there have never been cyberpunks per se, rather only hackers and other "netizens" who simply imitated in their lifestyles the imaginary concepts found in the novels of their day. If indeed there was a viable cyberpunk movement, its height surely came about in 1984 with William Gibson's novel *Neuromancer,* in which he coined the term cyberspace.[22] Cyberpunk culture was also evident in more recent popular movies such as *The Matrix* series, which depicted action-packed scenes in futuristic places with unbelievable although fascinating technological capabilities.

So, what does cyberpunk have to do with cybercrime? The answer to that question is complex and speculative and may well have to do with subculture and learning theories of crime. Cyberpunk was a social movement that for 20 years infatuated many young computer users and may have inspired some to commit daring crimes using computers. Cyberpunk may also have inspired characteristics and also negative connotations associated with the computer hacker subculture. Indeed, student computer geeks wearing dark-colored trench coats in the tradition of attire worn by fiction cyberpunk heroes such as Neo, played by Keanu Reeves of the *Matrix* series, can still be observed on some college and university campuses as if they were imitating fictional heroes.

## 7.2.2 *The Open Source Community*

The **Open Source Community** consists of people throughout the world committed to the principles of information sharing through the development of freely available software that is validated, used, and improved by members of the community. Active participants of this online community who are adept at software development constantly write, share, and update source code of applications, which are then posted online for other members of the community to examine, try out, and further improve upon. Free **open source software** is typically made available on any number of open source servers or forums, provided that users agree to abide by the primary community edict that the code used will not be stolen or copyrighted as being original.

The open source initiative originally sprouted from Richard Stallman's Free Software Foundation (FSF), which started a project in 1989 to develop a free version of the then-popular commercial operating system UNIX. While the FSF did manage to create many extremely important and powerful freeware tools, they never managed to complete a working kernel, the core of an operating system. Richard Stallman inspired the concept of **freeware**, and thus the concept for what would later become the Open Source Community. Linus Torvalds developed the Linux operating system kernel and then distributed it online, after which innumerable other computer enthusiasts improved it in the spirit of what by that time had become a viable Open Source Community. Today Linux is widely regarded as a stable operating system alternative to Microsoft Corporations's Windows® for use on PCs, and to the Mac OS operating system used in Apple/Mac computers. On this basis, firms such as IBM and Sun Microsystems have reportedly pledged millions of dollars for further development of Linux, and Apple may rely on open source software for its OS X operating system.[23] Other large corporations with interest in commercial and open source software development include Ericsson, 3Com, Intel, Motorola, Hewlett Packard, and Nokia.

The **Open Source Initiative** (OSI) is a nonprofit corporation dedicated to managing and promoting development of software for the good of the cyber society. Formed in 1998 with the goal of bridging the business and commercial sectors with non-criminal aspects of the hacker subculture, OSI is now an integral aspect of a growing initiative. Its work centers on access to source code while requiring that users adhere to several "Open Source Definition criteria" that are actually principles specifying rationale and terms of agreement for using and innovating code.[24]

Proponents of open source software call attention to the fact that security and other programming flaws are usually quickly discovered when an application source code is openly shared for public scrutiny. Although it is possible for programming errors to remain or be inserted into open source software, in theory these will be discovered, exposed, and corrected by the users of the software in the Open Source Community. People with adequate technical skills can, in addition to fixing programming problems, add features or otherwise improve upon software functionality. Of course learning your way around the Open Source Community, and the maze of free programs and their capabilities, is not exactly a plug and play endeavor. Most typical Linux installations require some technical knowledge to complete successfully. However, as an attempt to increase the Linux user base, most Linux distributions are now incorporating both detailed instructions and more user friendly installation procedures. Some users find that the experience of installing and using Linux

deepens their understanding and love for how computers work.

The main obstacle confronting the open source movement is getting mainstream computer users to know about and trust open source software. Movement participants are often unfairly labeled as "computer geeks" or "hackers" not to be trusted, even though they are motivated to create completely trustworthy computing software through open creation and free distribution of source code. Additionally, in capitalist societies the idea of creating and giving away potentially valuable software is viewed with suspicion. However, millions of people throughout the world now use open source software free of charge thanks to the contributions of vast numbers of people who volunteer their time and technical expertise because they believe in the fundamental notion that information, software, and computing should be as free and accessible as possible. Other users may not even realize that the software they are using is open source, much less known about the worldwide community effort that has gone into its creation and innovation. In reality, safe use of open source code is predicated on several factors, including: (1) being aware of available software that is compatible with your operating system and other applications that you wish to use it with, (2) knowing how to download and install the software; and (3) having sufficient time, interest, and technical competence to maintain the software and fix problems with assistance from other Open Source Community members.

For these reasons, the vast majority of nontechnical computer users are likely to prefer some if not all of their software to be of the commercial variety. Simply put, the majority of computer users (including those working in government agencies and not-for-profit and private sector firms) do not have sufficient time, technical interest, or acumen to check out all the operating systems and applications they may need, could use, or intend to use. Nor do they have time or expertise to fix and maintain open source applications, though increasing numbers of service technicians can be hired for this purpose. For the vast majority of computer users, it is more convenient and economical to purchase commercially available software that is reasonably warranted against problems and that can be easily upgraded and patched online or even returned to the distributor for replacement or refund.

## 7.2.3  *Electronic Gaming Enclaves*

Millions of people of all ages have been turned onto computer game playing: console, desktop, or online versions of action, adventure, arcade/shooter, board/puzzle, card, RPG, simulation, sports, or strategy games. What began to gain popularity with the development of *Space War* by a few MIT students in the early 1960s has led to a worldwide gaming culture supported by a $14 billion software development industry.[25] Recognizing the popularity of online computer gaming and the existence of **electronic gaming enclaves**, some corporations have even begun to utilize video games as potential advertising exposure points, hoping that a corporate logo advertising products and services plastered on a virtual wall or billboard will catch the eyes of gamers.

The military is also using computer games in its recruiting efforts. **Simulation technology**, once used only for training personnel and planning mission strategies, has in recent years been incorporated into exciting shooter and strategy games to attract a generation of young men and women who grew up playing computer games into military service. Beginning with *Marine Doom*, a modified version of the revolutionary first-person shooter game *Doom*, the military then created *America's Army: Operations,* followed by *Full Spectrum Warrior*.[26] Reflecting innovations in computer gaming technology, each of the military's games were successively more realistic and popular among gamers. It is also noteworthy that *America's Army* was released by the military to the public for free as a recruitment tool.[27] Another game, called *Soldiers*, that features role playing

adventures about being in the armed services rather than shooting enemy targets, is also available for free and is being used for recruiting. In addition, *Full Spectrum Warrior* was modified by a private third party developer to include a storyline that resulted in its becoming one of the most eagerly anticipated electronic game releases of 2004.[28]

Another form of online recreation with connections to the real world involves remote computer-controlled target practice, shooting competitions, and even live animal "hunting" experiences. Live Shot of San Antonio, Texas, has established an interactive shooting environment in which members can shoot computer-controlled rifles at real animals on ranges manned by people. The interactive service provider is also preparing shooting environments equipped with remote-controlled computers to provide people who are disabled or otherwise not able to participate in conventional hunting trips with opportunities to kill real animals on the firm's property in Texas via a home computer. The firm's Web site, like those of other online gaming and adventure content and service providers, explains membership signup procedures, target practice and hunting rules, pricing information, and demonstration videos, among other types of information.[29] How is this form of recreation, which combines elements of target practice, real hunting, and electronic and computer gaming strike you?

Computer gaming has also become integral to interactions and activities played out by people in virtual worlds, and this sometimes leads to tangible profits in the real world. For example, players involved in virtual worlds like *Everquest* now sell their virtual possessions for real currency via online auction sites such as eBay.[30] In other words, some people who interact in virtual-world adventure stories spend real-world money to purchase virtual-world property rights. One amazing study of this phenomenon showed that online sales from interactions in the virtual world, enabled by Sony's multiplayer online game *Everquest*, resulted in tangible earnings equal to an average hourly wage of about

$3.42 per hour for every player. on the basis 9 this wage rate, the number of players and their hours interacting online, and the volume and prices of virtual property sales, *Everquest* was estimated to be the 79th largest (national) economy on Earth.[31] One student recently reported how he was able to make real money through computer gaming by taking several months to create virtual shadow armor that sold later sold for $400 online. He complained that his side business was wrecked when people found an item duplication they used to copy his cyber creation, along with those of many other game players.

Beginning in 2001, a component of the popular computer game *The Sims Online* (TSO) morphed into a virtual dystopia, replete with unreal misery and wretchedness, including murder, drug abuse, child sex rings, and shadow governments. Apparently, Alphaville, as the cyber community was dubbed by its game participants, was originally intended to be a perfect world in cyberspace.[32] However, the virtual environment provided a forum through which people created and then acted out despicable behaviors, all reported online by the virtual game community newspaper called the *Alphaville Herald*, staffed by virtual game reporters in the form of a blog managed in a different online forum by philosophy professor Peter Ludlow of the University of Michigan. Real people, using pseudonyms and play-acting through cyber characters, engaged in many forms of conduct that would be considered legally obscene, indecent, or criminal except for occurring in an imaginary world (and as a form of free expression).[33] However, certain cyber sex services provided via an Alphaville brothel, including sex services performed by real adult characters pretending to be underage minors, reportedly resulted in real money payments from online clients, from which sex performers were paid handsomely.[34] When Professor Ludlow, himself a participant-observer of Alphaville and blog facilitator for discussion of the online community's activities, reported such questionable activity to game organizers, his account was reportedly suspended for unknown reasons.[35]

The ability to make money in the real world by selling virtual services or property raises unprecedented real-world ethical and legal issues. Another case resulted in the creation of a short-lived cyber gaming sweatshop in Tijuana, Mexico. In this city just across the U.S. border from San Diego, California, Mexican laborers were reportedly hired by a firm called Black Snow Interactive to play computer games for a living.[36] Their assignment was to find rare items in the massively multiplayer virtual gaming worlds of *Ultima Online* and *Dark Age of Camelot* in order to amass virtual wealth that could be converted through online auction sales into real money and profit. However, Mythic Entertainment, Inc., the developer of *Dark Age of Camelot*, suspended Black Snow Interactive's gaming activities for alleged copyright infringement. Black Snow in turn sued Mythic in federal court to reclaim its revenue stream. Before the case could be settled, the U.S. Federal Trade Commission slapped a $10,000 fine on Black Snow for allegedly "auctioning off nonexistent computers in a previous business incarnation." Thereafter the firm's operators shut down its operations and skipped town, allegedly leaving $23,000 in unpaid bills.

Although this case was exceptional in its outcome, bizarre electronic gaming interplay is already occurring throughout cyberspace and across the real world according to rules established by commercial developers and hosts of virtual gaming environments, with little or no government oversight. With relatively high real-world prices set for certain types of virtual gaming characters and property, cases alleging fraud and virtual property theft are already beginning to show up in civil courts and administrative hearings of various kinds in the United States and beyond. One student at the Rochester Institute of Technology reportedly asked for an extension to take a final exam because he needed to participate in an online mitigation hearing to resolve a virtual gaming property dispute. Perhaps the Black Snow Interactive versus Mythic Entertainment case will prove not to have been an aberration. Will courts begin hearing cases centered on illegal taking of property that does not actually exist but has value nonetheless because people are willing to pay for it? Can you imagine situations in which one person assumes the identity of multiple fictitious players in a gaming environment in order to fraudulently inflate the prices of virtual property in order to reap higher real-world profits? Is it also possible that gaming environments in which distinctions between real and virtual money and property could be used to launder funds associated with black market exchanges?

**Virtual gaming worlds**—online worlds where millions of people come to interact, play, and socialize—represent a new social order and economic dimension that is not without legal pitfalls.[37] Business transactions associated with virtual gaming worlds are reminiscent of many so-called dot com firms of the 1990s, which were perceived to have substantial value despite having few tangible assets, products, or services. The specter of virtual gaming worlds in which millions of participants from numerous nations having distinctive cultures and differing types of legal systems has disturbing implications for the administration of both civil and criminal justice. Legal experts throughout the world are attempting to unravel complex issues surrounding the creation of imaginary property created in virtual worlds that has tangible value in the real world and may be simultaneously implicated in physical and cyber aspects of crimes.[38] In March 2005, Qui Chengwei stabbed to death fellow online gamer Zhu Caoyuan in Shanghai, China, for selling a virtual cyber sword for 7,200 yuan that the men had jointly won in an online auction. Reportedly Chengwei had loaned the dragon saber to Caoyuan but reported it to police as being stolen after learning that Chengqwei resold it for the equivalent of $870. At the time of the murder, Chinese intellectual property laws had no provisions for determining rightful ownership of the virtual sword or its value, because although players must invest time and money to acquire virtual

property, such assets constitute data, for which there exist no legally admissible proof of ownership or legally recognized estimates of market value.[39] However, Qui Chengwei was convicted of murder and received a suspended death sentence for his crime from the Chinese government. This means that although he may spend the rest of his life in prison, the sentence could be reduced to as little as 15 years if Qui Chengwei behaves well.[40] Can you imagine spending the rest of your life in prison for killing someone because they stole virtual property from you that did not even really exist?

The legal basis for establishing ownership of **virtual property** is likely to remain unresolved for a long time. What do you think? Would the rightful owner of virtual gaming property be the player whose hard efforts in virtual reality created it or resulted in acquiring the items, other players who later purchased it either in the virtual or real world using fictitious or real forms of money, or the gaming technology developer who created the play-space in the first place? (One has to wonder if lawyers specializing in such cases will accept virtual property as payment for real-world legal services!) Given the potential for huge profits through employment of juveniles in countries with varying labor laws, is it also possible that organized crime is already or could become involved in the orchestration and perpetuation of online gaming worlds? What are the implications for government import and export regulation, tax policy, and international criminal investigations and prosecutions? One student reported that a friend spends about 100 hours per week gaming (not gambling) online and earns a sufficient amount of income to live on partly because he does not pay taxes on his gaming income as required by state and federal tax laws. Bizarre situations in which the virtual and tangible are interconnected in ways that complicate legal meanings and distinctions are no longer strictly hypothetical—they are unfolding in the real lives of real people with unpredictable consequences.

Finally, it must be noted that games featuring violence and nudity, even if only of animated characters, are controversial and gaining the attention of groups opposed to their being purchased or played by minors. Released in October of 2004, *Grand Theft Auto: San Andreas* is among the latest in the *Grand Theft Auto* series of games that feature adventurous violence in which players are awarded points for killing police officers, stealing cars, and committing other types of crimes. Another game denounced by the National Institute on Media and the Family for showing video of topless women is *The Guy Game*.[41] Other games also feature violent and other controversial content, including *Manhunt* (banned in New Zealand) and *Grand Theft Auto III,* implicated in two gang-related murders in California in which the accused were reportedly fascinated with the video game.[42] Recall that in Chapter 5 we considered arousal and behavioral theories of crime, and the unfortunate reality that some gamers spend inordinate amounts of time playing electronic games to their own detriment. On August 6, 2005, police in Seoul, Korea, investigated the death of a 28-year-old man who died apparently of heart failure after playing computer games in an Internet cafe for 50 hours straight, stopping only periodically to use the toilet and take brief naps. The man reportedly quit his job in order to spend more time playing computer games.[43]

The notion that sexually suggestive or violent computer and video games turn impressionable children, adolescents, and young adults into immoral sociopaths is controversial, at least in part because research on the effects of electronic gaming on human decision-making and behavior is limited and inconclusive. In addition, watchdog groups, applauded by many for monitoring electronic gaming content, do not always employ consistent standards when selecting or scrutinizing particular gaming products. In November 2004, the Interfaith Center on Corporate Responsibility released a list of what it considered to be the 10 most violent video games.[44] Included on

the list were *Hitman: Blood Money* (which had not yet been released), *Gunslinger Girls Volume II* (which could only be legally purchased and played in Japan), and *Manhunt* (of questionable popularity). By including these three games on its list of the ten most violent video games viewable by American adolescents, the ICCR's claims were hotly challenged and lost credibility among many online consumers of electronic gaming news. Meanwhile, many gamers periodically exhibit tremendous social responsibility, as evidenced by the gaming Web comic *Penny Arcade*, which in 2004 hosted the Child's Play charity toy drive via Amazon.com, resulting in more than $250,000 in cash (through PayPal) and toy donations to children's hospitals across the United States.[45] Thus, for a variety of reasons, harm associated with gaming content as well as the amount of time spent gaming is controversial. Do you think some games are over the top with respect to the amount of violence, sexuality, or other content they include? Would you agree that appropriate content and time spent playing electronic games is relative to age and other social factors, such as a person's ability to maintain balance in other areas of their lives? Can you think of any computer or video games that have little or no redeeming social, scientific, or even entertainment value given the subject or object of the game? Are some electronic games inherently obscene, pornographic, or simply in such poor taste that they should never be commercialized even if their content is not legally banned?

In November 2004, *JFK Reloaded* was released on the Internet and billed as an educational game that allowed players to assume the role of President John F. Kennedy's assassins. Relatively few potential consumers are even aware of its existence because it was not released by major game manufacturers in retail stores or advertised on television. At the time of its release people could only buy it off the Internet using a credit card. The game was widely criticized, primarily by nonplayers, as being despicable, and it was singled out by critics of overly explicit electronic games. Some observers think the game is an example of how some firms within the gaming development industry will not self-censor gaming content. Do you think the development of *JFK Reloaded,* which took players back to one of the most distressful days in modern American history so they could pretend to kill the president of the United States, was appropriate? How in principle does this game differ from, for example, games that feature WWII battles in which soldiers and innocent civilians are killed? Do you think games like these could have any substantial effect on crime-related behaviors of *some* juvenile or adult players?

The U.S. Secret Service and U.S. Department of Education has concluded that there exists "no useful profile of students who have engaged in school violence. "Further, although 59 percent of adolescents aged 11 to 21 responsible for major school shootings in recent years exhibited an interest in violence prior to their attacks (such as Eric Harris and Dylan Klebold, who killed 12 fellow students and a teacher in the 1999 Columbine High School massacre), their curiosity was demonstrated through watching movies (in 27 percent of 37 cases studied), reading violent books (in 24 percent of cases), and electronic gaming (in only 12 percent of cases). In fact, adolescents responsible for major attacks in schools who had prior interest in violence most often demonstrated this through their own writing of poems, school essays, or personal journals.[46] Hence, connections between playing electronic games and committing acts of school violence appear tenuous. Regardless of these research findings, do you think it matters that violent games such as *Doom 3*, *Halo 2*, and *Half-Life 2*, among many other titles, are marketed and sold via mainstream retail outlets often frequented by unsupervised minors? Should gaming content be censored or more closely regulated by government?

The gaming industry currently relies on voluntary compliance by retailers to abide by the Entertainment Software Rating Board's (ESRB) system of **age rating symbols** and **content descriptors** when selling games such as those labeled as "M" (intended for mature players not under 17 years of age) and "AO" (adults only). This means that not abiding by the ESRB system cannot result in criminal prosecution—selling adult only video games to minors cannot result in criminal prosecution unless for instance a local jurisdiction explicitly prohibits this under the auspices of a criminal pornography statute. In 2003 the ESRB established a partnership initiative to help retailers, parents, and other consumers determine if particular games are appropriate for intended players. The industry organization reports that as of 2004, it had rated over 10,000 games including 400 online games. The ESRB also publishes a newsletter, maintains an interactive Web site, and hosts a hotline through which consumers may acquire information, pose questions, and register complaints about software products.[47] Do you think this is an adequate system? What responsibilities do parents have for monitoring computer games purchased by their children? To what extent do you think today's parents are aware of electronic gaming content and actively supervise the purchase and playing of games by their kids? To what extent do you think retail outlets have established selling policies and train personnel to refrain from selling electronic games to children not of a product's rating age? What if any adverse effects occur as the result of playing explicit electronic games, and by extension, how might these relate to violence or crime in society?

### 7.2.4 Online Pornography

The human sex drive is natural, compelling, and satisfied in a variety of ways, including through fantasizing about romantic encounters and sexual activities. Explicit depictions of people engaged in sexual activities have existed for centuries as an integral if suppressed aspect of culture in many places throughout the world. It is also true that curiosity about sex and prurient interests have historically been accommodated by various information technologies.

Consider that **IT-facilitated sex** (i.e., phone sex) occurred as early as the late 19th century and became the first national pornography network during the 20th century as the number of dedicated personal telephone lines expanded.[48] Prior to that, telegraphers also reportedly sent flirtatious and potentially obscene messages to one another using Morse Code, along with jokes, stories, and local gossip. Even an operator's gender was usually detectable among experienced telegraphers on the basis of their key touch. This original form of online courting and romances naturally involved intimate erotic messaging, sometimes conveyed in code with Morse Code, and via the touch and corresponding rhythm and sound produced by telegraph machines as they transmitted electronic messages over great distances.[49] In fact, **pornography** in various forms has been long considered an innovating force for technology and vice versa, which helps explain why porn is often associated with innovative deviance, social abuse, and crime. Online pornography is widely regarded to have been the first significant and enduring form of e-commerce. Estimates of the amount of pornography sold via adult video stores, the Internet, pay per view movie channels, books and magazines, and paraphernalia vary widely, ranging from a few to several billion dollars in sales. Reputable sources usually put the combined value of porn sales in the United States at considerably less than $10 billion annually.[50] Legal pornography, as determined by local community standards, is now widely available in print via snail mail, on cable and satellite television, and online. Proponents argue that legal pornography provides a way for people not offended by such material to explore human sexuality for personal, social, and even professional reasons having nothing to do with deviance, abuse, or crime. Nonetheless pornography remains controversial, substantially because of the inherently private nature of sex, and because of obvious harm experienced by children groomed into sexual encounters for molestation by pedophiles

or criminally forced into pornographic modeling or prostitution, as well as potential harm inflicted on children exposed to porn of any nature. In June of 2005 FBI agents searched the San Jose, California, home of Arthur Schwartzmiller, a convicted repeat child molester, to find child pornography and other evidence that throughout 35 years when not in prison he may have molested hundreds or even thousands of boys in several states, Mexico, and Brazil.[51] Dubbed by police as being the worst child abuser on record in the United States, Schwartzmiller, as of this writing, was being held without bail in California on multiple counts of sex crimes, which, if he is convicted, could result in a maximum 105-year prison term.[52] Worldwide there is near universal condemnation of child pornography, generally defined as sexually explicit materials depicting individuals who are less than 18 years of age. Note that child pornography is often distinguished from **erotica**, in which adolescents are *legally* depicted in sexually suggestive poses without exposing of genitalia or female breasts. A common practice of pedophiles grooming intended child crime victims is to initially socially engineer them into posing in erotic pictures or videos, and then make these available online to fellow child pornographers, and so on. It is important to note that condemnation of child porn and child erotica is supported by above board adult entertainment trade organizations that seek to protect freedom of speech and expression rights and profit by selling legal pornography. To put it another way, the ability of the adult entertainment industry to profit from pornography-related materials and services depends on protecting speech, expression, and commercialization rights. Hence, morality aside, it is not in the political or long-term financial interests of adult porn providers to condone much less promote illegal conduct, especially that which involves exploiting children.

The Free Speech Coalition (FSC), founded in 1991, is a trade association of the adult entertainment industry. Located in Canoga Park,

California, the organization consists of members concerned about cyber-related laws and regulations governing development, distribution, and accessibility of legal sex toys and other products and services such as risqué online chat, phone sex services, and so on. FSC members are concerned about interpretations by government agencies and courts of constitutional provisions protecting freedom of speech and expression. Although many people have ill regard for the FSC and for people involved in the adult sex entertainment industry, FSC members support efforts to combat illegal child pornography and responsible adult use of pornographic materials whether off or online.

Other organizations that promote legal and responsible adult sex and entertainment practices include but are not limited to Adult Video News, the Adult Industry Medical Health Care Foundation, the Association of Club Executives, and the American Society Against Child Pornography (ASACP). The National Center for Missing and Exploited Children (NCMEC), which specializing in collecting, analyzing, and reporting child pornography available on the Internet to law enforcement is another major player in this arena (see NCMEC and the NetSmartz Workshop which it sponsors listed in Appendix A). In addition, the Internet Content Rating Association (ICRA) is a nonprofit organization that seeks to protect children online while respecting the rights of adult content providers. This organization has developed a 45-element questionnaire that Web masters can voluntarily use to evaluate content and then assign a corresponding ICRA label to Web sites. However, the ICRA itself does not rate Internet content.[53] Moreover, Internet content is not directly regulated by the government except to the extent that it has been criminalized with respect to child pornography or other types of content prohibited by state or local crime laws, combined with local community standards and interpretation of what is inappropriate. These and other legal aspects of pornography are addressed further in Chapter 8, and issues pertaining to investigating online child pornography cases are discussed in Chapter 9.

Online computing has created unprecedented access to pornographic materials for millions of people, including adolescents and children. Explicit photographs and movies, real-time pay-to-view streaming sex shows, chat and stories about men and women engaged in every imaginable form of sexuality, along with Web sites featuring animated characters in imaginary 3D settings are now ubiquitous on the Internet. Anecdotal evidence including a surge in new Web sites featuring **toon porn** (i.e., animated pornography originally popularized by the Japanese as **hentai**) is rapidly becoming a popular form of alternative adult entertainment. Some people pay nearly $40 per month to access such sites, which may be generally categorized as cartoon Asian hentai (meaning "perverse" in Japanese), Americanized hentai gaming figures, and Web sites featuring anatomically correct three-dimensional figures. As some people who engage in cybersex fantasies come to discover that sexually explicit animated figures can be arousing, the art form has crossed into both computer gaming and mainstream media as exemplified by Americanized gaming figures depicted nude in an October 2004 *Playboy* magazine pictorial. According to one hentai artist, the appeal of such art rests in unrestricted imaginative sexual situations and activities that exceed real human experience.[54]

There may also be a naturally occurring gender-driven market appeal of pornography to the extent that males tend to be more aroused by sexually explicit visual images than females, and women tend to respond more to emotional interactions and text that describes intimate relationships and romantic experiences. Certainly women are depicted in pornography to a much greater extent than are men, regardless of sexual positioning, activities, and gender orientations featured. This situation supports arguments that women and children are widely exploited financially and in other ways by legalized pornography, and by illegal prostitution services, both of which are increasingly being advertised and facilitated transnationally by criminals using computers, other electronic IT devices, and the Internet.[55]

Notwithstanding these important concerns, the 2004 survey of 873 college students conducted by the author and colleagues at the Rochester Institute of Technology substantiates that men view considerably more pornography than women. Findings from that study reveal that

- Overall, 31 percent of all students who responded to the survey used computers to view porn at least once per week for an average of 3.3 hours, which means that 69 percent of students reportedly do not view any porn online.
- Thirty percent of males reportedly viewed porn online at least once per week, whereas only three percent of female students viewed porn online that often. Thus, male students are ten times more likely than female students to view porn online.
- Males who reported viewing porn averaged doing so 3.2 times per week for an average of 5.5 hours per week. However, females who reported viewing porn did this on average only once every two weeks for about thirty minutes total. Thus, male students who view pornography online average viewing approximately 22 times as many hours of pornographic content per week, month, or year than female students do.
- Males also vary considerably more than females in the amount of hours they view porn online, ranging from one to ten hours per week (for 97 percent of males surveyed) compared with females who almost never view porn for an hour at a time.
- In rare instances, males and females report viewing more than 50 hours of pornography online per week—the equivalent to a full-time job plus 10 hours overtime.

Given these research findings, how much viewing of pornography do you consider deviant (i.e., socially abnormal behavior)? Would you agree that regarding any amount of porn viewing as deviant may depend on a person's gender along with social, religious and cultural factors? Let's face it: most people are curious about sex, many people are more curious and/or desiring of

sex in one form or another than other people, some people are consumed with satisfying their sexual urges periodically, and a relatively small number of people are consumed with seeking sexual gratification even to an extent that negatively affects their overall lives. Depending on an individual's circumstances, too much or too little sexual activity, or that which causes harm to oneself or others, may be classified as a mental disorder according to the Diagnostic and Statistical Manual of Mental Disorders published by the American Psychiatric Association. Pornography can factor into all these possibilities for people who do not object to viewing or otherwise experiencing such content. However, porn is not without controversy surrounding its legitimacy as art and the potential harm caused to individuals who voluntarily help produce or consume it, as well as to groups of people in society who may be completely or relatively powerless to prevent being exploited by the enormous online market demands for sex-related content. Online pornography in particular is controversial because of its ubiquity and affordability (much of it is free) and because it makes possible otherwise inaccessible, criminal, and even unimaginable sexual fantasies, viewing, and interactive experiences. So extreme is some content that even in the adult entertainment industry there exists cultural and ethical divides for what constitutes acceptable online depictions of cartoon figurines and their activities (e.g., depictions of adult cartoon figures having sex with children, corpses, animals, and forcibly upon people incapable of resisting in situations not involving domination and voluntary bondage, or even with tentacle-laden monsters).[56] Some hentai artists who commercially produce realistic sexually explicit images of virtual characters, for example, have their limits and will not link to hentai sites that typically feature graphically perverse images of human-like alien or monster characters engaged in extraordinary violence and humanly impossible sex.[57] Less to more graphic forms of porn, whether depicting real persons, morphed holographic human images, cartoon characters, or combinations of them are designed to satisfy if not

DADDY, THERE'S AN IM FROM MISTRESS NATASHA —
YOUR VOYEUR VIDEO STREAMING SESSION IS READY.

also fuel real sexual fantasizing by real people willing to pay for access to Web sites featuring the images and stories of real or imaginary actors.

Some people have favorite pornographic actors and follow their adventures in ways similar to that practiced by fans of conventional cartoon characters or television drama stars. Other people consider all forms of pornography, however "soft" or "hard," to be obscene, offensive, disgusting, revolting, or sinful. Some people believe pornography in all its forms should be criminalized or at least more stringently regulated than it is currently in the United States and in other nations. However, the U.S. Supreme Court has decided to balance free speech and other rights of producers and consumers of pornography with those of people who object to the availability of such materials in their community. Controversy about pornography often centers on the reality that obscenity is a subjective concept. In other words, people differ in their views about what materials are obscene as compared to merely sexy, and the extent to which such materials should be available in communities with differing overall public tolerance for pornography.

How much online pornography is there? Given the dynamic, inventive nature of the Internet as well as increasing amounts of discontinued Web content, it is doubtful that any reliable estimates of the number or proportion of Web sites featuring porn of any kind could be generated, although clearly thousands, and perhaps tens of thousands of porn sites exist. Collectively these sites feature millions upon millions of unique web pages containing graphic images and other explicit sex-related content, and more are being created all the time. So how much porn do you think exists online? Do you think there could be a million porn sites on the Net? On August 17, 2000, *Guinness Book of World Records* officials announced that glamour star, Danni Asche, was the most "downloaded woman on the web." Reportedly, between February 1996 and June 2000, her image had been downloaded "more than 840 million times—excluding pirated sites and newsgroups."[58] The announcement spurred further downloading of the former exotic dancer turned businesswoman, and by December 2000 her image had reportedly been downloaded more

**BOX 7.2 • *A Discredited Study on the Amount of Internet Pornography***

A once hailed but soon discredited study conducted in 1995 by Marty Rimm, an undergraduate student at Carnegie Mellon University, estimated that as much as 83.5 percent of images on the Internet were of sexually explicit content.[60] In its July 3 issue, *Time* magazine featured a several-page story on "Cyberporn"[61] that was based substantially on unconfirmed data reported by Rimm.[62] Two days later the ABC television show *Nightline* aired a story about pornography on the Internet during which Rimm's research became alternatively known as the "Carnegie Mellon survey" or "Carnegie report." The news story resulted in calls for restrictions on Internet content by Senator Charles Grassley (R–Iowa) and Christian Coalition executive director Ralph Reed. Only afterwards was Rimm's previously non–peer reviewed study examined by competent scholars Donna Hoffman and Thomas Novak of Vanderbilt University, who concluded that Rimm had grossly exaggerated the extent of pornographic images on the Internet.[63] How if at all do you think the amount of pornographic materials available on or offline influences deviant, abusive, or criminal behavior?

than one billion times.[59] This is just one indication of the enormous appeal of online adult entertainment, especially that featuring nude or scantily clothed women in seductive poses.

Whatever the claims about ubiquitous online pornography and the amount of available child pornography among other sex products and services available on the Internet, the truth is that a considerable amount of it consists of market-driven adult membership Web sites. Typically these sites feature a certain number of "free tour" Web pages that purport to show examples of the quality and variety of available content in order to lure people into subscribing for limited trial or monthly subscription viewing privileges and related services. Viewers typically must provide a valid credit card account number and certain personal contact information and affirm they are of legal viewing age in order to be admitted access. This or a similar procedure is now required in the United States by the Child Online Privacy Protection Act of 1998. Many people register for monthly subscription services, while others "pay as they go," sometimes incurring expensive 1-900 (or some other numerical prefix) telephone dialing charges. It has also been reported that some porn seekers have incurred enormous phone bills by calling normal-appearing area code numbers that connected via combinations of legitimate U.S.-based and shady overseas telephone companies not regulated by the U.S. Federal Communications Commission

(FCC). When this happens, viewers of porn and phone sex chatterers often receive charges from the U.S. phone companies that helped connect their calls, as well as hefty bills from the foreign firms that are not limited by various government-regulated fee rates existing throughout America.

### 7.2.5 Information Privacy Protections and Infringement

When you use your computer to browse for information online, send or receive a message, or make an online purchase, a record of the event will be stored on your hard drive and also in one or more databases that people you do not know may access, manipulate, and redistribute to other people you do not know. That is fact. Merely logging onto an information system with your username and password triggers electronic recording and potential monitoring in some form. The same holds for making purchases with a credit or debit card, whether the transaction occurs online or in person. Items scanned in stores can also be linked to your purchasing card number and used to create a profile of your purchasing preferences and habits. This information can be shared with (or more likely sold to) advertisers who may then target you to receive paper advertisements, spam, or telemarketing phone calls tailored to your shopping interests.

When walking to or from your car in a private or public parking lot day or night, your movements may be watched and recorded via a closed circuit television camera system. Similarly, when you drive down a road too fast, pass through a toll booth, sit waiting at a traffic light or run a red light at an intersection monitored by a surveillance camera, a picture of your vehicle, its license plate number, and everyone inside the car with you may be taken and used in an automated enforcement action of a police agency or for use in any other type of lawful investigation. Make a cell phone call from anywhere in the world, and the date, time, and approximate location where the call was placed, as well as the number and location of the phone number called, will be recorded. Visit a doctor or become hospitalized for any reason, and you may need to sign a form allowing release and comparison of your medical records to other physicians or insurance companies before being treated. This information may be used to determine your eligibility for future medical, life, or auto insurance, how much you will pay for insurance coverage, and so on. Similarly, your credit rating, as determined by firms that track and score your history of making payments, substantially determines the interest rate on future loans you are eligible to receive and therefore how much you will ultimately pay for items such as a new or used car purchased on credit. Where you live, the school you attend, and where you are employed, as well as the make and model of car you drive, and where you go can be rather easily determined and used for myriad purposes. Personal information collected about you, without your knowledge, could even be used in deciding whether you will be hired for a job.[64]

Has computing and the Internet rendered privacy impossible to retain? How is the amount and availability of data changing our expectations of privacy and the way people interact with one another both on and offline? By what authority or right can government agencies, your employer, or your school search the Internet, your computer, or snoop into its own information systems for evidence of wrongdoing by *you or those with whom you associate*? To the contrary, under what circumstances is your online searching to learn information about other people invasive, unethical, abusive, or even criminal?

In this subsection we will focus on **privacy infringement** as an aspect of computer abuse related to cybercrime. As we go forward it is important to understand several key points. First, people with access to important information about us and sometimes but not always entrusted with its safekeeping, can greatly influence if not control key aspects of your life, using fallible computers and information systems. Second, violating someone's privacy in the United States is not a crime, although it may be a civil tort for which snoopers can be sued civilly and be severely sanctioned by courts. In addition, an increasing body of federal legislation and regulation requires government agencies, firms, and nonprofit organizations within certain sectors (e.g., health and financial services) to provide security of information systems. Third, there are important interconnections between computer abuse, information security that affords legally mandated privacy protections, and IT-enabled crime, which often involves privacy infringement. As such, we will be butting up against legal issues that relate to potential computer abuse and cybercrimes, along with information systems security requirements. (More in-depth discussion of interplay and distinctions between criminal and civil law are taken up in Chapter 8.) Fourth, that which constitutes privacy infringement varies widely and is not universally recognized by state or federal courts. However, violating privacy now generally includes misappropriation of a person's name or likeness, intrusion into a person's personal affairs or solitude, publicly disclosing embarrassing facts, or causing negative publicity about a person.[65] Fifth, when determining civil culpability, courts are much less concerned with motives for violating privacy than with actual privacy infringement. In addition, courts will sanction private firms and nonprofit organizations for deceiving employees about the true purposes of information gathering (e.g., tricking them into sharing medical or other personal information), not keeping personnel information confidential, conducting secret or intrusive monitoring of purely private matters (e.g., using a company restroom), and intruding into an employee's private life.[66]

Government agencies as employers are generally held to the same privacy standards as employers in other sectors. This means that agency officials may legally monitor, log, and analyze email, keystroke, and Web browsing activities of employees. They may also legally examine any data saved on an employee's hard drive or archived anywhere on a government owned or controlled network. This applies to all local, state, and federal government agencies regardless of the nature of the work performed by the agency or its employees, unless laws in a given jurisdiction specifically prohibit such activities. Similarly, students in school, on school grounds, or using a computer, information system, or other equipment (such as a locker) have significantly diminished rights of privacy. Hence, students' clothing, personal property, and material records may be systematically or randomly searched by school officials who fear security problems or violations of either school policy or crime laws.

Remember that just as we discussed in Chapter 2, if you do not own and possess an electronic IT device or information system and the data it contains, chances are someone else claim legal ownership. Moreover, just as courts do not universally agree on what constitutes violations of privacy, neither are sanctions for violating privacy consistently applied. Employers, school officials, and members of the media in particular have historically been given considerable latitude in privacy-related policy, procedural, and publication matters. Now let us consider in turn research (or snooping) by individuals; privacy practices and infringement by firms, employers, and schools; and the activities of government agencies as they simultaneously seek to enforce crime laws, provide security, enforce regulations pertaining to privacy and other requirements of administrative laws, and monitor government employees for computer and information privacy abuses.

### 7.2.5.1 Snooping and Privacy Practices of Individuals.

When does legitimate research by an individual for lawful purposes begin to violate expectations of privacy held by other people? Under what circumstances should all of us be allowed to be left alone and tell someone in a respectful manner that something we consider private is none of their business? In 2004 developers of the Internet search engine Google™ allowed the public to purchase investment stock in the company. Today Google is the most popular search engine in the world as evidenced by the fact that **googling** has become a verb that means browsing the Internet. Googling for just about everything is now a hobby for many people, as well as a means for conducting legitimate research on any imaginable topic. Googling to find scholarly materials for incorporation of ideas into a college research paper is a legitimate activity. This book is chock-full of recent cybercrime examples conveniently located by using Google, along with other effective browsers. Many people engage in searching the Internet for the names of friends, prospective dates, coworkers, doctors, and potential employers. All this is generally legal and, depending on your point of view, may be ethical if not also helpful and even fun. On July 14, 2005, cnetnews.com used Google to conduct a thirty minute search of the Internet and then published a considerable amount of personal information about Google CEO Eric Schmidt in order to make two points: (1) that information archival firms and their Internet browsers such as Google, Yahoo, Microsoft's MSN, and Amazon.com's A-9, along with many other search and e-commerce companies, collect vast amounts of information on everyone and make substantial amounts of it available for free to anyone with a computer and Internet access; and (2) that personal data of the kinds described above can be improperly used for all sorts of illegitimate purposes by anyone, including unethical insiders or hackers who penetrate information systems security. Schmidt reportedly was not happy that his personal affairs were made public, but he defended Google's data handling and privacy policy.[67]

Let us now turn the googling table around and see how you like it from the perspective of being found out about. How does is make you feel knowing that anyone capable of using a computer Web browser can likely find out personal information about you anytime they wish? To some extent this has always been true, but IT has fundamentally changed the amount and variety of information that can be quickly gathered on people and distributed at minimal cost. Finding out information on others is so easy and convenient that people I now rarely stop to reflect on what they are doing and why, or what the potential consequences of their online searching activities may be. Have you ever found something out that upon reflection you wish you had not discovered? More than once a student using a laptop computer during one of my lectures has gotten online to confirm or refute what I have just said to the class or to check me out with respect to my former employment, research accomplishments, and other professional activities. Goodness knows what else they may be trying to find out about me, or for that matter, what else they may be using their computer for during class. Once I was informed that instant messaging between a couple of students in class was disrupting their ability to concentrate on the lecture. It is somewhat unnerving to me that this occurs, yet I do not want to discourage use of computers in my classes (except for exam purposes). I would rather encourage responsible and productive use of computers. Besides, I have to admit that students' wireless searching of the Internet during a lecture and then contributing what they have found periodically enriches the class discussion in ways beyond what my intellect, group facilitation skills, charm, and good looks alone can do!

Students at the Rochester Institute of Technology are also able to informally rate instructors anonymously online, which of course results in all sorts of positive and negative comments of questionable value. Part of the problem, of course, is that there is no real way for other students to verify the content, except by doing their own investigation (e.g., speaking with my current or former students, meeting me, and checking out course syllabi). Students have always been able to investigate faculty before investing their time and money in taking a class, and they should. Yet postings of information about people over which they have no control gives rise to privacy concerns, and may lead to additional unauthorized and inaccurate information being posted without their knowledge or permission of persons being depicted or described. When this happens, a person's options are to (1) ask the poster to reword or take down the incorrect or offensive content, (2) post information about himself or herself to refute or clarify what has been said, (3) seek a civil court order to have the material taken down, (4) sue for libel and/or slander and seek damages, or (5) resort to unscrupulous or even illegal behavior to get the poster to take down and stop posting the content. All these alternatives are a hassle to some extent for a person whose privacy has been violated, and may require some level of technical knowledge and skill as well as time and money to correct, although once a person's reputation is sullied it is very hard to repair regardless of the facts or circumstances leading up to the slander. All of this means that if people find Internet content about them offensive, they may consider themselves victims, and civil courts may agree with them. Material records about information systems (e.g., access logs and permissions, messages sent or received, and posted content) are subject to discovery and use in legal claims alleging violations of privacy. Therefore, you should be very careful about what you say about others online or, as IT professionals, what you allow others to convey or post via information systems that you are responsible for managing.

In February 2004 Paris Hilton filed a $30 million federal lawsuit against Panama-based Kahatani Ltd. for violating her privacy, illegal business practices and inflicting emotional distress, in connection with this firm's allegedly releasing a video of her having sex with a former boyfriend onto the Internet without her knowledge or consent.[68] Then in March, 2005, attorneys for Limp Bizkit rock star Fred Durst filed a $70 million federal lawsuit, asking for a temporary restraining order and writ of seizure requiring forfeiture of copyrighted and privacy infringement content, against 10 Web site operating firms, including Gawker Media, LLC, of Delaware, for releasing a homemade sex video of him and a lover onto the internet without authorization. The video, which was reportedly made in 2003 and stored on Durst's home computer, was allegedly stolen by hackers and released onto the Internet, where it was subsequently found and redistributed by the firms named in the lawsuit. Durst's attorney, Ed McPherson, revealed that neither the singer nor his former girlfriend depicted in the sex tape intended for the video to be shown, marketed, sold, or distributed to the public, and that federal agents were investigating whether the hackers were the same persons responsible for breaking into T-Mobile's server and distributing onto the Internet a month earlier Paris Hilton's personal information, along with that of numerous other celebrities (as described in the introduction of Chapter 9).[69] These tawdry incidents, involving violations of privacy in connection with cybercrimes and/or breaches of information systems security, are indicative of celebrities being targeted by cybercriminals because their personal data is inherently valuable. They also dramatize the potential for personal information about everyone being illegally revealed publicly.

Celebrities and government officials are public figures who have relatively few privacy expectations regarding their public affairs and who may be legitimately held to account and criticized on the basis of closed or open source material which is legally acquired and revealed about them. As a former employee of the U.S. Department of Justice, my name is associated with several publicly funded research projects, information about which is easily found online. My name, which is shared by other people on the planet, is also associated with events about which I have no knowledge. Nonetheless, an unwary reader of this information might assume it pertains to me and that I was involved in certain events. Many people agree that employees of the government have no **expectation of privacy** regarding their official duties, yet some investigators, for example tax auditors and undercover agents, are allowed, encouraged, and may even be required by their agencies to adopt a pseudonym in order to protect their identities and privacy. Concerns for privacy and employee safety are the reason for employees of government agencies and private sector firms identifying themselves only with ID numbers and why many people working in retail establishments or restaurants also adopt pseudonyms. Perhaps you agree that personal information about government employees is none of the public's business (e.g., President Clinton's affair with Monica Lewinski) or that an individual's privacy expectations necessarily depend on a variety of circumstances not limited to a person's employment status. What is considered private varies among individuals, as well as firms, schools, and government agencies. Historically, courts have disagreed about when people have reasonable expectations of privacy—the legal bright line that professionals often want and need to apply in administrative and operational situations.

What do you regard as private? What if someone without your permission intentionally posted true or false information about you online that resulted in you becoming the victim of a crime? What would you do? In 1998 Darren S. Kochanowski was arrested for aggravated harassment in Poughkeepsie, New York. His crime involved conspiring with a computer savvy coworker to create a Web site featuring photographs of his former girlfriend in sexually suggestive positions, as well as false messages alleging her willingness to meet with strangers for sex. The Web site included the victim's home address and both her residential and work telephone numbers. Posting of this information resulted in her receiving phone calls at work from men who desired her company. Only then did the victim learn about the Web site. Frightened and angry, she called investigators of the New York State Police who, utilizing computer forensics techniques, traced the Web site to Kochanowski. He was subsequently prosecuted and found guilty, but the victim was traumatized by the experience.[70] Hopefully you are beginning to appreciate:

- Potential problems of unscreened, unauthorized, and readily available personal information posted online
- Interconnections between (1) desires, needs, and rights for personal and information privacy, (2) human and technical aspects of information security, and (3) possibilities for IT-enabled abuse and crime as these pertain to civil violations of copyright and privacy
- Significant implications of these interconnected issues for determining what behaviors and actions involving use of IT should be illegal, what needs to be considered when investigating incidents of computer abuse and cybercrime, and what matters for designing information systems, and security policies and procedures.

Much more will be said regarding this very important theme throughout the remainder of the text. For now, please reflect seriously on the reality that weak information security may enable confidential information to be acquired about you or an organization you are associated with in ways that may violate civil and/or crime laws, or at the very least, would be deemed deviant and/or unethical. (Recall from discussion in Chapter 1, and particularly as depicted by Figure 1.1, that these concepts though different are interrelated and scalable.) Violations such as those described above may occur more often than we realize. What steps can you take to ensure that information about you

remains private? A large part of what can be done rests in keeping your personal and valuable data secure, locked down behind firewalls, in systems protected with strong passwords, routinely checked for malware, and so on. We will take up the topic of good information security practices in Chapter 10. However, here are a few other things you should know about at this juncture, and can do to protect your personal and information privacy:

- Do not indiscreetly post personal information about yourself such as your full legal name, address, social security number, or a photograph of yourself online.
- Be extremely careful about sharing confidential information with anyone you do not completely trust. Employ a personal "need to know" policy and verify as soon as possible who you are actually interacting with online.
- Periodically google for information about yourself online and investigate what pops up and then take legal steps to have it removed or to correct incorrect or inappropriate information about yourself.
- Report violations of privacy, such as the unlawful display of your image, to ISPs or other organizations with technical control over the network on which the private content resides.
- Seek legal counsel to determine what if any legal recourse is possible and appropriate.
- Be respectful of the private information of other people and, above all, be ethical in your own use of computers, other electronic devices, and information systems.

### 7.2.5.2 Privacy Practices and Infringement by Firms, Employers, and Schools.   Another controversial area of information privacy involves policies, IT systems capabilities, and the information monitoring activities of firms, employers, and schools. This is because (1) courts in the United States have established that workers have substantially reduced expectations of privacy while on an employer's property or using facilities including an employer's information

systems and (2) many firms have been slow to understand or have demonstrated little regard for the ways and extent to which IT can facilitate violation of privacy expectations of employees or customers. When it comes to managing IT, organizations including employers and schools often act responsibly within the framework of existing civil privacy laws, but this is not always the case. Sometimes managers of organizations mess up inadvertently in ways that result in law suits from the very people they may be trying to serve, collaborate or establish trust with, or they intentionally abuse information and systems despite their professional, ethical, and oft legal responsibilities.

We discussed the use of search engines and the Internet to quickly discover information about people. Regardless of how helpful, ethical, or legal this may be, the fact is that you might not get your next job without a clean "google history" because an increasing number of firms now check out prospective employees online. There is nothing illegal about conducting background investigations on prospective employees. To the contrary, there are many benefits and even legal requirements to conducting background checks, provided waivers are properly signed by job applicants. Problems arise, however, when information sought is not specific to the job applied for, when nonpertinent online information is inadvertently discovered and improperly used in hiring decisions, and when safeguards are not in place to verify that online information is accurate and complete before being acted upon. We have already discussed the problem of inaccurate, inappropriate, and even fraudulent information about people being posted online without their knowledge. Now we must consider possible consequences of abuse stemming from violations of *evolving* federal and state tort law having to do with privacy protections.

It turns out that the existence of readily available online information is potentially problematic for prospective employees as well as employers. Imagine a lawfully conducted online background check that turns up unfavorable information about a job applicant and how easy and expedient it would be to simply excuse a person from further consideration without verifying the information. How could that be accomplished legally? Legally prepped employers know better than to provide any negative employment information about an existing or former employee, as doing so could be grounds for a civil suit. Further, calling a candidate directly to seek clarification about information discovered online or calling someone who may know the candidate to ask about such information, but without the candidate's knowledge, is tricky at best. It's better to keep quiet and find somebody else for the job than risk getting bogged down in legal complications, right? Meanwhile, as this situation may recur with the increasing practice of Internet-based background checks, the candidate could be excused from consideration in other job application situations without ever knowing why and could even have additional information posted or shared online about him or her without ever knowing it, all of which combines to exacerbate and perpetuate the original problem.

Certainly a person improperly excused from a hiring process on the basis of inaccurate online information could sue someone if he or she knew what had occurred and had the gumption, time, and money to pursue legal action. However, by the time the case was investigated and processed in civil court, significant and irreparable damage to a person's reputation might already have occurred. Alternatively, an unwary job candidate may be unfairly excused from several positions for which he or she was completely qualified and suited without ever realizing this happened on the basis of unfavorable false Web information. If a candidate did discover what was occurring, might his or her only recourse be to take legal action against the firms involved as part of an overall strategy to stop the madness? Unfortunately, most working class people, especially if they are young and recently degreed college students just entering the job market, have relatively few financial resources to tap in order to bring and successfully prosecute civil actions. Suppose however, you were already employed and assigned to conduct a background check (with or without the benefit of a company policy for guidance) and you encountered information on the Internet that conflicted with information provided by a candidate on an application form, what would you do? Suppose instead you were the manager in an organization whose subordinates engaged in this type of legal activity. What would you do to avoid vicarious liability (i.e., being sued for the actions of your subordinates)?

The point is that legal practices do not necessarily make good business sense. Firms, employers, and schools can and do get themselves into all sorts of unnecessary management, ethical, and legal problems by intentionally or inadvertently doing things that end up violating the privacy rights of job candidates, employees, and customers. This may include collecting but not safeguarding or improperly distributing data, implementing polices or procedures that enable privacy infringement, failing to adequately train or supervise personnel regarding privacy expectations and what constitutes acceptable exchange of information, or maintaining insecure IT systems. Here are a few examples of what can go wrong when organizations are greedy, naïve, or irresponsible in their use or management of information about customers, job applicants, employees, students, and so on.

- On March 2, 2000, the Federal Trade Commission ordered Trans Union Corp. to stop selling personal credit data to junk mail companies. FTC oversight of the credit reporting firm's selling activities had been ongoing since 1992, even as its two competitors, Equifax and Experian, had complied with the intention of the Consumer Credit and Fair Reporting Act of 1970 to limit distribution of personal information to decisions about getting a loan.[71] Then in April of 2001 a federal appeals court in Washington, DC, ruled that credit reporting agencies do not have a right to sell names, addresses, and financial information to junk mailers.[72]

- In March of 2003 consumer rights groups informed the U.S. Treasury Department that tax preparation firms participating in the Free File program sponsored by the Internal Revenue Service were requiring taxpayers to sign a release allowing confidential tax information to be used in financial products and services marketing campaigns.[73]

- In November 2004 paranoid hospital officials in Las Vegas declined for two days to acknowledge that a 12-year-old boy, who had witnessed the killing of his mother and was himself stabbed in the chest, was a patient in a county hospital where he was being treated for his wound. The actions of hospital officials, who cited concerns about their interpretation of the Health Insurance Portability and Accountability Act (HIPAA), which authorizes up to a $250,000 fine and 10 years imprisonment for flagrant nonprotection of medical records, caused considerable angst for friends and members of the community who were aware of the incident but denied access to visit and comfort the boy. Nothing in HIPAA specifically requires not acknowledging that a patient is being treated in a medical facility.[74]

As evolving public concern about and tort laws protecting privacy continue to expand into new areas of IT policy and management practices, officials of firms, including employers and school administrators, need to stay abreast of potential IT-enabled abuse carried out in furtherance of organizational objectives, as well as by people whose actions they are responsible for, regardless of why they are using IT and information. In other words, lawsuits may result from privacy infringement stemming from the official policies or actions of an organization or unendorsed abuse or misuse of IT and information by employees or students with access to information systems. It is better for managers and IT professionals to stay abreast of legal and technological security requirements to protect privacy than for them to face costly law suits, public humiliation, and lost confidence by otherwise supportive customers, employees, and other stakeholders.

### 7.2.5.3 *Government Intelligence Gathering and Analysis.*

In Chapter 2 we addressed the fundamental importance of trust in relation to ensuring information assurance and the need for information security professionals to simultaneously distrust technology and people while ensuring protection of data and information systems. Here we will briefly revisit the issue of trust as it relates to the inseparable concepts of cybercrime, information security, and expectations of privacy surrounding data. Said differently, we will explore how trust, and therefore also distrust, relates to the interplay of these issues. We will focus on legal responsibilities, capabilities, and activities of the government. In Chapter 9 we will expand on this foundation to consider legal and operational considerations when undertaking physical and cyber surveillance.

To begin, it is useful to remind ourselves that Americans are deeply suspicious of government in many respects, due substantially to its periodic violations of privacy and heavy-handed law enforcement tactics. Indeed, the federal government has an unfortunate history of violating constitutionally protected rights of privacy, although often in mistaken beliefs about how best to interdict perceived threats to national security, including large-scale activities of organized crime, and insurrect political activism by individuals and groups concerned about various national policies. In 1976, in the wake of a decade of public protests and violence surrounding civil rights violations and America's involvement in the Vietnam War, congressional hearings into intelligence operations of the federal government concluded in part that

*Too many people have been spied upon by too many government agencies and too much information has been collected. The Government has often undertaken the secret surveillance of citizens on the basis of their political beliefs, even when those beliefs posed no threat of violence or illegal acts on behalf of a*

*hostile foreign power. The Government, operating primarily through secret informants, but also using other intrusive techniques such as wiretaps, microphone "bugs," surreptitious mail opening, and break-ins, has swept in vast amounts of information about the personal lives, views, and associations of American citizens. Investigations of groups deemed potentially dangerous—and even of groups suspected of associating with potentially dangerous organizations—have continued for decades, despite the fact that those groups did not engage in unlawful activity. Groups and individuals have been harassed and disrupted because of their political views and their lifestyles. Investigations have been based upon vague standards whose breadth made excessive collection inevitable. Unsavory and vicious tactics have been employed—including anonymous attempts to break up marriages, disrupt meetings, ostracize persons from their professions, and provoke target groups into rivalries that might result in deaths. Intelligence agencies have served the political and personal objectives of presidents and other high officials. While the agencies often committed excesses in response to pressure from high officials in the Executive branch and Congress, they also occasionally initiated improper activities and then concealed them from officials whom they had a duty to inform.*[75]

According to this 1976 Congressional Committee to Study Governmental Operations with Respect to Intelligence Activities (i.e., the **Church Committee findings**), examples of federal government violations of privacy known to have occurred include the following:[76]

• From 1953 to 1973 nearly a quarter of a million first class letters were opened and photographed in the United States by the Central Intelligence Agency (CIA), producing a CIA computerized index of nearly 1.5 million names of people and who they corresponded with.
• From 1940 to 1966 at least 130,000 first class letters were opened and photographed by the FBI in eight U.S. cities to record what people were corresponding with each other about.
• From 1967 to 1973 over 300,000 people were indexed in a CIA computer system, separate

files were created on approximately 7,200 Americans, and records were kept on over 100 domestic groups in connection with Operation CHAOS.

- From 1947 to 1975 millions of private telegrams sent from, to, or through the United States were obtained by the National Security Agency under a secret arrangement with three U.S. telegraph companies.

- From the mid 1960s to 1971 an estimated 100,000 Americans were the subjects of U.S. Army intelligence files.

- From 1969 to 1973 intelligence files on more than 11,000 individuals and groups were created by the Internal Revenue Service, which initiated tax investigations on the basis of political rather than tax criteria.

- At least 26,000 individuals were at one point during this period catalogued on an FBI list of persons to be rounded up in the event of a national emergency.

The Congressional Review Committee also concluded that government officials whose principal duty was to enforce the law had violated or ignored the law over long periods of time and, incredulously, had advocated breaking the law and even defended their right to break the law. In addition, the U.S. constitutional system of checks and balances had not adequately controlled intelligence activities. For example, whereas the executive branch of the federal government for many years had neither delineated the scope of permissible activities nor established procedures for supervising intelligence agencies, Congress had failed to exercise sufficient oversight, seldom questioning matters of intelligence gathering policies or technological capabilities being used in furtherance of those policies. Consequently, most domestic intelligence issues never reached the courts for judicial review, and in cases that did reach the courts, judges were reluctant to grapple with specific legal issues, much less try to stop the government from illegally spying on its own citizenry.[77]

It is important that current and future law enforcement officers, intelligence agents, prosecutors, and information security professionals understand that abuses of the past can recur, when government officials and others in power feel threatened by technology and behaviors they do not understand and when national security is perceived to be at stake. Indeed, as evidenced by the aggressive and rather uninformed investigation carried out by the U.S. Secret Service and arguably overzealous prosecution by U.S. attorneys in the early 1990s in connection with **Operation Sundevil**, government overreaction in response to computer-enabled crimes has already occurred, and not without substantial public backlash. Details of instances involving questionable actions by federal law enforcement agents, prosecutors, and IT and information security professionals are richly described in Bruce Sterling's *The Hacker Crackdown: Law and Disorder on the Electronic Frontier*. This book describes federal prosecutions against Robert J. Riggs, Craig Neidorf, and others accused of computer hacking and other IT-enabled crimes.[78]

In case you do not know about Operation Sundevil, Riggs and Neirdorf were accused in 1990 of conspiring, hacking, and distributing via *Phrack Magazine* a proprietary and sensitive E911 call system document belonging to Bell South. Federal prosecutors alleged that by using the manual, which was indeed taken via hacking and distributed via the Internet, hackers anywhere could control emergency telecommunications throughout the country. Although Riggs pleaded guilty and was sentenced to 21 months imprisonment and ordered to pay a substantial fine for his role in stealing the document, federal prosecutors dropped their case against Neirdorf during his trial (in which Riggs testified against him) in large part because it turned out that the twelve-page document (which became only six pages long after being edited by Neirdorf), purportedly worth $79,449, was actually worth about $13. Hence, its original theft by Riggs and distribution over the Internet failed to meet any meaningful basis for charges of interstate wire fraud. In addition, the document consisted principally of administrative information that could not have enabled hackers to affect any control or damage to telephone systems. Moreover, facts revealed at trial that surprised even the prosecution revealed that much more extensive technical Bell South documents were publicly available at negligible cost long before the federal investigation of Riggs and Neirdorf was even initiated.[79]

Sterling's true story about Operation Sundevil also details the related investigation and questionable raid on Steve Jackson Games, Inc., of Austin, Texas, based on federal agents' mistaken belief that a manual for the computer game *Cyberpunk* was actually a cryptic instruction book on how to commit computer crimes.[80] The case is revealing of what can go wrong when law enforcement investigators and information security professionals are unsure of their facts or the technology used to carry out legal and illegal activities and then conduct searches that violate federal privacy laws. Subsequent to a federal raid on March 1, 1990, that negatively affected the legitimate computer game development firm's assets and business operations, a federal lawsuit was filed against the U.S. Secret Service in May of 1991. Specific allegations were that Secret Service agents violated the Privacy Protection Act (42 U.S.C. Section 2000), the Federal Wiretap Act as amended (18 U.S.C. Sections 2510-2521), and the Electronic Communications Privacy Act of 1986 (an update to the Wiretap Act codified at 18 U.S.C. Section 2701-2711).[81] The federal district and appeals courts hearing the case found in favor of Steve Jackson Games and awarded the firm, its employees, and attorneys more than $300,000 in damages and fees.[82]

The actions of federal agents and prosecutors were intended to be a legitimate crackdown on the unlawful activities of hackers, but their efforts turned out to be in many respects rather clumsily carried out and resulted in what many

perceived to be an attack on a legitimate emerging computer gaming subculture and industry, not at all in the overall interests of justice, particularly considering that many private sector firms and government agencies then as now seek the expert computing skills of young adults for IT administration and information security purposes. The hack on Bell South was not particularly different from numerous others that had been taking place for over two decades, except perhaps that the youths involved ended up divulging something trivial that hundreds of other people already possessed. That the government would stage expansive raids without understanding the cyberpunk and computer gaming scene, and overestimate the value and importance of a simple document having little to do with national telecommunications vulnerabilities, was appalling to many law-abiding people. This episode remains a source of irritation for many computer enthusiasts as well as some seasoned computer crime investigators who appreciate the importance of properly estimating the value of documents and being more than just a little familiar with the groups targeted for investigations.

Fortunately considerably better-informed awareness of cybercrime issues and professional development now exists within federal, state, and local law enforcement agencies.[83] Even so, federal government actions in Operation Sundevil did inspire creation of the Electronic Freedom Foundation (EFF) and resurgence of concerns from the 1970s regarding government overstepping its constitutional powers. Based in San Francisco, the EFF is one of several donor-supported membership organizations working to protect fundamental rights relating to the use of IT. The organization also works to educate the press, policymakers, and the general public about IT-related civil liberties. The EFF seeks to defend the civil liberties of persons and groups whose rights have been violated, oppose what it sees as misguided legislation, initiate and defend court cases preserving individuals' rights, spearhead public campaigns and foster critical thinking in the area of IT-related rights, host educational events, maintain a Web archive, and encourage public debate and exchange of information regarding these issues.[84]

The EFF's efforts, along with other privacy and civil liberties organizations, helped temper some overzealous investigations and prosecutions throughout the remainder of the 1990s. However, the September 11, 2001, terrorist attacks on the World Trade Center and Pentagon changed much for Americans and millions of other people throughout much of the world. Following the attacks, the federal government enacted the **USA PATRIOT Act**, which provided government intelligence and law enforcement agencies unprecedented surveillance, search, and seizure authority. In the months that followed, it was revealed that the Department of Defense and its contractors were developing powerful counterterrorism data mining and analysis capabilities. The **Total Information Awareness Program**, as it was originally referred to (and re-dubbed the **Terrorism Information Awareness Program**, apparently to help appease congressional and public concern over potential government snooping), will if implemented use facial recognition and data integration analysis technology to identify individuals as well as behavioral and other patterns, trends, relationships, and anomalies indicative of terrorism. Personal information about millions of people, such as their driver's license records, telephone calls, financial transactions, recorded contacts with police, visas and work permits, and so on could all be tracked via a super-networked database. Privacy advocates, and especially the American Civil Liberties Union (ACLU), along with certain members of Congress, have expressed grave concerns about the potential for government abuse of such computer-enabled analysis capabilities.[85] Such concerns were validated in July of 2005 when General Accounting Office (GAO) investigators revealed that the Transportation Security Agency (TSA) of the U.S. Department of Homeland Security (DHS) had violated the Privacy Act of 1974 when in 2004 it secretly collected personal information on 250,000 people in order to test capabilities for computerized matching of airline passenger information with terrorist watch list data as part of the agency's Secure Flight program. The GAO reported that approximately 100 million records were illegally acquired from commercial data archival firms rather than airline passenger lists as the agency had previously announced, without notifying affected individuals as required by law. Rather astonishingly, the TSA official responsible for managing the Safe Flight program and overseeing the computer matching test, rationalized and trivialized the agency's violation of federal law. The incident which, drew sharp criticism of DHS from members of the Senate Homeland Security Committee, is reminiscent of discoveries by the Church Committee about privacy violations committed by the federal government throughout a good deal of the 20th century. The incident should serve as a reminder and warning about the propensity of actions government officials to illegally acquire and use information even if their gathers are well intentioned.[86]

In these times of heightened concern about terrorism, combined with the potential for cybercrime and attacks to cripple national critical information infrastructures and needed intelligence capabilities improvements (deficiencies paradoxically resulting in part from past curtailing of excesses in intelligence gathering), we need to vigilantly balance support of the government's ability to provide information and national security and ferret out criminals and terrorists against ensuring constitutional privacy protections.[87] This is not easy, and the stakes for miscalculating threats to either security or civil liberties do not get much higher, because American society is based upon ideally balancing security and privacy along with other civil rights. To these extraordinary ends, criminal justice and information security professionals, along with other clear-thinking members of society, should *periodically* ask a series of questions originally suggested 30 years ago by Congress in the course of investigating unethical and illegal spying by agencies of the federal government:[88]

1. Which government agencies actually engage in domestic spying?

2. How many citizens are targets of government intelligence activities?
3. What standards govern the opening of intelligence investigations and how can it be known when intelligence investigations have been terminated?
4. Where do current targets fit on the spectrum between those who commit violent criminal acts and those who seek only to dissent peacefully from government policy?
5. To what extent does information being collected include intimate details of the targets' personal lives or their political views, and has such information been disseminated and used to injure individuals in their personal, social, or professional affairs?
6. What actions beyond surveillance are intelligence agencies taking, such as attempting to disrupt, discredit, or destroy persons or groups who have been the targets of surveillance?
7. Are intelligence agencies being used to serve the political aims of presidents, other high officials, or the agencies themselves?
8. How are agency officials responding either to proper orders or to excessive pressures from their superiors? To what extent are intelligence agencies disclosing or concealing information to or from outside bodies charged with overseeing agency policies and actions?
9. Are intelligence or law enforcement agencies acting outside the law? What currently is the attitude of officers and officials in such agencies toward the rule of law?
10. To what extent is the executive branch and the Congress controlling intelligence and law enforcement agencies and holding them accountable for their surveillance activities?
11. Generally, how well is the federal system of checks and balances between the branches of government working to control intelligence activity?

You may be thinking that if you have nothing to hide, you have nothing to fear from the government. Besides, someone in authority must be paying attention to these issues, right? Possibly, but as you have just read, violations of federal privacy laws by the federal government still occur periodically. Of course, government agencies have intelligence gathering and analysis responsibilities, and their accomplishment requires gathering information about people and using it to achieve legitimate ends, some of which will invariably be detrimental to individuals and groups. In criminal prosecutions, courts have historically struck a balance between protecting the rights of persons accused of committing crimes and protecting society, which suffers the consequences of crime. Essential to balancing these goals are the rules of criminal law that specify intelligence gathering and analysis methods and procedures for introducing evidence of wrongdoing. In addition, rules of evidence provide for criminal defendants discovering evidence to be used in their own defense and for challenging the legality of how information and other evidence collected by the government is to be accomplished.[89] These issues will be explained in Chapter 9 when we discuss investigating and prosecuting cybercrimes.

### 7.2.5.4 Ethical and Legal Use of Surveillance Technologies.

Increasingly affordable, interoperable, and compact surveillance technologies make possible and help to perpetuate human desires, needs, capabilities, and willingness to engage in monitoring of virtually any activity, location, or process. Indeed, surveillance technologies now allow ubiquitous watching in many public and private places such as government buildings and courtyards and in airports, train and subway stations, shopping malls, and schools. Today, some parents even monitor their children remotely via a CCTV system and computer when they are at child care establishments. Have you ever thought about all the ways and places in which you are monitored? In 1949 George Orwell described a world in which everyone could be monitored all the time in his classic sci-fi novel *Nineteen Eighty-Four*.[90] Since publication of that book, people throughout the computerized world, particularly Americans concerned about protecting privacy rights, have become increasingly anxious about the technology-enabled surveillance capabilities of law enforcement, security, and intelligence agencies. Are we approaching a state of living in which our every movement can be tracked?

For nearly a hundred years, the military has developed increasingly sophisticated technologies with which to monitor and intercept electronic communications of various kinds. During World War I, for example, radio-telegraph signals emitted by ships were capable of being detected by more than one source and triangulated to plot the location of the message sender. In the late 1920s, law enforcement officers were beginning to tap into telephone lines to discover evidence of crimes. Initially, the police were not required to have a search warrant to listen in on or record telephone calls, although this changed with enactment of the Communications Act of 1934. Throughout the remainder of the 20th century U.S. courts steadily increased privacy expectations, and then following the terrorist attacks of 9-11 relaxed legal requirements for conducting searches, for using electric surveillance technology and for seizing evidence of crimes. This unfolding situation has tremendous implications for investigating cybercrimes while ensuring protection of the civil rights guaranteed in the U.S. Constitution. Nonetheless, worldwide concerns about transnational organized crime and terrorism has given

## BOX 7.3 • *Real-Time Electronic Surveillance, Tracking, and Recording Capabilities Relative to Behavioral, Investigative, and Security Functions of Law Enforcement and Intelligence Agencies*[91]

**Activities:** Observation of physical behavioral patterns such as with CCTV in private property or open public spaces.

**Biometric Verification:** Identification of an individual with fingerprints, palm prints, voice prints, iris/cornea scanning, or DNA typing in combination with determining or tracking physical locations at particular times.

**Contraband Detection:** Systematic scanning of people and shipping containers passing security checkpoints involving use of x-ray, gamma ray, and thermal or density imaging.

**Conversations:** Clandestine listening to people talk via room or space bugging, telephone or cell phone wiretaps, or remote laser vibration-sensing equipment.

**Emotions:** Measuring combinations of psychological and physiological reactions to circumstances and stimuli, as with polygraph testing, voice stress analyzers, and brain wave analyzers such as those used in airport security checkpoints to gauge the nervousness of passengers and/or level to which they are masking deceit.

**Financial Transactions:** Tracking credit/debit card purchases, ATM deposit and withdrawal activity, wire transfers, computerized payroll payouts and deductions, automatic bill payments, lottery and gambling winnings, and taxes owed and paid.

**Electronic Person-to-Person Communications:** Monitoring computer-mediated communications or telecommunications between two or more people, such as text or voice communications via commercial telephone, cell phone, teleconferencing, paging, email, and instant messaging services.

**Person-to-Electronic Device Activities:** Monitoring electronic activities such as Web site browsing, downloading, cable and satellite television-watching patterns, or hacking behaviors.

**Movements:** Plotting locations occupied via GPS/GIS monitoring systems attached to or embedded within vehicles, persons, cell phones, PDAs, laptop computers, and other tangible articles routinely carried such as purses and briefcases.

Here it is useful to mention that personal information available online can also be used to help bring about civil and criminal justice. After going on a date, a computer savvy woman did a routine check using Google to discover that a man she went out with, LaShawn Pettus-Brown, was wanted by authorities in Cincinnati, Ohio, on suspicion of wire fraud in connection with a failed project funded by that city. Pettus-Brown was subsequently arrested by the FBI in New York City.[97] For several years, law enforcement officers have also been using search engines such as Google to get clues pertaining to the whereabouts of fugitives, witnesses, and even victims of crimes who may have relocated to another state or elsewhere. Personal data available online also helps authorities track down deadbeat dads who fail to pay child support. For example, Rob Smitty was located and arrested for allegedly not paying $8,100 in child support after participating in an online dating service and being ratted out by his new acquaintance.[98]

Offices of medical examiners and coroners, among other types of criminal justice organizations, have also begun placing sketches or photos of missing persons and unidentified persons or bodies online in the hopes of someone making an identification.[99] The Doe Network is one of many online volunteer organizations that have formed to assist law enforcement in doing just that. Comprised of civilian volunteers and private investigators, the organization searches for the identities of missing and dead persons using Internet search tools. Since forming in 1999, The Doe Network claims to have solved 17 cases and assisted with four others by searching through photographs and trading leads and networking with law enforcement.[100] These are just a few examples of how computers are increasingly being used to track the identity and whereabouts of people in the interest of civil and criminal justice, in ways that do not violate legal expectations of privacy.

It is notable that in addition to having tremendous investigation and privacy responsibilities, most officials in agencies at all levels of government are deeply concerned about privacy protections and have been for many years. For example, shortly after presidential pronouncements of promise regarding the National Information Infrastructure in the early 1990s, the National Telecommunications and Information Administration of the U.S. Department of Congress issued a report on safeguarding privacy in the information age.[101] Since that time the National Academy of Sciences has also produced a number of reports with important privacy policy recommendations.[102] Many state government agencies have also promulgated privacy protection laws and regulations, notably in California, which now requires businesses and government offices to notify people about security breaches of databases containing their personal information. The California Breach Law, which went into effect on July 1, 2003, is intended to curb identity theft while also holding agencies and firms more accountable for protecting the privacy of individuals from whom personal information is collected. Firms found to not comply with the law face civil suits and Federal Trade Commission fines up to $25,000 for each day that notification is not made or that the security breach persists. The law applies to firms licensed to conduct business in California, as well as to firms in other states that have customers in California.[103]

As the result of new legislation and public concerns about privacy in connection with the need for information security to prevent cybercrimes, many government agencies and organizations have developed protection policies and employee training programs to declare and reinforce ethical and responsible use of computers and data. This subject is taken up in Chapter 11. Some nations, such as Australia, have also enacted policies and national legislation affording specific privacy protections to citizens or residents. Indeed, regardless of organizational and national differences, most people agree on basic principles for protecting the privacy of computerized information. The United States provides certain privacy protections, which when it comes

## BOX 7.4  •  *Basic Principles for Safeguarding Information Privacy*

**Openness:** The existence of record-keeping systems and practices regarding collection of data should be publicly available.

**Individual Participation:** Individuals should have control over collection of their personal data (except in instances of national security and law enforcement investigations).

**Collection Limitation:** No more information should be collected than is needed to complete a transaction for a specific purpose and agreed to in advance by parties involved.

**Use Limitation:** Information should not be used for purposes other than those for which it was expressly collected. So-called routine uses should be specified.

**Data Retention:** Data should be retained no longer than necessary, and individuals should be notified of retention limits in advance (e.g., the duration that records of long distance telephone calls, email, instant messaging, Internet browsing activities, etc., will be kept).

**Data Quality:** Information that is kept needs to be accurate and complete. For example, credit information should reflect all efforts made by consumers to pay their bills, not just delinquency activity, and criminal investigative records should reflect exonerating information and when charges were dropped by prosecutors. (This can be important for securing and retaining employment and good credit. Federal law provides for the right to review and have credit records corrected.)

**Access Controls:** Individuals should have the right of access to information being kept about them. Exceptions include ongoing national security and criminal investigations specific to particular events, not broad societal circumstances. In all instances, access to records should be controlled, logged, and periodically audited to ensure that inappropriate examination, analysis, or distribution is not occurring.

**Security Controls:** Keepers of data have a responsibility to keep it secure from loss, inappropriate access, manipulation, and destruction and to notify persons whose information may have been affected by security breaches or other events such as a fire or natural disaster.

to matters of criminal investigations by the government, are indirectly addressed by amendments to the U.S. Constitution and are described in a substantial body of criminal and civil case law (which we will talk more about in Chapter 8). Privacy principles are also included in various policies of government agencies and contained within Federal Information Processing Standards established by the National Institute for Standards and Technology (see Box 7.4).

## 7.3 Summary

In this chapter, we discussed the emerging potential for IT-enabled abuse and cybercrime and controversial issues related to cybercrime and information security. Ongoing transformations in areas of academic research and education, online banking and e-commerce, meeting

and courting significant others online, and IT-enabled democratization all present potential opportunities for new forms of IT-enabled crime. Internet blogging, smart mobs, and electronic voting each present opportunities for crimes to be committed with computers or other electronic IT devices via information systems. Who can say how, if at all, blogging, smart mobs, and other types of activities enabled by IT devices and information systems will affect future crimes, information security, and justice? Cybercrime affects computer users everywhere, in both physical and cyber realms, implying that we all need to be concerned about information security everywhere we go and in everything we do. Meeting someone online may result in a sex crime, but official or informal tracking of individuals may lead to the arrest of a wanted person or to civil justice such as paying bills that are owed.

E-commerce has many implications for cybercrime, many of which are financial in nature. Not everyone prefers to participate in e-commerce, although information security vulnerabilities related to financial cybercrimes can be reduced by practicing sound information security techniques (discussed later in the text) in combination with being an informed and reflective consumer. Reviewing monthly credit card receipts, for example, is today vital to detecting fraud and preventing identity theft.

Societies are comprised of institutions and private, not-for-profit, and government organizations that often collaborate to accomplish shared goals for the common good. Stakeholder groups, however, may have differing and overlapping interests and concerns about computers, computerization, and the many controversial issues regarding cybercrime and information security. Hence, cybercrime and information security laws, regulations, policies, programs, and acceptable practices are often controversial. Stakeholder groups help shape the organization of and rules for cyber society. Important stakeholder groups include government agencies, industrial sectors, not-for-profit organizations, advocacy groups, and various groups of computer users, all of which are affected by cybercrime. Many important organizations along with their primary interests and capabilities are listed in Appendix A.

Activities of the computer hacking subculture, Open Source Community, electronic gaming enclaves, and the online pornography industry are notably controversial and are related to opportunities for committing cybercrimes. Hackers have been increasingly branded and demonized by mainstream media. Many people do not understand the underlying ideologies of this subculture that inspire legal and illegal computing behaviors of its members. The goal of the Open Source Community is to promote creation, innovation, distribution, and use of software applications for free use, provided copyright protections of individual code writers are observed. Electronic gaming now provides exciting entertainment for people of all ages and gaming preferences. Many, but certainly not all, games feature violence and sexually suggestive content that is scrutinized by the gaming industry as well as watch dog organizations. Online pornography is also very controversial and has implications for computer abuse and cybercrime, especially with respect to illegal exploitation of children.

In the United States, where privacy infringements are often not legally defined as crimes, people are right to be worried about the extent to which information about them is being used without their knowledge, authorization, or control by individuals, groups, firms, and government agencies. Certain intelligence and law enforcement agencies within the U.S. government have during periods of intense concern over national security systematically violated privacy laws. The potential for this to recur during modern times, with heightened concerns over the potential for international physical and cyberterrorism coupled with the need for greater intelligence gathering and analysis to ensure homeland security, should give criminal justice and security professionals pause to reflect on the need to balance the privacy and security goals of free societies, as determined by laws and constitutionally required checks and balances within government. Controversial issues such as these that emerge with technological changes in society reveal the need to continually create new laws and regulations in order to better manage information security issues and prevent cybercrimes. This is will be our focus in Part III of the text.

## *Key Terms and Concepts*

Age rating symbols, 242
Blogs and blogging, 227
Church Committee findings, 255
Computer hackers, 232
Content descriptors, 242
Culture, 233

Cyberpunk, 257
Cyber society, 220
DEFCON, 235
Electronic gaming enclaves, 238
Erotica, 243
Expectation of privacy, 251

Freeware, 236
Googling, 249
Hacker ethic, 233
Hacker subculture, 232
Hentai, 244
IT-facilitated sex, 243

N-Generation, 221
Open Source Community, 236
Open Source Initiative, 237
Open source software, 236
Operation Sundevil, 256
Pornography, 243
Privacy, 232
Privacy infringement, 248

Simulation technology, 238
Smart mobs, 229
Stakeholder, 231
Swarm mobs, 229
Subculture, 233
Terrorism Information
   Awareness, 258

Toon porn, 244
Total Information Awareness,
   258
USA PATRIOT Act, 258
Virtual gaming worlds, 240
Virtual property, 240

## *Critical Thinking and Discussion Questions*

1. Think about how computers have changed the college and university environment. What opportunities do these present for computer abuse and cybercrime?

2. Briefly describe how you do your banking (i.e., how your paycheck is deposited, how you get cash, and the extent to which you use credit/debit cards). Then explain the two ways in which you may be most vulnerable to either online or cyber theft.

3. Suppose you wanted to meet someone special online and then eventually meet him or her in person. In what ways would you be concerned for your safety? What precautions would you take to protect yourself, your data, your money, and others in your life from harm?

4. Explain what you think the advantages and disadvantages of IT-enabled democratization are? Be specific about ways in which computers, other electronic devices, and information systems may help or hinder legal and fair elections or other government processes.

5. Express your views about blogging by investigators or information security professionals. Explain possible disadvantages or potential problems arising from officers blogging as opposed to sharing investigative information in more traditional ways.

6. Weigh in with your feelings about whether online tracking of people and posting of information about then online without their knowledge or permission is ethical.

7. Do some Googling about yourself or someone you know. Describe what you find, whether it is accurate, and how you feel about it being available to any connected IT user.

8. In your own words, briefly explain the essence of the hacker ethic. With what aspects of this philosophy do you agree or disagree? Explain why you feel the way you do.

9. Conduct a little online research, then in your own words, briefly explain the underlying principles of the Open Source Community. Cite your online sources, and explain aspects of this model for technology innovation you like or dislike and agree or disagree with Explain why you feel the way you do.

10. Briefly describe your computer, online, or video gaming experiences (i.e., what you play, how you play, how often you play, for how long, etc.) Then describe your most interesting, delightful, ridiculous, or horrific computer gaming experience ever.

11. Explain why you think some people engage in computer gaming to excess. What could or should be done to prevent them for harming themselves?

12. Do you think computer gaming can contribute to violent behavior in some people? Explain your answer and what should or should not be done about this controversy surrounding violent or sexually graphic computer games.

13. What is your opinion of adult pornography? Comment on whether you think (1) it should be banned or regulated more stringently than it is (e.g., not viewable by minors under 18 years of age), (2) whether it can be so alluring that it interferes with normal living and therefore should be restricted in some way (e.g., software filters), and (3) whether you think it can inspire some people to commit abusive or criminal acts.

14. Suppose you are in the library of your college or university doing research or studying. Another student nearby is quietly working on a laptop (with a wireless connection) and the screen is in plain view to you and anyone else who happens by. On the screen appears image after image of what is clearly pornography. What would you do? Do you think school environments should ban students from looking at porn in public areas shared by others who may be offended by such content? Whose rights are more important: the student viewing the porn or other students who may incidentally view the content while sharing the physical environment?

15. Explain in your view what should be considered private information? Then explain what should be publicly available and why. Include in your explanations descriptions of how IT has changed the ways in which privacy can be violated.

16. Go online and either google your name or find an example of what you consider to be a violation of privacy involving someone's personal information. Explain how you feel about your findings, and the basis for your views and steps that could have been taken to prevent any privacy violations from occurring.

## References and Endnotes

1. Baase, S. (2003). *A Gift of Fire: Social, Legal, and Ethical Issues for Computers and the Internet* (pp. 2–6). Upper Saddle River, NJ: Pearson Education.
2. Tapscott, D. (1998). *Growing up Digital: The Rise of the Net Generation.* New York: McGraw-Hill.
3. McQuade, S.C., & Ruff, R. (2005). Information Security: Risk Perceptions and Protection Capabilities of U.S. College Students. Unpublished manuscript. Rochester Institute of Technology.
4. D. Chu and Y. Ackah (2004). Who is stealing your money? A cross-national examination of an ATM skimming crime. Presented at the Annual Conference of the American Society of Criminology, November 19, Nashville, TN.
5. Allen, C. A., et al. (2002). *The National Strategy for Critical Infrastructure Assurance: Banking and Finance Sector.* Washington, DC: National Institute of Standards and Technology.
6. Staff Author (2005) Budding Jordan cyber love ends in divorce. Yahoo! News. Retrieved February 17, 2005, from http://story.news.yahoo.com/news?tmpl=story&cid=1517&e=7&u=/afp/afplifestyle jordan.
7. Cohen, A. (2003, December 30). Blogging for Business Case Study: Western States Information Network. Retrieved December 8, 2004, from http://www.pcmag.com/article2/0,4149,1401289,00.asp.*PC Magazine.*
8. Baker, S. & Green, H. (2005, May 2). Blogs will change your business. *Business Week*, p. 57.
9. Baker, S. & Green, H., 2005; see p. 59, note 8.
10. Rheingold, H. (2003). *Smart Mobs: The Next Social Revolution.* Cambridge, MA: Perseus Books Group.
11. Taylor, C. (2003, March, 3). Day of the smart mobs. CNN.com. Retrieved December 8, 2004, from http://www.cnn.com/2003/ALLPOLITICS/03/03/timep.smart.mobs.tm.
12. Rheingold, H. (2003, May 31). Swarm crime in Rio. Smart Mobs. Retrieved December 8, 2004, from http://www.smartmobs.com/archive/2003/05/31/swarm_crime_in_.html.
13. BBC Staff Author (2003, April 16). Texting blamed for crime rise. BBC News. Retrieved December 8, 2004, from http://news.bbc.co.uk/2/hi/uk_news/scotland/2954045.stm.
14. Levy, S. (1984). *Hackers: Heroes of the Computer Revolution.* New York: Doubleday.
15. Levy, S., 1984; see note 14.
16. Levy, S., 1984; see note 14.
17. Denning, D. (1990). Concerning hackers who break into computer systems. Proceedings of the 13th National Computer Security Conference (pp. 653-664). Quotation on p. 1 of document retrieved in 1998 from http://www.cosc.georgetown.edu/~denning/hackers/Hackers-NCSC.txt/
18. Levy, S., 1984; see note 14.
19. Landreth, B. (1989). *Out of the Inner Circle.* Redmond, WA: Tempus.
20. Parker, D. B. (1989). *Computer Crime: Criminal Justice Resource Manual,* 2nd ed. Washington, DC: National Institute of Justice.
21. Levy, S., 1984; see note 14.
22. Gibson, W. (1984). *Neuromancer.* New York: Ace Books.
23. OSI News Weblog (2004). Apple is depending on open source for security. Retrieved November 7, 2004, from http://opensource.org/weblog/2004/09/02#AppleTigerOSSecurity.
24. Open Source Initiative (2004). Web home page. Retrieved November 20, 2004, from http://www.opensource.org/.
25. NPD Group (2004). NPD Group reports on sales of licensed video games titles. Retrieved December 5, 2004, from http://www.npd.com/dynamic/releases/press_040608.htm.
26. Eng, P. (2002, August 21). U.S. military pursues computer war games. ABC News. Retrieved December 8, 2004, from http://abcnews.go.com/sections/scitech/DailyNews/wargames020821.html.
27. Shachtman, N. (2002 July, 4). Shoot'em up and join the army. Wired News. Retrieved December 8, 2004, from http://www.wired.com/news/games/0,2101,53663,00.html.
28. Associated Press Staff (2003, October 3). Military training is just a game. Wired News. Retrieved December 8, 2004, from http://www.wired.com/news/games/0,2101,60688,00.html.
29. Live Shot (2004). Real time, online, hunting and shooting experience. Retrieved November 23, 2004, from http://live-shot.com/howitworks.shtml.
30. Dibbell, J. (2003, January). The unreal estate boom. *Wired.* Retrieved December 8, 2004, from http://www.wired.com/wired/archive/11.01/gaming.html.
31. Castronova, E. (2002, January 14). Virtual worlds: a first-hand account of market and society on the cyberian frontier. Social Science Research Network Electronic Library. Abstract document retrieved December 8, 2004, from http://papers.ssrn.com/sol3/papers.cfm?abstract_id=294828.
32. Ward, M. (2003, December 22). The dark side of digital utopia. BBC News. Retrieved April, 17, 2005, from http://news.bbc.co.uk/2/hi/technology/3334923.stm.
33. Feldman, C. (2005). Banned Sims blogger bites back. GameSpot.com. Retrieved April 17, 2005, from http://www.gamespot.com/all/news/news_6085767.html.

34. Staff Author - Urizenus (2003, December 8). Evageline: interview with a child cyber-prostitute in TSO. *The Second Life Herald*. Retrieved April, 17, 2005, from http://www.alphavilleherald.com/archives/000049.html.

35. Feldman, C., 2005; see note 33.

36. Dibbell, J. (2003). Surfing the web: Black Snow Interactive and the world's first virtual sweat shop. Retrieved December 8, 2004, from http://www.juliandibbell.com/texts/blacksnow.html.

37. Lastowka, F. G., & Hunter, D. (2003, May, 29). The laws of the virtual worlds. Social Science Research Network Electronic Library. Retrieved December 8, 2004, from http://papers.ssrn.com/sol3/papers.cfm?abstract_id=402860.

38. Bartle, R. A. (2004, April). Pitfalls of virtual property. The Themis Group. Retrieved December 8, 2004, from http://www.themis-group.com/uploads/Pitfalls%20of%20Virtual%20Property.pdf.

39. Haines, L. (2005, March 30) Online gamer stabbed over 'stolen' cybersword. *The Register*. Retrieved April 5, 2005, from http://www.theregister.co.uk/2005/03/30/online_gaming_death/.

40. BBC Staff Author (2005, June 8). Chinese gamer sentenced to life. Retrieved August 16, 2005 from http://news.bbc.co.uk/1/hi/technology/4072704.stm

41. Associated Press Staff Author (2004, November 23). Group wants to restrict violent games. Bell Globemedia Publishing Inc. Retrieved November 23 2004, from http://www.globetechnology.com/servlet/story/RTGAM.20041123.gtviolence1123/BNStory/Technology/.

42. P2pnet Staff Author (2004, November 22). *Shoot Jack Kennedy* video game. p2pnet.net. Retrieved November 23, 2004, from http://p2pnet.net/story/3084.

43. Reuters Staff Reporter (2005, August 9). Man dies after 50 hours of computer games: South Korean left seat in Internet cafe only to use toilet, take brief naps. Retrieved August 16, 2005, from http://www.msnbc.msn.com/id/8888579.

44. Rainey, R. (2004, November 24). Groups assail "most violent" video games, industry rating system. *LA Times*. Retrieved December 5, 2004, from www.latimes.com/technology/la-na-games24nov24,1,2144307.story?coll=la-headlines-technology.

45. Krahulik, M., & Holkins, J. (2004). Child's Play. Penny Arcade, Inc. Retrieved December 5, 2005, from www.childsplaycharity.org.

46. U.S. Secret Service and U.S. Department of Education (2002, May). *The final report and findings of the safe school initiative: Implications for the prevention of school attacks in the United States* (pp. 28, 31). Washington, DC: Government Printing Office.

47. Entertainment Software Rating Board (2004). Game Rating & Descriptor Guide. ESRB. Retrieved November 23, 2004, from http://www.esrb.org/esrbratings_guide.asp.

48. Lane, F. S. I. (2000). *Obscene Profits: The Entrepreneurs of Pornography in the Cyber Age*. New York: Routledge.

49. Standage, T. (1998). *The Victorian Internet* (Chapter 8, pp. 127–144). Markham, Ontario Canada: Thomas Allen & Sons.

50. Ackman, D. (2001, May 21). How big is porn? Retrieved August 16, 2005 from http://www.forbes.com/2001/05/25/0524porn.html

51. Curtis, K. (2005, June 19). Man may have molested 36,000. Democrat and Chronicle, p. 4A, as originally reported by Associated Press.

52. MSNBC staff and news service reports (2005, June 17). Thousands of boys molested? Cops seek victims. Retrieved August 16, 2005, from http://www.msnbc.msn.com/id/8247899/

53. Internet Content Rating Association (2005). Home page of the ICRA. Retrieved January 10, 2005, from http://www.icra.org/about/.

54. Brunker, M. (2004). 'Toon porn' pushes erotic envelope online: adult animation booming on Web, spreading to mainstream media. MSNBC.com. Retrieved October 19, 2004, from http://www.msnbc.msn.com/id/6227619/.

55. Hughes, D. M. (2001, May). *The impact of the use of new communications and information technologies on trafficking in human beings for sexual exploitation: A study of the users*. Report of the group of specialists on the impact of the use of new information technologies on trafficking in human beings for the purpose of sexual exploitation (EG-S-NT). Committee for Equality between Women and Men. Strasburg, Germany: Council of Europe.

56. Brunker, M., 2004; see note 54.

57. Brunker, M. (2004). Is anything taboo in 'toon porn'? Weighing the moral and legal questions. MSNBC.com. Retrieved October 19, 2004, from http://www.msnbc.msn.com/id/6282737/.

58. Sieberg, D. (2000). Claim of 'most downloaded woman' heats up. Retrieved October 26, 2004, from http://archives.cnn.com/2000/TECH/computing/08/31/downloadable/.

59. Dauphine, D. (2004). The most downloaded person in history. Retrieved October 26, 2004, from http://www.billiondownloadwoman.com/.

60. Rimm, M. (1995). Marketing pornography on the information superhighway. *Georgetown Law Review*, 83, 1849–1934.

61. Elmer-Dewitt, P. (1995). On a screen near you: cyberporn. *Time*, July 3, pp. 38–45.

62. Cohen, J., & Solomon, N. (1995). How Time magazine promoted a cyberhoax. Retrieved October 26, 2004, from: http://www.fair.org/media-beat/950719.html.

63. Hoffman, D. L., & Novak, T. P. (1995). A detailed analysis of the conceptual, logical and methodological flaws in the article: Marketing pornography on the information superhighway. Retrieved October 16, 2004, from http://elab.vanderbilt.edu/research/topics/cyberporn/rimm.review.htm.

64. Sykes, C. J. (1999). *The End of Privacy: The Attack on Personal Rights at Home, at Work, On-line and in Court.* New York: St. Martin's Griffin.

65. Sykes, C. J., 1999, p. 96; see note 64.

66. FindLaw for the Public (2002). What you need to prove if you want to sue your employer for violating your privacy at work. Nolo, Inc. Retrieved March 21, 2004, from http://public.findlaw.com/employment_employee/nolo/ency/88C141F2-2B0C-4525-B34B3FCC7494B4A2.html.

67. Mills, E. (2005, July 14). Google balances privacy, reach. Retrieved August 16, 2005, from http://news.com.com/Google+balances+privacy,+reach/2100-1032_3-5787483.html

68. Reuters Staff Reporter (2004, February 9). Paris Hilton sues over Internet sex tape. Retrieved August 16, 2005 from http://www.cnn.com/2004/TECH/internet/02/09/paris.lawsuit.reut/

69. Associated Press staff reporter (2005, March 9). Fred Durst sues over sex video. Retrieved August 16, 2005 from http://abclocal.go.com/kabc/ontv/030805_ent_durst_tape.html.

70. Loundy, D. J. (2003). *Computer Crime, Information Warfare and Economic Espionage* (pp. 610–612). Durham, NC: Carolina Academic Press.

71. ConsumerAffairs.com (2000). Trans Union ordered to stop selling consumer credit data. Retrieved November 12, 2004, from http://www.consumeraffairs.com/news/trans_union.htm.

72. Benner, J. (2001). Court: no selling credit data. Retrieved November 12, 2004, from http://www.wired.com/news/politics/0,1283,43097,00.html?tw=wn_story_related.

73. Consumer Federation of America (2003, March 19). Consumer groups alert Treasury of privacy violations by free file tax preparation web sites. Consumer Federation of America. Retrieved March 21, 2004, from http://www.consumerfed.org/032503taxwebsites.html.

74. Editorial (2004, November 13). 'Privacy' law fails brave boy. *Review Journal.* Retrieved November 13, 2004, from:http://www.reviewjournal.com/lvrj_home/2004/Nov-13-Sat-2004/opinion/25250558.html.

75. U.S. Congress (1976, April 26). Final Report of the Committee to Study Governmental Operations with Respect to Intelligence Activities (i.e., the Church Committee Report). Washington, DC: Government Printing Office.

76. U.S. Congress, 1976; see note 75.

77. U.S. Congress, 1976; see note 75.

78. Sterling, B. (1992). *The Hacker Crackdown: Law and Disorder on the Electronic Frontier.* New York: Bantam.

79. Sterling, B., 1992; see note 78.

80. Sterling, B., 1992; see note 78.

81. Loundy, D. J., 2003; see note 70; *Steve Jackson Games, et al. v. United States Secret Service, et al.* U.S. Court of Appeals for the Fifth Circuit. 36 F.3d 457. Described at pp. 132–137

82. Loundy, D. J., 2003; see note 70.

83. See evidence of federal, state, and local cybercrime-fighting capabilities supported through R&D as supported by National Institute of Justice (2004). Electronic crime program. Retrieved June 14, 2004, from http://www.ojp.usdoj.gov/nij/sciencetech/text/tecrime.htm.

84. Electronic Frontier Foundation (2005). EFF home page. Retrieved March 26, 2005, from http://www.eff.org/.

85. Hudson, A. (2003). Report stirs fears of privacy violations. Article originally published by *Washington Times.* Retrieved on November 13, 2004, from: http://www.washtimes.com/national/20030624-101720-5150r.htm. Washington, DC: News World Communications.

86. Miller, L. (2005, July 24). Congress: Government broke privacy laws by collecting commercial data. Retrieved August 17, 2005, from http://informationweek.com/story/showArticle.jhtml?articleID=166401991.

87. 911 Commission (2004, July). *Executive Summary of Final Report of National Commission on Terrorist Attacks Upon the United States.* Washington, DC: Government Printing Office.

88. U.S. Congress, 1976; see note 75.

89. U.S. Congress, 1976; see note 75.

90. Orwell, G. (1949). *Nineteen Eighty-Four,* a Novel. London: Secker & Warburg.

91. Inspired by and adopted from Office of Technology Assessment, as described by Ibid., Gardner, 1988, p. 451; see note 90.

92. Society of Photo-Optical Instrumentation Engineers (2002). *Sensors, and Command, Control, Communications, and Intelligence (C3I) Technologies for Homeland Defense and Law Enforcement.* Conference Proceedings of the SPIE, April 1–5, Orlando, FL. Bellingham, WA: SPIE.

93. Goold, B. (2002, Winter/Spring). Privacy rights and public spaces: CCTV and the problem of the unobservable observer. *Criminal Justice Ethics,* 21–27.

94. See, e.g., discussions by Hunter, R. (2002). *Into the World Without Secrets: Business, Crime and Privacy in the Age of Ubiquitous Computing.* New York: Wiley; and Lyon, D., & Zureik, E. (1996). *Computers, Surveillance and Privacy.* Minneapolis: University of Minnesota Press.

95. Sussman, D. (2004). Just 1 in 5 feels rights violated. ABC News. Retrieved November 13, 2004, from http://abcnews.go.com/sections/us/DailyNews/liberties_poll021001.html.

96. U.S. Department of Homeland Security (2004). Department of Homeland Security Appropriations Act of 2005. Press release retrieved November 1, 2004, from http://www.dhs.gov/dhspublic/interapp/press_release/press_release_0541.xml.

97. Horn, D. (2004, January 28). Pettus-Brown done in by savvy date, Google. *Cincinnati Enquirer.* Retrieved December 8, 2004, from http://www.enquirer.com/editions/2004/01/28/loc_pettusbrown28.html.

98. Staff Author (2004). Kidney donation leads to arrest. *Democrat and Chronicle*, October 24.

99. Dotinga, R. (2003, April 19) Web helps ID John and Jane Does. *Wired News.* Retrieved December 8, 2004, from http://www.wired.com/news/culture/0,1284,58410,00.html.

100. The Doe Network (2004). International center for unidentified and missing persons. Retrieved December 8, 2004, from http://www.doenetwork.us/.

101. U.S. Department of Commerce (1995). *Privacy and the NII: Safeguarding Telecommunications-Related Personal Information.* Washington, DC: National Telecommunications and Information Administration.

102. See, generally, www.nap.edu.

103. Rupley, S. (2003, July). California's two-fisted privacy stance. *PC Magazine.* Article retrieved November 13, 2004, from: http://www.findarticles.com/p/articles/mi_zdpcm/is_200307/ai_ziff44513

# Part III

# *Managing Cybercrime*

*Cybercrime Investigator in Action* Photo by Nathan Fisk

In Part I we explored cybercrime as a technologically-evolving social construct consisting of combinations of behaviors enabled by computers and other types of electronic IT devices via information systems. In the process we discovered fundamental aspects of information assurance, as well as the myriad interrelated ways in which computer abuse and cybercrime takes place. In Part II we built on this foundation of knowledge to learn who cybercriminals are, why they commit abusive and criminal acts, how much cybercrime there may be, and the difficulties associated with measuring the impact on victims. We also discussed controversial and emerging issues related to computer abuse and cybercrime and how various stakeholders in society work to influence political and legal processes to their advantage. In essence, Parts I and II were devoted to understanding cybercrime. Now in

Part III we focus on managing and preventing cybercrime. We begin by examining cyber-related laws and regulations and then move on to learn about investigating and prosecuting cybercriminals. After this you will learn about security practices for protecting information systems, as well as steps that managers and IT professionals can take to improve the security posture within their organizations. The last chapter is devoted to understanding what the federal government is doing to address cybercrime, threats to critical information infrastructures, and computer ethics education as a foundation for preventing computer abuse and cybercrime.

# 8

# Cyber Laws and Regulations

## 8.0 Introduction: How Does Society Prohibit Cybercrime?

What are laws? What are regulations? How many different kinds of laws and regulations are there? How do they differ, interrelate, reflect, and affect society's views and responses to computer abuse, cybercrime, and protection of information systems? What differences exist between laws and regulations created at local, state, national, and even international levels of governance? How are laws and regulations pertaining to cybercrime and information security created? In addition, why should criminal justice and information security professionals care? After all, is it not their job to manage cybercrime, which essentially pertains to preventing and controlling illegal use of computers and other IT devices via information systems? Moreover, what possible role can we as individuals, not directly involved in political processes have, in the formulation of laws and regulations? At most, ought we not to concern ourselves with understanding the essence of crime laws and leave the rest to lawyers and politicians?

The short answer to all these questions is that laws and regulations are extremely important because to some extent they affect virtually every aspect of administering criminal justice and increasingly to managing the security of

data, information systems, and facilities that operate critical information infrastructures. In addition, information security and criminal justice professionals, among professionals in other fields who do not understand legal concepts, legal processes, and substantive aspects of several different bodies of law and regulations governing technology-related practices, quickly become vulnerable to inadvertently violating people's constitutional rights or having their investigations into wrongdoing challenged and cases dismissed by courts. They also unnecessarily risk losing data, having information systems compromised, and being successfully sued by individuals, groups, or organizations who have suffered losses as the result of inappropriate or illegal actions or inactions. In a nutshell, laws and regulations matter a lot. As criminal justice and security professionals, we must know what they are, how they are created, and how they can be used to help or hurt our interests and those of everyone else in society.

Laws and regulations can be thought of as tools government uses to maintain societal order, productivity, and well-being. Ensuring public safety and security and protecting the legal rights of citizens are among the most important functions of any government. Laws and regulations, however, are often complex, controversial, and difficult to administer within the government itself, as well as within private and nonprofit sectors consisting of stakeholder groups concerned about differing aspects of computer abuse, cybercrime, and information security issues. The importance of many bodies of laws and regulations combined with complex aspects of their formulation, interpretation, and administration is a primary reason law schools are notoriously difficult to enter and graduate from and why only qualified attorneys are allowed to practice law. This situation is exacerbated by cybercrime and information security being international concerns shared by many nations having different legal systems, traditions, and laws. Hence a single chapter devoted to cyber laws and regulations is barely sufficient for learning introductory legal information relevant to understanding and managing cybercrime.

With this disclaimer, we will begin the chapter by considering the rationale and jurisdictional reach of cyber laws. Here you will learn about the concepts of due process and legal jurisprudence. You will also learn the primary purposes of U.S. federal laws and regulations pertaining to computer abuse, cybercrime, and protection of information systems. This information will be useful when reflecting on controversial political and ethical issues, which you may be involved in or concerned about (e.g., equal opportunities and legal rights of "computer have-nots" or government agencies providing needed information security potentially at the expense of personal privacy). Most of the legal issues discussed, however, also pertain to the creation and implementation of laws and regulations within state and local levels of government. You will also learn about international bodies of law, as well as certain treaties (also known as conventions or agreements) between nations for preventing and controlling cybercrime, and for ameliorating its negative social and economic impact throughout the world.

In the second section we will distinguish between several bodies of U.S. law, namely constitutional and case law, criminal law, administrative law, intellectual property law, and civil and tort law. This will be done with respect to their general applicability to cybercrime and information security issues. You will learn how courts have thus far dealt with many of the legal issues posed by IT, particularly with respect to IT-enabled cybercrime and threats to information security. However, it is important to understand from the onset that construction and enforcement of cyber-related laws and regulations is rapidly evolving in ways that cannot be fully anticipated, and that analysis of these issues depends on understanding the challenges computing and telecommunications technology pose relative to legal standards of behavior, and with respect to due care and diligence in the design and management of information security products and systems.

The third section of the chapter is a refresher about how laws and regulations are created and administered in the United States, a subject of increasing importance to criminal justice and information security professionals in these rapidly changing times. You will be provided with a brief overview of legislative bills and executive approval processes, budget appropriations, and processes surrounding the propagation of regulations by federal and state government agencies responsible for helping to ensure enforcement of cybercrime laws and protection of information systems including those deemed vital to critical information infrastructures and national security. Then in the last section of the chapter you will be provided with a succinct overview of the most recent and important laws and regulations bearing on the prevention and control of crimes enabled with computers or other electronic devices. Specifically we will examine federal laws that (1) specify illegal use of computers and electronic IT devices, (2) facilitate or limit cybercrime investigations, (3) protect children from online pornography, (4) specify information security requirements for government agencies and private sector firms, and (5) afford privacy and consumer fraud protections.

The chapter summary provides a review of constitutional provisions for protecting freedom of expression and association and expectations of privacy in cyber society; and roles and responsibilities of government and criminal justice officials, IT administrators, and information security professionals in protecting information systems. A primary goal of this chapter is to help students understand laws and regulations, how they differ among geopolitical jurisdictions, processes by which they come about and change, differing bodies and types of laws, and key federal statutes governing cybercrime and information security standards and practices. This general approach offers students insights into how computer technology is changing law and the legal system, and conversely, how technology is being adapted to traditional standards and definitions of the law.

## 8.1 The Rationale and Reach of Cyber Laws and Regulations

Most people agree that an individual who sends a worm, Trojan, or virus into cyberspace, wreaking worldwide havoc on information systems and infrastructures, should be punished severely. No doubt an individual who uses a computer to commit white-collar crime; create, download, or disseminate child pornography; or plan an illicit drug deal and then launder money should also be investigated, apprehended, and punished. These and innumerable other similar kinds of behavior that are clearly criminal in nature call for the application of coercive powers of government and criminal justice systems. Other matters of law arising from using, misusing, and even abusing computers, other electronic IT devices, and information systems are not as clear cut. When, for example, is it permissible to acquire and distribute personal information without the knowledge of the person whose privacy is at stake? As indicated in Chapter 7, violating someone's privacy is not a crime, in the United States and the right to privacy is not expressly guaranteed in the U.S. Constitution. In fact, the word *privacy* does not appear in the Constitution or any of its 27 amendments. If not written down in laws, how

are people to know what their rights are, what society expects of them, and what the penalties for not obeying laws are? To answer these questions we must first realize that the concept of law is much more complicated than most people understand it to be.

The concept of law has various definitions and applications but is essentially a set of rules that defines standards of behavior and use of technologies by and among individuals in society. In the United States laws are created in legislative bodies of government, approved and administered by executive branches of government, and reviewed and ruled upon with respect to interpretation and application by judicial branches of government. Regulations are also rules that are effectively extensions of laws—rules created by executive branch agencies of government. More will be said about regulations later. Laws and accompanying regulations reflect the values, needs, and beliefs of the members of a society and they are designed to provide for the continuity of society, as well as safe, predictable, and reliable relationships among its members under changing conditions. The concept of **the rule of law** pertains to legal underpinnings for preservation of civil societies and essentially means that laws and regulations are to be created and enforced fairly and that punishments for violating laws are not meted out arbitrarily.

All societies impose formal and informal sanctions for violations of their laws and regulations. Recall from Chapter 1 how informal social sanctions may be imposed when people use technology in a deviant manner. In this chapter we focus on formal sanctions, the severity of which depends on the nature of the offense, the intentions of the perpetrator, the extent of harm done, and other factors that judges or juries may consider when sentencing convicted offenders of crime laws or defendants in civil cases. Specifying appropriate and inappropriate behaviors, and punishing individuals who violate legally expected standards of behaviors, is essentially what law accomplishes. For example, our society expects that when an individual agrees to purchase a computer system from another person or retail outlet, both parties will do as they promised or face paying monetary damages to the wronged party. The same legal principle applies to purchasing a car on credit, contracting for Internet services, and paying for a college education—all parties involved have legal rights and responsibilities.

Laws are also intended to deter people from committing wrongs; to protect individuals, groups, and organizations from harm; and to inform members of society of desirable behaviors and preferred courses of action as well as punishments for not voluntarily complying with society's rules. Regulations in particular can help many private sector firms and nonprofit organizations look to the government for guidance and assistance in legal matters (e.g., to assure that their policies, procedures, and technologies for protecting facilities and information systems are what they should be). Hence, none of us question that we are obligated to stop our cars at an intersection when a traffic light turns red. We also usually voluntarily obey speed limits, we try to maintain our cars in good working order for the safety of everyone on networks of public roadways spanning legal jurisdictions, and we resolve disputes arising from traffic accidents without resorting to violence or taking the law into our own hands. Similarly when we marry, give birth, or adopt a child, society defines for us the rights and responsibilities we owe in undertaking such important relationships, and the government may be able to provide assistance to ensure that our rights are not violated or help us out if we get into a jam.

By the same token, laws and regulations pertaining to illegal use of computers or other electronic IT devices are designed for the protection of everyone in computerized societies. Cyber laws and regulations also provide for ranges of penalties and compensation that may be owed to victims of cybercrimes. They also typically specify legal remedies for victims of computer abuse or cybercrimes to seek damages for losses associated with damaged, manipulated, stolen, or destroyed data or information systems. It is important to understand that administrative processes and ranges of penalties and compensation associated with violations of laws and regulations vary within the United States and even more so in other nations affected by cybercrime. Differences in crime and the administration of criminal and civil justice among nations are rooted in legal philosophies that serve as the basis for societies formulating laws and regulations. Let us therefore consider these philosophies, along with the concepts of due process and legal jurisprudence, primary purposes of federal laws in the United States, and international agreements pertinent to managing and preventing cybercrime.

### 8.1.1  Legal Philosophies

The history and ongoing evolution of technology, crime, and society makes clear that laws, regulations, and judicial processes surrounding their creation and administration did not appear overnight. Our current legal system reflects centuries of religious, philosophical, and political influences not limited to the American experience. Put differently, American laws incorporate legal principles spanning history and places beyond U.S. borders. At their core, laws in the United States are based on Judeo–Christian principles. The dictates of the Ten Commandments and the Golden Rule in particular form the basis for many contemporary local, state, and federal laws. Origins of American jurisprudence also date to 1066, when William the Conqueror began his attempt to unify England following the Norman Conquest. The Magna Carta of 1215, emanating from the brutish rule of King John of England, is also widely regarded as a staple for thinking about fairly administered justice systems, and its provisions were not forgotten by American colonists who revolted against oppressive English rule in this nation's Revolutionary War.[1] American laws also reflect social norms and principles for civil society as practiced by Native American tribes. For example, Irondequoit Indians practiced and imparted to early white settlers of North America many principles for democratic governance that are today reflected in the U.S. Constitution and its amendments. Cesare Beccaria (1738–1794) of Italy, as well as other 18th century European crime and justice thinkers, also influenced the Constitution by recognizing the importance of laws that they said set conditions under which otherwise independent and isolated men could unite to form societies.[2] Much of Louisiana's state legal system is derived from the Napoleonic Code, the civil law of France following Napoleon Bonaparte becoming emperor of that nation in 1804.[3]

The point is that legal customs and laws and regulations do not magically spring forth, as if from the mouth of Athena, the mythical Grecian goddess famous for providing her wise advice, protecting the state, and guarding the liberties of citizens. To the contrary, legal traditions are established over long periods of time by conscientious people working hard amidst political controversy and with limited resources. Despite their efforts, people and their governments do not always get laws right, and even when they do, laws periodically need to be updated in ways corresponding to social, economic, and technological changes. Laws also vary from one nation to another, which is a major reason why policing cybercrime not constrained to U.S. borders is so problematic. More will be said later about international agreements for managing cybercrime, but first you should know about three legal philosophies that are often incorporated into state and national laws, as well as international treaties. These are natural law, positive law, and the historical school of legal thinking, each of which consists of different concepts that influence how governments differ in their creation, interpretation, and administration of laws.

**Natural law** is the concept that moral and ethical principles are inherent in human nature, if not ordained by God, and are therefore naturally included in rules established by societies. The opening phrases in the U.S. Declaration of Independence, including "We hold these truths to be self-evident, that all men are created equal, that they are endowed by their Creator with certain unalienable Rights, that among these are Life, Liberty and the pursuit of Happiness," reflect the essence of natural law—that certain rights are so fundamental and obvious they need not even be written down. Proponents of this concept believe, for example, that civil and human rights are universal and that crimes such as murder, assault, and stealing or that involve damaging property are universally wrong. Indeed, laws and rules ranging from those of primitive computerized to societies generally proscribe such behaviors.

**Positive law** maintains that there are no God-ordained or universal laws. According to this view, the only laws or regulations that exist in a society are those that are socially constructed, written down, and administered by governments. Therefore, civil and private rights are not universal or "unalienable" as indicated in the Declaration of Independence. Rather, rights are given and may effectively be taken away by combinations of formal legal and informal social processes. Lawmakers and judges with positivist school leanings tend to rely exclusively on the existing laws and customs of a society rather than their own personal or professional sense of justice when rendering legal decisions. Similarly they are very reluctant to read into the meaning of the U.S. Constitution or accept anyone else's sense of what is inherently right, wrong, moral, or immoral. For them, if a law is not written down, it does not exist in practical legal terms, and if a new law is needed, it is up to the legislative and executive branches of government to get busy and create it.

The **historical school of legal thinking** emphasizes that past laws and court decisions, otherwise known as case law, are the best sources for ruling on legal matters in specific instances. Proponents of this view are most likely to apply decisions in past cases to resolve current legal conflicts, regardless of whether the laws alleged to have been violated emanate from natural or positive law traditions. In so doing, jurists provide legal continuity while helping shape future legal authorities, requirements, and protections for the betterment of society. More will be said about the importance of case law later. For now you should remember that all three philosophical views are useful for understanding the importance of laws and regulations and for administering justice in matters having to do with IT-enabled abuse and crimes. This is true throughout the United States and in other nations to a lesser or greater extent regarding criminal, administrative, intellectual property, and civil disputes.

### 8.1.2  Concepts of Due Process and Legal Jurisprudence

**Due process** refers to the administration of legal proceedings "according to those rules and principles which have been established in our systems of jurisprudence for the enforcement and protection of private rights."[4] The due process clause of the Fifth Amendment of the U.S. Constitution, combined with its application to states via the Fourteenth Amendment, obligates all governments within the United States to ensure that each defendant in a criminal case and every litigant in a civil case receives a fair trial. In cyber cases this means that parties accused of violating state or federal computer crime laws are entitled to impartial evidentiary hearings and other fairly

administered legal procedures and processes. Similarly, in administrative law proceedings on matters involving compliance with information security regulations, due process means that litigants must receive a fair hearing before an administrative law judge. A fair trial or hearing mandate that each person be afforded the same rights, protections, and procedures without regard to their race, religion, socioeconomic class, sexual orientation or the severity of the alleged activities or inaction. Understanding the concept of due process and the judicial system designed to uphold it is essential for law enforcement officers who routinely collect evidence of crimes and for prosecutors who seek to have evidence admitted at trial. Due process is also important for IT administrators and information security professionals to understand, as they may be called upon to defend themselves and the actions or inactions of their organizations in relation to technology standards or legal and illegal use of information systems.

Figure 8.1 illustrates that the U.S. judicial system consists of state and federal trial and appellate courts. Each of these court systems operates separately and creates different sets of case law precedents. Disputes, or cases, enter either the state or federal trial court system depending on the nature of the alleged violation within the

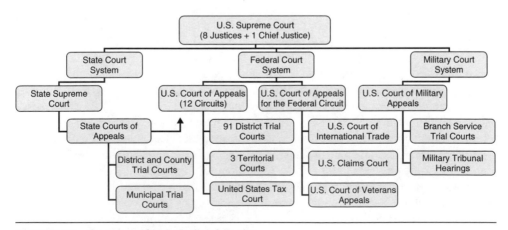

**FIGURE 8.1  *Overview of U.S. Judicial System***

affected geopolitical jurisdiction. For example, a defendant accused of violating a state computer crime law would ordinarily be charged in a state district or county trial court. If the defendant is also suspected of violating a federal crime law, he or she may be charged separately for the same offense by a federal prosecutor. This rule applies to members of the military who may also be charged under provisions of the U.S. Code of Military Justice (UCMJ) in addition to or in lieu of criminal charges brought in federal or state courts. Military cyber cases, including military tribunals involving suspected terrorists (and conceivably cyberterrorists), would fall under the jurisdiction of the federal military court system. None of these instances, however, constitute **double jeopardy**, which means being illegally tried a second time by the same court system for the same offense after being found innocent.

**Jurisdiction** pertains to the general authority of a specific court to accept and resolve a dispute. Traditionally, a court's jurisdiction is based on geographic factors such as the location of a defendant's residence or place of business, where a crime or civil wrongdoing allegedly took place, or the placement of disputed property, and so forth. Asserting geographic jurisdiction over a case also requires that a court have specific knowledge regarding the identity of the plaintiff and defendant, as well as control over identified tangible property involved. Laws of jurisdiction make it easy for a legal conflict to be aired and resolved. In the United States, it is a fundamental legal right and cultural expectation that everyone is entitled to their day in court, and everyone also has a legal right to a speedy trial and other expeditious legal proceedings. Except on weekends and holidays, for example, a person is entitled to be arraigned by a judge within twenty-four hours of being arrested by police. The legal system is organized to accommodate this need.

**Legal jurisdiction** pertains to a court's authority to accept a case and to make a decision that the litigants are legally bound to follow. In other words, a court cannot resolve a dispute unless it

has legal jurisdiction over the people or property involved. In practice the terms jurisdiction and legal jurisdiction amount to the same thing, although technically speaking they are somewhat different concepts. Internet-based computing presents special challenges in determining legal jurisdiction. Without a doubt, one of the most attractive features of the Internet is the ability of a user to communicate across boundaries of legal jurisdictions with any number of individuals and at minimal or no direct cost to the parties involved. Additionally, individuals are free to properly identify themselves or interact with other users with complete or pseudo anonymity, unless they are investigated for criminal or civil wrongdoing and exposed for who they really are. Cloaked with a stolen identity or disguised with an obscure IP address, a user can with near impunity download music, access child pornography, threaten a politician, or defame the quality of a product or business unless they become the focus of a determined investigator, prosecutor, and court, willing to assert jurisdiction, investigate, and hear such cases.

In criminal matters, legal jurisdiction is asserted by prosecutors after police have filed the case. It is rare for state and federal courts to hear the same case technically filed under different levels of crime laws. In civil and tort claims cases, a litigant must choose the appropriate court based upon case circumstances and laws of jurisdiction. Keep in mind that the accusing party (i.e., the plaintiff in a civil suit or the prosecution in a criminal matter) initially decides upon a court having jurisdiction over the accused (i.e., the person being sued or accused of committing a crime). Periodically, for political or tactical reasons, litigants may prefer to have their case heard by a court in a different location and possibly having a different type of jurisdiction because they believe interpretation of laws and rules of evidence will work in their favor. They seek what is known as a **change of venue**, which may result in the opposition having to spend additional time, effort, and money or possibly drop the case altogether. In cases involving cybercrime and information security, legal jurisdiction is often complicated by actions that transcend the geopolitical borders of states and nations. Therefore, it is useful to know about other types of jurisdiction established in law.

**Personam jurisdiction** is the ability of a court to make decisions regarding defendants who reside or conduct business within specified geographical boundaries. For example, a county-level district court would normally hear cases stemming from actions within that county. **Long arm jurisdiction** refers to the authority of a court in one state to have jurisdiction over an out-of-state (nonresident) defendant when that defendant has sufficient minimum contacts within that geographical area. Courts have also held that an out-of-state corporation doing business in another state is under the jurisdiction of the courts in which it primarily does business. However, individuals committing a crime, causing an accident, or breaching a contract in a state other than the one they live in will find themselves subject to the jurisdiction of the state in which the harm was done, regardless of where they primarily live or conduct most of their travels or business.

**Rem jurisdiction** has to do with a court's authority over property located within its geographical boundary. Thus, an Ohio-based firm with a computer system located in Pennsylvania would be subject to Pennsylvania courts on the basis of rem jurisdiction. **Subject matter jurisdiction** describes the type of cases that courts of limited jurisdiction may accept. For example, bankruptcy cases are heard in bankruptcy courts, disputes regarding the validity of a will are litigated in probate courts, and intellectual property cases are heard in federal claims courts, which have jurisdiction over patent, copyright, trade mark, and trade secret cases. **Original jurisdiction** refers to the jurisdictional requirements of a court when a dispute first enters the judicial system. **Appellate jurisdiction** defines the types of cases accepted by the intermediate and final, or supreme, levels of appellate courts. **Concurrent jurisdiction** exists when both federal and state courts have the legal authority to hear the same case. Federal courts also have jurisdiction when a case involves litigants with different state citizenship. To qualify for *diversity of citizenship* under federal court rules, litigants must be residents of different states and the dispute must involve a controversy involving $75,000 or more. When a case can only be tried in state court or only be tried in federal court, **exclusive jurisdiction** exists. Federal courts have exclusive jurisdiction over federal crimes, intellectual property, and certain other types of cases involving interstate rights or claims of wrongdoing. Federal and state courts may have jurisdiction in cases of bankruptcy depending on the nature of interstate loans and claims made by creditors of differing states. State courts have exclusive jurisdiction over disputes regarding traffic violations, divorce, adoption, state crimes, and interpretation of a state constitution.

Within the United States, the general rule is that a person may be charged with a cybercrime by every state alleging a violation of its law. In criminal matters, the state in which the crime was committed or from which it was launched will normally claim original jurisdiction. In civil matters, original jurisdiction is normally determined on grounds of where harm occurred. Typically a person or entity will answer to charges made against them and stand trial first in the state that first files formal charges or in the state in which the defendant was apprehended and is being held in custody. After the first state has finished its legal business with the accused, a convicted defendant may then be extradited to stand trial in a second state. However, if the defendant was found innocent in the first trial, he or she may be subpoenaed to appear or be rearrested and transported to a different state to stand trial on new charges. In international criminal and civil cases, legal jurisdiction also depends on laws of affected nations, as well as on international agreements between nations, such as **extradition agreements** specifying the conditions under which an accused person may be forcefully transported from one country to another in order to stand trial for a crime. People are not extradited in civil cases. However, defendants may be tried in absentia in either criminal or civil cases, depending on existing laws and legal precedents.

**BOX 8.1 • *Determining Jurisdiction in Cyber Suits: Zippo Manufacturing v. Zippo.com***

The Federal Court for the Western District of Pennsylvania wrote a well-cited opinion in *Zippo Manufacturing Company v. Zippo Dot Com, Inc.*, 952 F. Supp. 1119 (W.D, Pa. 1997). This case addressed challenges of interpreting jurisdiction in Internet-related cases. The plaintiff was the Pennsylvania corporation that held the trademark for and manufactured the popular Zippo® brand of cigarette lighters. The defendant was a California corporation that sold subscriptions for an Internet news service. It had exclusive rights to use the domain names zippo.com, zippo.net, and zipponews.com. Naturally Zippo Dot Com, Inc. used these domain names to advertise subscription news services to residents of Pennsylvania, among other states, via the Internet. It turned out that 2 percent (3,000) of Dot Com's 140,000 subscribers were Pennsylvania residents and that the firm had contracts with seven other Pennsylvania-based Internet service providers (ISPs). Zippo Manufacturing sued Zippo Dot Com for trademark infringement, but the defendant challenged the suit on jurisdictional grounds.

In making its ruling, the federal court carefully reviewed the traditional concepts of jurisdiction and a specific Pennsylvania statute creating a right for firms of that state to sue nonresidents and out-of-state firms. The decision created a sort of sliding scale to determine jurisdiction based on how much online business occurs and where. Specifically, jurisdiction over an entity was ruled to be "directly proportionate to the nature and quality of commercial activity" conducted over the Internet. Defendants who enter into contracts with out-of-state residents that "involve the knowing and repeated transmission of computer files over the Internet" clearly trigger jurisdiction of courts in the state in which the residents reside. However, a "passive Web site that does little more than make information available to those who are interested in it is not grounds" for a court to assert its jurisdiction to hear a case. Ultimately a court's jurisdiction to hear a case is determined by examining the level of interactivity and the commercial nature of information exchanged via Web sites or other Internet-based communications.[5]

## 8.1.3 International Agreements for Managing Cybercrime

The trans-border nature of cybercrime presents additional conditions and challenges to concepts of jurisdiction. Administering justice in international cases is predicated on identifying, and charging or arresting defendants suspected of committing crimes and/or civil wrongdoing and finding a court system with legal authority to bind litigants to its authority that is also cost-effective and geographically accessible. This can be enormously difficult. Consider the illegal transmission of a virus unleashed in a developing nation that infects computers and compromises data in information systems worldwide. What nations would have jurisdiction over the perpetrators? Could the defendants, if identified, be tried in the nation from which the malware was originally distributed or in one or more nations to which the malware was bounced and subsequently redistributed? Would prosecution depend on the number of victims involved and amount of harm caused within one nation as opposed to others? What if the transgressors resided in a country that did not have computer crime laws? Could they be charged under the laws of nations or states that do?

Similarly in what nation would a plaintiff in a civil suit claiming breach of contract sue when a defendant corporation is headquartered in a different country? If cyberspace extends beyond the geopolitical boundaries that traditionally define legal jurisdiction, what responsibility do governments have to protect individuals interacting in this transient realm? In any of these situations, what would be the financial costs associated with pursuing the case, and who would be responsible for paying the legal costs? The short answer to all these questions is, it depends on several factors because cyber society lacks all of the requisite attributes of a state as outlined in the 1933 Montevideo Convention on the Rights and Duties of States, which specifies that a bona fide country must have a permanent population, a defined territory, a government, and the capacity to enter into relations with other states.

This definition implies that cyber society is not a distinct and sovereign state. Rather, it is a composite of loose associations that transcend traditional geopolitical nation-state boundaries. Jurisdiction in cyberspace is therefore contingent on the laws of individual countries and on international agreements between countries that govern human activities in physical places.[6] **International agreement** is a generic term widely used to label agreements between nations and, as such, means the same thing as articles of agreement, charter, concordant, convention, declaration, pact, protocol, and treaty. Several additional terms are periodically used within the international community to describe agreements between nations. This is primarily the result of diplomatic traditions regarding references to human rights, friendship, commerce, navigation, crime fighting, and so on. Regardless of the specific term used, international agreements are intended to commit nations to particular foreign policies. Nations enter into agreements with each other when it is their interest to do so. Since the world community is without a centralized law-making institution, several international organizations are involved in facilitating the formulation of agreements between nations.[7] (You will be reading about the cybercrime fighting efforts of a few of these organizations shortly.)

International agreements are created often, as evidenced by the more than 25,000 treaties that have been recorded by the United Nations (UN) since its first General Assembly meeting in 1945. Once the wording of an agreement is hammered out by the affected nations, a treaty must be ratified through the separate legal and political processes of the signatory countries. Nations may approve a treaty in whole or part by modifying certain aspects of an agreement in their own interest. In the United States Article 2 of the U.S. Constitution empowers the president to establish treaties with other nations after receiving advice and a two-thirds consenting vote from the Senate. However, the president is also authorized to establish executive orders directing matters of foreign policy with or without senate approval. Executive orders are the functional equivalent of formal treaties, provided they are carried out and maintained by subsequent elected administrations.[8] International agreements about managing crime are usually very difficult to establish because nations often have very different views as to what constitutes justice. This is reflected in the structure and legal processes of various national criminal justice systems throughout the world. For example, a nation that does not endorse capital punishment is not likely to sign a treaty that obligates it to extradite prisoners to a nation such as the United States that can impose the death penalty in capital cases such as murder or treason. Conversely, Americans are opposed to extraditing people accused of crimes to nations that do not honor the right to legal counsel and to not self-incriminate. Thus, establishing international agreements on cybercrime has not been easy.

The history of efforts to establish international standards for investigating and prosecuting computer crimes, computer-related crimes and cybercrimes dates to 1976 and involves several international bodies consisting of numerous nation-state members. In 1976, under the auspices of the European Union, efforts were made to standardize international laws bearing on personal data privacy protections and information security. In 1981 the Council of Europe Convention for the Protection of Individuals with regard to Automatic Processing of Personal Data added to this effort. However, successful moves to internationally harmonize administrative and civil privacy laws were more difficult in the area of criminal law. Indeed, the transnational nature of computer-enabled crime and abuse throughout the world presented many unique legal challenges. Nonetheless, beginning in the mid-1980s, many nations, through the efforts of other key international organizations, began paying attention to an increasing variety and number of computer-enabled crimes and the social and economic impact they were having throughout the world. In 1983, the Committee of Experts on Computer Related Crime of the Paris-based Organization for Economic Cooperation and Development (OEDC) became the first international group to study what could be done to prevent, control, and reduce the harmful impact of computer-enabled abuse and crime internationally.[9]

The committee's report, released in 1986, specified several types of computer-enabled activities that countries should consider making illegal, such as computer-enabled fraud and forgery, unauthorized alteration of computer programs or data, interception of communications, theft of trade secrets, and computer hacking. The report also noted several barriers to international management of computer-enabled crime problems, including[10] (1) lack of global consensus regarding a legal definition of criminal conduct and by extension behavior constituting computer-related crime; (2) lack of expertise of police, prosecutors, and the courts to understand computer-enabled activities in relation to existing national laws and legal principles; (3) inadequacy of international legal powers to investigate and access computer systems and seize intangible data needed as evidence in national criminal hearings; (4) inconsistent bodies of national laws applicable to computer-related crime matters and for guiding, supporting, or mandating investigation of computer-related crimes; and (5) the transnational character of many computer crimes coupled with lacking extradition and mutual assistance treaties, plus the inability of existing treaties to take into account the dynamics and special requirements of computer-enabled crime investigations and prosecutions. In issuing its report, the OECD committee called attention to the world's enormous computer-enabled abuse and crime problem, made worse by limited and incongruent legal mechanisms among nations for preventing and controlling such high-tech crimes.

From 1985 to 1989, the Select Committee of Experts on Computer-Related Crime of the Council of Europe also examined legal problems presented by computer-enabled crimes internationally. On September 13, 1989, member nations of the Council adopted a series of recommendations that specified a list of offenses to be criminalized, including computer-enabled fraud and forgery; interference with or damage to computer data, programs, or systems; and unauthorized access to, interception of, or reproduction of data. Member nations also adopted a somewhat overlapping *optional list* of computer offenses that nations could ban if they chose to, including alteration of computer data or computer programs, computer espionage, unauthorized use of a computer, and unauthorized use of a protected computer program. However, the rather incomplete and overlapping list of mandated and optional offenses, combined with the council's lack of legal authority to make nations abide by its recommendations even if nations agreed to adopt them, effectively rendered the agreement useless.

The OECD and Council of Europe initiatives were followed in 1990 by an exploration of legal aspects of computer crime by the UN. The Eighth UN Congress on the Prevention of Crime and the Treatment of Offenders, held in Havana, Cuba, resulted in member nations adopting another resolution on computer-related crime. This document invited national governments throughout the world to help guide formulation of appropriate international legislation and policy directives to fight computer crime in accordance with the economic, social, legal, cultural, and political circumstances of each country.[11] In 1997 the European Ministers of Justice, at their 21st Conference in Prague, recommended international cooperation to support cybercrime prevention and control efforts being carried out by the European Committee on Crime Problems (CDPC) in order to standardize domestic criminal law provisions.[12] Also in 1997 the UN published its *Manual on the Prevention and Control of Computer-Related Crime*, a 70-page document that provided an overview of computer crime issues including types of attacks and crimes as they then existed, estimates of social and economic impact on crime victims, and guidelines for undertaking criminal investigations and prosecutions. The manual also provided another assessment of the limited abilities of existing national laws to address the problem, called for standardization of computer crime laws internationally, and sought to rally nations to take seriously the emerging transnational cybercrime threat.[13] As with other previous initiatives, however, the UN was and remains essentially powerless to make nations abide by its agreements.

It was also in 1997 that the President's Commission on Critical Infrastructure Protection's recommendations led to Presidential Decision Directive (PDD) 63 on Critical Infrastructure Protection. This first step taken by the United States toward developing a framework for responding to cyber threats against national information infrastructures directed the FBI to create an interagency National Infrastructure Protection Center (NPIC).[14] Also in 1997 the G-8 countries, consisting of the United States, England, France, Germany, Canada, Russia, Japan, and Italy, teamed up to further explore ways to prevent computer-enabled crime and mitigate its impact in nations throughout the world. Known as the Subgroup of High-Tech Crime, it held its first meeting in Washington, D.C., to declare that inadequate cyber laws make the world more dangerous and create difficulties in prosecuting cybercriminals. The subgroup held subsequent meetings and adopted 10 principles to combat cybercrime, the first of which called for worldwide development of comprehensive substantive and procedural computer crime laws. The goal of this initiative was to ensure that no cybercriminal receives safe haven anywhere in the world.[15]

In 1999 the Hoover Institution, the Consortium for Research on Information Security and Policy (CRISP), and the Center for International Security and Cooperation (CISAC) at Stanford University held a conference on international cybercrime and the need for an international convention. This conference was attended by approximately forty representatives of governments, industries, nongovernment organizations (NGOs), and academia from throughout the world.[16] The conference resulted in a proposal calling for an international agreement on cybercrime, acknowledging the inextricable nature of cybercrime, transnational organized crime, and terrorism. The final proposal, which relied in part on an analogy to civil aviation protections against cybercrime and terrorism, attempted to overcome legal disparities among nations by defining types of conduct that should be banned rather than specific laws that nations should enact.[17] The proposal also called for agreements pertaining to investigating, extraditing, and prosecuting cybercriminals and recommended that development and execution of laws be left up to the individual nations. The proposal did not, however, address controversial issues such as free speech or communications containing political content. These issues were left to individual nations to ban and enforce on their own absent multilateral support unless it could be negotiated separately between affected countries.

In February of 2000 Michael Vatis, then director of the US NPIC, gave testimony before both the Senate Judiciary Subcommittee on Criminal Justice Oversight and the Crime Subcommittee of the House Judiciary Committee in which he outlined the major cybercrime and critical infrastructure protection threats facing the United States.[18] These included information warfare, foreign intelligence services, terrorists, and organized criminal groups, all increasingly enabled by computing and telecommunications technology. In the months that followed, debate ensued in the United States and in other nations about the merits of an international treaty on cybercrime prepared by the Council of Europe.[19] A key issue pertained to balancing privacy protections with the need for parity of authority among nations conducting investigations of suspected cybercrimes and threats to critical national information infrastructures.

In September of 2001 the Council of Europe held a convention on cybercrime in Budapest, Hungary, that resulted in a final proposed treaty consisting of 48 articles defining computer-related terms, recommending development of criminal and procedural law, clarifying legal jurisdiction in cases of computer-enabled crimes, and spelling out principles for international cooperation between nations for investigating and prosecuting cybercrimes.[20] Although intended to be a comprehensive legal framework for the prevention and control of cybercrime in Europe and abroad, strong industry protest alongwith social and cultural differences resulted in political concerns about the agreement by several nations. The World Information Technology and Information Services Alliance (WITSA) and the Internet Service Providers Association (ISPA) were critical of the treaty because of requirements it placed on ISPs. The agreement was specially faulted for criminalizing certain IT tools that systems administrators and security specialists use for testing and securing computer systems.[21] Several of these were discussed in Chapter 3. Concerns also pertained to costs businesses would incur in order to maintain detailed system logs required by the convention document,[22] especially given the lack of police skills in most nations for investigating computer-enabled crime.[23] The American Civil Liberties Union (ACLU), among other legal rights and privacy advocacy organizations, argued that while providing additional powers to law enforcement, such as the ability to monitor individuals' online traffic, the treaty was thin in its provisions for protecting individuals' privacy rights.

The Council of Europe is not the only international organization that has sought to facilitate creation of international agreements on cybercrime. Immediately following announcements by the U.S. Department of Justice and other national law enforcement agencies about Operation Buccaneer (see Cyber Case 8.1) and

the signing by several nations of the Council of Europe's Convention on Cybercrime in November 2001, the unaffiliated European Union, consisting of 15 nations, announced plans to create another international agreement to prevent and control cybercrime. In 2002, another international organization, the UN Economic and Social Commission for Asia and the Pacific (UNESCAP), released a *Draft Action Plan on Cybercrime and Information Security* for the Asia–Pacific region. The document outlined a framework of actions needed to boost information security in that region of the world. Included were specific guidelines regarding the necessity of strict sanctions against cybercrime, cooperation in transnational investigations and prosecutions of offenders, and creation of secure methods for the exchange of information between investigatory bodies.

Also in 2002, the Commission of the European Communities (CEC) released *The Proposed Council Framework Decision on Attacks Against Information Systems,* which defines the various types of attacks that can occur on information systems and the necessary responses. The CEC recognized the varying degree of threats posed by several categories of cybercrime and made suggestions for standardizing baseline minimum laws across multiple European countries. The Commission also recognized the importance of protecting e-commerce capabilities for transnational economic stability and recommended that nations implement minimum security standards for online financial transactions.[24] In 2003 several international counterterrorism meetings were convened throughout the world by organizations such as the UN, the EU, and the Association of South East Asian Nations (ASEAN). These meetings generally resulted in pledges for greater international cooperation in the sharing of crime-related and intelligence information and conducting analyses of Internet traffic for indications of impending terrorist attacks, the existence of terrorist organizations, and evidence of ongoing financial support for criminal operations, etc.[25]

## *Operation Buccaneer Targets International Warez Groups*[26]

On December 11, 2001, the 19 field offices of the U.S. Customs Service, in coordination with its law enforcement counterparts in the United Kingdom, Australia, Finland, Sweden, and Norway, executed approximately 70 search warrants worldwide in the initial phase of Operation Buccaneer, the most significant law enforcement penetration to date of international organizations engaged in the criminal distribution of copyrighted software, games, and movies over the Internet. This coordinated law enforcement action was the result of a 14-month-long undercover operation that began in October 2000.

By July 12, 2002, 16 defendants had been convicted in the United States on felony charges of criminal copyright infringement, conspiracy, and/or aiding and abetting criminal copyright infringement. Of those convicted, 9 were sentenced to federal terms of imprisonment ranging from 30 to 46 months for crimes involving copyright infringement by suppliers, crackers, and leaders of multiple top-level warez groups that specialize in distributing pirated music, movies, or software. So-called release groups included DrinkOrDie, Razor1911, RiSCISO, MYTH, and POPZ. Additionally, the investigation successfully targeted members of several leading "courier groups" that specialized

in the illegal distribution and trading of copyrighted works over the Internet, including the groups RequestToSend (RTS), WeLoveWarez (WLW), and RiSC. Collectively, these warez groups were, according to the U.S. Department of Justice, responsible for illegally reproducing and distributing hundreds of millions of dollars worth of copyrighted works over the Internet.

The Computer Crime and Intellectual Property Section of the Department of Justice, the U.S. Customs Service (then still a component of the U.S. Treasury Department and now part of the Department of Homeland Security), and 19 U.S. attorney offices worked closely with law enforcement in the United Kingdom, Australia, Finland, Sweden, and Norway to effect 17 searches of foreign subjects simultaneously with the execution of the U.S. searches. In addition, law enforcement agencies seized several of the world's largest and most significant warez archive sites consisting of highly secured computers that were used to store and distribute massive quantities of copyrighted works throughout the world. Many of the sites contained 2,000 gigabytes or more of pirated music, movies, or software applications estimated to be worth hundreds of millions of dollars in potential retail sales.

All these attempts to create international agreements to manage cybercrime have been more or less effective. Clearly they indicate that progress is being made toward overcoming legal barriers to investigating and prosecuting cybercrime internationally. Yet, despite 30 years of progressive effort to establish uniform laws and standardize investigative and prosecution practices among nations, there exists no universally agreed upon set of civil or criminal laws, government regulations, or technology standards for the prevention and control of cybercrime. In many respects, the Internet has obscured the question of national sovereignty and jurisdiction. Consequently governments must

often continue to act unilaterally to protect their critical information infrastructures for purposes of foreign trade, domestic commerce, national defense, and so on. As described in Chapter 3, civilian law enforcement and military institutions are sorting out their respective roles and capabilities to take action in the new technological paradigm of cybercrime and network-centric warfare with the prospect of cyberterrorism looming (see Figure 3.1). However, considerable legal ambiguity is bound to remain as long as national and international laws addressing crimes enabled with IT via information systems are not clearly specified and consistently enforced. In pragmatic political

### *International Computer Gaming Bust*

In July of 2004 the FBI, Scotland Yard, and German authorities, acting in part on information received from members of the international computer gaming community, arrested individuals in several nations for allegedly releasing Valve Software's source code for its long-anticipated *Half-Life 2* computer game. "Having accessed Valve's server through a security-bypassing loophole in Windows, the hackers were able to download an early and hugely incomplete version of Half-Life 2 and post it on the Internet for downloading via Usenet. A boxed version of the code was even on sale on the Ukrainian and Russian black markets." Company officials equated the loss of its code to stealing and then distributing throughout the world an outline for an envisioned Harry Potter book. The cyber vigilantism coordinated by Valve resulted in the primary instigator contacting the firm to admit his responsibility. After being duped by company officials to fly to their corporate headquarters in Seattle, he was later arrested on German soil. Afterwards Valve prepared to sue other hackers and software pirates implicated in the case, while other computer gaming development firms throughout the world took steps to reassess their information security vulnerabilities.[27]

terms, this may never be universally possible. By the time international agreements are created and ratified, social, economic, and technological changes render aspects of crime-related treaties obsolete. Hence, international diplomacy concerning new treaties is driven by forces larger than the criminal justice systems of any given nation, each of which must perpetuate its own laws and regulations to combat cybercrime as best as it can. Nonetheless, transnational cybercrimes are being investigated and prosecuted as never before as the result of improved international cooperation and formal agreements between nations.

## 8.2 *Bodies of Law Pertaining to IT and Cybercrime Issues*

At a very general level, laws may be categorized as being either criminal or civil, and either substantive or procedural in nature. Criminal laws specify illegal conduct for which people may be fined or imprisoned. Civil laws specify wrongs for which people may be sued monetarily. **Substantive law** pertains to what is prohibited or determined to be wrong. Procedural law determines how substantive criminal and civil laws are to be administered. Substantive aspects of crime laws provide for (1) *definitions* of what a given law pertains to, (2) *labels* for prohibited conduct, (3) *elements* that specify prohibited behaviors or conditions, and (4) ranges of *penalties* for violating various aspects of the law. For example, substantive computer crime laws typically define what a computer is, signal that computer trespassing is against the law, explain what constitutes computer trespassing, and specify ranges of penalties for hacking into systems or exceeding authorized permissions. A given crime law may consist of many definitions, labels, and explanations for several different prohibited behaviors, each with different ranges of penalties. Substantive laws of a regulatory nature may also specify *required actions* in certain circumstances and penalties for noncompliance. For example, a health services provider in the United States must provide security for medical records of patients. If they do not, they are subject to being fined or having their license revoked by government agencies. Conversely, health services providers must not release medical records unless authorized to do so by patients.

By contrast, **procedural law** outlines processes governments must follow to ensure that due process provisions of constitutional amendments are abided by. This means that no one can be punished or deprived of any property without being informed of the charges against them and having an opportunity to retain legal counsel and respond to the charges, confront witnesses, and present evidence of their innocence in a court of law or administrative hearing. The most familiar examples of procedural laws are those that dictate certain investigative procedures such as when it is permissible to search a person, home, business or place of employment, vehicle, or IT device or information system. Procedural law in the United States also includes the legal requirement of police officers to advise someone under arrest and before questioning of their constitutional right to remain silent, that anything they say can and will be used against them in a court of law, that they have the right to the presence of an attorney acting on their behalf before any questioning if they wish, and that if they cannot afford a lawyer, one will be appointed to serve on their behalf at no cost. (These specific rights are often referred to as Miranda Warnings, and will be discussed further in Chapter 9.) Procedural law also applies to actions taken by judges in court proceedings such as also advising defendants accused of crimes of their Miranda Warnings, and allowing or disallowing certain evidence; to state and federal officials overseeing regulatory processes such as those pertaining to issuance of a state vehicle registration or drivers license; and to IT professionals as when financial institutions and health care providers must ensure information systems security on behalf of clients.

Substantive and procedural law is conceptually straightforward. In practice, however, society's rules are differentiated beyond substantive and procedural aspects of criminal and civil law. In the United States alone there are several interrelated bodies of federal, state, and municipal laws pertaining to IT, cybercrime, and information security that litigants may use while trying cases on behalf of their clients. For example, defendants charged with a single or series of cybercrimes may be prosecuted for violating one or more state computer crime laws, be sued under tort law based on alleged violations of federal intellectual property law, and have their professional license suspended or revoked under regulatory provisions of federal or state administrative laws and regulations. Many other hypothetical examples of applying different combinations of laws and regulations to either try or defend people of alleged criminal or civil wrongdoing are imaginable.

In this section you will be introduced to five bodies of law: constitutional and case, criminal, administrative, intellectual property, and tort laws. Each of these major categories of law is explained in general terms and with respect to cybercrime and information security issues. The intention is to provide an introduction to these types of laws and legal issues, which non-criminal justice students in particular may find very valuable. Then in Section 8.3 you will be presented with several federal crime laws and major regulations grouped in ways that relate specifically to managing cybercrime or information security.

## 8.2.1 Constitutional Law and Case Law

**Constitutional law** is a general reference to interpreting and applying legal principles of the U.S. Constitution and its amendments to criminal or civil matters in dispute. In the United States the Constitution is the fundamental and overriding law of the land. All laws and regulations, whether civil, criminal, substantive, or procedural, whether they are established by the federal government, state governments, or local governments, are derived from the U.S. Constitution and its amendments, as interpreted by trial and appellate courts. For this reason, constitutional law is often considered to be the most important body of law. Every day criminal and civil cases are won or lost on substantive and/or procedural grounds based on how litigants and judges interpret and apply constitutional law. Every day, government agencies and agents are found to have acted properly or improperly on the basis of constitutional law. Indeed, it is the U.S. Constitution that structures the organization and powers of the executive, legislative, and judicial branches of the federal government. Nothing is more fundamental to the rule of law, to the administration of criminal justice, and to lawful security management practices than legal principles established in the U.S. Constitution and its amendments.

Ultimately it is the United States Supreme Court when granting a *writ of certiorari,* indicating it will hear an appealed case, that decides the legality of provisions in substantive law or procedures followed by a lower court in a given case. Each year approximately 5,000 cases are submitted to the high court, of which about 200 (4 percent) are reviewed in order to clarify key issues of constitutional law on behalf of the entire nation. Throughout its history, the Supreme Court has interpreted the Constitution and its amendments on myriad issues of substantive and procedural criminal and civil law issues, sometimes fundamentally changing ways in which criminal justice is administered by local, state, and federal government agencies. The Miranda Warnings mentioned earlier, stemming from the 1966 U.S. Supreme Court ruling in the case of *Miranda v. Arizona* (384 US 436), and prior

rulings in the 1964 case of *Escobedo v. Illinois* (378 U.S. 478), forever changed investigative procedures pertaining to self-incriminating statements made to law enforcement officers. History reveals that several amendments, including certain ones contained in the Bill of Rights, are fundamental to ensuring information privacy, for not violating due process in the course of investigating and prosecuting cybercrimes, for regulating information security technology standards and practices, and for affording protections for our using computers and other IT devices in ways not *illegally* proscribed by law. For example,

• The *First Amendment* guarantees free speech and expression and the right to assemble and freely associate with whomever we wish, to protest, and to petition the government for redress of grievances. As such, the First Amendment protects the rights of U.S. citizens to create (but not release) potentially harmful computer code, to join subcultures and social and political movements, to sue for violations of copyright, and so on. Note, however, that not all forms of speech, expression, and assembly are protected. Communities may regulate protests

## BOX 8.2 • *The U.S. Constitution and its Amendments*

The U.S. Constitution was signed on September 17, 1787, by representatives of the thirteen original American colonies. In 1791 ten amendments specifying particular rights of individuals were added to the U.S. Constitution. Known as the **Bill of Rights**, these first ten amendments are as relevant today as they were when the nation was founded over 200 years ago. Since that time, 17 additional amendments have been added to the Bill of Rights so that today there are 27 amendments to the U.S. Constitution. Periodically a new constitutional amendment will be proposed by members of Congress or the President in response to lobbying efforts of stakeholder groups. For example, an amendment specifying the rights of crime victims has been proposed several times, as has a ban on burning or defacing the American flag. However, new amendments are rarely proposed and enacted, and only when there is a compelling national legal issue at stake. The last amendment, enacted in 1992, established that salary compensation for members of Congress can be made only after they are elected. Prior to that, the Twenty-Sixth Amendment enacted in 1971, granted U.S. citizens over 18 years of age the right to vote. Although no constitutional amendments specifically address IT, cybercrime, or information security, several elements of the Bill of Rights plus the Fourteenth Amendment pertain to these issues.

or parades on public property or streets. Use of "fighting words" that may be threatening, or yelling "fire" in a crowded theater, thereby creating panic and threatening public safety, are classic examples of speech that is not protected. U.S. courts including the U.S. Supreme Court have also ruled that obscene language as determined by local community standards is not protected speech, nor is receiving, possessing, transporting, or distributing obscene material via electronic or other means if it is considered obscene by the community from which it is sent or in which it is received or possessed. This issue will be discussed in more detail later.

- The *Fourth Amendment* concerns our right to privacy in our persons, homes, papers, and effects against unreasonable searches and seizures. Hence, the Fourth Amendment requires government investigators to apply for and receive search warrants on the basis of *probable cause* before conducting searches unless there are certain exigent circumstances or exemptions granted in law. For example, the controversial USA PATRIOT Act enacted into law following the 9-11 terrorist events makes it legal for federal agents to search homes and businesses, and computers, IT devices and information systems located within these and other places, without first acquiring a warrant in cases of suspected terrorism or association with terrorist groups. We will discuss this controversial law later as well.

- The *Fifth Amendment* requires formal filing of criminal charges when we are arrested, protects us from double jeopardy (as discussed above), preserves our right to not self-incriminate, prohibits punishment without due process of law, and requires the government to compensate us for converting our private property for pubic use. Hence, the Fifth Amendment ensures that we cannot be compelled to say things indicative of wrongdoing against our will and establishes due process provisions in law. This means we may not be incarcerated, have any

form of property taken from us, or be the subject of another form of punishment as the result of arbitrary actions of government.

- The *Sixth Amendment* guarantees us the right to a speedy trial by an impartial jury, to be informed of charges, to receive legal counsel when being investigated or tried for violating laws or regulations, to confront accusatory witnesses, and to present evidence in our own defense. However, these rights do not necessarily extend to non-U.S. citizens, residents, or to individuals being held under the jurisdiction of the U.S. Military Judge Advocate General who are suspected of being terrorists or enemy combatants and may threaten the national security of the United States.

- The *Eighth Amendment* prohibits cruel and unusual punishment and setting of excessive bail, thereby requiring a person to sit in jail while awaiting trial (although bail may be denied if a defendant is determined by a judge to be a flight risk or danger to the community).

- The *Ninth Amendment* says that rights indicated in the Constitution may not be construed in ways that disparage or deny other rights we have, such as those listed elsewhere in the U.S. Constitution, its amendments, or state government constitutions and amendments. Some legal scholars view the Ninth Amendment as the legal mechanism for protecting certain natural or "unalienable rights" (previously explained) that are not expressly granted in the Constitution, such as the right to privacy.

- The *Tenth Amendment* indicates that powers not expressly granted by the U.S. Constitution to the federal government are reserved for states. This is the basis for state governments to establish their own constitutions, criminal and civil laws, and criminal justice systems inclusive of policing, courts, and correctional agencies.

- The *Eleventh Amendment* prohibits people and organizations not of the United States from using U.S. law to advance their own legal interests against citizens of the United States. Thus, international investigations of cybercrimes involving U.S. citizens in America must rely on the laws of the nation alleging that an offense took place or international agreements as ratified by the nations involved, including the United States.

• The *Fourteenth Amendment* extends due process requirements established by the preceding amendments to all government agencies within the United States. This means, for example, that governments may not enact substantive computer crime laws or regulations, or procedural rules, that violate rights indicated in the U.S. Constitution or specified in any constitutional amendments. The Fourteenth Amendment also guarantees that all U.S. citizens are entitled to equal protection under the law. Accordingly, judges throughout the United States seek to uniformly apply constitutional principles of procedural law when rendering legal decisions in criminal and civil matters.

What a wonderful set of rights Americans have—unique in all history and throughout the world in their scope, jurisdiction, and applicability to situations resulting from inevitable social, economic, and technological changes. Nations have different legal philosophies that translate into very different types of organizational structures for government; very different sets of laws and regulations affecting the lives of people who live, work, or travel in various countries; and very different relationships between individuals and their countries' institutions including but not limited to government agencies. Consequently, social customs and cultures are influenced by the process of making and enforcing laws in addition to the substantive and procedural aspects of the laws themselves. Over time such influence, combined with court rulings that reflect interpretation of laws, has the effect of reinforcing state and national identities while also accentuating differences among people throughout the world. This situation further explains why it is so difficult to establish international agreements for investigating and prosecuting cybercriminals who are not constrained to national borders in carrying out their crimes via information systems such as the Internet.

Court decisions that have accumulated in the United States set legal precedents for every

CYBER CASE **8.3**

### ACLU v. Reno: Striking Down of the Communications Decency Act

In 1996 Congress passed the Telecommunications Act, inclusive of Title V, the Communications Decency Act (CDA), which banned sexually explicit material from online sites where children could easily find it. Specifically the CDA banned "indecent" online communications available to minors, including those available in emails, online newsgroups, Web sites, and so on. The CDA defined indecency broadly to include words, images, or ideas that depicted or described sexual activities or organs if such were determined to be "patently offensive" by "contemporary community standards." The American Civil Liberties Union (ACLU) was joined by several other free speech advocacy organizations in a federal lawsuit against then U.S. Attorney General Janet Reno. The suit resulted in certain sections of the CDA being ruled unconstitutional on grounds that they violated First Amendment free speech rights of adults to write, publish, or consume online material only fit for children.[28] However, the case was appealed by the U.S. Department of Justice to the U.S. Supreme Court, which in June of 1997 upheld the lower federal court's decision thus striking down key provisions of the law.[29] The case reveals how legal disputes involving controversial national public policies that clash with constitutional provisions may be processed expeditiously by courts when necessary.

aspect of living and collectively have come to be known as **case law**. American case laws date to pre-Colonial times and to England, where **common law** was developed and administered on the basis of societal rules commonly practiced and usually understood by laypersons. Eventually commonly administered substantive and procedural rules (i.e., Old English common laws) were written down, added to, and given formal recognition in deciding individual cases. Thus, common laws became the historical and legal foundation for modern American case law rulings. Case law is another extremely important foundation for litigants to base their arguments upon and for courts to consider when rendering decisions in matters of criminal or civil law. The extensive set of existing case laws, numbering in the tens of thousands, and reliance on legal precedents set in these cases to interpret how the law should be applied to new circumstances, underscores the importance of the historical school of legal thinking for managing contemporary cybercrime and information security practices. To this point we have mentioned *Miranda v. Arizona* and *Escobedo v. Illinois* as merely two among innumerable case laws that are added to virtually every day by courts throughout the nation and that collectively help to establish and reinforce our laws and national culture.

Common law doctrines and case law precedents apply to cases not specifically addressed by legislative acts or administrative law bearing on cybercrime law and information security regulatory issues. During the past 20 years combinations of legislated acts, government regulations created and administered in response to requirements of law, and subsequent rulings by courts in specific cases have matured into what some attorneys now informally refer to as **cyber law**. However, lawyers working on contemporary cases related to cybercrime and information security issues conduct legal research just as they always have into how laws have been previously interpreted and applied in circumstances similar to their case, and they carefully examine how rulings in

earlier cases relate to legal principles established in the U.S. Constitution and its amendments. Note that it is not essential that prior cases involved computers, IT devices, or information systems in order to be applicable to cases that do. Effective attorneys are often those who are able to make logical connections between physical and cyber technological realms, and then present convincing arguments based on legal principles identified in prior case law rulings. With this in mind, let us now consider criminal law as another major body of law of particular importance to managing cybercrime and information security.

### 8.2.2  Criminal Law

Crimes are behaviors that violate **criminal law**. You already know this, but if you are not majoring in criminal justice you may not know that crimes are typically categorized by law enforcement officials as being either **crimes against persons** or **crimes against property**. These are, respectively, also referred to as violent and nonviolent or property crimes. **Violent crimes** involve attacks on people. Murder, rape, robbery, and assault that result in bodily harm are examples of violent crime. **Nonviolent crimes** or **property crimes**, including burglary, larceny, fraud, embezzlement, vandalism, and trespassing, involve unlawful taking, damaging, or otherwise violating the property of a person, business, or entity such as a government agency. As explained in Chapter 6, crimes result in many types of primary, secondary, and tertiary harm to individuals, organizations, groups, or society as a whole, including emotional, psychological, and physical injuries and damage to or loss of property, including information and intellectual property.

Violent and nonviolent property crimes may each be subcategorized into specific violations of federal, state, or municipal crime laws depending, for example, on where crimes originated or the type and amount of harm caused. For example, the general crime of assault is usually subcategorized into aggravated assault if it involved the use of a weapon or resulted in significant physical injury to a person, and simple assault that would ordinarily involve only minor or no injury (as in a threat) to a victim.[30] Cybercrimes such as computer hacking, denial-of-service attacks, and releasing malicious computer viruses, worms, and Trojans onto the Internet would be considered property crimes unless they also indirectly result in physical harm to one or more persons.

Crimes are also categorized as being either felonies or misdemeanors depending on their seriousness, gauged in terms of potential or actual harm caused. In the United States a **felony** crime is a relatively serious offense punishable upon conviction by more than one year in a state or federal prison or corrections facility. Felonies generally include all violent crimes in which victims are physically harmed, plus nonviolent crimes in which the value of stolen or damaged property exceeds $1,000. A **misdemeanor** is a relatively less serious offense punishable upon conviction by incarceration for up to one year in a county jail or detention facility. Misdemeanors generally include all nonviolent crimes in which there was no physical harm to victims and the value of stolen or damaged property is less than $1,000. Distinctions between felonies and misdemeanors, as well as contract arrangements for housing prisoners convicted of crimes, vary among federal, state, and local criminal justice jurisdictions. Criminal penalties imposed by a judge or jury on an individual convicted of either a misdemeanor or felony crime may, in addition to or in lieu of incarceration, include paying a fine, performing community service, being placed on probation, and/or paying restitution to crime victims.

All crimes committed against an agency, facility, or asset (e.g., computer, information system or critical infrastructure) of the federal government are considered felonies and are potentially punishable by a monetary fine and/or more than one year in federal prison. Federal criminal statutes pertaining to illegal use of computers or other electronic devices are listed primarily in Title 18 of the United States Code (U.S.C.). This is where you can find, among other types of crime, detailed legal descriptions of wire fraud, computer fraud and abuse, and various financial crimes such as money laundering. Certain sections of other titles within the code also define crimes. For example, Title 17, governing intellectual property law, specifies criminal aspects of violating copyright and trademark laws, and Title 71 includes several statutes on what constitutes illegally receiving, possessing, sending, or transporting obscene materials electronically or in other ways. Specific key laws and regulations bearing on managing cybercrimes are discussed in Section 8.3 below.

Before leaving this introduction to criminal law, it is important to briefly contrast how the criminal justice system in the United States views and treats juvenile versus adult offenders. A **delinquent act** is a crime or **status offense** committed by a juvenile who is normally legally defined in law as a person who was under 18 years of age at the time the offense was committed. Within the U.S. criminal justice system, juvenile offenders are thought of and treated differently than adult offenders. This is evident in terminology used to describe juvenile offenders as opposed to adult offenders. For example, whereas adult offenders are arrested, convicted, and incarcerated in jails or prisons, juvenile offenders are apprehended, adjudicated, and housed in detention facilities. However, these and other terms such as *correctional facilities* are technical and legal distinctions that have little bearing in practice on understanding and managing cybercrime, except that, for example, juvenile offenders will generally be treated more leniently by officials in state and federal justice systems, and some courts have ruled that juveniles must be accompanied by a parent or legal guardian while being interviewed by police when their legal counsel is not physically present. The different terms and treatment of juvenile offenders stems from government policies in the United States designed primarily to treat and rehabilitate juvenile offenders

### Code Writer Faces Federal Prosecution

In August of 2003 the infamous Blaster worm and several variants were released onto the Internet, infecting more than a million computers worldwide. The Federal Bureau of Investigation (FBI) was quick to investigate, and within days 18-year-old Jeffrey Lee Parson, a high school senior living in Hopkins, Minnesota, fell under suspicion. On the September 2, 2003, episode of *The Today Show*, Parson's parents said impressions that their son was a loner and nerd who was obsessed with being overweight were unfounded and that Jeffrey was a responsible son who received "B" grades in school and who kept them apprised of his whereabouts.[31] Later that month, on September 17, the 18-year-old was arrested by the FBI and charged with intentionally causing and attempting to cause damage to a protected federal computer system in violation of Title 18, United States Code, Section 1030.[32] Initially, after pleading not guilty, Parson, known also by his Internet handle as Teekid, was placed under house arrest, monitored with an electronic tracking device, and forbidden to access the Internet.

Different versions of the Blaster worm (also known as the LovSan virus because of a virtual note left on infected computers saying "I just want to say, LOVE YOU SAN!") crippled networks throughout the world during the summer months of 2003.[33] The variant created by Parson caused a distributed denial-of-service (DoS) attack against Microsoft's Windows® update Web site, as well as personal computers. Government officials estimated that Parson's DoS attack affected more than 48,000 computers. Parson also admitted committing cyber assaults against other organizations, including the Motion Picture Association of America (MPAA) and the Recording Industry Association of America (RIAA), organizations resented by many for their anti-pirating policies and lawsuits. In November 2003 at a news conference that included national and international law enforcement officials, Microsoft announced a $5 million antivirus reward program to encourage people to report information about malicious code writers to authorities, "with initial rewards of $250,000 for evidence leading to the capture and conviction of the original authors of the MSBlast and SoBig programs" recently distributed.[34] A year later, on August 12, 2004, Parson plead guilty in federal court to modifying and distributing the original Blaster worm. When asked in court why he had released the Blaster variant, Parsons indicated he was unsure. In January of 2005 he was sentenced to 18 months in federal prison for his crime.

rather than punish them. In addition to punishing offenders, corrections facilities for adults as well as juveniles usually provide a range of education and job-oriented training programs intended to create new employment opportunities and encourage future decisions not to commit crimes.

### 8.2.3 Administrative and Regulatory Law

We often hear about "laws and regulations" as if they were two sides of the same coin. In a way they are. Administrative laws and regulations are directly interrelated, and each pertains to government oversight of information systems security and other business-related practices. **Administrative law** is the body of law that authorizes state and federal government agencies to create and enforce regulations governing licensed activities (e.g., driving a car, selling liquor, hunting and fishing, practicing law or medicine, and manufacturing certain technologies that must conform to safety standards). A state's Department of Motor Vehicles is an example of a regulatory agency that usually has authority to create and enforce rules having to do with registering cars, trucks, and watercraft, as well as issuing, and if necessary, revoking vehicle registrations and drivers' licenses. Government rules are known as **regulations**, and they may be binding on private firms, nonprofit organizations, and even other government agencies, depending on the power granted to the agency to create and enforce regulations. Conversely, government agencies may only create and enforce regulations authorized by law even though they may pertain to many different kinds of issues (e.g., pollution levels, worker safety, technology standards, and protection of information systems).

On January 14, 2005, University of Texas at Austin student Ryan Pitylak was sued by the Texas State Attorney General for allegedly sending hundreds of thousands of misleading spam emails to residents in that state. Reportedly, Pitylak and his business partner, Mark Trotter of Encinitas, California, operated the fourth largest spamming operation in the world, allegedly in violation of the federal CAN-SPAM Act of 2003. The suit filed on behalf of Texas residents also alleges that the defendants operated their business under as many as 250 different names and that by sending email with misleading headers that induced respondents to provide personal information that was then sold to online advertisers, the defendants violated Texas laws prohibiting deceptive trade practices.[35] Note how this case allegedly violated federal and state crime laws, as well as government regulations within the State of Texas.

Within the federal government, numerous agencies and offices within cabinet-level departments such as the Department of Justice, the Department of the Treasury, and the Department of Homeland Security have congressionally authorized rule-making and regulatory authority as specified in laws. Increasingly, private sector firms and NGOs are being regulated by government in the area of information security. Widespread recognition of personal privacy rights, combined with the realization the most components of the U.S. national information infrastructure are owned or operated by private and nonprofit sectors, has brought about greater government oversight of information systems security policies, procedures, and technology. Three laws with attendant regulatory provisions for information security include the Health Insurance Portability and Accountability Act of 1996, the Financial Services Modernization Act of 1999, and the Sarbanes-Oxley Act of 2002. Each of these laws is explained later in this chapter. For now you should know that regulations created and enforced by government agencies, as authorized by these laws, exemplify many regulated issues, ranging from technology development and protection of information systems to healthcare administration and consumer protections.

### 8.2.4 *Intellectual Property (IP) Law*

Most people enjoy a good book, movie, or sound track. People also appreciate a funny cartoon, a detailed illustration, a helpful diagram, or a beautiful photograph that captures an image in just the right lighting and circumstances. People who become sick may benefit from taking cold or flu remedies, and on a hot summer day a soft drink or cold beer can be mighty refreshing. Society also depends on inventions and technological innovations that include product designs, chemical compositions, manufacturing processes, the inner workings of electromechanical devices, and so on, all of which are forms of intellectual property protected by law because the knowledge that goes into making products represents real wealth. It has been estimated that wealth represented by intangible intellectual property exceeds the total value of all tangible properties combined. In 2002, the U.S. Department of Commerce indicated that[36]

- The IT sector accounts for 7 percent of all businesses in the United States, but from 1996 to 2000 IT drove 28 percent of economic growth in America, represented two-thirds of new productivity growth, and created twice as many jobs as other sectors while paying workers twice as much on average.

- Innovations in healthcare technologies and services have increased life expectancies, resulting in annual net gains of about $2.4 trillion to the U.S. economy.
- New bio-agriculture technologies can increase crop yields by 25 percent while reducing reliance on herbicides and pesticides, thus diminishing environmental pollution.
- New technologies help provide homeland security by detecting and preventing terrorist attacks and are improving how education is delivered as well as how people learn.
- The market for nanotechnology products and services may reach over $1 trillion by 2015 in the United States alone, and "leading experts gathered by the National Science Foundation [have] predicted nanotech's impact will be at least as significant as antibiotics, the integrated circuit and man-made polymers were in the 20th century. From genomics to quantum computing, from pervasive networks to proteomics, there will be more change in the next 30 years than we saw over the last 100."[37]

Indeed, America conducts more R&D and generates more patents per capita than any other nation in the world while funding 44 percent of worldwide R&D investments—equal to the amount of research undertaken by Japan, the United Kingdom, Canada, France, Germany, and Italy combined.[38] America built and maintains its economic and military superpower status on the basis of technology inventions and innovation, and as the old saying goes, there is nothing quite like good old Yankee ingenuity. National labs and universities are attractive destinations for foreign students, many who remain in the United States after completing their studies because it provides a better place to live and do business than offered in their home countries. American society encourages and rewards risk-taking while upholding the rule of law, including **intellectual property (IP) laws** for technology inventions and copyright and trademark protections. As a

nation, America provides the world's most rational, predictable, and transparent legal framework for protecting intellectual property rights. In so doing, the United States encourages invention, innovation, and investment in these processes and delivers the widest variety of technology products and services on the planet.

IP law is the branch of civil law that makes all of this innovation possible and as you can probably imagine has very important implications for computing, information security, and cybercrime. After all, knowledge, as discussed in Chapter 2, is a valuable source of power and wealth that may be generated, leveraged, shared, and kept secure as needed with IT. Copyrights, trademarks, patents, and trade secrets are specific types of IP, each protected by federal laws that are grounded in legal rights established by the U.S. Constitution. Patent and copyright protections are specifically addressed in Article 1, Section 8 of the Constitution, which says that Congress has the power "to promote the progress of science and the useful arts, by securing for limited times to authors and inventors the exclusive right to their respective writings and discoveries." Although primarily civil in nature, certain federal IP laws include criminal penalties for violators based on the theory that violating IP rights harms all of society. State governments have comparatively limited authority to protect IP and punish law violators. Nonetheless, understanding IP in relation to the potential for IT-enabled abuse, cybercrime, and information security is really important for local and state criminal justice and information security professionals, because federal IP laws extend to all jurisdictions throughout the nation (i.e., states, territories, districts, counties, and municipalities). Let us therefore consider each of these four types of IP and the associated legal protections in relation to the potential for computer abuse, cybercrime, and breaches of information security.

### 8.2.4.1 Copyright Law.

A **copyright**, as the word implies, is the legal right to copy a literary or artistic work. Copyright as a legal concept has existed for centuries, predating the printing press, and was originally incorporated into a written law in 1710 by England's Statute of Anne, which provided protections for original authors of written works.[39] The foundation for copyright law in the United States is established in the Constitution. The first explicit federal copyright law was enacted in 1790 and was thereafter amended numerous times, notably in the Copyright Act of 1909. Today copyright is defined and enforced primarily on the basis of the Copyright Act of 1976 as amended by several other statutes. For example, the Computer Software Act of 1980, the Semiconductor Chip Protection Act of 1984, the Audio Home Recording Act of 1992, the No Electronic Theft Act of 1997, and the Digital Millennium Copyright Act of 1998 have all amended the primary copyright law passed in 1976 to address the potential for innovations in IT to facilitate copyright infringement.

Collectively these laws make it illegal to use computers or other devices to copy original or reproduced works of authorship such as literature, illustrations, diagrams, photographs, musical or dramatic works, sculpture, motion pictures or other audiovisual works, architectural works, and software, and so on, or to distribute these or other expressions fixed in a tangible form without express permission of the legal copyright holders.[40] In other words, if concepts or images of any kind are recorded in any form onto any medium, they are copyrighted and may not be reproduced or distributed without the consent of the legal copyright holder. Note that such items are presumed copyrighted upon their creation by the author, and that notice of any item being copyrighted is not necessary in order to bring legal action against persons or organizations suspected of copyright infringement. Thus, any original work of authorship created after January 1, 1978, is automatically copyrighted under U.S. law, regardless of any copyright label. However, ideas, procedures, processes, systems, methods of operation, concepts, principles, and discoveries, regardless of how these are recorded, are not copyright protected.[41] After all, how can someone

own an idea? A nation trying to ensure wealth through innovation seeks to have good ideas imagined, acted on and replicated, but not suppressed, so the legal goal is to create incentives for artists and authors to create, and for entrepreneurs to invent and innovate, by providing copyright protections and thus exclusive financial incentives on certain items for limited periods of time.

Copyright protections enable publishers and authors of protected materials to profit through sales and royalties. Copyright duration extends for the life of an original author, plus seventy years, unless they release their copyright to another party such as a publisher. While developing the manuscript for this book I retained the copyright. However, Allyn & Bacon (a Pearson Education Company), which published the book, now owns the copyright, which in turn could be sold or released to yet another publisher in a business acquisition, and so forth. Publishers of authored materials retain copyright rights for ninety-five years from the date of first publication, or 120 years from origination, whichever comes first. Federal criminal penalties for violating copyright *for altruistic purposes* as opposed to financial gain were first authorized in the No Electronic Theft Act of 1997.[42] Under this law a violator may receive five years imprisonment and be fined up to $250,000. Criminal provisions for copyright violations involving intent to gain financially are codified in U.S.C. Title 17, Section 1204. Violators are subject to five years imprisonment and a $500,000 fine for a first offense and up to ten years in prison and a $1 million fine for additional offenses.[43]

The intention of copyright laws is to provide deterrence to law violators and legal protections as well as monetary rewards and other incentives to authors, artists, photographers, and programmers so they will continue to develop original works and thereby help to advance and enrich society. When copyrighted materials are illegally copied and distributed, creators, publishers, and authorized distributors of the materials suffer financial losses, as do law-abiding consumers who may end up paying higher prices for particular items or be denied choices in products or materials made available in the marketplace as the result of copyright law protections. Perhaps no post-Internet IP law is more protective of copyright than the extremely controversial Digital Millennium Copyright Act of 1998 (DMCA), which critics have labeled the brainchild of the big American record labels, movie studios, and book publishers.

The DMCA makes it illegal to manufacture, distribute, or sell technology that enables circumvention of copyright protections. However, the **fair use doctrine** provides narrow exceptions for legally reproducing copyrighted works without paying royalty fees to authors, artists, or their publishers. Section 107 of the Copyright Act of 1976 allows limited copying for purposes of criticism, commentary, news reporting, teaching, scholarship, or research. In determining fair use, the law requires courts to consider (1) why the material was copied and whether copying involved commercial motives, (2) the nature of the works copied, (3) the amount and proportion of materials copied, and (4) the effect that copying the material had on its commercial value.[44] Note that because courts decide fair use on a case-by-case basis, anything you copy that does not qualify as one of these exceptions may be construed as a violation of federal copyright law. This is why libraries commonly post notices of federal copyright law prohibitions. U.S. copyright legislation and case law rulings have generally established that

- Unpublished as well as published works are protected, regardless of their quality, usefulness or country of origin, provided the United States has signed an international agreement honoring copyright protections of the foreign nation or the president has recognized that the country honors U.S. copyright laws.[45]
- For the good and advancement of society, information of a factual nature absent some degree of originality is not protected by copyright law.[46] Thus, facts in the public domain are not

copyright protected, and it is permissible to paraphrase even for commercial purposes existing literary works that contain facts or convey ideas, although attribution of original authorship is customary and recommended.

- Fair use allows reproduction by libraries and archives and free use of copyrighted materials for instructional purposes in nonprofit educational institutions.[47]
- It is permissible for an individual who owns a legal copy of software to make a backup copy for archival purposes, provided that the backup copy is destroyed if the original copy is sold or otherwise disposed of.[48]
- No technological means may be used to circumvent protections of copyrighted works.[49] For example, posting encryption cracking programs on the Internet to allow easier downloading and copying of music or movie files is not a protected form of free speech or expression.[50] So far, however, manufacturers of computers, other IT devices and software primarily intended for *legal copying* of copyright protected materials have not been held criminally or civilly liable by courts in the United States, nor is it likely that they would be unless they purposely facilitated copyright violations. This was the legal principle upon which, in June of 2005, the U.S. Supreme Court unanimously decided for MGM Studios and against Grokster and StreamCast Networks, respectively the makers of the p2p applications Grokster and Morpheus, that purportedly facilitated massive illegal downloading of copyrighted movie, music, software, and other materials. Note however, that the high court did not address whether p2p technology, which can also be used to legally share copyrighted materials and non-copyrighted data, is inherently illegal.[51]
- Applying the same legal reasoning, the U.S. Supreme Court also reaffirmed in the case of *MGM v. Grokster and StreamCast Networks*, that ISPs are not liable for copyright infringement by their customers unless they are aware

it is happening and fail to terminate Internet access of the person violating copyrights (e.g., customers illegally sharing music or movie files).[52]

- Firms that maintain databases of archived articles must obtain permission from authors before making them publicly accessible online, via CDs, and so on.[53]

### 8.2.4.2 *Trademark Law.*

Think of a company you know. What comes to mind? Many people when thinking about a company's product line or services imagine the firm's logo. In the area of IT the logos of firms such as Intel, Apple, Dell, Microsoft, and Napster are well recognized and thus valuable for marketing purposes. (Can you imagine each of these logos?) Over time logos become more valuable as they help to foster label recognition in advertising, distinctions made by consumers between name brands, perceptions of product or service quality, and customer loyalty. Conversely, if products or services are of poor quality, logos can foster customer disloyalty and thus marketplace competition, which is also in the public interest. This is why distinctive logos are allowed to be registered with the U.S. Department of Commerce or state trademark offices and receive protection under IP laws from being illegally used. In short, a **trademark** protects a designer's right to profit from an article recognized by a unique word, name, symbol, device, or a combination of them. Cars and trucks made by the Ford Motor Company are identified with a unique, oval-shaped, blue and white emblem that in script writing reads "*Ford.*" McDonald's bright yellow arches are unmistakable, whether designed into the architecture of a restaurant or printed on the firm's advertising correspondence. Every major music recording firm and motion picture studio has its own one-of-a-kind trademark. Who in America is not familiar also with the Playboy bunny, the Energizer battery bunny, and RCA's cute little white puppy with black ears sitting next to an old-style phonograph? New logos

and accompanying slogans are continually emerging, but once established rarely change, a further indication of their market value as a form of intellectual property. Computer scanning/imaging devices and software capable of altering valued logos slightly and incorporating them into marketing campaigns for services or products that compete with those of the original trademark holder increasingly present legal challenges and claims of trademark infringement.

Trademark protections, like copyrights, are rooted in Article I, Section 8 of the Constitution and were originally outlined in U.S. legislation by the Lanham Act of 1946. This law made it illegal to "dilute" the market value of a distinguishing product label. The Lanham Act was amended by Congress in 1995 with enactment of the Federal Trademark Dilution Act, which extended trademark protections to goods or services that are *not* intended to compete with particular products and services provided by other firms. Today the protected trademarks are defined in U.S.C. Title 17 (copyrights), Chapter 13 (protection of original designs), Section 1301 (designs protected). Items *excluded* from trademark protections are described in Section 1302 and include articles that are (1) not original; (2) staple or commonplace in society, such as a standard geometric figure, a familiar symbol, an emblem, a motif, or another shape, pattern, or configuration that has become standard, common, prevalent, or ordinary; (3) different from a staple or commonplace design only in insignificant ways; (4) part of the functioning aspects of the embodying article; or (5) even if embodied in a useful article, made public by the designer or owner more than two years before trademark registration was filed with the U.S. Patent and Trademark Office of the Department of Commerce in Washington, D.C.[54]

Trademarks registered with the federal government pertain to items used in interstate commerce and are typically indicated as such with the symbol ® or ™ located next to the company logo on its advertising. Intrastate products and services may be registered with the trademark offices of state governments. However, it is not necessary that a firm have its trademark officially registered with either the federal government or a state government office in order to make a legal claim and sue for trademark infringement.[55] On a more technical level, trademarks and **trade names** distinguish products, service marks distinguish services, and **cyber marks** are trademarks, trade names, or service marks widely recognized in cyberspace.

In recent years trademark dilution on the Internet has become an important concern of courts, especially when it involves (1) incorporation of trade names into Internet domain names; (2) so-called *cyber squatting*, in which parties not affiliated with a protected trade name firm use its name in an obvious domain name, effectively denying the legitimate trade name firm from using its own identifying label in online advertising; and (3) *meta tagging*, which pertains to improper use of trademarks in conjunction with how Internet search engines prioritize and display hits in response to key word searches. These matters are addressed, and relief may be granted litigants, by, respectively, the Internet Corporation for Assigned Names and Numbers (ICANN), the Anticybersquatting Consumer Protection Act of 1999, and a relatively small but increasing body of case law rulings.[56]

### 8.2.4.3 *Patent and Trade Secrets Laws.*
Patent laws are designed to protect the financial interests of inventors, and as indicated above, to help ensure national economic and military security through technology innovation. Thus a **patent** is a legally recognized claim of technology invention. As with trademarks, applications for patent protections can be made to the federal government. Since it began issuing patents in 1790 as authorized by the Constitution, the U.S. Patent and Trademark Office has issued over 7 million patents for unique inventions. Three types of patents are identified in the federal

patent law as explained in Part II of U.S. Code Title 35: utility patents, design patents, and plant patents. As these labels imply, **utility patents** pertain to a unique process, the way in which something is utilized, manufactured, or its materials composition; **design patents** are awarded to truly innovative plans for how something is intended to work; **plant patents** cover biological engineering of new plants including hybrids and their reproductive components (e.g., spores or seeds).[57] Every patent issued by the federal government is given a patent number. Many combinations of patents are legally used in invention and manufacturing processes, provided originating inventors are paid in amounts determined in business contracts. It is common for technological devices such as computers and other electronic devices to list several patent numbers to indicate specific underlying designs and manufacturing processes used in bringing a product to market.

What is important to understand for our purposes is that spying within the private sector and stealing designs for new technologies and impending products in order to achieve market advantages has always occurred, but IT has made this situation far worse. First, patent protections are closely related to protecting trade secrets which, unlike copyrights and trademarks, are valuable because they are kept confidential. Further, trade information may only be secret if the owners take precautions to keep it confidential. This has important implications for information systems security design, policies, and procedures. Historically, legal remedies for patent infringement as well as stealing trade secrets primarily relied on civil law. However, the patent registration system maintained by the U.S. Patent and Trademark Office, combined with the reality that new products can be inspected for evidence of patent infringement, and even steep financial judgments imposed on patent violators, dissuaded few individuals and firms from patent infringement and stealing advance product information. Monitoring the enormous international marketplace for potential evidence of stealing trade secrets is simply not practical, especially for small firms with limited resources.

By the early 1990s advancements in computing enabled corporations and even governments to spy on each other in new ways and with unprecedented frequency. Many federal and state law enforcement agencies and private investigation firms recognized that disgruntled employees or others gaining access to controlled facilities or information systems could easily download sensitive and extremely valuable impending patent information and other types of trade secrets onto disks or off-site computers. If employees planning to leave a firm can defect with such knowledge, they may be able to start their own firm, or surreptitiously supply a new employer or competing firms with secrets that at once propel their standing in the marketplace while decreasing that of the rightful information owner. By 1996 this increasingly egregious situation caused Congress to enact the Economic Espionage Act, which criminalized theft of trade secrets in certain instances. Criminal penalties for violating this law can include 25 years imprisonment plus a $10 million fine if the act is intended to benefit a foreign government, or 15 years imprisonment plus $5 million in fines if the act is committed on behalf of a foreign or U.S corporation. The law applies to all U.S. citizens, even if they violate the law from outside American borders.[58]

## 8.2.5  *Tort Law*

A **tort** is a wrongful act that results in some type of harm to a person, organization, or their property. **Tort law** is the body of law that enables individuals and organizations to seek legal remedies and compensation for wrongs committed against them. Torts may occur as the result of negligence or indifference or failing to act or not act in a manner required by law, regulation, or social custom. Tort law is the legal basis for suing someone. Anyone can sue anyone else, nearly any time, and in any legal jurisdiction for alleged wrongful acts. As examples, a person can sue someone for **negligence** (doing something inappropriately or not doing something they should have done), **slander** (spoken insults or false accusations resulting in disrepute), **libel** (written slander), or **defamation** (a combination of slander and libel). People can also sue firms and individuals for not adequately protecting their information under contract or when there was an expectation that they would.

Civil suits may also accompany commission of crimes that result in personal injury or damage to property. This means that in addition to being charged with a crime, a suspected criminal may be sued by one or more victims independent of their being prosecuted, much less convicted, of violating a crime law. It also means that criminal justice officials and IT professionals

## BOX 8.3  •  *Types of Intellectual Property Law Protections*

| | |
|---|---|
| **Trademark:** | Any word, name, symbol, color, sound, product shape, device, or combination of them used to identify goods and distinguish them from those made or sold by competitors. |
| **Copyright:** | Original works of authorship—the expression of ideas rather than the ideas themselves. |
| **Patent:** | A legally enforceable right to exclude others from using an invention. |
| **Trade secret:** | Confidential proprietary business or technical information that is protected as long as the owner takes certain security actions. |

may be sued for not doing their jobs properly or for violating the legal rights of people with whom they interact. Savvy police officers anticipate the possibility of being sued, which helps them remain professional and responsible in their duties. Security professionals are also cognizant of the possibility of being sued for misconduct and failing to perform duties as required by laws, regulations, and contract requirements. Failure to abide by organizational policies, established procedures, and training instructions are also grounds for being sued if a person's actions result in harm to another person.

On December 18, 2004, U.S. District Judge Charles R. Wolle awarded a $1 billion judgment to Robert Kramer of Davenport, Iowa, for losses associated with 300 companies alleged to have sent 10 million spam messages per day to approximately 5,000 customers of his ISP firm—an average of 2,000 spam messages per day per ISP customer—enough to make most people discontinue processing email. No wonder civil action was taken. Specific judgments levied in this case included $720 million against AMP Dollar Savings Inc. of Mesa, Arizona, $360 million against Cash Link Systems Inc. of Miami, Florida, and $140,000 against TEI Marketing Group, also of Florida. Kramer's suit alleged violations of an Iowa Ongoing Criminal Conduct Act, which allows for damages of $10 per unsolicited spam message, and the Federal Racketeer Influenced and Corrupt Organizations (RICO) Act, which provides for triple damages. Hence, the judgment was at the time the largest of its kind.[59]

The Kramer case indicates that understanding and applying tort law can be important for managing cybercrime. Law enforcement officers conducting investigations must know the legal limits of their authority and potential liability for exceeding their powers to search, seize property, arrest suspected law violators, or use physical force. Information security professionals must also know the legal requirements, standards of due care and diligence, and limits to what is permissible regarding use and management of information systems. Computer users everywhere should know what is legally permitted with respect to sending messages, accessing systems, and possessing or using various types of data. Libel, slander, defamation, wrongful interference with a business relationship, and product liability are a few examples of torts for which you can be sued, if you act improperly and/or illegally with a computer or other electronic device. Copyright, trademark, and patent infringement also constitute wrongful acts for which persons or organizations may be sued and held liable by courts. Torts also include violations of privacy, online harassment, and failure to exercise due care and diligence when developing and managing information systems security (discussed in Chapter 10).

The legal standard for being found by a judge or jury to have committed a tort is known as **preponderance of evidence**, which means that it is more likely than not that a person did or did not commit an egregious act and cause the alleged harm. As discussed in Chapter 6, harm experienced by victims of crime, or anyone else, may be emotional, psychological, social, financial, and/or physical in nature. In the course of civil legal proceedings judges rely on constitutional law and case law precedents to make rulings, just as they do in criminal court legal proceedings. If a civil trial judge or jury finds in favor of the plaintiff who brought a lawsuit, he or she may impose a financial judgment on the defendant(s) in the case. **Civil judgments** are essentially fines imposed on persons found to have committed a tort. Judgments may be compensatory or punitive in nature, and often provisions for these are written directly into laws passed by legislative bodies as way of deterring wrongful acts.

Remember that, in general, laws are either criminal or civil in nature and that wrongful acts that negatively affect society as a whole are ordinarily considered crimes even if the harm is only tertiary in nature (see Chapter 6). Periodically, harm caused by certain types of torts warrant the abusive behavior being criminalized through

THANK YOU FOR CALLING SAL'S. OUR RECORDS SHOW
YOU'VE GAINED SOME WEIGHT SINCE YOUR DIVORCE ...
WOULD YOU LIKE TO TRY OUR NEW LOW CARB CRUST?

creation of new crime laws. This is consistent with the theory of technology-enabled crime, policing, and security discussed in Chapter 5. Recall, for example, that IT-enabled corporate espionage was criminalized when Congress enacted the Corporate Espionage Act of 1996. Prior to passage of that crime law, spying on firms to discover trade secrets was purely a civil matter that in theory individuals or organizations responsible for could be sued. Now responsible parties may be sued, fined, and imprisoned. Criminal justice and IT professionals must understand when they are operating within potential civil and/or criminal legal claims of wrongdoing, which continually change in the course of (1) legislative bodies creating new crime and civil laws, (2) government agencies creating regulations and enforcing crime laws and regulations, and (3) judges interpreting existing laws and rendering new case law rulings in

matters of crime and civil law inclusive of matters involving government regulations. Hence, criminal law and civil law are inseparable mechanisms through which society manages problems that cause harm. Managing cybercrime therefore requires fundamental understanding of IT-enabled torts, such as violations of cyber privacy, cyber harassment, and not exercising due care and diligence in the performance of professional responsibilities. Thus, if you wish to avoid being sued as a criminal justice or information security professional, know the laws and regulations bearing on your areas of responsibility and actions.

## 8.3  How Laws and Regulations Are Created and Administered

A recurring theme throughout this book is that the rapid pace of technological change continually challenges society to define deviant, abusive, and criminal behavior involving use of computers and other electronic systems via information systems. The U.S. Constitution, adopted by the colonies in 1789, established a framework for a federal form of government (i.e., federalism) in which the national and state governments share powers to make laws that govern the behaviors of citizens, residents, and visitors. The Constitution, in addition to establishing the framework of the federal government and sharing of power between the federal and state governments, also established the system by which laws and government regulations are made and enforced.

Understanding how laws are made and enforced is central to understanding government efforts to continually define and regulate computer abuse and illegal use of IT. In this section, we briefly describe this process as a foundation for providing an overview of key major federal cybercrime laws and regulations. You may already be familiar with some of the introductory information that follows, but in case you are not, the material will provide useful background information that will enable you to better understand what may be looming on the legal horizon and the implications of impending and new laws for implementing or revising information security policies, procedures, and technology standards in the organizations that you will one day help manage. The sharpest college grads and managers in criminal justice, information security, and other fields needing to better manage cybercrime threats understand how law-making occurs and even

*Continually evolving IT and other forms of technology adopted for abusive and criminal purposes require local, state, and national governments to update or create new laws and regulations. Throughout the summer of 2005 the United States Congress regularly held hearings to investigate new legal requirements for securing information held by credit and data archiving firms.* AP Wide World Photos

become involved in the process when possible. Currently, however, there is no professional membership association that systematically tracks emerging laws and regulations and their implications, or that directly represents the interests and concerns of information security professionals to Congress. Nor are information security professionals licensed or consistently regulated in their provision of services, yet they are required to comply with numerous government rules for ensuring information systems security. Hence, they must be keenly aware of legal issues and do what they can within the framework of ad hoc professional organizations to educate and exert influence for construction of new laws and regulations. Understanding the following material will help you to do this, and also play heads up ball when it comes to managing cybercrime and information security issues in changing legal environments and thereby avoid being sued for reasons discussed in the previous section.

### 8.3.1 Legislative Bills and Executive Approval

Article One of the Constitution authorizes Congress to make federal laws, which, after being enacted, generally apply to all people in the United States having legal residence status. Congress is composed of two law-making chambers: the U.S. House of Representatives and the U.S. Senate. The House has 435 members who serve two-year terms and represent congressional districts in their home states. The number of House members is based upon the number of residents in the states as a proportion of the national population. The Senate consists of only 100 members, two from each state regardless of population. All but one of the 50 states (or "commonwealths" as some states are called), have their own constitutions, and each state government is modeled after the federal congressional structure with its own separate House and Senate.[60]

Ideas or needs for new laws continually arise, often as the result of stakeholder interests or crises that require governmental action. Initially ideas for new laws that represent alternative approaches to resolving societal problems are researched, sponsored, and then proposed as a **legislative bill** by one or more members of either the House or Senate. Typically, a bill being formulated in one chamber will be matched by a companion bill in the other chamber. Eventually the two bills will be scheduled for a vote in their separate chambers. If and when both bills are passed with a simple majority, they are then sent to a bipartisan conference committee consisting of several House and Senate members. It is the conference committee's job to make revisions to the language and provisions contained in the two bills and then combine them into a single final bill that is presented in exactly the same language to both the House and the Senate. Again, if passed by a simple majority in both chambers, the final bill is sent for signature to the president.

Once signed by the president, the bill becomes law. If the president does not sign the legislation, it will be sent back to Congress, which must then achieve a two-thirds vote in both chambers to override the presidential veto. If Congress cannot accomplish this, the legislation will die unless resurrected by starting the process all over again. This is essentially how laws are made in the United States, although there are many other things involved, and the process may vary in certain situations. For example, the president can also suggest specific legislation by forwarding a sample bill to either the House or Senate. Also, in certain tax and extremely important national matters, the U.S. Senate may need to pass legislation with a supermajority (i.e., 60 votes). Each state government relies on a similar overall process, and the governor of the state, as chief executive, must sign a bill into law or veto it.

During the legislative process, bills traditionally become labeled as acts with catchy titles and the year of enactment (e.g., the Cyber Security Enhancement Act of 2002). In many instances, several bills and thus several acts will be combined into a single large law consisting of several titles, each identified as a separate act. This can be confusing, especially as bills are revised to reflect preferences of political parties and special interest groups representing industrial or business sectors, the views of professional membership associations, as well as concerns of government regulators and consumers. Lobbying firms are often retained to inform and influence legislators in the House and Senate about needed legislation, although by law, government agencies, while often consulted about impending legislation through offices of congressional affairs, are prohibited from lobbying Congress. Impending legislation can often be tracked online via any number of Web pages or chat forums, but the Thomas Directory of the Library of Congress and the *Federal Register* are official sources of information about proposed and existing federal legislation and regulations.

Once a law is signed by the president or a state governor, it is given a public law (PL) number and published in the *Federal Register* (see, http://www.gpoaccess.gov/fr/). Each new law is also added as an amendment to the parent statute in existing U.S. code. For example, if new crime legislation is enacted, it will be added as an amendment to United States Code 18, which is the primary body of federal crime statutes. Over the years, amendments accumulate and effectively change underlying aspects of the nation's laws. When trying to understand current federal or state crime laws, it is important to determine that you are reading the most recent version of a statute as reflected in amendments. You will also need to be familiar with case law rulings in order to determine how laws as amended have been interpreted by courts, and thus how they may apply to the situation you are researching.

### 8.3.2 *Implementation and Enforcement of Laws and Regulations*

After a law is enacted and made public, it is up to the executive branch of government to implement and enforce it. Directors of federal executive branch agencies report to cabinet-level department heads, such as the Attorney General of the Department of Justice or the Secretary for the Department of Homeland Security. Department or cabinet-level directors in turn report directly to the president in matters of federal policy, law, or regulatory enforcement. They must also answer to certain congressional oversight committees comprised of elected officials from the House of Representatives or Senate. Equivalent reporting structures exist within state governments, with a state's governor presiding as the chief executive and law enforcement official. The duty of the president or governor is to supervise each of their cabinet-level departments and by extension all organizational components within departments with respect to their promulgation of regulations and enforcement of these and crime laws.

The judicial branch of government, through federal- and state-level trial and appellate court systems, oversees the enforcement of statutes. This is accomplished through judicial resolution of factual disputes and interpretation, analysis, and application of statutes and regulations. If a law enforcement officer oversteps his or her legal authority during an investigation, it is the responsibility of courts to discover this. Trial and appellate court judges must then make legal rulings that hold government agents or others conducting investigations accountable for their actions. As indicated above, case law is made when a judge issues a decision that is binding on parties in a legal dispute, whether of a criminal or civil nature. The body of case law continues to accumulate along with new legislation, promulgation of regulations, and enforcement of regulations and crime laws.

Whereas the purpose of trial courts is to hear the facts of a case and determine who is guilty or innocent or otherwise discern who is responsible for wrongful actions, appellate court judges try to interpret what the legislature intended when it created and passed a law. In other words, appellate courts ensure the law was fairly applied by trial courts, but they do not retry cases. Appellate court judges also rule on the constitutionality of new statutes when necessary and thereby effectively oversee decisions made at the trial court level in the making of laws by the legislature. Case precedent is case law that must be followed by lower courts. A decision made by the highest state appellate court is mandatory case law for all trial courts within that state but is not binding on the decisions made in other states or on the federal judicial system. However, a decision made by one U.S. Circuit Court of Appeals is binding on all federal and state courts within its jurisdiction, but not to federal courts in other circuits. A decision made by the U.S. Supreme Court is binding on all federal and state courts throughout the country.

The concept of case precedent, especially in decisions made by the U.S. Supreme Court, has had a profound impact on American society. The collective power of the judiciary in state and federal court systems to declare a law or executive action unconstitutional (thereby nullifying it) has repeatedly changed the course of history, politics, and the administration of justice in the United States. For example, the U.S. Supreme Court has required police officers to inform suspects questioned in criminal cases of certain rights, mandated procedures for warrantless searches, and established information privacy rights. Many of these rulings have affected how cybercrimes are investigated and prosecuted, as well as how information security is now being provided for in organizations everywhere as required by federal legislation and regulations.

### 8.3.3 Federal Regulatory Agencies with InfoSec Oversight Responsibilities

Federal and state regulations are promulgated by government agencies often in response to requirements set forth in anticrime laws. For example, the Communications Decency Act, passed in 1996 and signed into law by President Clinton, authorized the Federal Communications Commission (FCC) to develop and enforce specific regulations pertaining to pornographic content on the Internet. Regulations have the full force of government law. This means that government regulatory agencies can take enforcement action against corporations, public utility and transportation companies, and other types of proprietary firms and subsidiary contractors if they violate regulations, such as legally required standards for information systems security technology and practices. Investigations must center on suspected violations of specific existing regulations. All government regulations are a matter of public record, and regulations of the federal government are codified in the Code of Federal Regulations.

In many instances, regulatory agencies have legal power to impose steep fines, issue stop-work orders, mandate reforms, and revoke business and operating licenses held by corporations, public utility and transportation companies, and other types of private and nonprofit organizations. Regulatory agencies also coordinate investigations with law enforcement agencies in cases involving suspected violations of regulations and crime laws. Examples of federal agencies with regulatory authority relating to potential computer abuse, cybercrime violations, and information security issues including protection of critical infrastructure and information infrastructure include the following:

**8.3.3.1 Federal Aviation Administration (FAA).** The Federal Aviation Act of 1958 created this agency, originally under the name Federal Aviation Agency, which changed to the Federal Aviation Administration in 1967 when it became a part of the U.S. Department of Transportation. Major roles of the FAA include regulating civil aviation to promote safety; encouraging and developing civil aeronautics, including new aviation technology; developing and operating a system of air traffic control and navigation for civil and military aircraft; researching and developing the National Airspace System and civil aeronautics; developing and carrying out programs to control aircraft noise and other environmental effects of civil aviation;

and regulating U.S. commercial space transportation. The FAA issues and enforces regulations and minimum standards covering manufacturing, operating, and maintaining aircraft and certifies pilots and airports that serve air carriers. It also operates a network of airport towers, air route traffic control centers, and flight service stations. It develops air traffic rules, assigns the use of airspace, controls air traffic, and sustains information systems to support air navigation and air traffic control, including voice and data communications equipment, radar facilities, computer systems, and visual display equipment at flight service stations. Accordingly the FAA is very concerned with the security of information systems for controlling civilian, commercial, and military aircraft all vital to the nation's critical infrastructure.[61]

### 8.3.3.2  Federal Communications Commission (FCC).

The FCC was established by the Communications Act of 1934 as an independent agency of the federal government, directly responsible to Congress. The FCC is charged with regulating interstate and international communications by radio, television, wire, satellite, and cable. As such, the commission is concerned with obscene, fraudulent, or other illegal or inappropriate broadcasts and communications carried out over the nation's IT communications network. The agency's jurisdiction covers the 50 states, the District of Columbia, and U.S. territories. The FCC is directed by 5 commissioners appointed by the president and confirmed by the Senate for 5-year terms, except when filling an unexpired term. The president designates one of the commissioners to serve as chairperson. Only 3 commissioners may be members of the same political party. None of them can have a financial interest in any commission-related business. The commission staff is organized by function, according to 6 operating bureaus and 10 staff offices. The bureau's responsibilities include processing applications for licenses and other filings, analyzing complaints, conducting investigations, developing and implementing regulatory programs, and taking part in hearings. Even though the bureaus and offices have their individual functions, they regularly join forces and share expertise in addressing Commission issues.[62] Since telecommunications is integral to critical information infrastructure, the FCC is a key regulatory agency for the prevention and control of cybercrimes.

### 8.3.3.3  Federal Deposit Insurance Corporation (FDIC).

The FDIC was created in 1933 in response to the thousands of bank failures that occurred in the 1920s and early 1930s. Its charge is to preserve and promote public confidence in the U.S. financial system by insuring deposits in banks and thrift institutions for up to $100,000; by identifying, monitoring, and addressing risks to the deposit insurance funds; and by limiting the effect on the economy and the financial system when a bank or thrift institution fails. As such, it is very interested in scrutinizing financial institution rating systems, lending practices, and the veracity of financial information systems security standards and practices. Since its creation, no depositor has lost a single cent of insured funds as a result of a failure. The FDIC receives no congressional appropriations. Instead, it is funded by premiums that banks and thrift institutions pay for deposit insurance coverage and from earnings on investments in U.S. Treasury securities. With insurance funds totaling more than $44 billion, the FDIC insures more than $3 trillion of deposits in U.S. banks and thrifts—deposits in virtually every bank and thrift in the country. Savings, checking, and other deposit accounts, when combined, are generally insured up to $100,000 per depositor in each bank or thrift the FDIC insures, but the agency does not insure securities, mutual funds, or similar types of investments that banks and thrift institutions may offer.

The FDIC directly examines and supervises about 5,300 banks and savings banks, more than half of the institutions in the banking system. Banks can be chartered by the states or by the federal government. Banks chartered by states also have the choice of whether to join the Federal

Reserve System. The FDIC is the primary federal regulator of banks that are chartered by the states that do not join the Federal Reserve System. In addition, the FDIC is the backup supervisor for the remaining insured banks and thrift institutions.[63] Since a substantial number of cybercrimes are also financial crimes and/or involve attacks on financial institutions, the FDIC is another key agency involved in protecting the country from harm caused by cybercriminals. Other key federal agencies with regulatory authority over financial institutions and banking systems include the Board of Governors of the Federal Reserve System, the Office of the Comptroller of the Currency (OCC), and the Office of Thrift Supervision (OTC).

### 8.3.3.4 Federal Elections Commission (FEC).

In 1975 Congress created the Federal Election Commission (FEC) to administer and enforce the Federal Election Campaign Act (FECA), the statute that governs the financing of federal elections. The duties of the FEC, which is an independent regulatory agency, are to disclose campaign finance information, to enforce the provisions of the law such as the limits and prohibitions on contributions, and oversee the public funding of presidential elections. The commission is also very concerned about the administration of fair elections and prevention of election fraud, such as that made possible by electronic voting machines and hacking into information systems containing voting records. The commission is made up of six members, who are appointed by the president and confirmed by the Senate. Each member serves a six-year term, and two seats are subject to appointment every two years. By law, no more than three commissioners can be members of the same political party, and at least four votes are required for any official commission action. This structure was created to encourage nonpartisan decisions. The chairmanship of the commission rotates among the members each year, with no member serving as chairman more than once during his or her term.[64]

### 8.3.3.5 Securities and Exchange Commission (SEC).

The laws and rules that govern the securities industry in the United States derive from a simple and straightforward concept: all investors, whether large institutions or private individuals, should have access to certain basic facts about an investment prior to buying it. To achieve this, the SEC requires public companies to disclose meaningful financial and other information to the public, which provides a common pool of knowledge for all investors to use to judge for themselves if a company's securities are a good investment. Only through the steady flow of timely, comprehensive, and accurate information can people make sound investment decisions. Hence, the primary mission of the SEC is to protect investors and maintain the integrity of the securities markets. The SEC also oversees other key participants in the securities world, including stock exchanges, broker-dealers, investment advisors, mutual funds, and public utility holding companies. Here again, the SEC is concerned primarily with promoting disclosure of important information, enforcing the securities laws, and protecting investors who interact with these various organizations and individuals. Crucial to the SEC's effectiveness is its enforcement authority. Each year the SEC brings between 400 and 500 civil enforcement actions against individuals and companies that break the securities laws. Typical infractions include insider trading, accounting fraud, and providing false or misleading information about securities and the companies that issue them.[65]

In 1974 Congress created the Commodity Futures Trading Commission (CFTC) as an independent agency with a mandate relating to that of the SEC to regulate commodity futures and option markets in the United States. The CFTC's mandate has been renewed and expanded several times, most recently by the Commodity Futures Modernization Act of 2000 (CFMA). The current CFTC mission is to protect market users and the public from fraud, manipulation, and abusive trading practices related to the sale of commodity and financial futures and options, and to foster open, competitive, and financially sound futures and option markets. Hence, cybercrimes involving insider trading, price fixing, and financial fraud are of particular interest to this agency, as are insecure information systems and practices that would enable such crimes to occur.[66]

### 8.3.3.6 Federal Trade Commission (FTC).

Originally the FTC was the Bureau of Corporations, which was created on February 14, 1903, under legislation sought by President Theodore Roosevelt to guard against price fixing by corporate cartels.[67] In 1914 Congress reconstituted the bureau into the FTC with enactment of the Federal Trade Commission and Clayton Act. Over several decades the mission of the FTC evolved to being among the most important in the federal government for combating cybercrime. This is accomplished through promotion of information security standards, spamming and identity theft fraud investigations, and regulatory oversight of corporations with regard to fair market practices. The FTC maintains consumer fraud (e.g., phishing and identity theft) reporting hotlines and Web sites, investigates regulatory violations, and refers

and supports cybercrime investigations undertaken by agencies such as the FBI and U.S. Secret Service. To these ends the agency has established a special Criminal Liaison Unit to expand criminal prosecution of consumer fraud. The Criminal Liaison Unit identifies enforcement agencies that may bring specific types of consumer fraud cases, educates criminal law enforcers in areas of FTC expertise, and coordinates training with criminal authorities to help the FTC prepare cases for referral and parallel prosecutions. Since 1996, dozens of FTC civil cases have resulted in concurrent or subsequent criminal prosecutions.[68]

### 8.3.3.7 U.S. Nuclear Regulatory Commission (NRC).

The U.S. Nuclear Regulatory Commission is an independent agency established by the Energy Reorganization Act of 1974 to regulate civilian use of nuclear materials. The NRC's primary mission is to protect the public and the environment from the effects of radiation from nuclear reactors, materials, and waste facilities and to promote the common defense and national security against acts of terrorism and, conceivably, cyberterrorism. Figure 8.2 gives an overview of

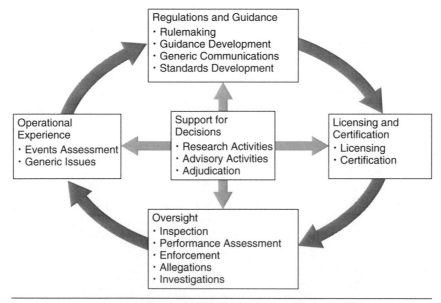

**FIGURE 8.2   *Regulatory Processes of U.S. Nuclear Regulatory Commission***
*Source:* U.S. Nuclear Regulatory Commission.

the NRC's regulatory process, which has five main components: (1) developing regulations and guidance for applicants and licensees, (2) licensing or certifying applicants to use nuclear materials or operate nuclear facilities, (3) overseeing licensee operations and facilities to ensure that licensees comply with safety requirements, (4) evaluating operational experience at licensed facilities involving licensed activities, and (5) conducting research, holding hearings to address the concerns of parties affected by agency decisions, and obtaining independent reviews to support regulatory decisions. These functions are fairly typical of most federal and state government regulatory agencies.[69]

## 8.4 Key Federal Cybercrime Laws and Information Security Regulations

Each year thousands of new laws are enacted by local communities, state governments, and the federal government. Consider that each township, city, and county in the Unites States has separate legislative and executive branches of government, each possessing law- or rule-making authority. When I worked for the U.S. Department of Justice, I was utterly amazed to walk through the law library in the Main Justice building. Each state in the union seemingly had its own room containing shelves full of its own law books. Of course computer systems also contained massive databases of laws, regulations, and legal decisions bearing on every topic imaginable. Every case ever decided anywhere in the United States conceivably could be found there, which explains why there were many thousands of federal government attorneys who worked out of this five-story city block-sized building.

With so many laws and regulations continually being created, how can we sort out what is really important for purposes of investigating and prosecuting cybercrimes and protecting information systems? The good news is that only a small proportion of laws and regulations actually pertain specifically to illegal use of computers or other electronic devices, not all laws or regulations are equally important in the big scheme of things, and new ones tend to modify old ones in minor ways.[70] Only rarely does a particular set of circumstances, a case, or a new law or regulation emerge that really requires our attention, *provided we understand existing government rules* bearing on our professional conduct and technology and generally pay attention to legal debates and developments surrounding the creation of new laws and regulations. As previously stated, it is vitally important as criminal justice officials, information security professionals, and IT administrators that we pay as much attention to laws and regulations coming down the pike as we do the technology being rolled out onto the market.

In the past several years Congress has enacted a number of key federal laws that contain provisions for addressing many of the issues described above and elsewhere in this text. This final section of this chapter examines legal provisions of the most recent, influential, and controversial cyber-related laws. Although not intended to provide definitive legal education by any stretch of imagination, the federal laws described here are those that all IT administrators, information security professionals, and public law enforcement officials in the United States should thoroughly understand. To begin, you should know that when it comes to preventing and controlling cybercrime, federal laws serve four primary purposes:[71]

1. Protect individual privacy and provide access to government information
2. Secure federal government information and information services
3. Ensure national critical infrastructure availability and reliability
4. Define IT-enabled abuse and crime

Federal regulations associated with these laws are much more varied and specific to various sectors including health care, financial services, and academia. Full descriptions of every federal law and regulation pertaining to cybercrime and information security issues exceed the scope of this text, as do the myriad important state crime laws and regulations bearing on cybercrime and information security issues. The remainder of this section describes many of most important federal laws for managing cybercrime and information security. These are grouped into sets of laws that (1) establish illegal use of computers and electronic devices, (2) facilitate or limit computer abuse and cybercrime investigations, (3) protect children from online pornography, (4) specify information security requirements, and (5) afford privacy and consumer fraud protections. Bear in mind that, as indicated above, each of the laws described below have already been enacted, assigned public law numbers, entered into the Federal Registry, incorporated into preexisting federal statutes as amendments, and stand to be further amended with passage of new legislation.

## 8.4.1 Laws Specifying Illegal Use of Computers and Electronic Devices

### 8.4.1.1 Mail, Bank and Wire Fraud Acts.
Before the invention of modern computers, the Mail Fraud Act of 1948 made it illegal to conduct, promote or carry out via the postal service fraud involving assumption of a false title, name, or address. A close read of the statute codified at 18 U.S.C. Section 1342 reveals that the Mail Fraud Act was the forerunner to federal prohibitions against identify theft, and as amended prohibits computer- and telecommunications-enabled frauds involving delivery of goods via delivery services such as United Parcel Service (UPS) and Federal Express. Fraud by wire, radio, or television was criminalized by Congress beginning in 1952, and prohibited transmitting an electronic signal such as writings, signs, signals, pictures, or sounds in order to obtain money or property under false or fraudulent pretenses.

Violators of this law, codified at 18 U.S.C. Section 1343, are today subject to fines and/or imprisonment not exceeding 20 years' incarceration. Bank fraud was expressly made illegal in 1984. To be convicted of this crime, a person has to knowingly execute or attempt to execute a scheme or document that results in defrauding a financial institution or obtaining money, funds, credit, assets, securities, or other property owned by, or under the custody or control of, a financial institution, by means of false or fraudulent pretenses, representations, or promises. According to 18 U.S. C. Section 1344, a person convicted of federal bank fraud may be fined not more than $1 million or imprisoned not more than 30 years, or both.

### 8.4.1.2 Access Device Fraud and Computer Fraud and Abuse Acts.
The Access Device Fraud Act of 1984 was the first federal computer crime law. Defined in 18 U.S.C. Section 1029, this law prohibits creating, distributing, possessing, or using counterfeit-making equipment or devices such as a counterfeit credit card to commit fraud. This law is complemented by the Computer Fraud and Abuse Act of 1986 (CFFA), which, as codified at 18 U.S.C. Section 1030, prohibited unauthorized accessing of federal government computers containing classified information, as well as computers of either the federal government or financial institutions that contained financial or credit data. The CFFA was amended to include all "federal interest computers," which effectively made it a felony to hack into or exceed permissions within any computer system of the federal government, its contractors, or grantees. Thus, for example, hacking into a computer system of a university funded by federal research grants is a felony under the CFFA, as amended, and punishable by up to twenty years imprisonment.

The CFFA was again amended by the National Information Infrastructure Protection Act of 1996 to include all "protected computers" connected to the Internet and used to support interstate commerce regardless of the federal government's possession, ownership, or interest in data stored on an information system. In 2000 the Federal Circuit Court for the Western District of Washington ruled in *Shurgard Storage Centers v. Safeguard Self Storage*, that the CFFA applies criminally and civilly to disloyal or departing employees who use computers to reveal trade secret information to competing firms (i.e., as in cases of insider corporate espionage).[72] In 2001 Congress again amended the CFFA, extending its reach to include computers located outside the United States involved in interstate or foreign commerce or communication. More recently the CFFA has also been used by major IT corporations in combination with other laws to sue spammers. Hence, the CFFA remains among the most important, evolving, and expansive federal anti-cybercrime statutes.

### 8.4.1.3 The Violent Crime Control and Law Enforcement Assistance Act.

The Violent Crime Control and Law Enforcement Assistance Act of 1994 is perhaps best known for authorizing federal funding to support hiring of an additional 100,000 community-oriented police officers by state and local law enforcement agencies. The law also created two new insurance and telemarketing fraud categories and enhanced punishments for fraudulent telemarketing phone calls aimed at elderly persons over 55 years of age. Additionally, the law made tampering with credit card access devices illegal if financial transactions within a single year exceed $1,000.

### 8.4.1.4 The Economic Espionage Act.

The Economic Espionage Act of 1996 represented the first time the theft of trade secrets, by any method, was declared a criminal violation. Prior to passage of this law, corporate spying and stealing trade secrets was merely a violation of civil law for which persons or organizations responsible could be sued. The law also criminalized informed possession, reception, or purchase of trade secrets. Hence, corporate officials and managers of firms who commission, condone or know of spying by their employees may be culpable under this act. Corporations may also be criminally fined as entities separate from punishments imposed on individuals for violations of the law. Firms claiming to have been victimized must demonstrate the approximate value of items stolen and demonstrate that reasonable efforts were taken to keep the trade secrets secure. As a practical matter, many federal district offices of U.S. attorneys have established minimum thresholds of $100,000 in alleged losses involving cases of white-collar crime, so not all violations of the EEA will necessarily be prosecuted criminally. If a case is prosecuted, steps must be taken to safeguard the secrecy of proprietary information to the extent it has not already been publicly revealed as the result of the alleged crime.

### 8.4.1.5 The No Electronic Theft Act.

The No Electronic Theft Act of 1997 authorized imposition of criminal fines and incarceration for people convicted of intentionally distributing copyrighted works over the Internet. Under previous statutory schemes, those who did not profit from distributing music, movies, or applications software over the Internet did not face criminal penalties, but the "NET Act," as it is sometimes referred to, extended criminal liability even to people (e.g., file sharers) who do not profit from unauthorized distribution of code. In July 1999 the Justice Department initiated an extensive effort to combat the growing challenge of piracy and counterfeiting of intellectual property, both domestically and abroad. Subsequent to this initiative, 17 defendants from across the United States and Europe were indicted by a federal grand jury for allegedly conspiring to commit copyright infringement of thousands of software items located on a server located at the University in Quebec in Canada. All 17 defendants were charged with one count of conspiracy to infringe copyrights. Twelve of the defendants were allegedly members of an international underground software pirating organization known as the Pirates with Attitudes. "The remaining five defendants were employees of Intel Corp., four of whom allegedly supplied computer hardware to the piracy organization in exchange for obtaining access for themselves and other Intel employees to the group's pirated software, which had a retail value in excess of $1 million."[73]

### 8.4.1.6 The Identity Theft and Assumption Deterrence Act.

The Identity Theft and Assumption Deterrence Act of 1998 brought sweeping protections to potential and actual victims of identity theft. Codified at 18 U.S.C. Section 1028, this law makes it illegal to knowingly (1) produce or transfer a false ID; (2) possess five or more false IDs with intent to use them for a fraudulent purpose; (3) use a false ID to defraud the United States; (4) produce, transfer, or possess a device used for making false IDs or other documents with the intention of using it to create false identity documents; (5) possess an ID that is or appears to be an identification document of the United State that is stolen or produced without lawful authority knowing that it was stolen or produced without such authority; and (6) transfer or use, without lawful authority, a means of identification of another person with the intent to commit, or to aid or abet, any unlawful activity that constitutes a violation of federal law or that constitutes a felony under any applicable state or local law.

Essentially the "Identity Theft Act" makes it illegal to create, transfer, possess, or use a fake or someone else's real ID to commit, promote, carry out, or facilitate a crime, including acquisition of money, property, or credit under an assumed name. The law pertains to any form of unique electronic identification, including biometric identification cards and verification technology. Persons convicted of identity theft or conspiracy to commit identity theft may be imprisoned for up to 20 years, especially if violations involve other serious crimes such as drug trafficking or crimes of violence. Between 1998 and 2001, there were 100 prosecutions of identity thieves under this legislation, with punishments ranging up to 15 years in prison and a fine.[74]

### 8.4.1.7 The Digital Millennium Copyright Act of 1998.

As indicated earlier in this chapter, the DMCA is a controversial law that makes it illegal to manufacture, distribute, or sell technology intending that it be used to circumvent copyright protections. Some additional highlights and specific provisions of the act are that it[75] (1) prohibits the manufacture, sale, or distribution of code-cracking devices used to illegally copy software but allows cracking copyright protections to conduct encryption research, assess product interoperability, and test computer security systems; (2) provides exemptions from anti-circumvention provisions for nonprofit libraries, archives, and educational institutions under certain circumstances; (3) limits ISPs from copyright infringement liability for simply transmitting data over the Internet; (4) limits liability of nonprofit institutions of higher education when they serve as ISPs regarding copyright infringement by faculty and students; and (5) allows for reproduction of copyrighted materials under the Fair Use Doctrine.

### 8.4.1.8 The CAN-SPAM Act.

The Controlling Assault of Non-Solicited Pornography and Marketing (CAN-SPAM) Act of 2003, which came into effect on January 1, 2004, represents the first U.S. national standard for the sending of commercial email and requires the Federal Trade Commission (FTC) to enforce its provisions. The act permits email marketers to send unsolicited commercial email only if it contains an opt-out mechanism by which recipients can prevent future emails, a functioning return email address, a valid subject line indicating it is an advertisement, and the legitimate physical address of the person or organization sending the email. The law is not applicable to foreign emailers, nor does it allow email recipients to sue spammers directly. However, the act does not prohibit the FTC, state offices of attorneys general, and ISPs from doing so. The first lawsuit filed under this statute alleging illegal spamming practices was in March of 2005 by the California ISP Hypertouch against the owner of BobVila.com, BlueStream Media Inc.

## 8.4.2 Laws that Facilitate or Limit Cybercrime Investigations

### 8.4.2.1 Conspiracy to Defraud and Making False Statements.

Conspiracy involves planning by two or more persons to commit a crime, followed by one or more of the confederates making at least one overt act in furtherance of the crime. If that happens, everyone involved in the original planning group may be charged with conspiracy and are subject to being punished in a manner consistent with the planned crime just as if the group had been successful in carrying it out prior to being found out, arrested, and prosecuted. Another law intended to aid criminal investigations prevents individuals from making false statements to federal agents. Although the Fifth Amendment to the Constitution guarantees that individuals suspected of committing crimes cannot be compelled to incriminate themselves and are entitled to the presence of legal counsel prior to questioning if they wish, if suspects lie while being questioned, they may be charged with making false statements even if it turns out they were innocent, not involved, or even unaware of a crime being investigated.

### 8.4.2.2 The Racketeer Influenced and Corrupt Organizations Act.

Enacted in 1961, this landmark statute delivered a substantial blow to organized crime by making it a federal crime to own, operate, or be involved in an organization engaged in perpetuating crime. RICO (pronounced reeko) provided a specific legal tool with which to prosecute individuals merely affiliated with criminal organizations, rather than only on the basis of specific crimes personally committed. In this way, by investigating the illegal activities of junior associates involved in criminal organizations, higher-ups who actually managed criminal organizations could also be indicted, prosecuted, and punished without direct evidence of their being involved in any specific crimes. RICO has been used to incarcerate numerous mob bosses, drug dealers, and their associates in cases often involving analysis of computerized records showing long-standing patterns of transnational drug smuggling, organized prostitution and other vice crimes, money laundering, bank fraud, and illegal gambling supported by telecommunications (a form of wire fraud).

### 8.4.2.3 The Foreign Intelligence Surveillance Act (FIS).

The Foreign Intelligence Surveillance Act of 1978 was created as an extension to laws of war and national defense (50 U.S.C. Section 1801) and as an amendment to privacy protections against unauthorized wire tapping as specified by the Communications Act of 1934 (47 U.S.C. Sections 551, 605, and 1008). The FIS allows federal law enforcement agencies to petition for a surveillance warrant to monitor electronic communications of persons suspected of espionage against the United States. The act created a special administrative court consisting of seven judges, which meets in secret to decide on the basis of a majority vote to either accept or deny applications for electronic surveillance warrants in suspected cases of espionage. The law also provides for a prosecutorial appeals court consisting of three judges who are empowered to review and overrule warrant applications denied by the seven-member court. Since its original enactment, the statute has been amended several times to keep pace with evolving computing and telecommunications technologies and the potential for them to be used for criminal purposes. Following the 9-11 commercial airline terrorist attacks on the World Trade Center and Pentagon, the FIS was amended by the USA PATRIOT Act to include an eleven-judge FIS Court in anticipation of increasing intelligence gathering and surveillance activities of the federal government.

### 8.4.2.4 The Federal Wiretap Act.

Officially known as the Wire and Electronic Communications Interception and Interception of Oral

Communications Act, this law provides for (1) interception and disclosure of wire, oral, or electronic communications (Section 2511); (2) prohibitions on the manufacture, distribution, possession, advertising, and confiscation of wire, oral, or electronic communication intercepting devices (Sections 2512 and 2513); (3) the admissibility of intercepted wire or oral communications as evidence (Section 2515); (4) authorizations, disclosures, procedures, and reports required for or relating to interception of wire, oral, or electronic communications (Sections 2516–2519); and (5) criminal imprisonment and civil damages and injunctions in connection with illegal communications interceptions (Sections 2520 and 2521). In practice, and in the big scheme of criminal law enforcement, authorizations for federal wiretaps are rarely sought and nearly always granted. Each year the Director of Federal Courts publishes a detailed wiretap activity report that includes information about the amount, duration, and costs of electronic communications interception by federal and state law enforcement agencies. Table 8.1 shows summary data for calendar years 1993–2003 as reported by the Administrative Office of the U.S. Courts.[76]

### 8.4.2.5  The Electronic Communications Privacy Act.

In 1986 Congress passed the Electronic Communications Privacy Act to update the Federal Wiretap Act to apply to all forms of electronic communications, whether by telephone, cell phone, computer, or other electronic device. The law specifically enabled ISPs to intercept and read suspicious emails, and granted nationwide one-party recording consent to law enforcement officers conducting criminal investigations. This means that police can today also monitor email with cooperative assistance from ISPs, who might well report messages indicative of criminal activity to authorities. However, the law also requires  that federal agencies fulfill a specific set of procedures before a monitoring search warrant is granted in such cases.

### 8.4.2.6  The Communications Assistance for Law Enforcement Act.

The Communications Assistance for Law Enforcement Act of 1994 expanded the ECPA to obligate telecommunications carriers to assist law enforcement in executing electronic surveillance. Prior to passage of this law ISPs were often reluctant to cooperate in criminal investigations due to concerns over customer privacy expectations and rights. This law provided needed legal protections to telecommunications companies. However, information sharing capabilities required to facilitate investigations by law enforcement agencies required technology upgrades in many instances, resulting in several major telecommunications and ISP firms seeking extensions to compliance deadlines set in the statute. Today, virtually all firms are in compliance with the law and regulated by the FCC, and startup ISPs or other types of firms offering telecommunications services are required to demonstrate their ability to assist law enforcement monitoring and surveillance needs prior to receiving an operating license.

### 8.4.2.7  The USA PATRIOT Act.

In the months following the terrorist attacks of September 11, 2001, there was a flurry of federal legislation that greatly increased the authority of law enforcement and intelligence agencies to conduct electronic counterterrorism monitoring and surveillance activities. The Uniting and Strengthening America by Providing Appropriate Tools Required to Intercept and Obstruct Terrorism (USA PATRIOT) Act of 2001 was passed just six weeks following the attacks, with extraordinarily little congressional debate. The law gave broad discretion to ISPs and law enforcement agencies to intercept communications of suspected terrorists, persons suspected of having affiliations with terrorist organizations, or other individuals such as hackers determined to pose potential threats to national security. With only a letter from police agencies rather than an affidavit and court order documenting suspicions of the above, ISPs were required by the law turn over electronic records of suspect communications sent or received by such groups or individuals to police. The act also allowed for real-time monitoring of such communications, but prohibits ISPs or others

**TABLE 8.1** *2003 Federal Court Wiretap Report Data*

*Authorized Intercepts Granted Pursuant to 18 U.S.C. 2519 as Reported in Wiretap Reports for Calendar Years 1993–2003*

| Wiretap Report Date | 1993 | 1994 | 1995 | 1996 | 1997 | 1998 | 1999 | 2000 | 2001 | 2002 | 2003 |
|---|---|---|---|---|---|---|---|---|---|---|---|
| **Intercept applications requested** | **976** | **1,154** | **1,058** | **1,150** | **1,186** | **1,331** | **1,350** | **1,190** | **1,491** | **1,359** | **1,442** |
| **Intercept applications authorized** | **976** | **1,154** | **1,058** | **1,149** | **1,186** | **1,329** | **1,350** | **1,190** | **1,491** | **1,358** | **1,442** |
| Federal | 450 | 554 | 532 | 581 | 569 | 566 | 601 | 479 | 486 | 497 | 578 |
| State | 526 | 600 | 526 | 568 | 617 | 763 | 749 | 711 | 1,005 | 861 | 864 |
| Avg. days of original authorization | 28 | 29 | 29 | 28 | 28 | 28 | 27 | 28 | 27 | 29 | 29 |
| Number of extensions | 825 | 861 | 834 | 887 | 1,028 | 1,164 | 1,367 | 926 | 1,008 | 889 | 1,145 |
| Average length of extensions (in days) | 29 | 29 | 29 | 28 | 28 | 27 | 29 | 28 | 29 | 29 | 29 |
| Location of authorized intercepts* | | | | | | | | | | | |
| Personal residence | 410 | 451 | 428 | 434 | 382 | 436 | 341 | 244 | 206 | 154 | 118 |
| Business | 124 | 118 | 101 | 101 | 78 | 87 | 59 | 56 | 60 | 37 | 35 |
| Portable device | – | – | – | – | – | – | – | 719 | 1,007 | 1,046 | 1,165 |
| Multiple locations | 92 | 97 | 115 | 149 | 197 | 222 | 287 | 109 | 117 | 85 | 95 |
| Not indicated or other* | 350 | 488 | 414 | 465 | 529 | 584 | 663 | 62 | 101 | 36 | 29 |
| Major offense specified: | | | | | | | | | | | |
| Arson, explosives, and weapons | – | – | 4 | – | 3 | 3 | 8 | 5 | 5 | – | 5 |
| Bribery | 1 | 6 | 4 | 10 | 13 | 9 | 42 | 21 | 1 | 3 | 9 |
| Extortion (includes usury and loansharking) | 9 | 8 | 18 | 9 | 24 | 12 | 11 | 10 | 28 | 18 | 6 |
| Gambling | 96 | 86 | 95 | 114 | 98 | 93 | 60 | 49 | 82 | 82 | 49 |
| Homicide and assault | 28 | 19 | 30 | 41 | 31 | 55 | 62 | 72 | 52 | 58 | 80 |
| Larceny and theft | 13 | 18 | 12 | 7 | 22 | 19 | 9 | 15 | 47 | 8 | 48 |
| Narcotics | 679 | 876 | 732 | 821 | 870 | 955 | 978 | 894 | 1,167 | 1,052 | 1,104 |
| Robbery and burglary | – | 6 | 5 | 4 | 5 | 4 | 4 | 4 | 8 | 3 | 3 |
| Racketeering | 101 | 88 | 98 | 105 | 93 | 153 | 139 | 76 | 70 | 72 | 96 |
| Other or unspecified | 49 | 47 | 60 | 38 | 27 | 28 | 37 | 44 | 31 | 62 | 42 |
| **Intercept applications installed**** | **938** | **1,100** | **1,024** | **1,035** | **1,094** | **1,245** | **1,277** | **1,139** | **1,405** | **1,273** | **1,367** |
| Federal | 444 | 549 | 527 | 574 | 563 | 562 | 595 | 472 | 481 | 490 | 576 |
| State | 494 | 551 | 497 | 461 | 531 | 683 | 682 | 667 | 924 | 783 | 791 |

*continued*

317

**TABLE 8.1** *Continued*

*Authorized Intercepts Granted Pursuant to 18 U.S.C. 2519 as Reported in Wiretap Reports for Calendar Years 1993–2003*

| Wiretap Report Date | 1993 | 1994 | 1995 | 1996 | 1997 | 1998 | 1999 | 2000 | 2001 | 2002 | 2003 |
|---|---|---|---|---|---|---|---|---|---|---|---|
| For intercepts installed: | | | | | | | | | | | |
| Total days in operation | 39,819 | 44,500 | 43,179 | 43,635 | 48,871 | 53,411 | 63,243 | 47,729 | 53,574 | 50,025 | 60,198 |
| Avg. number of persons intercepted | 100 | 84 | 140 | 192 | 197 | 190 | 195 | 196 | 86 | 92 | 116 |
| Average number of intercepted communications*** | 1,801 | 2,139 | 2,028 | 1,969 | 2,081 | 1,858 | 1,921 | 1,769 | 1,565 | 1,708 | 3,004 |
| Average number of incriminating intercepted communications*** | 364 | 373 | 459 | 422 | 418 | 350 | 390 | 402 | 333 | 403 | 993 |
| Authorizations where costs reported | 912 | 1,042 | 983 | 1,007 | 1,029 | 1,184 | 1,232 | 1,080 | 1,327 | 1,193 | 1,236 |
| Average cost of intercepts for which costs reported | 57,256 | 49,478 | 56,454 | 61,436 | 61,176 | 57,669 | 57,511 | 54,829 | 48,198 | 54,586 | 62,164 |
| Intercept applications authorized but reported after publication**** | 206 | 46 | 82 | 48 | 90 | 118 | 196 | 196 | 200 | 161 | – |
| Total authorized by year (reported through Dec 2003) | 1,182 | 1,200 | 1,140 | 1,197 | 1,276 | 1,447 | 1,546 | 1,386 | 1,691 | 1,519 | 1,442 |

\* Starting in 2000, location categories were revised to improve reporting and reduce the number of instances in which "other" location was reported.

\*\* Installed intercepts include only those intercepts for which reports were received from prosecuting officials.

\*\*\* As of 1998, the average excludes those reports in which the number of persons intercepted, the number of intercepts, or the number of incriminating intercepts was not reported or could not be determined.

\*\*\*\* Some wiretaps terminated in a given year are not reported until a subsequent year because they are part of ongoing investigations.

receiving search authorization letters from police agencies from disclosing to anyone that an investigation is underway. This provision effectively banned ISPs, other types of firms, or administrators of online chat forums from consulting with their own attorneys, although the provision was challenged and as of this writing is under review.

The Patriot Act also expanded the type and amount of information that could be collected by law enforcement officers through the use of pen registers, phone tap, and phone trace technology including routing and addressing information [see U.S.C. Section 3121(c)]. In addition the law allowed police to conduct "roving wiretaps" of *individuals* using any fixed computer or portable communications device such as a cell phone or PDA if that individual was determined to pose potential threats to national security. Furthermore, the Patriot Act allowed warrantless searches of homes and businesses in instances involving suspected terrorist planning or other activities and the seizure or copying of any tangible or electronic records therein without leaving notice that a search was conducted or that any evidence of possible criminal wrongdoing was seized. As in cases involving ISPs, persons aware of such police actions were prohibited from talking about the investigation with anyone, including their attorneys, although that legal provision was also challenged in court.

As originally legislated, the Patriot Act made it a federal crime to not cooperate in these types of investigations and in the interest of national security prohibited business owners and others from consulting their own legal counsel. Since passage of the law, however, one federal appeals court has ruled this to be a violation of the First Amendment, effectively restoring the right to legal counsel during investigative proceedings. Nonetheless, as of this writing the Patriot Act remains an extremely controversial law, unprecedented in its relaxing of Fourth Amendment protections against unreasonable search and seizure and the right to freedom of speech and to confer with legal council during a criminal

investigation. Congress was not fully unaware of risks associated with the law, which is why it wrote into the statute requirements for legislative review after five years (i.e., in 2006). However, other counterterrorism monitoring and surveillance laws were proposed or enacted to build on Patriot Act provisions, including the Cyber Security Enhancement Act of 2002, the Domestic Security Enhancement Act of 2003, and the National Security Intelligence Reform Act of 2004.

### 8.4.2.8 Other Counterterrorism Monitoring and Surveillance Acts.

In 2002 the Cyber Security Enhancement Act was enacted to supplement parts of the USA PATRIOT Act of 2001. The law adjusted sentencing guidelines upward in cases of cybercrime including for punishments imposed on first-time and repeat computer hackers. The law also further expanded certain police powers to conduct real-time Internet and telephone taps in cases of suspected threats to national security. Also in 2002, the Homeland Security Act created the Department of Homeland Security (DHS) by combining numerous existing federal agencies into a single cabinet-level agency. Agencies combined into DHS included the U.S. Coast Guard, U.S. Secret Service, the Immigration and Naturalization Service (INS) inclusive of the U.S. Border Patrol, and the FBI's National Information Protection Center (NIPC). Notably the Act transferred investigative authority of federal computer crimes to DHS, but the FBI's Computer Investigations and Operations Section (CIOS) retains authority within the U.S. Department of Justice to also investigate computer crimes. (In practice, many federal, state, and local law enforcement agencies investigate various types of IT-enabled crimes.) In January of 2003 the U.S. Department of Justice, under the direction of then Attorney General John Ashcroft, proposed new legislation called The Domestic Security Enhancement Act. Leaked as a draft in February of that year by a Justice Department staffer to the Center for Public Integrity, and thereafter dubbed "Patriot Act II" by many civil rights watchdog groups, this proposed legislation would have permitted, among other provisions,[77] (1) retroactive revocation of American citizenship for individuals determined to have contributed material support to terrorist organizations, (2) instant deportation of any noncitizens found to pose a threat to national security, even in the absence of a criminal charge, (3) development of a national DNA database inclusive of interior cheek swab samples collected without a court order on the basis of an arrest on suspicion of criminal wrongdoing, and (4) expanded government wiretap and surveillance authority along with prohibitions against releasing the identities of persons arrested in connection with suspected terrorist plots.

Organizations that contributed legal analysis and widespread public condemnation of the Domestic Security Enhancement Act of 2003 included the Center for Public Integrity, the ACLU, and the Electronic Freedom Foundation (EFF).[78] Although the Domestic Security Enhancement Act was defeated through public discourse, in August of 2003 another controversial law, called the Vital Interdiction of Criminal Terrorist Organizations Act, was proposed by leading Republicans serving on the Senate Judiciary Committee. This law sought to link the wars on drugs and terrorism by creating a new criminal construct for "narco-terrorism," which actually had existed since the early 1990s. Provisions of this legislation would have further broadened police wiretap authority while relaxing procedural rules of evidence regarding the admissibility of wiretap evidence in court, restricted sentencing discretion of judges in drug cases while increasing penalties for selling drugs by persons under 21 years of age, expanded government access to financial records in drug investigations, allowed easier asset seizure in money laundering cases, and allowed the FBI rather than courts to self-issue subpoenas for electronic and other records in terrorism investigations.[79] This proposed legislation was also defeated.

The National Security Intelligence Reform Act was, however, enacted in December of 2004

and authorized creation of a director of national intelligence (DNI), who has overall responsibility for coordinating counterterrorism intelligence gathering, analysis, and sharing among all federal agencies and with state and local law enforcement agencies. The law also authorized funding for an increase in the number of border patrol and immigration agents, the creation of an oversight board on civil liberties, and establishment of minimum standards for states issuing drivers licenses. The act supports new aviation security programs and contains even more provisions for expanded cyber surveillance by intelligence and law enforcement officers.

### 8.4.3 Laws Protecting Children from Online Pornography

Historically issues of privacy, morality, personal and public health, and suspected links to deviant and criminal conduct have all contributed to controversy surrounding pornographic materials as a source of adult entertainment. The United States and other nations have sought to ban or at least limit the type, amount, and means of distributing pornographic materials.[80] For example, moral crusader and U.S. Postmaster General Anthony Comstock late in the 19th century orchestrated the criminalization of sending obscene materials through the U.S. mail. Until America amended its tariff laws in 1930, several literature classics, such as James Joyce's *Ulysses* (which you may have been required to read in an English class), were banned on grounds that they contained indecent content. Legal prohibitions over creation, distribution, and possession of pornography were thereafter steadily relaxed, although not without additional cultural and legal controversy. During the 1960s publisher Ralph Ginzburg was convicted and sentenced to five years in prison for distributing via U.S. mail what was then widely considered obscene materials.[81]

In 1973 and again in 1987 the U.S. Supreme Court ruled that state and local courts could restrict materials that were patently offensive, appealed to prurient interests, and were without serious literary, artistic, political, or scientific value as determined by local community standards.[82] This interpretive standard was effectively reiterated by the U.S. Supreme Court in 1997 when it overruled portions of the Communications Decency Act of 1996 (CDA) that sought to ban sexually explicit material from online sites where children could easily find it.[83] Meanwhile, in 1996, Congress enacted the Child Pornography Prevention Act (CPPA), which expanded the federal prohibition on child pornography to include not only pornographic images made using actual children, 18 U.S.C. § 2256(8)(A), but also "any visual depiction, including any photograph, film, video, picture, or computer or computer-generated image or picture" that "is, or appears to be, of a minor engaging in sexually explicit conduct," §2256(8)(B), and any sexually explicit image that is "advertised, promoted, presented, described, or distributed in such a manner that conveys the impression" that it depicts "a minor engaging in sexually explicit conduct" §2256(8)(D).[84] However, on April 16, 2002, the U.S. Supreme Court struck down the CPPA on First Amendment grounds.[85]

Congress, the Justice Department, and President Bush responded to the high court's ruling by enacting the Child Online Protection Act of 1998 (COPA). Written as a replacement law for the CDA, COPA was more narrowly focused on commercial providers of content potentially harmful to minors. Specifically, COPA prohibited unrestricted Internet access to materials deemed harmful or obscene to minors under a three-part standard already upheld in earlier rulings by the U.S. Supreme Court, including (1) whether, according to contemporary community standards, the communication was designed to pander to prurient interests, (2) whether the content depicted or described sexual acts or nudity in a manner patently offensive with respect to minors, and (3) whether it lacked serious literary, artistic, political, or scientific value for minors.[86] The law required persons accessing sexually explicit materials to demonstrate they were over 18 years of

age via a valid credit card number, adult access code, or other digital certificate. COPA also precluded ISPs that did not provide their customers with Internet filtering technology from receiving a telecommunications tax moratorium. Finally, COPA threatened anyone who distributed obscene and potentially harmful content to minors online with a $50,000 fine and six months imprisonment.

In short, COPA, unlike the CDA and CPPA, applied only to material displayed on the World Wide Web, covered only communications made for commercial purposes, and restricted only material deemed harmful to minors. By targeting profiteers as sources of content potentially harmful to minors, Congress hoped to avoid judicial problems. However, COPA was immediately challenged by the American Civil Liberties Union and other freedom of speech and privacy advocacy organizations. Reminiscent of the CDA case several years earlier, the lawsuit against COPA worked its way through the federal court system to be heard by the U.S. Supreme Court in November of 2001. On May 13, 2002, in a five-to-four decision the Supreme Court remanded the case to the U.S. District Court for the Eastern District of Pennsylvania (in Philadelphia) to determine whether "COPA's reliance on community standards to identify what material is harmful to minors" is substantially too broad for First Amendment purposes.[87]

The net result of this ongoing battle over freedom of speech, expression, and privacy means that local prosecutors, trial court judges, and juries are free to decide on a case-by-case basis what according to local community standards is legally obscene or appeals to prurient interests or exposes unwilling adults to images they regard as being offensive. Thus, federal obscenity laws and case rulings have decreed that

- Depictions of real people (but not holographic images of human-appearing or cartoon characters) less than eighteen years of age, who are nude or engaged in explicit sexual activity (i.e., child pornography) may not be created, distributed or possessed although adolescent erotica not depicting sex organs is legal.

• Obscene material (e.g., adult pornography depicting persons over eighteen years of age in nude, lewd, or sexually explicit acts) may be restricted outside of private homes by local or state governments, but such material possessed inside private homes is not illegal.

• Creation or distribution of adult pornography even to individuals in their private homes and by any means may be criminalized or regulated by states and municipalities based on local community standards regarding what constitutes obscene material defined as that without serious literary, artistic, political, or scientific value.

Two other federal laws enacted in recent years have sought to work with and around these general legal principles to tighten online access to pornography by children and to deter violations involving child pornography and other cyber sex crimes. The Child Internet Protection Act of 2001 (CIPA) requires schools and libraries in poor and rural school districts receiving federal support through the FCC's E-Rate Internet funding program to develop safe Internet use policies and procedures to include monitoring Internet access and browsing by children, plus implementation of filtering technology to remove objectionable content. Under FCC regulations, American schools and libraries not part of the E-Rate program must show that they have policies in place, while school districts not participating in the program must certify that they are enforcing the policy.[88] In addition, the PROTECT Act of 2003 added significant protections for children engaged in online browsing and chat by establishing programs such as the AMBER alert and removing the statute of limitations on the abduction, physical abuse, or sexual exploitation of a child. The act affords law enforcement officers with easier attaining of wire taps warrants to monitor online activities suspected of involving child pornography or abuse and affirmatively declares any obscene materials depicting children to be illegal. The act also increased penalties for persons convicted in cases

involving child pornography, cyberstalking, or pedophilia and encourages voluntary reporting of suspected child pornography found online.[89]

### 8.4.4 Laws Specifying Information Security Requirements

**8.4.4.1 Computer Security Act of 1987.** The Computer Security Act of 1987, obviously created after the Computer Fraud and Abuse Act of 1986, expanded the definition of computer security protection and required that every government system with sensitive information have a custom security plan that should include training. The law required that the National Bureau of Standards (now the National Institute for Standards and Technology) develop standards and guidelines for federal computer systems with the ability to draw upon the National Security Agency for technical assistance in the area of IT and information security.

**8.4.4.2 Information Technology Management Reform Act of 1996 (ITMRA).** The Information Technology Management Reform Act of 1996 requires creation of a chief information officer (CIO) position within federal government agencies to ensure that information systems are acquired and managed properly. It also requires the secretary of commerce to create standards and guidelines to improve efficiency of computer operations, security, and privacy of federal computer systems and made the Office of Management and Budgeting (OMB) responsible for overall federal IT procurement, investment, and security.

**8.4.4.3 Health Insurance Portability and Accountability Act of 1996 (HIPAA).** The Health Insurance Portability and Accountability Act of 1996 (HIPAA) introduced important new protections for millions of working Americans and their families who have preexisting medical conditions or might suffer discrimination in health coverage based on a factor that relates to their health. The law also requires that all providers of medical services take steps to protect the privacy and security of patient treatment records.

#### 8.4.4.4 Financial Services Modernization Act of 1999.

Also known as the Gramm-Leach-Bliley Act (or simply GLB), this law repeals restrictions on banks affiliating with securities firms and allows them to create a financial holding company to underwrite insurance and securities services. Provision of such services may be limited, suspended, or repealed if the bank fails to pass financial or security audits. The law allows federal regulators to specify prudential safeguards for banks offering new financial services and removes FDIC assistance to bank subsidiaries and affiliates while providing for national treatment of foreign banks. Other provisions include protection of consumers' personal financial information held by financial institutions. There are three principal parts to the privacy requirements of GLB: the Financial Privacy Rule, the Safeguards Rule, and pretexting provisions.

The GLB Act gives authority to eight federal agencies and the states to administer and enforce the Financial Privacy Rule and the Safeguards Rule, which are federal regulations pertaining to privacy expectations of personal and commercial financial information. These two regulations apply to financial institutions, which are broadly defined to include banks, securities firms, insurance companies, and other entities providing many other types of financial products and services to consumers such as lending, brokering or servicing any type of consumer loan; transferring or safeguarding money; preparing individual tax returns; providing financial advice or credit counseling; providing residential real estate settlement services; collecting consumer debts; and an array of other activities. Firms providing these types of services are required to have information security policies, procedures, and technological capabilities in place to protect privacy of financial information.

#### 8.4.4.5 Sarbanes-Oxley Act of 2002.

The Sarbanes-Oxley Act of 2002 is a direct result of corporate misconduct such as the Enron scandal. The law requires compliance with a comprehensive reform of accounting procedures for publicly held corporations to promote and improve the quality and transparency of financial reporting by both internal and external independent auditors. Specific titles within the act address public company accounting oversight boards, auditor independence, corporate responsibility, enhanced financial disclosures, analyst conflicts of interest, commission resources and authority, studies and reports, corporate and criminal fraud accountability, white-collar crime penalty enhancements, corporate tax returns, and corporate fraud and accountability. Section 404 requires annual reporting by management regarding internal controls and procedures for financial reporting and an attestation as to the accuracy of that report by the company's auditors. While none of the sections specifically address information security, Section 302 addresses corporate responsibility for financial reports, Section 404 pertains to management assessment of internal controls, and Section 409 discusses real-time disclosure of financial data.

### 8.4.5 Laws Affording Privacy Protections

Concerning issues of privacy, there is one constitutional amendment in particular that protects citizens' rights: the Fourth Amendment. The actual text of the amendment reads,

*The right of the people to be secure in their persons, houses, papers and effects, against unreasonable searches and seizures, shall not be violated, and no Warrants shall issue, but upon probable cause, supported by the Oath or affirmation, and particularly describing the place to be searched, and the persons or things to be seized.*

Originally, this amendment was interpreted by the courts in a manner that set limits on the government's ability to *physically* search our homes, persons, or property. Of course, when the amendment was written, the technology to electronically monitor and record audio and video from remote locations did not exist. As new technologies allowing law enforcement to perform these types surveillance developed, the outdated interpretation of the amendment was challenged in court. The landmark case was that of *Katz v. United States* (1967) in which the FBI used an electronic bugging device on a bank of public pay phones that Charles Katz routinely used for illegal gambling purposes. While this action would have been acceptable under the original interpretation due to the lack of physical intrusion into the phone booth by the FBI, the defense successfully argued that privacy rights should apply to people, not places. Under this new interpretation of the amendment, it was decided that privacy rights could be protected if the person in question had a "reasonable expectation of privacy" at the time of the supposed violation of rights. The definition of "reasonable" is defined on a case-by-case basis in the courts.

While the *Katz v. U.S.* decision in 1967 was certainly in favor of retaining privacy rights for changing technology, cases that followed since that time have been slowly defining what is and is not protected by the Fourth Amendment. For example, court cases have decided that your bank records, car movements, garbage on the street, and anything that can be seen with the naked eye by the police from an aerial flyover are not protected by the Fourth Amendment. More recently, court cases have also been decided recently that email senders and recipients have a reasonable expectation of privacy while the email is in transit. However, chat rooms, bulletin boards, and open email are not protected by the Fourth Amendment.

### 8.4.5.1 The Freedom of Information Act of 1966.

The Freedom of Information Act (FOIA) of 1966 establishes a presumption that records in the possession of agencies and departments of the executive branch of the U.S. government are accessible to the people. This was not always the approach to federal information disclosure policy. Before enactment of the FOIA in 1966, the burden was on the individual to establish a right to examine these government records. There were no statutory guidelines or procedures to help a person seeking information. There were no judicial remedies for those denied access. With the passage of the FOIA, the burden of proof shifted from the individual to the government. Those seeking information are no longer required to show a need for information. Instead, the need to know standard has been replaced by a right to know doctrine. The government now has to justify the need for secrecy.

The FOIA sets standards for determining what records must be disclosed and what records may be withheld. The law also provides administrative and judicial remedies for those denied access to records. Above all, the statute requires federal agencies to provide the fullest possible disclosure of information to the public. The history of the act reflects that it is a disclosure law. It presumes that requested records will be disclosed, and the agency must make its case for withholding in terms of the act's exemptions to the rule of disclosure. The application of the act's exemptions is generally permissive—to be done if information in the requested records requires protection—not mandatory. Thus, when determining whether a document or set of documents should be withheld under one of the FOIA exemptions, an agency should withhold those documents only in cases where the agency reasonably foresees that disclosure would be harmful to an interest protected by the exemption. Similarly, when a requestor asks for a set of documents, the agency should release all documents, not a subset or selection of those documents. Contrary to the instructions issued by the Department of Justice on October 12, 2001, the standard should not be to allow the withholding of information whenever there is merely a "sound legal basis for doing so."

### 8.4.5.2 The Privacy Act of 1974.

"The Privacy Act of 1974 is a companion to the FOIA. The Privacy Act regulates federal government agency recordkeeping and disclosure practices. The act allows most individuals to seek access to federal agency records about themselves. The act requires that personal information in agency files be accurate, complete, relevant, and timely. The subject of a record may challenge the accuracy of information. The act requires that agencies obtain information directly from the subject of the record and that information gathered for one purpose not be used for another purpose. As with the FOIA, the Privacy Act provides civil remedies for individuals whose rights may have been violated. Another important feature of the Privacy Act is the requirement that each federal agency publish a description of each system of records maintained by the agency that contains personal information. This prevents agencies from keeping secret records."[90]

### 8.4.5.3 The Right to Financial Privacy Act of 1976.
The Right to Financial Privacy Act of 1976 protects the confidentiality of private financial records by requiring government agencies to notify the individual before viewing their records. The USA PATRIOT Act amended this to exclude intelligence agencies. State government agencies can get financial records if reasonably described and (1) the customer authorizes access, (2) there is an appropriate administrative subpoena or summons, (3) there is a search warrant, (4) there is an appropriate judicial subpoena, and (5) there is an appropriate written request from an authorized government authority.[91]

### 8.4.5.4 The Computer Matching and Privacy Act of 1988.
The Computer Matching and Privacy Act of 1988 amends the Privacy Act to add several new provisions [see 5 U.S.C. § 552a(a)(8)-(13), (e)(12), (o), (p), (q), (r), (u) (2000)] that federal government agencies are to follow when engaging in computerized data-matching activities. The law also guarantees, with certain exceptions, that individuals who have been identified through computerized data matching analysis receive notice of this and are able to review and refute information before having a benefit denied or terminated. The law also requires that agencies engaged in matching activities establish data protection boards to oversee computer and database matching activities. It is notable that this law had the effect of restricting a certain amount of intelligence sharing among law enforcement and intelligence agencies that maintained and operated different information and analysis systems.

### 8.4.5.5 The Paperwork Reduction Act of 1995.
The Paperwork Reduction Act of 1995 created the federal Office of Information and Regulatory Affairs to oversee development and implementation of policies, principles, standards, and guidelines on privacy, confidentiality, security, disclosure, and sharing of information collected or maintained by or for federal agencies.

### 8.4.5.6 The Fair and Accurate Credit Transactions Act of 2003.
The Fair and Accurate Credit Transactions Act of 2003 is designed to help consumers build good credit and confront identify theft. Specific provisions of the law ensure that lenders make loan decisions on complete and accurate credit histories and that lenders and credit agencies take action to inquire about and warn possible victims of fraud and identity theft even before it is confirmed that a crime has occurred. The law also grants consumers the right to receive an annual credit report free of charge for purposes of detecting possible identify theft and correcting errors in their credit history. Credit reporting agencies are required to place alerts on consumer credit histories when fraud is alleged, and merchants are prohibited from using all but the last five digits of a credit card number off store receipts. The act also creates a national fraud reporting and detection system that allows consumers to make a single call to report suspected fraud rather than making separate calls to every credit card company. In addition, the law requires regulators (e.g., the FTC) to devise a list of red flag indicators of identity theft, drawn from the patterns and practices of identity thieves, and use these in compliance examinations of financial institutions.[92]

## 8.5 Summary

Laws are societal rules that govern human behaviors. They are created by the federal government and by state, county, and municipal governments.

Creation and interpretation of laws typically reflect one of three legal philosophies, either natural law, positive law, or the historical school of legal thinking. Additionally, laws are administered by courts based on several specific types of jurisdiction which pertains to legal authority to render decisions in cases brought before courts. Jurisdiction to investigate and try cybercrime cases is significantly related to legal philosophies and structures of nations which historically have sought to establish international agreements, also known as treaties among other terms. International efforts to prevent and control IT-enabled abuse and crimes is increasing and improving. American laws are based on Old English common laws, statutory laws that may be amended periodically, and accumulating bodies of case laws based on legal rulings within local, state, and federal court systems. The five main bodies of laws pertaining to cybercrime are constitutional and case, criminal, administrative and regulatory, intellectual property, and tort law. Constitutional law is based on the U.S. Constitution and its amendments, as well as the interpretation of them by judges at the trial, appellate, and supreme court levels of states and the federal government. Criminal law specifies illegal conduct classified as either misdemeanors or felonies for which, if convicted, perpetrators may be incarcerated, fined, and/or receive other types of sentences. Administrative law pertains to the issuance and revocation of licenses and is the basis for government agencies promulgating regulations, which are rules imposed on businesses. Regulatory authority is authorized by laws, and regulations enacted and enforced by government agencies are in effect extensions of laws for which violators may be fined or sanctioned in other ways determined by administrative law judges or hearings officials. Intellectual property law defines copyright, trademark, patent, and trade secret protections, violations of which may be civil or criminal in nature. Tort law specifies civil wrongdoing for which organizations and individuals may be sued monetarily.

Laws are created through a consensus-building and political process within separate legislative chambers in state governments and within the federal government. Laws often are created and passed in joint packages simultaneously voted on by elected officials of the legislature and then forwarded to the executive office for approval or veto. Override provisions are specified in laws as an aspect of governmental checks and balances. After being enacted, laws are implemented and enforced by government agencies, some of which further enact and enforce regulations. Cybercrime laws are enforced by federal, state, and local law enforcement officers. Federal regulatory agencies with specific cybercrime investigation and information security-related charters include the Federal Aviation Administration (FAA), the Federal Communications Commission (FCC), the Federal Deposit Insurance Corporation (FDIC), the Federal Elections Commission (FEC), the Securities Exchange Commission (SEC), and the U.S. Nuclear Regulatory Commission.

Federal laws and regulations related to preventing and controlling cybercrime date back several decades, nearly to the invention of modern computers. These may be categorized as laws that (1) specify illegal use of computers and electronic devices, (2) facilitate or limit cybercrime investigations, (3) protect children from online pornography, (4) specify information security requirements for government agencies and private sector firms, and (5) afford privacy and consumer fraud protections. Several laws within each of these categories were briefly summarized in this chapter. Collectively they provide law enforcement officers, government regulators, and prosecutors, as well as IT professionals and organizational managers with rules to investigate and live by. The state of laws and regulations in society continually evolves, driven by combinations of technological, social, economic and political forces that exceed the ability of any single group, vendor, or institution to unduly influence their formulation and enforcement. For this reason, varieties and extensive bodies of laws provide for a remarkably stable system of governance and commerce despite rapidly changing crime and security threats. Laws also specify inappropriate behaviors requiring investigation and potential criminal prosecution, the subject of the next chapter.

## Key Terms and Concepts

Administrative law, 294
Appellate jurisdiction, 280
Bill of Rights, 289
Case law, 292
Change of venue, 279
Civil judgments, 302
Civil law, 277
Common law, 292
Concurrent jurisdiction, 280
Copyright, 296
Crimes against persons, 292
Crimes against property, 292
Criminal law, 292
Cyber law, 292
Cyber mark, 300
Defamation, 301
Delinquent act, 293
Design patents, 300
Double jeopardy, 279
Due process, 274

Extradition agreements, 280
Exclusive jurisdiction, 280
Fair use doctrine, 298
Felony, 293
Historical school of legal
  thinking, 277
Intellectual property (IP) law, 296
International agreement, 282
Jurisdiction, 279
Legal jurisdiction, 279
Libel, 301
Long arm jurisdiction, 280
Misdemeanor, 293
Natural law, 277
Negligence, 301
Nonviolent crimes, 292
Original jurisdiction 280
Patent, 300
Personam jurisdiction, 280
Plant patents, 300

Positive law, 277
Preponderance of evidence, 302
Procedural law, 287
Property crimes, 292
Regulations, 295
Rem jurisdiction, 280
Rule of law, 275
Slander, 301
Status offense, 293
Subject matter jurisdiction, 280
Substantive law, 287
Tort, 301
Tort law, 301
Trademark, 299
Trade name, 300
Trade secret, 301
Utility patents, 300
Violent crimes, 292

## Critical Thinking and Discussion Questions

1. There has been a growing call for homeland security and critical information infrastructure over the past 10 years, with new organizations and studies being done regularly. Critical information infrastructure and homeland security has been necessary for much longer than that, during multiple periods in the history of the United States. Do you believe that the recent creation of new committees and organizations (such as the Department of Homeland Security) will help strengthen international security and infrastructure protection? If so, explain how the forming of the new Department of Homeland Security will provide added security over the previous system. If not, explain possible reasons for creating the Department of Homeland Security outside of security reasons.

2. How has American life been affected by the USA PATRIOT Act? Provide examples of impact on the online community, the tech industry, and law enforcement.

3. The Patriot Act has caused a huge uproar among civil libertarians yet has many strong supporters within the government. What exactly is the problem?

4. Keeping the cyber community in mind, explain at least three problems with the Patriot Act from the point of view of a privacy advocate and explain at least three beneficial tools gained from the point of view of the government and law enforcement. As a

citizen or resident of the United States, why are you for or against the Patriot Act?

5. Out of the five bodies of law that pertain to IT and computer crime issues, choose three and give an example (a law, act, or trial) of each. For each of your answers, provide a brief description of the law and explain why you do or do not believe that it is helpful in fighting computer crime.

6. Recently the RIAA sent ex-police officers wearing FBI-style RIAA raid jackets onto the streets to confiscate bootleg CDs from street vendors (http://www.laweekly.com/ink/04/07/news-sullivan.php). Do you believe this kind of action by the RIAA is warranted?

7. What legal conditions would lead the RIAA to take such an action? What kind of precedent does this kind of action from the private sector set? Should the RIAA be held accountable for impersonating law enforcement? Should there be stricter legislation for copyright violation?

8. The current legal system is having trouble keeping up with the constantly evolving nature of technology. Few legislators possess the technological knowledge to completely understand the complexities of computer crime. Do you believe that this knowledge gap creates a feeling of isolation from the government in the cyber community? How does this gap affect the

hacker subculture? How does this gap affect the Open Source Community? As technology becomes more complex, do you believe it is necessary to have more technology-oriented people in government?

9. Is it possible for the United States or any other country to completely follow the Council of Europe Cybercrime Agreement pertaining to investigation of computer crimes? Why or why not? Explain what changes would have to be made in order for the international standards to be met. Give specific examples from U.S. laws that meet standards set in the Council of Europe agreement.

10. When the Digital Millennium Copy Right Act (DMCA) was introduced in 1998, academics and civil liberty activists spoke out against it. Write a position piece from the point of view of academics, activists, the government, or industry in support for or against the DMCA. Provide references to support your position.

11. A nationally known public figure who resides in Virginia sues a nonresident for defamation as a result of

statements the defendant made on his Web site at a URL bearing the plaintiff's name. The defendant challenged the jurisdiction of the Virginia court, stating that he did not specifically target Virginia Web surfers. Using the Zippo standard, who will prevail? See *Jerry L. Falwell v. Gary Cohn* and God, Info Civ, Act. No 6:02CV0040 (W.D. Va. March 4, 2003).

12. A respondent in the Electronic Crime Needs Assessment published by the U.S. Department of Justice mentioned the importance of keeping in close contact with legislators about technology being used in crime. Do you believe that taking this sort of initiative would help prevent and/or control cybercrime? Why or why not?

13. What kind of management issues would be involved with bringing law enforcement and lawmakers closer together in their understanding of IT-enabled crime threats? What effects can collaboration between agencies, firms, academic institutions, and professional organizations have on formulating government policies, regulations, and laws?

## References and Endnotes

1. British Library (2005). *Magna Carta.* The British Library Board. Retrieved March 17, 2005, from http://www.bl.uk/collections/treasures/magna.html.

2. Beccaria, C. (1764). On crimes and punishments. In Joseph E. Jacoby (Ed.), *Classics of Criminology,* 2nd ed., 1994 edition (pp. 277–285). Prospect Heights, IL: Waveland Press.

3. Falcone, D. N. (2005). *Dictionary of American Criminal Justice, Criminology, & Criminal Law.* Upper Saddle River, NJ: Prentice Hall.

4. Black, H. C. (1979). *Black's Law Dictionary.* St. Paul, MN: West Publishing.

5. *Zippo Manufacturing Company v. Zippo Dot Com, Inc.,* 952 F. Supp. 1119 (W.D. Pa. 1997).

6. Hwee, T. K. (2000). Prosecuting foreign-based computer crime: International law and technology collide. Attorney-General's Chambers, Singapore. Retrieved March 14, 2004, from http://www.un.org.

7. See Chapter 16 in Chen, L. C. (1989). *An Introduction to Contemporary International Law: A Policy-Oriented Perspective.* New Haven, CT: Yale University Press.

8. Chen, L. C., 1989; see note 7.

9. United Nations (1997). *Manual on the Prevention and Control of Computer-Related Crime.* New York: United Nations.

10. Organization for Economic Co-operation and Development (OECD) (2003). Broadband access in OECD countries per 100 inhabitants (underlying data). Retrieved March 12, 2004, from http://www.oecd.org/sti/telecom.

11. United Nations, 1997; see note 9.

12. Council of Europe (2001). *Convention on Cybercrime.* Budapest, Hungary: Council of Europe.

13. United Nations, 1997; see note 9.

14. Moteff, J. (2001). *Critical Infrastructures: A Background and early Implementation of PDD 63.* Washington, DC: Congressional Research Service.

15. United Nations, 1997; see note 9.

16. Goodman, S. E., & Sofaer, A. D. (2000). The transnational dimension of cyber crime and terrorism. Retrieved February 8, 2004, via http://www-hoover.stanford.edu.

17. Cuéllar, M., Drozdova, E. A., Elliott, D. D., Goodman, S. E., Grove, G. D., & Sofaer, A. D. (2001). *The Transnational Dimension of Cyber Crime and Terrorism,* Abraham D. Sofaer and Seymour E. Goodman (Eds.). Stanford, CA: Hoover Institution Press.

18. Vatis, M. A. (2000). Statement to the Senate Judiciary Committee, Criminal Justice Oversight Subcommittee and House Judiciary Committee, Crime Subcommittee. Washington, D.C. Retrieved March 12, 2004, from http://www.usdoj.gov/criminal/cybercrime/.

19. Knight, W., & Thorel, J. (2000, May 18). G8 nations team up to fight cyber-crime. Retrieved March 11, 2005, from http://news.zdnet.co.uk/internet/security/0,39020375,2079018,00.htm.

20. Council of Europe, 2001; see note 12.

21. Allen, C. A., et al. (2002). *Compendium of Supporting Documents to the National Strategy for Critical Infrastructure Assurance: Banking and Finance Sector.* Washington, D.C.: National Institute of Standards and Technology.

22. Hwee, T. K. (2000). Prosecuting foreign-based computer crime: international law and technology collide. Attorney-General's Chambers, Singapore. Retrieved March 14, 2004, from http://www.un.org.

23. Goodman, S. E., & Sofaer, A. D. (2000). *The Transnational Dimension of Cyber Crime and Terrorism.* Retrieved February 8, 2004, from http://www-hoover.stanford.edu.

24. Commission of the European Communities (2002). *Proposal for a Council Framework Decision on Attacks Against Information Systems.* Brussels, Belgium: Commission of the European Communities.

25. Privacy International (2003). 14th ASEAN-EU meeting, Joint Declaration on Co-operation to Combat Terrorism. Retrieved March 21, 2005, from http://www.privacyinternational.org/article.shtml?cmd[347]=x-347-122006&als[theme]=Cyber%20Crime.

26. U.S. Department of Justice 2000 #72911

27. Korda, M. (2004, July 15). The net's sleuths. *Guardian Unlimited.* Retrieved November 4, 2004, from http://www.guardian.co.uk/online/story/0,3605,1260989,00.html.

28. *Reno v. American Civil Liberties Union, 117 F. Supp. 2329 (1997)*

29. *ACLU v Reno, 521 U.S. 844, 1997*

30. Many jurisdictions define and criminalize making threats to harm persons or property separately from the crime of simple assault. In other jurisdictions, threatening harm is a specific or implied element of the crime of simple assault and aggravated assault, so making threats may constitute its own form of assault.

31. Staff Author (2003). Hopkins teen charged with Blaster worm. About.com. Retrieved November 3, 2004, from http://minneapolis.about.com/cs/crime/a/blasterworm.htm.

32. Becker, D., & Hines, M. (2003). FBI arrests MSBlast worm suspect. CNET News.com. Retrieved November 3, 2004, from http://news.zdnet.com/2100-1009_22-5070000.html.

33. Staff Author, 2003; see note 31.

34. Schwartz, J. (2003, November 6). Microsoft sets $5 million virus bounty. *New York Times* (Section C, Page 4 , Column 3). Retrieved August 23, 2005, from http://query.nytimes.com/gst/abstract.html?res=F4071EF73C5D0C758CDDA80994DB404482.

35. Associated Press Staff Author (2005, January 14). Texas college student named in spam suit. Fox News. Retrieved April 11, 2005, from http://www.foxnews.com/story/0,2933,144368,00.html.

36. Mehlman, B. P. (2002). *The Changing Wealth of Nations: Intellectual Property and American Competitiveness in the Age of Innovation.* Washington, D.C.: U.S. Department of Commerce.

37. Mehlman, B. P., 2002; see note 36.

38. Mehlman, B. P., 2002; see note 36.

39. Girasa, R. J. (2002). *Cyberlaw: National and International Perspectives* (p. 156). Upper Saddle River, NJ: Prentice Hall.

40. Girasa, R. J., 2002; see note 39.

41. U.S. Code, Title 17, Chapter 1, Section 102.

42. Clarkson, K. W., Miller, R. L., Jentz, G. A., & Cross, F. B. (2004). *West's Business Law* (p. 153). Mason, OH: Thomson South-Western.

43. U.S.C Title 17, Chapter 12, Section 1204.

44. Clarkson, K. W., et al., 2004, p. 151; see note 42.

45. Girasa, R. J., 2002, p. 157–158; see note 39.

46. Girasa, R. J., 2002, p. 160; see note 39.

47. Girasa, R. J., 2002, pp. 168–169; see note 39.

48. U.S. Code, Title 17, Chapter 1, Section 117 (a)(2).

49. U.S. Code, Title 17, Chapter 12, Section 1201 (a)(1)(A).

50. *Universal City Studios, Inc. v. Corley* (2001). 273 F.3d 429. Federal Court of Appeals.

51. Crawford, K. (2005). Hollywood wins Internet piracy battle: The U.S. Supreme Court rules against file-sharing service Grokster in a closely watched piracy case. Retrieved July 24 from http://money.cnn.com/2005/06/27/technology/grokster/

52. See specific provisions of Digital Millennium Copyright Act, and further discussion of the DMCA later in this chapter.

53. *New York Times Co. v. Tasini* (2001). United States Supreme Court. 533 U.S. 483.

54. U.S. Code, Title 17, Chapter 13, Section 1302.

55. Clarkson, K. W., et al., 2004; see note 42.

56. Clarkson, K. W., et al., 2004; see note 42.

57. Girasa, R. J., 2002, pp. 243–250; see note 39.

58. Chapter 15 in Loundy, D. J. (2003). *Computer Crime, Information Warfare and Economic Espionage.* Durham, NC: Carolina Academic Press.

59. Associated Press Staff Author (2004, December 18). ISP awarded $1B in spam lawsuit. Fox News. Retrieved April 11, 2005, from http://www.foxnews.com/story/0,2933,141950,00.html.

60. Nebraska is an exception because it is the only state with a unicameral legislative system. It combines traditional house and senate bodies and their respective functions into a single legislative body.

61. Federal Aviation Administration (2005). FAA home page. Retrieved March 25, 2005, from http://www.faa.gov/about/mission/activities/.

62. Federal Communications Commission (2005). FCC home page. Retrieved March 25, 2005, from http://www.fcc.gov/aboutus.html.

63. Federal Deposit Insurance Corporation (2005). FDIC home page. Retrieved March 25, 2005, from http://www.fdic.gov/about/learn/symbol/index.html.

64. Federal Elections Commission (2005). FEC home page. Retrieved March 25, 2005, from http://www.fec.gov/about.shtml.

65. Securities Exchange and Commission (2005). SEC home page. Retrieved March 25, 2005, from http://www.sec.gov/about/whatwedo.shtml.

66. Commodity Futures Trading Commission (2005). CFTC home page. Retrieved March 25, 2004, from http://www.cftc.gov/cftc/cftcabout.htm.

67. Winerman, M. (2003). The origins of the FTC: concentration, cooperation, control and competition. *Antitrust Law Journal, 71*(1).

68. Federal Trade Commission (2005). FTC home page. U.S. Department of Commerce. Retrieved April 21, 2005, from http://www.ftc.gov/.

69. U.S. Nuclear Regulatory Commission (2005). USNRC home page. Retrieved March 25, 2005, from http://www.nrc.gov/.

70. Chambliss, W. J. (1993). On lawmaking. Chapter 1 in *Making Law: The State, the Law and Structural Contradictions*. William J. Chambliss and Marjorie S. Zatz (Eds.)., Indianapolis: Indiana University Press.

71. Science Applications International Corporation (1995). *Information Warfare: Legal Regulatory, Policy, and Organizational Considerations for Assurance*. Report for the Chief, Information Warfare Division (J6K) Command, Control, Communications, and Computer Systems Directorate. Washington, D.C.: Joint Staff, the Pentagon.

72. Musto, D. F. (1997). Historical perspectives. *Substance Abuse: A Comprehensive Textbook*, 3rd ed. (pp. 1–10). London: Williams and Wilkins.

73. U.S. Department of Justice (2000). U.S. indicts 17 in alleged international software piracy conspiracy. Retrieved online March 22, 2005, from http://www.usdoj.gov/criminal/cybercrime/pirates.htm.

74. Butterfield, F. (1929, March). Reason for dramatic drop in crime puzzles experts. *New New York Times* (Late Edition).

75. Online Institute for Cyberspace Law and Policy. (2001, February 8). University of California at Los Angeles. Retrieved April 21, 2005, from http://www.gseis.ucla.edu/iclp/dmca1.htm.

76. Administrative Office of the U.S. Courts (2004, April 30). 2003 wiretap report (see Table 7, p. 32). Washington, D.C.: U.S. Department of Justice.

77. Welch, M. (2003, April 2). Get ready for Patriot II. AlterNet. Retrieved April 8, 2005, from http://www.alternet.org/story/15541.

78. American Civil Liberties Union (2003, February 14). Interested persons memo: section-by-section analysis of Justice Department draft "Domestic Security Enhancement Act of 2003," also known as "PATRIOT Act II." Retrieved April 8, 2005, from http://www.aclu.org/SafeandFree/SafeandFree.cfm?ID=11835&c=206.

79. Singel, R. (2003, August 21). Patriot Act II resurrected? Wired News. Retrieved August 21, 2002, from http://www.wired.com/news/poltics/0,1283,60129,00.html.

80. Underwood, B. B. (2001, May). Reply brief for writ of certiorari to John Ashcroft, Attorney General of the United States, petitioner v. American Civil Liberties Union, et al. Submitted to the U.S. Supreme Court by Acting Solicitor General and Counsel of Record for the U.S. Department of Justice. Washington, D.C.: U.S. Department of Justice.

81. Infoplease (2004). History of censorship in United States. Retrieved October 23, 2004, from http://www.infoplease.com/ce6/society/A0857225.html.

82. Infoplease, 2004; see note 81.

83. See, 521 U.S. 844.

84. *Ashcroft, Attorney General, et al. v. Free Speech Coalition et al*. United States Supreme Court. Washington, D.C.

85. McCullagh, D. (2002, May 3). Round two on 'morphed' child porn. Wired News. Retrieved April 18, 2005, from http://www.wired.com/news/poltics/0,1283,52285,00.html.

86. Newsday (2004). U.S. law on Web porn is blocked. High court sends back case on measure to protect children. *Democrat and Chronicle*, June 30.

87. U.S. Supreme Court (2002, May, 13). *Ashcroft, Attorney General v. American Civil Liberties Union et al*. U.S. Supreme Court. Retrieved March 25. 2005, from http://caselaw.lp.findlaw.com/scripts/getcase.pl?court=us&vol=000&invol=00-1293.

88. Cyber Telecom (2005, March, 2). Children's Internet Protection Act. Retrieved March 3, 2005, from http://www.cybertelecom.org/cda/cipa.htm.

89. U.S. Department of Justice (2003). Fact Sheet PROTECT Act. Retrieved March 3, 2005, from http://www.usdoj.gov/opa/pr/2003/April/03_ag_266.htm.

90. U.S. Congress (2003). *A Citizen's Guide on Using the Freedom of Information Act and the Privacy Act of 1974 to Request Government Records*. Report of the U.S. House of Representatives, 108th Congress, 1st Session. Washington, D.C.: U.S. Government Printing Office.

91. Encryption and evolving technologies as tools of organized crime and terrorism (1997). Washington, D.C. National Strategy Information Center, U.S. Working Group on Organized Crime (WGOC).

92. White House (2004, December, 4). Fact sheet: President Bush signs Fair and Accurate Credit Transaction Act of 2003. Retrieved April 21, 2005, from http://www.whitehouse.gov/news/releases/2003/12/20031204-3.html.

# 9

## *Investigating and Prosecuting Cybercrime*

### 9.0 Introduction: What Happens When Cybercrime Laws Are Broken?

In February 20, 2005, socialite Paris Hilton had the contact information of her personal friends, including many other celebrities, posted to a Web site frequented by hackers. Phone numbers, addresses, and personal emails of rapper Eminem, actor Vin Diesel, actress Lindsay Lohan, singers Christina Aguilera and Ashlee Simpson, as well as tennis players Andy Roddick and Anna Kournikova were suddenly available to anyone in the world with an Internet access device. This also was true for many other famous individuals until authorities of T-Mobile, the firm which stored Hilton's personal information for online retrieval purposes, found out about the security breech and notified the FBI, which initiated a cybercrime investigation. The case may have involved either hacking into T-Mobile's server, unauthorized release of information by an employee of the firm, or someone temporarily accessing Hilton's Sidekick device in order to download the contact data before posting it onto the Internet. In 2003 T-Mobile was hacked by Nicholas Jacobsen, who reportedly accessed names and social security numbers of over 400 customers before being arrested. Two days after the Hilton incident, in which Jacobsen was apparently not involved, he pled guilty to computer trespassing to face a potential punishment of five years imprisonment plus a $250,000 fine for violating federal computer crime law. If investigators are able to solve the Hilton case, the person or persons responsible may face the same or a similar fate.[1]

If you were an investigator who was asked to solve the Hilton case, how would you begin? Where would you go and what precisely would you do when you got there? Who would you interview first, second, third, and so on? What types of evidence would you look for, and how would you retrieve it for purposes of analysis and potential prosecution? By what authority would you conduct your investigation, and what if any legal restrictions would you be mindful of as you examined one or more crime scenes, computers systems, and electronic IT devices? For example, would you need to get search warrants in order to examine electronic evidence on computers or would certain people providing you with their consent be sufficient? If the latter, who could grant you legal consent to search and under what circumstances and who could not? Who if any-one would you notify about your ongoing inves-tigation, how would you record investigative actions, and who would you look to for technical assistance or other support if you needed help? These questions are indicative of the many possi-ble issues that may arise during the course of a computer abuse or cybercrime investigation.

This chapter provides an overview of is-sues that pertain to what happens after incidents of computer abuse or cybercrimes occur. Our focus is on certain legal issues and investigative processes and how these relate to prosecuting people for having committed cybercrimes. Many of the issues and basic procedures discussed also apply to administrative or internal organizational investigations of computer abuse that may not constitute a violation of crime law. We will begin with a brief overview of the types of criminal justice system agencies and other organizations typically involved in cybercrime investigations that often collaborate to solve cases. You will learn about the different and overlapping roles of public law enforcement and private security firms, and the relationship of these organizations to offices of local, state, and federal prosecutors. You will also learn about dedicated cybercrime investigation and prosecution units, factors af-fecting creation of these within organizations, and several key national organizations and feder-al government agencies that can assist state and local information security professionals, law en-forcement investigators and prosecutors, in solv-ing cases.

We will also cover legal issues governing investigative procedures, including evidentiary challenges faced by law enforcement and infor-mation security professionals undertaking a vari-ety of physical and cyber surveillance operations among other investigative activities. Because cy-bercrimes may and often do involve both physi-cal and cyber dimensions, investigators need to be concerned about tangible, electronic, and other forms of evidence that are also discussed. We therefore will address issues pertaining to responding to and securing crime scenes, identi-fying evidence indicative of crime, and managing evidence collected at crime scenes in preparation for computer forensics analysis and prosecution. This general information will be especially bene-ficial to students who are not majoring in crimi-nal justice but who nonetheless may in future careers conduct or be responsible for overseeing computer abuse investigations in organizational settings. You will also learn basic concepts of computer forensics and how to go about inter-viewing victims, witnesses, and suspects in com-puter abuse and cybercrime cases. In the final section we will consider issues pertaining to prosecuting cybercrimes, including requirements to prove elements in law with legally acquired evidence from crime scenes and from individuals with knowledge of the facts, circumstances, and events of cases being tried in court. You will learn the basics of how to present evidence in court and about criminal appeals and alternatives to formal criminal prosecution that are increas-ingly being employed at all levels of government in order to promote justice while reducing incar-nation levels.

A major theme of this chapter is that all the hype often found in books, magazine articles and news reports about cybercrime, its, investigation and prosecution does not differ substantially from that of other types of crime. Indeed, as we have es-tablished in earlier chapters, many types of tradi-tional crime increasingly involve use of computers or other types of electronic devices, a general con-dition that tends to confound understanding about the evolving nature and extent of cybercrimes. To put it another way that also ties in with earlier dis-cussion, computers, other types of electronic IT devices, and information systems are so ubiqui-tous in society that they have become integral, or at least of tangential evidentiary importance, to many forms of crimes depending on the technolog-ical preferences and SKRAM (**skills**, **knowledge**, **resources**, **authority**, and **motives**) of individual crime perpetrators. This means that today's inves-tigators can never know in advance when or how important IT will turn out to be even in routine non-cybercrime cases, or by extension, when a given case will turn out to involve cybercrimes. The idea that cybercrimes are fundamentally different from many other conceptual categories of crime with respect to human factors, technologies involved, or legal issues is utter nonsense, and believing this myth contributes to sensationalizing cybercrimes. Seasoned cybercrime investigators know this to be true, while also understanding that IT is of particular interest as a potential means of committing crimes in new ways and as repositories of electronic evidence of old as well as innovative forms of crime. This all continually combines to challenge interpretation of laws as technology evolves to create new opportunities for social abuse and crime involving varying amounts of IT used in simple to complex ways. We discussed in Chapter 5, the interplay of these issues as addressed by the theory of technology-enabled crime, policing, and security. And through the art and science of computer forensics, computers and other types of electronic IT devices and specialized investigation software are also providing new means of solving cybercrimes and convicting cybercriminals.

Criminal justice students will find much of the material in this chapter useful because it applies essential information about longstanding case law, investigative procedures and prosecution principles to new and emerging forms of cybercrimes. Students who are majoring in other subjects and who are possibly taking only one or a few criminal justice courses will also find the information contained in this chapter useful, if not completely new. Regardless of whether this is your first exposure to investigative procedures and prosecution principles or supplemental to what you have already learned in another course or perhaps through professional experience, information covered in this chapter will help you to better understand, investigate, and manage incidents of computer abuse and cybercrimes with an attitude of getting the job done in a way that will likely withstand legal scrutiny in both criminal and civil court proceedings.

## 9.1 Collaborative Criminal Justice System Responses to Cybercrime

The criminal justice system in the United States is composed of policing, courts, and corrections agencies at local, state, and national levels of government. Tens of thousands of criminal justice agencies exist (over 18,000 in policing alone), often with overlapping authority and responsibilities as established in laws, regulations, and mutual aid agreements. As indicated in previous chapters, international cooperation among agencies to combat cybercrime is increasing often with guidance provided in agreements, treaties, or conventions pertaining to protocols for investigating and prosecuting IT-enabled crimes. This is important because concern about information security and jurisdiction over cybercrime exists throughout the world and is not the purview of any single agency or set of criminal justice organizations. Rather, as discussed in Chapter 8, legal jurisdictions are determined on a case-by-case basis according to combinations of applicable crime laws, procedural laws, and related case law rulings. By law, certain government agencies also have regulatory authority for overseeing specific types of business practices and standards deemed to be in the public interest. Moreover, pervasive IT inherent to cybercrimes means that several geopolitical jurisdictions, and criminal justice system components, may be affected by or involved in investigating and prosecuting a given combination of IT-enabled abuse, attacks, and crimes.

Policing agencies must investigate crimes that increasingly involve computers, other types of IT devices, and information systems; courts struggle to interpret and apply longstanding but evolving bodies of law to technologically inventive cybercrime cases; and corrections agencies are required to house convicted cybercriminals as well as prisoners awaiting trial in cases involving computers and other types of electronic devices. Criminal justice and security agencies must also maintain computerized management information systems, and managers are concerned with the security of these systems in order to ensure the confidentiality, integrity, and availability of the data they contain. Correctional agency officials must also constantly be aware of possibilities for cybercrimes to be committed by prisoners.

In 1999 inmates operating from within Federal Bureau of Prison facilities located in various states engineered and carried out a sophisticated income tax fraud scheme. Using official forms of the Internal Revenue Service, actual Fortune 500 tax payer ID and social security numbers, and employee demographic information retrieved off the Net, a team of prisoners prepared and submitted false federal and state tax forms and received government refund checks. The checks were deposited in banks with assistance from conspiring family members, then converted to money orders to disguise the origins and sources of funds, and finally used to purchase consumer items, pay bills, and so on.[2] Note from lessons on information systems assurance discussed in Chapter 2 the interrelated issues presented in this case: (1) potential threats posed by insiders and/or outsiders who may conspire to commit crimes; (2) the need to provide information systems security in order to prevent cybercrimes; (3) combinations of physical and cyber methods of attack and assets in need of assurance, and (4) money, a special form of data, may be converted quickly in various locations into different forms.

The specter of cybercrime is unprecedented in the history of deviant, abusive, and criminological behaviors, owing only to the IT that makes it possible. Cybercrime has no regard for the systems it impacts, even though specific abuses, attacks, and crimes involving computers and other types of IT may be used to target individuals, organizations or their devices, data, and information systems on the basis of the actual or perceived value of assets and other factors. Additionally, the nature of information systems, ranging from relatively simple home PC–based networks, to incredibly complex critical information infrastructures relied on by regional populations, implies that government alone cannot fully manage, much less prevent, all IT-enabled abuses and threats of attacks and cybercrimes. Seasoned scholars and practitioners understand that everyone in society, especially IT administrators and information security professionals employed in public, private, and nonprofit sector organizations, along with associations of high-tech crime investigators and prosecutors, plays an important role in combating cybercrime. Professionals in the business of fighting cybercrime must work together to stay abreast of IT-enabled threats to protect people and information systems from harms and prevent and deter cybercriminals to the extent possible while also solving cybercrime cases.[3]

In this section we will expand on this theme in three ways. First we will examine the differing and collaborative roles of public law enforcement and private sector security firms for investigating cybercrimes and the intermediary technical assistance role that high-tech crime investigator associations and other entities have in promoting information assurance and combating cybercrimes. Then we will consider dedicated cybercrime investigation and prosecution units (CIPUs) that exist within larger government agencies. These will be considered with regard to their establishment, scope of operations, management, and resource requirements. Last, several key national cybercrime investigation and technical assistance agencies will be described with respect to their capabilities for assisting investigators, prosecutors, and information security professionals. The major goal of these three subsections is to enlighten readers about the roles, relationships, and capabilities of agencies involved in promoting information security, and investigating and prosecuting cybercrimes. In this way, you will understand the big picture and how key players interact, this in preparation for learning about more the technical issues of investigating and prosecuting cybercriminals.

### 9.1.1 Roles of Public Law Enforcement and Private Security

Criminal justice agencies including city police departments, county sheriffs' offices, state-level police and investigation agencies, and components of federal government departments are tax-funded and empowered to carry out investigations of criminal wrongdoing. Officers, deputies, and agents employed by these organizations are empowered to arrest people who have violated crime laws within their jurisdiction. Their **investigative and arrest powers** may extend beyond specific geographic boundaries. For example, a deputy sheriff of a county in Arizona can arrest a juvenile or adult anywhere within that state for violations of state crime laws. Similarly, federal agents are empowered to conduct criminal investigations in all states, districts, and territories of the United States in order to enforce federal crime laws. Federal agents may also conduct investigations of transnational crimes depending on provisions in international laws, treaties, and conventions established between the United States and other nations, and in manners consistent with policies of their organizations. Agents of the Bureau of Immigration and Customs Service, the Secret Service, and the FBI have all taken lead investigative roles in international cybercrime cases. In any case, it is government empowerment to initiate criminal investigations and to arrest people suspected of violating crime laws that distinguishes public police from private sector security professionals. Cases involving violations of laws are therefore the domain of police, who may also assert legal authority to investigate any incident involving computer abuse, an attack on information systems, or misuse of other IT devices which could potentially constitute a violation of law.

Private sector security firms also provide vital protection and investigation services to individuals, groups, and organizations on a contract basis. In the realm of cybercrime, these services include but are not limited to facilities and information systems protection, data recovery, and computer forensics. Services provided by security firms sometimes are provided even for large public law enforcement agencies. For example, various security firms provide facilities protection and/or information security services under contract to law enforcement and other types of agencies of state governments and the federal government. Private security firms also provide physical and information security for critical infrastructure facilities and information systems throughout the country, such as for nuclear power plants and airports and the computerized systems they rely on. Some private sector security and nonsecurity firms employ public police for security functions, although publicly employed police officers are usually restricted in the types of investigative assignments or tasks they can perform off-duty or that fall outside the scope of their primary employment with a government agency.[4] In addition, private sector security officers may investigate computer abuse and even cybercrimes on behalf of their employer in cases not reported to the police or other government authorities. This periodically occurs in cases when financial institutions wish to avoid publicly revealing a financial loss or weakness in information systems to avoid risking reduced confidence of investors in the security of their funds. For many years however, financial services and other private sector firms have realized the importance of reporting information about cybercrimes to police and also sharing of security threat information with other firms. To aid information sharing about cybercrimes, businesses and organizations in the Philadelphia-area have created a new Cyber Incident Detection & Data Analysis Center (CIDDAC). Founded in April, 2005 with $100,000 from participating organizations along with $200,000 in federal seed money contributed by the U.S. Department of Homeland Security, the Center is pilot testing real-time computer system attack sensing and reporting technologies.[5]

The extent to which public policing and private security overlap to provide facilities protection, information security, investigation of wrongdoing involving computers, and cybercrime prevention services is not really known. Although the number of criminal justice and security organizations can be determined with reasonable accuracy, research mechanisms for determining the number or relative capabilities of units or investigators within organizations do not currently exist. Nor is there currently available a complete list of private sector security and investigative firms or nonprofit organizations with infosec expertise. Knowing such overall numbers and corresponding capabilities is less important than knowing what agencies, organizations and firms are willing and able to provide assistance when it is required. In this regard investigators may be constrained for certain technological or legal reasons from sharing information, although most professionals can generally count on longstanding mutual aid agreements and interprofessional relationships developed over years of cooperation and trust-building. Since professionals now recognize that investigating cybercrimes requires greater understanding and shared resources, they are in most instances more willing than ever to collaborate, regardless of their being employed by public policing agencies versus private or nonprofit sector security or investigation firms. Joint government, nonprofit and private sector initiatives are now improving information systems security throughout society and helping solve many types of cybercrime cases while also enhancing information security capabilities. The Philadelphia based CIDDAC mentioned above, is one of many examples of improved information sharing and collaboration occurring throughout the nation.

In this and several other instances, collaboration between organizations is fostered through legislative or other government initiatives. Following the 9-11 terrorist attacks and passage of the USA Patriot Act, Electronic Crimes Task Forces (ECTFs) were established throughout the United States to bring together law enforcement, industry, and academia to fight high-tech terrorism and IT-enabled interstate and transnational crime. These regional task forces now operate as R&D and information-sharing networks with support and guidance from the U.S. Secret Service, which is a component of the U.S. Department of Homeland Security.[6] ECTFs are designed to share information with private sector partners. The Federal Bureau of Investigation (FBI) maintains a separate organizational network known as Infragard that fosters sharing of critical infrastructure protection information with state and local law enforcement agencies, private corporations, and academic institutions. The FBI has also established cybercrime task forces (CCTFs) to investigate intrusion cases, denial-of-service attacks, and large-scale malware incidents capable of impacting regional and national critical information infrastructures. CCTFs often coordinate with computer emergency response teams (CERTs), such as the one located at Carnegie Mellon University, to quickly provide expert information systems diagnostic and analytical assistance, as well as regional computer forensics laboratories for technical investigative support. Other organizations, such as Secunia (see Appendix A), identify software exploits and new Internet threats and list these online for public consumption and as a resource to the entire community of law enforcement and information security professionals.

The U.S. Secret Service has also joined ranks with the FBI to provide cooperative programs with state and local agencies to gather and share information, as well as resources for investigating cybercrimes and protecting critical information infrastructures against potential acts of cyberterrorism. Many chapters of high-tech crime investigator associations now provide forums for sharing information about new laws and regulations, new criminal and investigative methods, and technologies for securing information systems. In numerous locations the mission of HTCIA chapters are supported by other joint public-private sector information security professional organizations. For example, the Rochester Area Information Security Forum (RAISF) frequently holds meetings at the Rochester Institute of Technology and other locations in New York State for training workshop and information-sharing purposes. In addition, the Financial Crimes Task Force (FATF), spearheaded by the Financial Crimes Enforcement Network (FinCEN) of the U.S. Department of the Treasury, has generated greater reporting by private sector firms of money laundering and other types of cybercrime. The Office of the Inspector General of the Federal Emergency Management Agency (FEMA) leads fraud task forces that can include several agencies such as the U.S. Small Business Administration, the FBI, and the U.S. Army, which may conduct fraud investigations involving information crosschecks with even more government agencies and private insurance companies.[7] Inspector General offices have government oversight and investigative responsibilities existing within and transcending all departments of the federal government. Organizational alliances and networks such as these at all levels of government, and throughout the private and nonprofit sectors are increasingly helping to build capacity for securing facilities, information systems, and infrastructure and for investigating and prosecuting cybercrimes nationally, regionally, and locally.

## 9.1.2 Dedicated Cybercrime Investigation and Prosecution Units

Since the late 1980s some criminal justice and security professionals have advocated for dedicated organizational units to investigate and prosecute cybercrimes.[8] Many of these units exist throughout the nation, within federal, state, and large metropolitan policing agencies. However, relatively few of America's 18,000-plus police agencies (over 80 percent of which consist of twenty-five or fewer officers) possess the financial, personnel, and technological resources to establish high-tech crime investigation or prosecution units. Publicly funded offices of local, state, and federal prosecutors are typically resource constrained. Why is this? Besides the obvious answer that no one likes to be taxed more than necessary to maintain government services, consider that police administrators and prosecutors tend to be more concerned about violent and other street crimes featured in the media than with high-tech crimes that often go undetected, do not demand immediate attention, or originate from beyond or exceed local geopolitical jurisdictions. Imagine high-ranking police officials, sitting at their desks early each work day morning, sipping coffee, and reading their local newspapers in order to stay abreast of community affairs. What in particular do you suppose they are scanning for as they prepare for their workday? Although they are certainly interested in community affairs and perhaps also catching up on sports scores, seeing the weather forecast, and knowing about other matters of community interest, I can guarantee you that they are most concerned about stories of local crimes involving physical injury or tangible property damage experienced by individual crime victims, and news reports pertaining to local crime patterns or trends, as well as how investigation of these by their agencies are being publicly portrayed. For its part, the media is interested in getting the news out, and often only large-scale cybercrimes attained from wire services such as the Associated Press or Reuters, or those involving local cases of child pornography, are reported. As the old expression goes, "If it bleeds it leads"— a reference to images of physical injury or property damage, rather than harm to information systems or even people as the result of losing data. Unfortunately for cybercrime aficionados, this means that police chiefs and sheriffs who are politically aware and media sensitive are mostly concerned with street and violent crimes. In the broad scheme of things this is not necessarily bad. Crime reported by the media raises public awareness and heightens concerns among other government officials, which may translate into supplemental financial support for investigating specific cases or broader crime problems facing communities. Although reporting of sensational cybercrimes, or patterns and trends of these could also increase community awareness and lead to greater investigative resources, it is still generally true that cybercrimes tend to fascinate, confuse and intimidate people, including reporters, who oftentimes do not understand the underlying combinations of IT and human factors issues involved in specific crimes. Individual reporters can readily explain ordinary crime incidents and the public can readily understand forms of crimes with which they are familiar, but many people have difficulty comprehending high-tech crimes with which they are less familiar. Unfamiliarity with numerous types of cybercrimes exists among many law enforcement agencies and officers as well as the media and public. Reduced awareness of cybercrimes and how to prevent or investigate them perpetuates problems associated with high tech crimes.

The stark reality about cybercrime is that most members of the general public, as well as high-ranking police and other public officials including prosecutors, pay more attention to crime problems in human and legal terms than with respect to the technological ways in which they are committed. This general condition, along with the fiscal and political reality that few police executives can afford or are willing to turn their investigators loose on crimes exceeding local jurisdictions, means they are also disinclined to create special high-tech crime investigation and prosecution units that require investment in special equipment and training and thus divestment of personnel and other resources that could be used to fight higher priority street crimes. State-level and large metropolitan police agencies are nonetheless increasingly creating high-tech crime units that investigate cybercrimes within their jurisdictions while providing technical investigative support for smaller agencies on either a mutual aid or contract-for-service basis.

Sometimes, especially at the state level and in very large cities, these units consist of several personnel who are equipped with full-service computer forensics laboratories in which to process IT devices for evidence of cybercrimes. In other locations, the unit may consist of a single investigator who uses limited and even outmoded equipment to process electronic evidence. For several years, a single expert computer crime investigator in the Monroe County, New York, Sheriff's Department has provided computer forensics support for all police agencies in the entire county including the City of Rochester Police Department (serving a combined population of 1.4 million people), plus support for agencies in thirteen additional counties on a contract basis. How would you like to have this investigator's job? Fortunately additional resources in the form of multiple agency cybercrime task forces and an increasing number or private sector computer forensics labs now provide relief services and technical assistance for many smaller agencies that do not have their own high-tech crime investigation units.

Dedicated prosecution units have also been created in recent years to process the increasing volume of cybercrime cases being referred by police agencies for formal charges. In the mid-1990s the Computer Crime Unit of the U.S. Department of Justice consisted of *three* very overwhelmed federal prosecutors. Unable to prosecute many individual cases, they primarily provided policy development and legal advice assistance to offices of U.S. attorneys located throughout the country. The reconstituted U.S. Computer and Intellectual Property Crimes Section now employs several dozen attorneys and investigators who actively help coordinate and prosecute important national and international cybercrime cases. In addition, the FBI has created a computer crime unit within each of its regional offices that is staffed with agents trained in computer forensics analysis who routinely work with assistant U.S. attorneys designated to prosecute IT-enabled crimes. This basic organizational trend is occurring throughout the United States and in other nations cracking down on the illegal activities of cybercriminals.

### 9.1.3 Key Investigative and Technical Assistance Agencies

As criminals become more technologically sophisticated, so must our ability to investigate and prosecute cybercrime. Despite lack of awareness and responsiveness to cybercrime in many places, an increasing number of investigators and prosecutors now specialize in cybercrime cases. Also, the barriers that once separated organizations are disintegrating as professionals encounter more complex crimes that span jurisdictions and require technical computing expertise in order to successfully investigate and prosecute them. Hence, specialized and collective investigation and prosecution strategies and units, as indicated in the previous subsection, are already the norm in many places. Let us now consider the general roles, capabilities, and activities of several key organizations involved in combating cybercrimes. As you read about these organizations, periodically refer to Appendix A and look up their home pages online to become even more familiar with their missions, structure, and operational capabilities.

#### 9.1.3.1 CERT Coordination Center. The CERT Coordination Center (CERT/CC) was originally formed by the Software Engineering Institute (SEI) and the Defense Advanced Research Projects Agency (DARPA) in 1988. The CERT/CC is a nongovernment entity located at Carnegie Mellon University, with primary funding coming from the U.S. Department of Defense and the U.S. Department of Homeland Security. The center coordinates closely with the FBI on specific cases in which its assistance is requested, and it will provide technical assistance to other agencies when requested, as resources allow. The center provides other noninvestigative services including tracking trends in malware design and intruder activities, researching and publishing solutions to information security problems, and providing professional training in several topics relating to the investigation of

cybercrime.[9] Several other entities in the United States and other nations have adopted the "CERT" label in their organizational names, including for example, AusCERT (the Australian Computer Emergency Response Team), which emulates the U.S. CERT/CC in its technical capabilities, services, reporting, and coordination with law enforcement and security firms nationally and even internationally when necessary.

#### 9.1.3.2 FBI Cyber Division. The FBI has two important roles related to the prevention and control of cybercrime. First, it is the lead law enforcement agency for investigating cyber attacks by foreign adversaries and terrorists. Second, the division conducts high-profile investigations involving interstate and international cybercrime involving fraud, cyberstalking, corporate espionage, defacement of Web sites, large-scale releases of destructive malware, and so on. The primary objectives of the cyber division are to (1) coordinate, supervise, and facilitate the FBI's investigation of federal violations in which information systems are exploited or are the instruments or targets of terrorist organizations, foreign government–sponsored intelligence operations, or organized criminal activities; (2) form and maintain public and private alliances in conjunction with enhanced education and training to maximize counterterrorism, counterintelligence, and law enforcement cyber response capabilities; and (3) coordinate with the U.S. Secret Service of the Department of Homeland Security and other federal law enforcement and regulatory agencies regarding protection of critical national information infrastructures. Specific enforcement and prevention programs operated or supported by the Division include InfraGard and the National Center for Missing and Exploited Children.[10]

#### 9.1.3.3 High Technology Crime Investigators Association. The High Technology Crime Investigators Association (HTCIA) is a national

and international professional membership organization that has approximately 30 chapters worldwide consisting of police officers, investigators, attorneys, and management and security professionals who specialize in cybercrime. The mission of HTCIA is "to encourage, promote, aid and affect the voluntary interchange of data, information, experience, ideas and knowledge about methods, processes, and techniques relating to investigations and security in advanced technologies among its membership." Regional chapters often maintain active restricted online chat forums for their members, who discuss emerging cybercrime-related issues. Some chapters also archive information about various types of cybercrime and information security issues, have developed professional codes of ethics for high-tech crime investigators, and share investigative and research findings with their members and the public in certain unrestricted situations.[11]

### 9.1.3.4 International Criminal Police Organization (Interpol).
Interpol was established in 1923 to facilitate cross-border criminal police cooperation and today has dozens of units within member nations spread over five continents including Europe, Asia, Africa, and the Americas. Interpol supports and assists all criminal justice organizations, authorities, and services whose mission is to prevent or combat international crime. Interpol is comprised of the General Assembly, the Executive Committee, the General Secretariat, the National Central Bureaus, and the Advisers. With general secretariat headquarters in Lyon, France and four continental regions the organization provides a fast and reliable communication system that links police around the globe to combat terrorism, organized crime, financial crime, international drug smuggling, and trafficking in human beings. Interpol provides direct assistance in international fugitive and other types of criminal investigations spanning national borders and world regions. It also maintains an IT crime working party consisting

of the heads or experienced members of national computer crime units.[12]

### 9.1.3.5 National White Collar Crime Center.
The National White Collar Crime Center (NW3C), with headquarters in Richmond, Virginia, is a federally funded nonprofit corporation that provides nationwide support to law enforcement, prosecution, regulatory, and other investigative organizations involved in the prevention, investigation, and prosecution of what it considers economic and high-tech crimes. NW3C has no investigative authority; its job is to help law enforcement agencies better understand and utilize tools to combat IT-enabled crime, which it does through public education, professional training workshops and symposia, and posting onto its Web site research on many varieties of white collar crime. The NW3C has instituted the Internet Crime Complaint Center (IC3), which intakes, tracks, and refers complaints of telemarketing and Internet-based fraud, among other types of IT-enabled crimes, to authorities for investigation. NW3C sponsors a small amount of research through the White Collar Crime Research Consortium (WCCRC), a collective of more than one hundred academic scholars and practitioners committed to promoting increased public awareness of white-collar crime and its impacts on society.[13] The organization also sponsors the National Cybercrime Training Partnership, whose goals are integrated with other aspects of NW3C services.

### 9.1.3.6 SANS Institute.
The SysAdmin, Audit, Network, Security Institute, simply referred to as SANS, was founded in 1989 as a cooperative research and education organization. Since its inception, SANS has become one of the largest and most trusted sources of information security training and certification in the world. SANS has trained over 165,000 professionals in a variety of information security areas including auditing procedures, computer forensics, legal issues, and security management and operations. SANS has

an extensive collection of information security research documents and manages the Internet Storm Center for tracking infosec threat trends on the Internet. Through training workshops, professional symposia, and a widely recognized set of certification courses, SANS aids in the development of industry minimum standards and best practices, providing a framework for how information security professionals conduct investigations, manage information, and write policy.[14]

### 9.1.3.7 U.S. Computer Emergency Readiness Team.

The United States Computer Emergency Readiness Team (US-CERT) of the U.S. Department of Homeland Security represents a public–private partnership in the fight against cybercrime and information security threats to critical infrastructures. Established in September 2003, US-CERT is the nation's focal point for preventing, protecting against, and responding to cyber security vulnerabilities. US-CERT is responsible for (1) analysis of and reduction of cyber threats and vulnerabilities, (2) disseminating cyber threat warning information, and (3) coordinating large incident response activities of federal law enforcement agencies. US-CERT also provides a way for citizens, businesses, and other institutions to communicate and coordinate directly with the U.S. government about cyber security.[15]

### 9.1.3.8 U.S. DoJ Computer Crime and Intellectual Property Section.

The Computer Crime and Intellectual Property Section (CCIPS) is an organizational unit within the Criminal Division of the U.S. Department of Justice. Founded in 1991, the DoJ Computer Crime Unit was upgraded to section status in 1996 and now oversees dozens of prosecutors and investigative staff who focus exclusively on crimes involving illegal use of computers or other electronic devices. The section conducts follow-up investigations, litigates cases, provides legal training, coordinates for and supports large-scale national and international cybercrime investigations, develops cybercrime-related policies for the Justice Department and other components of the federal government, and proposes legislation and regulations for possible enactment by Congress. The section also chairs the international G-8 subgroup on High-Tech Crime and makes known on its Web site extensive information about cybercrime including material pertaining to ongoing and resolved cases.[16] This is done to educate the public and deter cybercriminals from violating federal cybercrime laws and regulations.

## 9.2 Legal Issues Governing Investigative Procedures

Investigative procedures are governed by established statutory and case laws, coupled with organizational policies and procedures based on academy, in-service training, and special technical training of law enforcement and security officers. Several of the national organizations discussed above were indicated as offering professional technical training relating to information systems security, cybercrime investigations, and legal issues for law enforcement officers, prosecutors, and information security professionals. All of these sources of training are important for establishing knowledge and for building skills for investigating computer abuse and cybercrimes. Equally if not more important are legal issues governing investigative procedures.

In Chapter 8 we alluded to legal issues governing investigative procedures in the context of criminal and civil laws applicable to cybercrime and investigation of these. In particular, we explored issues having to do with constitutional rights bearing on freedom of speech, expression, and association; self-incrimination, legal counsel, speedy trial, and the abilities to confront witnesses and produce evidence in one's defense; and personal privacy extending to confidential information versus the rights of employers and government officials to search and seize evidence of wrongdoing. Here we will build on that foundation to consider additional legal issues regarding the specific types of evidentiary challenges faced by investigators and prosecutors involved in physical and cyber surveillance operations and the gathering of tangible and electronic evidence pursuant to legally acquired consent, stipulation, and search warrants.

## 9.2.1 Evidentiary Challenges Faced by Investigators and Prosecutors

Law enforcement officers and security professionals investigating computer abuse and cybercrime are obligated to determine how case facts and circumstances, including the behaviors of persons involved in incidents, relate to evidentiary challenges of bringing a case to court and thereafter securing a conviction. Regardless of the specific kinds of tangible or electronic evidence involved in a case, prosecutors will insist that three sets of issues be addressed and that legal procedures be well documented as a prerequisite to filing formal charges against individuals suspected or committing crimes. For all types of crime cases these pertain to (1) motive, opportunity, and means to commit crimes; (2) *mens rea,* which has to do with mental states and legal intentions of committing crimes; and (3) standards of proof that must be established during investigations and at trial in order to bring a case to a successful conclusion. In practice, law enforcement officers and prosecutors often work together to establish these things as investigations unfold. Let us now consider each of these core issues in more detail.

### 9.2.1.1 Motive, Opportunity, and Means.

On September 20, 2001, Aaron Caffrey launched a denial-of-service attack against "Bokkie," a South African chat room user, in revenge for defamatory remarks she made about the United States during a period when Caffrey had an American girlfriend named Jessica. Caffrey routed his cyber attack through the unprotected Port of Houston, Texas, server system, which crashed as it processed and attempted to bombard Bokkie's

computer with more than 100,000 messages. This meant that vital weather and navigation data was unavailable to the crews of ships entering and leaving the busy harbor. Federal investigators traced the source of the attack to Caffrey's home computer in the United Kingdom, where he was charged in Southwark Crown Court on October 7, 2003. Chat room logs presented at trial revealed that Caffrey wrote, "She [Bokkie] hates America. She was probably one of the people cheering when Bin Laden attacked the USA. I want to see her time-out. If she hates America, she hates Jessica. That is a no no." In his defense Caffrey claimed his computer was taken over by someone using his name, but his claim was disputed by a British computer forensics examiner and he was convicted of the cybercrime under British law.[17]

**Motives for committing cybercrimes** are nearly as varied as the technologies involved and are the same as those that have always existed: greed, actual or perceived need, revenge, curiosity, malice, excitement . . . you name it. People are motivated by many things to commit crimes using computers and other electronic IT devices. Although motives for committing cybercrimes are essentially no different than those of other crimes, investigators and prosecutors need to understand what they are while theorizing why crimes occurred, so that they may be explained in court to the judge and/or jury who will ultimately need to be convinced of a person having adequate motivation to commit the crime in question. Consider a hypothetical cybercrime involving insider corporate espionage. It would matter significantly that the accused was a disgruntled employee who was motivated to steal proprietary information in order to profit while also getting revenge for what he considered ill treatment by the firm's management. The specific motives do not matter, provided they can be discovered and fit the overall facts of a case as discovered through investigation.

Investigators, prosecutors, judges, and juries are also concerned with establishing that people accused of committing crimes had the opportunities to carry them out. This is conceptually more complicated than it may seem, because **opportunity to commit crimes** may depend on several factors. First, opportunity means that the suspect was physically able to commit the crime in question, through physical and/or cyber activities. This implies that the suspect could not have been incapacitated in some way (e.g., being in a jail or passed out from drugs or alcohol). Second, establishing opportunity requires determining that the technology needed to carry out particular acts was available to the suspect and working properly at the time the cybercrime was committed. Third, opportunity to commit a crime can also mean that various protective mechanisms were absent. This means that human, technological, or environmental factors were conducive for committing the crime in ways corresponding to available evidence. Recall that the opportunity to commit crime in the absence of capable guardians was previously addressed in the Chapter 5 discussion of routine activities theory.

**Means to commit a crime** refers to technology plus an individual's skills, knowledge, resources, and technical authorities and permissions to access the physical and cyber environments in which the crime took place. In Chapter 2 we introduced Donn Parker's SKRAM model for understanding the overall potential of individuals to commit particular cybercrimes. By understanding the required skills, knowledge, access, and resources needed to commit given crimes, plus potential motivations involved, investigators can focus on certain individuals or groups and eliminate other possible suspects. Also, investigators need to be aware of technological innovations as potential means of committing cybercrimes in relation to enhanced or expanded opportunities to commit cybercrimes. Thus, regardless of motivation, ability and proficiency to commit a cybercrime are based on the perpetrator's technical skills and knowledge of tools and techniques, combined with available resources to access physical spaces and cyber places.

### 9.2.1.2 Criminal Intent and Culpable Mental States.

In law there exist several types of intent, including common, criminal, general, specific, and transferred intent.[18] Criminal intent refers to a perpetrator's culpable state of mind before and/or during the commission of a crime. Note that intent to commit a crime is not the same as motive to commit a crime. Whereas motive pertains to what prompts a person to commit a crime (e.g., greed, need, revenge), criminal intent for our purposes refers to a person's guilty state of mind when a cybercrime is committed. There are four culpable states of mind we need to be concerned with, each generally corresponding to the seriousness of crimes and/or the extent of harm caused by cybercriminals when violating crime laws. These are frequently referred to as *mens rea* (which in Latin means a guilty mind or wrong purpose) and generally pertain to behaving

- **Intentionally:** With premeditation and determination to commit a crime with full awareness of what is occurring and with cognizance of the impacts or harms that certain illegal actions may cause
- **Knowingly:** With full awareness that what is being planned or occurring is wrong or illegal and with cognizance of the impacts or harms that certain actions may bring about.
- **Recklessly:** With gross disregard for the law and likely impacts that doing something or not doing something may result in
- **Negligently:** In an unreasonable manner likely to endanger persons or property or that accidentally causes harms as the result of violating criminal law

Thus, a person may commit a cybercrime intentionally, knowingly, recklessly, or negligently. Each of these legal concepts represents the level of a person's **culpability**, or if you prefer, the extent to which she or he had a guilty mind while contemplating and carrying out violations of the law. The four culpable mental states described above are listed in descending order of seriousness.

Hence, intentionally committing a crime is treated more seriously by justice officials than crimes committed knowingly, recklessly, or negligently. Knowingly committing a crime is a more serious violation of law than committing a crime with only recklessness or negligence, and committing a crime in a reckless manner is more serious than doing so with mere negligence.

Often the degree of a guilty mind required to commit a specific crime will be reflected and even expressly stated in crime laws. For example, first degree murder is defined in many states as killing someone with premeditation. Undoubtedly you have also heard of reckless driving, which is typically defined in laws as driving with gross disregard for potentially causing harm to persons or property. In comparison, negligent driving is typically defined as driving in a manner likely to endanger persons or property. Notice how the language used in these examples of decreasingly serious crimes corresponds to the definitions of declining degrees of culpable mental states described above. Ordinarily a person convicted of first degree computer trespassing (i.e., hacking into a system from outside a network environment) will receive a harsher punishment than someone convicted of second degree computer trespassing (exceeding permissions within a network system to which they had legal access). Culpable mental states apply to all criminal violations, including cybercrimes, and will ultimately affect (1) specific types of evidence that need to be collected at crime scenes and from persons involved in cases under investigation, (2) elements of crimes that must be established by investigators and prosecutors in order to prove their cases in court, and (3) the amount of punishment imposed on violators.

The implication is that investigators must know specific elements of crime laws and be able to determine a suspect's state of mind on the basis of case-related facts, circumstances, events, and evidence. Only in this way can prosecutors determine the appropriate violations of law with which to charge perpetrators of crimes. In the famous case of *United States v. Robert T. Morris Jr.*, defense counsel argued that the defendant did not have the requisite culpable mental state because he did not intend to cause damage by releasing the first Internet worm, which he never realized could rapidly invade and cause damage to thousands of interconnected computers. However, the court ruled that the federal computer crime statute only required intent to enter into a computer system unlawfully and that it did not matter whether resulting damage was caused intentionally or accidentally.

Establishing the culpable mental state of all suspects in a given case, in addition to every individual's motives, opportunities, and means to commit specific illegal acts, is vitally important to the success of criminal investigations and prosecutions. Culpable mental states can be established in numerous ways involving collection and analysis of tangible physical and electronic evidence. For example, while conducting a search of an online child stalker's residence pursuant to a warrant, investigators in Rochester, New York, discovered a paper map of directions from the suspect's house to the prearranged meeting place with a child victim. This evidence, found in the suspect's computer printer tray, was invaluable for helping to establish his premeditated state of mind, as were sex-related paraphernalia and numerous photos of young girls hung up around his house and computer work station. Data seized during a forensic analysis of the suspect's computer system further revealed his mental state (e.g., the number and names of files saved and search terms typed into the Internet browser all revealed that he was prowling the Internet for child porn). For example, activity logs showing search terms like "child sex" entered into the browser application on several occasions indicated that the perpetrator did not accidentally stumble across several Web sites featuring child pornography, with only a negligent state of mind. When investigating cybercrime, numerous other sources and types of evidence may help establish that a suspect knew what he or she was doing when violating the law, including: authorized user and nondisclosure agreements, employee manuals, intellectual property agreements, splash screens, log-in warnings, user names and passwords, and so on. The goal is for investigators to understand the total physical and electronic environment in which a crime occurred with respect to what a suspect could and did know before committing a cybercrime. Showing the means of access as well as the degree of rights and privileges a perpetrator possessed can provide significant evidence indicative of the level of their guilty mind. We will be discussing other types of evidence and computer forensics in more detail later.

No matter what type of case is being investigated (e.g., illegal online gambling, fraud, sex-related crimes, or cyberstalking), an important challenge is to match the culpable mental state with specific evidence of acts prohibited by crime laws. Often this can be done by examining computers and other types of electronic devices, even in cases in which such devices were not directly used in furtherance of illegal acts. On Monday, March 21, 2005, Jeff Weise of Bemidji, Minnesota, shot his grandfather and grandmother with a .22 caliber gun and then drove to his school. As he passed through a metal detector, Weise shot and killed the on-duty security officer. He then went on a shooting rampage, killing a teacher and five students and wounding seven other people before committing suicide.[19] Follow-up investigation revealed that Weise was adept with computers and used his home PC extensively to chat with friends online about violence, including violent acts in schools. For example, one of his messages made reference to the Columbine High School shooting on April 20, 1999, in which 13 people were killed and 21 wounded by two gun-bearing students. Not coincidentally, Weise also used his computer to create an animated film of a gun-toting figure firing a rifle at people and then killing himself. These were among several indications found on Weise's computer that he was upset and had apparently been planning the shooting at

At this residential crime scene investigators located extensive physical evidence of child pornography and clues about the perpetrator's guilty mind in the form of sex-related trophies and paraphernalia, including a female mannequin surrounded by pictures showing sexually explicit images of young girls. Notice the photos on the wall, images in the mirror, trinkets lying about, and condoms hanging from the holiday pine tree— all evidence of the suspect's intentions.
Photo courtesy of: Detective Joe Hennekey, Monroe County Sheriff's Department, New York.

his school for several weeks. Thus, examination of IT devices may yield important information about a subject's state of mind, as well as their motives, opportunities and, means to commit cyber- and non-cybercrimes.[20]

***9.2.1.3 Standards of Proof.*** The third fundamental legal issue that investigators and prosecutors are concerned about when initiating and

*The number, type and placement of evidentiary items within a crime scene may help an investigator understand the extent of crimes involved, as well as perpetrator's motive, opportunity, and means to commit crimes. In this crime scene the number of television and computer screens that could be viewed simultaneously by the perpetrator, along with video tapes and DVDs later found to contain child pornography, reveals premeditation.*
Photo courtesy of: Detective Joe Hennekey, Monroe County Sheriff's Department, New York.

bringing crime cases to a successful conclusion are standards of proof pertaining to investigative hunches, preponderance of evidence, reasonable suspicion, probable cause, and proof beyond a reasonable doubt. Each of these five legal concepts are widely recognized to mean increasing levels of evidence of wrongdoing that warrants correspondingly increasing actions by law enforcement or security officers, regulatory agency officials prosecutors and Judges. Let us briefly distinguish between each of these legal standards of proof.

An **investigative hunch** is a suspicion, formulated in the mind of an investigator or prosecutor, in reaction to encountering facts and circumstances that have been interpreted on the basis of expertise developed through education,

training, and experience. Formulating investigative hunches is the primary way in which cases are initiated. Investigators see something unusual that commands their attention precisely because it is unusual, perhaps unobvious to an untrained person, and they become curious to learn more about what is going on. Courts have determined that investigative hunches may legitimately come about through sensory perceptions (i.e., seeing, hearing, smelling, tasting, or touching things), as a matter of deductive reasoning as in situations when things do not seem to make sense, or with experts, on the basis of their professional instincts that something is amiss and warrants looking into. Investigators are paid to develop hunches that pan out, and often the investigators are individuals known for their ability to sense when things do not add up. Once an investigator develops a hunch regarding something suspicious, he or she is legally entitled and may be obligated under the law to investigate. This is not the same thing, however, as an investigator who is merely suspicious by nature.We are referring to a particular legal standard for initiating an investigation into misuse of computers or other electronic IT devices for harmful purposes based on articulate facts or circumstances and even inarticulate things that causes an investigator to become suspicious. Investigative hunches are routinely developed by investigators in criminal and civil cases of wrongdoing. Obviously the more experience and training an investigator has, the more investigative hunches of quality they are likely to develop in any particular case, and to be believed when later testifying in court regarding the basis of their hunch.

The second standard or level of proof developed during investigations is referred to as **reasonable suspicion**, defined as facts and circumstances that would lead a reasonable *law enforcement officer* (also known as **peace officers** in some jurisdictions) to believe that a crime has been or is about to be committed and that persons to be *detained and questioned* are somehow involved. Reasonable suspicion is the legal standard required to formally investigate possible criminal wrongdoing and to detain and question persons who may have knowledge of suspicious circumstances. This legal standard of proof is derived from the famous incident in 1963 in which a police detective in Cleveland, Ohio, observed two men standing on a sidewalk and lurking into a store in a manner not consistent with window-shopping. To the detective they were acting suspicious, so he approached them, identified himself as a police officer and began to question them about what they were doing. When a third man apparently known by the other two suddenly appeared, the detective spun one of the men around, frisked all three, and found two concealed pistols. Evidently the men had been casing the store before robbing it. Upon review of this

case (i.e., Terry v. Ohio) the U.S. Supreme Court determined that the officer acted properly on his investigative hunch; that reasonable suspicion to formally investigate, detain and search the suspects for weapons existed; and ruled therefore, that the guns were admissible evidence.[21] To this day, legal conditions justifying police frisking for suspected weapons following on a legally initiated investigation on the basis of reasonable suspicion is known as a "Terry stop".

Bear in mind that there is nothing inappropriate or illegal about an officer speaking to anyone in conversation, and people are free to respond or not as they choose. However, if a law enforcement officer declares he or she is investigating suspicious circumstances indicative of a crime or another matter pertaining to public safety, individuals are obligated to comply with lawful orders to provide reasonable proof of identity and contact information (e.g., name, address, occupation, place of employment, and phone numbers) and an explanation of their presence in a given location. Failure to provide satisfactory identification and explanation of one's presence and activities, if not expressly illegal, will certainly raise further suspicion and lead to more in-depth investigation and potentially an arrest for crimes such as obstructing justice or interfering with a criminal investigation. Courts have ruled that in general, law enforcement officers in the United States may detain a person for up to twenty minutes for purposes of establishing their identity and possible connections to a crime.[22] However, the length of time an officer can legally detain an individual or group of people depends on the totality of circumstances, which may change even during the initial period of contact. This means that if more suspicion develops within the first twenty minutes of an investigative detention, an additional ten or twenty minutes or even longer detention period may be justified, depending on the nature of additional evidence discovered.

In rare circumstances a person may be detained for up to several hours without being formally arrested for a crime. However, technically speaking, and for purposes of in-custody questioning relative to the need to advise people of their constitutional rights not to answer questions and have an attorney present during questioning, arrest occurs at the moment the people being detained feel they are not free to leave.[23] During investigative detentions based on reasonable suspicion, officers in some states may demand written proof of identification and if none is produced, search a person for an ID. However, this is not a universal rule of law. In addition, police may ask a person to voluntary accompany them to another location to continue an investigation, but people cannot be forced against their will to go with police anywhere, unless they have been placed under arrest for committing a crime. If they are forced without having been placed under arrest any evidence that results will be considered tainted and inadmissible in court.[24] In addition, lying to federal agents, or other law enforcement officers in certain states or local jurisdictions, may constitute a separate crime such as obstructing justice or hindering prosecution.

The third standard or level of proof developed during investigations is referred to as **probable cause**, which police officers customarily refer to simply as PC. Probable cause is similar to reasonable suspicion and is defined as facts and circumstances that would lead a reasonable *law enforcement officer* to believe that a crime has been committed and that the person to be arrested did it. Probable cause may be established in many ways and through many different combinations of evidence such as personal observations and other experiential factors; reports or orders made by other law enforcement officers; statements provided by informants, victims, or witnesses; or combinations of physical and electronic evidence. Probable cause is the legal standard that allows officers to arrest people and take them into custody on suspicion of their having committing a crime and to search them and their immediate

surroundings (including the passenger compartment of a vehicle) incidental to the arrest for weapons or further evidence of the crime for which the arrest was made.[25] If in the process of a search incident to a lawful arrest evidence of other crimes is discovered, the person already under arrest may be charged with additional crimes. More will be said about this later. At this point you should know that in addition to establishing probable cause, a lawful arrest requires the following four elements: (1) legal authority to make an arrest, (2) assertion of arrest authority and informing a person that they have been arrested, (3) understanding on the part of the person that he or she have been arrested, and (4) physical restraint of a person, meaning he or she is not free to leave or move around.[26] Thus, for example, if a person did not comprehend they had been placed under arrest and were not free to move about, then a legal state of arrest would not exist.

It useful to realize that arresting a person is comparable in law to seizing property. Both involve taking evidence related to a crime into custody and require an officer to have first established probable cause. Hence, probable cause is also the legal standard required for an officer to obtain a court-issued warrant for either the arrest of a person suspected of committing a crime or a warrant to search a home, business, vehicle, or computer system. Arrest and search warrants are essentially court orders commanding law enforcement officers who apply for them to produce the persons or other items as evidence of suspected crimes. However, police officers are not obligated to arrest persons who are suspected of having violated the law even if probable cause for doing so exists, unless a court has issued an arrest warrant or statutory law specifically requires that an arrest be made. This flexibility allows officers to bide their time and even use the threat of arresting someone to their investigative advantage. This flexibility is also what enables investigators to carry out major investigations over long periods of time before rounding up multiple suspects in a single operation spanning many jurisdictions.

In general, people cannot be arrested inside their homes unless officers have both an arrest warrant and a search warrant. This rule varies somewhat among states. In New York and several other states, for example, a police officer only needs an arrest warrant to enter premises in which he or she reasonably believes a suspect may be located, but law enforcement officers may periodically also seek search warrants for suspects when they develop circumstantial evidence to build probable cause to search a residence for a suspect. Note also that there are hot pursuit and other exceptions to the exclusionary rule (described below) that allows an officer to pursue and arrest a suspect in his or her home without an arrest or search warrant. In other instances officers seeking to arrest a suspect for whom they do not posses a search warrant must ask him or her to step outside the home, or entice him or her to do so in order to make an arrest. To avoid complications, officers will often simply stop subjects while they are driving cars, arrest them as they arrive at or leave school or work, or "take them down" in a discrete location such as when they are out jogging, going into a convenience store, and so on.

**Proof beyond a reasonable doubt** is the legal standard required to convict a person of crime in the United States. For many people, including jurors empanelled to determine a person's innocence or guilt in a cybercrime trial, this concept can be confusing. In lay terms, proof beyond a reasonable doubt essentially means that in order to find a person guilty of a crime, a judge or *all* members of a jury, depending on whether a bench or jury trial was chosen by the defendant, must be substantially convinced that the accused violated one or more specific crime laws for which they have been accused. This does not mean that however, jurists may not have some doubts about a person's guilt in order to find them guilty, only that they cannot

have doubt that exceeds reason or sound thinking. In other words, if the evidence presented in court is within the bounds of common sense and ordinary understanding, a verdict of guilty must be rendered. Feeling sorry for a defendant, empathizing with his or her motives for committing a crime, or inventing possible alternative explanations not presented as evidence is not allowed.

A determination of wrongdoing in a civil case is based on the fifth and final standard of proof. Known as a **preponderance of evidence**, this level of proof exists when it is more likely than not that a person accused of a wrongdoing is responsible. Preponderance of evidence is normally interpreted to mean that a person or firm was negligent in doing something or not doing something they were required to do as a matter or law or regulation or simply that they should have known that either doing something or not doing something would result in harm. Accusations of civil harm are often made along with criminal prosecutions. In other words, if a person commits a crime against the state, he or she may also be sued for causing harm or violating the property or civil rights of others. To make a determination of civil wrongdoing on the basis of a preponderance of evidence, the judge or jury hearing a case must think that, on the basis of the evidence presented in court, it is more likely than not that the defendant irresponsibly did what he or she is being accused of and that harm resulted.

To put this a little differently, evidence of civil wrongdoing must indicate a greater than even chance of culpability (i.e., more than a 50-percent likelihood that someone committed an act or failed to act in a way that resulted in harms to a person or firm). In short, preponderance of evidence is the legal standard used to determine fault in a civil action. The standard can also be used in internal investigations of suspected employee wrongdoing, such as violating organizational policies, required procedures, or technology standards. Since a person can be held civilly liable (i.e., sued for libel, negligence, or violating rights or legal protections such as copyright) and be charged criminally in separate court actions, investigators need to remember that evidence of civil wrongdoing may be admissible in criminal proceedings and vice versa. Periodically, law enforcement officers involved in criminal proceedings are also required to testify in civil actions. In addition, evidence of criminal wrongdoing is often presented in civil proceedings regardless of whether a defendant in a criminal trial is found guilty or innocent of specific crimes.

## 9.2.2  Physical and Cyber Monitoring, Surveillance, and Investigative Operations

Throughout the summer of 2004, unbeknownst to millions of Internet users, the FBI was leading a multi-agency task force in a nationwide crackdown of crimes occurring via the Net. Dubbed **Operation Web Snare**, the task force conducted over 150 investigations of myriad cybercrimes in which an estimated 870,000 people were victimized and collectively experienced $210 million in financial losses in the United States and abroad. The operation involved federal agents serving more than 130 search warrants that resulted in 100 arrests and 116 indictments for crimes that involved spamming, phishing, spoofing, reshipment schemes, cyber extortion, credit card and online auction fraud, copyright infringement, hacking, theft of trade secrets, money laundering, and identity theft. Federal components of the U.S. Secret Service, the U.S. Postal Inspection Service, the Bureau of Immigration and Customs Enforcement, and the Federal Trade Commission were all involved in Operation Web Snare. In addition, the IC3 of the NW3C and numerous state and local law enforcement agencies participated in ways designed to demonstrate the far-reaching capabilities of government to carryout physical and cyber monitoring and surveillance.[27]

As indicated in Chapter 7, a primary societal role of law enforcement, security, and intelligence officers is to observe physical and cyber environments for patterns, trends, relationships, and anomalies indicative of security threats and crimes. Essentially, police and security and intelligence officers engage in routine systematic monitoring of persons, places, and things for suspicious activity. Once something deemed suspicious is discovered, officers will slip into a surveillance mode, which may involve combinations of relatively simple to complex physical and cyber tools and techniques carried out from within or outside criminal organizations or settings. If this sounds familiar, it is because law enforcement use of technology is the conceptual analog of technologies used by criminals for countervailing purposes (as discussed in Section 2.3, and elsewhere throughout our text). Hence, whereas **monitoring** involves systematic and continual active or passive in-person or electronic observation of persons, places, things, or processes, **surveillance** involves *targeted monitoring* of suspicious activities for purposes of obtaining specific evidence of crimes or other wrongdoing. Thus, when something is deemed suspicious, investigators intensify their operations. Depending on circumstances, they will immediately intervene to make one or more arrests or begin and then maintain physical and/or cyber surveillance as long as necessary in order to collect additional and specific evidence of criminal wrongdoing. Surveillance may take place over time spans ranging from a few minutes, to several hours, days, weeks, or for even longer periods of time.

Physical surveillance operations normally focus on the movements and interactions of individuals or groups occupying vehicles, buildings, or other spaces. In contrast, cyber surveillance may combine targeted wiretapping of telephone conversations; electronic eavesdropping of cellular phone conversations; "bugging" of people located in rooms, vehicles, or open spaces; tracking keystroke, Web browsing, downloading, cable or satellite television-watching patterns, or hacking behaviors; intercepting computer-mediated communications such as email or instant messaging between two or more people; and plotting locations via GPS/GIS monitoring systems attached to or embedded within vehicles, persons, cell phones, PDAs, laptop computers, or other routinely carried articles such as purses and briefcases. (These possibilities were previously listed and discussed in Chapter 7 in the context of government intelligence gathering and analysis capabilities; see Textbox 7.3).

Whether physical or cyber in nature, the goal of surveillance in criminal investigations is to acquire evidence of crimes that will be admissible in a criminal prosecution. Physical and/or cyber surveillance operations carried out by properly equipped investigators may

- Be stationary or mobile and require various types of technologies to enhance visual or hearing capabilities of officers
- Involve recording of events, locations, days or times, and patterns of behaviors or activities inclusive of persons contacted, locations visited and technologies used for illegal purposes
- Include listening to and tracing phone, or in-person conversations, as well as electronic correspondence such as email or instant messaging exchanged between individuals or groups of people.

Surveillance is usually carried out by security or law enforcement officials in covert ways, and in criminal investigations this must always be done with legal authority so as to not violate the targeted person's privacy rights against unreasonable searches and seizures as prohibited by the Fourth Amendment of the U.S. Constitution. Sometimes surveillance will uncover evidence of criminal planning of specific crimes, impending acts of terrorism, or other physical or cyber threats to homeland, infrastructure, information systems or organizational security. At other times surveillance may be of ongoing crimes committed by individuals or criminal activities of organizations or of terrorist cells operating anyplace in the world. Remember, law enforcement officers are generally

not required to make an arrest even when they know laws are being violated, although officers do have a responsibility to intervene in criminal activities in order to prevent serious physical harm from being inflicted on crime victims, witnesses, or other innocents. Surveillance operations may also be undertaken on or within criminal subcultures, such as criminally prone groups of hackers for whom committing particular types of computer-enabled crimes is integral to the group's overall behavioral patterns. Conducting surveillance can be dangerous, especially when undercover agents attempt to gain entry and fit into organized crime or terrorist cells. Thus, the overriding goal of investigators is to legally and safely employ monitoring and surveillance to detect suspicious circumstances and then when possible interdict cybercriminals before they act or afterwards, depending on what is most useful for preventing harm and controlling the greatest amount of crime in society. In all cases, carrying out physical and cyber monitoring, surveillance, and investigative operations is about acquiring legally admissible evidence in ways that do not unduly compromise officer or community safety.

### 9.2.2.1 Exclusionary Rules of Evidence.

This text provides you with a mere overview of the legal issues deemed fundamental in cybercrime investigations. It is not possible in the space available to provide you with in-depth legal explanations of evidence gathering and analysis or presenting evidence of crime in criminal prosecutions. Therefore, we must concentrate on the most important things criminal justice and information security professionals must know. Exclusionary rules of evidence are important to understand because they underpin modes of legal surveillance and evidence gathering usable in prosecuting cybercriminals. In a nutshell, the **exclusionary rule of evidence** establishes rules for law enforcement officers and prosecutors to legally acquire evidence of crimes and bars illegally obtained evidence from being used in criminal prosecutions. The **fruit of the**

**poisonous tree doctrine** (also known as the derivative evidence rule) dictates that evidence of criminal wrongdoing indirectly found as the result of illegally discovered evidence is inadmissible, with certain exceptions that we will discuss below. For now you should know that rules of evidence are based on constitutional principles and case law rulings, and they are intended to deter law enforcement officers from violating privacy rights and other civil liberties during monitoring, surveillance, and other investigative operations.

The exclusionary rule and fruit of the poisonous tree doctrine did not always exist. The exclusionary rule was first used in federal courts in 1914 but was not universally adopted by state courts until mandated by the U.S. Supreme Court in the famous 1961 case of *Mapp v. Ohio*. In this case police officers were determined to have illegally forced their way into a private residence without permission or a search warrant and then seized evidence used to convict the defendant.[28] As such, the exclusionary rule is a relatively new legal concept, and because it is not based on earlier Roman Law, Napoleonic Law, or even on the Common Law of England, it is not universally recognized by legal philosophies or adhered to by many national criminal justice systems. In many places outside the United States, even evidence of criminal wrongdoing that is *intentionally* illegally acquired by police may still be used in proceedings against persons accused of committing crimes. Prior to formulation and consistent enforcement of the exclusionary rule by American courts, obtaining criminal evidence in violation of privacy and civil rights was considered a violation only of civil law. Today, officers in the United States who violate the exclusionary rule risk loosing their evidence if not their entire cases at trial and being sued personally for civil rights violations. In extraordinary cases involving intentional violation of constitutionally protected civil rights, American law enforcement officers may also face federal prosecution. These matters are typically investigated by the FBI in concert with the civil rights division of the U.S.

Department of Justice. Given the importance of this issue, let us consider gathering evidence legally in more detail.

Evidence of crime abounds. To a trained and experienced investigator, evidence of criminal wrongdoing may be found on the streets and other public places and in businesses, factories, schools, homes and so on. Evidence of crimes also exists within computers and other electronic IT devices and in information systems including the Net, over which criminal messages and content flow unabated. In many instances, evidence of crime is stumbled upon accidentally in physical realms or in cyberspace and then acted upon by officers who having recognized a crime in-progress, criminal condition, or suspicious circumstances, initiate an investigation. Often investigative hunches turn into reasonable suspicion, and then probable cause, leading to the arrest of one or more persons. Regardless of how it is legally obtained, new-found evidence may cause investigators to intensify their ongoing efforts, change focus, or initiate one or more additional investigations.

Given adequate investigative resources, operations will likely produce tangible and electronic evidence of criminal activity that can be observed, tracked, recorded, and analyzed through surveillance, and other investigative tactics. In all cases analysis of physical and electronic evidence involves determining the criminal who, what, when, where, how, and why of things and their interrelationships. In addition, as discussed in Chapter 2, crime, security and intelligence analysis undertaken by government agents or private security professionals necessarily involves determining the reliability and validity of evidentiary data in order to make informed decisions about how best to direct investigations or otherwise respond to emerging crime or security threats. The challenge for investigators is to conduct lawful and safe investigations that result in legally obtained evidence. For this reason, law enforcement officers receive extensive training in substantive and procedural aspects of criminal

## BOX 9.1 • *Mapp v. Ohio Results in Nationwide Exclusionary Rule*

Many cases from long before computers and other types of contemporary electronic devices were commonplace, important case law rulings established principles for investigating and prosecuting crimes which are just as relevant today in instances of cybercrime as they were decades before in cases involving earlier forms of technology or no IT at all. On May 23, 1957, police officers in Cleveland, Ohio, acting on information that a fugitive wanted for questioning in a recent bombing was hiding out in a local residence in which there was also illegal paraphernalia, responded to the home of Dorlee Mapp. Initially the officers knocked and requested to be admitted, but Mapp demanded to see a search warrant and denied them entrance. Several additional officers arrived on the scene and took up surveillance to prevent the subject wanted for questioning from escaping.

Eventually, officers forced their way into the residence and when asked by Mapp to produce a search warrant, held up a sheet of paper that Mapp grabbed and stuffed into her bosom. In an effort to retrieve the paper, a struggle ensued, Mapp was handcuffed, and the officers retrieved the paper and then conducted a thorough search of the residence.

During the search police officers found materials located in a trunk in the basement that were deemed to be obscene under Ohio law, so Mapp was formally arrested and charged with this crime. The only other people present during the incident were Mapp's young daughter and her attorney, who she had called shortly after police initially arrived on the scene, but who was never allowed to confer with Mapp or see the warrant, which could never be produced by prosecutors or be determined to have been issued by a court.[29]

As a result of police tactics employed in this investigation, the exclusionary rule already used by federal courts and by some state courts was mandated for use in all criminal investigations and court proceedings by the U.S. Supreme Court.[30] It is interesting to note that in some states courts enforce more stringent exclusionary rules than required by federal law, while other states such as California and Florida have simply abolished their own original exclusionary rules in favor of directing courts to abide by the Fourth Amendment of the Constitution as interpreted by the U.S. Supreme Court.[31] Today the exclusionary rule, and fruit of the poisonous tree doctrine, apply to criminal prosecutions of all types of crime regardless of technology used by offenders or law enforcement officers.

law, especially regarding exclusionary rule provisions and exceptions.

### 9.2.2.2 Exclusionary Rule Exceptions.

In the American criminal justice system, *all* evidence of criminal wrongdoing is assumed to be *inadmissible* unless it is seized pursuant to a court-authorized search warrant. Further, the exclusionary rule applies to all forms of evidence in criminal actions (but not to civil cases), including tangible items such as weapons or computer hardware; electronic evidence such as computer logs and telephone or cell phone records; verbal and written confessions, incriminating admissions,

and other statements made by anyone involved in a case; and eyewitness, voice, and biometric identifications. This means that police officers engaged in physical or electronic surveillance operations must be constantly aware of the legal grounds they have for taking specific actions because they can never be sure when, where, or how evidence of criminal wrongdoing will appear. In the interest of balancing justice on behalf of the state and those accused, courts have recognized several exceptions to the exclusionary rule—conditions in which evidence discovered by police even in the absence of a search warrant may be admissible.[32]

**9.2.2.2.1  Plain View Exceptions.**   If police officers can plainly observe readily apparent evidence of a crime from a position they are lawfully occupying, they can immediately seize the evidence without a warrant and initiate further investigation. Depending on circumstances, officers *may* be required to obtain a warrant before searching for additional evidence. Consider the following hypothetical example. A police officer makes a traffic stop after observing a traffic violation. The driver says his license is in the trunk of the car. In order to produce his driver's license he opens the trunk, exposing to the officer what is clearly child pornography—bingo! That is admissible evidence because the officer, who had already made a legal traffic stop, was lawfully positioned to see the porn when the driver opened the trunk lid. Hence, the driver will be arrested for illegal possession of child pornography. The officer may also apply for a search warrant and continue to search the car and any computers or other IT devices and medium found therein. Depending on what is found during this secondary search of the car and its contents, the officer may search other locations such as the person's home or business and computers, IT devices and medium therein after acquiring additional search warrants.

Suppose the officer while searching the suspect's home legally examines closets and drawers—anywhere child porn in hardcopy or electronic form could be hidden. As he opens a desk drawer, he finds a large bag containing a green leafy substance appearing and smelling like marijuana—bingo! If the crime lab confirms that the green leafy stuff is marijuana in an amount exceeding that allowed by state law for personal use or medical purposes, the person may also be charged with illegal possession of marijuana. These examples demonstrate how follow-up investigations involving traditional or cybercrimes can result in expanded investigations into other acts of criminal wrongdoing on the basis of tangible and/or electronic evidence. You can just as easily imagine that if a forensic examination of the home computer suspected of containing child

porn revealed evidence of selling marijuana, the person originally arrested for possessing child pornography might be facing charges of conspiracy to illegally distribute a controlled substance in addition to merely possessing a small amount of dope and the child porn in the trunk of his car.

The plain view exception extends to police officers using flashlights, binoculars, and certain other technologies to aid in their sensory perceptions. However, as established in the 2001 case of *Danny Lee Kyllo v. United States*, use of thermal imaging technology to spot relatively warm marijuana-growing greenhouse operations is not permissible because infrared radiation is not visible to the naked eye.[33] Utilization of laser listening devices that can detect and enhance sound waves of conversations emitting off of glass is also not permitted without a warrant, as was ruled in the 1967 case of *Charles Katz v. United States*. In this case, FBI agents attached a listening device to the outside of a public phone booth that the defendant was using to transmit illegal gambling information. Katz was convicted, but on appeal, the U.S. Supreme Court effectively ruled that telephone conversations transmitted from in the phone booth carried an expectation of privacy and that seizing the conversation via electronic means without a search warrant violated the Fourth Amendment against unreasonable search and seizure.[34] After the Katz ruling, specific requirements for acquiring warrants to monitor electronic communications and penalties for illegal wiretapping were specified in federal law and in many state laws governing wiretapping and electronic surveillance. This is the same legal rationale that allows law enforcement officers to rely on witnesses reporting a crime that was not personally observed by officers, and allows use of drug- and bomb-sniffing dogs to detect contraband also (in effect) on behalf of officers.

**9.2.2.2.2  Poisonous Tree Exceptions.**   Three exceptions to the derivative evidence rule are (1) attenuation of causal links resulting from the passage of time, (2) police learn of the evidence from an independent source, or (3) police would have inevitably discovered the evidence.

The first exception essentially means that if the police, while executing a warrantless search, discover evidence of criminal wrongdoing that is in no way related to the case at hand, even if the search is ruled to be improper, the evidence obtained indicating the other crime may still be admissible, especially if a significant time lapse has occurred between the commission of the crime and finding of evidence. With regard to the second point, even if police discover evidence of a crime during a warrantless search deemed improper by a court, it may still be admissible if there was independent information that the evidence existed, upon which the police could have legally acted to search or obtain a search warrant. The third exception, which relates closely to the second point, is easier to understand. It simply means that even if the law enforcement officers conducted an improper warrantless search, the incriminating evidence in question would eventually have been legitimately discovered anyway.

### 9.2.2.2.3 Automobile, Fleeting, and Destruction of Evidence Exceptions.
The U.S. Supreme Court has ruled that probable cause alone, absent a search warrant, is sufficient grounds to search an automobile that is mobile and does not equate to a home or business in terms of privacy expectations.[35] By extension, evidence suspected of existing anywhere and also suspected of being ruined or destroyed before officers can secure a search warrant, may be searched for and seized immediately without a warrant. In practice, officers will often secure a crime scene to prevent evidence from being destroyed by inclement weather, the intentional efforts of suspects, and so on and then apply for a telephonic search warrant before actually searching a vehicle, premises or open locations.

### 9.2.2.2.4 Protective Sweep Exceptions.
Policing is dangerous work, and officers have a right to protect themselves. They also are responsible for protecting other people in the immediate area of their investigations. Therefore, as indicated above in the description of *Terry v. Ohio*, courts have ruled that police officers are allowed to conduct warrantless searches of people, vehicles, premises, and property within the immediate reach or lunging area of known or unknown subjects where weapons may be located *if* they already have or formulate reasonable suspicion that weapons may be present. Incriminating evidence that is discovered in the process of conducting a protective pat-down search of outer garments and handbags of individuals lawfully detained in a criminal investigation, or during a protective sweep of an area in which weapons could be accessed or hostile persons located, will be admissible in court.

### 9.2.2.2.5 Incident to Arrest Exceptions.
Whenever an officer makes a lawful arrest, he or she may search the person and their immediate surroundings including a vehicle if the person was driving it just prior to being stopped and arrested. Any evidence found during a search incident to arrest is admissible.[36] In order to qualify as being incidental to an arrest, a search must take place immediately following the taking of a person into custody.[37] The search may not extend beyond the area immediately accessible to the person arrested. Searching their person or the driver's compartment of a vehicle is permissible; searching a closed trunk or engine compartment would not qualify. Similarly, during booking procedures, it is permissible to record contents of electronic devices that were in the possession of a person at the time of arrest, just as prior to the existence of PDAs it was permissible to record or make copies of written documents, notes or contact lists found in the possession of those arrested. Such information can provide invaluable leads for advancing investigations later on. It is not permissible however, to use a portable electronic device to gain access to another device not in the possession of a suspect at the time of their

arrest, or to remotely search through records of a networked computer.

### 9.2.2.2.6 Private Search Exceptions.

The exclusionary rule only applies to law enforcement officers. Searches conducted by employers, school officials, security officers, and other private persons not acting as agents of the police are not subject to procedural laws of criminal evidence. If in the process such people discover evidence of crime, they may seize it and give it to police, and it will probably be admissible if corroborated with other evidence and no laws were broken. Hence, if as an information security professional you discover evidence of cybercrime on a computer assigned to a particular employee, you may present this evidence to police officers, who may then initiate a criminal investigation that could involve forensic analysis of the computer hard drive, system logs, and so on, plus interviewing of various employees of your organization including, most likely, the worker to whom the computer containing the evidence was assigned. By extension, the exclusionary rule does not apply to evidence in civil cases or to private investigations into violations of organizational policies and procedures. Moreover, the Fourth Amendment protects against unreasonable searches of people, not places, except to the extent that people put things in locations that society generally considers to be a private (i.e., a place in which there exists a reasonable expectation of privacy).

### 9.2.2.2.7 Discarded and Abandoned Property Exceptions.

A improper search occurs when a person's reasonable privacy expectations as determined through interpretation of constitutional language or case law rulings are infringed upon. For this legal condition to exist, a person must actually expect privacy and believe that this expectation is reasonable. This means that if people discard or deny ownership of computer equipment or storage media, they effectively relinquish their expectations of privacy. Thus, if evidence of criminal wrongdoing were found on a computer donated to charity, the evidence would be admissible in a criminal prosecution. Similarly, expectations of privacy are relinquished when property is sold or abandoned. Thus, if computer disks were left inside a car that was sold or abandoned and found later found to contain evidence of a crime, the evidence would be admissible.

### 9.2.2.2.8 Other Exclusionary Rule Exceptions.

Local, state, and federal law enforcement officers are not the only government officials who periodically conduct searches that may result in discovery of incriminating evidence. Consequently several other exclusionary rule exceptions are recognized by courts, including routine searches conducted by common carriers (e.g., airlines, railroad, and freight companies), the U.S. Customs and Border Protection Service at border crossings and ports of entry, probation or parole officers in connection with revocation hearings, detention and correctional officers in their supervision of prisoners, child protective workers, school officials including teachers, and searches by employers of offices, desks, file cabinets, and computers along with information systems not owned by an employee. Search by police officers on the basis of permission voluntarily given by a person with legal authority to grant consent to search is another exclusionary rule exception, although the burden for proving this in court falls on police officers and prosecutors. More will be said about this important exception to the exclusionary rule, the only one in which property owners rather than the police decide what will be searched, will be discussed shortly.

### 9.2.2.3 Search and Electronic Monitoring Warrants, Subpoenas, and Consent to Search.

Since officers cannot and should not count on exceptional circumstances to legally search, they must go about collecting evidence of crimes in ways that protect their cases from accusations of legal impropriety. Law enforcement officers who conduct an illegal search may lose criminal evidence in court, if not their entire case, and incur civil liability, especially in egregious situations that result in substantial violations of privacy or other civil rights. Law enforcement officers are very concerned about conducting proper searches, and they are trained to secure a search warrant, a court order authorizing electronic monitoring, or at least receive voluntary consent before conducting a search if at all possible. At this point you may be asking yourself several fundamental questions such as: What is a warrant? How are they obtained? What do search warrants actually allow law enforcement officers to do? How do warrants to search for tangible evidence differ from warrants to search for electronic evidence of crimes? These are very good questions that will now be answered.

To begin, recall that in Chapter 8 we discussed the U.S. Constitution and several amendments that are of particular importance in cybercrime investigations and that pertain to providing security of information systems. The Fourth Amendment states that the government can issue no warrants except "upon probable cause, supported by oath or affirmation, and particularly describing the place to be searched and the person or things to be seized." In effect, the Fourth Amendment equates people and things as items that may be taken into custody by law enforcement officers who are armed with a warrant. So, what is a warrant? Essentially a warrant is a court order directing officers to carry out the law. A "search warrant" as the term is used, consists of three documents, including

1. The **affidavit:** A sworn and signed application by a law enforcement officer that explains the basis of probable cause to search a specific location and property inclusive of information systems (typically a street address and physical description of the premises and a general statement about computing devices and storage media)
2. The **warrant:** An order signed by an impartial judge commanding the officer who petitioned the court for the warrant, along with his or her agents, to search for and bring forth, normally within three to ten days, evidence of the crimes indicated in the affidavit
3. The **inventory:** A sworn, signed statement by an officer indicating that the search warrant was served, along with an itemized list of all property seized during the search.

The inventory must be completed and returned to the court within the specified time period even if no evidence of crimes is seized. The court and the officer will keep copies of all three portions of the search warrant, and the property owner is entitled to a copy of the warrant and the inventory. Property owners are not, however, entitled to receive a copy of the affidavit at the time of the search, because it will contain investigative details giving rise to probable cause and suspected crimes that could be used by suspects to figure out what exactly the police are up to and destroy or hide additional evidence of crimes. This is also why separate warrants authorizing the search of several different locations are often simultaneously executed by teams of officers. In this way, suspects are not able to tip each other off. If a property owner is not present when the police show up to search the premises specified in the warrant, they may legally search the premises anyway and leave a copy of the warrant and completed affidavit showing what they seized. This list would include any computers, other electronic devices or storage media, as well as hardcopy records, photographs, money or contraband taken as potential evidence. If the owner is present but declines to let the police onto the property or inside buildings or vehicles specified in the warrant, the officers can (and will) forcibly enter and may arrest the owner and anyone else who obstructs or interferes with the investigation. Also, if in the process of conducting a search the police develop probable cause to arrest the property owner or someone else present for a crime, whether or not the new-found probable cause directly relates to the suspected crimes for which the search warrant was issued, they may make the arrest on the spot. This does not contradict the earlier statement concerning officers not being able to arrest people inside their homes unless they have both an arrest and search warrant, because in this situation the arresting officer possessing only a search warrant is already legally within the home. The same applies to a business or other workplace setting.

While serving search warrants, police may legally look into every nook and cranny that may conceivably conceal the item or evidence they are looking for. If they are searching for a flash drive, they may legally look into very small spaces or containers in every portion of every room including the attic, basement, and furnace ducts if they so choose. Sealed pet food bags are fair game, as are pillow stuffing and furniture cushions. They may even look into toilet reservoir tanks and sump pump drains, which may conceal water-proofed evidence. Police may also search the grounds, outbuildings, and every compartment of every vehicle on the premises, provided these are also specified in the search warrant. If in the process of conducting a search, police discover unanticipated evidence of a different crime, they are generally advised to stop the search and acquire an amended or secondary search warrant, usually by phone (i.e., a telephonic search warrant).

There is nothing very remarkable about **telephonic search warrants**, which are routinely applied for by law enforcement officers in situations when it is not practical to get a search warrant in the traditional manner described above. Typically, telephonic search warrants are applied for during a tactical search or other field operation that occurs unexpectedly at night or on weekends when the court having jurisdiction is not open for normal business or whenever time is of the essence. In these situations, a judge is typically paged or called at home, and then following an oral briefing by the officer applying for the search warrant, she or he will orchestrate a formal approval process over the phone, conforming to

affidavit procedures of a traditional warrant application. This means the officer will give a sworn verbal statement of probable cause (often written out in advance and read aloud to the judge), which is normally tape-recorded and later transcribed to become part of the investigative record. The judge or court will receive a copy of the transcribed telephonic affidavit and warrant after the fact, along with a search warrant inventory as usual, and the tape recording will usually be submitted into evidence in case the legitimacy of the transcript or search is questioned after the fact.

While searching, police officers may damage property (e.g., break locks, knock holes into walls and hidden compartments, rip open furniture upholstery) in order to access spaces. They may or may not be held civilly liable for damages in a subsequent legal action brought by the property owner. In practice, if a criminal prosecution and conviction ensues, officers will not be found liable. Also in practice, judges tend to frown on overly aggressive police tactics except in the most violent or heinous situations. Moreover, police themselves tend to be very respectful of property being searched, recognizing that often innocent people live in the house or work at the business being searched, that there may be children present, and so on. In other words, many law enforcement officers are not insensitive to the human factors involved in search and arrest situations. In addition, officers rarely destroy property, and even if in the absence of a property owner, will make good faith efforts to secure broken doors and locks before leaving the search premises and may even be required to do so according to their agency's search warrant policy.

Any premises, vehicle, computer, or information system searched must be treated as if it were a crime scene. In the next section, we will explore issues pertaining to processing crime scenes for evidence and handling evidence after it is discovered. For now, you should know that evidence of crimes found during the execution of a search warrant will be seized, taken into custody, and then prepared for further analysis and long-term storage pending presentation at a criminal trial. As noted, following a fruitful or unsuccessful search, the police officer who applied for the warrant is legally responsible for returning a copy of the completed inventory. If he or she fails to do so without cause, the judge who issued the search warrant could declare any seized evidence inadmissible. Judges could, in theory, also hold officers in contempt for failing to obey a court order and have them arrested. Of course, this never happens. Officers are generally anxious to serve search warrants, and those who do routinely "know the drill" quite well and make sure they get inventories back to the court on time.

To this point, I have not mentioned prosecutors' having any role in the investigative or search process. In practice, direct involvement by prosecutors will vary on a case-by-case basis according to its legal complexities, the seriousness of crimes involved, the public profile of suspected offenders, and their workload, among other factors. Sometimes officers like to confer with prosecutors during the search and arrest phases of investigations, but not always, and rarely will prosecutors respond to crime scenes to oversee investigations that they may have no legal authority to intervene in.

The application and other legal procedures involved in electronic monitoring, or "wiretapping," warrants differ in specific ways from conventional search warrants and are extensively used in certain types of cybercrime investigations. The Fourth Amendment, as interpreted by the U.S. Supreme Court in *Katz v. United States*, "protects people, not places. What a person knowingly exposes to the public, even in his own home or office, is not a Fourth Amendment protection . . . But what he seeks to preserve as private, even in an area accessible to the public, may be constitutionally protected."[38] Facts surrounding this ruling (described above) established *Katz v. United States* as the seminal case preceding enactment of the Federal Wiretapping and Electronic Search Act of 1968. Following

the U.S. Supreme Court ruling in this case, telephone conversations transmitted from inside a closed phone booth were deemed to carry an expectation of privacy and that seizing a conversation via electronic means without a search warrant violated Fourth Amendment rights against unreasonable search and seizure. Thus, specific requirements for acquiring warrants to monitor electronic communications and penalties for illegal wiretapping are now specified in federal law and in many state laws governing wiretapping and electronic surveillance. (For details, see Section 8.4.2.4 in Chapter 8).

It is interesting to note that federal wiretap laws restricting law enforcement monitoring of telephone calls existed in the early 1930s, and that wiretapping laws adopted or amended in the late 1960s and 1970s were designed to cover all electronic forms of communication that predated widespread use of computers, cellular phones, and other types of electronic devices. However, the federal wiretap law has been amended following the 911 terrorist attacks to include all electronic devices, as well as safeguard against police use of sophisticated listening technology to monitor conversations and other communications in situations where a person would have a reasonable expectation of privacy. However, courts have ruled that not all forms of electronic communications have equal protection. For example, widely broadcast radio signals and other wireless communications, such as cordless phone conversations, are inherently less protected than dedicated phone line conversations. As WiFi networks such as those used in airport terminals and Internet cafes become more popular, and as new forms of IT emerge and are adopted for criminal use, this will remain an evolving area of police practices and law. Discussion of wireless devices and WiFi networks will be taken up again in the next chapter.

The old saying of the police, "When in doubt, get a warrant" makes very good sense from the standpoint of preserving case integrity, especially in questionable legal circumstances, very important cases, or those involving protected electronic communications. However, many times it is not practical or necessary to get a warrant before searching, as indicated above by several exclusionary rule exceptions. Periodically a **subpoena** will suffice, as in instances where an investigator needs IT-related data maintained by a suspect's ISP, employer, or school. A subpoena is another type of court order. They are applied for by police or prosecutors, delivered by investigators, and compel an entity to cooperate by giving up information deemed material in an ongoing criminal investigation. Subpoenas provide entities that receive them with legal protections against civil law suits alleging privacy violations. For example, if a law enforcement officer serves an ISP with a subpoena that orders it to relinquish Web site visitation and other traffic data for certain clients, they are legally bound to comply with the court order and thus insulated from any privacy infringement claims later brought by those individuals. The same holds true for colleges and universities that receive subpoenas to reveal student names associated with computer IP addresses and suspected illegal downloading of music or movie files. Technically however, a subpoena can only be used to obtain **administrative records** or testimony including subscriber account information such as a suspect's name, physical or email address, phone number, and so forth. Web site visitation records, uploads, and downloads are considered **transactional records** and require a search warrant for purposes of criminal prosecution.

It is also possible for law enforcement officers who receive **voluntary consent** to search a person, location, vehicle, or computer system to discover incriminating evidence of crimes that will be admissible in court. The concept of voluntary consent refers to someone's legitimate authority to grant officers permission to search. A person cannot grant officers permission to search any property that he or she does not either own or have an exclusive expectation of privacy regarding. For example, a homeowner can allow police to search his or her house, but a property owner or manager cannot grant police permission to search somebody else' apartment or other type of rental unit. Similarly, children cannot grant law enforcement officers permission to search their parents' home, but adult children and roommates may grant police permission to search areas of a residence that they regard as private or as communal living areas (e.g., their own bedroom, or the kitchen, family/day room, or shared garage, etc.). They may not grant permission to search other areas they do not control, such as their little brother's bedroom, dad's office or their roommate's private bedroom, closet, furniture, or other belongings.

It follows that people cannot grant law enforcement officers permission to search other types of locations, vehicles, and computers or other electronic devices that are not within their legal control or for which other people have an exclusive right of privacy. However, a person who has *joint* ownership, occupancy, or control over property may grant law enforcement officers permission to search, although this could become grounds for a legal challenge depending on other factors involved, which we will consider below. The decision to search based on permission is a judgment call made by officers. If they judge wrong about a person's legal authority to grant permission, they may lose the evidence and potentially their entire case in court. Note also that voluntary consent may be given orally or in writing and revoked at anytime. Law enforcement officers are trained to always get a permission to search in writing after they have established the legal basis of the person granting permission to do so. This ordinarily involves establishing the person's identification and age, legal authority over property and locations within a given premises, and information about other people who share the domain and can legally access or use particular locations and property such as vehicles and computers. When all of this type of information has been ascertained, a warrantless search may commence, and any evidence of criminal wrongdoing discovered in the process will be admissible unless it is successfully challenged after the fact in motions to dismiss the evidence.

When the item to be searched is a computer seized from a structure, then the follow-up analysis of the computer is comparable to a search of another entire structure—a search within a search. Each physical drive (hard disk), logical partition (virtual drive), folder, file, and unused space is analogous to another physical building, room, or cabinet. Depending on the scope of search provided for in the search warrant, these areas may require further, in depth, digital analysis. Further complicating searches of computers and electronic devices is the reality that a suspect's personal data may be digitally stored among personal electronic files belonging to other people, as well as among applications, tools, games, and artifacts. Searching the suspect's data amidst other data stored on the same device is similar to searching a residence for which a search warrant only specifies half the house, or particular types of evidence within an entire dwelling. Thus, when and where during the course of a search expectations of privacy regarding electronic data begins and ends is rather complex and subject to legal interpretation. Courts continue to struggle with this issue and continually try to apply physical metaphors and case law rulings involving tangible evidence to electronic evidence in cybercrime investigations.

In the simplified hypothetical examples stated earlier, it makes sense to look in drawers and other small places for computer disks or flash drives containing evidence of child pornography or other electronic contraband. However, looking into small places for large items authorized by a search warrant is not permissible. By analogy, certain areas inside a hard drive or on a controlled access network may be off limits in searches for specific electronic evidence. Investigators must know what these boundaries are and know when to stop the search based upon reasonable expectations of privacy as established via common understandings, case law rulings, and other information ascertained prior to commencing their search. Knowing the law and being able to apply legal principles in practical investigative circumstances is especially important for electronic evidence analysts, as well as field investigators of traditional crimes. The difference between knowing when to stop and apply for a warrant, or being able to articulate legal justification to continue a search under an existing scope of authorization, may be the difference between admissibility or suppression of evidence in any given case.

## 9.3 Crime Scene Processing and Evidence Management

The first thing to understand about processing evidence in cybercrime cases is that any traditional crime scene may have electronic evidence. Conversely, cybercrime investigations are likely to yield substantial amounts of nonelectronic evidence of equal or greater value to proving violations of specific crimes. In all cases, the ultimate goal of investigators and prosecutors is to match case facts, circumstances, and evidentiary artifacts to specific illegal behaviors of individuals in accordance with their motives, means, and opportunities to commit crimes. In this section we will discuss crime scene processing and the management of criminal case evidence. We begin by considering the oft overlooked issues of responding to and protecting scenes of cybercrime investigations. Then we will consider issues pertaining to the collection, preservation, and analysis of different kinds of physical and electronic evidence common in various types of cybercrime investigations. Here you will be provided with an overview of chain of custody issues and computer forensics. The section ends with a discussion about interviewing victims, witnesses, and cybercriminals to acquire testimonial evidence.

### 9.3.1 Responding to and Protecting the Crime Scene

What is a crime scene? What is a cybercrime scene? Given the intermingled nature of physical and cyber attacks and assets, is there really any difference between traditional crime and cybercrime scenes and the evidence to be found in tangible spaces versus cyber places? The answers to these questions are really quite straightforward. First, a **crime scene** is any location where a crime or suspected crime took place. Crime theory holds that a criminal will always bring into the crime scene and/or take away evidence of themselves or other items that can be located and connected to form investigative leads or conclusions about causal relationships and events. Sometimes many separate locations contain evidence of one or more crimes, all of which will need to be processed for clues and evidence at some point in an investigation. In complicated cases, it is not uncommon for a few separate crime scenes to need to be processed for clues and evidence simultaneously, implying the potential need for more than one investigative team consisting of officers and analysts who possess a variety of expertise. Major crime scenes are processed by more than one investigator, and perhaps as many as a third of all crimes involve more than one location that will requiring searching, especially if vehicles are counted separately.

Second, a **cybercrime scene** may be regarded as any location, computer, or electronic IT device or information system containing potential evidence of a cybercrime. In practice, there is not any practical difference between a modern crime scene and a cybercrime scene because, as we have stressed throughout this text, cybercrimes, and therefore evidence of cybercrimes, are not limited to cyberspace. Cybercrime scenes may also yield tangible or electronic evidence of of traditional crimes. Conversely, traditional crime scenes may yield evidence of electronic crime. To put this another way, electronic evidence of crimes crosses into and out of cyberspace and the real world in which people live, and therefore evidence of cybercrimes and non-cybercrimes is often inextricably commingled with tangible things, people, places, and historical events. Thus, cybercrimes are not fiction—they result in real harm, as well as many forms of evidence of varying degrees. Hence, the answer to the third question above ("is there really any difference between traditional crime and cybercrime scenes?") is, "no, not really" except that obviously, electronic or so-called digital evidence of crimes can only be found in tangible computers or other electronic IT devices, or within information systems also contained within tangible devices locatable within actual places.

The implication is that responding to and protecting cybercrime and non-cybercrime scenes involves essentially the same concerns: adequate preparation plus a tactically safe response and arrival, securing the scene from loss of evidence including electronic evidence unseen within computers and other electronic devices, and making necessary incident notifications, including to computer forensics specialists when needed.

Circumstances will dictate what is appropriate. For example, in the case of a worm transmitted over the Internet, there could be millions of victims in separate locations and jurisdictions with one or more release points of origin. This may require a very different set of investigative protocols than a simple cybercrime scene resulting from a citizen calling to report contraband found on the family computer, or a Fortune 500 company reporting that millions of dollars have been siphoned off of its accounts and electronically transmitted elsewhere by persons unknown over an extended period of time.

The multiple crime scenes, multiple jurisdictions, and anonymity involved in some cybercrimes can make investigating them very complicated. Nevertheless, cybercrimes are investigated just as any other type crime, by following processes for obtaining information in logical ways. There are no absolute rules here but generally, investigating different types of crimes requires following different but relatively standard procedures. Let us now discuss some of the basics.

### 9.3.1.1 Preparation, Tactical Response, and Arriving Safely.

Suspected cybercrimes come to the attention of law enforcement officers in one of three ways: (1) police officers may discover cybercrimes while "patrolling" the Net, while working other cases or undercover sting operations; (2) victims, witnesses, or informants may report cybercrimes they have become aware of; or (3) criminal investigations may be referred from one law enforcement agency to another have primary jurisdiction or adequate resources to handle a given case. Once an investigator becomes aware of a possible cybercrime, he or she will typically "pull a case report number" and begin documenting facts. If the case turns out to be unfounded, a short report is often filed anyway as a means of documenting the incident, or that no leads or credible evidence could be established. Assuming, however, that a crime is confirmed to have occurred and leads are generated, the investigator will add the case to his or her other ongoing investigations and work leads as fast as possible.

It is not uncommon for a single detective in a mid- to large-sized police agency to investigate, on average, thirty or more new cases per month and to unfound or close out an additional 100 cases monthly for lack of evidence. Perhaps ten percent of cases reported to and investigated by law enforcement agencies lead to formal charges. The number of new cases added to an investigator's case load will depend on the amount of crime in the community, how crimes are categorized for assignment within investigative units, and the number of unsolved cases already being worked in comparison to case loads of other available investigators. Since investigators never know when a new case will suddenly appear on their radar screen and require an immediate response, they must at all times be prepared to respond to a crime scene or go into action if they unexpectedly find themselves amidst evidence of a crime, as during a traffic stop or while working on another case. Preparation means having crime scene processing equipment at the ready (see Textbox 9.2)

With equipment inspected and restocked after processing every crime scene, investigators are ready to go into action at the next crime scene they encounter. Whenever possible, investigators should do as much advance intelligence gathering and analysis about the physical layout of crime scenes and the people who are likely to be there before responding. After all, cybercriminals may be involved in several different kinds of criminal schemes, be operating under different types and levels of strain, and have various criminal backgrounds and violent tendencies. In addition, crime scenes may be indoors or out-of-doors, and consist of any combinations of buildings, vehicles, and electronic equipment, and so forth, all of which may contain some form of evidence. (Can you think of a cybercrime that could involve one or more outdoor crime scenes?) Knowing this, experienced investigators never take their response to crime scenes, nor the potential threats posed by cybercriminals, for granted. Instead, they will approach scenes carefully, being cognizant of needed backup and locations offering tactical cover and concealment in case it becomes necessary to suddenly assume an operationally defensive stance or offensive action.

### 9.3.1.2 Securing and Evaluating Cybercrime Scenes.

After gaining entry to a crime scene forcibly or with permission, officers will ordinarily conduct a protective sweep for weapons and people. This is done very quickly, and caution is taken to ensure that persons present cannot lunge for weapons or destroy evidence. Persons present must be identified and are often assembled in one location where evidence is not likely to be found. Officers will normally then interview anyone present to discover their identities and evaluate the scene for potential evidence. This involves informing persons present why the police are investigating, learning from those present what has been going on, and explaining search and evidence collection procedures and how long crime scene processing will take, if they intend to search. At this point persons with knowledge of contraband being sought, possibly

## BOX 9.2 • *Typical Crime Scene Processing Equipment*

Since investigators must conceivably process traditional and cybercrime scenes for both tangible and electronic evidence, basic and specialized tools, equipment and supplies are needed in crime scene processing kits. The items listed below, while not exhaustive, are typical of what may be needed to process a crime scene. Note that analysis of electronic devices will ordinarily not be accomplished at crime scenes. Instead, devices are normally packaged and sent to a computer forensics lab for analysis after a physical crime scene has been processed.

| | |
|---|---|
| **Crime scene protection and notification checklist**: | Used by investigators to remind themselves of everything they need to pay attention to and do after initially securing a scene |
| **Crime scene barrier ribbon, traffic cones and roadway flares**: | Used to mark perimeters and access points |
| **Digital camera** | plus an extra memory card, an extra rechargeable battery, and a battery charger |
| **Evidence packing equipment**: | Includes waterproof markers and storage envelopes, boxes,and bags along with packing/sealing tape and labels |
| **Flashlight** | and mini tape recorder, with extra batteries for each |
| **Medically approved blood and fluid vials**, | used for collecting evidence by licensed medical technicians at the scene of crime |
| **Paper and pencil (and space pen)** | for sketching crime scenes and taking quick notes even on wet paper at wet outdoor crime scenes |
| **Plastic tarps** | for protecting areas explosed to inclement weather |
| **Portable generator with auxiliary lighting and extension cords** | (a nice luxury) |
| **Sanitary equipment**: | Such as rubber gloves, bleach disinfectant solutions, paper towels and sanitary wipes |
| **Standardized forms** | used for case reports and evidence processing |
| **Mini tape or digital recorder** | (and backup tapes as necessary) for transcribing notes and conducting on-scene interviews of victims or witnesses. |
| **Toolbox**: | 25-ft. steel tape measure, 100-ft. wind-up cloth tape, screw drivers, pliers, wire cutters, claw hammer and other miscellaneous tools needed to access locations, pickup or move items |
| **Video camcorder**, | also used for documenting the appearance of crime scenes and potentially interviews of victims, witnesses or suspects. |
| **Wireless communications** | devices including both a portable radio and cell phone |

realizing its inevitable discovery by officers who may have arrived with a search warrant, will often retrieve the items rather than have their premises "turned upside down."

If officers establish probable cause to arrest anyone during their preliminary evaluation of the scene or a search they may immediately arrest and take individuals suspected of committing crimes into custody or arrange to have them charged with violating crime laws after the fact through an investigative filing by a prosecuting attorney. Officers armed with a search warrant may opt, however, to continue searching for additional contraband at the scene if a precise

*In this crime scene, the property owner suspected of cyber sex crimes, had placed several different weapons in readily accessible areas throughout the house. Here, a large hunting knife is shown hanging next to the doorway. Investigators learned after the fact that the suspect had planned to fight his way back through the house if confronted by police. In this case, he was not at home when the warrant was served.* Photo courtesy of: Detective Joe Hennekey, Monroe County Sheriffs Department, New York.

warrant (e.g., checking out a location in which cybercrimes or other types of crimes are reportedly occurring). In the course of an initial response and investigation, officers may decide there is nothing to the report or that further investigation is warranted. If officers conducting an initial investigation spot contraband or other physical evidence of crime in plain view, they may as previously indicated seize a scene and request consent to search or apply for a telephonic search warrant. Law enforcement officers are normally required to complete searches during daytime hours, although depending on circumstances, they will process crime scenes anywhere day or night, and for several days without stopping if necessary. Patrol officers in particular, as opposed to plain clothes detectives, will normally process crime scenes on the spot as they discover them and, depending on agency procedures, secure telephonic warrants in situations when consent to search is not granted. In fact, many small local law enforcement agencies may not even have officers assigned as plain clothes detectives, so all cases and required follow-up investigations befall patrol officers.

Nonpolice investigators and information security professionals, depending on their organizational policies, may conduct searches of work areas or computers during business hours or at other times, with or without employees giving consent or being present. This is because, as previously discussed, courts have ruled that employees do not have legal expectations of privacy regarding their offices, cubicles, work stations, or computer equipment, or of data stored on information systems owned by the employing organization. Decisions of managers, IT administrators, and information security professionals to search will often depend on the nature of the case and investigative strategy, in conjunction with policies, established procedures and other circumstances. The main point here, with respect to searches carried out by law enforcement officers or private sector mangers and IT professionals is that investigations are initiated

quantity of evidence sought was not specified in the search warrant. Remember that in the course of routine police work officers frequently investigate potential and actual crime scenes without a and unfold in different ways and there is no set way to respond to a crime scene. Every situation is different and requires investigators to employ sound judgment about how to protect themselves and other persons involved and how best to go about legally identifying, seizing, and preserving evidence of crimes.

### 9.3.1.3 Making Incident Response Notifications.
If an initial investigation establishes that one or more major crimes or that those of a sensitive nature have occurred, most agencies have incident response notification procedures that must be adhered to. Who should be notified will usually depend on the seriousness of the crime, tactical circumstances, condition of the crime scene, and anticipated evidence that will need to be collected and analyzed. Obviously emergency notifications will be made to treat injured persons,

and tactical units may be requested to help secure crime scenes or suspects if violence is anticipated. In addition, the number of victims and harm experienced, unusual circumstances, and involvement of public officials as potential suspects are factors that may trigger required notifications to supervisors, managers, and media relations personnel who may respond to a scene. It may also be conventional practice in some jurisdictions to notify prosecuting attorneys of certain types of cases or developments while investigating cases. In some instances, prosecutors may also elect or need to respond to crime scenes to offer legal advice and direction.

Other notifications may need to be made to investigative experts and crime scene technicians, as well as to investigators in other jurisdictions, government regulatory agencies, and so on. Family members, landlords, employers, and

---

**CYBER TALE 9.1**

### Searching for Physical and Electronic Evidence of Counterfeiting

Several years ago as law enforcement agencies were beginning to see a marked increase in computer-related crime, I was asked to assist with the service of a search warrant at a residence where a computer was believed to have been used to counterfeit $20 bills. The suspects were young men, one of whom had admitted that a family computer had been used to make the bills. The warrant authorized search of the entire residence for evidence of counterfeiting. After initially presenting the warrant and securing the home with the aid of other officers, I began a field analysis of the computer as part of my search team responsibilities. As I dismantled the computer, carefully noting and marking all the connections, I noticed that the rest of the search team was standing behind me watching in awe.

At that moment, one of the other investigators said; "So this is how you seize a computer. Is there anything we can do to help you?" I

immediately responded with, "Well, you could search the rest of the house for evidence of counterfeiting." One of the officers remained with me to take notes and photos of the computer work station as the others began searching the residence. It wasn't long before one investigator returned, having found two floppy diskettes that had been secreted between the suspects' mattress and box springs. Another officer soon discovered numerous bill trimmings and failed print attempts in the trash containers located in the garage. Subsequent forensic analysis of the diskettes showed that each one contained a document file that consumed almost the entire storage area of the diskette with graphic images of the front and back of a counterfeit bill saved with a misleading file extension. This experience taught the officers not to be too focused on the computer work station, and the importance of searching for both physical and electronic evidence of cybercrimes.

*Anonymous High-Tech Crime Investigator*

friends of individuals involved in a case may also need to be notified of an arrest, or about a victim's injury status or that children of injured or arrested adults need to be cared for. In cases affecting the welfare of children a child protective services agency may need to be summoned to the scene or police station to take children into temporary protective custody pending other housing and supervision arrangements. Similarly, an animal protective services agency may need to be called to take custody of unattended pets or to arrange for care and feeding of livestock. To many readers, these sorts of notifications in cybercrime cases may seem strange, but investigating traditional or cybercrimes uncovers and results in all sorts of very odd circumstances.

### 9.3.2 Collecting and Preserving Physical and Electronic Evidence

In any investigation it is imperative to preserve all or as much of the evidence as quickly as possible, before it is inadvertently deleted, altered, or destroyed thereby rendering it useable in criminal or administrative proceedings. In sex crime investigations it is imperative to get an accurate disclosure from the victim. Because of the nature of sex crimes, such as in instances involving child exploitation, victims may be too embarrassed or fearful to disclose all the facts known to them. Or for any number of reasons victims may intentionally or unintentionally distort case facts. The overt acts involved in a case must usually be corroborated through witness statements, medical examination and/or forensic analysis of physical or electronic evidence. Homicide investigations, on the other hand, start with thorough background investigations to find out who the victim associated with and what his or her lifestyle patterns were and to identify intense personal problems that might lead to clues about motive, and then an identified suspect's opportunity and means to commit the crime. Here as in sex crimes and other types of criminal investigations, data stored on computers and other

electronic devices can be very revealing. Electronic evidence can also help investigators trace stolen property and follow the money trail in embezzlement, fraud, and money laundering cases. Each type of criminal investigation relies on somewhat different processes, but all cases necessarily involve making connections between various types of evidence. What other forms can evidence take? How exactly is evidence collected, analyzed, and preserved for purposes of criminal prosecution? How does collecting evidence for use in criminal prosecutions differ from procedures employed in administrative investigations? Who is authorized to collect evidence, and how can judges, attorneys, defendants, and jurors be convinced of the authenticity of evidence presented in court?

In this subsection we will answer these questions, initially by considering other types of evidence typically collected and analyzed in cybercrime cases. We will also discuss what is commonly referred to as the chain of custody, which is a set of conventional practices to ensure the safekeeping and authenticity of evidence. Of course we will also consider computer forensics as an emerging extension of criminalistics that focuses on analyzing electronic evidence in computers and other electronic devices. We will also explore many other issues related to collecting and preserving physical and electronic evidence. When you are finished reading this portion of the text you will be ready to learn about interviewing victims, witnesses, and crime suspects to acquire testimonial and other types of evidence.

**9.3.2.1 Types of Evidence.** Increasing levels of evidence correspond to increasing levels of proof. A little evidence is a sufficient basis for a trained experienced investigator to formulate a hunch. More facts and circumstances may lead a police officer to establish reasonable suspicion, and more evidence still may result in probable cause, the legal basis for making an arrest. Ultimately, proof beyond a reasonable doubt is required for a judge or jury to find someone guilty of committing a crime. Each of these levels of evidence is subjective, may increase or decrease relative to the amount and type of evidence discovered through investigation, and is subject to being scrutinized by lawyers or a trial judge. The five basic kinds of criminal evidence are physical, electronic, circumstantial, testimonial, and demonstrative. Note that these types of evidence may be interrelated. For example, an investigator may find an article of physical evidence and suspected electronic evidence at a crime scene and later at trial provide testimonial evidence about how she located it and submitted it for forensics analysis. To understand what each kind of evidence is, let us now consider them in turn and further discuss how they may interrelate and also differ.

**Physical evidence** consists of tangible artifacts. Documents including those produced by computers, photographs and diagrams, weapons and tools, intoxicating beverages and drugs, and computer hardware and media such as CDs, DVDs, and flash drives are examples of physical evidence because they can be looked at, touched, and manipulated during a crime scene examination or laboratory analysis. Latent physical evidence is that which is very difficult or too small to see with the naked eye. Hair, very small drops of blood or other fluids, DNA, and small synthetic fibers are also examples of physical evidence, as are pieces of broken glass or other materials, including tire, tool, and bite marks linked to crime suspects or victims. In short, any tangible item may become evidence of crime or, conversely, evidence of someone's innocence which is known as **exculpatory evidence**.

A primary responsibility of crime scene investigators is to identify, locate, and process physical evidence. The term *locate* as used here means to plot items of evidence relative to their location within a crime scene. This can be accomplished with crime scene sketches, photographs, or video recordings. Processing evidence means to locate items and preliminarily understand their interconnections and links to people and their overall relevance to violations of crime laws. Processing physical evidence also involves protecting items from being damaged and securing them from being tampered with. Later we will discuss processing electronic evidence in computer forensics analysis.

Identifying, locating, and processing physical evidence at crime scenes requires training and experience, along with basic and specialized equipment, a healthy amount of curiosity, and patience. Searching crime scenes ranges from being very easy to extraordinarily difficult, depending on the location and overall state of the scene and amount of potential evidence that needs to be sifted through. Most investigators prefer a neat and orderly indoor crime scene over outdoor scenes subject to inclement weather or that contain messy and even unhealthy piles of potential evidence. Searching scenes for evidence of crimes is especially onerous and even dangerous when drug paraphernalia such as used syringes, along with other sharp objects and bodily fluids, are present.

Officers who practice methodical processing of crime scenes for small and large pieces of evidence and who attempt to make connections between evidence found at multiple crime scenes usually solve more cases than investigators who approach, enter, and search scenes haphazardly. Aside from the basic truism that things done carefully are more apt to be done well, careful searching is important because an investigator cannot always know while processing a crime scene what evidence will ultimately prove most crucial in solving a case. Rubbing a pencil back and forth over text impressions left on a notepads may reveal very important clues, as may searching through a waste basket, refrigerator, or hamster cage. So might the make, model, age, and ways that computer hardware is connected, as well as articles being strewn about versus being neatly stacked, labeled and placed on shelves or in drawers. Computer-related documentation such as software user manuals may also provide clues needed to help profile cybercriminals and solve cases.

*Crime scenes range from being clean, neat, and easy to process to being filthy, cluttered, and extremely difficult to process for evidence. In this scene a variety of potential physical evidence including computer hardware, documents and storage media are strewn about. Sexually suggestive and explicit photos and other paraphernalia are also present in abundance. Do you see any tangible items which may contain electronic evidence? Which items do you think might be important for solving a cybercrime case?* Photo courtesy of: Detective Joe Hennekey, Monroe County Sheriffs Department, New York.

What does it say about a suspect who has an *Internet for Dummies* book located nearby his work station with pages marked? Conversely, what would a Linux OS/Red Hat manual indicate about the relative SKRAM of the suspect an investigator is dealing with? Sometimes the number, placement, and general appearance of articles within an overall crime scene, in addition to their substantive content, can prove valuable in understanding a suspect's lifestyle and modus operandi with respect to technological preferences. Items can also reveal a crime perpetrator's intent and the extent of his guilty mind (i.e., whether he committed illegal acts with premeditation, knowledge, recklessness, or negligence as specified in crime laws).

**Electronic evidence** is merely an extension of physical evidence in concept, law, and with respect to processing items at crime scenes. Electronic evidence pertaining to content, identification and authentication and levels of access, and configurations or permissions may be found within central processing units (CPUs), on hard drives, network components, memory cards and diskettes, and/or access control devices. Electronic evidence (and physical evidence such as latent fingerprints) may also be located on peripherals such as printers, scanners, copy machines, credit card imprinting devices, lamination machines, digital watches, routers, hubs, and switches, as well as on digital cameras, answering and fax machines, cellular phones, pagers or PDAs, GPS/GIS devices, and so on. Electronic evidence may consist of[39]

- **User-Created Files** such as address books, audio and video files, calendars, database files, documents or text files, email files, image and graphics files, Internet bookmarks, and spreadsheet files

*Hardcopy documents, mail, legal papers, and books including IT user manuals, among many other types of documents, constitute physical evidence that may provide important clues for understanding a suspect's skills, knowledge, needed resources, access to facilities or information systems, and motivations (i.e., SKRAM)—all of which may be helpful or necessary for proving their guilt in a court of law. Sometimes documents and similar materials are referred to as "documentary evidence", but in the computing age, this term can be confusing because documents of evidentiary value may simultaneously exist in several hardcopy and/or electronic forms.* Photo courtesy of: Detective Joe Hennekey, Monroe County Sheriffs Department, New York.

- **User-Protected Files** such as those that are compressed, encrypted, hidden, misnamed, password-protected, or encoded as steganography (i.e., hiding of images or other data within images)
- **Computer-Created Files** including backup, configuration, cookies, hidden, history, log, printer spool, swap, system and temporary files
- **Other Data** such as bad clusters, computer date and time stamps, deleted files, free space, lost clusters, metadata, slack space, structured and hidden partitions, and unallocated space or memory

A thoroughly processed crime scene will be examined for all these types of equipment and corresponding electronic evidence. Another important thing to understand about electronic evidence is that clues of its existence, and places in which it may be found, are infinite, yet investigators typically have only a limited amount of time and other resources with which to process a crime scene. As indicated in Cyber Tale 9.1, a printout found crumpled up in the waste basket may contain information indicative of criminal activity undertaken on particular computers or via other electronic devices and information systems. An investigator who does not recognize the potential value of a PDA or flash drive when searching a drug dealer's home or place of employment may be missing critical physical or electronic evidence containing phone numbers, contacts, and/or transaction records of money laundering, all tying into crimes previously undiscovered. However, an investigator who knows the potential evidentiary value of discarded hard copies and media storage devices can routinely target these in their investigations in order to obtain electronic data needed to solve their current case and other crimes that would otherwise go undetected.

---

**BOX 9.3 • *Controversy and Evidentiary Challenges of Child Porn Morphing***

Federal law prohibits distribution of child pornography in interstate commerce and on federal property. The federal child pornography statute, codified at 18 U.S.C. 2256, defines child pornography as any visual depiction of a minor under 18 years old engaging in sexually explicit conduct including actual or simulated (1) sexual intercourse, including genital-genital, oral-genital, anal-genital, or oral-anal contact, whether between persons of the same or opposite sex; (2) bestiality; (3) masturbation; (4) sadistic or masochistic abuse; or (5) lascivious exhibition of the genitals or pubic area. However, IT has made production and distribution of illegal child pornography easier and cheaper with less risk of detection than traditional paper-based illegal porn. Using digital graphics software, pornographers can now merge portions of images of real children into a single image depicting virtual children posing in sexually explicit ways. This process, called **morphing**, is extremely controversial.

Freedom of expression advocates insist that even if morphed images are socially despicable, legally they differ little from movies that depict killings and other atrocities without violating crime laws.[40] In addition, youthful sex appeal is promoted commercially and socially glamorized in the United States and several other countries.[41] Proponents of criminalizing child porn morphing argue that such images (1) improperly aid in sexual arousal and gratification, (2) validate fantasies about having sex with children, (3) are used to blackmail or seduce children and lower their inhibitions about sexual activity, (4) are used to convince children that sexual contact between them and with adults is OK, thereby building trust between child victims and pedophiles, and (5) are created for commercial purposes, collected as trophies, and used to gain entrance into private clubs, thereby perpetuating demand for more traditional high-tech illegal child pornography.[42]

On April 16, 2002, the U.S. Supreme Court *struck down* the Child Pornography Prevention Act of 1996 (CPPA), which expanded a federal prohibition on child pornography to include not only pornographic images made using actual children, 18 U.S.C. § 2256(8)(A), but also "any visual depiction, including any photograph, film, video, picture, or computer or computer-generated image or picture" that "is, or appears to be, of a minor engaging in sexually explicit conduct," §2256(8)(B), and any sexually explicit image that is "advertised, promoted, presented, described, or distributed in such a manner that conveys the impression" it depicts "a minor engaging in sexually explicit conduct" §2256(8)(D).[43] Consequently morphed child porn images are legal in the United States, although they are illegal in England and many other nations.

Today cybercrime investigators and prosecutors must substantiate that child porn images depict real children, despite law enforcement beliefs that pedophilia is highly correlated with creation and possession of such images.[44] To do so, investigators can: (1) match aspects of morphed image evidence with archived sources of child pornography created from the 1960s–1980s, such as the infamous Helen and Gavin series; (2) attempt to locate a real child victim locally using school picture books or other sources to match aspects of morphed images, on the theory that pedophiles often prey on relatives or children close to where they live or work; (3) induce testimony of child victims or codefendants who may have exchanged pornography with major offenders; (4) employ physicians and other expert witnesses to testify about the age of children depicted, or that digital photos have been morphed or altered to depict nude portions of more than one child as evidenced by different bone structure, skin tone, hair color, lighting or shading conditions, and so on. Prosecutors are urged to pursue cases even if only a portion of a single photo can be verified as belonging to a real child victim, such as when parts of scars, marks or tattoos can be positively identified.[45] Additionally, background details contained in a single or series of child porn photos, whether morphed or not, can provide valuable clues about the geographic location in which the pictures were taken.

**Circumstantial evidence** consists of intangible facts, events, and associations that happen to be related in some way and point to an individual's guilt. For example, if a computer disk found at the scene of homicide scene were analyzed to reveal an IP and MAC address traced back to your computer, this may be purely circumstantial because months earlier your laptop backpack containing several disks was stolen. The fact that the disk turned up later in a place that you have never been, in the presence of a homicide victim you did not know, is purely circumstantial. Countless possibilities for the existence of particular circumstantial evidence often cause people unfamiliar with criminal investigations and prosecutions to discount its value by saying things like, "Oh well, that is just circumstantial" in reference to someone or something simply being in a particular place and time. In practice however, circumstantial evidence can be powerful in court, especially if there is an abundance of coincidental facts, events, or associations that are best explained, or perhaps cannot be explained in ways other than, by a prosecutor's theory of how a given crime occurred. It is like asking, what are the odds that all given circumstances could exist if the defendant did not commit the crime? Each year thousands of people in the United States are convicted solely or substantially on the basis of circumstantial evidence. Such cases may be relatively difficult to prove beyond a reasonable doubt, but not impossible. In many instances, circumstantial evidence is all that investigators are able to produce. The

implication is that while in the course of processing crime scenes, interviewing people about crimes, and gathering background information, investigators should document anything that may remotely constitute circumstantial evidence because it will bolster if not add up to a solid case against cybercriminals.

**Testimonial evidence** consists of oral and/ or written statements provided by victims, witnesses, or suspects. Testimonial evidence may be obtained by first responders to crime scenes who naturally confront and ask questions of people present or by detectives conducting follow-up interviews of witnesses or victims, or by any other law enforcement officer who conducts interrogations of suspects or persons already arrested for crimes. Typically individuals are initially asked to orally explain what happened and answer questions. Depending on the value or suspicion of what they report, individuals will be asked by investigators to complete a written statement and sign and date it. If a person is incapable of writing his or her own statement, investigators will often write down what a person dictates, after which the person may leave his or her personal mark on the statement form, which is witnessed and countersigned by one or more officers present. In these instances, officers may also write down questions asked and in the course of interviewing a person pass the statement form back and forth so that an interviewee's responses are in their own handwriting, or at least acknowledged as being true with initials or a other written mark. Interviews and statements may also need to be undertaken with assistance provided by a translator, and/or be tape or video recorded. In some states in-custody interviews must be video recorded to be admissible in court.

Testimonial evidence also includes confessions and spontaneous exclamations of suspects or persons arrested. For example, if a cybercriminal caught in the act of counterfeiting utters an incriminating statement such as, "The other guy copied all the documents, all I did was get the paper and printer cartridges," this would likely be considered admissible testimonial evidence depending on other case circumstances. This would be true whether the utterance occurred before or after the suspect was advised of their right to remain silent, provided it was made of their own volition without promises of threats of any kind being made by investigating officers. If a case goes to trial, anyone interviewed during the investigation may be called as a witness to provide testimony under oath about the oral or written statements they previously provided to investigators, and vice versa. All such statements are considered testimonial evidence, which may ultimately be accepted or excluded by a judge in the course of criminal proceedings. Testimonial evidence, including eyewitness accounts of crimes, is often given considerable weight by jurors making decisions about the credibility of people involved in a given case as well as the guilt or innocence of persons accused of committing crimes. For this reason, prosecutors and defense attorneys carefully scrutinize police records of statements provided by victims, witnesses, and suspects to ensure they were voluntarily and legally obtained.

New investigators should be aware that testimonial evidence is often flawed. Research has shown that crime victims and witnesses frequently are mistaken about what they remember. This is particularly true of situations involving violence, poor lighting or visibility, inclement weather, and other factors that may impede recognition or memory. In addition, victims and witnesses who may be involved in crimes or otherwise have

something to hide may not tell the whole truth or employ sophistry, exaggerate, or lie. Obviously suspects will also frequently attempt to conceal or lie about their involvement in a crime, as well as their connections to other persons, places, or things. However, in general, a deceiving statement, regardless of how it is made and recorded, can be invaluable to investigators in unpredictable ways, including later demonstrating that a person intentionally tried to throw them off the trail, which is ordinarily very condemning evidence of criminal wrongdoing.

The final type of evidence that we will consider is **demonstrative evidence**, which consists of aerial photographs, scale models, illustrations, time charts, drawings, technical diagrams, certain types of forensic depictions, and other items that are presented in court to help clarify aspects of a crime, crime scene, evidence or its processing, or investigative procedures, and so forth. This type of evidence demonstrates important aspects of a case. Since attorneys must exchange in advance lists of the evidence they intend to introduce at trial, judges will often rule on the admissibility of demonstrative evidence (as well as other specific evidentiary items) before a trial begins. Rarely is demonstrative evidence excluded unless it would tend to have an undue prejudicial effect on a jury. The same is true for all the other types of evidence previously discussed.

### 9.3.2.2 Chain of Custody.

It is usually pointless to locate and process evidence of a crime if it cannot later be introduced by a prosecutor at trial to demonstrate some aspect of criminal behavior or association. To this end, investigators and prosecutors must work together to ensure that evidence is legally obtained, processed with integrity, and brought to court in an acceptable condition. The concept of **chain of custody** refers to documenting the complete process leading to the identification, collection, analysis and producing at trial of physical, electronic, and certain types of testimonial evidence such as a confession in the suspect's own handwriting. The essential idea underpinning chain of custody is that, whenever possible, evidence presented at trial should be the actual evidence located and seized at a crime scene. To this end, investigators who seize evidence are responsible for initiating a chain of custody by documenting the date, time, location, and precise description of each piece or bundle of evidence collected.

All law enforcement agencies use standardized evidence forms for this purpose, as well as special envelopes, bags, boxes, sticky labels, and tags to put evidence into and track its shipping and storage. After being initially bagged and tagged evidence is normally retained by the officer or crime scene technician until being submitted into evidence, perhaps in an evidence locker at a police station. Typically an evidence technician will later remove the evidence from the locker and place it into long-term storage to await trial or forward it to a crime lab for analysis as directed by the investigating officer. An increasing number of law enforcement agencies use bar-code scanning labels to mark and track evidence and associated investigation reports. Printouts can usually be provided by these types of semi-automated records management systems.

Regardless of technology used to track and inventory evidence, any time an article of evidence switches hands or locations, the responsible party is required to update the chain of custody documentation electronically or via a hand-written form. This includes analysts who work at crime labs and detectives or other officers who may for some reason sign evidence out in the course of conducting follow-up investigations (e.g., to have a victim identify certain property). This way there will always be a written record for every piece of evidence introduced at trial. If a record to establish the chain of custody revealing who had possession of an item from the time of seizure to its presentation in the courtroom cannot be provided, the evidence will likely be ruled inadmissible, or at a minimum, defense attorneys may question its authenticity

with regard to its not having been tampered with between the time it was seized and its introduction at trial. Over the years, many items of evidence improperly seized or not properly documented with respect to the dates, times, and locations of transference have been lost at trial, resulting in guilty persons going free.

Sometimes it is not practical or physically possible to seize, transport, store, and produce the exact evidence of a crime at trial. For example, cars are never towed into courtrooms—neither are large computer systems consisting of many CPUs, monitors, and keyboards. Instead, photographs and/or diagrams that depict cars of importance in a given case are introduced as evidence. In cybercrimes, it may be permissible to do likewise with extensive amounts of hardware that were originally connected when found and seized at a crime scene. In cases where it is not possible or practical to produce the actual evidence of a crime, the **best evidence rule** will normally apply. In cybercrime cases involving corporate or business victims, duplicating data and preserving it for trial as if it were the original will often suffice as the best *available* evidence. Courts recognize this as being a fair compromise to producing the original (best) evidence, a solution that also encourages reporting of cybercrimes to law enforcement agencies because it allows firms to conduct business as normal in the months surrounding a criminal trial. In addition, investigators need not seize and necessarily store and safeguard all the hardware, software, or working data belonging to victims, or make voluminous images of electronic data, provided (1) victims establish adequate safeguards to protect the items from future attacks or damage, (2) they are available if needed for inspection by a court, and (3) can be authenticated by computer forensics experts as being in original condition, or at least not tampered with respect to their evidentiary value in the case being heard. Moving the data to a protected area on a victim's network or verifying it through technical means such as an MD5 has value prior to saving a copy (known as a mirror image) to alternative media may also be a sufficient way to protect and later present evidence if court rules allow for this. In some cases a third party, such as an ISP, may be directed to retain data pending police obtaining a court order to examine it forensically, a subject to which we now turn.

### 9.3.2.3 Computer Forensics.

Criminal forensics, also known as criminalistics, or simply forensics, involves using tools and techniques to identify, collect, analyze, preserve, and present evidence of crimes. There are many types of forensic methods, each corresponding to the types of evidence being analyzed. *Ballistics* is the study of firearms, ammunition, bombs, explosive materials, bullets and other projectiles. Other types of forensics include, but are not limited to, *forensic anthropology* (reconstructing likenesses of decomposed or dismembered bodies), *forensic odontology* (matching bite marks with dental records), forensic entomology (the study of insects feeding on decomposing flesh to determine the approximate time of death), *forensic psychology and psychiatry* (to mentally profile criminals), and *forensic toxicology* (analysis of drugs and poisons).[46] **Computer forensics** is an important emerging specialization within the field of criminalistics. It applies scientific principles to processing electronic evidence of cybercrimes. In this portion of the text you will learn about the fundamental concepts and important issues of a nontechnical nature having to do with criminalistics and computer forensics, in particular. If after reading this overview you wish to know more about processing electronic evidence, you are encouraged to read any number of good books on the subject or take a course in computer forensics which is increasingly being offered by colleges and universities as well as professional training organizations.

Most cases involving electronic evidence will necessitate the involvement of a field agent who will manage the overall crime scene and ensuing investigation, and a trained computer forensics analyst who will focus on processing electronic evidence at crime scenes and/or at a computer forensics lab. Other personnel with specialized expertise may be called in to assist in an investigation according to the physical size of crime scenes and the number of persons and electronic devices involved, and the overall complexity of the affected computer network and case. Note that depending on contractual relationships established between law enforcement agencies and private sector computer forensics labs, investigators working on a cybercrime case may be employed by either the private or public sector. Sometimes, but not always, computer forensics experts providing analysis in a case are commissioned police officers with arrest powers, but this is not always the case. Private sector investigators will not have powers of arrest, and only in rare instances will the field agent and the computer forensics expert be the same person. Generally this is because of the amount of training and technical expertise required of computer forensics specialists not ordinarily possessed by field investigators (i.e., regular patrol officers, agents, deputy sheriffs, or other types of law enforcement officers), and because of the amount of time, special equipment, evidence handling procedures and laboratory facilities required to support many investigations simultaneously and on an ongoing basis.

The overriding goal in criminalistics is to verify and refute connections between physical evidence such as prescription and illicit or illegal drugs; metals; glass; plastics; fuels; paints; finger, tire, and shoe prints; tool marks; and latent substances such as synthetic fibers, human hair, and animal fur, *and* among electronic, circumstantial, and testimonial evidence regardless of the specific type of crime being investigated. The legal challenges that all forensics specialists are concerned with have to do with establishing the overall validity, reliability, and credibility of evidence to be presented in court. Thus, forensic analysts must help protect evidence from harm, conduct professional analysis, follow strict chain of custody procedures, and truthfully present their findings in legal proceedings while also working to improve their expertise through professional training while maintaining laboratory equipment in proper working order. Failure to do these things consistently has contributed to charges that forensics is a type of **junk science** that overly relies on human judgment rather than scientific principles combined with probability sampling and calculations to match-up evidence seized at crime scenes and other locations, and to determine that a crime unfolded in a certain way to the exclusion of all other possibilities and suspects implicated.[47]

Although criminalistics has in recent years greatly improved with respect to the types of analyses possible and quality of analyses undertaken, and the field has generally established legitimacy in courts of law, it is not an exact science. Every case centers on professional judgment employed by the forensics analysts involved who are responsible for matching up

evidence characteristics and when possible establishing as range of probability supporting a suspect's exoneration (i.e., the odds that items appearing to match up even under a microscope in fact do not). Arguably computer forensics, like DNA "fingerprinting" offers experts greater ability to precisely match particular items of evidence. However, even a unique IP address assigned to a user or node on a computer network, or the unique MAC code assigned to every computer, does not mean that a particular subject used a computer on a given day and time to commit a crime. In many respects computer forensics is like investigating a hit-and-run traffic collision in which an offender leaves the scene without providing his or her drivers license information. In such cases, the investigating officer will attempt to locate the suspect vehicle, perhaps on the basis of a witness reporting its license plate number. After locating a suspect vehicle, and perhaps matching damage on it to the victim's car on the basis of paint transfers or other physical evidence,

*Cartoon 9.1    The Mad Computer Forensics Examing*

the investigator must investigate further to put a driver behind the wheel of the car at the time of the crime. He cannot assume the registered owner of the suspect vehicle was driving it as it left the scene of the collision. Neither cars or computers do not commit crimes—people do. Hence, field agents and computer forensics investigators must work together to place an individual at a computer keyboard or in control of an electronic device used in the commission of cybercrime in order to solve these types of cases.

The job of a computer forensic analyst is to overcome such concerns by locating and tracing electronic evidence of cybercrimes in contexts of physical and other types of evidence. Much of their work involves processing electronic crime scenes that exist within physical crime scenes (e.g., computers and other electronic devices and information systems located within buildings). Computer forensic analysts help place an individual at a computer work station or in possession of an electronic device in locations and at times that incriminating data was created, transmitted, downloaded, or stored. Whether employed by or on behalf of police agencies or private firms, cyber sleuths are required to understand computer technology, terms, and functionality, as well as the legal aspects of discovering, analyzing, and transferring evidence according to chain of custody procedures. It is enormously advantageous if analysts also understand criminal law and investigation procedures inclusive of legal rules of evidence, as well as human aspects of crime from the standpoint of victims and perpetrators with respect to generating, transmitting, and utilizing the data they are required to analyze. For example, simply knowing whether the hard drive they are analyzing was seized from a suspect's CPU versus belonging to a crime victim and other background information concerning the suspected computer-using habits of both the suspect and victim may be crucial in determining what tests the analysts will conduct, what specifically they will look for, and the probative value of electronic evidence discovered in particular types of cases.

CYBER CASE **9.1**

### The Challenge of Putting a Cybercriminal Behind a Keyboard

Solving a cybercrime requires determining who was in control of a particular computer or electronic device at the time of a crime. This may be straightforward or overwhelmingly difficult, depending on circumstances involved. Consider the following case: a female college student receives harassing email on her home computer and reports the crime to the local police agency. An investigator trained in computer forensics responds to her house, examines the harassing email, and determines that although the suspect's identity has been spoofed, the IP address traces the computer used to send the email to the college attended by the victim. At this point the investigator realizes that the perpetrator could be any student, staff or faculty member, or visitor to the college capable of accessing the email server. The investigator obtains a subpoena from a court requiring the college to produce login data for the crime date, time, and IP address of the computer used to send the email.

The records show that the IP address is assigned to a particular computer in the library accessible by anyone, but that a particular username and password were used to access the network for the session during which the harassing email was sent. Since there is no specific subscriber information associated with that session, however, a second subpoena must be obtained to acquire the personal information associated with the username and password. Hence, the identity of one student becomes known, but the investigator still cannot be sure that someone else was not using his username and password at the time of the crime. (After all, many students foolishly share this information with each other.) It also occurs to the investigator that the computer used to commit the crime may have incriminating evidence on it, so he obtains consent to search it from the librarian. Sure enough, a field examination of the imaged hard drive reveals log records, file names and other information for the same date and time that can be tied to assigned school work the suspected student was also using the computer for. At that point the officer seizes the hard drive and computer logs as evidence, and the college technical services unit is able to restore the CPU to operating condition by installing a new hard drive. However, the officer's work is far from complete.

Library records reveal the identity of other potential students using computers in the immediate area of the one used by the suspect. Perhaps one of them knows the suspect and if necessary could verify his presence and use of the seized computer on the date and time of the crime. Having entered the original hard drive into evidence at police headquarters, the investigator is working fast in his computer forensics lap to further analyze the imaged hard drive in order to capture and make sense of as much potential electronic evidence and data linking the suspect and as many potential witnesses to the computer and library crime scenes as possible. He also obtains a photo of the student based on a drivers license check, and recontacts the victim to determine if she knows him. She recognizes the person depicted in the photo as being that of a male student in one of her classes, who she declined to let copy her homework two weeks earlier. Now armed with reasonable suspicion, and a plausible theory inclusive of motive, opportunity and means, the investigator confronts the male student, who subsequently confesses to the crime.

---

The general challenges of processing electronic evidence are twofold. First, investigators must protect the integrity of electronic data. They must take care when discovering computers and other electronic devices to leave them exactly as found: with power on or power off, connected or not connected, and in precise locations relative to other evidence. Second, investigators must find evidence of cybercrimes by conducting a thorough search of the entire crime scene which may contain one or more electronic devices that may be connected to one or more information systems. When a device is seized as evidence at a crime scene it will ordinarily be removed to another site or computer forensics lab where it can be properly analyzed and searched by a qualified computer forensics analyst. The first step in an analysis of a computer or other type of electronic device is to ensure the integrity of electronic evidence by forensically acquiring a duplicate copy known as an **image**. This is accomplished via specific procedures and techniques including verification of a digital data signature such as an **MD5 hash value**. In this way, a unique image of the data is created and used for forensic analysis while preserving the digital integrity of the actual electronic evidence. In other words, in a computer forensics analysis the original data is secured and left untouched. Compared to the actual analysis to follow, imaging data with proper training and tools is rather easily accomplished.

It is fortunate that, unlike many traditional types of crime, cybercrimes provide unique evidence trails for investigators to follow although these may be fairly obvious or very obscure, depending on the number and type of hardware, software, and information systems involved. The form of data involved in a given cybercrime case may also present particular challenges, such as when it is encrypted. Frequently computer forensic analysis involves tracing **Internet Protocol (IP) addresses** or analyzing system access logs to determine who acquired, manipulated, or damaged particular data, where and when. It is critical to distinguish between electronic evidence resident on devices and systems not belonging to or under the legal control of suspects from evidence that is under their control or to which they may have a legal expectation of privacy. For example, data resident on the server of an ISP used by a suspect to access the Internet is not owned or controlled by him, but he may still have a legal expectation of his transaction records (e.g., Web sites visited) remaining private.

Distinguishing data ownership and possession with respect to levels of reasonable privacy expectations is vital in all cybercrime forensics analyses and has significant bearing on the level of proof needed to obtain subpoenas, consent, or warrants to search computers, other electronic devices, and information systems. Subscriber information and customer records are seldom maintained in paper form or stored in filing cabinets, so legal requests for such documents amount to seeking copies of electronic data in a readable format. Data of this type typically include names, addresses, phone numbers, email addresses, level of service provided, payment history, methods of payment, and log-in records. Such data may be obtained with a subpoena based on reasonable suspicion if it is in the possession of a person or organization not implicated in a crime (as in Cyber Case 9.1). Acquiring data residing on a suspect's computer, however, will invariably require a search warrant based on probable cause or a valid consent to search. Understanding when a warrant is required versus mere consent or a subpoena on the basis of statutory law and case law rulings often means the difference between winning or losing a cybercrime case in court.

Since electronic evidence cannot be observed without special equipment, it is necessary to document the state in which it is seized. For example, if a flash drive is seized as having suspected contraband on it, such as forged checks in digital form, then the location the drive was found, the time and date of the seizure, and a physical description of the drive brand and model if available are all important for ensuring the forensic integrity of the evidence. Forensic analysts must also consider whether data sought is in archived and/or real-time status. Computerized communication has made possible a variety of different protocols for exchanging messages and data (e.g., IM, IRC, mIRC, voice mail, and text messaging), any of which may be encrypted, or even double or triple encrypted and with varying levels of deciphering key and algorithm strength (e.g., 56 or 128 bit DES encryption). In some jurisdictions, acquiring an electronic monitoring (wiretap) warrant may require that, in addition to establishing probable cause to search, all other means of acquiring the electronic evidence without jeopardizing the case or violating privacy rights have been exhausted.

In organizational settings, if a wiretap warrant by police is not acquired in connection with a criminal investigation, an employee's privacy expectations regarding their real-time voice and electronic communications may need to be relinquished with a signed agreement indicating they are aware that communications are subject to monitoring. Even in these cases, investigators should proceed cautiously to avoid legal pitfalls such as accusations of illegal wiretapping or, if they are police officers, claims that private investigators were acting as their agents. Further complicating electronic data searches and analysis is the reality that personal files and communications may be stored in and among nonsuspect and hidden files, as well as with digital tools, games, and artifacts resident on a given computer system that more than one person can legally access or has a reasonable expectation of privacy to. The nature of the investigation and scope of a warrant or consent will dictate the parameters of a search, but just as investigators of traditional crimes must anticipate when they are beginning to infringe on privacy expectations, so too must computer forensics analysts as they explore the inner workings of information systems, electronic devices, hierarchies of data files, and so on.

The fragile nature of electronic evidence requires a high degree of attention to technical and legal procedures throughout the course of a forensic analysis. Investigators need to be concerned with chain of custody and the "forensic integrity" of electronic evidence. Even though they necessarily make investigative judgments about the potential value of evidence they find, analysts conducting computer forensics do not make final determinations about the forensic value of the evidence for purposes of securing convictions; this is the responsibility of attorneys prosecuting or defending those accused of crimes, as well as judges or juries who hear the case and consider evidence as it is presented at trial. To the contrary, forensics investigators are legally bound to document potential **exculpatory evidence** that may help prove the *innocence* of persons accused of crimes. All this is accomplished by taking notes and photographs and drawing sketches of hardware configurations and file storage arrangements, as well as writing reports, maintaining computer forensics analysis logs, dutifully completing chain of custody forms for all evidence processed, and rendering professional judgment on the basis of training and experience.

Analysis of electronic data is only one aspect of what computer forensics technicians are responsible for. They are also required to testify about the forensic merit of the processes and equipment used in their analyses. This may be just as important as the discovery and processing of evidence in the first place. Technicians must also continuously validate analytical processes, certify the good working order of software examination tools and hardware, and stay abreast of new analysis methods even as they maintain and update their professional qualifications. Since one person can rarely attend to everything, professionals in this field frequently rely on other computer forensics analysts and equipment service contractors to assist with equipment validation testing and certifications. This also provides for professional information-sharing about emerging forms of cybercrimes, information security technologies, computer forensic tools and

laws, and so on. Government agencies such as the National Institute of Standards and Technology (NIST) and organizations such as the Scientific Working Group for Digital Evidence (SWGDE) produce guidelines and best practices (see Appendix A).

### 9.3.3  Interviewing Victims, Witnesses, and Cybercriminals

To this point in the chapter section we have explained issues surrounding crime scene and evidence processing used to solve cybercrime cases and support prosecution of cybercriminals in court. We have focused a good deal of our attention on the interconnections between physical and electronic evidence but we have not considered how to go about collecting testimonial evidence in any depth. As you now realize, cybercrime investigations involve considerable field work and human interaction—good 'ol fashion gum shoe police work—to discover and process all sorts of evidence in no way limited to physical and electronic evidence. Think about it: criminal investigations typically begin and end with people, including the investigators themselves. Even if a case is initiated through electronic data mining, investigators look for patterns, trends, relationships, and anomalies in data that are indicative of suspicious, abusive, or illegal behaviors. Hence, cybercrimes are first and foremost about *people* violating crime laws and causing harm to other *people*. They are not about damage inflicted on data, devices, and systems only.

This reality underscores the importance of what we stressed earlier in Chapter 2 about human factors, distrust and attack dimensions, and now our emphasis on testimonial evidence and its interconnections with physical and electronic evidence, all of which may combine to form circumstantial evidence and levels of proof needed to successfully investigate and prosecute cybercrime cases. Cross-jurisdictional issues combined with the prophylactic scope and anonymous nature of many cybercrimes make it nearly impossible for investigators to do their work without inducing and managing cooperation, coordination, and communication. Victims and witnesses, private security firm investigators, law enforcement officers, prosecutors, and government policy makers are some of the primary stakeholders who may be needed to cooperate and facilitate aspects of a cybercrime investigation. Cooperation, communication, and coordination between these and other types of individuals and their respective organizations depend on investigators being able to speak and write clearly and to be professionally engaging in personal ways. A bit of charm—or social engineering if you prefer—for legitimate purposes never hurts in accomplishing what is needed to bring solid investigations to successful conclusions.

### 9.3.3.1 Interview Preparation and Legal Considerations.

Many law enforcement investigators are intimidated by the technological aspects of cybercrime. Conversely, some IT professionals may not be comfortable interacting with people in interviewing situations, yet depending on circumstances, they may need to ask people who are involved in a case questions of a technical or personal nature. Much insecurity can be overcome by using the Internet to conduct case-related research prior to interviewing, when possible. Online searches for names, addresses, phone numbers, email addresses, user names, and other personal identification information may provide valuable information related to the people involved in an investigation. (Just remember from our discussion in Chapter 7 the potential pitfalls of googling names of people when conducting background investigations.) There are also subscription services for public records checks that can provide a wealth of information on people and places. Mapping, satellite imagery, and live-feed video cameras can also provide information valuable to investigations with regard to crime scenes and potential sources for recorded video. Even photographs of potential

suspects may be available online through pictures posted to a personal Web site. Online research may also help an investigator prepare for a field interview by providing technical information concerning a software application or terminology that may surface during the interview. Encyclopedic Web sites such as Wikipedia.com can provide a wealth of information to investigators who are unfamiliar with certain technical terms or concepts.

Other Web sites can help debunk hoaxes or provide step-by-step instructions for obtaining technical information such as procedures for obtaining long-header information from email clients. List-serves, news groups, and chat rooms can also provide specific types of information relevant in computer forensics investigations. Information security or law enforcement groups frequently assist investigators on matters pertaining to modus operandi, jurisdiction, investigative techniques, and subject matter experts who may be available to provide assistance in particular types of cases. Traditional law enforcement databases are another invaluable source of information for acquiring criminal history, drivers license or vehicle registration information, and so on. For example, the National Criminal Information Center (NCIC), and state-level criminal records databases, and the growing National Fingerprint File (NFF) are valuable resources with which to link evidence and advance a case investigation. These are just a few examples of helpful information which may be available via the World Wide Web. Accumulating as much advance information as possible about a case, and the technology and people involved, is likely to make interviews much more productive.

Many good books have been written about techniques and legal issues pertaining to interviewing of victims, witnesses and suspects. In the limited space available in this text to address interviewing, there are a few specific things you should know about getting evidence from persons suspected of committing crimes. Recall that investigations begin with investigative hunches that may rapidly evolve to reasonable suspicion, the level of proof required for police to stop, frisk (if warranted), and formally interview a person in connection with a crime. Anything an interviewee says at this juncture is admissible evidence, provided the stopping of the person was legal. However, once a person becomes the focus of a criminal investigation, whenever probable cause is established related to an individual, or whenever suspects are arrested for a crime and questioning ensues, they must be advised of their constitutional right to remain silent and have a lawyer present before questioning. If they waive those rights, anything they say, write down or do can be used as evidence against them. A notable exception to this sequence involves the **spontaneous utterance** made by a suspect before (or after) being advised of and/or invoking their constitutional rights. If a person blurts out incriminating evidence, this will normally be admissible as evidence. Officers are not required to gag people who insist on talking. To the contrary, experienced investigators understand the value of *not* questioning suspects in certain circumstances, or allowing them to ramble on after advising them of their constitutional right to remain silent. In one-party consent jurisdictions, doing so with a tape recorder on can be useful in follow-up interviews with the suspect or other people, as well as providing damning evidence for use in court.

### 9.3.3.2 The Importance of Understanding Technological Terms and Concepts.

Few investigators need to know the explicit details of electronic devices, whether of analog or digital technological design. However, in today's high-tech environment all investigators need to know basic terms and the types of devices used by criminals, as well as potential ways in which devices and information systems can be abused. This knowledge is critical to performing the interviews and follow-up work necessary in computer abuse and cybercrime investigations. The language and culture of "computer people" may

be considerably different in certain respects from that of common street criminals. A high-tech crime investigator unfamiliar with such terms and cultural nuances will be just as disadvantaged as a gang investigator who does not understand the terms, hand signs, and graffiti used by gang members. Learning the language of the real and cyber streets in order to understand and relate to a range of criminals can be very important because many different types of criminals use IT to commit their crimes. Even common street criminals are today employing IT for purposes of communicating, record keeping, moving money, and planning their operations. Cyber sleuths must be prepared to engage all types of crimes, criminals, and crime scenes in order to assemble physical, electronic, and testimonial evidence in preparation for making arrests and bringing offenders to trial.

From the initial report of a cybercrime though the entire investigation, understanding basic IT and street jargon, as well as the correct meaning of technical terms, is necessary. If an investigator does not understand the terms a victim is using to explain an intrusion, the original investigative report may be inaccurate, incomplete, or unacceptable in later phases of an investigation (e.g., as a basis for securing a search warrant). Similarly, if the investigator is unable to speak with confidence and thereby earn a suspect's respect during an interview, the suspect is more apt to attempt deceit. However, with understanding of IT-related terms and concepts, and being able to speak in terms an interviewee can relate to and respect, investigators can establish ethos, empathy and understanding which enables them to ask clarifying questions, develop clues, and advance cases in ways otherwise not possible. In addition investigators will eventually need to be able to explain on a witness stand, while being cross examined, why they did what they did and how they arrived at certain conclusions. If they do not know what talking about, or are unable to articulate in precise but understanding ways what they did and why, the case will be jeopardized.

### 9.3.3.3 *Interviewing Strategies and Practices.*
Unless they are dispatched to or encounter a crime in progress, law enforcement officers and other investigators will normally have considerable flexibility in deciding when and where to interview people involved in a criminal case. This can be enormously important and potentially advantageous because picking the interview time and location allows investigators to assemble and understand background information on technology, people, and other aspects of cases before conducting key interviews. Intentionally delaying interviews also provides time to decide on precise questions to which answers may provide important clues or fill in gaps in a case. In other circumstances, it may be important for investigators to move quickly to interview and secure statements of persons involved in a case. A well-timed surprise interview of suspects or their associates, as well as interviewing persons in a particular sequence, can also be very important for achieving and maintaining control of an interview and the overall investigative processes. Equally important is deciding who will be present at an interview. Sometimes it is appropriate to have more than one investigator ask questions or to have more than one investigator present during questioning merely to witness the session. When interviewing juveniles, it can be important as a matter of policy or law to have a parent or guardian present. When interviewing victims of sex crimes, it can be important to have a medical technician or counselor present or available to provide support or guidance. It is also important to control what information about a case is made known during the unfolding of an investigation. At times it can be useful to let certain information about a case "leak" either to persons involved or to the media as a way of prompting guilty parties to come forward, take revealing actions, or make admissions during an upcoming interview.

Unlike on television, police inducing a suspect to voluntarily accompany them "down to the station for questioning" without first placing them under arrest for a specific crime rarely happens because doing so constitutes an arrest. Remember from our earlier discussion, that if the suspect believes they are not free to leave the presence of the law enforcement officers, an arrest situation requiring advisement of constitutional rights to remain silent and to have an attorney present during questioning exists. However, it is common practice to ask crime victims, witnesses, and even suspects to come into a police station at a predetermined time in order to complete a statement or be interviewed and perhaps also look at photographs, identify evidence, reclaim property, and so on. Most people, if asked politely, will cooperate with investigators, especially if a visit to the investigator's office can be scheduled around employment, child care, or other obligations. In practice, however, most interviews are done in the field at the time of an investigator's choosing, but less often in place of their choosing. Typically, if an investigator is fortunate, a quiet room at an interview subject's residence or place of employment can be found with or without advance notice.

If you plan to become a successful investigator or prosecutor, you will need to develop savvy interviewing skills. In particular, you will need to learn how to formulate and ask precisely the right questions of key people, in just the right way, about specific issues, and at a time and place likely to elicit crucial information needed to solve cases. This is no easy task. Interviewing crime victims, witnesses, and, especially, suspects is an art form requiring significant understanding of laws, investigative procedures, types of evidence, human nature, and, simply put, the way of things. Expert interviewers possess and are able to employ many qualities for managing their environment, and of effective communication, interviewing, and interrogation simultaneously, including patience, empathy, active listening, directing conversation, echoing responses to questions, summarizing an understanding of what is being said, and controlled verbal aggression without planting ideas or illegally coercing admissions. In short, investigators need to be able to stylize their interactions and take copious notes on what people say and how they respond to questions under various circumstances.

Experienced cybercrime investigators know that when interviewing, they must focus their attention on the person being questioned, rather than on a computer, other electronic device, or data contained in an information system. Victims need to be listened to, witnesses need to be clearly understood, and suspects need to be figured out. In all interviews, investigators must seek to discover the classic who, what, when, where, how, and why of things. Each person spoken to must be gently or sternly prodded to voluntarily provide as much information as possible. Bear in mind that coerced confessions are inadmissible as evidence in court, that victims and witnesses cannot be unduly lead to formulate what they think are good answers to questions, and that people being interviewed may not be completely forthcoming about what they know. Some people honestly forget or misconstrue facts. Suspects may try to baffle investigators with technical details, claim ignorance about how IT works, or impress them with superior knowledge (which they may actually possess—never underestimate suspects). A well-orchestrated and managed interview will usually reveal tell-tale signs of a suspect's guilt or innocence. Investigators armed in advance with plenty of case information, and who are prepared to psychologically engage a suspect, will elicit more valuable information than investigators who are not as prepared. Remember, the objective is to put suspects at the keyboard or in possession of an electronic device at the time of crime, and discover why and precisely how they committed a crime online and/or offline whether using an IT device or not. In other words, they must establish the motive, opportunity and means of committing a crime. If this requires coddling, prodding, or appearing sympathetic to a suspect, so be it.

In addition to interviewing crime victims, witnesses, and suspects, investigators often seek information from other people with knowledge about these persons or from technical experts and service providers who are able to shed light on key aspects of a case. Here again, investigators need good interviewing skills in order to understand what they are being told and to make connections between sources and types of evidence. For example, once during an intrusion investigation, an investigator was interviewing the system administrator of an attacked network. The system administrator provided a print-out of the network directory on which a common hacking tool, NetBus, was easily identified. He told the investigator that he had no knowledge of what the program was or what it could do and further indicated (with a bit of coaxing and empathy by the investigator) that his span of control over the network was severely strained, that he was working on a shoestring budget with obsolete attack prevention and network diagnostic tools, and that there was no one else he could rely on for help. (If you are an IT professional, perhaps this scenario sounds familiar.) Through careful interviewing and appropriate coaching that did not unduly taint the system administrator's thinking or statement, the investigator also learned that as the result of inadequate security measures, the network had often been targeted by novice hackers who acquired step-by-step attack instructions off the Internet. Can you see how knowledge of technical terms combined with good interviewing skills, along with effective coordination, communication, and cooperation during investigations are among the key elements underpinning successful cybercrime investigations?

## 9.4 Prosecuting Cybercriminals

In February of 2000, Juan Vargas was stopped by a city of Liberal, Kansas, police officer for driving a car with a defective rear license plate light. In the ensuing investigation, Vargas presented the officer with false identification, namely identification cards from the state of Missouri and the National Beef Packing Company. The officer conducted a routine records check and received identical "hits" from five other states, implying that either Vargas traveled a lot, that more than one person had the same name and numerical identifiers (e.g., date of birth), or that Vargas was not the individual's real name and other individuals may have also assumed the false identity. When confronted by the officer about these possibilities, Vargas admitted his true identity, saying that he was an illegal immigrant and purchased the false ID in order to get the job at National Beef. The officer arrested Vargas and charged him with the defective equipment violation, failure to wear a seat belt, not having a valid drivers license, and one count of *identity theft* on the basis of his having obtained employment and an economic benefit on false pretenses. He was found guilty in a district trial court of the first charges and innocent of identity theft. The city appealed this verdict to the Kansas State Court of Appeals, which affirmed the lower court's verdict on grounds that because Vargas had been paid for actual labor, he did not defraud the National Beef Packing Company.[48]

This simple case reveals several important aspects of investigating and then prosecuting cybercrimes. First, the cyber aspects of a case may not be addressed by actual violations of crime laws that a defendant is charged with. In this case, creation of the false Missouri ID card was accomplished with a computer, probably in a manner described in Chapter 4 (see Cyber Tales 4.4). Second, cybercrime cases may involve various types of evidence. In this case, the officer encountered physical evidence in the form of the false ID and testimonial evidence in the form of the admission made by Vargas. Third, police and prosecutors must apply facts, circumstances, and evidence to technical elements of evolving statutory crime laws in order to successfully prosecute criminals. In this case, the 1998 Kansas law prohibiting identity theft defined the crime as

*knowingly and with intent to defraud for economic benefit, obtaining, possessing, transferring, using or attempting to obtain, possess, transfer or use, one or more identification documents or personal identification number of a person other than that issued lawfully for the used of the possessor; [and that] Intent to defraud means an intention to deceive another person, and to induce such other person, upon such deception, to assume, create, transfer, alter or terminate a right, obligation or power with reference to property.[49]*

On the surface, the Kansas law may appear to cover the actions of Juan Vargas, who used a false ID to obtain employment. However, the appeals court ruled that there existed no evidence that Vargas intended to defraud National Beef by stealing money, other property, or services because he actually exchanged (i.e., sold) his labor to the firm for payment. Fourth, this case reveals potential multijurisdictional claims and implications posed by crimes that may violate the laws or regulations of more than one governing body. Vargas admitted he was an illegal alien, not entitled to employment in the United States. Under federal law, he was subject to deportation before or after conviction. In addition, National Beef was subject to being investigated for unlawfully employing an undocumented migrant worker. Finally, this case is representative of thousands of cases involving illegal use of IT and the reality that the vast majority of cybercrime cases involving differing degrees and combinations of simple to complex tools and techniques are committed in local and state jurisdictions. Although we often hear about sensational cybercrimes and cybercriminals busted by federal law enforcement agencies and prosecuted by offices of U.S. attorneys, it is actually state and local police and prosecutors who do the bulk of America's traditional and cybercrime fighting.

In this last section of the chapter we briefly explore issues having to do with prosecuting cybercriminals. We will begin by examining postarrest, pretrial procedures including police booking of suspected law violators, arraignments, preliminary hearings, and grand jury proceedings. In this subsection you will learn what initially happens to people who are arrested and charged with crimes and how evidence is determined to be admissible or inadmissible even before commencement of criminal trials. In the next subsection you will learn about basic trial procedures and the art of presenting evidence in court. This involves many factors, including good planning and preparation such as reviewing elements of crime laws, as well as police reports, victim, and witness statements, and retrieving evidence in accordance with chain of custody procedures. In the third subjection, we will discuss how court decisions are made and appealed, and alternatives to formal criminal prosecution, which you may be surprised to learn happens quite often in the interest of justice and saving taxpayers considerable sums of money. When you have completed this chapter you will be ready to study ways to prevent cybercrimes by effectively using information security technologies.

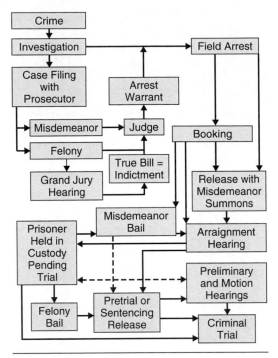

**FIGURE 9.1**  *Pretrial Procedures*

### 9.4.1  Pretrial Procedures and Hearings

Long before a criminal trial can begin, several pretrial procedures and court proceedings need to occur. These are set into motion when the police arrest a person and arrange for him or her to be arraigned by a judge on specific charges. Following arraignment, several types of court hearings may occur depending on the nature of case and decisions made by prosecution and defense attorneys about how to best proceed in what will unfold as an adversarial process designed to promote justice. This subsection provides an overview of that process beginning with what happens when someone is arrested, booked, arraigned, and awaits trial by either a judge or jury.

#### 9.4.1.1  Arrest and Booking.
What happens after an investigation and arrest depends on several circumstances and possible sequences of pretrial events. In misdemeanor cases, an officer usually has the prerogative according to state law

or agency policy to issue a **summons** to appear in court to answer charges on a date to be determined by the court. This is just like receiving a traffic ticket and promising to either pay a fine or appear in court, except that in most criminal matters defendants must appear before a judge initially to declare guilt, innocence, or no contest (which means defendants do not dispute charges against them and give up their right to trial just as if they had plead guilty; this can be important for avoiding blame in a subsequent civil proceeding). If a person is issued and signs a summons promising to appear in court and then fails to do so, a judge will issue an **arrest warrant**. The warrant will be a hardcopy document kept on file by the court and entered into the state's fugitive database and probably the National Crime Information Center (NCIC) system maintained by the FBI. When electronic arrest warrants are issued, a notation is made as to whether the issuing jurisdiction will provide or otherwise pay for **extradition** of a defendant back to the jurisdiction in which charges are pending. Rarely will state and local jurisdictions extradite a person apprehended in another state for an outstanding arrest warrant alleging a single misdemeanor violation.

Police officers usually may also choose whether to physically take a person into custody after arrest. In these instances, persons suspected of committing a crime will be transported to a holding or detention facility, such as a police station or county jail, to be **booked** on specific charges. The term *booked* derives from officers entering the name of person arrested into the prisoner log or arrest book typically maintained in the holding facility. It is there, in the **booking facility**, that the person is photographed, fingerprinted, asked a battery of identification-related questions, given a breath test (in DUI cases), and so on. Frequently a person is also re-interviewed about aspects of a case during booking procedures, assuming of course that he or she has already been advised or is readvised of his or her **Miranda Warnings**. At this time, a suspect may be asked or given an opportunity to provide a written statement about his or her involvement in a crime. After the police are through with booking procedures, a suspect will be allowed to make one or more phone calls to an attorney, employer, family member, friend, and so on. If the person arrested is a juvenile, law enforcement officers are normally required to ensure that a parent or guardian is contacted and informed of their child's arrest status and location. As previously indicted, some jurisdictions also require that in-custody interviews of juveniles or adults be video taped.

### 9.4.1.2 Arraignments.
In misdemeanor cases, a law enforcement officer may cite and release a person following booking procedures by issuing a summons, which when signed by a suspect becomes a promise to appear later in court for **arraignment**. This is often done by suburban law enforcement agencies to save money and time associated with transporting prisoners to a county jail and having to pay for overnight or longer-term housing costs of prisoners awaiting arraignment on the charges against them. Normally a person will be brought before a judge and arraigned within one business day. However, if a person is arrested on a weekend, arraignment may not occur until the following Monday (or Tuesday if it is a holiday weekend—tough luck for some folks). Some large metropolitan jurisdictions, such as those that maintain night and weekend court sessions, allow officers to physically arrest and book prisoners and then immediately transport them to court for an arraignment. This also happens in smaller jurisdictions if there is an opportunity to schedule a person for an arraignment on the same day as the arrest. Some judges in smaller rural jurisdictions are still known to arraign defendants in the evening and on weekends as a public and civic courtesy and as a way to save local law enforcement agencies overnight and weekend prisoner housing costs.

An arraignment is the first court hearing in a criminal case. The **purposes of an arraignment** are for a judge to (1) make a formal determination of probable cause to believe a crime was committed and that the accused committed it; (2) officially notify defendants of the charges against them; (3) advise defendants of their right to confer with an attorney before pleading to any and all charges against them; (4) determine whether defendants are indigent and entitled to a court-appointed lawyer (e.g., a public defender); (5) determine if there are any other outstanding charges or arrest warrants for the defendants and whether or not they are on active probation or parole or away without leave (AWOL) from the military (for which warrants are also issued); (6) hear prosecutor recommendations and defense arguments regarding bail (in felony cases only; see further explanation below); and (7) decide whether to release a defendant pending trial or sentencing and by what means a person should be released (see next paragraph). Note that if a person pleads guilty to a crime, he or she may be sentenced on the spot by the presiding judge and/or remanded to the custody of a law enforcement agency (usually a county sheriffs office) pending completion of a presentencing report. In these situations, defendants will be scheduled to reappear before the judge for sentencing, which may occur several days or even weeks after arraignments in which they plead guilty (or following a trial in which they are convicted).

Here it is important to explain the ways in which a person may be released from custody pending trial or sentencing. Persons charged with *misdemeanor crimes* must normally be either (1) released on their own recognizance (e.g., by signing a summons and promising to appear for later court proceedings); (2) released to a responsible third party (such as a parent or guardian in juvenile cases); or (3) held in custody until they can post bail. An individual's promise to appear for later court proceedings is either explicitly required or implicit in each of these options. **Bail** is an amount of money paid to the court to help guarantee that a defendant will appear for trial. Bail is based on the premise that persons are innocent until proven guilty in court and therefore should not remain in custody unless they present flight risks or are dangers to themselves or others in the community. This is true for both felony and misdemeanor defendants. Bail amounts have nothing to do with punishment (which cannot be imposed unless a person is convicted of a crime) and are often predetermined amounts set equal to the maximum amount of a fine that could be imposed following a conviction on specific charges. For example, if person were to be found guilty of computer trespassing in violation of a state misdemeanor crime law and subject to being fined $500 in addition to being incarcerated for up to a year in jail, bail for their pretrial release might be set at $500. This is not always the case, however, and judges frequently have flexibility to raise or lower bail amounts and even deny people their right to post bail depending on case facts and circumstances.

Bail amounts in felony cases vary considerably more than in misdemeanor cases according to the seriousness of alleged crimes, potential punishments that a person convicted of crimes may receive, and correspondingly higher pretrial flight risks. Persons suspected of murder are usually denied bail. The author once investigated an aggravated assault case in which bail was set at $1 million. A **bail bond** is provided by a private (usually licensed) **bail bond company**, which ordinarily will post the full bail amount with a court on behalf of a defendant. Bail bonds are essentially loans, fully guaranteed with a percentage prepaid in cash (usually 10 percent of the total bail amount) plus collateral in the form of real property. In this way, if a defendant skips bail, the court keeps the bail posted and the bail bond company can sue for claim of the property pledged as collateral. Hence, a word of caution: if you post bail to get a family member or friend out of jail, make sure that person does not skip town, or you will find yourself out your money, your car, your house, or any other property you put up as collateral.

### 9.4.1.3 Preliminary, Grand Jury, and Motion Hearings.

In general, every effort is made within the criminal justice system to process prisoners expeditiously, to ensure that investigative needs and legal rights of defendants are equally accommodated according to statutory and case laws, and to ensure that unnecessary incarceration, associated expenses, delays, and inconvenience to everyone involved are avoided. However, cases involving felony charges normally offer considerably less flexibility to arresting officers and everyone else involved in processing a defendant. Typically police investigators have two choices. They may either arrest and book suspected felons, who will then go through the arraignment process as described above without an immediate right to post bail pre-arraignment or they may file their case for review and formal charging by a designated prosecutorial office. In these situations, depending on state and local laws and customs, the prosecutor in the case may either pursue a grand jury hearing or seek an arrest warrant through a judge and later convene a preliminary hearing after the defendant is arrested, booked, and arraigned. The grand jury or preliminary hearing will determine if sufficient grounds exist to formally charge a defendant with specific felony crimes. Preliminary hearings in misdemeanor cases are also convened in some jurisdictions, but this occurs rarely because of the trouble, time, and expense involved. Conversely, grand juries are only convened for suspected felony crimes.

Although preliminary hearings and grand jury hearings are routinely convened by the jurisdictions who use them, and they have the same outcome (i.e., formal determination of probable cause to charge one or more persons with a crime), these are very different types of proceedings that offer different advantages, primarily to prosecutors who choose which type of hearing they will employ. In brief, a **preliminary hearing** (called a P.H.) is like a mini trial in which the prosecutor calls essential witnesses in a case, including crime victims, police officers, and laboratory technicians such as computer forensics experts, to testify and substantiate that a crime was committed by the accused. Defendants are entitled to be present during a preliminary hearing and to present witnesses or other evidence of their not committing the crimes of which they are accused. Testimony presented at preliminary hearings are transcribed, which is beneficial for documenting peoples' recollection and accounting of events within relatively short periods after crimes have occurred.

**Grand jury proceedings**, in contrast, are usually held in secret, often without defendants knowing they are being investigated for felony crimes. Grand juries often consist of 23 citizen members, who are called to serve in the same manner as other citizens periodically summoned to appear for jury duty. Grand jury hearings are one-sided affairs, with no defendant or defense counsel present, in which the prosecution presents witnesses and other evidence to the empanelled jurors for purposes of securing a **true bill**, which is nothing more than a majority vote by jurors in favor of formally charging the accused with crimes for which there exist probable cause. When this happens, persons suspected of committing felonies are said to have been "indicted." Therefore, an **indictment** is a legal finding by a grand jury of probable criminal wrongdoing. Grand juries may, in rare instances, choose to conduct their own expanded investigations into criminal wrongdoing with judicial guidance and involvement of a prosecutor's office. However, in practice, grand jury proceedings are short hearings, not protracted investigations, and they nearly always result in a true bill and subsequent issuance of felony summons or arrest warrants for persons accused of committing felony crimes.

If a presiding judge at a misdemeanor arraignment or preliminary hearing, or a majority of jurors at a grand jury hearing, finds that there are insufficient grounds to charge a person with the crimes as alleged, the charges will be dismissed and no trial will take place. Otherwise the case will advance to the trial phase and several additional legal hearings may take place. These may involve motions by either the prosecution or defense for discovery or suppression of evidence, dismissal of charges on grounds of insufficient evidence, a continuance or change of trial venue, severance of offenses or defendants (i.e., to consider these in separate hearings or trials), or a bill of particulars having to do with notifying defendants in detail about charges and evidence they are facing. At any time during the pretrial phase, a defendant may elect to plead guilty to the charges levied or to lesser charges in a **plea agreement**. The vast majority of criminal cases are disposed of prior to a trial with plea agreements between prosecutors and defendants in consultation with their attorneys. Plea agreements are generally regarded as a way of saving the state the time, trouble, and expenses associated with criminal trials. Typically, if a defendant agrees to plead guilty to lesser charges, the prosecutor will recommend to the judge that they impose a comparatively lenient sentence.

On February 4, 2005, Jason Smathers of Harpers Ferry, West Virginia, pled guilty in a Manhattan, New York, U.S. District Court to conspiracy in connection with sending an estimated seven billion spam messages to Internet users. Smathers, a former America Online employee who was fired for stealing a list of 92 million AOL multiple email addresses belonging to the firm's 30 million customers, admitted that he accepted $28,000 to help market an offshore Internet gambling service to the AOL members in violation of a federal law prohibiting interstate transportation of stolen property and the nation's CAN-SPAM Act, which was enacted in 2003. Under the plea agreement Smathers faced eighteen months to two years imprisonment and a court order to repay AOL between $200,000 and $400,000 in restitution. In accepting the guilty plea, Federal District Judge Alvin Hellerstein informed Smathers that he personally had discontinued his AOL service because of excessive SPAM. Judges are not obligated to accept either plea agreements or sentencing recommendations made by prosecutors, but they usually do so. If a plea agreement acceptable to both the prosecution and defense or cannot arranged, a case will proceed to trial. In Smather's case, Judge Hallerstein originally rejected a plea agreement in December of 2003 because he was not convinced the defendant had actually violated the CAN-SPAM Act.[50] At final sentencing in August of 2005, twenty-five year old Jason Smathers received a term in federal prison of one year and three months incarceration.[51]

### 9.4.2 Trial Procedures and the Art of Presenting Evidence

During the trial phase of a case police officers and prosecutors present their theory about how and why the accused violated one or more crime laws. In the American criminal justice system, the burden for proving guilt beyond a reasonable doubt is the responsibility of a prosecutor, a trained lawyer who represents the interests of the state. As in the Vargas case described earlier, prosecutors employed or contracted by cities or counties try violations of either municipal, county, or state misdemeanor or felony crime laws. U.S. attorneys prosecute violations of federal crime laws. The court in which a case is heard will depend on issues of legal jurisdiction as discussed in Chapter 8. It is also during the prosecution phase of a case that persons accused of crimes get their proverbial day in court to confront witnesses such as law enforcement officers or other investigators, to challenge and present evidence, and to offer alternative explanations for how a crime may have occurred and who else may be responsible for harm caused during an illegal incident.

Defendants in felony and serious misdemeanor cases prosecuted in the United States are usually represented by an attorney, who may be a public defender if the accused cannot afford to hire a lawyer of his or her own choosing. Sometimes people represent themselves if they desire to do so and convince a judge they are competent to serve as their own legal counsel. Judges scrutinize these requests carefully and typically recommend against self-representation unless a person has legal experience or training. Even then, most people experienced in the law would recommend that people never represent themselves in court, because there are too many legal technicalities, tactical nuances, and other matters that detached and competent council are more likely to be aware of than defendants.

In theory, the job of a prosecutor is more difficult than that of a defense lawyer (or team of attorneys), but in practice most people arrested and formally charged with crimes, and especially cybercriminals, whose cases typically involve substantial amounts of finance-related hardcopy and electronic documentation evidence, either plead guilty or are found guilty. However, as discussed in Chapter 6, the majority of crimes, including white-collar crimes and many other categories of crime involving extensive use of computers or other types of electronic devices, are never reported to police. As well, the majority of nonviolent crimes that are reported never result in an arrest, much less a conviction. This is true of cybercrime cases investigated and prosecuted in foreign nations, as well as in the United States. Nonetheless, the increased attention authorities are paying to threats posed by cybercriminals to IT devices and information systems, coupled with international cooperation for investigation, prosecution, and extradition of cybercriminals is mounting worldwide.

### 9.4.2.1 Bench Trial or Trial by Jury?

Defendants have the right to decide whether their cases will be heard by a judge or by a jury of their peers. It is common practice for defendants to choose the former, which is also known as a bench trial, if they wish to have their cases heard very quickly or if their case involves legal technicalities that a trained judge would recognize and favorably rule on. Bench trials are also often selected in cases where the stakes for an individual are not that high (e.g., not involving much likelihood of incarceration or significant punishment) or when presenting a case to jury is perceived to be

MANILA, PHILIPPINES: Security officials led by Philippine Air Force chief Major General Jose Laroza Reyes (2nd-R) display seized computer and communication equipments used by hackers during a press conference at the air force headquarters, in Manila 20 July 2004. Two Indian nationals, a Bangladeshi and five Filipinos were arrested in series of raids against cyber crime syndicates especializing in hacking into Philippine telecommunications systems to make unauthorized overseas calls. Authorities said the Philippine Long Distance Telephone Co. lost 197 million pesos (3.5 million USD) in income from the cyber crime syndicates. ROMEO GACAD/AFP/Getty Images, Inc.

risky for some reason. Conversely, jury trials can be advantageous to defendants accused of crimes in which the evidence is only circumstantial and relatively weak. Jury trials are also sometimes opted for in cases involving questionable reliability of prosecution witnesses, the appearance of police misconduct, or when the government's prosecution is seen as tantamount a miscarriage of justice. Trial type decisions may also hinge on the background, criminal and civic history, appearance, and mannerisms of defendants, some of whom are naturally innocent-looking and appear forthcoming when answering questions. When it comes to defending against charges of cybercrimes, additional factors that may be considered are the technological and technical aspects of a case (e.g., whether similar criminal actions have previously been prosecuted, the systems and IT complexity involved, and the likelihood that suitable expert witnesses who can explain complicated aspects of a defense can be retained).

The Sixth Amendment guarantees that anyone charged with a crime in the United States is entitled to a trial by an impartial jury. However, defendants opting for a trial by jury will be required through their attorney to provide a speedy trial waiver to allow the court scheduling time. During this period, which may take several weeks, the defense will prepare its case even as the accused may be ordered by the judge to remain in custody pending trial. Historically the jury trial system has been praised and critiqued by legal observers and the general public.

Proponents point out that jury impartiality can be controlled with from the onset by court ordered excusal of jurors based on their personal or professional backgrounds (e.g., working in law enforcement), and by careful instructions to and oversight of jurors as provided by judges during trials. Controlling the makeup of juries also occurs through **voir dire questioning** of prospective jurors just before a trial begins, during which defense lawyers and prosecutors have a certain number (usually three) of **peremptory challenges** that they may exercise to have prospective

jurors excused for any reason whatsoever. In addition, the attorneys for the state or defense may ask a judge to excuse a prospective juror for cause, as when a person is unable to serve impartially because of his or her philosophical beliefs. In addition, both defendants and prosecutors are allowed to choose jurors with specific or varying backgrounds (e.g., knowledge of computers, electronic devices, and information systems). Potential jury bias attributable to community demographics may result in the granting of a change in trial venue.

Critics of jury trials insist that only people who are similar to a defendant and who may have had their own experiences with the criminal justice system are capable of rendering a fair verdict. Opponents also point out that most people regard jury duty as an inconvenience that may negatively impact their ability to earn money. Many people summoned to appear for jury duty (usually on the basis of having registered to vote) attempt to be and sometimes are excused from serving by a court administrator or judge for various reasons. Consequently, jurors available and actually selected for duty in a given trial tend not to include persons who must maintain a business or work at one or more jobs, adult students, severely handicapped persons, and the very wealthy who claim that executive responsibilities preclude their serving. Police officers, other criminal justice employees, and their family members are also often excused from serving on juries as a matter of course. Opponents of the jury trial system also point out that in addition to not being truly representative of communities, individual jurors and even entire juries can be fickle in their judgments about evidence and may even base their decisions regarding guilt or innocence on the appearance or mannerisms of defendants or lawyers involved in a case. In numerous cases juries were discovered after a trial to have followed their hearts or their own senses of justice rather than the law as instructed by the presiding judge. Furthermore, jurors do not equally pay attention during trials (the author has even witnessed a juror sleeping during witness testimony), nor do all jurors weigh evidence carefully and deliberate responsibly. In extended or complicated trials, there may be a sense of exasperation, especially if jurors are cloistered during the trial. In these instances, less committed jurors will often think, if not say outright, "Lets just get this over with and get back to our normal lives." All such possibilities need to be considered when deciding between bench and jury trials *before* a trial commences.

When it comes to picking members of a jury, lawyers for the prosecution and defense desire to weigh the need for computer-savvy jurors versus individuals who know relatively little to nothing about electronic devices, data, and information systems. Can you imagine situations when a defense team may not want a jury to know too much about how computers work? Conversely, can you imagine technically complicated cases where the defense or prosecuting attorneys would desire jurors to know a considerable amount about the inner workings of computer systems? During voir dire it may be essential to question prospective members of a jury regarding their personal use of computers and other types of electronic devices in order to determine how capable they are of understanding technical computer forensics evidence. A juror employed as a computer programmer or IT administrator may be capable of helping other members of the jury to understand the intricacies and the meaning of electronic evidence during deliberations.

A jury will often rely on one or two of its members to interpret testimony on foreign subjects. Even though this sort of auxiliary expert testimony is not acceptable conduct, it does occur sometimes in overt or subtle ways simply because it must. Suppose a cybercrime case involves possession of child pornography and the defense posits a Trojan horse scenario wherein the illegal pornography could have been planted by an unidentified suspect. A technically illiterate juror may develop reasonable doubt of the defendant's guilt based upon their personal suspicions of Internet viruses and intrusions—this despite testimony provided by a computer forensic analyst that a thorough examination turned up no malware. Nonetheless, the computer-illiterate juror may think to himself, "This could happen to me" and disregard the facts as presented during the trial. Then again, a jury that is computer literate may not duly consider certain evidence on the grounds that it did not meet their understanding of the technology involved.

### 9.4.2.2 Courtroom Procedures.

Trials begin with **opening statements** made by the prosecution and defense. During opening statements the prosecution describes, from its point of view, how crimes occurred and what it intends to prove with respect to the defendant's motive, opportunity, and means to violate the law. An opening statement by the defense always follows that given by the prosecution and may, at the discretion of defense attorneys, occur after prosecutors have presented all their evidence and rested their case. It is intended to provide an alternative explanation for how a crime may have occurred and an overview of evidence that will be presented to prove a defendant's innocence. Opening statements are carefully crafted, because it is here that jurors formulate their first impressions of a case, the defendant, and lawyers involved on both sides.

Opening statements are followed by the prosecution's **presenting witnesses**, usually in an order that chronologically explains how a crime and its investigation occurred. The first witness called by the prosecution in its **direct examination** is usually the crime victim or person who discovered or first reported a crime to the police. These witnesses are typically followed by questioning of law enforcement officers who originally responded to, observed, or investigated the crime. Laboratory and expert witnesses are often called next to provide the technical details needed to substantiate the validity of evidence and so on. After each witness testifies on behalf of the prosecution, the defense is allowed to **cross examine** about any topic already brought up or alluded to during direct examination by the prosecutor. As witnesses testify, each item of evidence is introduced, and if it is admitted by the judge into evidence, jurors will be allowed to see it up close and even handle it. After the prosecution has presented all of its witnesses and evidence, it will rest its case, and the defense will be allowed to present its witnesses and evidence. When the defense rests its case, the prosecution may call rebuttal witnesses, and then the defense may also call rebuttal witnesses.

During questioning, both prosecutors and defense lawyers are allowed to object to questions asked by the opposing counsel on several grounds (e.g., an item or topic has not yet been recognized or admitted into evidence by the judge, answering would require a witness to speculate, or the form of a question is leading a witness to answer in a biased way). Counsel on either side may also object to evidence being introduced on various grounds (e.g., that it is not relevant, that suitable foundation for it to be considered as evidence has not been established, that it would unduly bias the jury, etc.). Judges are required to either sustain or overrule objections pertaining to testimony or evidence of any kind. In the process, the judge may ask counsel to approach his or her bench in the courtroom to discuss or quietly argue subtleties of law that jurors are not allowed to hear. If a complicated legal issue is involved, a judge may temporarily recess the court and confer with the lawyers in chambers before making a ruling. Judges also periodically grant recesses for other reasons as they oversee and manage court proceedings and keep a trial on schedule. Remember, many cases are being processed by the courts, so it is important to keep a trial moving forward at a steady pace.

### 9.4.2.3 Presenting Evidence at Trial.
Trials are all about presenting the most credible, legally obtained evidence in convincing ways. Testimony provided by witnesses is invariably the primary source of evidence in any trial, although it may not always be the most convincing. Jurors judge witnesses according their appearances, what they say in relation to facts already in evidence, their responsiveness to questions asked of them, and their mannerisms and reactions to statements made to or about them. The value of testimony comes down to the believability of witnesses. To this end prosecution and defense attorneys interview their own witnesses prior to trial and make suggestions for how they should talk about issues but not what they should say, as that would constitute the crime of witness tampering. For example, it is common for prosecutors to remind police officers to speak to the jury when answering questions and to make eye contact with individual jurors in order to convey their truthfulness about investigative matters. Witnesses may testify to anything they personally know, but they may not normally comment on things they heard from someone else, as that would constitute **hearsay** and not be admissible as evidence.

Persons who qualify in court as **expert witnesses** may testify about what they know personally and give opinions on matters that directly pertain to their areas of expertise. Thus, computer forensics experts may explain what they discovered in the course of analyzing a system, explain how particular software works, or express an opinion as to why an electronic device was used on the basis of the evidence at hand. To qualify as an expert witness a person will normally be required to possess extensive education, professional training, and experience. It may be necessary for experts to produce documentation of their qualifications prior to or during court. When investigators and experts such as computer forensics experts testify, it is important that they answer questions directly and speak slowly and in plain language easily understood by everyone in court. If technical computing terms are referenced, they should be immediately explained so that jurors, attorneys, and the judge are not confused. Investigators should also be careful not to volunteer information but to answer just the questions being asked and trust that the attorneys who subpoenaed them to testify know what they are doing. However, with regard to technical matters, it can be useful prior to a trial for an expert to help a prosecutor or defense attorney understand what to ask and why.

The best witness may, in a manner of speaking, be the electronic devices used to perpetrate crimes, although it is difficult to get these to actually take the stand and testify about what they know! In a sense, however, the device testifies by proxy through investigators and computer forensic analysts who take the witness stand to interpret what an electronic gadget or information would say if it could. Therefore, a significant part of any trial preparation is for the prosecutor to understand the technology involved in the cybercrime and figure out how it can best be described in plain English to the judge and jury. A number of logistical issues must also be considered during preparation for trial. For example, getting expert testimony may require locating and arranging for payment and travel of qualified witnesses who can validate particular computing processes. Sometimes hardware and software firms will supply such expertise at no cost as way to guard against ill-repute stemming from the abuse of a company product. Other experts may require remuneration for their professional testimony. Both prosecution and defense attorneys must also be aware that presenting electronic evidence in court may require special provisions for computer equipment to be set up in courtrooms (e.g., digital projectors, projection screens, network connections, and additional sources of electrical power).

As for actually proving a case beyond a reasonable doubt, note that every criminal statute contains at least two elements: a culpable mental state and an overt act. Having already discussed culpable mental states, let us now consider types of overt actions that must also be proven in cybercrime trials. Practically every cybercrime involves accessing data (also known as computer-related

material). What is done to the data by the perpetrator will ordinarily constitute the overt act prohibited by law. Whether the data is accessed, copied, moved, altered, or added to illegally will often depend on the degree of system rights and privileges possessed by the defendant at the time of the cybercrime. Thus, once the electronic evidence trail has been followed to implicate the defendant, it is still necessary for investigators and prosecutors at trial to legally establish their employee, access, and data possession or ownership rights and privileges, as well as put the defendant in control of affected computers or other electronic devices and media at the time of offense.

This is when having documented insider system users' rights and privileges during an investigation will really pay off. Authorized use and nondisclosure agreements, employee manuals and training records, intellectual property agreements, splash screens, log-in warnings, user names, and passwords are significant for determining legal rights to access and manipulate data as well as for establishing a defendant's culpable mental state at trial. Meanwhile, for a suspect who hacks into the system, a history of due care applications, security patches, and countermeasures to prevent intrusion can be critical evidence to establish that the rights and privileges to externally access a given system by an unauthorized defendant. Organizational policies that explicitly deny rights and privileges to unauthorized people may also provide excellent evidence in court.

Next, unauthorized and illegal access to a victim's system and data must be proven. Suspecting a hack occurred, establishing that a hack actually occurred, and showing in court who is responsible for particular hacking violations are very different legal challenges. Fortunately for investigators and prosecutors, even in cases of simple computer trespass, it is nearly impossible for a cybercriminal to enter a computer system without generating or altering data in some way. In many cases of intruder attacks a system administrator "plugs the hole" and will not report the hacking unless there is a significant loss of data, a major security compromise, or substantial computer or network loss while repairs are made. This course of action is risky because it presumes that all tampering can be discovered. Even so, illegal trespassing into a system or exceeding of authorized access permissions can usually be determined through an analysis of logs, comparing system benchmarks, or comparing backup tapes or other media. Of course this is only possible if such data are recorded and maintained.

In other types of cases, possession of electronic contraband, whether it is copies of forged documents, counterfeit currency images, or child pornography, will weigh more heavily. Regardless of the type of physical and electronic evidence involved in a case, showing that a defendant had exclusive rights and privileges, was not authorized to access systems or certain data, or was in possession of contraband will often be the crux of a cybercrime prosecution. Thus, the electronic trail that led investigators to each suspect charged with crimes will need to be demonstrated in court. Internet usage by logged-in users coupled with paths of downloaded and saved digital contraband files to user-created folders is one example. Log-in user names with links to print media and paths to forged instruments is another example of how electronic evidence trails can lead to cybercrime suspects.

After all the witnesses and evidence are presented in a trial, lawyers for the prosecution and defense will provide their **closing arguments**. The defense always presents their closing before the prosecution, and it is important to note that closing arguments may only summarize a case and facts in evidence and point out the strengths, weaknesses, or inconsistencies of testimony and evidence admitted by the judge. Following closing arguments, the judge will give the jury instructions on the law and how they must go about rendering a verdict. Afterwards juries retire to deliberate the case. During deliberations jurors are allowed to review witness statements that have been entered into evidence, including,

for example, police reports and confessions made by the defendant. There are no limits on how short or long deliberations can be, although judges will keep close track of a jury's progress and will answer questions of law that may arise (this occurs rarely). Juries often decide cases within an hour. Other times they may deliberate for several days.

### 9.4.3 Trial Verdicts, Sentencing Policies, and Appeals

Juries are required to render a **verdict** of guilt or innocence on every charge by a unanimous vote. If jurors become deadlocked and unable to reach a unanimous decision, judges will ordinarily instruct them to further consider evidence and may also explain that obstinate jurors for or against a conviction may need to articulate, on the basis of the evidence, why they believe as they do. If after further deliberations a jury remains deadlocked (known as a **hung jury**), the trial will be declared a draw. Prosecutors then have the right to retry the case on behalf of the state, but they are not obligated to do so. If defendants are found innocent, they are immediately free to leave the court unless charges are pending in other jurisdictions, and they may never again be charged for the same crimes by the same court system. However, if they are found guilty of one or more crimes defendants may continue to be held or they may be immediately taken into custody by a court, released on their own recognizance, or released to a third party pending sentencing.

#### 9.4.3.1 Purposes of Offender Sanctions.
On March 7, 2005, Parvin Dhaliwal became the first person in the United States sentenced to jail for illegally downloading and selling music. In a deal struck with prosecutors, the eighteen-year-old student, who was seventeen at the time of his crimes, received a three-month suspended jail sentence. In addition, he was sentenced to 200 hours of community service, fined $5,400, and required to take a course on copyright law at the

University of Arizona. On top of that he was given three years probation and ordered not to use peer-to-peer file sharing applications. Although illegally downloading music is a violation of federal copyright law, U.S. attorneys referred the case to the Maricopa County Prosecutor's Office in Phoenix, as a way to avoid mandatory incarceration of the youth. In addition, by prosecuting the low-level felony in a state-level court, the copyright charge against Dhaliwal could be reduced to a misdemeanor after he successfully completing probation (in 2008).[52]

The Dhaliwal case indicates the considerable variety of sentences that a person convicted of committing crimes may receive. Sentences are often intended to accomplish several purposes, including (1) **punishment** of the offender, (2) **compensation** to crime victims for their financial losses and other types of harm experienced, (3) **retribution** on behalf of crime victims and society, along with a sense that justice has prevailed, (4) **deterrence** of others who would commit similar crimes, (5) **protection** of crime victims and other people from being further harmed by offenders, (6) **rehabilitation** of offenders through education and training, as well as through counseling and drug treatment when required, and (7) **restoration** of offenders as law-abiding and contributing members of society who, having been truly reformed, are accepted by or back into caring communities to lead crime-free lives.

Formal sentencing is normally preceded by a presentence report and sufficient time for a judge to reflect on the nature of crimes committed, the harm experienced by victims and others including family members, and the criminal history, motivations, criminal actions, attitudes, and likelihood of re-offending by the defendant. Prosecutors and defense attorneys will normally make sentencing recommendations, and in some jurisdictions juries may be permitted or required to make sentencing recommendations to a trial judge. On April 8, 2005, Jeremy Jaynes of Ralieigh, North Carolina, was sentenced on the recommendation of a jury to nine years' imprisonment for running a spamming operation that specialized in selling pornography and fraudulent products and services including a Federal Express refund processor. The operation, which grossed as much as $750,000 per month in sales, sent millions of spam email and advertisements via an America Online server located in at the firm's headquarters in Loudoun County, Virginia, where the prosecution also took place. Because the conviction was the first such in United States resulting in a prison term, Loudoun County Circuit Court Judge Thomas Horne decided to postpone Jaynes' incarceration until defense attorneys can appeal the case on constitutional grounds.[53]

As we have stressed throughout this book, legal violations of laws that are defined as cybercrimes on the basis of the technology used in their commission range in harm caused and may be either misdemeanors or felonies. As a rule, cybercrimes do not *directly* result in physical injury or death to crime victims and in many cases cause financial harm and/or may also be considered white-collar, financial, or organized crime. Thus, sentencing for crimes in which computers or other electronic devices are used via information systems vary greatly. Historically, individuals convicted of classic computer-enabled crimes such as hacking, piracy, and Web site vandalism have received what many observers feel are lenient sentences. (Do you think the sentences imposed in the cases mentioned in this chapter were too lenient, fair to too harsh?). In recent years this has been steadily changing as the result of the number and variety of cybercrimes committed, the increasing amounts and varieties of harm caused, and the threats posed by the actions of cybercriminals to critical information infrastructures that are seen as potential aspects of the war on terrorism and the need to crack down on cyber offenders while deterring cyberterrorists.

### 9.4.3.2 Indeterminate versus Structured Sentencing Policies. Sentencing of cybercriminals

is geared differently by states and the federal government according to **indeterminate and structured sentencing policies**. What does this mean? Prior to the 1970s federal and state courts imposed widely ranging sentences for all types of crimes, such as ten to twenty years imprisonment for burglary, that depended on myriad case circumstance. In addition, the amount of time actually served by offenders, irrespective of their sentence, varied greatly according to their behavior while incarcerated, determinations by parole boards regarding offender rehabilitation progress, and prison overcrowding conditions. During this period there was growing recognition throughout the United States that in many cases early release decisions by parole boards were unfortunately based on an offender's race and resulted in inherently unequal potentials for offenders to quickly acquire gainful employment that, it was hoped, would help prevent recidivism. There was also wide recognition that a majority of offenders committed crimes even while on active parole, thus indicating a level of failure in corrections policies. In the 1980s, fueled by the war on drugs and widespread violent crime, a get tough on crime and criminals mood pervaded most of the United States, resulting in vigorous prison construction in many jurisdictions.

Also during this general period, some states began to abolish their parole systems and replace indeterminate sentencing practices with four new types of structured sentencing policies: (1) **determinate sentencing**, consisting of legislatively mandated fixed terms of incarceration with time off allowed good behavior while in prison, (2) **advisory sentencing guidelines**, consisting of sentences recommended by advisory boards to judges on the basis of past sentencing practices, (3) **presumptive sentencing**, consisting of compulsory guidelines established by law or sentencing commissions that judges are required to follow as when imposing sanctions unless they articulate exceptional circumstances justifying a deviation from what the legislature or commission, and thus the people, expect offenders to receive for their

crimes; and (4) **mandatory sentencing**, in which all judicial discretion is removed, such as exists under three-strikes laws that require life imprisonment without possibility of parole for offenders convicted of three felonies. Although structured sentencing policies are intended to compensate for arguably lenient sentencing and early release practices under indeterminate sentencing policies, structured sentencing policies, and especially mandatory sentencing, are often criticized because they prevent judges from adequately considering aggravating and mitigating circumstances in all cases and generally matching punishments imposed to crimes actually committed. Today there remains substantial variance within the federal court system and among states with regard to their sentencing policies and actual types and levels of offender sanctioning, as well as with regard to early-release decision criteria and methods of postrelease supervision.

*9.4.3.3 Appeals.*    An **appeal** is a challenge to the ruling of a trial court or an appellate court. As a general rule, a litigant has an automatic right of appeal to the intermediate level appellate court but must apply for the right to appeal to the highest level of appellate court. In other words, the U.S. Supreme court and the highest appellate-level state courts are generally not obligated to hear any case, although death penalty cases are legally mandated for appellate court review in most states. If application for appeal is denied by the U.S. Supreme Court or its state-level equivalent, the intermediate appellate court's decision is the final resolution of the dispute. If an appeal is accepted for review, the highest court's decision establishes case precedent by deciding the issues presented by the litigants. A litigant with a final decision at the highest state appellate court may apply to the United States Court if the litigant's legal issue involves a federal law or an interpretation of the U.S. Constitution. Appellate courts do not retry cases per se. For instance, they do not listen to the testimony of witnesses or examine physical evidence of a crime. Instead, the role of state and federal appellate courts is to ensure that the law was properly administered at the trial court level.

## 9.5 Summary

When cybercrimes are committed, investigators and prosecutors, along with other elements of the criminal justice system, respond into action. Many federal, state, and local government agencies, along with private sector firms and nonprofit organizations now collaborate to protect information systems, investigate incidents involving abuse of computers and other electronic devices, and prevent cybercrimes. Partnerships between government agencies, private sector firms, academic institutions, and professional membership associations all contribute to the growing need for effective and comprehensive electronic crime fighting. There is an important distinction between the investigative roles of public law enforcement officers and private and nonprofit sector information security professionals and investigators. Whereas police officers, also known as peace officers, investigate crimes on behalf of government agencies and are empowered to arrest suspected law violators, other information security professionals focus on cases of computer abuse within organizational settings. Some large government jurisdictions have established dedicated cybercrime investigation and prosecution units to manage the growing number of criminal cases involving unlawful use of computers and other types of electronic devices.

The overriding goal in all cybercrime investigations is to discover, collect, analyze, and present in court evidence of crimes committed by individuals or groups of offenders. Evidentiary challenges faced by investigators and prosecutors pertain to establishing the motive, opportunity, and means of crime suspects to violate crime laws. It is also essential that investigators and prosecutors determine the criminal intent and culpable mental states of law violators, as this will dictate the level of crimes and specific laws that a person can be charged with violating. The four culpable mental states specified in crime laws pertain to committing crimes *intentionally* and with premeditation, *knowingly* with foreknowledge that behaving illegal is wrong, with *reckless* indifference to causing harm, or with *negligence,* as in cases in which a person should have known that his or her actions would cause harm. These states of guilty mind reflect decreasing levels of criminal culpability and thus less significant violations of crime laws.

Police officers and prosecutors are also concerned with undertaking physical and cyber monitoring and surveillance operations in the course of their investigations. Whereas monitoring of open public spaces is routinely accomplished using a variety of technology to detect and prevent crime, surveillance involves targeted watching of persons suspected of abusing IT or committing cybercrimes. Surveillance can be an effective means of gathering evidence, although police investigators must be continually aware of statutory and case laws governing their search for and seizure of evidence. The exclusionary rule is an important legal principle that requires police to obtain a search warrant before looking in protected locations for evidence of crimes, with several notable exceptions. Regular search warrants and electronic monitoring warrants are different legal instruments that authorize law enforcement officers to conduct different types of evidence-gathering operations in the course of criminal investigations. The nature of the investigation and the scope of the warrant will dictate the parameters of any search in physical and cyber environments.

An important concept regarding response to and processing of crime scenes for evidence is that cybercrimes invariably involve physical and electronic evidence. Investigators who discover crimes or respond to reports of crimes must exercise tactical precautions to ensure their own safety and guard against contaminating evidence.

Securing and evaluating crime scenes, inclusive of computers, other electronic devices, and information systems must be done efficiently so that evidence is not lost and persons suspected of crimes who may be present at the time of the search are properly controlled and not allowed to interfere with investigations. Prudent case law rulings and decisions by officers about these matters will always depend on all the circumstances with respect to the nature of evidentiary items sought versus reasonable expectations of privacy by everyone who has data contained within an information system. Investigators will often make notifications about certain types of crimes being investigated, including to computer forensics and other types of technical assistance experts capable of helping process crime scenes for evidence. Whenever physical or electronic evidence of criminal wrongdoing is found, it must be carefully located within the scene and processed with careful attention to documenting the chain of custody. This is important during field collection and laboratory analysis of evidence such as occurs during computer forensics examinations of hardware, software, and data.

Victims and witnesses of crime, as well as suspected offenders, subject matter experts, and other people familiar with aspects of a case may all provide important information needed by investigators to solve crimes. Testimonial evidence is provided throughout investigations orally and in writing and will later become the primary basis through which prosecutors present their cases in court. Interviewing persons with knowledge of cybercrime or the technology used in their commission requires preparation and substantial legal knowledge regarding the admissibility of statements and different ways of legally eliciting information from people. Effective interviewing is an art form that requires an understanding of human nature and outstanding communication skills. Acquiring background information about persons suspected of crimes, and planning the time, location, and who should be present during an interview, among other issues, are also important considerations. Investigators must also possess a working knowledge of computer-related terminology used by IT professionals and criminals in order to understand the technical aspects of cybercrimes.

Procedures for arresting and prosecuting cybercriminals are well established in law and by policies and working agreements of criminal justice agencies. Persons the police suspect of committing crimes are typically taken into custody, booked, and then scheduled for an arraignment. At arraignments defendants are formally apprised of the charges against them, afforded legal counsel and allowed to enter a plea. Case circumstances will dictate whether a person is remanded to custody to await trial or released on his or her own recognizance, to a third party, or allowed to post bail. During the pretrial phase investigators will continue to conduct interviews, collect additional evidence, and arrange for computer forensics and other crime lab analysis. Prosecutors meanwhile must confirm what specific laws have been violated, evaluate legal aspects of crime cases, and interact with defense attorneys to establish an acceptable plea agreement. If a case is destined for trial, attorneys will seek one or more motion hearings that may pertain to the admissibility of evidence, severance of charges or defendants in a case, or other legal matters.

Defendants are legally entitled to choose a trial by judge or jury, each having certain advantages depending on the nature of the case. Jurors are selected from a pool of citizens subpoenaed to appear for jury duty who have not been excused by a court administrator or trial judge. Trial procedures include opening statements made by prosecutors and defense lawyers. These are followed by the prosecution presenting its case by calling witnesses, usually in a way that provides a chronological explanation for how and why crimes occurred. When the prosecution has rested its case, the defense is then permitted to present its case. Witnesses called by the prosecution and defense are directly questioned and may also be cross examined. Investigators and prosecutors who present evidence in court must do so in ways that comply with rules of evidence established in law and administered by judges in the interest of serving justice on behalf of the state and with regard to the rights of the accused. Judges are also responsible for ruling on objections made by attorneys during trials, and for ensuring that trials are carried out in an orderly manner and kept on schedule. Jurors have the responsibility to render verdicts of guilt or innocence on each specific charge of criminal wrongdoing. If a jury becomes deadlocked and is unable to reach a verdict, a new trial may or may not ensue at the discretion of a prosecutor.

Judges sentence persons convicted of crimes according to the statutory seriousness of offenses, extent of harm caused, criminal history of the offenders, and other mitigating and aggravating factors. Historically persons convicted of cybercrimes as opposed to violent crimes resulting in

deaths or physical injuries received relatively lenient punishment. This is now changing as the number of cybercrimes and the harm caused by cybercriminals throughout society have increased and in the context of potential cyberterrorism that threatens to affect critical information infrastructures. Also, increasing numbers of people are being investigated and prosecuted for many different types of cybercrimes. This movement represents an important sea change in how cybercrimes are seen and managed by the criminal justice system. Sentencing practices and policies are governed by indeterminate or structured sentencing policies established in states and within the federal government. Since 1970 a get tough on crime mood as swept over much of the United States, resulting in a shift toward determinate, presumptive, and mandatory sentencing policies designed to decrease the flexibility that judges have in sentencing.

## Key Terms and Concepts

Administrative records, 360
Advisory sentencing guidelines, 398
Affidavit, 357
Appeal, 398
Arraignment, 387
Arrest warrant, 386
Bail, 388
Bail bond, 388
Bail bond company, 388
Best evidence rule, 374
Booked, 387
Booking facility, 387
Chain of custody, 373
Circumstantial evidence, 372
Closing arguments, 396
Compensation, 397
Computer forensics, 375
Computer-created files, 370
Crime scene, 362
Cross examine, 394
Culpability, 343
Cybercrime scene, 362
Demonstrative evidence, 373

Determinate sentencing, 398
Deterrence, 397
Direct examination, 393
Electronic evidence, 369
Exclusionary rule of evidence, 351
Exculpatory evidence, 380
Expert witnesses, 394
Extradition, 387
Fruit of the poisonous tree doctrine, 351
Grand jury proceedings, 389
Hearsay, 394
Hung jury, 396
Image, 378
Indeterminate and structured, 398
Investigative and arrest powers, 335
Sentencing
Indictment, 389
Intentionally, 343
Internet Protocol (IP) addresses, 378
Inventory, 357

Investigative hunch, 346
Junk science, 376
Knowingly, 343
MD5 hash value, 378
Mandatory sentencing, 398
Means to commit a crime, 343
Mens rea, 342
Miranda Warnings, 387
Monitoring, 350
Morphing, 371
Motives for committing cybercrimes, 342
Negligently, 343
Opening statements, 393
Operation Web Snare, 350
Opportunity to commit crimes, 343
Other data, 370
Peace officer, 347
Peremptory challenges, 392
Physical evidence, 368
Plea agreement, 389
Preliminary hearing, 389
Preponderance of evidence, 349

Presenting witnesses, 393
Presumptive sentencing, 398
Probable cause, 348
Proof beyond a reasonable
   doubt, 349
Protection, 397
Punishment, 397
Purposes of an arraignment, 387
Reasonable suspicion, 347
Recklessly, 343

Rehabilitation, 397
Restoration, 397
Retribution, 397
Spontaneous utterance, 382
Structured sentencing
Subpoena, 360
Summons, 386
Surveillance, 350
Telephonic search warrants, 358
Testimonial evidence, 372

Transactional records, 360
True bill, 389
User-created files, 369
User-protected files, 370
Verdict, 396
Voir dire questioning, 392
Voluntary consent, 360
Warrant, 357

## *Critical Thinking and Discussion Questions* _____

1. Refer to Appendix A for the Web home page for the High Tech Crime Investigator's Association, then go online to find the HTCIA chapter nearest your school and home town. Pick one of these chapters. Describe its basic mission, activities and collaboration with other local, state and federal law enforcement agencies.

2. Many authors of malware create their code for the sheer intellectual challenge of doing so. For them there is nothing better than inventing something that is really cool, unlike anything previous, and to which they can embed their own coding signature in some way. How would you classify the culpable mental state of code writers who distribute harmful programs onto the Internet?

3. The Electronic Crime Needs Assessment published by the U.S. Department of Justice found that most electronic crimes get low to middle priority attention within state and local law enforcement agencies. Responding participants in the study mentioned that although management realizes a cybercrime problem exists, they don't know what to do about it. When cybercrime is investigated, child pornography and exploitation cases nearly always get higher priorities. Explain how social and managerial issues affect resource allocations for dedicated investigation and prosecution of cybercrimes.

4. Refer to Appendix A for the Web site home page for the CERT Coordination Center, the Cyber Division of the FBI, the High Tech Crime Investigators Association, the National White Collar Crime Center, the SANS Institute, the U.S. Computer Emergency Readiness Team, and the USDOJ Computer Crime and Intellectual Property Section. Visit three of these organizational Web sites to discover something new or interesting that the agency is doing or involved. Report your findings.

5. Review the crime scene photos displayed earlier in the chapter. Do you believe that someone with only an IT background could adequately investigate the crimes portrayed and discussed? Explain why or why not. Conversely, would someone with only a criminal justice background have sufficient expertise to be able to process such crime scenes?

6. Referring to the crime scene photos displayed earlier in the chapter, pick out examples of evidence where IT and other investigative knowledge, skills, and expertise could be beneficial.

7. Do some online research to discover training programs, conferences, and other opportunities for investigators and prosecutors to learn more about cybercrime and information security issues. Briefly describe three examples with regard to who sponsors the training, what it cover and costs, and when and where criminal justice and information security professionals may attend.

8. Briefly define the key elements and authority and purposes of the investigative hunch, reasonable suspicion, and probable cause. Provide a hypothetical example of each of these levels of proof.

9. Briefly explain the difference between intentionally, knowingly, recklessly, and negligently committing crimes. Provide a hypothetical example of a cybercrime involving each of these guilty states of mind.

10. Explain basic challenges and precautions involved with collecting evidence at crime scenes. What is meant by the "chain of custody"?

11. List, define, and provide examples of physical, electronic, testimonial, circumstantial, and demonstrative evidence.

12. Provide two hypothetical examples of exceptional circumstances in which police officers would not be required to acquire a search warrant before looking for evidence in a location in which people have reasonable expectations of privacy.

13. What are the basic purposes of and differences between search warrants, arrest warrants, subpoenas, and summons? Explain how an electronic monitoring warrant differs from an ordinary search warrant.

14. Explain the basic challenges faced by investigators, expert witnesses, and prosecutors when presenting complex technical evidence to average unskilled jurors and judges?

15. What kind of impact do you suppose technically skilled law enforcement officers have on the average citizen? Do you believe that having more officers with technical skills would help prevent computer crimes to an extent that the public would take notice? How does public opinion influence creation and management of computer crime investigation and prosecution units?

16. Computers are becoming smaller, faster, and more powerful. They are also integrated into more devices, systems, and infrastructure. Currently it is possible to purchase a refrigerator with a built-in screen for World Wide Web access, and other home appliances are also available for incorporation into newly constructed or retrofitted "smart houses." What kind of security risks might these devices pose? As computers become more integrated into our daily lives, how does the job of computer crime law enforcement units change? Provide two specific examples.

17. Go online to the National Criminal Justice Reference Service (NCJRS) located at www.ncjrs.org. Locate a copy of Electronic Crime Scene Investigation Guidebook published by the National Institute of Justice in 2001. Review the booklet and then provide examples of old technology and new types of technology not listed as potential evidence. What do you conclude?

18. In 2004 the Recording Industry Association of America initiated "Jane/John Doe" lawsuits in which the real names of persons accused of copyright infringement via peer-to-peer file sharing was not known. Instead, an IP address was listed in court documents filed by the RIAA, which insisted that an IP address could be used as a unique identifier for file sharers. Write a short paper arguing for or against this practice on the basis of legal and evidentiary implications. Comment on what basis such cases would stand up in criminal and civil proceedings.

19. Explain the purposes of an arraignment and differing investigative and procedural circumstances that may lead up to the convening of this type of hearing.

20. Describe the basic differences between preliminary hearings and grand jury hearings. Under what conditions may these two alternative approaches to considering criminal cases be employed? What are the advantages to each approach?

21. Refer to Appendix A and locate the URL for the U.S. Department of Justice Computer Crime and Intellectual Property Section. Go to the section home page and review several examples of prosecuted cybercrimes. List the two least and two most substantial punishments imposed on cybercriminals. Then explain how these sentences compare in your view to the relative seriousness of the crimes committed. What do you conclude?

## References and Endnotes

1. Musil, S. (2005, February 21). Paris Hilton's cell phone hacked? Retrieved February 27, 2005, from http://news.com.com/Paris+Hiltons+cell+phone+hacked/2100-7349_3-5584691.html.

2. *United States of America v. Janet Bifield et al.* U.S. District Court for the Middle District of Pennsylvania (Indictment/Case no. 4:CR-97-0195); and/or 42 F. Supp. 2d 477 via 1999 U.S. Dist. LEXIS 3663 (1999).

3. President's Commission on Critical Infrastructure Protection. (1997, October). *Critical Foundations: Protecting America's Infrastructures.* Final report of the President's Commission on Critical Infrastructure Protection. Washington, DC: Government Printing Office.

4. Reiss, A.J. (1988). *Private Employment of Public Police.* Washington, DC: National Institute of Justice.

5. Greenemeier, L. (2005, August 24). New cybersecurity center to warn law enforcement of critical infrastructure attacks. Retrieved online August 26, 2005 from http://informationweek.com/story/show Article. jhtml?articleID=170000319.

6. U.S. Secret Service. (2004). *Electronic Crimes Task Forces.* U.S. Department of Homeland Security. Retrieved December 24, 2004, from http://www.ectaskforce.org/Regional_Locations.htm.

7. Federal Emergency Management Agency. (2003). Guarding against disaster fraud. U.S. Department of Homeland Security. News release No. 1490-59. Retrieved January 3, 2005, from http://www.fema.gov/news/newsrelease.fema?id=6348.

8. McEwen, J.T., Fester, D., & Nugent, H. (1989). *Dedicated Computer Crime Units.* Washington, DC: National Institute of Justice.

9. CERT Coordination Center. (2005). CERT home page. Retrieved March 5, 2003, from http://www.cert.org/.

10. Federal Bureau of Investigation. (2005). FBI Cyber Division investigative and prevention programs.

Retrieved March 27, 2005, from http://www.fbi.gov/cyberinvest cyberhome.htm.

11. High Technology Crime Investigation Association. (2003). HTCIA home page. Retrieved March 27, 2005, from http://www.htcia.org/.

12. Interpol. (2005). Interpol home page. Retrieved April 21, 2005, from http://www.interpol.int/Public/Icpo/default.asp.

13. National White Collar Crime Center . (2005). NW3C home page. Retrieved March 27, 2005, from http://www.nw3c.org/.

14. SANS Institute. (2005). SANS home page. Retrieved March 27, 2005, from http://www.sans.org/aboutsans.php.

15. U.S. Department of Homeland Security. (2004, November 22). U.S. Computer Emergency Readiness Team home page. Retrieved March 27, 2005, from http://www.us-cert.gov/.

16. USDOJ Computer Crime and Intellectual Property Section. (2004, June 29). CCIPS home page. Retrieved March 27, 2005, from http://www.cybercrime.gov/ccips.html.

17. McCue, Andy. (2003, October 7). 'Revenge' hack downed US port systems. Retrieved March 5, 2005, from http://news.zdnet.co.uk/internet/security/0,39020375,39116978,00.htm.

18. Black, H.C. (1979). *Black's Law Dictionary*. St. Paul, MN: West Publishing.

19. USDOJ Computer Crime and Intellectual Property Section. (2004, June 29). CCIPS home page. Retrieved March 27, 2005, from http://www.cybercrime.gov/ccips.html; see also School gunman stole police pistol, vest. CNN.com. Retrieved March 23, 2005, from http://www.cnn.com/2005/US/03022/school.shooting/index.html.

20. Davey, M., & Wilgoren, J. (2005, March 24). Signs of danger were missed in a troubled teenager's life. *The New York Times*. Retrieved March 24, 2005, from http://www.nytimes.com/2005/03/24/national/24shoot.html?ex=1112331600&en=67e7e64dcf50caed&ei=5070.

21. *Terry v. Ohio. U.S. Supreme Court*. 392 U.S. 1. Washington, DC.

22. *United States v. Sharpe*. U.S. Supreme Court. 470 U.S. 675. Washington, DC.

23. *U.S. v. Mendenhall*. U.S. Supreme Court. 446 U.S. 544. Washington, DC.

24. See Gardner, T.J. (1988). *Criminal Evidence: Principles, Cases and Readings,* 2nd ed. Chapter 8: The rule of exclusion of evidence (pp. 213–228). St. Paul, MN: West Publishing.

25. *New York v. Belton*. U.S. Supreme Court. 453 U.S. 454. Washington, DC.

26. See cases discussed in Gardner, T.J., 1988, pp. 293– 294; see note 24.

27. Federal Bureau of Investigation. (2004, June). Operation Web Snare. U.S Department of Justice. Retrieved March 28, 2005, from http://www.fbi.gov/cyberinvest/websnare.htm.

28. Gardner, T.J., 1988, p. 213; see note 24.

29. *Mapp v. Ohio*, 1961; see note 30.

30. Harrison, M., & Gilbert, S.E. (2003). *Criminal Justice Decisions of the United States Supreme Court*. Mapp v. Ohio, pp. 37–47 Carlsbad, CA: Excellent Books.

31. Gardner, T.J., 1988; see note 24.

32. Gardner, T.J., 1988; see note 24.

33. *Danny Lee Kyllo v. United States*. United States Supreme Court. 533 U.S. 27. Washington, DC.

34. *Charles Katz v. United States*. U.S. Supreme Court. 389 US 347. Washington, DC.

35. *Carroll v. United States*. U.S. Supreme Court. 267 U.S. 132. Washington, DC.

36. *Chimel v. California*. U.S. Supreme Court. 395 U.S. 792. Washington, DC.

37. *Preston v. United States*. U.S. Supreme Court. 376 U.S. 364. Washington, DC.

38. *Charles Katz v. United States*. U.S. Supreme Court. 389 US 347. Washington, DC.

39. NIJ Technical Working Group for Electronic Crime Scene Investigation. (2001, July). *Electronic Crime Scene Investigation: A Guide for First Responders*. Washington, DC: National Institute of Justice.

40. Perianwyr. (2002, July 2). The regulation of fantasy. Kuro5hin. Retrieved April 18, 2005, from http://www.kuro5hin.org/story/2002/7/2/11558/71439.

41. Court TV Staff Author. The media and pedophilia. Court TV. Retrieved April 18, 2005, from http://www. crimelibrary.com/criminal_mind/psychology/pedophiles/6.html?sect=19.

42. ECPAT Staff Author. (2001). Questions and answers about commercial sexual exploitation of children. ECPAT International. Retrieved April 18, 2005, from http://www.ecpat.org.uk/child%20pornography.htm.

43. *Ashcroft, Attorney General, et al. v. Free Speech Coalition et al.* United States Supreme Court. Washington, DC.

44. McCullagh, D. (2002, May 3). Round two on 'morphed' child porn. Wired News. Retrieved April 18, 2005, from http://www.wired.com/ news/politics/0,1283,52285,00.html.

45. Heimbach, M.J. (2002). Hearing before the Subcommittee on Crime, Terrorism, and Homeland Security, Committee on the Judiciary United States House of Representatives, May 1, 2002. Retrieved April 18, 2005, from http://www.fbi.gov/congress/congress02/heimbach050102.htm.

46. Brown, D.T. (2002). Pornography after the fall of the CPPA: Strategies for prosecutors. American Prosecutors Research Institute. Retrieved April 18, 2005, from http://www.ndaa apri.org/publications/ newsletters/ update_volume_15_number_4_2002.html.

47. McQuade, S.C. (2005). Forensics. In *Encyclopedia of Science, Technology, and Ethics*. New York: Macmillan Reference USA.

48. Park, R. (2000). Judgment day in which the courts confront junk science. In *Voodoo Science: The Road from Foolishness to Fraud* (pp. 162–171). New York: Oxford University Press.

49. *City of Liberal, State of Kansas v. Juan Vargas*. (2001). Kansas State Court of Appeals. 24 P.d 155. Case described in Loundy, D.J. (2003), *Computer crime, information warfare and economic espionage* (pp.336–338). Durham, North Carolina: Carolina Academic Press.

50. (Ibid 2001, see note 49).

51. Associated Press Staff Author. (2005, February 4). AOL spammer pleads guilty. Fox News. Retrieved April 11, 2005, from http://www.foxnews.com/story/ 0,2933,146460,00.html.

52. Associated Press Staff Author (2005, August 18). Seller of AOL data is sentenced. Retrieved August 18, 2005 from http://www.nytimes.com/2005/08/18/ technology/18spam.html.

53. Associated Press Staff Author. (2005, March 7). Teen convicted under Internet piracy law. Forbes.com. Retrieved online April 6, 2005, from http://www. forbes.com/business/manufacturing/feeds/ap/2005/ 03/07/ap1868015.html.

54. Associated Press Staff Author. (2005, April 8). Judge sentences spammer to nine years. Fox News. Retrieved April 11, 2005, from http://www.foxnews. com/story/0,2933,152889,00.html.

# 10

# *Preventing Cybercrime with Information Security*

## *10.0 Introduction: How Can We Better Protect our Computer Systems and Data?*

In July of 2004, after 60 years of continuous operation, the national laboratory located at Los Alamos, New Mexico, famous for its central role in the Manhattan Project of WWII and postwar development and testing of nuclear and other forms of weapons, shut down operations in order to get to the bottom of information security leaks. Two weeks after zip disks were reported missing, officials investigating their disappearance still were uncertain what happened to them, what information they contained, and whether or not data contained in them compromised national security. This was the *third* incident of missing disks within the past year from the lab, which contains over 40,000 computer devices containing classified information. Security problems at the lab date back several years and include incidents allegedly involving spying on behalf of other nations, misappropriation of funds for personal use, and missing door keys to lab facilities containing nuclear materials. Furor over the security leaks raised questions about management of the lab, which since its creation has been under the direction of the University of California with a contract from the U.S, Department of Energy and its predecessor agencies. Several employees interviewed about the situation indicated that operations, attitudes and culture surrounding security at the lab had slipped over the years.[1]

How is it possible that a national laboratory, charged with inventing and safeguarding the nation's most guarded technological secrets, under the management of a prestigious university, and with oversight by the federal government, could allow such deterioration of physical and information security? After all, we are talking about nuclear materials and the information needed to process these into weapons of mass destruction. You would think that nothing on the planet would be more closely inventoried, controlled, and guarded—physically and electronically. Perhaps the most positive spin that can be put on this situation and the lesson to be learned are that valuable assets are inherently at risk, and if lax security and loss of assets can happen at Los Alamos, they can happen anywhere, to anyone, and at anytime when adequate physical and information security measures are not in place, utilized, and periodically audited to ensure they afford the required assurance levels.

Every day an increasing number of people and firms purchase computers or upgrade information systems and proceed to connect to the Internet without adequately understanding the threats to their data and the range of human and technological countermeasures that may be employed to safeguard valuable physical and information assets. Consequently, they fail to apply the crime prevention concept of **target hardening**, long associated with protecting homes, businesses, and other types of physical facilities to the protection of their computer systems and information. Additionally, people often fail to learn about new techniques being used by cybercriminals. In many instances, within just a few weeks, days, or even hours of using their new devices and systems, problems begin to emerge. At first, the problems are likely to be quite minor nuisances really—not worth bothering with. In time, as problems compound, more components of IT-enabled human systems are affected, causing technological and operational slowdowns. Often the worsening situation will be exacerbated by continued unawareness, inattention, and tolerance of growing inefficiencies as individuals settle into their personal and work routines, merrily using their IT devices and data with declining efficiency. Ultimately, if not corrected, defective hardware, software, and data processing, combined with and causing unproductive interactions between people and organizational units, will lead to a disastrous systems security and operational meltdown.

If you are among the *lucky* ignorant, this is what you have to look forward to. If, however, you are ignorant of security risks and among the many less fortunate, your system or its data will without warning suddenly cease to perform or be stolen, degraded, or ruined. This can and does happen as the result of intentional attacks and theft and unintentionally as the result of natural disasters like hurricane Katrina which on August 29, 2005 struck several Southern states with devastating effects. In such events, loss of systems capability and/or data will often be unexpected, untimely, frustrating, embarrassing, and costly, if not also impossible to repair technologically and

politically, in terms of lost customer confidence and damaged public image. Hopefully, whether you loose your systems capability and data slowly or all at once, you can recover most or all your data and get back into action, perhaps with affordable technical advice and assistance. You may even do so while avoiding a lawsuit for not adequately protecting valued professional or confidential personal data for which you were responsible. Many firms, NGOs and government agencies are not this fortunate.

This chapter is about securing your facilities, information systems, electronic IT devices and data at home, school, and work. This chapter presents essential information that *every* computer user must know and continually practice. It is written for you and for your family members, friends, classmates, coworkers, and managers—everyone who uses computers and other types of IT devices at home, school, at their place of employment, or while traveling. The goal is to explain how individuals (of all ages), families, groups, organizations, and community sectors can prevent cybercrime. Prevention methods include several technical and not very technical solutions that are described in easy-to-understand terms and in ways that make sense for implementing, whether on small or large scales. We will begin by discussing personal and organization information security protocols. This will include what every person should know to protect their equipment and data at home, school, and work. You will also learn about assuring systems and information integrity in organizational settings by using security assessments, designing and implementing security controls, and making sound technology investment and purchasing decisions.

In the second section, we will explore how to go about advancing the security posture of organizations, beginning with preparing to implement better information security. This includes defining missions and scopes of authority of key personnel, understanding alternative ways to structure organizations for enhanced facilities and information security, and designating individual and unit priorities and responsibilities. Next, we will discuss concepts of risk management, including risk analysis and mitigation of security threats, security policies, and procedures and data and business recovery planning. We will also address managing organizational culture and change for enhanced information security. This portion of the discussion will describe the managerial leadership needed to foster responsible use of IT and information systems, which can be accomplished in part through training, supervising, and inspiring personnel.

In the third and final section, you will learn about the purposes and value of security and systems auditing. Specifically, we will address program operations, technology, security and financial audits with respect to what they are and have to do with protecting facilities, information systems, and data. We will also consider auditing decisions— whether or not to undertake certain audits and whether these should be accomplished internally by organizational personnel or under contract to an external auditor. Then we will discuss auditing phases including announcing, preparing for, and following procedures during and after auditing. Types of information assurance standards often utilized in auditing will also be briefly described. After reading this chapter, you should have a good sense of what you and those with whom you interact need to know to better protect computers, other types of electronic IT devices, information systems, and data.

## 10.1 Personal and Organizational Information Security

How often in the course of a week do you hear someone complain about receiving a virus, losing data, or experiencing a system crash? Information systems vulnerabilities are so commonplace that many firms in the IT industry, including major ISPs, are now finally advertising and offering information security as part of the services they provide for their customers. Indeed, the personal computer has become such an integral part of our daily lives that virtually all students in modernized nations now use computers at school and many have one or even more personal computers at home. Depending on the nature of a person's work, people are issued a desktop, laptop, or other portable computing device by their employer with which to access company information, communicate, conduct research, and accomplish tasks while traveling. People also often utilize systems belonging to other people or organizations, such as when visiting a public library. On the home front, Americans increasingly access the Internet with high-speed connections, as opposed to the slower dial-up modems, allowing, if not helping to drive, even greater computer usage throughout society. Everyone who uses networked computers or other types of IT devices is vulnerable to becoming a victim of cybercrime. People who use computers more often and for more purposes are at greater risk according to the amount of time they spend online engaged in various activities. But as you know, people who use IT offline are also vulnerable to being victimized to the extent they share data via various media and do not physically secure their equipment and facilities in which these are located.

Whose responsibility is it to protect your computer and data from harm? If you are using your personal computer at home, or even at school or work, you probably understand that you are expected to ensure its security. How much do you know about information security? How confident are you that what you are doing provides adequate security for the device and the data it contains? Approximately 50 percent of several hundred college students asked this question in the Computer Use and Ethics Survey administered at the Rochester Institute of Technology (RIT) in April of 2004 indicated that they had a good or excellent ability to protect their computer and data, while the other half of students surveyed indicated that they were either unsure or had only an average, poor, or no ability to protect their equipment and the information stored on

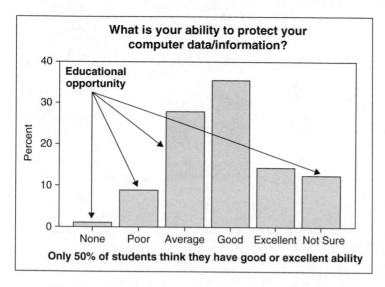

**FIGURE 10.1**  *Students' Ability to Protect Their Systems and Data.*

*Source:* 2004 RIT Computer Use and Ethics Survey.

them (see Figure 10.1). When asked about specific information security techniques they routinely employ, only 53 percent of students indicated that they use personal firewalls, 57 percent restrict Internet browser and cookie default settings, and 54 percent change software manufacturer default settings to higher security levels (see Table 10.1). As listed in Table 10.2, students asked about other information security practices reported relatively infrequent or insufficient updating of

antivirus protections (31 percent), changing system passwords (87 percent), updating security patches (34 percent), backing up data (70 percent), and checking system operating and security logs (66 percent). Many students indicated that they were unsure, how often they did any of these things, indicating that they are very vulnerable to becoming a cybercrime victim.

What do you make of these statistics? How competent do you think the average college

**TABLE 10.1**  *Routine Use of Security Techniques by College Students*

| Computer Security Technique | Yes I do/use | No I do not/use | Not Sure |
|---|---|---|---|
| Antivirus software (n = 866) | 759 | 79 | 28 |
| | 87.6% | 9.1% | 3.2% |
| Personal firewall (n = 855) | 456 | 264 | 135 |
| | 53.3% | 30.9% | 15.8% |
| Restrict Internet browser or cookie settings (n = 844) | 480 | 234 | 130 |
| | 56.9% | 27.7% | 15.4% |
| Avoid opening unsolicited email attachments (n = 858) | 765 | 60 | 33 |
| | 89.2% | 7.0% | 3.8% |
| Change software manufacturer default settings to higher security levels (n = 840) | 449 | 213 | 178 |
| | 53.5% | 25.4% | 21.2% |

*Source:* 2004 RIT Computer Use and Ethics Survey.

**TABLE 10.2**  *Use of Other Security Techniques by College Students*

| Security Procedure or Update Method | Never | Annually | Every Few Months | Monthly | Weekly or More Often | Not Sure |
|---|---|---|---|---|---|---|
| Update virus definitions (n = 861) | 125 | 53 | 129 | 163 | 310 | 81 |
| | 14.5% | 6.2% | 15.0% | 18.9% | 36.0% | 9.4% |
| Change passwords (n = 863) | 389 | 173 | 192 | 67 | 14 | 28 |
| | 45.1% | 20.0% | 22.2% | 7.8% | 1.6% | 3.2% |
| Update security patches (n = 861) | 126 | 50 | 117 | 200 | 229 | 139 |
| | 14.6% | 5.8% | 13.6% | 23.2% | 26.6% | 16.1% |
| Backup data (n = 862) | 260 | 131 | 215 | 102 | 86 | 68 |
| | 30.2% | 15.2% | 24.9% | 11.8% | 10.0% | 7.9% |
| Check operating system and security software logs (n = 863) | 383 | 71 | 116 | 100 | 87 | 106 |
| | 44.4% | 8.2% | 13.4% | 11.6% | 10.1% | 12.3% |

*Source:* 2004 RIT Computer Use and Ethics Survey.

student is when it comes to protecting his or her own computer system and data? How secure do you think the overall network of *your* college or university is, given the percentage of students at RIT who do not practice all of the security procedures listed in Table 10.1 and 10.2? If you were the official responsible for ensuring the confidentiality, integrity, and availability of data on your school's network, what steps would you take to raise information security awareness and precautions?

### 10.1.1  What Every Person Should Know about Information Security

At school and at our workplaces most of us operate computers and other IT devices in network environments that serve up software that enables us to do our work. This software includes word processing, database, accounting, presentation, scheduling, statistical analysis, imaging, email, and other types of special applications including software for accessing and exploring the Internet. If something goes wrong, we can call the help desk and request assistance from support staff. It is, after all, their responsibility to ensure that our systems are functional and secure, right? At what point should we as individual users take

responsibility and be held accountable for securing our own or assigned computers and the data they contain? After all, systems are only as secure as their weakest link or user. Consequently, we are all at risk due to the security negligence of all system users. Given that accessing school or work networks from home effectively extends networks into and from these environments, are we not all responsible for the overall security of the systems we use and depend upon? Even from our homes, do we not jointly share responsibility to protect our work and school networks from computer abuse, attacks, and cybercrimes? The answer of course is that we most certainly do, and when it comes to doing your part, there is nothing you need to be intimidated by even if you are not a "computer person". Responsibly using computers in the information age is akin to driving a car safely— learn how, practice, and adopt safety and security practices into your technological lifestyle.

### 10.1.1.1 Technologies Needed to Protect Your System and Data.

To become a safe and security conscious user of IT devices, it is useful to first review the technologies you will need to acquire, and potentially also install and learn to use correctly. Before buying a new whiz-bang PC with an ultra high-speed processor, gigaton hard drive, magic music player, super-dooper graphics, separate CD and DVD recorder drives, and always-on Internet capability you should carefully consider basic system security requirements (along with figuring out what you actually need and will use the computer for). Many purchasers of new computers and other IT devices are oversold or they over-purchase items and features they do not need, while overlooking basic security functions that they do need. Fortunately, for the majority of computer users who are not technically inclined, there is no need to learn about technical specifications to adequately protect a home PC or portable device. In addition, there are great advantages to keeping your system architecture simple. A house with 1 door and 2 windows to which you alone have access is much easier to protect than a commercial building with 5 doors, 10 ground-floor windows and lots of people with keys. The same concept is true of computers, their features, and the locations in which they are set up to be operated within.

Many people complain about all the avenues of cyber attack and the multitude of defenses needed to prevent cybercrimes, while more than half of the programs on their computers sit unused, poorly maintained, and open to attack. If you decline to purchase unneeded applications in the first place or remove unused pre-installed software at your earliest opportunity and keep your operating system patched-up and free of malware, you will immediately and forever afterwards reduce your exposure to harm. Similarly, I recommend that you do not install any free or "bonus" software that comes with hardware purchases or that you receive in the mail or online because they may contain spyware or adware. In August of 2004, the Federal Trade Commission accepted a regulatory oversight settlement offer from Advertising.com Inc., a component of media giant Time Warner Inc.'s popular American Online ISP, for reportedly embedding adware

into its free *SpyBlast* anti-spyware application without sufficiently revealing this to customers.[2] In Chapter 3, we discussed the potential security-related risks of adware that often comes bundled with spyware and other types of promotional software applications. Two months earlier, in June of 2005, Intermix Media Inc. agreed to a $7.5 million settlement with the office of New York Attorney General Eliot Spitzer that it also illegally distributed adware.[3] These examples reveal why you should scrutinize offers for free and packaged software carefully while striving to keep your system architecture and security practices as simple as possible. By doing so, you will have less hardware that can malfunction, fewer cyber closets accumulating data clutter and that may become infected, as well as fewer things to backup and security-related processes to manage. In short, good information security consists of: (1) knowing what sorts cybercrimes and information security threats exist; (2) becoming aware of what hardware and software you actually need to purchase, install, and maintain; and (3) keeping all this as simple as possible so that you can enjoy computing with as few security-related hassles as possible.

Let us now consider three generally affordable levels of home computer security. First is a low-level security set-up that will provide novice users and people with very little money or essential security products that no one should be without. The mid-level security option will provide a higher level of security for average computer users and at somewhat greater expense but still well within the budgets of most college students and computer users. The high-level security option will afford advanced users or individuals who are very concerned about protecting their data with products to make their systems extremely secure. Table 10.3 provides a guide to specific information security technologies, sample product vendors, and approximate costs for all three security levels. In general, the low-level is recommended for basic home usage including limited Internet exploration via dial-up connectivity. Mid-level

**TABLE 10.3**   *Technology Security Investment Options*

| Security | Technology | Sample Vendors | Pricing |
|---|---|---|---|
| **Low-Level** | Antivirus software | McAfee, Norton | $50 |
| | Antispyware | Microsoft, Spybot, Ad-aware | $0 |
| *Total Cost =* | | | **$50** |
| **Mid-Level** | Antivirus software | McAfee, Norton | $50 |
| | Personal firewall | McAfee, Zone Alarm, Norton | $0–50 |
| | Antispyware | Microsoft, Spybot, Ad-aware | $0 |
| *Total Cost =* | | | **$50–100** |
| **High-Level** | Antivirus software | McAfee, Norton | $50 |
| | Router w/firewall | Linksys, Belkin, NetGear | $30–60 |
| | CD/DVD burner | Sony, Memorex, Pioneer | $35–80 |
| | Antispyware | Spybot, Ad-aware, Microsoft | $0 |
| | Antikeylogger | Spycop, PestPatrol | $60–200 |
| | Password manager | RoboForm, Compelson | $0–60 |
| | Encryption | GnuPG, PGP, Sony Puppy, SanDisk Cruzer Profile | $0–200 |
| *Total Cost =* | | | **$175–650** |

security is generally recommended for users who frequently browse the Internet with a high-speed connection from home, school, or work. Obviously, recommended security levels increase with greater Internet access and usage, as well as the amount and value of data in need of being secured. The high-level security category is for people who use their systems for work-related tasks or keep financial, client, or similarly important confidential records on their systems. The high-level security option is also a good choice for people who desire strong security for any reason but who must also contend with a modest budget. As Table 10.3 indicates, security technology for individual user systems, even if networked to other computers via the Internet, does not need to cost very much. This is especially true if you are willing to rely on certain freeware products available through the Open Source Community, as we discussed in section 7.2.2 of Chapter 7. Users purchasing new computers or upgrading their systems can choose between different technology investment packages and pricing options. However, note that, in general, the quality of technology you buy is correlated

with its price. Be careful about skimping if you can afford not to. As revealed in Cyber Tale 10.1, skimping on even something as seemingly unimportant as a combination power cord plug-in with electrical surge protector can be disastrous.

As indicated in Chapter 3, dozens if not hundreds, perhaps even thousands of new malicious codes are written and released onto the Internet every week. As of this writing, Symantec and McAfee, both firms specializing in computer security software development and online antivirus services, had detected, inventoried, and designed programming fixes for several thousand strains of malicious code known to exist in the public domain. These and other firms offering antivirus protection services often provide virus definition updates online, if not also automatically on a periodic basis to some operating systems. If infection prevention, virus definition updates, and operating system patch-up programs are not installed, used, and updated frequently, new as well as old computer systems and other types of IT devices (depending on their programming vulnerabilities) will be exposed to malware infection immediately upon being connected to

**CYBER TALE 10.1**

### A Security Lesson about Purchasing Inferior Technology

Protecting computer and information assets necessitates using the highest-quality technology you can afford, right down to the power strip used to plug in your CPU, monitor, and peripherals. One student unfortunately learned this lesson the hard way. The apartment he lived in was part of an older complex that periodically experienced localized brown- and blackouts. A couple of electrical outlets seemed to be particularly problematic as evidenced by new lamps that, in relatively short periods of time, would begin flickering and eventually burn out. At the time, he didn't think too much about it, so it never occurred to him after purchasing an expensive computer system to use a different electrical outlet or at least a good quality surge protector. Sure enough, within the first month of using his new computer, the monitor and CPU began flickering intermittently.

The inexpensive surge protector he purchased at "a dollar store" did its job and he experienced nothing but minor irritation with periodic flickering of his computer, until one day when he smelled something burning. His worst fear had come true: components on the inside of the CPU, including the motherboard itself, had literally melted. Both his computer and his data (which had not been properly backed up) were completely destroyed. It turns out that the inexpensive surge protector was not guaranteed to work more than once. To make matters worse, the building superintendent hired an electrician to fix the problem but he refused to replace the computer (especially since the student failed to bring the electrical problem to his attention earlier). The lesson for information security is clear and simple: buy good-quality technology including reusable surge protectors, disconnect your system at the first sign of electrical difficulty, and do not use your computer, at least from the same outlet, until electrical problems can be thoroughly investigated and fixed by a certified electrician. Can you think of other electronic devices that people are tempted to skimp on, and that could jeopardize their systems and data?

other computers, as the result of loading files from portable media, and especially by connecting to the Internet. One source estimated that an unprotected computer running an operating system made by Microsoft Corporation would become infected with malware within twenty minutes of connecting to the Internet.[4]

Unprotected systems remain susceptible to becoming infected at any time and in several ways until adequate precautions are taken, and in the interim they are also at risk of infecting other computers and devices. Malware can remain undetected or dormant on infrequently used and even updated systems, then re-emerge online in their original or modified strains long after an initial widespread infection, detection, and cleaning processes throughout cyber society has taken place. This is all the more reason to invest in, install, use,

and regularly maintain information security technologies and practices. How do know that storage devices such as diskettes and flash drives that you receive from your friends in order to quickly exchange files are not infected? Do you run a virus scan on files before downloading them, whether from the Internet or another source? I remember once in graduate school using a friend's floppy disk which he had just used in the university's computer lab in order to get a homework assignment. Three days later, a computer retail and service center technician declared my "computer dead on arrival", having been infected by several known and malicious Trojans, worms and viruses that were evidently on my friend's diskette. His PC also died, forcing both of us to immediately purchase new computers in order to finish the homework assignment by the due date—a very expensive lesson in information security. Remember, everyone must be responsible for protecting their own systems, and they should do their best to help others to do likewise. People should also be held accountable for helping to protect the networks they use by employing sound information security practices. After all, not maintaining a secure and clean computer system is a form of social abuse because this endangers the operating systems, files, and data of all computers and other types of IT devices connected to a given network. In retrospect, my friend and I both acted very irresponsibly within the community of university computer users of which we were a part. We also neglected to simultaneously distrust people and technology, as was discussed in Chapter 2, and I had not updated by antivirus definitions in a long time thereby making my system vulnerable to known variations of malware. Thus, information security is not a program or activity—to become effective it must become a shared lifestyle of everyone using a computer network.

### 10.1.1.2 *Protecting Your System and Data at Home, School, and Work.*

On March 11, 2005, an unattended laptop computer was stolen from an unlocked office in a restricted area at the University of California, Berkeley. The laptop contained the names, social security numbers, and other personal information of 98,369 students, student applicants, and alumni. In response, the university made a public apology, established a 1-800 number that people could call for information and security advice, and to comply with California law, began notifying all persons affected to begin monitoring their credit card purchasing records for signs of fraud and identify theft. Earlier at the Berkeley campus, in September of 2004, confidential information on more than 600,000 California residents was compromised after a hacker gained access to a computer system being used for research on behalf of the state's Department of Social Services.[5] These examples illustrate that good personal information security begins with good physical security of your office, workstation, and

hardware. Physical security must then be accompanied with sound information security investments and practices. There is after all, an old saying: If a competent hacker can get to your keyboard, they own your data. This is probably true. Even if they cannot access your data immediately, they can resort to simply stealing your computer or other electronic device. *Never* leave your system unattended, even for a moment, because that is all the time a competent thief needs to steal your hardware or make a copy of data from an unsecured IT device.

Bearing in mind the need to continually practice good facilities protection and physical security, and to guard against social engineering, let us now consider several important information security practices. Note that additional and updated information on what follows is generally provided online by several of the law enforcement and security oriented organizations listed in Appendix A.

### 10.1.1.2.1 Use Strong Passwords.

Your password is the means of accessing an information system. Unauthorized system access by a hacker, internal trespasser, or *person you allow to have access* may control your computer or device operating system, its applications, logs, folders, documents, files, email account information, and all attendant personal information. If they also possess your network username and password, they will also be able to access your school or employment network resources (e.g., file servers, printers, and special applications). Is your password constructed so simply that a casual observer of your workspace could guess it, or find other passwords within your system after they gain access to it? Picture an office cubicle with a large poster of the Dallas Cowboys on one wall. OK, let's guess the password: "dallas"—access denied. Let's try "cowboys"—again, access denied. How about, "dallascowboys"—bingo, hacker in the box! Basic tenants of good password selection and use have changed little in several years. The real challenge has been convincing users to embrace proven practices, such as not picking an obvious password and regularly changing it.

A **strong password** consists of a mixture of at least eight upper and lower case letters, symbols, or numbers. Passwords should never consist of proper names or defined words listed in an dictionary or encyclopedia published in any language. However, it is easy to convert any name and word into a strong password. For example, the word *potential* can be converted to "P0tEnT1@L". The password "P0tEnT1@LLernor" is even better because it substitutes characters as in the first example and adds a second misspelled word in a way that is easy to remember. Now the password pronounced "potential learner" combines several alphanumeric characters plus at least one other keyboard character in a very strong way. You would hope that it also cannot be intuitively associated with tangible items, pictures, or other intelligence known on the basis of items locatable in a user's workstation, or that pertain to the names of family members or pets, or their hobbies, other commonly known lifestyle activities, and favorite sports teams (e.g., dallascowboys). Using and frequently changing a strong password can eliminate significant risk of system manipulation and loss of data. In review, here are five basic rules for selecting a strong password:

• Make your password at least eight characters long, consisting of a mix of lower and upper case letters, numbers, and symbols.
• Do not use proper names or words from a dictionary or encyclopedia, including those printed in foreign languages.
• Make sure the password does not contain data of a personal nature, such as birthday, anniversary, street address, part of your social security number, or pet's name.
• Change your password often. In general, 8–16 week intervals are satisfactory.
• Do not repeat use of a password. Many systems administrators rightfully configure networks to prevent this practice.

Unfortunately, many people do not employ sound password practices. Referring again to the RIT Computer Use and Ethics Survey, after being shown an example of a strong password comprised of randomly selected alphanumeric characters, 60 percent of the college students surveyed reported that their current system password was not strong. In addition, 55 percent of the students reported that they had shared their network password with someone else within the previous twelve months, and of those who did, over 70 percent reported that they had not changed their password after sharing it. It is not known with whom the RIT students shared their network passwords—for example whether it was with fellow students or persons not authorized to use the university system or both. What is clear is that substantial sharing of passwords results in a computing environment that is less safe and less secure for everyone who uses a network.

What is in your files, documents, and email? Website bookmarks and notes to a friend that you may not wish to be public knowledge? Purchasing orders placed online that contain your confidential credit card information? Perhaps a really important school project or a company report indicating a major revenue generator for the upcoming marketing cycle? Does your position at the company provide access to the organization's payroll data or to the medical records of fellow employees? If so, and without adequate password protection of your system, and prohibitions on sharing and revealing passwords, data such as this may become an intruder's information as well, and possibly even shared online with the rest of the computing world. Let's hope you do not have elevated rights to a system machine, such as "power user" or "administrator" status, because if you do, an intruder who gets your data will also. With root authority, a cybercriminal can do anything to the system: copy, manipulate, distribute, or destroy data; create and install backdoors or malware; or assume genuine username identities and carry out malicious pranks and even cybercrimes in other users' names or yours, or create original illegitimate user accounts, usernames and passwords.

As described in Chapter 3, a malicious hacker may alternatively simply lie in wait, patiently monitoring, recording, and analyzing keystrokes and data traffic patterns before deciding what actions to take and *who else* to grant access to. These are very simple and brief examples of what could and does happen when passwords are compromised.

### 10.1.1.2.2 Practice Efficient Password Management.

Many people have several computers or electronic IT devices, along with legitimate access to one or more networks and online accounts, each of which may require a different password. This brings up the important issue of practicing effective **password management** (e.g., keeping track of multiple passwords but not recording them in an easily discovered location or way). Researchers in June of 2003, in a survey of 3,000 IT administrators, executive management users, and information security professionals, found that 55 percent of respondents write their passwords down at least once, 9 percent write down every password, 40 percent share their passwords, 51 percent periodically require assistance from help desk staff to re-access their systems, 80 percent have implemented stronger password protection policies, and on average, users have five passwords. Researchers also found that users frequently employ combinations of usernames and passwords that are insecure and that if changed may become counterproductive and costly as a means of user authentication.[6] What then is a person with multiple passwords to do?

First, try to minimize the number of passwords you need. Second, realize that passwords for less critical systems can be duplicated or only slightly different. Third, some passwords may need to be stronger than others, implying that some can deliberately be made easier to remember and type on a keyboard or otherwise enter with an input device such as keyboard. Passwords for Web sites that provide nonprivate information can have passwords set the same.

Do not, however, use the same password to access human resources or financial data systems at work as one used for accessing a Web site that maintains bulk mailing lists. Long passwords or frequently changed ones do provide higher levels of security, but to be effective, passwords also need to be easy to remember, use, and change. They should also be recoverable in ways consistent with the level of security needed for particular data. Security policies taught and reinforced through personnel training should prohibit people from writing down or recording passwords used to protect certain kinds of data, or storing a password in a place easily discovered, such as on a note stuck to a computer monitor or under the keyboard, which is like leaving the key to your front door under the welcome mat. Password policies can also be tailored to fit varying employee ranks or assignments according to the type of information employees access. For example, a government official who is authorized to access classified information should be prohibited from saving system passwords in PDA devices, especially if the data is unencrypted.

A 2002 survey that mobile security firm Pointsec conducted of 332 people working in IT and sales positions (43 percent in large corporate environments) revealed that 10 percent of PDA owners stored financial data on their device but without password protection or encryption. Six percent of the surveyed PDA owners reported having lost their device, yet nearly a third of those individuals, even after replacing their device, did not bother with passwords or encryption. The study also revealed that 25 percent of PDA owners who store passwords and PINs on their devices do not have them configured to require a password to access data. In addition, while 65 percent of PDA owners surveyed store unencrypted financial data on their portable device, approximately 25 percent do not require a password to access the data. Moreover, 23 percent of survey respondents indicated that the PDAs they use are company owned, yet 66 percent of firms issuing the devices did so in the absence of policies or guidelines governing password protection and encryption. This is about the same percentage of respondents who reported that although they use their PDA to store confidential corporate data and access corporate networks, they do not restrict access to the little gadgets with a password.[7] Fortunately you are smarter than these corporate big shots, right?

A low-tech way of recording passwords is to write them down and lock them up in a safe or file cabinet to which you alone have the combination or key, and which you do not put in an unlocked desk drawer. Alternatively, simply put your list of passwords inside a book on a shelf. This method is not perfect, but it can be sufficiently protective when simultaneously managing numerous passwords governing access to different systems and networks containing data of relatively low value. (Just make sure nobody is watching you when you grab the book off the shelf to remove and look at your password list.) What is not recommended is mixing portions of passwords for the sake of remembering them, except if they protect very low-level non-financial Web accounts of some kind. Separating passwords used on the job from those needed at school and while at home, however, can be helpful, as can isolating passwords used to access financial or other types of very important data. One way to manage several sets of account usernames and corresponding passwords is to put them in a text file, name the file with an innocuous label, and encrypt the file contents. In this way, even if your system is compromised, a cursory search by the attacker for such data will not be easily located and will be even more difficult to crack. By that time, you hope, you will have discovered that your system was or may have been compromised and taken steps to resecure it.

It is important to know where all of your passwords are and when you last changed them, rather than guess about these matters and end up losing passwords or changing them too infrequently or never. Password management software can help by creating a single master password for you

to remember (and write down if you must) and by encrypting all other passwords. Password management software can also facilitate easy access and backing up passwords while ensuring that they remain out of sight even if the system on which they are installed is compromised. KeePass is a free open-source password management application that can help you manage your passwords in a secure way. You can put all your passwords in one database, which is locked with one master key or a key-disk. In this way you only have to remember one master password or insert the key-disk to unlock the whole database. Then you can encrypt the database with products that utilize proven encryption algorithms (e.g., AES and Twofish).[8] Other products such as the Sony Puppy, SanDisk Cruzer Profile, and Authenex A-Key allow users to create encrypted files that can only be accessed with a special USB token. The Sony Puppy and Cruzer Profile devices use biometric fingerprint technology to further authenticate access to systems only by an authorized user. Smartcards, such as the ChipDrive, manufactured by SCM Micro, are now also available for password storage and are beginning to include biometric authentication technology. More generally, technology can now be used in network environments to force users to change their passwords regularly and employ strong naming configurations.

As discussed in Chapter 3, software cracking and recovery tools are available for purchase and as open-source applications off the Internet. These tools can be used for legitimate and illicit purposes, and they work on a wide variety of electronic devices, operating systems, and applications that may all have different levels of specific passwords. Some of these tools are very powerful and are capable of generating millions upon millions of possible passwords in very short periods of time in what amounts to automated guessing (also known as brute force attack). Cracking tools combined with the powerful computers available to cybercriminals underscores why passwords need to be strong and changed often.

**10.1.1.2.3 Repeatedly Use and Update Anti–Virus, Trojan, and Worm Software.**  Elsewhere in the text, I have mentioned the importance of using and updating **antimalware software** also commonly called antivirus software, although in addition to ridding our systems of viruses, Trojans, and worms we are also interested in defending against and eliminating spyware and adware. Let us now talk specifically about repeatedly using and updating software designed to detect harmful programs. First, make sure you install reputable antivirus/antimalware products *before* ever connecting to the Net; otherwise your computer could be compromised even before you finish downloading needed product upgrades and patches (discussed shortly). The U.S. Computer Emergency Response Team and Coordination Center (CERT/ CC) provides a guide for home computer users, *Before You Connect a New Computer to the Internet*, which provides excellent specific suggestions on this topic.[9]

Antivirus software protection can be purchased from different reliable firms, including, for instance, Symantec and McAfee, which also provide operating system problem detection services for modest annual fees. Some software development firms and ISPs are now also providing anti-malware services to their customers. Use and updating of known virus, Trojan and worm definitions should occur at least weekly, and during

---

**CYBER TALE 10.2**

### A Case of Sloppy Password Administration

Attitudes towards cybercrime differ. Recently, a high school installed a new network and hired a system administrator to maintain it as well as provide technical support to students, staff, and teachers. Full access to the network was naturally limited to the system administrator, who used a lock-down program to help manage permissions and so on. Unfortunately, the particular application she used for this purpose had several known bugs and work-arounds that allowed computer-savvy students to run a hexadecimal reader in order to view configuration files, disable the lock-down application, and discover passwords for everyone except the system administrator.

One day, a student tried guessing the system administrator's password and within minutes discovered it was "cat"—a password only three characters long and straight out of the dictionary. The student was so amazed by his discovery that he shared it with several of his computer pals who, in the spirit of ethical hacking, set out to discover all the vulnerabilities on the network. Soon they had an extensive list of usernames, passwords, and other incendiary data they proudly shared with their computer science teacher, who was himself aware of certain flaws on the network. Armed with the information provided by his students, the computer science teacher reported all that he knew to the administration.

Unfortunately, the information was not well-received, and everyone involved was reprimanded. The system administrator got in trouble for using a weak password, the science teacher was scolded for praising his students' criminal accomplishments, and the students were all verbally warned, except for the ringleader. One day soon after the incident, this student was officially confronted by school administrators and the police. The computer he was working on was seized and rumor had it that a mirror image of his system's hard drive was made for investigative purposes. In the end, he didn't receive any punishment other than being banned from working on any computer at school for the remainder of the school year (but it was only October).

*Anonymous Student*

pronounced periods of malware releases, even daily. Granted, this can be tiresome and difficult to remember, but many of the major antivirus vendors provide automated updates that can perform their detection and cleaning routines while you are having lunch, working out, or sleeping. Enabling auto-updates, and periodically running them with manual commands, is a great way to keep your system free of viruses, Trojans, and worms.

When opening email you can improve the effectiveness of your antivirus software by;

- Using your antivirus protection software to scan email (some products will do this as a configurable setting and some will only scan attachments after they are saved to disk.).
- Never opening email attachments from strangers, regardless of how enticing the subject line or attachment, because you are probably being socially engineered.
- Being suspicious of any *unexpected* email attachment from someone you *do* know because it may have been sent without that person's knowledge via an infected or bot machine.
- If your email program can be set to *not* download pictures, you should also enable this setting. This will prevent your computer from accidentally downloading spamming, spyware, or adware intelligence-gathering tools or other exploits not readily detectable.

System administrators worry more about vulnerability and possible infection of the networks they are trying to protect rather than individual computer nodes. However, individual nodes on a network can be a primary source of network problems if malware is introduced through them. For example, if an employee brings in an infected disk to the office, it may introduce a malicious virus, Trojan, or worm to the network. This general problem is expanded by people working from home on networks maintained by

their employers. If an organization has a virtual private network (VPN), which amounts to a type of protected information system within the Internet, employees may be allowed to configure their home systems to access their employer's network remotely. If this is not done properly, employees may expose the organization's network to attacks launched against their relatively insecure home systems. Widely available high speed connectivity exacerbates this potential problem, especially since few residential class users use the full array of security techniques discussed in this chapter and do not have the expertise needed to properly secure networked computing environments.

### 10.1.1.2.4 Install and Use a Software or Hardware Firewall.

A **firewall** is a set of access lists either installed on a computer or coded into an appliance that protects a computer or network from intruders. Firewalls effectively isolate a user's system from all others on the Internet, typically by electronically determining whether a message or request for information was initiated by the user or by an outside source. If, for example, a user browses the Net, return information is allowed to come back through the firewall. If an outside party probes a system, essentially making a request to enter a computer system, then the firewall will inspect, pass, or block those packets based on established rule sets. Firewall rules can be configured to detect and deny intruder probes in various ways (e.g., individually, by zone, or with a setting to deny all connections). Firewalls may be either less expensive software products or more expensive hardware products, each of which ranges in price according to product capabilities and features.

Using a software or hardware firewall will eliminate most risk of a computer break-in from hackers who do not already know access information. A software firewall is sufficient for a single computer but will not provide adequate protection and options necessary to protect a computer network. Some users employ both hardware and software firewalls in layered security to provide an even higher level of system protection. Many inexpensive software firewalls offer traffic monitoring features that will alert you anytime someone attempts to hack into your system. The popular ZoneAlarm firewall software, among other products, will also help protect laptop computers when being accessed wirelessly, as is common in Internet cafes and other locations that provide WiFi connectivity for their customers. If you want to learn the locations from which cybercriminals are probing your system, turn on the alerts feature of your firewall and, if it is so equipped, monitor and translate the top-level domain country name element codes in attacker message headers (e.g., RU is the Russian Federation, KR is the Korean Republic).[10] Many firewall products also have a prompt feature that asks, "What is this?" and other features that categorize the type and relative seriousness of probes and attempted attacks against your computer system.

Novice users of firewalls are often amazed to see dozens or even hundreds of cyber probes pinging against their firewall during any given work session, a terrific reminder of threats awaiting unprotected computers or other IT devices that are connected to the Net. After a while, most users will disable the audible and visual alert features of their firewall in order to avoid being bothered almost constantly with warnings of intruder probes, opting instead to let the firewall work silently to safeguard their system. Today the need for personal firewalls installed on every desktop and laptop computer connected to the Internet is essential. Eventually, the computer industry may incorporate firewalls as a standard tool into base operating systems such as Windows®, Unix®, Linux®, Netware®, or MacOS®. Portable devices offering Internet connectivity and/or wireless communications are also being enhanced with security features. For now, and for most users, it is critical to purchase, install, and periodically update firewall protections on every personal computer.

**10.1.1.2.5  Regularly Download Security Patches for your Software and Operating Systems.** To achieve and maintain excellent system performance and guard against harm resulting from programming vulnerabilities, you must patch your system with the latest available software updates. **Patching** must not be limited to updating your operating system; rather, all applications such as virus protection, word processing, databases, and communication packages need to be periodically updated, as does the operating code for peripherals such as printers and scanners. Patching needs to be a regular aspect of security maintenance because manufacturers are continually releasing new versions of their products as well as updates to guard against security vulnerabilities discovered as a consequence of ongoing testing, customer complaints, and exploits posted onto the Net. By upgrading to newer versions of software and downloading security patches (usually at no cost), you can fortify your system against a substantial number of security risks and operating problems.

Why is patching so important? Consider the SQL Slammer virus that doubled the number of infected systems every nine seconds. Virus protection product vendors were quick to respond and had security patches available within hours. Unfortunately, millions of users throughout the world did not practice patch management. If they had, the virus outbreak could have been much better controlled because security patches against the vulnerability exploited by Slammer were available months *before* the virus was released onto the Internet. The Blaster virus outbreak used a new technique for exploiting vulnerable systems, was (and still is) extremely prolific, and has the ability to bring legitimate network traffic to a complete halt. As with Slammer, Microsoft patches were available *before* Blaster was released, but millions of users who have not patched up remain vulnerable. It is notable that patch management rests on the premise that security researchers will find and fix software vulnerabilities before cybercriminals can

**CYBER TALE 10.3**

### *Software Firewall Programs May Not Provide Complete Protection*

One day, after installing a software firewall program, I began experiencing increasing problems with my CPU: slower and slower responses to commands, etc. My computer started complaining about the NTFS file system used by Windows XP® being corrupted, and then, all of a sudden, the whole system crashed. Since I was backing up data at the time, I presumed the crash was due to the data coming from the other computer I was backing up, so I simply rebooted, noticed everything seemed to be working properly, and went off to class and then on to work. From there, I checked my email later in the day to learn that the university had blocked my computer from accessing the network because it was spreading a virus.

As soon as I got home, I updated my virus definitions and ran a full diagnostic check. No problems were indicated, and I presumed the problem had been fixed. Later, I attempted to reboot, but the system refused, so I had to reinstall Windows®, losing nearly all my data in the process. (I should have backed up my data, but that is another story.) It turned out that I had been victimized by the W32.Witty worm that was designed to defeat virus definition updates by residing on random access memory (RAM), which is not normally actively scanned by virus protection service programs because powering down a system will normally remove a memory-resident infection. But that did not occur in this instance, nor did my inferior firewall program (which I had installed primarily to monitor attempted attacks rather than to provide solid protection) detect the worm.

The lesson here is that no product is infallible. Information security requires a combination of reputable hardware and software products, plus good anti-infection services coupled with solid infosec practices to ensure complete protection of your computer and its data. But even these combined prevention measures will not completely protect you in all instances, so you must routinely back up your data and store it off the local site or network where it cannot be corrupted by infections that manage to get onto your primary system.

*Anonymous Student*

create new versions of their malicious code, and that users will stay informed and take precautions by downloading security patches often and as quickly as possible when virus outbreaks become known. As cybercrime becomes more lucrative, some security researchers may become cybercriminals specializing in discovery of system vulnerabilities for which there are no patches. Layered firewall defenses combined with carefully scrutinizing of inbound traffic to your system may offer your best protection in these situations.

Typically, upgrade and security patch download links can be found at software developers' Web sites. Some manufacturers also send registered users of their products announcements of available updates. These may be sent electronically following a system scan that inventories what is currently installed and compares this information to available product upgrades and security patches. If you are not automatically notified of the need to patch, you should take the initiative to analyze and patch-up your system manually with correct free downloads available at manufacturer Web sites. Updates for Microsoft can be found at http://windowsupdate.microsoft.com. Note, however, that the "Windows Update Service" does not update your operating system or applications automatically, so be careful to opt-in for the particular upgrades and patches that you require. Microsoft also offers a separate "Office Update Service" that patches most of their applications, which is at http://office. microsoft. com/en-us/officeupdate/default.aspx. The software giant now also provides security scanning and remote installation of security software that can help protect your system. Other software developers such as Adobe also provide update services. Some vendors have also begun offering "middleware" update services, whereby their product will check your system against available upgrades and patches of other manufacturers and either alert you to this availability or fetch and install it for you. McAfee tried this in the late 1990s with their "Oil Change" product. BigFix (see www.bigfix.com) launched a similar product in 1997 and from 2003 to 2005 began to receive IT industry recognition. This firm offers extensive enterprise services for multiple platforms that will inventory, alert, patch, and report accomplishments for users' review.

### 10.1.1.2.6 Frequently Install and Use Antispyware and Adware Software Often.

Statistics published by Earthlink.net in 2005 indicate that of 4,610,738 computers remotely inspected, an average of 25 spyware applications were found on users' systems presumably without their knowledge; of the 100 million pieces of spyware detected, over 1.5 million were the highly invasive systems monitors or Trojans, indicative of very high information *insecurity*. Consequently, Earthlink researchers concluded that 90 percent of all computers connected to the Internet probably are infected with spyware.[11] Perhaps you like being spied on, or receiving unsolicited advertising messages and spam and using computers that run a little slower than honey poured from a cold jar. If not, then installation, regular use, and updating of antispyware and anti-adware software products will help you detect and remove these types of malware from your system, speed up system performance, and offer a level of protection from being re-affected when you browse Web sites.

Antispyware and anti-adware products, some of which are free to download off the Internet thanks to open-source programmers, can remove various market intelligence-gathering software capable of mining and sending your personal information back to Web sites that collect, process, and sell personal information to advertisers. Note, however, that some spyware

---

**CYBER TALE 10.4**

## The Importance of Patch Management

One student recently reported that upon returning home from summer vacation he began using the computer in his bedroom to email friends, and play games and so on. Within a few days, he noticed that CPU performance deteriorated to the point that several applications would not function properly and booting-up seemed to take forever. Even after he resinstalled the original Windows operating system from CD installation disks, the same problems soon resurfaced. He also noticed that the amount of data being uploaded from his machine exceeded the amount he was downloading, a sure sign that an outsider had gained control of his system. Only then, through some personal research, did he discover the importance of frequently updating his computer with Microsoft Service Packs and other patches. Over the next several days he updated his system with every available and appropriate patch, after which his computer ran fine. In his words, "ignorance is not bliss and it is important to know what you are doing. I now know that it is commonplace for operating system CDs to be insecure by the time they reach consumers' hands and that immediately after installing operating systems and other software users need to patch their computers."

*Anonymous Student*

programs actually purport to be antispyware scanners. Typically, these pop up while you are online to report something like, "PC running slow—Click here to have it checked." Of course, if you click to have it checked, you will inadvertently install the spyware that will check your system all right, over and over again as you are being spied on. One way of distinguishing these malicious programs from truly helpful software is to use only established, well-known software products or services of highly regarded firms. You may also wish to confer with someone you trust either in-person or online, perhaps participants in a respected technology review listserv, chat forum, or your ISP, who should have your best interests in mind or has already invested time, money, and effort to evaluate specific products in order to reduce security-related problems resulting in customers calling for assistance.

**10.1.1.2.7 Back Up all Your Data Often, Systematically, and in Different Ways.** When was the last time you lost some or all of your data? I have never met a person who at one time or another has not lost the latest version of a document, folder, or portions of saved media. The worst data losses are associated with crashed hard drives (which I certainly know about). Hard

drives rarely malfunction on their own but do frequently fail to respond because of a cyber attack, an accident such as dropping your laptop on the ground, or exposure to inclement weather. Some firms with headquarters or division offices located in the World Trade Center lost all their data during the terrorist attacks on September 11, 2001, because although backed up on site, they were not also backed up at another location. The point is that all users are vulnerable to losing data for various reasons including operator error and using media of inferior quality, thus requiring periodic, systematic, and divergent ways of backing up systems and data.

**Backing up data** can be accomplished in numerous ways. Occasionally, computer science students make fun of how I back up my system files, which they think is inelegant from a programming standpoint, but it works quite well, substantially because of its low-tech approach and my ability to easily understand and manage the process. As you might imagine, I have a tremendous amount and various kinds of valuable data on several personal and university-issued computers. I routinely work with three computers: my home desktop, my office desktop, and a laptop that I pack around most of the time and tend to use as my primary workstation

**CYBER TALE 10.5**

### *Backup Data Only on Trusted Media!*

One student was in the habit of periodically backing up her data files and then reformatting her computer and reinstalling applications as way of removing unneeded files and keeping her system working at maximum efficiency. This is a good maintenance routine, but unfortunately she once made the mistake of backing up her data files to a friend's contaminated server. After she resaved the data to her own cleaned computer she experienced

multiple errors, only to discover that she had inherited over 400 viruses from her friend, whose server turned out to have been banned by the university system for being so infected and the source of many viruses on innumerable university-owned computers. Fortunately, a combination of updated Norton antivirus definitions and additional online solutions enabled her to fully restore her system with no damage to any data files (no small miracle), and she no longer relies on any media but her own for backing up files—a very good rule indeed.

because it affords flexibility with regard to when and where I work, as well as what I sit in while I work (too many old policing and athletic injuries). Each day, I add research materials and new data to my laptop, which I then use to teach classes, write books and articles, conduct research, and so on. (I keep my personal consulting and finance data on a system not integrated with the university network.) My computers are all equipped with compatible operating systems and exactly the same legally licensed software, and the desktops all appear nearly identical. I have one folder saved on the laptop hard drive that contains a very organized directory of several other folders and all my data by subject (e.g., courses, research, publications).

I typically work with many documents open and different applications running simultaneously. I am generally not online unless I need to be, and I always operate from behind at least one firewall. As I work, I constantly save new versions of files across my directory system. In a four-hour writing or work session I may have acquired or updated twenty or more files and saved these versions to the hard drive of the laptop. Then once per day, *every day*, I back up the main folders containing multiple layers of subfolders and documents that I have been working with to a portable, reliable, yet inexpensive external hard drive. Then once per week I use the external hard drive to overwrite and thus update and backup all my data onto my other computers at home and work. This is easily accomplished because of the neat directory system that allows me to specify only the main folder into which all my other folders and files are saved. Meanwhile, I am patching up, updating virus definitions and conducting periodic virus checks, etc. I do not use CD or DVD recorders to backup because they do not have sufficient memory and are limited in the number of characters that a given folder or file name may consist of. (Given my extensive directory naming hierarchy some of my files are named with more than 150 characters + spaces.) Thus, my data is systematically and perpetually

backed up on *five* separate computers, under two different management systems, and physically located in three different places. In this way, if my alarmed house with a watchdog gets burglarized, and the university office building I work in burns down, and I drop and break my laptop *all on the same day* my data will still be backed up on the university network server located in a different office building on the other side of campus. At worst, I will loose one week's worth of work.

My backup procedures are not perfect, but they work for me, and that is what matters. You, too, need to establish a regular method of backing up your data on more than one machines, located in more than one place, and preferably under different management systems. Do not, however, make backing up your data more complicated than it needs to be, as this may confuse or discourage you from backing up frequently and effectively. Modern personal computers often come pre-equipped with applications that can facilitate efficient backing up or you may purchase these separately at a modest cost or find a reliable solution through the Open Source Community. Also take advantage of your system's archiving capability, transfer data often to alternative media, and *test your ability to restore important files.* Note that government, university, and corporate computer systems should have much more sophisticated enterprise-wide back up solutions and procedures, but these employ essentially the same goals that I have when backing up my own personal data: regular, routine, systematic, complete, automatic, and redundant saving.

Commercial data archiving services, such as those offered by firms like NeoScale Systems, Decru, Vormetric, and Kasten Chase, can provide technical back up procedures assistance and off-site vaulted, firewall, and encryption information security assistance. Firms managing financial, health, and other types of records may be required by state and/or federal regulations such as the HIPPA and Sarbanes-Oxley laws (see Chapter 8) to provide for **storage area network**

(SAN) security. SAN security involves extraordinary cyber protection of mission-critical and confidential information, as well as physical security controls to help guard against theft, natural disaster or harm to data caused in other ways, such as cyber attacks. Security protocols often extend to interim data storage and encryption, data transference to and transportation of backup tapes, and off-site, long-term data archiving. As a large disk repository that organizations use for mass storage, SAN facilities have no immediate relationship to security used within client facilities, but do require extra precautions associated with transferring data to and from SANs for systems restoration purposes, as in the aftermath of a natural disaster such as hurricane Katrina which in August of 2005 struck the Gulf of Mexico states of Louisiana, Mississippi, and Alabama, causing over $25 billion in damages. How many of the millions of individuals and organizations who experienced losses in that disaster also lost computers, other electronic devices, and data critical for sustaining their lives and operations? How many do you think can recover their data, perhaps from a source located outside the Gulf Coast region? Do you suppose many had special insurance coverage to compensate for personal or business losses caused as a direct result of losing data rather than as the result of property damage attributable to storm flooding?

**10.1.1.2.8 Consider Using Anti-Keylogger, Encryption and Digital Signature Technology.** As defenses have been strengthened on servers and for applications through the use of strong passwords along with tight access controls, targeting by cybercriminals has remained intently focused on acquiring account and password data of potential victims. Recall from Chapter 3 that hackers and employers will sometimes use **keylogger software** to remotely monitor key strokes of computer users in real time. Often the results are scanned-for usernames, passwords, credit card, and social security numbers, among other confidential information that can be used for identify theft and other types of fraud. Protection against the use of keylogging by hackers is becoming increasingly important.

Fortunately more antivirus applications are detecting keystroke logging attempts, especially ones distributed through worms. There are, however, intentionally planted commercial keylogger programs used in conjunction with spyware and adware. Hence, just as cybercriminals routinely employ multiple methods of attack, sound information security requires multifaceted defense strategies that employ good protection technologies and behavioral routines that protect against social engineering.

Even the most proactive infosec users, and government agencies and corporations concerned about information theft, may periodically experience unauthorized accessing and removal of classified or propriety data. This is when data encryption becomes a vital component of information security. **Encryption** is nothing more than encoding data with a cipher in a way that makes it unreadable except by using a decoding key. **Encryption keys** are generally regarded as being either paired **public keys** that users share with persons who they wish to be able to decipher data or **private keys** that users keep confidential for purposes of encoding data. With public key encryption, a user encrypts data using a private key and allows someone else to decrypt it with an authorized public key. The process also works in reverse: encryption with a public key can be decrypted with an authorized private key. Either way, the idea is for the encryption sponsor to make the public key widely available and keep the private key confidential. In this way, individual users and people working in agencies or firms can send encrypted messages back and forth and decode them upon arrival.

Encryption has a long and interesting history, including the fact that it is nothing new; military commanders since ancient times have found ways to encode secret dispatches. The same is true today, except that the science of **cryptography** has produced very complex computer algorithms for creation of encoding and decoding ciphers. The longer the key is in terms of bits, the more difficult it is to decipher. As of November 2001, the U.S. Government adopted the **Advanced Encryption Standard (AES)** for encoding money data, as during wire transfers. Certain intelligence agencies, such as the National Security Agency (NSA), specialize in intercepting and unscrambling encrypted messages for national security purposes. Encryption for private use is becoming a mainstream information security method, but in some ways is not yet ready to be used by everyone, even though reliable encryption software is readily available, easy to use, and inexpensive or even free.

General purpose encryption provided by **Pretty Good Privacy (PGP)** has been around since 1991 and provides an easy-to-use desktop icon interface. The Massachusetts Institute of Technology (MIT) and the Free Software Foundation have both developed several open-source PGP implementations and derivations. When PGP went commercial in 1996 (for use with Windows operating systems), it was acquired by security vendor McAfee and later remarketed as its own entity. All of this is to say that encryption, once the domain of secretive government agencies and financial institutions, still has a mystery about it that confuses and intimidates many nontechnical users. However, the commercial versions of PGP and other encryption applications are very easy to use and integrate well into desktop applications. Macintoshes have a similar encryption utility built into the OSX operating system. Encryption can also protect data on transportable devices such as USB drives, CDRs, DVD-Rs, and backup tapes and can make email and instant messaging useful for sharing sensitive information.

Problems with encryption are most often associated with managing private keys and pose challenges similar to managing multiple passwords. How can one or more long private encryption keys be remembered? If written down, private keys, like other valuable information assets, are susceptible to being stolen, whether saved in hardcopy or electronically. What if your private encryption keys were to become lost, damaged, or stolen? Say goodbye to all of your encrypted data. To guard against this, perhaps you would opt to create copies of your private encryption keys. The problem with doing so is storage and security of multiple key sets. Where and how can you safeguard them while assuring a level of reasonably convenient access? Would you do the cyber equivalent of hiding a private encryption key under an external doormat or in a flower pot next to the entrance of your residence? Technical and process-based solutions for securing private encryption keys do exist, such as **key escrow**, in which trusted sources store copies of private keys in off-site locations on behalf of their owners. However, if the holders of keys held in escrow become known to criminals, their facilities and information systems may instantly be targeted for physical, cyber, and social engineering attacks. Where better to get a job as a computer technician or a janitor than in the server area of a key escrow government agency?

If private keys are discovered, they must be canceled and reissued much like a credit card when it is lost or stolen. Additionally, all data must be re-encrypted with a new cipher, and intended users must then be informed of new access requirements. This is not straightforward because encryption sponsors may not know everyone who needs a new public key and/or they may not have maintained accurate lists of revoked public key holders. Suppose you sent very sensitive information months ago encrypted by your old private key to public key holders who need or want to decrypt it *after* you have issued a new public key. Things get complicated. Another problem has to do with properly signing encrypted messages. Suppose you want to send a confidential document to another person. To be safe, you must encrypt it with a unique public key; otherwise, anyone who intercepts your message and possesses a general-purpose public key can read the message. The implication is that just sending and receiving electronic messages securely is not straightforward, even though technology allows for easy encryption. Moreover, continually encrypting and decoding messages and data can be a hassle, inefficient, and costly in terms of time and effort required to do it properly. Ultimately, the effectiveness of encryption often comes down to determining who can be trusted with what data, further determining what must be encrypted, plus managing and protecting an **electronic key ring** in which private and public keys are stored, often with single, double, or even triple layers of encryption requiring different keys depending on needed security and levels and the extent of access authorization required.

**Digital signatures** are another information security measure used to establish the real identity of an email or instant messaging author. They can be used to defeat impersonation and social engineering in electronic messaging by using encryption in a very specific way combined with a one-way hash algorithm. **Algorithms** are mathematical formulas that combine file size and the relative position of bits to produce a unique **hash value** that cannot be regenerated as the original file (hence the "one-way") and will change its value whenever changes are made to the original file. Technical examples of common hash algorithms are MD5, SHA1, and SHA256. Digital signatures work with a **certificate authority** such as Thawte, Comodo, or Verisign, which can be purchased from commercial vendors or acquired for free online. The certificate contains a private key, which is only used for signing. The issuer holds the public key. When a person figures out where their mail reading application stores certificates for signing, they put the certificate in the folder and they set the email (or other messaging applications) to digitally sign correspondence. When messages are sent, the one-way hash is applied to the body of the correspondence and any attachments. Said differently, the results of the hash algorithm are encrypted with the private key in the certificate on the user's computer. When mail arrives at the other end, the email program retrieves the public key from the certificate authority, decrypts the value of the one-way hash function, computes the same one-way hash function on the message and its attachments, and then compares the sent value to the computed one. If they match, the person sending the message is identified and the integrity of the message is verified.

**10.1.1.2.9 Do Not Work from an Account with Root or Administrator Privileges.**    System administrators, information security professionals, and cybercrime investigators also have personal systems, devices, and data. If you are a member of this elite group, do not be tempted to work on your own data from an account with root or administrator privileges, as doing so may expose an entire network to a mistake you make. Even while diagnosing and servicing network-based operating systems, applications, and data files, work from a regular user account. That way if you get tricked into launching a worm or virus, it can only affect the regular user account you are using and not the entire network. Then when you need to install or remove software, login to the root or administrator account. Remember, a computer is only as secure as the administrator is trustworthy. Even as a professional, you will make mistakes. Moreover, since your job is to detect errors and problems, you are more exposed and in some ways more vulnerable than ordinary system users—the equivalent of primary school teachers who catch every bug young students contract. If other professionals need to use your computer, make sure they also login as a regular user to avoid inadvertently making system-wide mistakes.

**10.1.1.2.10 Adopt Information Security into Your Personal and Professional Lifestyles.**    It bears repeating that effective information security is not an activity, project, or program. Rather, as previously indicated, it must become a chosen lifestyle that transcends computing for personal and professional purposes. In this regard, there are several additional things you should strive to do. First, find ways to keep yourself and your technology current. Information security will continue to rapidly evolve along with innumerable technology-enabled threats, so find infosec sources that "speak your language" and check in with these periodically to discern how computer abuses, cybercrimes, and attack methods are changing. Then build a response and management process around these threats that you understand, can easily implement, maintain, and afford. Set a reminder in your calendar to back up, patch up, and check for security updates. Make an information security Web page your browser home page and spend a couple of minutes every day scanning for new threats, infosec products, and even emerging laws and regulations that may impact your professional responsibilities.

A few good choices are SecurityFocus (http://securityfocus.com/), which organizes content by topic, SecurityNewsPortal (http://securitynewsportal.com), which grabs infosec and cybercrime news from other online sources, and Gladiator Security Forum (http://www.gladiator-antivirus.com/), which offers discussion boards including a good "Security Newbies" moderated board. Also consider subscribing to a security newsletter such as *InfoSec News* (http://www.c4i.org/isn.html), which delivers content from a wide variety of sources to your mailbox. You may also wish to read a security blog, such as those of security expert Bruce Schneier (http://www.schneier.com/blog/) or virus expert Eugene Kapersky (http://www.viruslist.com/en/ weblog). PC expert "Donna," a Microsoft "MVP," has a "PC & Internet Security Blog" (http:// msmvps .com/donna/) that points to a lot of good security news links and has great resources listed on the sidebar. These are just a few of the many popular ways and locations through which you can stay informed, reevaluate your own security practices, and protect your systems and data.

Another thing that you should be mindful of is taking control of your applications with respect to their having minds of their own. Periodically,

programs will automatically open your Internet browser in order to fetch product upgrades or relay updated information about your data or browsing activities, as is the case with spyware. Many good firewall applications will monitor attempted outgoing activity of your computer along with inbound traffic. You should get in the habit of not allowing these updates to occur until you approve. For instance, ask yourself, why is this program attempting to access the Net? Do I approve, and if I do, can it wait until later when I can more closely monitor what is occurring? If you learn to take control of your system in these ways, you should certainly not allow incoming messages to control your thinking about information security and the dangers of social engineering. Never open (i.e., execute or double-click) an email or instant message attachment unless it has been sent by someone you know and trust. If you do, you risk installing a Trojan or other type of malicious code onto your system.

One student recently told me that he lives in rural Pennsylvania in an area for which there is currently no local broadband ISP, so he subscribes to America Online to which he can at least connect using a dial-up modem. One day, while his computer was dialing out, error messages popped up indicating that AOL had denied access to all his user names on the account. Subsequently, an AOL tech support person informed the student that the action was taken because his computer was being used to spam people, evidently as the result of its being hacked into and taken over for this purpose. The technician assisted him by issuing a new password consisting of several numbers and letters. He also told the student to change the passwords on all his computers, install one or more firewalls, and update both virus definitions and software patches on a regular basis. Today, the student pays attention to all these preventative measures. He is also very careful about his online activities, especially downloading files when interacting and purchasing things online.

You also need to be careful about what you do with your old system after purchasing a new

**CYBER TALE 10.6**

### Broadband Connectivity: Learn to be a Savvy ISP Customer

Many, but certainly not all, computer users are switching to high-speed broadband Internet connectivity as it becomes available in their community. Without a router or firewall, people connected to the Internet via broadband cable are completely and especially vulnerable to packet sniffing and hacking. Unfortunately, few ISPs disclose the full range of potential security vulnerabilities their customers will face once they connect to the Net. One student complained that within two months of acquiring high-speed Internet service through a cable company, his computer was hacked and subsequently used to distribute pirated software without his knowledge. The hacker responsible also accessed and changed the cable company's maximum modem traffic settings. As a result, the cable company reportedly sought $3,000 in damages from the student, who was not even aware that his computer had been compromised. Only after the firm realized that several of their customers had been similarly victimized was civil action against the student halted. Eventually, the suspect who committed these crimes was caught. He turned out to be a local teenager whose parents had signed up for the same cable service, but they had no idea what their son was able to do and actually accomplished online. As an apology for its own security ineptness, the ISP gave the student and other violated victimized customers a year of free high-speed Internet service.

**CYBER TALE 10.7**

### Avoid Being Swindled in Online Auction Fraud

When you are young and money is burning a hole in your pocket, you might as well spend it on something like beefing, up or tricking, out your ride in order to get attention from the ladies. I love my car; it's a manual transmission with just less than 200 horsepower (for now). After purchasing it in the summer of 2002, I wanted to start tricking it out, but I didn't have much money and I didn't want the standard after-market things. So I started conducting searches on a very popular online auction Web site to see what was out there and about how much it would cost. I've always wanted Lamborghini style doors that open up rather than out, but these cost too much. However, I did find for only $12.85, instructions and a few special parts that would allow my trunk to slide back and then open up. In this way, I could show off my sound system after I got one.

So I sent a check to some guy in San Jose, California, but did not receive my kit. After a couple of weeks, I became concerned and emailed him. There was no response, and thirty days after the sale the auction site deleted all the online transaction records. I contacted the site to inquire and complain, but was told I would only be compensated a dollar for my loss. So I contacted my bank which, sure enough, had already processed the check. Then I checked online for persons living in San Jose with names matching the endorsement on the check, but I couldn't find an exact match. I was so upset that I actually called phone listings having correct first initials and last names, but it was to no avail—I knew I'd been ripped off!

Although this incident did not involve much money (even with my long distance phone calls), it really shook me up and for a long while I was afraid to shop online. I have since resumed my faith in doing business online, even through auction sites, but in every instance I keep records of everything: dates, times, names, email and real addresses, and account and confirmation numbers, etc. I never planned on getting taken and now I take all these steps to ensure I don't get ripped off either by an online auction firm or its patrons.

*Anonymous Student*

one. It is nice to donate older systems to charity, but unless data stored on media is completely eradicated, it is potentially recoverable by an increasing number of savvy computer users and cybercriminals. Eradication of a hard drive can be effectively accomplished with at least seven wipes using tools like Autoclave, KillDisk, or QuickWiper. If the hard drive is very small and not really worth saving, even as a donation, or if you are paranoid about someone recovering your deleted data, drill three holes through the hard drive or cut it in half with an axe. While we are on the subject of paranoia, do not inadvertently bug your own residence or business. Remember that webcams, microphones, and other computer components have been successfully controlled remotely with programs like Subseven, Nimda, Netbus, and BackOrifice. Make sure your system

is adequately fortified and that you do not remain online unnecessarily. Close the shutter or unplug your webcam when it is not being used, and turn your system microphone off. Finally, remember to share all you know and learn about cybercrime and information security with your family, friends, and professional associates. There is no magic to information security and prevention of cybercrimes and no reason to be intimidated, overwhelmed, or stick your head under a blanket. Think and talk about infosec in this way and teach people how to protect their systems so they too can enjoy more trouble-free computing.

### 10.1.1.3 Practicing InfoSec while Traveling.

Computerized societies are also mobile societies, with people seemingly always on the go. For several years, while employed by government

HE DOES THIS WHENEVER I ASK ABOUT FIREWALLS, VIRUS PROTECTION, AND OTHER STUFF LIKE THAT.

agencies in Washington, DC, I traveled extensively throughout the nation, usually with a laptop computer and even a portable printer or LCD projector on occasions in order to conduct work-related tasks while visiting criminal justice agencies. Fortunately, during all those years, I never experienced an accident or information security attack that resulted in harm to my computer equipment or loss of data (that I know of), despite routinely connecting to the Internet from hotels and other places. Many people traveling for business or pleasure are not so fortunate because they are careless with their electronic equipment and storage media. To some extent, this is completely understandable because traveling often requires breaking personal, professional, and computer- and infosec-related routines. Unlike when working within the familiar surroundings of an employer's or home office, mobile computing frequently places people in fast-paced, congested, and cramped environments within airports, train stations, and various modes of transportation, each presenting unusual conditions and opportunities for harm coming to systems and data.

It is important to understand that for purposes of information security, the concepts of travel and mobile computing are relative to the normal activities and lifestyles of users combined with their security awareness and comfort operating within specific computing environments. Consider, for example, that many students "travel" around their college and university campuses, routinely engaging in stand-alone and connected wired and wireless computing. Whether using their own laptops or school computer nodes to work on- or offline, they are to some extent mobile even if only saving their work on disks and carrying them around to other workstations. If they are familiar with and comfortable within the physical and cyber environment in which they are operating any type of electronic device, it matters little whether or not they are traveling in the traditional sense of going from one location to another, as when going home for the holidays. The real danger in mobile computing, however

conceived, lies in taking physical and information security in any environment for granted. Let us therefore briefly consider some security practices for computing in unfamiliar places as well as those you may routinely occupy away from home, work, or school.

First, recognize that all the preceding security tips apply to mobile computing. These include keeping things simple and, as just indicated, being cognizant of your surroundings inclusive of human systems and technological systems operating in the places you occupy. Obviously, circumstances and security implications change from place to place and may affect your security practices even while you travel around. Thus, you should never take a given physical or cyber environment for granted. Rather, you should assume that your electronic devices and data are vulnerable in every location you occupy.

One student reported that, as a joke, he waited until his roommate left their dorm room with his laptop computer still operating. Within a minute, he was able to install a remote access program on his roommate's laptop and thereafter control it from anywhere on campus. His tricks included rearranging items on the desktop, moving the mouse icon around aimlessly, and popping up pornographic pictures at inopportune moments such as when the campus resident advisor was visiting dorm rooms. Reportedly, the student victim had no idea what caused these things until the perpetrator told him. Although the incident did not result in any permanent harm, the roommate victimized could have prevented from these pranks by using a password-protected screen lock whenever he left the presence of this computer.

Another student was less fortunate when a laptop computer was stolen from his mother's house. The laptop contained a considerable amount of personal family information including income tax filing forms and financial documentation. Because his mother was employed as a teacher and used the laptop for work-related purposes, the computer also contained her students' grades and other personal information. To make matters worse, the laptop was not configured to require entry of a bios-level or Windows password for accessing the desktop and applications. This meant the thief could access all her data simply by turning the computer on. Fortunately, theft of the computer did not result in additional cybercrimes being committed, though it was difficult and embarrassing to clean up the ensuing security concerns surrounding the compromised student information. These two incidents underscore the importance of using password protection options along with sound physical security practices. As previously indicated, if a competent attacker can get unsupervised access to a keyboard, he or she essentially owns your system and all your data if not immediately, then potentially afterwards from a remote location. With this in mind, make sure you never leave your devices unattended and set your screen locks to activate when you leave.

I am not a fan of laptop cable locks, but they can be effective in close-proximity, short-duration situations if the machine is locked down with a password re-entry screen prior to being left unoccupied. Alternative physical protection devices include the Caveo Anti-Theft motion sensor alarm that fits in a CardBus/PCMCIA slot and Mobility's TrackIT, which has a key fob transmitter and a receiver alarm that sounds if you are separated from your laptop by more than 40 feet. If you insist on momentarily leaving your computer unattended, at least make sure that you disable the auto login feature and require use of both a bios-level password in addition to a Windows-level password for signing on. If you use a newer Microsoft operating system, the NTFS file system contains access controls that let you also specify read, write, change, or full system control privileges for individuals or groups who may periodically use your portable device, as in instances in which a laptop is shared by coworkers.[12] Unfortunately, too many people simply leave their electronic devices unattended, activated when not in use, or do not require strong access passwords on their portable devices, thereby allowing

intruders access to their device and control of their data. I never leave my portable devices unattended when out of my office environments— they go with me everywhere. Even when I leave my office, the door is always locked, with the machine locked down. After all, it only takes me a moment to retype the password to renew a work session. The forgoing methods will prevent outright theft of your device and data. Here are some additional tips to think about when traveling or engaged in mobile computing:

- Back up all your data before traveling.
- Take only what you need so that you are not preoccupied and weighed-down by lots of stuff, and do not unnecessarily risk losing equipment you are not likely to use anyway.
- Do not show off expensive computer equipment. Name brand computer cases look sharp but have the effect of advertising your gear.
- If you must leave your laptop in your car, hide it in the trunk or at least put it in a gym bag or some other inconspicuous container rather than in a special laptop briefcase or name brand computer bag.
- Keep your laptop, PDA, cell phone and other devices and portable media with you, if at all possible. If you cannot, consider registering these items with a hotel security service for safekeeping.
- Consider carrying and backing up your data to a large-capacity flash drive while traveling. That way, if your electronic device is stolen you will still have your data.

Encryption can also be very useful while traveling, because then stolen devices, even if hacked, will not yield useful information. Sony, SanDisk, and other vendors make USB flash memory drives that unlock biometrically with a fingerprint. Some laptops now also require a fingerprint scan before the computer will boot. Authenex markets a USB hard drive encryptor (HDLock) that also does not allow the laptop to boot completely without its USB key connected. The Sony Puppy can store digital signature certificates, as well as regular files in its 64K memory. The encrypted partition of the Puppy is protected with 3DES (i.e., triple encryption). The Puppy, Cruzer Profile, and the Authenex A-Key provide convenient alternatives to storing files on a laptop, and the A-Key will aid in encrypting files as well. Sony also incorporates its Puppy biometric technology into memory sticks and authentication devices.

Finally, we need to briefly consider dangers associated with wireless computing made possible by **WiFi networks** that exist in Internet cafes, public transportation terminals, shopping malls and on college or university campuses, among other types of locations. Wireless devices combined with WiFi standards and the Internet have extended wireless connectivity into homes, businesses, and other types of facilities and grounds of relatively small size. But like all forms of technology, there are potential risks associated with abusive, unethical and even illegal use of

WiFi that consumers should be aware of. People who create local WiFi networks for residential or commercial use have limited control over the broadcast distance, normally varying between 150-300 ft. (or considerably further) depending on wattage output of their system and environmental factors such as wall density, terrain and other obstacles like trees or parked cars, along with atmospheric and weather conditions. If data is broadcast unprotected, it is subject to being intercepted by other people who accidentally or intentionally tune into the frequency. This is similar to using portable telephones or walkie-talkies that utilize unrestricted airwaves and that allow people to listen in on conversations. Uncontrolled WiFi networks enable other users with an electronic device equipped with a wireless access card to share the connection, oftentimes without the knowledge of the person hosting the WiFi network. Once extra access is achieved, the new user can achieve Internet access through the host

## CYBER TALE 10.8

### *A Security Conscious Traveling Executive*

A Fortune 100 executive frequently traveled to Europe with his laptop computer, PDA, and cell phone. As an information security–conscious leader of a major corporation, he considered it a professional management responsibility to back up his system frequently, employ strong passwords, be aware of his surroundings, and encrypt all his data as well as several passwords. One day while in Europe, he found himself without a workable cell phone and was forced to make a call at a public telephone. While talking on the phone and taking notes, he set his fancy leather laptop case that identified the brand of his computer on the ground between his feet. Momentarily a thief snuck up behind him, grabbed the computer case and rushed down into a nearby subway entrance. The executive gave chase, only to see his laptop and the

thief disappear behind the closing doors of a departing train.

"Thank goodness," he thought to himself. At least his data and passwords had been encrypted so none of the valuable trade secrets, client sales, legal contracts, and ongoing corporate expansion plans would be accessible to the thief. Suddenly, he felt numb and began to visibly shake as he felt around for the flash drive disk containing all the password and data encryption decoding keys . . . that he had always kept in the laptop case—so much for that data. It was a significant career-limiting move, and more than a little embarrassing when his staff found out about his overseas security blunder. The corporation quickly did what it could to fortify its information security systems, including a policy review and updated training for staff, but with the corporate intelligence effectively leaked, the damage was already done.

computer just as if they were using their own ISP connection. A single location affording WiFi connectivity to the Internet is known as an **access point**. **Hotspots** are geographic locations in which many access points are located. Internet/WiFi cafes and certain airport terminals, among other locations populated by many computer users, are considered access points. If co-located with other access points they would combine on a map to constitute a hot spot. **Wardriving and warwalking** are slang terms used respectively for driving or walking around with a laptop computer or other device in search of open WiFi access points. Sometimes the people who do this will leave chalk or paint marks (i.e., graffiti) to indicate a place in which others can potentially jump online. In June of 2004, the controversial Worldwide Wardrive.org completed its final survey of access points. From June 12-19, participants from around the world reported 228,537 open access points, of which only 87,647 were **WEP enabled** (i.e., protected by technology meeting Wireless Encryption Protocol standards), 140,890 were not WEP enabled, 71,805 host systems had not changed default configurations, and 62,859 reportedly had default configurations and were not WEP enabled.[13] Similar findings, although on smaller survey scales, are commonly reported by computer buffs and information security professionals.

Devices connecting via a WiFi connection can infect host systems with malware, such as viruses, and if an unknown person accesses your device and commits a crime via a WiFi connection, you could still potentially be found civilly and/or criminally responsible, although you could presumably muster a defense that you were unaware of what was taking place. In Chapter 3, we pointed out that accessing a WiFi network without permission is illegal. Indeed, in July of 2005, Benjamin Smith (41) was arrested by police in St. Petersburg, Florida for unlawfully accessing a computer network, allegedly after a resident experienced desktop problems and saw Smith sitting outside his home with a laptop computer.[14]

However, accessing WiFi networks without explicit permission is controversial on legal, technological, and cultural grounds, and an emerging area of law. Consider that many people living in computing societies are to a greater or lesser extent "computer people" who are familiar with laptops, PDAs, and other electronic devices. Social norms, values, and ethical standards vary among computer users and depend on various factors such as their knowledge of and expertise using computers, other electronic IT devices and information systems; the extent and purposes of their technology use; and their subcultural or social affiliations. In the cyber society, there exist shared ethos for information sharing, which implies networking for mutual benefit (e.g., communication, research, entertainment, purchasing, online banking and investment, etc.). As we learned in Chapter 7, the original hacker ethic espoused exploration with computers and unfettered access to and sharing of information even if it meant doing so illegally. Similarly, the Open Source Community consisting of myriad computer enthusiasts exists to develop and maintain high quality software which is substantially free to the public. Many WiFi networks are intentionally left open by individuals for free access by strangers, a sort of "help yourself" to what otherwise would be a wasted or under-utilized resource. In addition, commercial enterprises and even municipalities throughout the world are increasingly making free access point (i.e., WiFi networks) available respectively to create/expand their customer bases or provide a public service. Thus, throughout society there exists a growing expectation and market demand for high-quality and less expensive portable IT devices coupled with more access to lower cost and even free high speed connectivity. Freely accessing WiFi networks represents a new area for criminal and civil/tort law. Historically, attorneys, jurists, and legal scholars have always tried to apply existing case law rulings, and thus prior technological circumstances, to new situations brought about through technology invention and innovation. Oftentimes, analogies to other technological circumstances provide insufficient bases upon which to establish new legal principles.

Who owns a given WiFi connection? Who has a legal right to control or access the WiFi airwave? If a person pays for 100mb access, are they entitled to full high-speed connectivity even when they are not actually using the system and services? Who owns the data if it is broadcast in the clear (i.e., not encrypted)? Is this akin to shouting out your door or using a megaphone, where people passing by on the street can hear what is said? Or does it depend on whether the broadcast and data exceeds a person's property line?

Suppose a person's device on boot-up automatically but accidentally connects to a private WiFi while the user is in a public place. But the user is not technologically savvy enough to even notice that their device is connected to the Net, much less check the service set identifier (SSID) settings to realize they are on a foreign private WiFi as opposed to a public/community one—after all, the strongest signal strength will prevail in a given geographic location. What about instances in which a WiFi signal is transmitted into a neighbor's house and due to signal strength prevents the neighbor from connecting to the Internet via their own WiFi network? How can courts determine culpability when the user did not realize it was not a public WiFi, or in cases in which multiple users (e.g., children) share a single host computer system?

As we learned in Chapter 8, prosecution for theft of services often requires prior legal notice, as is often true for prosecuting computer trespassing cases. Providing legal notice of illegal conduct helps to establish an illegal intent. But could this also depend on the purpose or motivation for which unknown/unauthorized access was achieved? Perhaps merely accessing a WiFi network without permission and thereby denying a paying customer full access is akin to theft of services. However, if hacking activities were involved, this would obviously constitute computer/network trespassing. If other crimes were committed in conjunction with hacking, such as downloading child porn or theft of data for credit

card fraud or identity theft purposes, then additional charges would also be in order. Further, how are we to distinguish between what is socially normal, ethical, and legal? These are different concepts which arguably are of equal importance. Just because it is legal to do something does not make it right. Meanwhile, the IT industry, inclusive of hardware and software developers, manufacturers and retailers are not currently required by regulations to inform consumers of risks associated with product use. Developers, manufacturers, and retailers are interested in pushing products for money. Absent regulation, security-related costs are often avoided except to the extent marketing and provision of security can be linked to sales and profits. Some manufacturers are, however, beginning to set minimum authentication defaults on their products. However, most devices are preset to default settings that result in devices automatically searching for WiFi access points, and that enable file sharing and sending/receiving unencrypted messages. Consumers generally do not understand these information security risks, much less how to reconfigure their systems to enable and thus require security procedures. Until these legal, technological and cultural issues are sorted out by local, state, and federal courts, host and participate in WiFi networks with care. To minimize risks of cybercrime associated with wireless networks, information security professionals recommend that users: change default settings and passwords on their systems, restrict access to authorized users encrypt data, avoid making SSIDs public, install a firewall on the wireless network router, ensure that laptop computers of authorized users of the network also have firewalls installed, and maintain antivirus software.

## 10.1.2 Assuring Protection of Information in Organizations

To this point we have primarily focused on what individual users should do to protect their personal computer systems, other electronic devices, and data. The information security rules discussed also pertain to individual employees working in government agencies, private firms, or nonprofit organizations. However, information security in organizations is naturally more complex and, therefore, difficult owing to increased numbers of people combined with varying technologies and amounts of data involved. In addition, the stakes of insecure systems and data involving large government agencies and corporations are generally higher, although the loss of services, data, and revenue generation capability can render any size of organization dysfunctional or insolvent in very short order. Approximately 60 percent of companies that lose their data will cease operating within six months of a disaster, and 93 percent of firms that lose data center capabilities for ten days or longer file for bankruptcy within one year, while about 50 percent of firms without data management for this same time period will file bankruptcy immediately.[15]

While loss-related statistics are alarming, it is also true that technology salespersons generally desire to sell organizations every imaginable information management and security product. IT professionals also generally wish to purchase new products or upgrades for very good reasons. Obviously, the size of an organization; its product and service missions; the amount and type of critical data needed, generated, stored, used, and transmitted; and data availability requirements relative to confidentiality and integrity should help determine security investment decisions. A single unprotected PC could effectively render an entire network useless by absorbing all available bandwidth as a result of a virus attack or illegitimate downloading of music and movie files. A single failed device responsible for billing customers but not backed-up with redundant operating capabilities may cause revenues to suddenly and significantly drop off. Worse, a down server that houses patient information could delay delivery of critical information needed to make an emergency surgery decision.

All this implies that managers throughout organizations, not merely in IT departments, need to diligently consider technology and human factors as investments for reliable computing and thus enhanced information security. This is no easy task because every user and device on a network is important in maintaining the overall security secure posture of a given enterprise. What is needed is a general method for determining current and future states of information security within organizational settings.

***10.1.2.1 Security Assessments.*** Information security within organizational settings most often begins by determining the extent and effectiveness of information assurance controls already in place. **Security assessments** are inspections of hardware, software, data, and human factor controls to determine what is already in place and what needs to be changed to afford a satisfactory level of security. A **baseline security assessment** is the first of what should be many assessments conducted at regular intervals to identify weaknesses in security systems. The goal of these assessments is to track security status and improvements and make ongoing recommendations for security improvements in accordance with changing threat environments and **due care and diligence** standards determined on the basis of laws and regulations along with best practices exemplified within a given industrial sector. Although technical aspects of how to perform security assessments are not within the scope of this book, current and future IT professionals and managers employed throughout government agencies, private sector firms, and nonprofit organizations in today's information-driven society must understand what security assessments are and what they generally cost.

Not every organization will be able to achieve, much less maintain, the highest possible level of information security, nor is this necessary in all situations. The extent and quality of security controls to be implemented following a security assessment will logically depend on the nature of an organization and its mission; what its current and future operations will consist of; how large and spread out the physical plant and

*Security Assessment in Action* Photo courtesy of: Jack Finklea, Telperion Solutions Group, LLC.

information network systems are and may become; the types of most critical information and requisite confidentiality, integrity, and availability factors associated with these data; and how much a firm can afford to spend on information systems security upgrades inclusive of personnel training and so on. **Baselining** is the technique for modeling physical and information systems security against real, current, and future threats relative to in-place or available security controls protecting selected assets. By *available*, we mean attack prevention or countermeasures generally accepted as preferred methods of protecting assets as determined by information security

professionals working in closely related sectors and organizations of similar size. The idea is to gage appropriate levels of advance security and countermeasures to be deployed in attack situations and not to expend inordinate resources to protect assets of little value. This should take into account human and technological factors, which as you will recall from Chapter 2, must both be simultaneously trusted and distrusted to some extent in order to optimize information assurance.

### 10.1.2.2 Designing and Implementing Security Controls.
Security assessments and baselining provide reference points for making improvements

to information security systems. As such, they are essential components of continuous quality improvement programs for monitoring and enhancing security within organizations as needed according to evolving computer abuse, physical, and cyber security threats, and cybercrimes faced by all types of organizations, large and small. A college student reported that while working in a summer co-opposition, a disgruntled employee thought he could profit by changing customer account data in their favor and then charging an administrative fee that he would then siphon off to a personal account, but without actually increasing the bill. As the employee perceived his treatment by management to worsen, he hired a programmer to write malicious code that would freeze messages on users' computer screens at particular times. The employee also knew that the firm was lax in its data backup policies, so before resigning he apparently installed another malicious program that was timed to wipe out the firm's hard drive. The time bomb program took effect about three months after the employee's departure and required retaining technical experts at a cost of $75,000 to restore most of the customer account data. However, some of it was not recoverable, and it could not be substantiated that the disgruntled former employee had been responsible for the damage.

Managers today need structured ways to systematically pay attention to the physical and information security needs of their firms. Security assessments and baselining under the guidance of trained security professionals, who themselves remain abreast of current and unfolding threats and available security countermeasures, are as critical as the data in need of assurance. However, keeping pace with cyber threats and countermeasures is more than a full-time job in many organizations, especially given regulatory or policy requirements to meet due care and diligence standards to protect assets and reduce liability associated with compromised systems and denial, degradation, loss, or destruction of data. How is this accomplished in practice? Where

can managers, including those of smaller firms without the benefit of IT professionals on staff, go to learn about and begin the ongoing processes of designing, implementing, and evaluating security controls?

Most small- to medium-sized businesses cannot afford an information technology team that has the skill set and knowledge to dissect an operating system and analyze the vulnerabilities within that platform. The internal IT team will frequently rely upon outside assistance and may adopt many of the practices found in freely available resources from the National Security Agency (NSA) and affiliated agencies. The NSA resource pool has security guidelines for most of common network operating systems and supporting network devices and maintains a large library of instructional information for protecting information technology infrastructures. Outside consultants are another resource for conducting an assessment. They generally have very qualified staff members with credentials from the well-known International Information Systems Security Certification Consortium, Inc. (ISC$^2$), the Information Systems Audit and Control Association (ISACA), and the SANS Institute. All three of these organizations promote security programs and certifications that focus on protecting an organization's critical data. Additional resources are the manufacturers and vendors of services, which almost always have a large knowledge base of information specific to their products. Microsoft and Cisco, in particular, freely publish their recommendations for best security practices for configuring their software and hardware.

### 10.1.2.3 Technology Investment and Procurement Decisions.
Making information security technology investment and procurement decisions in dynamic threat environments is tricky, often frustrating, and, unfortunately, may also prove expensive and ineffectual. The Robert Hanssen treason case mentioned in Chapter 3 as an example of insider espionage proved embarrassing to

several Department of Justice officials, as well as to the entire FBI, which was already under congressional scrutiny for longstanding managerial, operations, and technological problems with its information management system and security. The Hanssen incident resulted in a major initiative to review and overhaul information security policies, procedures, and case management systems technologies within the FBI. However, in February of 2005, the Bureau announced that its virtual case file information system, which had already cost $104 million and was still in development to support organized crime and terrorism investigations, needed to be entirely scrapped and reinvented in order to meet changing administrative, operational, and security requirements.[16]

How can IT administrators, information security professionals, and other managers of organizations continually go about making wise infosec technology investments in order to stay in business and keep from being sued? There is no easy answer to this question, and it is an increasingly sore subject at management meetings and boardroom discussions because as cybercrime threats increase, state governments and the federal government are simultaneously promulgating information security regulations and cracking down on lax security practices. California now requires all organizations that experience an information security violation resulting in unauthorized release of confidential information to immediately notify clients or customers. Other states and the federal government may soon enact similar legislation. The obvious problem for mangers is that good security in organizational settings requires considerable time, money, and investment of personnel and technological resources in various appropriate combinations and amounts not easy to determine. This perplexing reality underscores confusion and even hostility toward IT administrators and information security professionals who are constantly advocating strong security protections amidst political and operating climates of constrained budgets, limited understanding of IT, and sophisticated cybercrime

methods versus available infosec countermeasures, plus undetermined *actual* threats faced by organizations. More will be said about this in the next section when we consider risk management.

## 10.2 Advancing the Security Posture of Organizations

Organizations require differing levels of physical and cyber security. Since the nature and extent of threats is continually changing, all organizations must continually monitor the effectiveness of their existing security systems and make changes when warranted. Unfortunately, it often takes a loss of data or an embarrassing episode before security problems are detected and remedies instituted. In July of 2004, as a direct result of former National Security Advisor Samuel R. Berger's removal of classified documents from the National Archives in preparation for his testimony before the 9-11 Commission, nongovernmental persons who are now granted access to classified materials must review documents under continuous monitoring in rooms equipped with surveillance cameras. New policies also prohibit any type of electronic device being taken into classified materials research rooms and restrict the type and amount of materials that may be reviewed at a given time.[17]

Arguably, security violations such as that reported in the Berger incident, come about in the natural course of agency and business operations and cannot always be predicted. If they could be, we could simply implement security precautions once and thereafter consider them good enough. Of course, this is not possible, and managers, on reflection, come to realize that many security incidents could have been anticipated and that measures should have been taken to reduce risks of loss. When government regulators, stockholders, and juries in civil suits also come to this realization, information security has a way of getting on radar screens. Had the U.S. National Archives & Records Administration conducted periodic reviews of its security policies, procedures, and practices, the embarrassing and politically charged incident involving former National Security Advisor Berger certainly could have been averted. Similarly, the University of California Berkeley, among numerous other academic institutions, government agencies, private sector firms, and nonprofit organizations should be learning from their past mistakes and those made by similar entities.

In this section, we explore how to plan, implement, and evaluate organizational changes for enhanced information security and cybercrime prevention. We begin by considering how managers can prepare themselves and organizational personnel for change processes. Specifically, we will address the importance of defining security missions in other business and operating contexts and different scopes of authority for overseeing information security change processes. We will also address alternative approaches for structuring security-related personnel positions within organizations according to varying general needs and designation of security improvement priorities and responsibilities of key personnel for ensuring that security improvements are accomplished. Next, we will discuss risk management with respect to creation and implementation of security policies and procedures. Then we will examine data and business recovery issues and vitally important processes having to do with managing organizational culture and change processes with and without technical contractor assistance. Finally, we will discuss security audits, with particular attention paid to auditing decisions, procedures, and information assurance standards. Although these very important topics are discussed at a general level, the following discussion cannot be regarded as a "how to" manual for accomplishing tasks described. Instead, this material is provided as an overview of what all aspiring criminal justice, security, and other types of organizational managers should know to ensure that their agency or firm is not caught off guard and suffers from preventable losses of data.

## 10.2.1 Security Change Procedures

There is an old saying that people do not plan to fail—they just fail to plan. This is certainly true, as is the necessity to plan how to effect organizational change processes. An IT administrator or information security manager who impetuously begins making systems changes without carefully considering alternatives and possible impacts on technology, personnel, and operations is borrowing trouble and will eventually find him- or herself in a disastrous situation. For this reason, let us now consider how to go about planning physical and information security changes in organizations.

### 10.2.1.1 Determining Priorities and Designating Responsibilities for Change.  For discussion's sake, let us assume that circumstances in an organization require security changes to be made as the result of either an actual or averted loss of data, because new laws or regulations require new security measures, or because a wise manager decided it was time to get serious about security and make needed improvements. The first step to take toward making security changes is to determine the nature of threats relative to differing assets in need of protection versus physical and cyber security measures already in place. This means security change processes begin with an understanding of what needs to be improved to varying degrees and what does not need to be changed at all. Hence, someone, hopefully working collaboratively across an organization, needs to make security *assessment* determinations in environments of threats versus best practices for meeting due care and diligence standards. In other words, managers need to determine and prioritize needed security improvements—someone must be empowered to call the shots.

An individual or team of managers charged with making security assessment determinations and recommendations for improving security technologies, policies, and practices must be selected on the basis of their technical skills, knowledge of technology, and ability to get things done with help from other people. The best IT administrators and information security professionals have considerable "people skills" and political savvy in addition to technological knowledge and skills, but to be truly effective they must be made responsible and held account- able for accomplishing security assessment and change tasks, with support from executives. This means they must be granted authority to make needed changes, and supplied with needed re- sources. Indeed, only when senior managers are seen to have authority and needed resources to effect changes, and also take personal interest in security will the majority of rank and file em- ployees typically get on board with security change processes. Conversely, if physical and in- formation security is merely espoused without genuine understanding and support from senior managers, organizational change processes for enhanced security are doomed. Hence, leader- ship at executive and managerial levels of an or- ganization is also critical. Many information security professionals complain that lack of un- derstanding and support from their bosses is of greater concern than the potential cyber security threats they face. All too frequently, inadequate resources in terms of money, time, technology, training, and support personnel are allocated for security upgrades and change processes. When combined with a lack of understanding and polit- ical commitment among competing managerial interests, the results are often fatal.

### 10.2.1.2 Alternative Approaches for Structur- ing Security Changes.

It is important to de- termine as early as possible the extent to which security change processes will be accomplished by employees or outsourced to contractors. In general, **in-sourcing** will cost less, be accom- plished faster, take operational nuances into greater consideration, and allow managers more personal involvement and oversight of change processes. Disadvantages of having designated employees effect security changes often include

their lack of broader perspectives and needed technical expertise, diminished respectability among or resentment by fellow employees, and being under-resourced and pulled away to per- form other "priority" duties by senior managers or other supervisors to whom they normally re- port. Conversely, **outsourcing** has the advantage of involving genuine security expertise, having technically complicated aspects of projects done right (although not always in the first attempt!), and providing accountability via a legally bind- ing contract. It is important to observe that, in practice, security improvements facilitated by outsourced vendors usually come about as the re- sult of contracts for IT systems upgrades rather than explicit contracts to improve information security. Disadvantages of outsourcing typically are the time, expense, and time management re- quired to prepare and bid contracts and provide contractor oversight and liaison, and the reality that upon completion of contracts, vendors may move onto new jobs with other clients, leaving organizations without ongoing technical support or resident expertise for managing new informa- tion systems.

Assuming that commitment and support for security changes are in place and that compe- tent personnel have been selected to design and engineer needed security change processes, the next step is to determine the best way to structure their positions within organizations. Many large firms have dedicated security units, although fa- cilities and information security functions typi- cally remain separated. This means special effort is required to bridge these inextricable organiza- tional functions. The implication is that the most successful overall security solutions will position personnel charged with implementing security changes with joint-unit input or oversight author- ity. However, ultimately one individual must be able and willing to make key and binding deci- sions so that needed changes can go into effect quickly, when necessary. Generally, the higher a change agent is positioned in an organization's chain of command, the more real and perceived power he or she will have to lead, push, and pull for needed security changes. Positioning of security-change managers in firms for maximum effectiveness also depends on technological, legal, political, and socio-cultural factors at work in the short, mid, and long terms.

Structuring of positions within organizations may also depend on the scope of intended authority. If a chief information security officer (CSO) is assigned to report directly to a chief executive officer (CEO) or president of a company, they are positioned and likely expected to provide a check and balance to both the firm's chief information officer (CIO) and chief financial officer (CFO). This can be advantageous for internal security and auditing purposes (discussed later). A CSO who reports directly to a CEO or president can communicate information security status and improvements status, while also arguing the business case for investing in security technologies and training. However, a CSO assigned to report to a CFO may be more empowered to recommend network security changes that reporting to a CIO would disallow. It is also possible that positioning a CSO to work under the direction of a CIO may bring technical expertise to an IT support unit and help to ensure appropriate technological integration in future procurement decisions and so on. This approach would also help a CIO to back security systems integration at the enterprise level. Many other personnel structuring possibilities will provide pros and cons that must be weighed against resources and challenges at hand.

### 10.2.1.3 Implementing Security Changes.

Security changes range from short lists of easily accomplishable tasks to major organizational changes such as indicated above in the discussion of alternative approaches to structuring security change agent positions. In any case, information security is important to the financial health and operational well-being of all organizations. As indicated in Chapter 2, infosec operates best in trusting environments, yet as we know, people

and technology must be simultaneously distrusted to some extent because either or both may fail under stress. Ideally, infosec is free from politics, but this is not realistic; mangers will guard their turfs and what they rightfully believe to be the best interests of their units and the overall organization, and many will not understand or appreciate the importance of information security policies, procedures, and technologies with respect to due care and diligence standards. Some will hold the mistaken belief that information security is something "techies" alone are suppose to pay attention to. To inspire confidence and maintain credibility of infosec change processes, senior managers, IT administrators, and information security professionals must lead by example. If a key role is review of security procedures and technology, then senior managers should mandate periodic infosec assessments. Similarly, if infosec is important, CEOs should build it into annual capital improvement and operating budgets. Such practices will reinforce the importance of information security and help infuse sound infosec practices into the culture of an organization. In all cases, the message from top management should be, "Infosec matters, and negligent security blunders constitute career limiting moves."

Implementing information security changes can be made easier for less technically-inclined employees and managers by dividing security technology upgrades and new practices into phases that each have specific goals and objectives. In this way, realistic expectations can be set and reported on to executive managers, with modifications to implementation strategies being made as needed. This concept fits nicely with the reality that information security needs to be continually reassessed given dynamic threat and technology innovation environments. Cybercriminals are not going to back off simply because an organization feels like "calling time out" in order to improve its security posture, or feels that it has already done so. To the contrary, insider and outsider attackers may become emboldened if they sense an organization's security is lax or is slipping, regardless of why this may be happening (e.g., we did an assessment last year, we need a rest, countermeasures are too expensive) To avoid **threat fatigue**, it is important recognize improvements and foster a sense of teamwork. Additionally, there needs to be an expectation set for everyone involved that as security baselining and controls *improve, detection of security problems may initially result in a greater number of discovered and/or reported* violations—a counterintuitive sign that information security is actually improving. This is often seen in policing: improved police-citizen relations and community crime prevention leads to more reporting of crimes and the perception that crime rates are increasing when actually they are decreasing. In short, many executives and senior managers need to be educated and "brought along" in their understanding, tolerance, and support of information security changes.

## 10.2.2 Risk Management

**Risk and threat analysis** is a controversial practice that attempts to qualify and quantify potential security threats for purposes of making cost–benefit technology and personnel investment decisions. Certainly return on investment considerations are necessary, however, it is seldom possible to make accurate benefit-to-cost assessments, because the benefit in terms of IT-enabled abuse and crimes averted is incalculable. Although *qualification* of threats to physical and information security are based on known physical and cybercrime attack methods, *quantification* of threats for purposes of making security investments is not straightforward or reliable. As explained by information security expert, Donn Parker, risk assessments necessarily involve estimating expected losses under varying circumstances on the basis of past losses for the full range of experienced and potential attack scenarios.

Parker also explains that credible risk analysis is impossible because, in considering both technology and human factors, "it involves trying to estimate the future misbehavior of unknown people, using unknown methods with unpredictable motives, against unknown targets that may cause unknown losses." Moreover, while risk analysis is based on probability theory, there exist "no statistically valid samples applicable to specific vulnerabilities for use in information security risk assessment."[18] Consequently, mangers, IT administrators, and information security professionals are without scientific means to accurately assess the threats they face. This underscores why they must stay abreast of potential threats, available security technologies, and best security practices in order to protect their networks and comply with due care and diligence standards applicable to their situation (review Textbox 10.1).

It is important to note that information security professionals, even those employed by government agencies, are divided in their views about the value of risk analysis and assessments, which must not be confused with security assessments, discussed earlier in the chapter. The National Institute of Standards and Technology (NIST) has a long history of referring to risk assessments in its official publications as if to endorse the practice. However, as reported by Parker, the National Security Agency (NSA) no longer helps develop risk assessment methodologies and has quietly ceased to espouse risk analysis, even though it continues to produce highly recommended information security practices.[19] Where does this leave IT professionals and managers who must make infosec technology investment decisions on an ongoing basis? First, recognize that we have already *qualified* the evolving nature of potential computer-enabled abuses, threats to information security systems, and cybercrimes. We did so explicitly in Chapters 2 and 3. We have also established in Chapter 6 that the amount of computer-enabled abuse and cybercrimes is not fully known and may be unknowable given changing conceptual and definitional problems and so on. However,

## BOX 10.1  •  *Due Care and Diligence*

Due care and diligence is an extremely important information security concept. It pertains to legal responsibilities that organizations and IT professionals have for protecting information systems and data. In short, company executives, system administrators, and information security professionals are liable for everything that occurs on the computer networks of their organization. Firms, IT professionals, and senior managers who fail to develop, implement, and enforce policies and procedures for adequately protecting information systems and data may be held civilly and even criminally liable. Organizations with effective physical and information security programs in place greatly reduce risks of security violations and attendant liability. Conversely, firms that are negligent with regard to their information security policies, procedures, practices, and technologies are exposed to both attacks and liability.

Due care and diligence standards vary according to industrial sector and type and size of organization and the types and amount of data maintained. Unfortunately, these standards are rarely, if ever, written down. Instead, they develop informally and through official actions in accordance with known security threats and available technology countermeasures including best practices for utilizing tools and techniques for enhanced physical and cyber security. In general, the larger the agency, company, or nonprofit organization, the more security it is expected to have. Large publicly-traded corporations and organizations with public fiduciary functions including security of health and financial records are expected to have higher security than smaller firms or those that do not have these responsibilities. Similarly, organizations that maintain and manage large amounts of confidential personnel, client, or customer account data are held to higher security standards than firms that do not control extensive amounts of data.

Managers and IT professionals who fail to make inquiries or decisions or act to address security deficiencies, or who are in any way negligent in their oversight and technical responsibilities, may be personally liable for civil law suits, criminal prosecution, and tax liability. In 1997, federal sentencing guidelines became applicable to cybercrimes, which resulted in senior officers now being personally liable for violations of information security–related laws and regulations. Management must also take reasonable precautions to prevent data losses occurring as the result of natural disasters involving fire, floods, and structural failures (e.g., archiving records in off-site locations). We live in a litigious society, and one vulnerable to the effects of computer abuse and cybercrimes. Students and practitioners of information security are well-advised to adopt the view that sooner or later they *will be* sued. Whether or not they and their attorneys can successfully defend against civil actions will substantially depend on their compliance with due care and diligence standards in the weeks, months, and years prior to alleged negligence.

we do know in specific technological terms measures that can be taken to prevent IT-enabled abuses and crimes, and these are being increasingly established in due care and diligence standards and codified in specific government laws and regulations.

Managers, therefore, can and must make reasonably informed decisions pertaining to information security investments based on what is known to be occurring offensively and with regard to available defensive countermeasures, even if they cannot rely on *quantifiable criteria* in their decision making. In other words, managers must exercise sound judgments about needed security with imperfect information about the nature of the threats they face. Alas, this is what they are paid to do, and it assumes they have or will acquire basic knowledge, understanding, and concern about cybercrime and information security issues as discussed throughout this text. Honest information security consultants can be very helpful to managers making investment decisions on the basis of emerging threats and technological countermeasures. Savvy managers should never discount the potential for loss of data. They must also recognize that some data losses are probably inevitable and that under- and over-investments to prevent security violations and loss of data will also likely periodically occur. Security investment and tradeoff concepts were introduced in Chapter 2 and by now should make even more sense with regard to why managers and IT professionals must weigh the types and amounts of security required in varying environments.

Traditionally risk managers and security managers are viewed and treated as either the same or separate functions depending on the size of an organization, its facilities, and the nature of operations. In the classic sense, security managers are primarily concerned with facilities protection, including the comings and goings of personnel, suspicious activities, and the adequacy of locks, lighting, alarm, and biometric and other physical access security technologies. Risk managers are traditionally viewed as a liability and safety officials who specialize in understanding laws and regulations governing work environments; operations, services, and product liability oversight; and creation of policies and procedures supported by employee training programs and effective supervision. Information security professionals in management roles are newcomer positions, that, as explained above, may be advantageously assigned to report to senior managers within organizations in different ways. However, in theory and practice there is increasing overlap between physical security, information security, and risk management functions, regardless of the size of an organization. In other words, all organizations must attend to these issues, so it is a matter of prioritizing and structuring these to ensure adequate overall security while minimizing differing kinds of risks.

### 10.2.2.1 Security Policies and Procedures.
The phrase "policies and procedures" is often bantered about with little regard for or understanding of what these different concepts mean, much less how to effectively design, implement, maintain, evaluate, and modify them when necessary. A **policy** is a written document that states management's position on taking actions toward the accomplishment of certain goals under varying conditions. Depending on their formality and length, policies often contain a set of *definitions*, a *purpose statement*, an *explanation* or examples of the types of activities governed, and *guidelines* pertaining to issues of adoption, implementation, evaluation, and modification. Organizational policies are often created to comport with laws or government regulations, agency or firm mission statements, insurance coverage limitations, risk analysis recommendations, and so on. Policies help managers understand what needs to be accomplished and why, and they are therefore rooted in organizational values.

By contrast, a **procedure** is an established way of doing something that may be written down in training documents and used as a basis for task instruction. Whereas organizations tend to have relatively few policies, they will often have dozens of interrelated, overlapping, and acceptable alternative procedures for accomplishing tasks. In essence, policies and procedures combine to specify what needs to be accomplished, how, by whom, and why under varying circumstances. It follows that security policies and procedures specify physical and cyber assets in need of protection and acceptable or required technologies (i.e., tools + methods) for safeguarding them. Computer-use policies and procedures are euphemisms for information security policies that declare how employees and other people may use IT devices, information systems, and data owned or controlled by the organization. Sometimes these policies and procedures may extend to the use of personally owned computers and other electronic devices. Does your employer, college, or university have computer use policies and procedures in effect? Do you know what they are? Are these written down? Do you know exactly where you could locate a copy? Do you know the extent to which you and those with whom you interact are generally in compliance with your organization's IT security policy? If your organization does not have an IT security policy in effect, what does this indicate?

All government agencies, private sector firms, and nonprofit organizations should have security polices and procedures that take IT into account, and these should be incorporated into employee training, serve as a basis for management oversight of employees and operations, and become infused into the cultures of organizations. In other words, security policies and procedures should matter in practical and symbolic ways and be guidelines for everyone in or visiting an organization to help protect assets by not abusing or misusing IT. As such, designing, implementing, and following policies and procedures are important aspects of effecting security changes within organizations. Each of these steps present separate challenges for managers, IT administrators, and security professionals, as well as for rank-and-file employees and other users of electronic devices and information systems. This is why management is often considered the art of getting things done through others, which implies the need for members of organizations to buy into, practice, and genuinely value polices and procedures.

Space limitations preclude going into detail about how to create, implement, oversee, evaluate, and modify security policies and procedures. However, the following principles and basic tips are revealing of what managers should generally know and pay attention to. Security policies must:

- Comport with laws and regulations
- Reflect core organizational values and mission
- Be designed and implemented with user needs, input, and buy-in in mind
- Stress positive behaviors as opposed to being expressions of "thou shall not"
- Be realistic and provide flexible procedures for accomplishing goals

- Be approved and espoused by senior management following legal review
- Be written down in a clear manner and referred to often in daily operations
- Be declared in employee orientations and reinforced through in-service training
- Be reinforced by acknowledging achievements of individuals and teams
- Be periodically reviewed, updated, and republished as needed

The structure of policies varies greatly. An excellent resource for information security policies and procedures comes from a book *Information Security Policies Made Easy,* by Charles Cresson Woods.[20] Now in its ninth edition, this book is advertised to have more than 1360 example policies. However, such extensive and detailed security policies are not required by every organization. In fact, organizations cannot benefit from cumbersome policies that may actually cause more trouble than they are worth. Employees who cannot digest or understand, much less practically incorporate, policies and procedures into their daily routines will simply not abide by or espouse them. Some security organizations churn out policies faster than organizational cultures can assimilate and accept them. Some organizations have 200 or more pages of security policies and procedures. How would you like to be the manager responsible for overseeing these? Imagine how difficult it would be to train personnel in all aspects of such extensive sets of policies. Pity the new employee who tries to get a hand on them all, as well as the policy analyst who must ensure that each policy comports with changing laws, regulations, and threats to information systems.

Finally, note that in security policy development there are usually two primary obstacles. The first has to do with knowing where to start and knowing when you are done. Remembering due care and diligence, an organization's overall security posture will be measured against that established and maintained by its competitors and peers. If other organizations of similar size and type make their policies available, they can provide a good starting point for developing one's own computer use and security policy. The second obstacle is the language. It needs to be precise, although there is value in limiting the number of policies and wording them loosely to provide flexibility within organizations. This is where examples from *Information Security Policies Made Easy* have extra value. This is a somewhat expensive product (about $795) consisting of a book, CD, and license to use examples of policy language without the need for a reference to the copyright holders. Several other very useful policy development products are also available to help managers get a jump-start on improving their organization's security posture.

### 10.2.2.2 Data and Operational Recovery Planning.

Suppose you were senior manager of an organization that just experienced a successful attack against its information system resulting in instant total loss of data. I mean everything—customer and advertising data, production and delivery scheduling data, financial and client billing data, human resources and personnel management data, even security-related data—everything. Suppose further that portions of your system consisted of customized programming platforms but that your organization had not made backups of either its data or applications. What would you do? Who would you call? Where could you possibly go for help? Of course you could contact a firm that specializes in data recovery, but they can be expensive and there are

---

**CYBER TALE 10.9**

### The Need for Computer Use and Security Policies

As high school students competent in basic computer systems administration tasks, "Duke" and "Pete" were given positions as computer lab assistants from which they provided helpdesk services and worked on special projects with faculty members. One day, a faculty member asked Duke to install *FoolProof*, a security application designed to prevent unauthorized users from accessing certain features on a computer. At the time of this incident, *FoolProof* came packaged with an optional install that would lockdown access to the computer's hard drive if the user did not know the password. Knowing the risks involved (e.g., that he would not be able to continue servicing the computer if something went wrong) Duke asked the faculty member if he was sure that he wanted this feature installed. The teacher said that he did because he wanted "maximum protection" on his system from students who might otherwise be able to access his computer.

So, Duke installed *FoolProof* along with the optional lock-down feature. Several weeks later, Pete performed a routine installation of an updated MAC operating system on the teacher's computer. As the teacher was getting familiar with the new system he suddenly exclaimed, "Where are all my data files?" Only then did Pete discover that the lock-down feature previously installed by Duke at the teacher's request was not compatible with later releases of MAC operating systems. Thus, no one could access the teacher's data files except through a recovery process that proved to be less than 100 percent effective – much of the teacher's critical data had been lost forever! The lesson here is that even being conscientious about protecting data can be disastrous if product limitations or warnings are not understood and followed, and if policies and procedures governing installation and use of applications are established and abided by.

*Anonymous Student*

no guarantees that data will be recoverable. Even if it is, trade secrets or other proprietary or confidential information must be assumed to be compromised.

Unfortunately, total loss scenarios happen frequently due to cyber attacks and natural disasters, and when they do, firms unable to recover their data typically go out of business within a period of weeks or months. Statistics also reveal that 34 percent of companies fail to test their tape backups, and of those that do, 77 percent have found tape back-up difficiencies or failures; and sixty percent of companies that perform tape backups will nonetheless fail in their efforts to restore data files critical to their operations. [21]

In today's world of cybercrime and threats to information systems, it is imperative that in addition to routinely backing up data, every organization should develop a **data recovery plan** and an **operating continuity plan**. Data and business recovery planning is just an acknowledgement that not all facilities and information security breaches, human and technology failures, and natural disasters can be anticipated or minimized in their effects. Therefore, data and operations recovery planning, policies, and procedures are necessary. One thing to remember is that when disaster strikes, everyone needs operations to resume as quickly as possible—time is of the essence. Without adequate planning, data availability concerns will completely obliterate data confidentiality and integrity concerns. In other words, survival may depend on getting back into action at the expense of confidentiality and integrity of data. Hence, the measure of a good operations continuity plan is the level of balance achieved with respect to confidentiality, integrity, and availability (CIA) of data, which were discussed in detail in Chapter 2.

An organization's IT data recovery plan is a key element of its comprehensive operations continuity plan, which must combine to ensure the recoverability of data and systems. This means that every scrap of data, including data about operating systems, applications, workstations, peripherals,

and other components of information systems needs to be archived (off site), updated frequently, and accessible immediately so that in the event of catastrophic data loss an entire enterprise including remote site locations can be brought back online within a few hours. Therefore, data recovery plans and comprehensive operations continuity plans must specify how to regroup following a disaster and, typically, will combine to address:

• Enterprise-wide backup solutions
• Asset management and systems inventorying tools
• Server and network device baselining processes
• Patch and critical update management procedures
• Virus protection server deployment standards
• Separation of local, domain, and super-user system administrator roles
• System services review for SSH, Telnet, FTP/TFTP, and HTTP
• Penetration testing (external and internal)
• Content filtering and monitoring activity
• Logon banner implementation

Provisions for off-site storage of critical infrastructure and data components are also needed and should include:

• Network device configurations
• Source software, customized applications, and media
• Operating platform software configurations
• Manuals and documentation (e.g., policy and procedures manuals)
• Backup media
• Change management documents

*An untested plan is potentially a defective plan. Therefore, it is essential to periodically test data and operations recovery planning models. Organizations can do this by simulating losses of data or actually turning off access to data and applications as a form of fire drill to determine if employees know what to do and if they are able to access off-site archives and restore data and systems. Testing can also involve social engineering and security awareness checks. Practice gained through testing will be more than worthwhile should the need arise.*

### 10.2.2.3 Managing Organizational Culture and Change.

Organizing a substantial change effort involving senior management, IT administrators, physical and information security professionals, risk managers, other employees, and technical assistance contractors involves issues having to do with organizational theory and change management practices. **Change management** requires astute understanding of the interplay between organizational factors and how alternative structuring of security responsibilities within organizations, along with situational management and leadership styles, can be applied given differing resources and circumstances to bring about efficacious security changes. For example, an organization that is instituting emergency security upgrades following a major loss of data, but also facing business continuity challenges, public outcry, and investigation by government regulators, is likely to assign employees and/or outsourced contractors to work with immediate access to and authority of executives to make rapid policy and procedural changes, technology procurement decisions, and so on. However, if a security change process is occurring under less demanding circumstances, and is more tempered with respect to swiftness and degree of changes immediately necessary, it may be satisfactory and even more appropriate to assign key personnel to less senior standing, access, and authority.

Effective security changes also require simultaneous management of technology, data, money, time, expertise, and other resources for enhanced information security and inspired leadership—the art of fostering commitment for enhanced information security and a sense of computer and IT ethics within organizations. This is important because nearly all organizations have individual employees, if not groups

and teams of people, who are not fully aware, who do not care about, or who are not equipped to support security missions. These individuals require special education, training, support, supervision, and leadership.

Senior managers who recognize the increasing importance of information security to maintain and improve operations, and to avoid law suits and special regulatory attention, must be cognizant of the reality that infosec cannot be only a project or program, marginally funded and periodically checked on. Instead, to be effective, infosec must be integrated into the core mission, priorities, and culture of organizations.

Ask seasoned managers about accomplishing lasting organizational reforms and they will usually become quiet, wrinkle their brows, and ultimately say something like, it is always tough and rarely possible to bring about meaningful change in organizations unless the stars in the night-time sky are lined up just right. Indeed, making significant security changes is rarely easy because it often requires rethinking of priorities, retooling technology with less than adequate funding, acquisition or reassignment of personnel expertise, and general and specialized training of employees across the organization. Meaningful change requires dynamic and committed executive leadership to bring about attitudinal and behavioral reforms. It also helps to develop enthusiasm and pride in what is being accomplished, overcoming labor and management tensions, and finding ways to involve people in what needs doing and reward them. Many years ago, the Ford Motor Company introduced its slogan, "Quality is Job 1" to aid in bringing out a better product, pride among employees, and consumer confidence. Reform initiatives comprised of slogans and not backed by real leadership and management action quickly become hollow words. However, many government agencies, private sector firms, and nonprofit organizations could benefit from adopting a variation of Ford's slogan to kick off genuine security reforms. "InfoSec is Priority 1" proclaims that without adequate ongoing protection of information systems there may be no product to make or service to provide!

The need for a formal **change management system** to accompany planned information systems security upgrades cannot be overstated. Change management provides a communication path between information technologists and application stakeholders, establishes baseline information if a recommended platform change corrupts an information system, acts as a reference source, and defines approval processes for changes to IT platform configurations. Change management considerations are needed at the onset of security systems upgrading and must remain intact as part of ongoing operations planning and technology upgrading processes. This is just another way of saying that managing change is inevitable and therefore is an integral aspect to managing organizations. After all, we must protect data and systems in dynamic threat and operating environments. An effective change management system

will ensure that IT-related and information security changes are appropriate to operating or business needs, approved, documented prior to and after implementation, and tested prior to and after full release.

Effective change management systems should also have designated team assignment responsibilities, authority, and clear chain-of-command reporting structures; a master change log with unique log identifiers; documented and understood approval processes; and fast-track data and operations recovery capability. The single key benefit of maintaining change management systems in place is the ability to roll a system back to its previous configuration should the update corrupt or render the system to a nonoperational state. Can you see how understanding information security best practices and security assessments; designing and implementing security controls; making wise technology procurement and investment decisions; determining security priorities and designating responsibilities

for change; having alternative approaches for structuring key IT, security, and risk management personnel; developing and implementing security policies and procedures; and assuring data and operations recovery capabilities all factor into change management processes? This is a lot to understand and remember, but the risks of not paying attention to all these issues are very high.

### 10.2.2.4 Security Audits.

**Audits** are formal processes involving inspection of facilities and information systems for compliance with laws, regulations, established policies and procedures, technology standards, and due care and diligence expectations for security practices and capabilities. Audits are a necessary aspect of information assurance, which, if properly viewed and managed, can be extremely helpful to managers of organizations, IT administrators, and information security professionals. Many people have the mistaken view that all audits are or should be adversarial in nature. This is not true, because the role of auditors is usually to conduct independent observations, assessments, and recommendations with input from managers and others working in organizations undergoing audits. Many types of organizations are subject to being audited by government regulators or independent accounting firms such as Ernst & Young, Pricewaterhouse Coopers, Deloitte Touche Tohmatsu, and KPMG International. As with other portions of this chapter, no attempt is made here to teach you how to go about arranging for or conducting audits, although students learning how to manage cybercrime in organizations and throughout society must have basic understanding about auditing that fundamentally pertains to information security as well as to crime prevention, detection, and deterrence.

You may be surprised to learn that there are several types of audits that go by different names but essentially pertain to areas of operations within organizations. These include program operations audits, technology audits, security audits, and financial accounting audits.

Each of these types of audits may be separate or combined and involve review of facilities, policies and procedures, training standards, hardcopy and electronic records, functionality of information systems, and personnel knowledge and performance capabilities. **Program operations audits**, such as those conducted during site visits by government program managers to criminal justice agencies that have received federal grants, often involve review of operational capabilities improvements tied to grant monies received. These may not involve review of actual expenditures, which occurs in **financial accounting audits** that are routinely conducted to ensure money was spent as reported and in appropriate ways. **Security audits** typically involve inspection and testing of information systems security combined with a review of facilities security. In practice, security and **technology audits** amount to the same thing, and, increasingly, this is true of financial audits as well, because computers provide the technological basis for budgeting, procurement, funds transfers, accounting, and so on.

Many organizations are mandated by laws and attendant regulations to have periodic audits. The Health Insurance Portability and Accountability Act (HIPAA) of 1996, the Financial Services Modernization Act of 1999 (Gramm-Leach-Bliley), and the Sarbanes-Oxley Act of 2002 in particular have substantially impacted healthcare providers and financial institutions with regard to assuring that standards for information security, privacy of confidential information, and responsible spending and investments are met. Additional laws and regulations regarding information security and protection of confidential personal information will be enacted as cybercrime threats evolve to impact other sectors throughout society. The implication is that managers of organizations in regulated sectors may not have a choice whether or not be audited. Either they comply with audit requirements, or the government may impose penalties and ultimately revoke an organization's operating license. However, some firms that are not required to conduct periodic audits can still benefit from having them done.

Decisions about audits not mandated by laws or regulations typically involve (1) deciding why an audit would be useful in given operating and political contexts; (2) the authority and independent reporting mechanisms to be afforded an auditing team; (3) the scope of an audit and extent to which various personnel, units, and organizational functions will be reviewed and involved; (4) whether to conduct audits utilizing in-house expertise or contract for an audit conducted by an external source; and (5) the timing and auditing procedures with regard to noninterference with existing operations. In any case, managers will need to consider how best to go about announcing auditing plans so as not to unnecessarily alarm employees. A successful audit is often one that is embraced by managers and employees because it is intended to be a means of improving security and operations rather than punitive in nature. To this end, it is important to develop a plan for announcing intentions to audit and inviting employee participation in an advisory role. Of course, this will depend on circumstances. Obviously, if malfeasance is suspected, announcing an audit in advance could cause cybercriminals to cover up their electronic tracks, or destroy data of ongoing embezzlement, and so on. Managers must also consider audit reporting issues and after-audit response plans. After all, it is assumed that good audits will uncover opportunities for organizations to improve, which presumably is exactly what mangers wish for.

Finally, information security audits are often intended to determine compliance with existing technology standards. Several of these have been developed over time by different organizations as a way to set minimum IT and information security standards for different types of organizations operating in varying environments. Unless you plan to specialize in auditing or become a CIO, it is doubtful that you will ever need to know the specifics of these standards. However, all managers, and especially information

security professionals, should be aware that the following standards may be used in a given organizational sector or may be commonly referred to or specialized in by an auditing firm:

*The Control Objectives for Information and Related Technology (CoBit):*  COBIT was developed by the IT Governance Institute as a generally applicable standard for good IT security and control practices. COBIT provides a framework for management, users, and information security audit, control, and security practitioners. Recently, the Information Systems Audit and Control Association (ISACA) released two new significant works. The first is the COBIT Security Baseline, which establishes minimum security practices and points the way of advancement. Also, seventeen information security standards and models were cross-referenced and harmonized in the 150-page *Information Security Harmonisation: Classification of Global Guidance.*

*The National Security Agency's InfoSec Assessment Methodology (IAM):*  NSA's InfoSec Assessment Methodology focuses on assessment (measurements) of information security processes and technology. The IAM grew out of the IA-CMM, and like all capability maturity models, focuses on organizational aspects, processes and documentation, and technology. In the case of the IAM, the focus was the capability to deliver an InfoSec assessment. In the scope of an information security program, it is a framework to support the consistent delivery of internal or external assessments.

*ISC 2's Certified Information Systems Security Professional Standard (CISSP):*  The CISSP is a coveted certification by information security professionals and is used to indicate essential awareness and technical competencies of individuals in information security positions. Earning the CISSP credential involves considerable preparation to understand ten "domain areas" of knowledge. To be eligible to take the CISSP exam, full-time work experience is mandated in one or more of the ten domain areas. The first three domains address security management, access control, and technology for securing data. The next three address the design and implementation of security architecture across infrastructure components. The last four domains address various aspects of integrating information security with other aspects of business, such as legal and ethical contexts, physical security, and business continuity planning. The CISSP standard is mentioned here because many information security and financial auditors now possess this credential, which through its domain areas of instruction provides very good information security standards for organizations to consider adopting to be in general compliance with due care and diligence.

*The Computer Emergency Response Team's OC-TAVE:* OTAVE and OCTAVE-S were developed by CERT in conjunction with the Carnegie-Mellon University Software Engineering Institute (CMU/SEI) as models for information security within healthcare organizations. Initial applications were in veteran's hospitals but have now been adopted by other healthcare providers in partial response to regulatory requirements mandated by HIPPA.

*International Security Standard (ISO) 17799:* ISO 17799 has many of the elements of the other models but is widely regarded to be an extremely useful, comprehensive, and detailed set of standards for information security. It consists of two basic parts: (1) A code of practice (ISO 17799) and (2) specifications for an information management system (BS 7799-2). Ten components of the standard pertain to business continuity planning, systems access controls, systems development and maintenance, physical and environmental security, compliance with laws and policies, personnel security, managing security within organizations, computer and operations management, asset classification and control, and development and implementation of security policies.

## 10.3 Summary

All users of computers, other electronic IT devices, and information systems have data they regard as relatively confidential or valuable and therefore in need of security. Good information security begins with understanding the technologies needed to protect data, combined with proven methods for utilizing computers and other IT devices while at home, school, work, and traveling. Good information security need not cost individual users a lot of money, although investing in quality technology is recommended. Best practices for safeguarding information include use of strong passwords and effective password management, frequent updating of antimalware definitions; installation and use of a software or hardware firewalls; regularly downloading security and other patches for operating systems and applications; installation and frequent use of antispyware and anti-adware applications; backing up data systematically and in different ways; using anti-keylogger, encryption, and digital signature technology; not working for routine purposes from an account with root or system administrator privileges; and adopting several other information security practices into personal and professional lifestyles.The concept of mobile computing in regards to employing sound information security tools and practices applies to working with IT devices in alternative locations as well as to long-distance traveling and wireless computing via WiFi networks.

Ensuring protection of information in organizations builds on the these measures and situations, and typically begins with a security assessment that determines baseline physical and information security status from which design and implementation of security controls may commence. These processes will shed light on the types of technology investments that need to be made in order to comply with laws, regulations, and appropriate standards of due care and diligence. To strategically advance the security posture of organizations, it is necessary for senior managers to periodically conduct security assessments; develop policies, procedures and employee training programs; and plan and carry out security change procedures. Lessons can be learned from mistakes made by other organizations and by keeping abreast of evolving cybercrimes and potential threats to information security. This helps managers set priorities for protecting their most critical data given available resources. Frequently implementing security upgrades and changes requires expertise from trained information security professionals who, if not already employed, typically need to be contracted. There are advantages and disadvantages to in-sourcing versus outsourcing technical assistance for information security changes, and there are also several alternative ways to structure IT administration, physical security, infosec, and risk management functions within organizations.

Implementing information security changes requires fundamental understanding of change management processes. Although qualitative risk and threat analysis is a useful practice that attempts to anticipate an organization's exposure to potential cybercrimes, quantitative methods for achieving this are controversial and of very limited usefulness. However, development of security policies and procedures is very important for bringing organizations into compliance with laws and regulations and due care and diligence standards. To these ends, it is important that security policies comport with laws and regulations, reflect core organizational values and mission, be designed and implemented with users in mind, stress positive behaviors, be realistic and afford flexible procedures for accomplishing goals, be approved and espoused by senior management following

legal review, be written down in a clear manner and referred to often in daily operations, be declared in employee orientations and reinforced through in-service training, acknowledge employee achievements, and be periodically reviewed, updated, and republished as needed.

Most organizations that experience a major loss of data or computing capability fail. Private sector firms that experience such losses often file for bankruptcy. Data and operational recovery planning pertains to being able to quickly and fully recover from a data or computing catastrophe due to a technology failure, cybercrime, natural disaster, and so on. Data recovery plans and operating continuity plans are used by IT administrators, information security professionals, and other managers to avert operational or business failure following a disaster. Key aspects of this include performing regular data backups, systems testing, utilizing off-site archiving services, training, and evaluating personal in cyber fire drills that test an organization's recovery readiness. Managing security changes is an ongoing process, driven by the technologically-evolving nature of cybercrimes and IT that make them possible. Several types of organizations including financial institutions and healthcare providers are mandated to maintain certain physical and information security standards and capabilities. Auditing is a process designed to help organizations meet their regulatory obligations frequently by comparing capabilities against external standards. Although audits are often viewed as adversarial and are intended to help detect, prevent, and deter cybercrimes, auditing can be very beneficial to managers who assume a responsible and proactive stance regarding their organization's security needs.

## Key Terms and Concepts

Access point, 434

Advanced Encryption Standard (AES), 426

Algorithms, 427

Antimalware software, 418

Audits, 451

Backing up data, 423

Baseline security assessment, 436

Baselining, 437

CERT - OCTAVE, 453

Certificate authority, 427

Change management, 449

Change management system, 450

CISSP, 452

CoBit, 452

Cryptography, 425

Data recovery plan, 448

Digital signatures, 427

Due care and diligence, 436
Electronic key ring, 426
Encryption, 425
Encryption keys, 425
Financial accounting audit, 451
Firewall, 419
Hash value, 427
Hotspot, 434
In-sourcing, 441
ISO 17799, 453
Key escrow, 426
Keylogger software, 425

NSA Infosec Assessment
    Methodology, 452
Operating continuity plan, 448
Outsourcing, 441
Password management, 416
Patching, 420
Policy, 445
Pretty Good Privacy (PGP), 426
Private keys, 425
Procedure, 445
Program operations audit, 451
Public keys, 425

Risk and threat analysis, 443
Security assessment, 436
Security audit, 451
Storage area network, 424
Strong password, 415
Target hardening, 407
Technology audit, 451
Threat fatigue, 443
Wardriving and warwalking, 434
WEP enabled, 434
WiFi networks, 433

## Critical Thinking and Discussion Questions

1. Name five specific things that users of computers and other types of IT devices can do to protect their data and systems. Briefly describe the essential elements or steps involved in each measure. Then prioritize the measures; that is, explain the order in which you would employ or accomplish them and your rationale for doing so.

2. Explain your personal procedures for routinely backing up your data. Then explain how these could be improved upon.

3. Explain how data at your place of employment is routinely backed up. Also explain what, if any, data and operations recovery plans are in effect for your organization.

4. What is an information security assessment, and what are the possible pros and cons of conducting one of these in an organizational setting? What factors should managers and information security professionals, in particular, consider when deciding whether and how to undertake an assessment?

5. Explain the general concept, key issues, and logical steps involved in a formal data management change process.

6. Compare and contrast a data recovery plan with an operations continuity plan. Explain key items, elements, and/or steps involved in developing and carrying out of these types of plans.

7. Previously, in Chapter 2 we considered the reality that information security professionals are required to do what they must and more of what they can with available resources and in consideration of inevitable tradeoffs. What is meant by each of the clauses within this statement? Support your answers with real or hypothetical examples of each clause (e.g., "doing what must be done"). Hint: Refer back to the principles of information assurance discussed in Chapter 2.

8. Explain the basic problem facing information security professionals or risk and threat analysts who would attempt to quantify vulnerabilities and potential losses from attacks to information systems.

9. On your home computer, what steps do you take to protect your system from outsiders (i.e., external attacks)? What about attacks from insiders to either your data or computer or device hardware? What additional steps can you take to make your computer or other IT devices more secure?

10. Do you believe computer codes of conduct can help improve information security? Explain and provide examples that reinforce your argument.

## References and Endnotes

1. Blumenthal, R. (2004). Idle at Los Alamos: A weapons lab as its own worst enemy. *New York Times.* Retrieved July 23, 2004, from http://www.nytimes.com/2004/07/22/national/22lab.html?th.

2. Associated Press (2005, August 4). AOL business unit settles FTC adware charges. Retrieved August 26, 2005 from http://informationweek.com/story/showArticle.jhtml?articleID=167100784.

3. Ibid., Associated Press 2005, August 4. See note 2.

4. Granneman, S. (2004). Infected in 20 minutes. *The Register.* Retrieved April 1, 2005, from http://www.theregister.co.uk/2004/08/19/infected_in20_minutes/.

5. Liedtke, M. (2005, March 29). Stolen UC Berkeley laptop exposes personal data of nearly 100,000. Associated Press/*The Detroit News.* Retrieved April 6,

2005, from http://www.detnews.com/2005/technology/0503/30/tech-132193.htm.

6. Rainbow Technologies. (2003, August 5). *Rainbow Technologies survey.* Retrieved April 13, 2005, from http://www.corporate-ir.net/ireye/ir_site.zhtml?ticker=rnbo&script=410&layout=-6&item_id=438314.

7. Leyden, J. (2002, May 28). PDAs make easy pickings for data thieves. *The Registrar.* Retrieved April 13, 2005, from http://www.theregister.co.uk/2002/05/28/pdas_make_easy_pickings/.

8. KeePass Password Safe. (2004). Official homepage of KeePass, the free, open-source, light-weight and easy to use password manager. Retrieved October 27, 2004, from http://keepass.sourceforge.net/index.php.

9. CERT Coordination Center. (2005). Before you connect a new computer to the Internet. Software Engineering Institute, Carnegie Mellon University. Retrieved April 16, 2005, from http://www.cert.org/tech_tips/before_you_plug_in.html.

10. International Organization for Standardization. (2005). English country names and code elements. ISO. Retrieved April 15, 2005, from http://www.iso.org/iso/en/prods-services/iso3166ma/02iso-3166-code-lists/list-en1.html.

11. Earthlink Staff Author. (2005). Earthlink spy audit. EarthLink.net. Retrieved April 16, 2005, from http://www.earthlink.net/spyaudit/press/.

12. Microsoft Staff Author. (2005). Five-minute security advisor: the road warrior's guide to laptop protection. Microsoft Corporation. Retrieved online April 17, 2005, from http://www.microsoft.com/technet/ community/columns/5min/5min-205.mspx.

13. Worldwide Wardrive (2005, June). Worldwide wardrive survey findings. Retrieved August 20, 2005 from http://www.worldwidewardrive.org/.

14. Lyman, J. (2005, July 8). Floridian faces wireless trespassing charges. Retrieved August 25, 2005 from http://www.technewsworld.com/story/FnWLg G0RqdfwZN/Floridian-Faces-Wireless-Trespassing-Charges.xhtml.

15. National Archives and Records Administration. (2004). Facts on demand. Retrieved March 1, 2004, from http://www.archives.gov/index.html.

16. Frieden, T. (2005, February 3). Report: FBI wasted millions on 'Virtual Case File.' CNN.com. Retrieved February 23, 2005, from http://www.cnn.com/2005/US/02/03/fbi.computers/.

17. Lichtblau, E. (2004, July 23). Archives put in cameras after Berger took papers. *New York Times.* Retrieved July 25, 2004, from http://www.nytimes.com/2004/07/24/politics/24berger.html.

18. Parker, D. B. (1998). *Fighting Computer Crime: A New Framework for Protecting Information* (p. 270). New York: Wiley Computer Publishing.

19. Parker, D. B., 1998, p. 271; see note 18.

20. Wood, C. C. (2002). *Information Security Policies Made Easy.* Houston, TX: PentaSafe Security Technologies.

21. Personal communication, Jack Finklea, Telperion Solutions Group LLC., November 3, 2004.

# 11

# *Future Opportunities for Managing Cybercrime*

## *11.0 Introduction: Where Can We Go from Here?*

Today's high-tech crime scene is characterized by widespread and evolving wire and wireless communications and information systems that link millions of private, government, and not-for-profit computers locally, regionally, nationally, and transnationally. Internet and satellite communications links now transcend international borders, economies and financial systems, governmental and political structures, legal and law enforcement processes, social organization and cultures, and technological conditions. Consequently, cybercrime and countervailing information security measures are global issues that present challenges of immense complexity. The following *partial* listing of headlines links posted *on a single day* in 2005 by infosecdaily (http://www.infosecdaily.net/) are indicative of the complexities associated with worldwide cybercrime and information security management challenges:

- Study Finds Spammers Use P2P Harvesting to Spam Millions

- UK Court Orders ISPs to Reveal IDs of 33 Filesharers
- Fraud Case Focuses Unwelcome Attention on Indian Outsourcing
- China Jails 2 U.S. Men for Piracy
- Apple Posts iSync Security Fix
- Sober.M: Spreading Worm, or Spammed Worm?
- The Dangers of Ad-Hoc Wireless Networking
- Banks Lash out at Security Study
- IM Security: The Worst Is Yet to Come
- LexisNexis Begins Notifying Possible Victims
- Open-Source CVS Project Plugs Security Leaks
- Prison Terms on Tap for 'Prerelease' Pirates
- iPods Valuable in the College Classroom?
- Controls on Internet Access, China
- Net Citizens with Good Intentions May be Caught Out
- Viacom Looking to Internet to Boost Revenue
- Symantec Releases Beta Anti-Spyware Software
- IRS Security Gaps Could Expose Taxpayer Data
- Spyware Could Cost You $2M in Washington State

These headlines refer to several nations and states within the U.S., different types of cybercrimes and victimization, release of new malware variants, new laws and regulatory issues, punishments for crime violators, emerging technologies and the IT industry, security vulnerabilities within systems as well as organizations, social norms and cyberspace, the Open Source Community, financial institutions and research studies, and more. Every subject indicated by this list of headlines has been addressed in preceding chapters of the text. How can people possibly hope to get their heads around and stay abreast of all these issues, much less manage the enormous, complex, and interrelated issues attendant to computer abuse, cybercrime, and information security?

The worldwide imperative to better manage cybercrime is exacerbated by the reality that IT-enabled crimes are routinely committed by people in all walks of life and of varying age, race, wealth, education, employment, professional and social status, technological ability, and so on. We have also learned that cybercriminals and those who abuse computers, other types of electronic IT devices, and information systems may be either organizational insiders or outsiders who use simple to complex tools and techniques to attack cyber and/or physical assets for any number and combinations of motives, and that real people and organizations suffer as a result. This general condition raises another fundamental question: What more can be done to improve information security to better prevent cybercrime and ameliorate its harmful impacts on society? In this final chapter of the book we will contemplate and attempt to answer that question and consider the importance and elements of computer ethics education, which is desperately needed throughout primary, secondary, and higher education.

In the first of two sections, we will focus on several specific things that the government can do in partnership with private sector and nonprofit entities and with other nations to prevent and control cybercrime, improve information security,

and protect critical information infrastructure. Within a general framework of getting ready, getting set, and moving forward, these include researching the nature and extent of the cybercrime threat; passing legislation, creating executive authority, and issuing presidential orders as needed; helping create and sign international treaties and conventions; appropriating funds to carry out authorized actions; improving coordination and implementation of planned initiatives; enhancing critical information infrastructure capabilities; carrying out and supporting technology R&D, testing, and evaluation; providing technical assistance to public and private sectors; offering market and investment incentives to enhance information security; creating technology market push and pull via procurement power; creating and enforcing regulations for greater information security responsibility; resolving contentious legal issues; cracking down on cybercrime offending; promoting public awareness about cybercrime and information security; and fostering infosec and computer ethics education and training. These courses of action reflect a classic public policy approach to better understanding and managing cybercrime.

In the last section of the book, we will carefully examine concepts in computer ethics education. Here you will come to understand the philosophy of ethics applied to the harmful use of computers and other IT devices. You will read about computer-enabled abuses and learn the extent to which some college students report being relatively ethical versus unethical in their use of computers, other types of IT devices, and data. You will have an opportunity to compare your attitudes toward responsible use of computers with those held by other college students. The hope is that you will contemplate the importance of using and espousing use of computers in ways that are not abusive or illegal, rather that are ethical, security-minded, helpful to others, and legal in addition to being productive and enjoyable. The book concludes with my arguing that all of us must work to foster greater intolerance of computer misuse and abuse and essentially create a new computing culture that is consciously aware of cybercrime prevention and ethical use of computers, other types of IT devices, and information systems.

## 11.1 What More Can Government Do to Prevent Cybercrime?

What sorts of cybercrime and infosec problems are you periodically hearing of, reading about, or experiencing? What more could be done to address these problems in small or large ways that are already not being done? Are local and state governments and the federal government doing enough to deter computer abusers and cybercriminals from harming individuals, groups, organizations, and even entire communities? What about homeland security—do you think that federal government agencies, are adequately working in partnership with those in state and local governments, as well as with private sector and nonprofit organizations, to protect the nation's critical information infrastructures? What in your view should different levels and branches of government (i.e., legislatures, courts, and executive agencies) do differently or perhaps do more or less of to prevent cybercrime? What role do private and nonprofit sectors currently have in managing cybercrime, and ought this to change? If you agree that governments alone cannot and should not attempt to solve all crime-related problems, what can they do to help improve information security, prevent cybercrime, and ameliorate the harmful impacts of cybercrime on society? These questions pertain to proper roles and responsibilities that government has in our society to help address many types of social, economic, and technological problems.

To begin to understand what more can and should be done to address complex and seemingly insurmountable problems associated with cybercrime, it is useful to briefly consider what government is designed and legally authorized to accomplish. Irrespective of subjective views about what should be done to prevent cybercrime and the well-understood reality that limited resources prevent the government from being all things to all people, it is important to understand that the government is equipped to carry out certain kinds of activities on behalf of the people but is not best suited to deal with all societal problems. The federal government is constitutionally empowered to protect all members of society in ways that do not infringe on the civil and economic rights of competing stakeholder groups. This is inherently political, yet governments are meant to serve and protect the people without playing favorites and with a certain amount of deference to free markets while recognizing that market failures can and periodically do arise. Therefore, government involvement in societal problems is often based on answering the following questions:

- Is there a problem?
- What is the nature and extent of the problem?
- Must the problem be solved, and if so when, to what extent and by whom?
- What are possible ways in which the problem can be solved?
- Which among alternative solutions are the most promising?
- Do circumstances require government involvement or intervention?
- What types of specific government interventions are indicated and possible?
- What will the indicated solutions cost taxpayers?
- Can society afford (or not afford) to solve the problem as defined?
- Who will or will not benefit and in what ways as the result of the government taking action?
- Who could be negatively impacted, and what spin-off problems could occur?
- What could be done to ameliorate harm caused by the negative spin-offs of a policy intervention?

These are the types of analytical questions often formulated by public policy analysts who specialize in recommending alternative courses of actions that government policymakers then consider in political contexts. Collectively such questions provide a logic model for thinking about how to solve many types of complex social problems, such as those pertaining to crime and criminal justice, without automatically assuming that government can or even should be involved in every situation even if the general problem concerns a fundamental role of government such as crime fighting. After all, governments must prioritize what they will address, when, where and how. Such challenges also imply that it is usually necessary to conceptualize how to solve smaller problems within larger problem arenas. Take another look at the headlines listed in the introduction and notice the multitude of issues at stake. Can you imagine ways to divide up the world's cybercrime and information security issues into manageable problems that one or more governments could afford to address? In essence this is exactly what criminal justice and IT professionals working in government, private, nonprofit, and academic sectors need to do in order to improve information systems security and cybercrime prevention capabilities in organizations throughout society. Hence, understanding how to manage cybercrime as a complex social problem in legally permissible and economically feasible ways depends on transforming humongous problems like cybercrime into smaller manageable ones that people can actually get their heads around and do something about in incremental and coordinated ways.

Before moving on to discuss the particular things that government is already doing and can potentially do better, let us briefly consider several general strategies that governments can employ when addressing crime, security, and other types of social, economic, or technology-related problems in society.[1] First, governments can provide assistance by **creating climates** that align labor and capital, organizational networks, and political and marketplace conditions that are conducive to addressing problems. Second, government can engage in **surveying** problems to promote understanding in society about what is occurring and raise public awareness to energize concern for solving problems. When government pays attention to a problem in society, divergent stakeholders will too and may offer to provide assistance in ways consistent with their interests. Third, government can help **link and coordinate** different types of resources and capabilities to help solve societal problems. This includes developing, maintaining, and facilitating rapid flexible responses to emerging security and crime threats by involving individuals, groups, and organizations that possess different expertise, skills, and abilities. Fourth, government can use its immense resources to **fill gaps** by providing assistance in areas that private and nonprofit sectors are incapable of addressing or that market forces alone are not likely to bring about.

Fifth, government may also provide problem-solving assistance by **supporting R&D** and **providing information** about the nature and extent of problems and ongoing problem-solving initiatives. Information security and counterterrorism technology R&D sponsored by the Department of Homeland Security, the Justice Department, and the Department of Defense are examples of this capability. Sixth, through legislation and regulation activity, government can provide **incentives** for organizations to change their policies and ways of doing things, to adopt technologies for enhancing information security and preventing cybercrimes, and so on. For example, tax credits can be offered as a positive incentive to procuring or upgrading information security technologies or as a means of offsetting information security training costs. Negative incentives may result from fines or other penalties imposed through regulatory actions. The federal government is also empowered to adjust intellectual property rights affecting patent, trade mark, copyright, and trade secrets protections. We have seen this accomplished through legislation enacted by Congress in recent years. Seventh, governments can provide monetary and technical assistance **resources** to industrial sectors and organizations, as when they sponsor professional development training through grants programs to criminal justice agencies. Finally, and as we discussed in Chapters 8 and 9, governments can create and **enforce crime laws, prosecuting suspected offenders and imposing stiff penalties on those convicted of unlawful acts**. Ultimately enforcement of laws control what people may, must, and must not do, while also inspiring voluntary compliance with what is deemed to be in the broad interests of society.

As you can see, government's ability to help address cybercrime and information security issues is not limited to patrolling the streets of cyberspace or to prosecuting cybercriminals or even to supporting development of new information and computer forensics tools. Although such measures are important and are already being accomplished, they are insufficient for solving the immense cybercrime and information security problems faced by society. Therefore let us examine a wider range of specific things government is doing to prevent and control cybercrime and ponder additional courses of action that could be taken to better manage cybercrime.

### 11.1.1 Preparing to Manage Cybercrime

Government is pretty good about talking and getting ready to do important things for the betterment of society. For decades a few agencies within the federal government paid some attention to emerging computer-enabled crime and information security problems. In recent years, we have seen a flurry of federal initiatives having less or more to do with getting ready to solve these problems. These include researching the nature and extent of the cybercrime threat; passing legislation, creating executive authority, and issuing presidential orders as needed; helping to create and sign international treaties and conventions; appropriating funds to carry out authorized actions; and coordinating and implementing planned initiatives. Let us briefly consider each of these courses of action.

---

**BOX 11.1 • *Actions Government Can Take to Prevent and Control Cybercrime, Improve Information Security Capabilities Nationally, and Protect Critical Information Infrastructure***

1. Research the nature and extent of the cyber threat.
2. Pass legislation, create executive authority, and issue presidential orders.
3. Help create and sign international treaties and conventions.
4. Appropriate funds to carry out authorized actions.
5. Improve coordination and implementation of planned initiatives.
6. Enhance critical information infrastructure capabilities.
7. Carry out and support technology R&D, testing. and evaluation.
8. Provide technical assistance to public and private sectors.
9. Offer market and investment incentives to enhance information security.
10. Create technology market push and pull via procurement power.
11. Create and enforce regulations for greater information security responsibility.
12. Resolve contentious legal issues.
13. Crack down on cybercrime offenders.
14. Promote public awareness about cybercrime and information security.
15. Foster infosec and computer ethics education and training.

### 11.1.1.1 Researching the Nature and Extent of Cybercrime.

To better understand and manage emerging cybercrimes, significant and increasing amounts of research have been undertaken in recent years, although government sponsored research has not focused on the *criminological aspects* of crimes committed with computers or other IT devices. For example, beginning in 1990 the National Academies of Sciences (NAS) began undertaking studies that included[2]

- Computers at Risk: Safe Computing in the Information Age (1990)
- Rights and Responsibilities of Participants in Networked Communities (1994)
- Cryptography's Role in Securing the Information Society (1996)
- For the Record: Protecting Electronic Health Information (1997)
- Realizing the Potential for C4I (1999)
- Trust in Cyberspace (1999)
- Digital Dilemma: Intellectual Property in the Information Age (2000)
- The Internet's Coming of Age (2001)
- Making the Nation Safer: The Role of S&T in Countering Terrorism (2002)
- Critical Information Infrastructure Protection and the Law (2003)

These reports are among the most in-depth, insightful, and informative studies ever undertaken on the topics indicated, all of which *relate* to cybercrime and information security issues, but do not with any depth investigate criminological issues of cybercrime, such as *why* people abuse IT. Even so the report titles are revealing of topical areas that the federal government has been concerned about and investigated, and many of the studies listed above include important recommendations for improving information systems security in order to prevent cybercrimes and for additional technology-related R&D. Several other studies, some of which were described in Chapter 6, have also been undertaken to inform societal understanding of computerization in relation to nature and extent of IT-enabled crime and conflict in the information age. Collectively this body of research paints a picture of information and cyber society concerns and has substantially helped people understand threats posed by cybercriminals as well as technological ways in which government, private sector firms, and nonprofit organizations can respond to prevent cybercrimes. Note that research, such as the NAS studies listed above, often lead to creation of new laws and regulations and may periodically also be undertaken as the result of legislation enacted by Congress. Hence, research is an integral aspect of government policy making for understanding, preventing, and managing technology-enabled crime.

With federal law enforcement agencies now cracking down on many types of cybercrimes, and businesses and professional membership associations such as the Recording Industry Association of America (RIAA) and the Motion Picture Association of America (MPAA) suing digital pirates, and Congress poised to mandate information security requirements on previously unregulated business sectors such as stockpilers and sellers and or personal information, it is clear that aggressive law and regulatory enforcement and prosecution of cybercriminals is already occurring, even as additional R&D of cybercrime prevention and information security technologies is also being undertaken. Can you think of certain types of cybercrimes or locations throughout the world or even within the United States that are inadequately policed with respect to how computers and other types of electronic devices are being used to violate crime laws? Do you think local and state investigation and prosecution of cybercrimes is on par with federal initiatives? What types of cybercrimes should state and local investigators and prosecutors concentrate on? Should they refocus their efforts or do more of the same? What would it take to effect changes in the focus of state and local cybercrime-fighting capabilities? Can you see how important research is to answering these types of questions?

According to a 2001 research report published by the National Institute of Justice (NIJ), the ten most critical needs for improved state and local investigation and prosecution of cybercrimes are[3]

- Public awareness
- Data and reporting
- Uniform training and certification courses
- Onsite management assistance for cybercrime units and task forces
- Updated laws and regulations
- Cooperation between law enforcement agencies and the IT industry
- Special research and publications
- Agency management awareness of investigative issues and support of investigators
- Investigative and forensic analysis tools
- Advice for structuring IT-enabled crime units

This is a very solid list of recommendations for criminal justice research, which are consistent with topics addressed and suggestions made throughout this book. The list above is also consistent with observations made by Richard Hollinger[4] and Kenneth Rosenblatt[5] in their written remarks presented at the Computer Crime Conference sponsored by NIJ on September 14–15, 1989, in Washington, DC. The inference is that for many years, the U.S. Department of Justice, and officials at NIJ in particular have known about emerging crime threats associated with computerization but have not always responded to help criminal justice and security professionals fight high-tech crime through research and evaluation. During the 1980s, NIJ, as the lead R&D agency for the U.S. Department of Justice, sponsored very little research on computer crime issues. During the 1990s, even as computer crime morphed into computer-related crime and further into cybercrime, the agency sponsored even less research to facilitate understanding and responses to these evolving crime threats. I know this personally, because for a few years during the mid 1990's I was employed as the NIJ program manager who was assigned to pay attention to emerging computer-related crime issues. However, despite my best efforts to get research of cybercrime issues funded, other priorities prevailed.

Historically the federal government as a whole has also been slow to recognize technological interconnections between criminological constructs such as white-collar crime and corporate crime, cybercrime, organized crime, and so-called "narcoterrorism," despite indications that collectively these can combine to undermine regional economies and even threaten national security. Fortunately that is changing. In Chapters 3–6 we explored the nature of cybercrime and threats to information security, along with types of cybercriminals and theoretical explanations for why they behave in abusive and illegal ways, as well as how much cybercrime exists to cause social and economic harms to individuals, groups, and organizations. Indeed, some research studies and routinely generated reports are now the result of government agency sponsorship. Chapters 5 and 6 identified several additional possibilities for criminological research, prevalence studies, and linking social and technological aspects of cybercrime. Other possibilities, such as those identified in solicitations for research issued by the National Science Foundation and agencies and offices of the Defense Department and Department of Homeland Security also exist.

### 11.1.1.2 Passing Legislation, Creating Authority, and Issuing Directives.

In Chapter 8 we learned in some detail about government's role and process for creating laws and regulations, and as you can see from the list of laws and their descriptions in the last section of that chapter, the federal government has been very active legislatively. In Chapter 8 we also learned that legislation authorizes creation of government agencies and grants to them authority as well as responsibilities for enforcing the provisions of laws, promulgating regulations, and generally being of public service. To this point we have not mentioned that the executive branch can issue orders to government agencies and their employees to carry out federal policies deemed to be in the interests of justice and national security. As long as policies do not countermand laws, agencies may and are expected to issue directives. A classic example is Presidential Decision Directive (PDD) 63, issued by President Bill Clinton on May 22, 1998, pertaining to critical infrastructure protection and calling for a national effort to ensure the security of vulnerable and interconnected telecommunications and computing systems. PDD-63 created the President's Commission on Critical Infrastructure Protection (PCCIP) and stressed the importance of cooperation between the government and the private sector because critical infrastructure in the U.S. is primarily owned and operated by the private sector. PDD-63 eventually resulted in the creation of the Office of Critical Infrastructure Protection.

Another example occurred in October of 2001, when President George W. Bush signed Executive Order 13231 pertaining to critical infrastructure protection in the information age, which created the President's Critical Infrastructure Protection Board (PCIPB) to recommend policies and coordinate programs for protecting information systems for critical infrastructure, including emergency preparedness communications and the physical assets that support such systems. The PCIPB consisted of senior officials from more than twenty federal agencies and departments. On September 18, 2002, the PCIPB, under the leadership of then White House National Security Director Richard Clark, released its draft report, *The National Strategy to Secure Cyberspace*, which contained recommendations for protecting America's information systems ranging from desktop computers to the Internet. (The final version of this report, along with the National Strategy for the Physical Protection of Critical Infrastructures and Key Assets is viewable at: http://www.whitehouse.gov/pcipb/). Following the release of the national strategy report, the National Cyber Security Partnership (NCSP) was created, consisting of the Business Software Alliance (BSA), the Information Technology Association of America (ITAA), TechNet, and the U.S. Chamber of Commerce in voluntary partnership with academics, CEOs, federal government agencies, and industry experts. (The National Cyber Security Alliance Web site is listed in Appendix A and is among the best sources of information about public–private policy coordination efforts to protect critical information infrastructures.)

As you can see, executive directives are a very effective way for government to accomplish things in more expedient ways than through legislation. Executive actions also have the benefit of not being directly tied to political parties, election platforms, or candidates for public offices. Thus, it was relatively easy for President Bush of the Republican Party to continue the basic information infrastructure assurance policies initiated by President Clinton, a Democrat. In addition, Presidential commissions, such as the PCCIP and the PCIPB, are normally designed to include representatives from both political parties and from the private sector as well as key federal agencies. In this way, recommendations are seen to be apolitical and in the broad interests of society. Commissions for investigating matters of national concern can also be created by Congress. The most recent national commission with a tenuous connection to potential cyber threats was the National Commission on Terrorist Attacks Upon the United States (i.e., the 9–11 Commission). It consisted of five republicans and five democrats selected by elected leaders of the nation.[6] A good listing of federal government initiatives, executive orders, and presidential directives related to cybercrime, information security, and terrorism prevention is maintained by the Homeland Security Institute, viewable at http:// www. homelandsecurity.org/library.asp?fmt=1&CatID=1 #1. Check it out, and plan to use these materials and additional information as it is added to the Web site in order to support your own research needed for future school or work-related assignments.

### 11.1.1.3 Acting Internationally.   Traditionally, international commerce has occurred through formal trade agreements established by governments

and channels for the exchange of commerce among private sector firms. The combined advent of the Internet and proliferation of personal computers has resulted in unprecedented informal channels for international commerce. Individuals in almost any country can now purchase goods and services from just about any other country with a few simple keyboard clicks. International and domestic commerce have also been facilitated by the advent of inexpensive and expedited international shipping services, such as those offered by Federal Express and United Parcel Service, all made possible by computerized labeling, inventory, and shipping systems. Although convenient for millions of consumers, new forms of free trade come with inherent dangers and unique problems. As easily as individuals in disparate countries can engage in healthy commerce, so too can individuals engage in illicit activities with little fear of retribution or apprehension. This state of affairs, however, is rapidly changing.

On April, 21 2005, federal agents revealed details of an investigation into international smuggling that also involved reselling of prescription drugs via the Internet. Twenty suspects, including two U.S. college students, were arrested after allegedly conspiring to advertise and distribute controlled substances via the Internet. According to federal court records and media reports, Akhil Bansal and his father Brij Bhusan Bansal, who is a physician in Agra, India, arranged to sell tens of millions of doses of narcotics, anabolic steroids, and amphetamines through largely unregulated online pharmacies with the help of Atul Patil and several other suspects.[7] The illegal operation, which reportedly began in July 2003, allegedly involved contacting online pharmacy owners via email or bulletin boards, then shipping the drugs from Chester, Pennsylvania, for distribution to approximately 200 pharmacies for online reselling via Web sites to more than 100,000 customers located throughout the world. Investigators seized 5.8 million drug doses and $6 million from bank accounts controlled by the suspects involved.[8] U.S. arrests in the case were

made in Florida, Texas, New York, Pennsylvania, and South Carolina. International arrests occurred in Australia, Costa Rica, and India.[9]

The above case and several other international cases mentioned elsewhere in the text reveal the international scope of many cybercrimes and the necessity for governments throughout the world to collaborate in order to prevent and control crimes committed with computers or other electronic IT devices via information systems. In Chapter 8, we reviewed international treaties such as the Council of Europe Convention on Cybercrime, which exemplifies multinational commitment to combat cybercrime in many ways. The United States is now a signatory to that agreement, and many recent cases indicate that federal law enforcement agencies are collaborating as never before directly with their counterparts in other nations and through Interpol when international communications assistance and transnational cooperation is needed.

Police agencies in dozens of nations are now involved in preventing and investigating many different forms of cybercrime, even as developing countries are looking for model approaches to managing and controlling IT-enabled social abuse and crime.[10] The central challenge that lies ahead is reducing international disparity of cyber laws and regulations and disbanding existing safe havens for cybercriminals including terrorists and clusters of organized criminals who use computers to facilitate operational planning, and money laundering, and so on. In addition, technical and educational resources must be allocated to update law enforcement skills and practices needed to enforce cybercrime laws throughout the world.[11] Perhaps more technologically developed nations can invest in the IT infrastructure and security of less developed nations in order to reduce risks associated with potential attacks on critical information infrastructure and transnational cybercrime.[12] Other investments in enhancing national and international law enforcement and prosecution capabilities should also be considered and revisited by internationally recognized policy planning bodies such as those mentioned in Chapter 8 as having been instrumental in developing international agreements to combat cybercrime.

### 11.1.1.4 Appropriating Funds to Carry Out Authorized Actions.

Chapter 8 also mentioned that even though Congress authorizes things in legislation, separate legislation that actually appropriates money to be spent is required before government agencies can act unless they are legally able to cover the costs of their actions with funds previously appropriated. In 2002 Congress passed the Cyber Security Research and Development Act, which authorized $900 million in new spending in that year for cyber security technology R&D and education to improve information security within the federal government, to help protect critical infrastructure, and to create new research centers and fellowship programs at or through the National Science Foundation (NSF) and the National Institute for Standards and Technology (NIST). Each year Congress approves appropriations, and these are subject to political processes. The main thing to understand as an emerging professional is that congressional funding is subject to change that sometimes occurs rapidly and radically and in ways that may seem not to make sense. Understanding and managing cybercrime effectively at federal, state, and local levels of government, and elsewhere in society, requires paying attention to funding cycles and program priorities. Here again professional membership associations have a vital role in helping elected officials understand key crime and security issues in need of government attention and public financial support.

## 11.1.2  Getting Set and Moving Forward

Government can also be pretty effective at getting set to do things for the betterment of society. As indicated above, government has been busy in recent years trying to address cybercrime threats in various ways. Let us now consider five more sets of activities that the federal government is less or more involved in. These pertain to supporting technology R&D, testing and evaluation, providing technical assistance to public and private sectors, offering market and investment incentives to enhance information security, and creating technology market push and pull via federal procurement power.

### 11.1.2.1 Supporting Technology R&D, Testing and Evaluation.

Technology R&D investments by the federal government for countermanding IT-enabled abuse and crime are underway principally at technology-oriented colleges, universities, and federally funded research and development centers (FFRDCs). Grant solicitations are routinely issued by the Defense Advanced Research Projects Agency (DARPA), the NSF, and the National Security Agency (NSA). In 2003, DARPA alone gave out $51 million in grant funding for critical information infrastructure protection research. Many technology R&D solicitations pertain to self-regenerative information systems, the concept of trusted computing, and for dynamic quarantine of viruses, Trojans, and worms. These and other agencies within the Departments of Justice, Homeland Security, and Defense are tackling cybercrime prevention and infosec technology R&D in different ways, frequently with involvement from private sector firms that help shape technology research agendas and carry out research with government funding in some instances.

NIJ exemplifies the types of technology R&D initiatives occurring within the federal government to aid in detecting, investigating, and prosecuting cybercrimes, as well as improving information security potential for individuals, organizations, and critical information infrastructure protection. As described on its program Web page, NIJ's Electronic Crime Program is designed to address crimes involving digital technology, including cybercrime and cyberterrorism. The program goal is "to enable criminal justice agencies to better address electronic crime by building capacity for and conduits among Federal, State, and local agencies, industry, and academia."[13] NIJ's program is based substantially on its 2001 needs assessment report, whose ten most needed criminal justice systems improvements for investigating and prosecuting cybercrimes are listed earlier. NIJ's Electronic Crimes Program has three components:

1. The **Electronic Crime Partnership Initiative** to establish working groups to help define the agency's research agenda and build partnerships between criminal justice agencies, industry, academia, and other resource providers to help the nation better combat cybercrime through technology R&D.
2. The **Office of Law Enforcement Standards,** which is operated by NIST to: (1) develop and evaluate computer forensic tools, (2) create a National Forensic Software Library, (3) establish a Computer Forensic Tool Testing Project, and (4) develop best practices for electronic-crime-scene investigation.
3. The **CyberScience Laboratory (CSL)** to coordinate outreach, awareness, technical analysis and assessment, and technology transfer required by the Electronic Crime Partnership Initiative (above).

The private sector is also capable of undertaking technology R&D to help prevent and control cybercrime. So-called cam-jamming technology that interferes with the use of video camcorders in theaters is now being considered by the Motion Picture Association of America (MPAA), which represents the intellectual property interests of all seven major Hollywood production studios. The devices, which would operate via WiFi networks, are designed to locate and disrupt camcorder functioning with either electronic signals or randomly emitted light beams that would not interfere with audience viewing. Another form of the technology would send and embed an electronic signature detectable on camcorder movies as a means of enabling data forensics tracking.[14] Another example can be seen in the area of electronic gaming. Shortly after the release of the long-awaited *Halo 2* computer game, hundreds of individuals with modified Xbox™ video game consoles reported that they were ejected from playing in the firm's online gaming environment Xbox Live. It appears that Microsoft was using its popular game as a vehicle to crack down on modified chips and other hacks of its Xbox video game console.[15] In the fall of 2003 Microsoft also set up a $5 million fund to pay for information leading to the arrest and prosecution of malicious code writers who target computers running its Windows® operating system. As of November 2004, $250,000 bounties had been announced for the creators of Blaster, Sobig.F, and Mydoom.B.[16] Hence, technology R&D can be linked to investigations and private enforcement activities as well as to those of public sector law enforcement agencies.

Technology is critical in crime fighting, but technology alone is never a silver bullet, and if not carefully considered, it can be ineffectual or even backfire. Consider the now defunct Regional Coding System once employed by "Digital not-so Versatile Disk" manufacturers to counter movie piracy. Once upon a time this group divided the world into six regions and created DVD players capable of viewing movie disks that were purchased only in the same region. In 2002 when the system was put in place, the United States was in one region, Western European nations were in another region, Australia and Pacific Island nations were in another region, and so on. Sometimes it would take a year for movies released on DVD in the United States to become legally available in nations located in other regions. This created black market opportunities throughout the world beyond U.S. borders for pirates capable of altering the read programming capabilities of DVD players. Consequently the ill-conceived technology intended as a way of preventing movie piracy turned out to be a great big dud.[17] Remember that technology is like a genie let out of its bottle: according to the theory of technology-enabled crime, policing and security (described in Chapter 5), criminals will always seek technological work-arounds to crime prevention barriers, implying that technology prevention strategies need to be logical and adopted broadly, be implemented fast and remain flexible in order to accomodate changes and further innovation as needed.

### 11.1.2.2 Providing Technical Assistance to Public and Private Sectors.

In coming years criminal justice and information security professionals may look forward to many new technology innovations bearing on national capacities to prevent and control cybercrimes and protect information systems inclusive of critical information infrastructure. In addition to funding and undertaking technology R&D, the federal government also advises and provides technical assistance to private firms and public sector agencies, including security firms and policing agencies. Now, as we near the end of the book, let's further contemplate what more can be done to improve information security and prevent cybercrime throughout society.

What types of new or improved tools and additional knowledge do *you* think criminal justice and security practitioners and policymakers need most? Are there particular interests or concerns that *you* have as an emerging professional related to needed research and technology development and the types of advising and assistance needed by security firms and law enforcement agencies? If you were a city police chief, county sheriff or director of security in a government, private or nonprofit organization, what types of IT would you want developed so you could better protect your agency or firm and investigate cybercrimes? Do you know where you can look to find out what is already being researched and developed by components of the federal government and within the private sector, and how you can find assistance? Here is where professional membership associations can really be helpful. Take a look at Appendix A to see the many sources of information and assistance that may be available to you.

### 11.1.2.3 Creating and Enforcing Regulations for Greater Information Security.

Despite increasing criminal and civil prosecutions and harsher sanctions imposed by courts, cybercrimes continue to flourish, as do breaches of physical and information security, resulting in confidential data on many tens-of-thousands of people being compromised. As you know, such data is used by cybercriminals to commit credit card and other forms of fraud, as well as longer-term identity theft on grand scales. Fears that over-regulation of the Internet would inhibit e-commerce and hinder rapid economic growth have thus far forced lawmakers to be relatively cautious about regulating cyber activities. The antitrust suits by the Justice Department and certain governments of European nations against Microsoft were notable regulatory exceptions. However, under-regulation of certain sectors is producing worry about safe environments for expanding e-commerce, keeping critical information systems secure, and keeping confidential information from the preying eyes of cybercriminals.[18] In late 2004 a rash of information security breeches occurred, resulting in hundreds of thousands, perhaps millions of instances of data theft. The following examples of security breaches illustrate the seriousness of large-scale cases that may in response to legislation require notification of clients and customers:[19]

- On April 12, 2005, LexisNexis, famous for its electronic inventory of legal and other research materials and provision of these through subscriber services, announced that personal information including social security numbers and drivers license and address data of approximately 310,000 people may have been stolen in 59 different incidents in which unauthorized users were able to login with the usernames and passwords of legitimate customers acquired through unknown means.[20]

- On April 18, 2005, officials of DSW Shoe Warehouse announced that cybercriminals had accessed a database containing sales records for 96,000 transactions. As of this writing, the firm was in the process of notifying thousands of customers of the security breech, even as the U.S. Secret Service continued its investigation of the case, in which more than 100,000 people may have had their drivers license, credit card, and checking account numbers compromised.[21]

- On February 18, 2005, officials at Bank of America announced that backup storage tapes containing data on 1.2 million customers, including many high-ranking government officials who participate in the U.S. Government's SmartPay charge card program, was lost or stolen during transit to a long-term storage facility. Federal law enforcement agents were immediately called in to investigate, and the incident could jeopardize the bank's SmartCard program contract status with the Government.[22]

Major information security breeches at firms such as ChoicePoint (see Cyber Tales 11.1), LexisNexis, and Bank of America, which prompted Congressional hearings in the Spring of 2005, inspired interest in creating national regulations pertaining to data protection requirements and notifications of data loss and revealing of legal distribution of personal information for product marketing and other purposes. Essentially there is now a nation-wide push for greater information security mandates and government oversight of what has been substantially unregulated industrial sectors. In response to state and national laws and regulations, many firms are now budgeting for, implementing, and maintaining information security programs and data assurance practices.[23] These include policy development coupled with personnel training, strong password and firewall protections, and routine data backup procedures that include

encrypting sensitive information along with offsite storage archiving.

### 11.1.2.4 Resolving Contentious Legal Issues.
In addition to promoting aggressive law enforcement, prosecution and regulatory strategies for preventing and controlling cybercrime, it is also important for society to resolve contentious legal issues. As discussed throughout this book, technology-enabled crime, countervailing policing, and security perpetuate legal challenges that require redress through new legislation and judicial interpretations of existing cybercrime laws. In Chapter 10 for example, we explored unfolding legal controversy surrounding the use of WiFi networks. Earlier in Chapter 9 we discussed controversy over the U.S. Supreme Court ruling that child porn morphing was protected in the United States as form of freedom of expression under the First Amendment. Since the invention of modern computers, and especially since the emergence of cybercrime made possible if not inevitable by the Internet and increasing broadband connectivity, governments have responded to help address if not resolve many contentious legal issues. Legislators and judges have also created or interpreted cyber-related laws pertaining to privacy, intellectual property rights, and investigative methods involving electronic monitoring along with search and seizure of incriminating data.

These and other legal issues, however, have not always been fully resolved to the satisfaction of everyone in society. Police and prosecutors remain disadvantaged to determine if child porn morphing involves real children as crime victims, and many opponents of this prurient practice claim that real children are victimized even if such images are merely digital images of naked, prepubescent, virtual girls and boys. In addition, controversy still surrounds provisions of the Digital Millennium Copyright Act, even as millions of people throughout the world continue to engage in piracy of music, among other largely unchecked violations of intellectual

## *Information Insecurity at ChoicePoint*

In 2004 ChoicePoint, a data aggregation firm that specializes in acquiring and then selling access to, personal credit reports, sold confidential information on about 145,000 Americans to an identity theft ring posing as legitimate business persons conducting employment background checks.[24] Data released may have enabled the cybercriminals to gain access to names, addresses, social security numbers, and credit reports of individuals living throughout the United States. ChoicePoint is among the nation's largest data aggregation firms and reportedly maintains a database containing 19 *billion* records pertaining to credit history, driving and insurance records, sex offender registration, and so on. Numerous employers pay to access this information, which provided the basis for the crime in this incident.[25]

In order to comply with the California Database Breach Act (SB 1386), ChoicePoint began notifying approximately 30,000 affected persons in that state of the information security breech in October, 2004. Public outcry lead to notification of persons in other states whose information was mistakenly released to masquerading criminals, although ChoicePoint has no loyalty to these individuals because its business is selling their personal information without their knowledge or approval. In March of 2005 ChoicePoint shareholders filed a class action lawsuit against the firm and its top executives because in the wake of the incident its stock prices took a 20 percent nosedive, declining from $47.85 per share value on February 4, to $37.65 per share within a month.[26] Subsequent Congressional hearings in April into data insecurity practices at ChoicePoint and other major firms including LexisNexis and Bank of America revealed that ChoicePoint had experienced *fifty* separate account breech incidents. Consequently it was several weeks before affected persons were informed that their personal information had actually been sold to thieves.[27]

By early 2005 the caper had resulted in 750 identity theft victimizations. Criminal investigation into the ChoicePoint data fraud incident resulted in the arrest and conviction of Olatunji Oluwatosin, who in April of 2005 was sentenced in Los Angeles to sixteen month imprisonment.[28] However, the number of additional victims of credit card fraud and identity theft, among other types of cybercrimes, may never be known. How does it make you feel, knowing that data aggregation firms collect massive amounts of personal information on people without their knowledge or approval, and then sell it for a profit while not having to comply with government enforced information security regulations? Do you agree that Congress is correct to consider passing legislation and authorizing promulgation of regulations to curb massive leaks of personal information?

property law. By the time this book is in print, Congress will decide whether to reauthorize controversial provisions in the USA Patriot Act that allow law enforcement officers to search private homes without warrants in cases of suspected terrorism or when national security is deemed to be at stake. Some observers, however, have called attention to the legal reality that hacking into computer systems containing government data may be construed as a threat to national security, thereby equating curious hackers with terrorists for purposes of search and seizure even if they are not malevolent in their intentions. Can you think of other legal issues and cyber-related controversies, perhaps relating to expectations of privacy, e-commerce, and security regulations mandates that are emerging and may require congressional, judicial or executive branch intervention in coming years?

### 11.1.2.5 Cracking Down on Cybercrime.

Criminal justice students are naturally inclined to think about preventing and controlling crime through criminal law enforcement combined with aggressive prosecution. Indeed, as we have read throughout the text, keeping up with criminal capabilities requires society to pursue aggressive policing and prosecution strategies, even as governments continually create new crime laws and regulations to address technologically evolving cybercrimes and other forms of illegal conduct. Recent reports that Islamic extremists may be organizing a hackers' jihad in cyberspace;[29] that Web sites in China are being used heavily to target computer networks in the Defense Department and other agencies of the U.S. government;[30] and that IT infrastructures could become the battlefields in future wars,[31] support the notion that in the never-ending cat and mouse game of cops versus crooks, innovative investigative methods and prosecution strategies in contexts of emerging legislation give hope for enhancing infosec and preventing cybercrimes, even as harsher sentences imposed by courts continue to reflect growing societal intolerance of would-be cyber terrorists and other types of cyber law breakers. The Family Entertainment and Copyright Act of 2005 authorizes three years' imprisonment for prerelease of one or more movies, songs, and other digital entertainment media having a total retail value of $1,000 or more. A second offense would result in a six-year prison term.[32] This is an example of the increasing seriousness of cybercrimes and intolerance of those who commit such offenses. In this subsection we will explore prospects for expanding ongoing aggressive policing and prosecution and international collaboration and the need for the judiciary to weigh-in on certain unresolved legal issues.

Cybercrime cannot be addressed by government alone, much less by only criminal justice and security firms. Yet investigations by public law enforcement agencies and private sector security firms, combined with civil and criminal prosecution of IT abusers and cybercriminals can be an effective means of arresting cybercriminals and deterring cybercrime violations. This is especially true when enforcement actions are widely publicized and viewed as a necessary and reasonable means of protecting society from criminals. Prosecution of cybercrime offenders who have committed a broad range of crimes utilizing computers and other IT devices via information systems has been ongoing for many years, and this book has mentioned several prosecuted cases. Beginning in late 2004, however, partially as the result of collaborating with other nations, the United States has seen a marked increase in the number and variety of cybercrimes prosecuted and increases in punishments imposed by courts. Consider these examples:

- On April 8, 2005, Jeremy Jaynes, of Ralieigh, North Carolina, was sentenced on the recommendation of a jury in Virginia to nine years imprisonment for running a spamming operation that specialized in selling pornography and fraudulent products and services including a Federal Express refund processor.[33]
- On April 19, 2005, two Americans and two Chinese residents were sentenced to prison for pirating and selling more than 180,000 DVDs via the Internet to purchasers in twenty-five other nations including the United States. Randolph Guthrie was ordered to pay a $60,500 fine and will spend up to two and a half years incarcerated. Codefendant Abram C. Thrush, who was convicted as an accessory, will spend one year also in prison and must pay a fine of $1,200. Both men will be deported after serving their prison sentences in China.[34]

With regard to civil actions alleging cyber abuses, many law suits in the past decade have centered on spamming practices, even if these were not yet criminalized under state crime laws or the federal CAN-SPAM Act of 2003. Specific cases have involved accessing commercial customer database records to acquire mass email distribution lists, using spoofed email return addresses in spam, taking control of servers through which to distribute spam, using a spoofed return address that results in damaging the reputation of a third party firm, and spamming with the intention to falsely advertise products, services, or get-rich schemes, among other actions.[35] Civil judgments rendered in disclosed cases further indicate that computer abuse and cybercrimes involving spamming, intellectual property rights, and other types of laws are being dealt with by courts in increasingly harsh manners. In April 2005 Symantec received a $3.1 million default judgment against Sam Jain for violations of federal copyright infringement in which he and several codefendants reportedly sold counterfeit versions of the firm's Norton SystemWorks, Antivirus, Ghost, and PC Anywhere software products in a false email and Web page phishing operation (customers were duped into believing their antivirus service needed updating and then responded to a Web site to renew the service with their credit card).[36]

### 11.1.2.6 Promoting Public Awareness about Cybercrime and Information Security.

Media reports and news casts featuring stories consistent with the headlines at the beginning of this chapter are a daily occurrence. Everyone knows that cybercrime is a big deal, but most of the nonprofessionals I know haven't a clue as to how vulnerable they and society at large really are. Computer servers of government agencies and universities are being hacked into, organizations are losing all their data as the result of manmade or natural disasters, and individuals suffer malfunctioning technology as the result of malware that periodically seems to be taking over. Even people who are not computer users and who do not own electronic data processing or communications devices other than a standard telephone are indirectly vulnerable to harm caused by cybercriminals. All of this is to say that public consciousness about the dangers of cybercrime and information insecurity are steadily

increasing. Why is this? Much public awareness is unfortunately attributable to harm already experienced. The 2004 Rochester Institute of Techonology (RIT) Computer Use and Ethics survey revealed that of a random sample of 873 college students, only 34% of respondents indicated that they had *not* been victimized in a computer-related incident during the preceding twelve months.

People are also becoming more aware of potential cybercrime by talking with family and friends who have also been victimized, through e-commerce and online banking activities, and via software industry and ISP advertising. Colleges and universities are beginning to provide information security briefings and copies of computer use policies to incoming first-year students. It is now common during an evening session of watching television to view one or more advertisements for cybercrime prevention and/or information security services or products. Certainly the IT hardware and software industries have incentives to market their wares, as do academic institutions to raise awareness about safe computing practices. Government also has a responsibility to promote public safety and security, which historically it has done in numerous areas of public policy. Often these are in connection with a prevention program of some kind, along with a slogan and a symbol with special appeal for children—indoctrinate good citizens early. For example, McGruff reminded many Americans beginning in the late 1970s to "take a bite out of crime," Smokey the Bear warns of forest fires dangers, Coastie is an animated robotic cartoon character that travels around the country to talk to children about water safety, and Woodsy Owl flutters about saying "Lend a Hand—Care for the Land." Each of these characters charms and persuades people on public policy issues related to safety, security or well-being. Today society could benefit from a "Cyber (something)" to further raise prevention awareness and increase information security practices among the computing public. Given the need to protect critical information infrastructures, initiatives of this sort have their place and should be considered. Whatever is done must exceed the helpful vulnerability warnings that malware control companies and organizations like CERT post online, which tend to be read only by people who already know how to protect their systems at a general level. What is needed is a government sponsored social movement for enhanced information security and cybercrime prevention.

Fortunately we are making progress. Did you know that October 2004 was dubbed the first official "Cyber Security Month"?[37] Indeed, the National Cyber Security Alliance has now assumed a major role in fostering greater public awareness about the need to improve information security. This is accomplished by establishing working relationships with industry partners, which of course have a vested marketing interest in promoting cybercrime awareness and prevention, but there is nothing cynical about this. The trick for government, as discussed earlier in the chapter, is to determine what role it can and should have given market and other forces at work in society. It is not a coincidence that some NCSA board members have ties to industry and government. This is true of many professional membership and industry associations. Hence, declaration by the federal government of a National Cyber Security Awareness Month should come as no surprise, rather just as an example of how public and private sectors can join forces to publicly promote cyber security and safety. When the new awareness month was announced and publicly supported by the U.S. Congress, the Business Software Alliance (BSA) also got on board, as did the Cyber Security Industry Association and other organizations, along with certain state governments, including New York State, where I live. Colleges and universities also are now supporting this national initiative, all in an effort to heighten information security awareness.

### 11.1.2.7 Fostering Infosec Transformations via Education and Training.     Another course of action that government can take is to foster

cybercrime prevention and information security education. For several years the National Security Agency in partnership with the National Science Foundation has sponsored a nationwide education initiative intended to increase the number of information security experts in the workforce. As part of this initiative, colleges and universities are encouraged to apply for federal grants to create new multidisciplinary programs of study in information security.

Grantees are encouraged to apply to become accredited as a Center in Academic Excellence for delivery of broad-based and technical courses in cybercrime and information security, which this textbook is designed to support at the introductory level. NSF also awards grants to academic institutions so that they may improve courses, curriculum, and instructional materials needed in these topical areas. In addition, a small number of fellowships and scholarships are competitively awarded to exceptional students desiring to pursue careers in information security and infrastructure assurance protection.

A good source of information about these programs activities, in addition to the NSF and NSA, is the National Colloquium for Information Systems Security Education (NCISSE). Headquartered at James Madison University in Virginia, NCISSE is a leading proponent for implementing courses of instruction in information security into American higher education (see Web site listed in Appendix A).

Donn Parker, in *Fighting Computer Crime: A New Framework for Protecting Information* (1998), argued strenuously for the need to transform the folk artistry of information security into a viable and recognized profession.[38] That is now beginning to occur with professional training and certification programs such as the Certification in Information System Security Professional (CISSP), the Certified Information Systems Auditor (CISA) credential, and the Certified Information Security Manager (CISM) credential, which provide recognized ways for existing and emerging professionals to become expert in their fields. Preparation courses to take certification examinations are offered by several organizations, notably the Information Systems Audit Control Association (ISACA) for the CISA and CISM credentials, and the International Information Systems Security Certification Consortium or (ISC)$^2$ for the CISSP. Other formal education and certificate training programs offered by colleges and universities, as well as other professional membership associations and organizations such as those discussed in Chapter 9 can also provide professional development resources and opportunities (see Appendix A for listings and Web site information).

## 11.2  Computer Ethics Education and Intolerance of Cybercrime

A key element to all cybercrime prevention and information security education and training is computer ethics coupled with a healthy dose of intolerance for cybercrimes and cybercriminals. In this final section of the book a short block of instruction explains the philosophy of ethics as another very important component of multidisciplinary studies in cybercrime and information security education and training. Here we explore how people rationalize the ways in which they use computers and go about deciding whether

---

**BOX 11.2  •  *Get Ahead by Joining a Professional Membership Association***

Joining a professional membership association is a great way for students to stay abreast of cutting-edge issues, learn new technical skills, and develop a network of colleagues from whom they can learn and stay informed over the course of their careers. Virtually every profession has at least one professional membership association, and it is no different for high-tech crime and information security professionals. In general, some associations are loose affiliations that require only that you pay annual dues or attend meetings every so often. Others have strict rules for obtaining membership, ranging from requiring members to pass tests or provide proof of education or work experience, and even acquire sponsorship by a current member.

Costs of joining an association vary and can be quite expensive. However, the benefits can be very worthwhile, especially if discount student or organization rates for joining are available and if membership provides entitlements such as a journal or newsletter, reduced conference fees, or discounted auto and health insurance. These are merely perks when compared to the real benefit of joining a professional membership association, which is building a professional network of colleagues with whom you can develop career-long relationships. Trusted colleagues can be sought out for advice during all sorts of problematic situations, provide insights into thinking about emerging technological developments, or provide suggestions if you find yourself looking for a new position within the field.

Continuing education and training will become very important when you're finished with your college studies, and professional membership association annual national or regional conferences can often provide an inexpensive way to keep your knowledge, skills, and resume current. Because professional groups range tremendously in their relative costs and benefits, students and young professionals are advised to carefully choose the ones they become involved in. They should also consider local, regional, and national groups and after joining think about volunteering to assist committees working on association affairs. Such experience will often complement a person's ongoing work, provide in-depth exposure to emerging issues, instill new management skills, and increase the size and diversity of a professional network, while also providing opportunities for you to demonstrate your expertise and potential contributions.

to cause harm with them or other types of IT devices. From the onset, it is interesting to note that not everyone likes using computers, and this alone can impact how and the extent to which they actually use, abuse, or misuse them (e.g., not employing good security on their computer systems). Perhaps they are apathetic about, confused, or intimidated by electronic gadgets or are simply into other things. We first discussed these ideas in Chapter 1 in the context of understanding the role of IT in evolving notions of social deviance. Now we will revisit this concept to further understand and manage cybercrime from the standpoint of ethics and ultimately what has come to be called computer ethics.

### 11.2.1 The Philosophy of Ethics

How do you think people should use computers? Have you ever done something with a computer or other type of IT device that you are not proud of, embarrassed by, or would take back if you could? Do you think we should *not* download music files simply because it is illegal to do so? Answers to these and many other questions pertaining to controversial issues can be guided by studying ethics. Ethics is essentially a "systematic endeavor to understand moral concepts and justify moral principles and theories."[39] The goal of ethics, therefore, is to understand what is right, wrong, permissible, good, or evil in social and moral contexts and thereby to guide formation of beliefs and attitudes as well as decision making and behaviors in myriad circumstances. Ethics is closely associated with principles of law, religion, social etiquette, and morality (i.e., promoting well-being and alleviating suffering).[40] As you will recall from Chapter 1, ethics also relates strongly to the concepts of social deviancy, abuse, and crime, which are all judged according to potential or actual harmful impacts on individuals,

---

**BOX 11.3 • *Not Everyone Likes Using Computers***

I have never been fond of computers and did not embrace them as most people of my generation have. My choice of colleges does not reflect my detestation of computers and most other technology. I dislike computers so much that until two years ago I used a word processor, which I suppose may be another type of computer, but how would I know something like that? After finally buying a computer I did find some benefits in using it, but somehow I managed to delete a forty-page term paper that I could never recover. I know this was my fault because I never back anything up and I rarely even save anything on a disk, only to my hard drive. I get these virus warning messages on my computer that essentially tells me everything on my computer is infected. What does that mean anyway? I just tell the computer that I will clean it later, which I never actually do.

I have had many experiences with computers and most of them have been negative. I also think there are many people who use computers for unethical purposes. Once I realized all the things people could do with computers and the things that computers could do to people, there is no way I can trust them. On the other hand, QuickBooks has made running my business a lot easier. Part of me just knows that I will always have a distrust and loathing for computers. I will never like using them to talk to people; the instant messaging annoys the crap out of me. I just think the phone is a lot more personal for catching up with my family and friends. I do see email as a good thing for contacting people with questions and what not. And I can shop a little on the computer, but I still like going to the store better, though I cringe every time I have to put my credit card or social security number into a computer.

*Anonymous Student*

groups, organizations, or society at large. Harm associated with computer abuse and cybercrime was discussed in Chapter 6. Here we further examine those concepts to reflect on what *is or ought* to be considered deviant, abusive, and legal or illegal with respect to our personal actions and professional practices.

Ethics as a field of study dates to the classic Grecian teachings of Socrates and his student Plato's views about moral imperatives and religion (ca. 428–348 B.C.) and those of Aristotle who, as Plato's student (384–322 B.C.), expanded earlier conceptions of morality to include ideas about moderation, reason, and justice in one's pursuit of an excellent life. Although detailed explanation of these and many other specific ethical concepts exceeds the scope of this book, it is important to understand that the philosophy of ethics is an immensely complex field of study with important implications for responsible, legal, and moral use of computers and other electronic devices and therefore also to our understanding and managing of cybercrime. However, the field of ethics consists of many coherent theories that are mutually inconsistent, inherently controversial, and supported more on the basis of logical arguments than empirical research.

At a general level, ethics involve several traditional philosophies, notably idealism, realism, pragmatism, and existentialism. Let us briefly consider each of these fundamental ethical concepts.

**Idealism** is the notion that human thoughts, spirit, and language have a crucial role in making the world the way it is and therefore have intrinsic value. A simplistic way to think about idealism is to view it as being the opposite of realism. Idealists believe in the redeeming nature of human beings and they typically wish the world would consist of relatively little evil, harm, or conflict. Idealists often characterize themselves as optimists. Most law enforcement officers, prosecutors, and information security professionals who deal with criminals and personally

experience the evils of the world regard idealism and idealists with skepticism.

**Realism** is a philosophy based on practical realities and political pragmatism. Realists are concerned with verifiable facts, common sense, and things that are obvious or proven. Realists tend to reject idealism, fantasy, mythology, and generally implausible explanations for causes or events. Most law enforcement officers, prosecutors, and information security professionals who deal with criminals and personally experience the evils of the world tend to be realists. However, many of these professionals also hope that criminals can be reformed if they are caught, punished, educated or trained, and given supervised opportunities. This also reveals that realism is not inconsistent with being trusting and compassionate with respect to securing information systems.

**Pragmatism** pertains to getting things done regardless of environmental constraints. Thus, pragmatism pertains to recognizing constraints over which you have little or no control, compromising your hopes or expectations when necessary, and making choices in an imperfect world consisting of scarce resources. An information security professional who, because of organizational budget constraints, is not able to completely retrofit or upgrade computer system security may need to prioritize and choose which hardware and software improvements are most important under particular circumstances. Similarly, a prosecutor who is unable to convict the perpetrator of a particular cybercrime may need to offer a plea agreement in order to settle a given case. Both examples involve the philosophy of pragmatism (i.e., being pragmatic).

**Existentialism** stresses the importance of individual human beliefs and values developed throughout life, and that the meaning of life depends on a person first being alive. In other words, existentialism pertains to the need for people to decide for themselves what is right or wrong because there are no acceptable predetermined standards for behaving properly. After all, nothing is really permanent, so who is to say what should be? Thus truth is merely a reflection of things that exist and is therefore collective experience. Existentialists argue that truth is a function of existence, and that what is considered good or evil depends entirely on what people who are living decide it is.

### 11.2.2 Classical Ethics Theories

Two reigning classical ethics theories exist within the philosophy of ethics. One is **utilitarianism**. The other is generally referred to as **Kantian ethics** or **deontological belief systems**. If you have ever taken a course in ethics you are bound to have studied these classic ways of rationalizing behavior. What you may not have realized is that they have a great deal to do with how and why people use technology and therefore with criminological theories, which as we learned in Chapter 5 seek to explain why people commit crimes and cause harm. Let us therefore briefly consider each classical ethical theory.

#### 11.2.2.1 Utilitarianism.  According to utilitarian theory, the best choice is that which, on balance, brings about the greatest happiness or good for the least cost, unhappiness, or harm to everyone affected. Utilitarianism recognizes that we live in a world of scarce resources, that everyone cannot have their complete way all the time, and that in any given situation alternative choices, each involving compromises, are inevitable. The theory is most applicable in situations involving group, organizational, community, or societal issues in which many people have a vested interest in the outcomes of a decision or course of action. The U.S. Supreme Court often employs utilitarian analysis in deciding which legal cases it will review and how laws should be interpreted in the future by lower courts so as to maximize benefits to society as a whole rather than to individuals involved in specific cases.

This explanation is rather simplistic. In practice, decision making on the basis of utilitarianism is more complex and depends on the following additional principles or assumptions:

- Actions are assumed to be voluntary.
- There is no preference for immediate versus delayed happiness realized.
- Unhappy as well as happy tradeoffs for everyone involved must be considered.
- Decisions may involve inevitable unhappiness (choosing the lesser of evils).
- Happiness is subjective and cannot be measured only in quantitative terms.
- Your happiness does not count for more than anyone else's happiness.

Utilitarianism is sometimes applied indiscriminately without considering all the potential consequences of a decision. For example, illegal downloading of music and movie files may seem ethical because many people benefit as the result of not having to pay for these types CDs and DVDs. However, if billions of dollars are not paid for these products, then certain artists and recording industry employees who hold the copyrights, along with law-abiding consumers, are effectively penalized as the result of losing royalties and jobs and having to pay higher prices for music media. Certainly pirates benefit, and many people complain and rationalize illegal downloading behaviors, and some are defiant in their attitudes toward recording and movie industry practices, as if to say "give us what we want or else." However, in the final analysis courts throughout the world are consistently ruling in favor of intellectual property rights holders and ruling that illegal downloading of music and movies are indeed violations of criminal and civil laws. In life people cannot always legally acquire all they may desire, all of which pertains specifically to perceptions of fairness and motivations for some people to behave illegally. Think back to Chapter 5, which discussed criminological theories underpinning IT-enabled abuse and cybercrimes. Which of those theories relate specifically to rationalizations made by music and movie file sharers?

OKAY, I'M GROUNDED. JUST BE ADVISED I CAN NO LONGER GUARANTEE THE INTEGRITY OF YOUR SYSTEM FILES.

To learn more about utilitarian ethics, students are encouraged to review classic readings in the subject, such as those written by

- Thomas Hobbes (1588–1679): Ethical egoism and the political theory of Leviathan
- David Hume (1711–1776): The idea that justice results from human selfishness and limited generosity
- John Locke (1632–1704): God bestowed people with inalienable natural rights
- John Stuart Mill (1806–1873): The best action is the one with the best consequences
- G.E. Moore (1873–1958): What is right must be defined in terms of what is "good," a non-natural indefinable property that can only be discovered through intuition

### 11.2.2.2 Kantian Theory and Deontological Belief Systems. **Kantian theory**, so named for the great German philosopher Immanuel

Kant (1724–1804), represents a second major way of viewing and applying ethics in decision making. According to this view, people should never be treated as a means of accomplishing things because their needs, feelings, and desires are also important moral ends. In other words, we ought to help others even as we fulfill our own needs. After all, Kant believed, people are special creations of God who possess dignity therefore have intrinsic worth and are therefore deserving of our respect, assistance, forgiveness, and love.

Kantian ethics addresses the reality that everyone in society depends on each other for virtually all their needs (e.g., food, clean water, shelter, safety, security, social networks, employment). It is right, therefore, to respect others who are involved in our lives, for example those who maintain the security and functionality of information systems. Respecting others is also pragmatic because we often need help from others, and they will be more inclined to offer and provide assistance if they are respected, appropriately compensated, and thanked by us. However, the moral imperative in Kantian ethics is to genuinely serve and support other people rather than manipulate them into helping us. In Kant's words, "Act so that you treat humanity, whether in your own person or in that of another, always as an end and never as a means only."

Kantian ethics are also known as deontological theories. **Deontologists** are ethicists who stress the importance of duty and rules in decision making, and they tend to be of two minds (or categories): act and rule. **Act deontologists** view every moral dilemma as a separate ethical situation in which we must decide what to do on the basis of our intuition. "Let your conscience be your guide" is a general principle held by act deontologists, who also believe in the concept of situation ethics (i.e., correct decisions are premised on moral perceptions of varying situations rather than on abstract rules to be generally applied in every situation). **Rule deontologists** believe in universally applying basic rules such as keeping promises, telling the truth, and obeying the law. However, even rule deontologists are divided in their views as to whether such prima facie rules should occasionally be overridden if choosing to obey them would result in a lesser good or greater harm.

Act and some rule deontologists recognize that there may be exceptions to every rule or law. For example, suppose that by truthfully telling on a friend because she cheated on a computer programming exam you caused her to fail the class and not graduate from college. To whom will the lesser good or (if you prefer) greater harm incur—to your friend who will not graduate and therefore may not be able to secure employment and help others with her technical skills, or to yourself, other students, and academia as a whole, which awards college degrees only to those demonstrating necessary knowledge, skills, and abilities sufficient to expertly assist others in their career fields? Many other situations present ethical dilemmas at school and at work and other

areas of our lives. When was the last time you experienced an ethical dilemma? When was the last time you experienced an ethical dilemma with regard to using computers or other types of electronic devices? What contributed to the circumstances? What choices were made, and on what ethical bases were they made? What happened as a result? If you could do relive the experience, would you do anything differently on moral grounds?

As with utilitarianism, Kantian and deontological theories consist of more complexities than can be considered in detail here. Students interested in these issues as well as views contradicting tenets of Kantian ethics are encouraged to read the writings of various ethicists including

- W. D. Ross, who wrote on **ethical intuitionism**, the notion that we inoftuitively know what is right and that moral decision making depends on perceptions and overriding necessities
- Phillipa Foot on **descriptivism**, the idea that certain facts logically entail value
- Thomas Nagel, who wrote that the opportunity and ability to be moral is actually a matter of luck (i.e., circumstances into which we were born, where and how we were raised and educated, and employment opportunities, which are based on factors largely beyond our control)

Can you think of situations in which these principles would apply to investigating or prosecuting cybercrimes or to securing information systems? For example, consistent with Thomas Nagel's hypothesis, if you happened to grow up in a family or school situation that stressed responsible use of computers, you may be more apt not to misuse computers. Do you agree? Why or why not? Formulating similar hypothetical situations and answering critical thinking questions alone or in small groups can be an excellent way to develop responsible and ethical use of

**CYBER TALE 11.2**

### *Unethical Employment Practices: Don't Get Burned!*

A student recounted an incident in which he agreed to design and stand up a Web site for a respected retail establishment. Because he wanted exposure for his fledging Web design business, he agreed to work for only $8 per hour. Over a three-week period he designed, tested, and implemented the Web page, which included attractive graphics, informative content, automated interactive responses to customers, and so on. During the process, the business owner who hired the student exhibited rude behavior in part by defaming a former Web designer. Then after the job was completed and accepted, the owner paid the student without so much as a "thank you." Several weeks later the owner requested special instruction in how to periodically update and maintain the site, so the student developed a basic instruction manual, only to be paid $20, again without even a "thank you."

Then one day in a multimedia design class the student went online to demonstrate some of his best work to the class, only to discover that his Web page had been significantly altered, that many of the functions no longer worked, and that his copyright, logo and designer credits had been removed. When the student confronted the owner in an email about his defaced work, the owner reportedly replied, "I'm not going to be held hostage by a college student" and then he promptly took the site down. The lessons here for technically skilled students just beginning to provide consulting services is not to under (or over) value your work, to regard all employment as legal agreements, the details of which are specified in a binding contract, and to understand that some people will attempt to take advantage of your relative inexperience.

computers in organizations. You should know that the study of ethics also includes an **analytic tradition** espoused by more contemporary philosophers who believe ethics are most useful when applied in our daily lives. Listed below are several examples of ethical concepts and theories applicable to cybercrime and information security–related decision making. Can you think of situations in your own personal, academic, or professional life that these are applicable to?

• J. Ayer: **Emotivism** versus logical positivism (e.g., merely hoping that information systems are adequately protected rather than knowing so on the basis of security assessments).
• Joel Feinberg: Rights are a valid moral claim and are essential for an adequate moral theory (as when computer users act in accordance with system rights established by organizational policies for information security).
• William Frankena: Virtuous character traits must be accompanied by moral principles in

order to bring about right actions or good consequences. (This theory holds that good security systems are achievable when good people behave in accordance with fair and just policies but also implies that people without an adequate moral compass jeopardize security within organizations.)
• R. M. Hare: Morality can be universally prescribed through our words and deeds. This means that officials, managers, and other professionals espousing justice and security must lead by example and verbally express what is important and what they stand for.
• Gilbert Harman: **Moral nihilism**, the idea that ethical theories cannot be proven because moral facts cannot be empirically observed as in scientific hypothesis testing.
• J. L. Mackie: It is better to do right than pursue goals or perform duty. According to this theory, there may be times when violating policies, regulations, and laws in the interest of justice is morally correct, although people

may experience negative consequences for doing so.

- John Rawls: Justice ought to be liberally and equally available to everyone, which, for example, is the moral basis for equal protection provisions of the U.S. Constitution and the rationale for ensuring that all users of a information system are treated equally with respect to their needs for access to data.
- Nicholas Rescher: Justice and rewards ought to be distributed on the basis of effort, need, and other circumstances. This theory posits that it is OK to reward people for good information security practices and to give someone special user permissions in warranted situations.

### 11.2.3 Computer Ethics

Beginning in the 1980s business ethics became a popular topic of courses, conferences, workshops, and seminars. Ethics was widely taught in business schools, philosophy departments, and theological seminars. As noted at the time by the famous management consultant Peter Drucker, principles of business ethics were also being incorporated into legislation as a means of preventing unscrupulous commercial corporate practices.[41] Today, numerous books and other materials pertaining to computer ethics and ethical use of information technologies are available in libraries, bookstores, and online. The subject is also often required in order to earn a degree at many colleges and universities, which increasingly mandate these courses in connection with academic institution accreditation requirements.

#### 11.2.3.1 How Ethical Are We in Our Use of Computers?
IT invention and innovation continually provides unscrupulous individuals with new ways to commit deviant acts, social abuse, and crime. Do you think all such acts are unethical? If you believe there are exceptions, under what circumstances would these be? For example, do you consider malicious forms of computer code released onto the Internet by hackers to

be unethical, when to them it is considered a form of art expression that is protected under the Free Speech Doctrine of the First Amendment of the U.S. Constitution? Some talented creators of malware (i.e., viruses, Trojans, and worms) insist they write the code merely for the intellectual challenge, that they would never risk prosecution by actually releasing their malicious programs onto the Internet.[42] Recall that writing malicious code is not illegal. Only releasing it is. However, malicious code, even if not activated by its author, is frequently posted onto Web sites where it is found by unscrupulous young hackers (often called "script kiddies") who do activate and distribute it widely onto the Internet via email attachments and so on. Therefore, even if not illegal in most nations, how ethical is it to write and then post malware onto Web sites, knowing that it will likely be distributed and cause harm to computer users throughout the world? Do you agree with some legal scholars who believe this is akin to criminal conspiracies in which perpetrators are supplied with the means to commit a crime? What about downloading music, movie, or application files for free and using these without authorization in violation of federal copyright laws? What if you knew that real people lost their jobs as the result of the effects of illegally downloading music and movie files?

Let us now consider an aspect of computer ethics that many students have first-hand experience with: unethically using computers or other IT devices to cheat, harass, or threaten. Using such devices to cheat on exams and assignments is perceived to be a huge problem at some if not most American colleges and universities. Plagiarism in any form is universally prohibited in academia, and students who do it may be expelled from their college or university for violating academic integrity policies. Yet at one Tennessee State University cheating is reportedly such a problem that one professor now makes students turn in their cell phones before taking exams to prevent them from sending text messages to each other.[43] He is not alone. Increasingly professors throughout the country are disallowing any type of electronic device into examination rooms. To counteract online plagiarism, many professors and/or their academic institutions now employ software tools to detect and validate plagiarism in preparation for academic integrity review hearings and meting out sanctions.

Another approach now used to combat dishonesty at many colleges and universities involves students helping faculty and school administrators develop, market, and institute cultural acceptance and reinforcement of academic honor codes.[44] Other means to curb cheating include disallowing use of all electronic devices, maintaining close watch for improper use of devices that are allowed, using test generation software to scramble the order of examination questions, and the age-old method of using more than one test version when administering an exam.[45] Some professors also believe that honor codes, including having students sign their names to research papers, homework assignments, and exams to indicate they did not cheat may reduce academic cheating while also acculturating students on college campuses into behaving more ethically.[46]

Some universities have hired contractors to survey their student populations to determine how extensive the cheating problem really is.[47]

Are today's college students, most of whom grew up with computers in their homes (and had them available to cheat with in high school if they were so inclined), less ethical than college students in former times? Do computers and other types of IT devices make it comparatively easy to plagiarize and/or cheat and then rationalize such behaviors? Several studies of high school students indicate that although a majority of students say it is wrong to cheat, a majority have plagiarized materials from the Internet using copy and paste software. Many students also admit they would commit insurance fraud, accept bribes, or engage in another type of crime in order to succeed in business.[48] Findings from the 2004 RIT survey are generally consistent with those of other studies. When asked how wrong it is to use a computer or other electronic device for various academic activities, nearly all respondents indicated that they thought it was at least somewhat wrong to (1) present someone else's thoughts as their own, (2) copy computer codes to use on their own assignments, (3) buy papers to use as their own, (4) cheat on school assignments, and (5) cheat on exams. Table 11.1 summarizes the mean student scores as reported on separate scales ranging from zero ("not wrong") to four ("very wrong").[49]

**TABLE 11.1**   *Student Survey Attitudes*

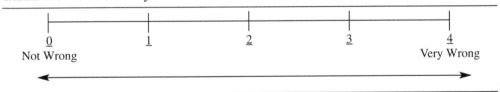

| Indicate how wrong is it for someone to do each of the following activities: | Mean Score |
| --- | --- |
| 1. Present someone else's thoughts, research, or writing as your own | 3.53 |
| 2. Copy computer code to use as your own in school assignments | 3.33 |
| 3. Buy papers to use as your own in school assignments | 3.51 |
| 4. Use a computer or other electronic device to cheat on school assignments | 3.48 |
| 5. Use a computer or other electronic device to cheat on exams | 3.58 |

A reasonable first impression of the data listed in Table 11.1 is that students are fairly honest. After all, their combined overall average score on the zero to four ethics attitude scales rounds up to 3.5 out of a possible 4.0, the equivalent of an "A" for honesty. However, upon closer examination, the data reveal that most students do not completely agree that all five forms of academic dishonesty asked about in the survey are "very wrong." This implies that as a group they believe some types of cheating are at least "a little OK." In fact, 97.4 percent of the students surveyed indicated that at least one of the five types of cheating was not "very wrong, and 14.5 percent indicated they had cheated in some way during the preceding twelve months. Mean scores listed in Table 11.1 also obscure the fact that 5.3 percent (46 out of 873 students surveyed) scored only one or zero on the ethics scale in three or more of the five behavioral items. This means that one in twenty students think most of the cheating behaviors are at least somewhat OK.

What is your reaction to these data? Are you surprised by any of the survey results? If this survey had been conducted on your campus, what do you think the average scores of each form of academic dishonesty would have been? How would you score your own attitudes on each question scale? How do you think the computer ethics of students in high school and junior high compare to those of college students? A student in junior high may not see the immoral nature of downloading MP3 files because he has learned it to be an acceptable behavior from his classmates. Do you agree that first-year college students who have never before had access to the resources and lightning-fast Internet connection that most universities provide, upon seeing the ease with which their roommates cheat on exams or illegally download pirated software with little fear of being caught or severely punished, may see this as justified or harmless and believe it to be perfectly acceptable and moral?

Many college students report that they learned how to illegally download music files after beginning college. What is your attitude toward this form of computer-enabled crime? Nearly all students surveyed at RIT, in responding to questions about illegal downloading of music or movies indicated that it was not wrong, or not very wrong. Across the board, approximately 80 percent of students indicated that any form of unauthorized file sharing was not at all wrong.[50] I know what you may be thinking: music file sharing is controversial and not a typical computer ethics issue, but, as previously discussed, thousands of innocent people in the entertainment industry have already lost their jobs because of illegal file sharing.

Another form of cybercrime involves using a computer or other electronic IT device to harass or threaten. In Chapter 5 we reported on ways in which this form of crime occurs and how much has been indicated to occur on college campuses. Again, according to the RIT study, 7 percent of students surveyed in April of 2004 indicated it was not that wrong to harass, 4 percent indicated it was not that wrong to threaten, and more than 1 percent indicated it was not at all wrong to either harass or threaten someone online.

### 11.2.3.2 The Need for Computer Ethics Education.

The huge number of people being exposed to an even greater number of new technologies, along with a lack of proper moral guidance for using computers and other types of IT devices, has resulted in a society in which individuals must often learn computer ethics from people who either have had no formal education or training in the subject and/or abuse these same devices. In the RIT study 50 percent of students surveyed reported that they taught themselves computer ethics. How is it possible for anyone to teach themselves to behave ethically? Another 34 percent of students surveyed said they learned computer ethics from their friends, more than half of whom also reported they regularly illegally download music. Go figure!

**BOX 11.4  •  *Is It Ethical to Use a Work Computer for Personal Reasons?***

There is some disagreement about whether using a computer at work to check a private email account or to send and receive instant messages is an abuse of the employer's time, equipment, and computer resources or whether it is an entitlement due every individual working in the cyber society. After all, what is the big deal about sending a personal email now and then, which is comparable to making a personal phone call on the company phone? OK, fine. Who then should be held accountable when an offensive joke or comment is sent to all employees of a firm by an associate from outside the firm or by an employer via the interoffice email network? If punitive action is taken, on what basis shall it be taken: causing an offense or improper use of network resources? If the latter, where do you draw the line with respect to the analogy of using the phone to make a personal call?

The need for teaching ethics relating to business practices has long been recognized and is today more pressing than ever, as evidenced by the national scandal involving Enron Corporation, the nation's largest wholesale distributor of electric power. In 2001, senior corporate officials and the firm's accounting agency were investigated for falsely reporting that the firm was not in financial jeopardy. Within months, Enron went bankrupt, causing thousands of employees to loose their jobs and many to lose years of retirement savings that had been invested in company stocks on the basis of fraudulent reports of company earnings and net worth.

The Enron scandal prompted Congressional hearings into the unethical practices of Enron executives and their accountants, and these resulted in sweeping regulatory and legislative reforms of the public utility and financial services sectors. In the wake of the Enron scandal Congress passed the Sarbanes-Oxley Act of 2002, which requires compliance with a comprehensive reform of accounting procedures for publicly held corporations to promote and improve the quality and transparency of financial reporting by both internal and external independent auditors (see Appendix A). This law directly bears on ethical business and accounting practices. By extension the law also addressed ethical use of computers to collect, monitor, and generate financial data and earnings-related reports.

Today, as in the early 1980s, there is considerable concern about the need to teach computer ethics along with or as part of business ethics education. So, how ethical are users of computers and other electronic devices, and in what other specific ways does unethical use of computers relate to cybercrime? Since the early 1990s several computer ethics studies focusing on the computer ethics of college students have been undertaken. Most of these studies are self-report surveys that typically investigate ethical attitudes as a basis for decision making in hypothetical situations. Studies have tended to survey and compare responses of undergraduate students in different types of colleges or programs of study (e.g., business versus computer science). Five studies compared students in the United States to students of Asian nations,[51] one compared U.S. and Australian students,[52] and another compared Canadian and Swedish students.[53] A second general category of studies compared illicit and unethical use of computers among college students majoring in technical versus nontechnical fields (e.g., computer science or information technology systems versus liberal arts or business).[54] A variation of this research approach compares self-reported attitudes and behaviors of students to employed computer professionals.[55]

Nearly all these studies involved asking respondents what they would do in given hypothetical situations and/or how right or wrong various courses of action would be under given circumstances. Very few studies have involved testing of hypotheses related to specific theoretical explanations of unethical computer conduct.[56] However, in 1996, the theory of reasoned action was tested in regard to computer ethics,[57] and in 2000, Adam and Ofori-Amanfo found gender differences in certain computer-related attitudes and behaviors, which provided a basis for arguing that aspects of feminist theory apply to computer ethics.[58]

In addition to studies involving college students as respondents, there have since 1990 been several studies of the computer ethics of business professionals but very few involving responses of the general public who were not identified as a particular type of working professional.[59] The majority of studies of business professionals explored the effectiveness and importance of professional and ethical codes of conduct on behaviors involving the use of computers.[60] However, one business-oriented study examined differences in computer ethics between end users and computer professionals,[61] and another explored frequencies and opportunities for unethical computer behavior.[62] Combined findings of all these empirical studies support the following general conclusions:

- Computer abuse and crime committed on college campuses and/or via college computer networks is ubiquitous and increasing in its volume, seriousness, and impacts.
- College students and professionals generally agree about what constitutes relatively ethical versus unethical behavior but respond to unethical behaviors inconsistently and often in ways contrary to those prescribed by professional codes of ethics.
- People tend to receive very little computer ethics education while in college and little to no professional computer ethics training afterwards. Moreover, best practices for teaching computer ethics have yet to be validated scientifically.

Thus, we live in an increasingly computerized society in which more computers and other types of electronic IT devices are available and being purchased for every imaginable task. Additionally, information systems that network these devices and make available vast amounts of information are ubiquitous and becoming more so every day. Children begin using computers earlier in life (average age for today's college students is ten years of age), and these are more powerful than ever in terms of processing speed, memory, Internet connectivity, and plug 'n play applications technology. Unfortunately too many children receive far too little supervision of their computing activities, which is hardly surprising since their parents are either baby boomers or the X-generation of computer users: aware but not savvy, familiar but not expert in knowing what to do to secure IT and data from being harmed or from being used to inflict harm. The paradox is that today's college-age adults are best positioned to assume greater responsibility and leadership for enhancing responsible use of computers and other electronic devices throughout society. Please be one of these individuals.

Finally, bear in mind that the primary mandate of any government is to protect its citizens from dangers both domestic and international. Nation-state motivations for managing and controlling cybercrime and the potential for cyberterrorism are as diverse as the cultures they represent, an understanding of which is necessary to develop an effective framework for combating transnational threats to social order. Acts of terrorism are designed to heighten awareness about perceived social, economic, religious, political, and/or cultural causes or injustice. Terrorists believe that messages of fear are powerful vehicles for influencing societal changes, and to the extent that acts of cyberterrorism are seen to accentuate the potential for this on scales grander than possible through traditional terrorist tactics they may be employed. Such threats present unprecedented strategic challenges for governments because, in part, they blur traditional boundaries

*Mother teaching son responsible use of computer* Photo by Nathan Fisk

between domestic and international intelligence gathering, policing, and security management while also testing the strength of existing international treaties, conventions, and cooperative agreements. In short, actual and potential cyber conflicts are challenging how we conceptualize crime, terrorism, and even warfare.

Throughout history and especially during these anxious times, people rightfully worry about the foreign policies of their national governments and whether everything possible is being done and in morally correct ways to protect human rights in all nations. These are complicated issues that go well beyond the scope of this text. Even so, the United States currently maintains military bases and operational capabilities throughout the world and collaborates with federal intelligence and law enforcement agencies to protect America's borders, critical infrastructure, and critical information infrastructure.

Ethical use of computers has never been more important. The field of computer ethics is derived from the philosophy of ethics, including classical ethical theories and the more modern analytical ethical tradition that seeks to apply fundamental principles of ethical decision making to contemporary issues. These are pertinent to understanding and managing cybercrimes and particularly for making ethical decisions in contexts of law enforcement, prosecution, and information security management. Research reveals that college students today may not be adequately educated or trained in computer ethics or information security. Fortunately society is working across government, private, and nonprofit sectors to redress this state of affairs. This book is dedicated to those students and this critical need in higher education.

## 11.3 Summary

Government has a fundamental interest and role in preventing cybercrime through promotion of information security through criminological and technology R&D; passing legislation, creating government agency authorities, and issuing directives; actively collaboratively with private and nonprofit sectors and internationally; appropriating funds to carry out expected and needed government interventions; and improving coordination of planned initiatives. The federal government can also work to prevent cybercrime by providing technical assistance to smaller governments and to private and nonprofit sectors and by creating and enforcing regulations for greater information security when necessary. For several years the federal government and state governments have been promulgating regulations for enhancing security of information systems and data. Law enforcement agencies and prosecutor's offices are also cracking down on many forms of cybercrime, and courts are increasingly taking a dim view toward cybercriminals as evidenced by harsh criminal and civil penalties.

A major opportunity to prevent cybercrime through enhanced information security is via public awareness, formal education, and professional training. Colleges and universities are increasingly offering introductory and specialized courses in cybercrime and information security

issues, and some academic institutions are or are becoming Centers of Academic Excellence in information assurance education, with grant assistance from the National Science Foundation and certification by the National Security Agency. These are bold initiatives that are beginning to pay off with high-quality college graduates prepared to join the workforce with education and skill sets urgently needed to secure information systems, protect organizations, and assure critical information infrastructures.

Our best evidence indicates that computer ethics education is most effective when infused into a variety of courses, over extended periods of time, taught in different ways perhaps not limited to case study approaches, and reinforced in formal and informal ways. We learned in this chapter that many college students, and others in society, do not always use their computers responsibly. Therefore a primary societal goal is to develop and promote widespread computer ethics education and training for everyone in society, appropriate to their age, social situation and professional position. This is a goal that government alone cannot accomplish but can foster through legal means discussed in this chapter.

## Key Terms and Concepts

Act deontologists, 479
Analytic tradition, 480
Creating climates, 460
Deontological belief systems, 477
Deontologists, 479
Descriptivism, 479
Emotivism, 480
Ethical intuitionism, 479

Existentialism, 476
Fill gaps, 460
Idealism, 476
Incentives, 460
Kantian ethics, 477
Kantian theory, 478
Link and coordinate, 460
Moral nihilism, 480

Pragmatism, 476
Providing information, 460
Realism, 476
Resources, 460
Rule deontologists, 479
Supporting R&D, 460
Surveying, 460
Utilitarianism, 477

## Critical Thinking and Discussion Questions

1. If you were the President of the United States, what technologies would you direct federal government agencies to invest in to help prevent cybercrimes and promote information systems security?

2. Under what circumstances, if any, do you thinking computer hacking is ethical? Is hacking by "black hats" ethically different than white hat hacking? Explain your answer and give real or hypothetical examples of white hat versus black hat hacking. Then contrast your answers thus far with the activities of so-called gray hat hackers.

3. Assuming there is an ethical difference between white hat and black hat hacking, do you think it is possible for an individual to be both at the same time? Explain why or why not, and give examples or explanations to support your answer.

4. How, if at all, do you think employment pay scales factor into decisions of ethical versus unethical behavior on the job?

5. Writing malware has been compared to studying subjects or developing technologies that are potentially dangerous (e.g., a nuclear device falling into the hands of terrorists). Explain why you think writing malware is or is not ethical, given the potential for particularly destructive code to be used for cyberterrorism.

6. Explain why you think writing malware and posting it to Web sites as a form of legally protected artistic expression is ethical or unethical?

7. In thinking about the "digital divide" (i.e., computer "haves" and "have-nots," is government ethically bound to address this problem, or is it more properly a matter to be addressed if at all via the not-for-profit or private sectors? What in your view would an appropriate public policy solution to this problem be?

8. This chapter briefly discussed professional standards of ethics. Find a professional computer code of conduct, read it, and write a short essay detailing your reaction to it. Think about how easy it would be to enforce, how easy it would be to comply with, and the potential effect it could have on an organization if it were adopted.

9. Computer hacking causes damage to the data (i.e., property) of other people whether the act involves destruction of Web sites or merely manipulating programming as in cases of posting "cyber graffiti" to the victim's site. What about hacking just to snoop? Is computer trespassing in addition to being illegal also unethical in your view? What about illegal music or movie file sharing? How do you explain any differences in your views?

## References and Endnotes

1. Kline, S. J., & Kash, D. E. (1992). Government technology policy: what should it do? *The Bridge, 22* (1), 12–18.

2. To obtain copies of these reports, contact the National Academy Press at http://www.nap.edu/.

3. Stambough, H., Beaupre, D. S., Icove, D. J., Baker, R., Cassaday, W., & Williams, W. P. (2001, March). *Electronic Crime Needs Assessment for State and Local Law Enforcement.* Washington, DC: National Institute of Justice.

4. Hollinger, R. C. (1989). Statistics on Computer Crime: A Review of the Research Questions. Paper presented at the National Institute of Justice Computer Crime Conference, September 14–15, Washington, DC.

5. Rosenblatt, K. S. (1989). Improving Techniques for Investigating and Prosecuting Computer Crime: Out of the Classroom and into the Field. Paper presented at the National Institute of Justice Computer Crime Conference, September 14–15, Washington, DC.

6. Note however, that the *Final report of National Commission on Terrorist Attacks Upon the United States* scarcely referred to cyber threats or information security issues.

7. Kaufman, M. (2005, April 21). Internet drug ring broken. *Washington Times.* Retrieved April 21, 2005, from http://www.washingtonpost.com/wp-dyn/ articles/A6180-2005Apr20.html.

8. Schmitt, R. B. (2005, April 21). Rogue Internet pharmacies targeted. *Los Angeles Times.* Retrieved April 21, 2005, from http://www.latimes.com/news/nationworld/nation/la-na-drugs21apr21,0,2620642.story.

9. Kaufman, M., 2005; see note 7.

10. McConnell International LLC. (2000). Cyber crime . . . and punishment? Archaic laws threaten global information. Retrieved March 14, 2004, from http://www.mcconnellinternational.com.

11. Goodman, S. E., & Sofaer, A. D. (2000). The transnational dimension of cyber crime and terrorism. Retrieved February 8, 2004, from http://www-hoover.stanford.edu.

12. Redo, as cited by Broadhurst, R. (2003). *Summary Report: 2nd Asian Cyber Crime Summit.* Hong Kong

University Council Chamber. Retrieved March 15, 2004, from www.hku.hk/crime/rapporteur'sreport. doc.

13. National Institute of Justice. (2005). Electronic Crime Technology R&D Program description. U.S. Department of Justice. Retrieved April 22, 2005, from http://www.ojp.usdoj.gov/nij/sciencetech/ecrime.htm.

14. Jardin, X. (2004, November 12). An eye on movie theater pirates. *Wired News*. Retrieved November 23, 2004, from http://wired.com/news/digiwood/0,1412,65683-2,00.html?tw=wn_story_page_next1.

15. Becker, D. (2004, November 12). Is Microsoft using 'Halo2' to thwart Xbox hackers? CNT News.com. Retrieved November 22, 2004, from http://news.com/Is+Microsoft+using+Halo+2+to+thwart+Xbox+hackers/2100-1043_3-5449160.html.

16. Thompson, C. (2004, February 8). The virus underground. *New York Times*. Retrieved November 10, 2004, from http://www.nytimes.com/2004/02/08/magazine/08WORMS.html?ex=1100235600&en=e27d746ecc37cfcb&ei=5070&oref=login.

17. Rubens, P. (2002, May 19). Border controls crumble in DVD land. BBC News. Retrieved November 23, 2004, from http://news.bbc.co.uk/1/hi/in_depth/sci_tech/2000/dot_life/2197548.stm.

18. Grabosky, P. (2000). The mushrooming of cybercrime. Retrieved March 18, 2004, from http://www.un.org.

19. Greene, T. C. (2005, April 14). It's official: ChoicePoint, LexisNexis rooted many times. *The Register*. Retrieved April 20, 2005, from http://www.theregister.co.uk/2005/04/14/privacy_invasion_is_good_for_you/.

20. Timmons, H. & Zeller, T. Jr., (2005, April 13). Security breach at LexisNexis now appears larger. *The New York Times*. Retrieved April 13, 2005, from http://www.nytimes.com/2005/04/13/technology/13theft.html?ex=1114056000&en=8a4c960dae9723ae&ei=5070.

21. Associated Press Staff Author. (2005, April 18). 1.4 million exposed in shoe data breach: 10 times as many as originally thought affected. MSNBC News. Retrieved April 20, 2005, from http://www.msnbc.msn.com/id/7550562.

22. Lemos, R. (2005, April 25). Bank of America loses a million customer records. cnetnews.com. Retrieved April 21, 2005, from http://news.com.com/Bank+of+America+loses+a+million+customer+records/2100-1029_3-5590989.html.

23. Robb, D. (2005, April 20). Corporate data leaks spur interest in storage security. Internetnews.com. Retrieved April 21, 2005, from http://www.internetnews.com/storage/article.php/3499266.

24. Gray, T. (2005, February 18). ChoicePoint data theft fallout spreads to 145,000. Internetnews.com. Retrieved April 21, 2005, from http://www.internetnews.com/security/article.php/3484501.

25. CNN Staff Author. (2005, February 17). ChoicePoint: more ID theft warnings. CNN. Retrieved April 21, 2005, from http://money.cnn.com/2005/02/17/technology/personaltech/choicepoint/.

26. Evers, J., & Roberts, P. (2005, March 7). Shareholders sue ChoicePoint: the company's share price has dropped more than 20% in a month. IDG News Service. Retrieved April 21, 2005, from http://www.computerworld.com/governmenttopics/government/legalissues/story/0,10801,100239,00.html.

27. Schneier, B. (2005, February 23). ChoicePoint. Counterpane Internet Security, Inc. Retrieved April 20, 2005, from Schneier security Weblog viewable at http://www.schneier.com/blog/archives/2005/02/choicepoint.html.

28. (Gray, T. 2005; see note 24.)

29. Waterman, S. (2005, August 26). Islamists seek to organize hackers' jihad in cyberspace. Retrieved August, 26, 2005 from the Washington Times at http://washingtontimes.com/national/20050825-111136-2852r.htm.

30. Graham, B. (2005, August 25). Hackers attack via Chinese web sites. Retrieved August 26, 2005 from the Washington Post at http://www.washingtonpost.com/wp-dyn/content/article/2005/08/24/AR2005082402318.html?referrer=emailarticle

31. Wait, P. (2005, August 26). IT infrastructures could be battlefields of future wars. Retrieved August 26, 2005 from Government Computer News, at http://www.gcn.com/vol1_no1/daily-updates/36688-1.html

32. Hachman, M. (2005, April). Prerelease pirates could receive jail time. ExtremeTech. Retrieved April 20, 2005, from http://www.extremetech.com/article2/0,1558,1788120,00.asp?kc=ETRSS02129TX1K0000532.

33. Associated Press Staff Author. (2005, April 8). Judge sentences spammer to nine years. Fox News. Retrieved April 11, 2005, from http://www.foxnews.com/story/0,2933,152889,00.html.

34. Associated Press Staff Author. (2005, April 20). Two Americans sentenced in DVD Piracy in China. *The New York Times*. Retrieved April 20, 2005, from http://www.nytimes.com/2005/04/20/business/media/20piracy.html?ex=1114660800&en=e23b54d8c7caad35&ei=5070.

35. SRBC Staff Author. (1998). Netlitigation: spamming and spoofing. Sugarman, Rogers, Barshak & Cohen Attorneys at Law. Retrieved April 20, 2005, from http://www.netlitigation.com/netlitigation/spam.htm.

36. Hines, M. (2005, April 20). Symantec wins piracy judgment. CNET News.com. Retrieved April 20, 2005, from .

37. National Cyber Security Alliance. (2004). NCSA home page. Retrieved April 1, 2005, from http://www.staysafeonline.info/home-news.html.

38. Parker, D. (1998). *Fighting computer crime: A new framework for protecting information.* New York: Wiley Computer Publishing

39. Pojman, L. P. E. (1989). *Ethical Theory: Classical and Contemporary Readings* (p. 1). Belmont, CA: Wadsworth.

40. Pojman, L. P. E., 1989, p. 2; see note 39.

41. Drucker, P. (1981). What is business ethics? *Across the Board* (pp. 22-32).

42. Thompson, C., 2004; see note 16.

43. Kerr, G. (2004). Honor code could boost collegiate integrity. *The Tennessean*, November 17.

44. McCabe, D., & Pavela, G. (2000). Some good news about academic integrity. *Change, 32–38*.

45. Read, B. (2004, July 16). Wired for cheating: some professors go beyond honor codes to stop misuse of electronic devices. *Chronicle of Higher Education.* Retrieved November 22, 2004, from http://chronicle.com/free/v50/i45/45a02701.htm.

46. Kerr, G., 2004; see note 43.

47. Kerr, G., 2004; see note 43.

48. As cited by Davis, S. F., Grover, C. A., Becker, A. H., & McGregor, L. N. (1992). Academic dishonesty: prevalence, determinants, techniques, and punishments. *Teaching of Psychology, 19*(1), 16–20.

49. McQuade, S, & Linden, E. (2005). college Student Computer Use and Ethics: An Empirical Analysis of Self-Reported Unethical Behaviors. Manuscript: Rochester Institute of Technology.

50. McQuade, S., & Linden, E., 2005; see note 49.

51. Swinyard, W. R., Rinne, H., & Kau, A. K. (1990). The morality of software piracy: a cross-cultural analysis. *Journal of Business Ethics, 9*(8), 655–664; Whitman, M. E., Hendrickson, A. R., Townsend, A. M., & Rensvold, R. B. (1998). Computer aversion and computer-use ethics in U.S. and Asian Cultures. *Journal of Computer Information Systems.*

52. Forcht, K. A., Brookshire, R. G., Stevens, S. P., & Clarke, R. (1993). The computer ethics of university students: an international exploratory study. *Information Management & Information Security, 1*(5), 32–36.

53. Kowalski, S., & Kowalski, H. (1990). Computer ethics and computer abuse: a study of Swedish and Canadian university data processing students. *Information Age, 12*(4), 206–212.

54. See e.g., Paradice, D. B., & Dejoie, R. M. (1991). The ethical decision-making process of information systems workers. *Journal of Business Ethics, 10*(1), 1–21.

55. Athey, S. (1993). A comparison of experts' and high tech students' ethical beliefs in computer-related situations. *Journal of Business Ethics.*

56. See e.g., Conger, S., Loch, K. D., & Helft, B. L. (1995). Ethics and information technology use: a factor analysis of attitudes of computer use. *Information Systems Journal, 5,* 161–184; Kreie, J., & Cronan, T. P. (2000). Making ethical decisions: how companies might influence the choices one makes. *Communications of the ACM, 43*(12), 66–71; Khazanchi, D. (1995). Unethical behavior in information systems: The gender factor. *Journal of Business Ethics, 14*(9), 741–749; Thong, J. Y. L., & Yap, C.-S. (1998). Testing an ethical decision-making theory: the case of softlifting. *Journal of Management Information Systems, 15*(1), 213–237.

57. Loch, K. D., & Conger, S. (1996). Evaluating ethical decision making and computer use. *Communications of the ACM, 39*(7), 74–83.

58. Adam, A., & Ofori-Amanfo, J. (2000). Does gender matter in computer ethics? *Ethics and Information Technology, 2*(1), 37–47.

59. Gattiker, U. E., & Kelley, H. (1999). Morality and computers: attitudes and differences in moral judgments. *Information Systems Research, 10*(3), 233–254.

60. See e.g., Peterson, D. K. (2002). Computer ethics: the influence of guidelines and universal moral beliefs. *Information Technology & People, 15*(4), 346–361 Harrington, S. J. (1996). The effect of codes of ethics and personal denial of responsibility on computer abuse judgments and intentions. *MIS Quarterly,* 257–278; Hilton, T. (2000). Information systems ethics: a practitioner survey. *Journal of Business Ethics, 28*(4), 279–284; Pierce, M. A., & Henry, J. W. (1996). Computer ethics: the role of personal, informal and formal codes. *Journal of Business Ethics, 15*(4), 425–437; Pierce, M. A., & Henry, J. W. (2000). Judgments about computer ethics: do individual, co-worker, and company judgments differ? Do company codes make a difference? *Journal of Business Ethics, 28*(4), 307–322.

61. Watson, R. T., & Pitt, L. F. (1993). Personal computing ethics: beliefs and behavior. *International Journal of Information Management, 13,* 287–298.

62. Vitell, S. J., & Davis, D. L. (1990). Ethical beliefs of MIS professionals: the frequency and opportunity for unethical behavior. *Journal of Business Ethics, 9*(1), 63–70.

# *Appendix A*

| Organization | Home Page | Interests and Expertise |
|---|---|---|
| **Banking, Financial and E-Commerce Services Sector Organizations** | | |
| American Bankers Association | www.aba.com/default.htm | Online banking |
| Consumer Bankers Association | www.cbanet.org | Online banking |
| ECLIPS | www.osc.edu | E-commerce |
| Internet Law and Policy Forum | www.ilpf.org | Cyber law, e-commerce |
| **Consumer Rights, Privacy, and Internet Safety Organizations** | | |
| Adult Industry Medical Health Care Foundation | www.aim-med.org | Public and personal health related to sexual orientation and lifestyle |
| Adult Video News (AVN) | www.avn.com | General adult entertainment information |
| American Civil Liberties Union (ACLU) | www.aclu.org/index2.cfm | Censorship and privacy |
| American Society Against Child Pornography | www.asacp.com | Prevention and reporting of sexual child abuse |
| Better Business Bureau | www.bbb.org | Scam alerts and advisories; truth and accuracy in advertising |
| Center for Democracy and Technology | www.cdt.org | Online banking, censorship, domain names, privacy |
| Computer Professionals for Social Responsibility | www.cpsr.net | Encryption |
| Electronic Frontier Foundation | www.eff.org | Censorship, crime, privacy |
| Electronic Privacy Information Center (EPIC) | www.epic.org | Banking, censorship, encryption, privacy |
| Free Speech Coalition | www.freespeechcoalition.com | Freedom of expression, adult entertainment, legal case decisions |
| Internet Society | www.isoc.org | General information |
| Internet Privacy Coalition | www.epic.org/crypto | Encryption policy, privacy |
| National Consumers League | toolbox@nclnet.org | Consumer protection; Internet and telemarketing fraud |
| National Fraud Information Center | www.fraud.org | Internet and telemarketing fraud |
| Privacy Rights Clearinghouse | www.privacyrights.org | Privacy |
| Privacy Times (Newsletter) | www.privacytimes.com | Privacy |
| Wired Safety | www.wiredsafety.org | Online child and adult safety |
| **Intellectual Property & Professional Associations** | | |
| American Society of Journalists and Authors | www.asja.org | Copyright |
| Authors Guild | www.authorsguild.org | Copyright |
| Business Software Alliance (BSA) | www.bsa.org | Copyright and software licensing |
| Entertainment Software Rating Board (ESRB) | www.esrb.org | Computer and console game ratings; consumer information |
| Information Tech Association of America | www.itaa.org | Domain names, software licensing, taxation |
| Licensing Executives Society | www.les.org | Software licensing and intellectual property |
| Motion Picture Association of America | www.mpaa.org | Copyright, movie ratings, economic reviews, legislation |
| Open Source Initiative | www.opensource.org | Open source software |
| Recording Industry Assoc. of America | www.riaa.org | Music copyright |
| Software & Information Industry Assoc. | www.siia.net | Software licensing |
| Software Publishers Association | www.spa.org | Copyright, encryption, software licensing |
| **Legal Aid, Counseling, Education, Training, and Awareness** | | |
| American Bar Association (ABA) | www.abanet.org/home.cfm | IP law, e-commerce, software licensing, telecommunications |
| American Intellectual Property Law Association (AIPLA) | www.aipla.org | IP law, software and trademark licensing |
| American Law Institute | www.ali.org | IP law, e-commerce, software licensing |
| Information Systems Audit and Control Association | www.isaca.org | CISA and CISM certifications and training |
| International Information Systems Security Certification Consortium | www.cissps.com | CISSP certification and training |
| National Colloquium for Information Security Education | www.ncisse.org | Education policy and planning |
| National Cyber Security Alliance | www.staysafeonline.info | Public awareness and advising |
| NetSmarz Workshop | www.netsmartz.org | Online safety training for children |

## Law Enforcement, Security, and Cybercrime Research Agencies

| | | |
|---|---|---|
| CERT Coordination Center at Carnegie Mellon University | www.cert.org | Infosec, attack assessments |
| Computer Emergency Readiness Team | www.us-cert.gov | Infosec and cybercrime capabilities of Dept. of Homeland Security |
| Department of Justice Computer Crime and Intellectual Property Section | www.usdoj.gov/criminal/cybercrime | Cybercrime law, regulation, and prosecution information |
| Federal Bureau of Investigation | www.fbi.gov | Crime and cybercrime investigation |
| High Tech Crime Investigators Association | www.htcia.org | Cybercrime investigation, state and international police training |
| Interpol | www.interpol.int/Public/Icpo/default.asp | International police investigation support and coordination |
| National Center for Missing & Exploited Children | www.missingkids.com | Child pornography and missing child data analysis |
| National Institute of Justice | www.ojp.usdoj.gov/nij | Technology and criminal justice research |
| National White Collar Crime Center (NWC3) | www.nw3c.org | Training, research, fraud reporting |
| SANS Institute | www.sans.org | Infosec training |
| Scientific Working Group for Digital Evidence | ncfs.org/swgde/index.html | Computer forensics best practices |
| Secunia | secunia.com | Software vulnerability and Internet security threat listings |
| Transnational Crime & Corruption Center | www.american.edu/traccc | Cybercrime research |
| U.S. Computer Emergency Readiness Team (US-CERT) | www.us-cert.gov | Infosec, attack assessments |
| U.S. Department of Homeland Security | www.dhs.gov/dhspublic | Critical infrastructure protection |
| U.S. Secret Service | www.ustreas.gov/usss/index.shtml | Cyber and financial investigations for Dept. of Homeland Security |

## Other Federal and State Government Regulatory and Policy Formulating Agencies

| | | |
|---|---|---|
| Federal Aviation Administration (FAA) | www.faa.gov | Aviation infrastructure protection and regulatory oversight |
| Federal Communications Commission (FCC) | www.fcc.gov | Communications policy development and regulatory oversight |
| Federal Deposit Insurance Corporation (FDIC) | www.fdic.gov | Financial guarantees against bank failure and regulatory oversight |
| Federal Trade Commission (FTC) | www.ftc.gov | Spamming and ID theft oversight |
| Federal Elections Commission (FEC) | www.fec.gov | Elections regulation oversight |
| Federation of Tax Administrators | www.taxadmin.org | Taxation |
| National Security Cyber Partnership | www.cyberpartnership.org/ | Private–public policy coordination |
| National Governors Association | www.nga.org | General IT-related policy |
| National League of Cities | www.nlc.org/nlc_org/site | IT-related tax policy |
| National Tax Association | www.ntanet.org | Taxation |
| National Association of Counties | www.naco.org | Telecommunications tech, taxation |
| Securities Exchange Commission | www.sec.gov | Stock market, securities, and bonds trading regulatory oversight |
| U.S. Nuclear Regulatory Commission | www.nrc.gov | Nuclear infrastructure protection |

## Technology Industry and Standards Setting Organizations

| | | |
|---|---|---|
| Association for Computing Machinery (ACM), U.S. Public Policy Committee | www.acm.org/usacm | Encryption |
| Information Technology Association of America | www.itaa.org | Trade organization representing broad IT interests |
| International Electrotechnical Commission (IEC) | www.iec.ch | Technical standards |
| International Organization for Standardization (ISO) | www.iso.org/iso | Domain names, technical standards |
| Internet Architecture Board (IAB) | www.iab.org | Domain names, technical standards |
| Internet Assigned Number Authority (IANA) | www.iana.org | Domain names |
| Internet Content Rating Association | www.irca.org | Voluntary Internet content rating procedures |
| Internet Engineering Steering Group (IESG) | www.ietf.org/iesg.html | Technical standards |
| Internet Engineering Task Force (IETF) | www.ietf.org | Technical standards |
| Internet Network Information Center (InterNIC) | www.internic.net | Domain names |
| Internet Policy Oversight Committee | www.gtld-mou.org | Internet architecture, domain names |
| National Institute of Standards & Technology | www.nist.gov | Technology standards and testing |
| World Wide Web consortium (W3C) | www.w3.org | Internet technology standards |

# *Index*

academia/academic cheating
  academic cheats and, 132
  cheating on exams and assignments,
    89–92
  emerging potential for abuse in, 221–22
  plagiarism and, 91
  scientific misconduct and, 93
  students admitting to abuse, 113, 198–99
administrative law, 294–95
adult entertainment industry, 244
adware
  bundling with software applications, 411
  defined, 64–65
  making computers run slowly, 83
  overview of, 78
  protecting against, 422–23
affidavits, 357
age, of computer abusers/cybercriminals, 130
alien servers, 103
Al Qaida, 104
anti-keylogger software, 425–27
antimalware software, using, 418–19
antispyware, installing and using, 422–23
anti-viral software, using, 418–19
appeals process, 398–99
appellate jurisdiction, 280
application fingerprinting, 80
ARPANET, 54
arraignment, 387–88
arrests, cybercriminal
  booking, 386–87
  criteria for, 348–49
  power to, 335
  warrants for, 386
ATMs, criminal opportunity and, 38, 223
attacks, 45–51
  cyber vs. physical, 46–47
  emerging trends, 99–102
  insider vs. outsider threats, 47–50
  overview of, 45–46
  responding to, 50–51
audits, security, 451–53
automated attack tools, 101

background checks, Internet-based, 253
backups, 45–46, 423–25
bail bonds, 388
banking
  fraud laws, 312
  reluctance to report theft, 193
  rip-off mortgage scheme, 49
baseline security assessments, 436
best evidence rule, 374
Bill of Rights, 289
bits, defined, 33
Blaster malware, 294, 420, 467
blogging, 226–27

booking, of cyber suspects, 386–87
bot, 99–100
bouncing, 89
broadband Internet connections, 429
BSA (Business Software Alliance), 207
bugs, defined, 64
bulletin-board reading, 115–16
business, cybercrime against, 200
Business Software Alliance (BSA), 207
byte, defined, 33

California Database Breach Act, 470
CAN (computer attack network), 106
carding technique, 68
career criminals, defined, 127
case law, 292
Central Intelligence Agency (CIA), 255–56
CERT (Computer Emergency Readiness
    Team), 341
CERT (computer emergency response team)
  guide for home computer users, 418
  observing recent attack trends, 100–101
  overview and *The CERT Summary*, 203
  tracking cybercrime, 201
CERT Coordination Center, 339
certificate authorities, 427
Certified Information Systems Security
    Professional Standard (CISSP),
    452–53
chain of custody, 373–75
change management, 449–51
child pornography
  evidentiary challenges, 371–72
  laws against online, 320–22
  worldwide condemnation of, 97–98,
    243–44
CIA (Central Intelligence Agency), 255–56
CIA (confidentiality, integrity and
    availability), 39–42
CIIP (critical information infrastructure
    protection), 55–56, 461, 464
CIIs (critical information infrastructures)
  conceptual and national differences, 55
  cyber security for, 57–58
  cyberterrorism against, 103–04
  defining, 53
  networks and services integral to, 54
  recent attack trends, 101
CIPUs (cybercrime investigation and
    prosecution units), 334
Circuit Court of Appeals, U.S., 307
circumstantial evidence, 372
CIs (critical infrastructures)
  conceptual and national differences, 55
  defining, 53–54
  PCCIP exploring, 38
  physical protection of, 57–58

CISSP (Certified Information Systems
    Security Professional Standard),
    452–53
civil judgments, defined, 302
CoBit (Control Objectives for Information
    and Related Technology), 452
code
  overview of, 33
  writing and distributing malware, 64–67
Code Red, 100, 104, 206
common law, defined, 292
computer abuse
  defined, 16
  differing views about, 20–21
  first recorded, 12
computer abuse and crime theories, 139–85
  anomie theory, 165
  arousal theory, 150–52
  behavioral theory, 153–55
  biosocial theory, 148–49
  cognitive theory, 152–53
  conflict theory, 166–74
  containment theory, 156
  control-balance theory, 157
  cultural deviance theory, 166
  differential association theory, 157–58
  differential reinforcement theory, 158
  general deterrence theory, 144–48
  general social structure theory, 164
  general strain theory, 165–66
  institutional anomie theory, 165
  Instrumental Marxism, 170
  integrated and technological theories,
    174–79
  labeling theory, 161–63
  Marxist criminology neutralization
    theory, 159–61
  people committing cybercrimes and,
    139–41
  practicality of, 141–43
  punishment theory, 158–59
  rational choice theory, 144, 148
  relative deprivation theory, 165
  routine activities theory, 147, 148
  self-derogation theory, 156–57
  social bond theory, 156
  social disorganization theory, 164–65
  social learning theories, 157–59
  social process theory, 155–63
  social structure theories, 163–67
  strain theories, 165–66
  structural Marxism, 170–71
  technology-enabled crime, policing and
    security, 175–79
  trait theory, 147–55
computer abusers/cybercriminals, 113–35
  adversarial SKRAM model, 117–22

computer abusers/cybercriminals (*Continued*)
  categorizing, 56, 124–33
  employments of, 130–31
  fears of, 122–24
  identifying traits of, 129–31
  interpersonal relationships of, 131
  lifestyles of, 131
  more comprehensive schema for, 131–33
  overview of, 124–26
  professional status of, 130–31
  social engineering tactics, 114–17
  stereotypical and other adversary
    profiles, 126–29
computer addiction, 151–52
computer attack network (CAN), 106
computer-based dating services, 224–25
computer crime
  concept of, 14
  defined, 16
  emergence of, 12–14
Computer Crime and Intellectual Property
    Section (CCIPS), Department of
    Justice, 338, 341
computer efficacy, 153–55
computer ethics, 474–86
  classical theories of, 477–78
  deontological belief systems, 479–81
  of hackers, 233–35
  Kantian theory, 478–81
  need for education, 483–86
  overview and philosophy of, 474–77
  utilitarianism, 477–78
computer forensics, 375–80
computer gaming
  arousal theory and, 151–52
  behavioral theory, 153–55
  cognitive theory and, 152
  enclaves, 238–42
computer hackers. *See also* hackers
  defined, 232
  and system trespassing, 83–85
computerization
  defined, 3
  globalization as result of, 53
  white-collar crime changing as result of,
    25–26
computer trespassing, 132
concentric zones concept, 164
concurrent jurisdiction, defined, 280
confidentiality, data, 40–41
consensus view of social organization,
    167–68
constitutional law, 288–91. *See also* U.S.
    constitution
consumer rights organizations, 491–92
copyright law, 296–99
corporate crime
  defined, 12
  emergence of computer crime, 12–14
  IT-enabled espionage and, 85–86, 132
Council of Europe's Convention on
    Cybercrime, 2001, 285
counterterrorism monitoring and surveillance
    legislation, 316, 319–20
courtroom procedures, 393–94
crackers, 127
credit card fraud
  distrust created by, 44
  as opportunity for criminals,
    223–24
  overview of, 68–69
  student victim of, 70

crime. *See also* cybercrime
  blogging for, 229
  clear definitions of, 16–20, 25
  crimes against persons, 292
  crimes against property, 292
  hi-tech, 13–14
  new IT-enabled crimes, 177–78
  prevention through environmental
    design, 165
  smart mobbing used for, 229–30
  theories of. *See* computer abuse and
    crime theories
  types of, 12–14
  victimization. *See* victimization,
    computer-related
crime scene processing, 361–84
  collecting and preserving evidence,
    367–80
  crime scene, defined, 362
  crime scene protection, 361–67
  equipment for, 364
  evaluating crime scenes, 363–66
  incident response notifications, 366–67
  notification and protection checklist, 364
  preparations, 362–63
  safe arrival, 362–63
  securing crime scenes, 363–66
  tactical response, 362–63
criminal intent, and culpable mental states,
    343–45
criminal justice system, 333–41
  investigation and prosecution units,
    337–38
  investigative and technical assistance
    agencies, 339–41
  missing persons online, 263
  overview of, 333–35
  public law enforcement *v.* private
    security, 335–36
criminal law, 292–94
criminology
  defined, 113
  new criminologies, 212
  of place, 164–65
criminology theories, 143–48
critical information infrastructure protection
    (CIIP), 55–56, 461, 464
critical information infrastructures. *See* CIIs
    (critical information
    infrastructures)
critical infrastructures. *See* CIs (critical
    infrastructures)
cross examination, 394
cruel and unusual punishment, 290
cryptography, 425–27
cryptoviruses, 100
CSI (Computer Security Institute), 201–02
culpable mental states, 343–45
culture
  defining, 233
  organizations, information security and,
    449–51
cyber activists, 127
cyberbullying, 94
cyber conflict continuum, 106
cybercrime
  computer abuse theories. *See* computer
    abuse and crime theories
  defined, 16
  federal regulations against. *See* federal
    laws and regulations
  international agreements, 281–87

investigating and prosecuting. *See*
    investigation and prosecution
  managing, 271–72
  overview of, 16–18
  vs. physical attacks, 46–47
  social and economic impacts of. *See*
    social and economic impacts, of
    cybercrime
  technology fusion bringing about, 14–16
  viewpoints on, 25
  widespread adoption of term, 212
cybercrime, as new paradigm
  computer-related crime emerges, 12–14
  defining, 2–4, 16–18
  financial crime, 11–12
  law and regulation enforcement, 18
  organized crimes, 12
  preventing, 24
  principles for, 20–24
  research and justice systems
    improvements, 19–20
  social construction concept, 10–11
  technology fusion and, 14–16
  white-collar crime, 11
cybercrime, controversial issues, 219–69
  computer hacker subculture, 232–36
  electronic gaming enclaves, 238–42
  online pornography, 242–47
  Open Source Community, 236–38
  privacy. *See* privacy infringement
cybercrime, emerging trends, 98–108
  crime and attacks, 99–102
  futuristic forms of conflict, 102–05
  information and network-centric warfare,
    105–08
cybercrime investigation and prosecution
    units (CIPUs), 334
cybercriminals. *See* computer
    abusers/cybercriminals
cyber law, 292
cyberpunks, 127, 236
cyber sex offenders, 132
cyber society, 220
cyberspace
  defined, 3
  normalcy, deviancy and crime in, 10,
    24–25
cyber squatting, 300
cyberstalking
  as limited form of terrorism, 103
  overview of, 95–96
  pedophilia as, 96–97
cyberterrorism
  defining, 102–04
  overview and managing, 103–07
cyber terrorists, 127, 132

*Danny Lee Kyllo v. United States*, 354
data
  availability, 41–42
  backing up, 423–25
  confidentiality, 40–41
  as evidence, 370
  integrity, 41
  knowledge management vs., 33–35
  loss, from cybercrime, 190
  money as special form of, 36–38
  physical security of, 414
  possession vs. ownership, 35–36
  recovery plans, 447–49
dating services, computer-based,
    224–25

DDOS (distributed denial of service) attacks, 76
Declaration of Independence, 277
defamation, defined, 301
DEFCON, 235
delinquent acts, criminal definition of, 293
democratization, IT-enabled, 226–31
  blogging for crime and justice, 226–29
  political activism, 229–30
demonstrative evidence, 373
denial-of-service (DoS) attacks, 76, 99–100
deontological belief systems, 479–81
  Intellectual Property Section), 338, 341
descriptivism, 479
design patents, 300
detaining suspects, 347–48
deterrence, 397
deviant behaviors
  in cyberspace, 10
  differing views about cybercrime, 20–21
  in most of us, 113
  overview of, 5–8
  use of IT, 8–10
digital piracy, 207–09. *See also* piracy
digital signatures, 425–27
direct access revolution, 88
direct examination, 393
distributed denial of service (DDOS) attacks, 76
distrust, principle of, 43–45
DNS (Domain Name System), 54–55, 101
Domain Name System (DNS), 54–55, 101
double jeopardy, 279
due care and diligence standards, 436, 444
due process
  in cyber law, 278–79
  in U.S. Constitution, 290

e-commerce
  IT-enabling abuse and crime, 222–25
  online pornography as main form of, 243
  service sector organizations, 491
economic crime, defined, 12
economic impacts, of cybercrime. *See* social and economic impacts, of cybercrime
ECTFs (Electronic Crimes Task Forces), 336
education
  computer abusers/cybercriminals, 130
  cybercrime requirements, 22–23
  IT-enabled abuse and crime, 221–22
  need for professional, 21–22
  and training in cybercrime management, 473–74
  and training organizations, 492–93
effects-based operations (EBOs), 106
EFF (Electronic Freedom Foundation), 257–58
election fraud, 230
electricity, security and, 51–53
electronic crime
  defined, 19
  Electronic Crime Partnership Initiative, 467
  Electronic Crime Program of NIJ, 466–67
  Electronic Crimes Task Forces (ECTFs), 336
electronic evidence, 369–71
electronic gaming enclaves, 238–42
electronic key rings, 427

email
  hoaxes, 73–74
  spoofing, 71–72
Emergency Preparedness and Response (EPR), DHS, 56
emotional harm, 190–92
emotivism, 480
employees, and computer crime, 130–31, 223
employers
  privacy infringement by, 252–55
  surveillance technologies of, 262
  unethical practices, 480
encryption
  algorithms, 417
  illegally acquired entertainment files, 89
  online banking and e-commerce using, 222–23
  personal information security, 425–27
encryption keys, 425
enforcement. *See* laws and regulations, enforcing
Entertainment Software Rating Board (ESRB), 242
environmental criminology, 164–65
epistemology, 35
equal protection under the law, 291
erotica, 243–44
espionage, 85–86, 132
ethical intuitionism, 479
ethics. *See also* computer ethics
  morality and, 6
  of surveillance technologies, 261–62
ethnicity, of computer abusers/ cybercriminals, 130
Europe, Council of, 282–85
evidence, 342–80. *See also* crime scene processing
  chain of custody, 373–75
  collecting and preserving crime scene, 367–80
  computer forensics and, 375–80
  data as, 370
  evidentiary challenges, 342–50
  exclusionary rules of, 350–61
  images as, 378
  IP addresses as, 378–79
evidence, in trial procedures, 390–96
  bench trial vs. trial by jury, 391–93
  courtroom procedures, 393–94
  overview of, 390–91
  peremptory challenges, 392
  presenting, 394–96
  voir dire questioning, 392
evidence, types of, 367–73
  circumstantial, 372
  demonstrative, 373
  electronic, 369
  exculpatory, 368, 380
  images, 378
  physical, 368
  testimonial, 372–73
exclusionary rules of evidence exceptions, 353–61
exclusive jurisdiction, defined, 280
exculpatory evidence, 368, 380
existentialism, 476–77
expert witnesses, 394
extradition, 387

fair use doctrine, 298
FBI (Federal Bureau of Investigation)
  CIOS (Computer Investigations and Operations Section), 319
  Cyber Division, 339
  Hanssen case, 439
  Infragard, 336
  investigative and arrest powers of, 335
  Operation Web Snare, 350
federal laws and regulations
  Access Device Fraud Act, 312
  Audio Home Recording Act of 1992, 297
  CAN-SPAM (Controlling Assault of Non-Solicited Pornography and Marketing) Act, 314–15
  Child Internet Protection Act (CIPA), 322
  Child Online Privacy Protection Act of 1998, 247
  Child Online Protection Act (COPA), 321
  Child Pornography Prevention Act (CPPA), 321
  Communications Assistance for Law Enforcement Act, 316
  Communications Decency Act of 1996 (CDA), 291, 307, 321
  Computer Fraud and Abuse Act (CFFA), 308, 312–13
  Computer Matching and Privacy Act of 1988, 325
  Computer Security Act of 1987, 322
  Computer Software Act of 1980, 297
  conspiracy to defraud and making false statements, 315
  Consumer Credit and Fair Reporting Act of 1970, 254
  COPA (Child Online Protection Act), 321
  Corporate Espionage Act of 1996, 303
  counterterrorism monitoring and surveillance legislation, 316, 319–20
  Cyber Security Enhancement Act, 319
  Cyber Security Research and Development Act, 466
  Digital Millenium Copyright Act (DMCA) of 1998, 297–98, 314, 469
  Domestic Security Enhancement Act of 2003, 320
  Economic Espionage Act, 313
  Electronic Communications Privacy Act, 316
  Family Entertainment and Copyright Act, 471
  Federal Wiretap Act, 315–18
  Financial Services Modernization Act of 1999, 323
  FIS (Foreign Intelligence Surveillance) Act, 315
  Foreign Intelligence Surveillance (FIS) Act, 315
  Freedom of Information Act (FOIA) of 1966, 324
  future regulations, 468–69
  Gramm-Leach-Bliley (GLB) Act, 323, 451
  HIPAA (Health Insurance Portability and Accountability Act), 254, 322–23, 451
  Homeland Security Act of 2002, 56–57, 262
  Identity Theft and Assumption Deterrence Act, 314
  information security requirements, 322–23

federal laws and regulations (*Continued*)
    Information Technology Management
      Reform Act (ITMRA), 322
    ITMRA (Information Technology
      Management Reform Act) of
      1996, 322
    legal issue resolution, 469–70
    Lanham Act of 1946, 299
    Mail Fraud Act, 312
    National Information Infrastructure
      Protection Act, 312
    National Security Intelligence Reform
      Act, 56, 320
    No Electronic Theft Act, 313–14
    Paperwork Reduction Act of 1995, 325
    Privacy Act of 1974, 325
    RICO (Racketeer Influenced and Corrupt
      Organizations) Act, 315
    Right to Financial Privacy Act of 1976,
      325
    Sarbanes-Oxley Act of 2002, 323
    Semi-Conductor Chip Act of 1984, 297
    USA Patriot Act, 316, 319
    Violent Crime Control and Law
      Enforcement Assistance Act, 313
    wire fraud, 312
federally funded research and development
    centers (FFRDCs), 466
*Federal Register*, 306
federal regulatory agencies, 307–11
Federal Trademark Dilution Act, 299
Federal Wiretap Act, 315–18
felony crimes
    bail, 388
    defined, 293
    preliminary hearings and grand jury,
      387–89
feminist criminology, 172–74
file sharing illegally
    economic impacts of, 206–09
    mass-distributed, 90
    unauthorized and illegal, 86–89
filters, spam, 207
financial accounting audits, 451
financial crimes, 190
    defining, 11–12
    emergence of computer-related, 12–14
    harm experienced by victims of, 190–91
    online banking and e-commerce, 222–25
    white-collar crime researched as, 205
financial organizations, 491
firewalls
    attacks through, 101
    installing and using, 419–20
forensic sciences, 375
fraud
    electronic voting, 230
    Internet Fraud Crime Report, 202–03
    online auction sites, 224
fraud, IT-enabled, 67–72
    academic dishonesty, 89–93
    credit card, 68–69
    cybertales, 70, 75
    high-tech disaster, 73
    hoaxes, 73–74
    identity theft, 69–71
    IM spimming, 72
    laws governing, 312–13
    reverse engineering vigilantism against,
      74–75
    Web and email spoofing, 71–72
fraudsters, 132

freedom of speech, 289–90
freelance espionage, 132
Free Software Foundation (FSF), 236
Free Speech Coalition (FSC), 243–44
freeware concept, 236
fruit of the poisonous tree doctrine, 351–52
gambling
    illegal online, 189
    trait theory and, 149–50
gaming. *See* computer gaming
gaming hackers, 234
gender
    of computer abusers/cybercriminals, 130
    online pornography driven by, 244–45

GIGO (garbage in, garbage out), 33
globalization, 53
googling, 249–50, 252
government espionage, 85–86, 132
government intelligence gathering, 255–59,
    262–64
government interventions, 459–74. *See also*
    federal laws and regulations
    education and training, 473–74
    enforcement, cracking down on, 471–72
    funding, 466
    international agreements, 464–66
    legal issues, resolving, 469–70
    legislation, authority, and directives,
      463–64
    overview of, 459–61
    preparing now, overview, 461
    public awareness, 472–73
    regulating information security, 468–69
    research, 462–63
    technical assistance for public and
      private sectors, 468
    technology R&D, testing, and evaluation,
      466–68
grand jury hearings, 388–90
gray hat hackers, 132
*Grokster and Streamcast Networks v. MGM*,
    87–89, 298

hacker ethic, 233–35
hackers
    categorizing, 127, 132
    corporate and government espionage,
      85–86
    differential association theory and, 158
    distributing programming vulnerabilities,
      85
    electronic voting frauds and, 230
    government overreaction to, 256–58
    online banking and e-commerce, 223
    overview of, 83–85
    subculture, 232–36
*Hackers* (movie), 234
hactivists, 127
harassers, 127, 132
hardware firewalls, 419–20
hardware hackers, 234
harm
    crime causing wide range of, 187
    to data, property and finances, 190
    emotional and psychological, 190–92
    physical, 190
    from primary victimization, 187–88
    social, professional and organizational, 192
    summary, 214
harassment
    cyber threats and, 93–95

illegal pornography, 97–98
    online stalking, 95–96
hash values, 427
Health Insurance Portability and
    Accountability Act (HIPAA), 254,
    322–23, 451
hearsay testimony, 394
hentai, 244–45
high-tech crimes, 13–14, 16
High Technology Crime Investigators
    Association (HTCIA), 336, 339–40
historical school of legal thinking, 278
hoaxes, 73–74
Homeland Security Institute, 464
home, protecting system and data at, 414
hotspots, 434
HTCIA (High Technology Crime
    Investigators Association), 336,
    339–40
human factors, 43
hung jury, defined, 396

IA (information assurance), 29–62
    characteristics of information, 31–33
    data availability, 41–42
    data confidentiality, 40–41
    data integrity, 41
    data vs. knowledge management, 33–35
    overview of, 38–39
    pragmatism about, 42–45
IA (information assurance), attacks, 46–51
    cyber vs. physical, 46–47
    insider vs. outsider threats, 47–50
    overview of, 45–46
    responding to, 50–51
IA (information assurance), for
    infrastructure, 51–58
    critical information, 55–56
    defining, 53–55
    differences in, 55
    overview of, 51–53
    vulnerability of Net, 56–58
IAIP (Information Analysis and
    Infrastructure Protection), DHS, 56
IANA (Internet Assigned Numbers
    Authority), 55
ICANN (Internet Corporation for Assigned
    Names and Numbers), 300
ICRA (Internet Content Rating
    Association), 244
idealism, 476
identity theft fraud
    Federal Trade Commission survey on,
      201
    overview of, 69–71
    Vargas case of, 384–85
IIPA (International Intellectual Property
    Alliance), 207
illegal file sharing. *See* file sharing illegally
images, as evidence, 378
IM (Instant Messaging), 72, 73–74
impulse control disorders, 149–50
incentives, for cybercrime prevention, 460
incident response notifications, 366–67
incident to arrest exceptions, 355–56
indeterminate sentencing policies, 397–98
indictments, 389
informal sanctions, 145–46
information
    defining, 34
    primary characteristics of, 31–33
    privacy. *See* privacy infringement

information age conflict, 106–07
information assurance. *See* IA (information assurance)
information dominance, 105–06
information ownership, 35–36
information possession, 35–36
information security
    avoiding root or administrator privileges, 427
    discussion questions, 455
    in future, 468–69
    government actions supporting, 461
    introduction, 406–08
    key terms and concepts, 454–55
    laws and regulations. *See* federal laws and regulations
    organizational. *See* organizational information security
    overview of, 408–10
    public awareness of, 472–73
    references and endnotes, 455–56
    requirements for, 322–23
    summary, 453–54
information security, personal, 408–35
    anti-keylogger software, 425–27
    anti-spyware and anti-adware software, 422–23
    anti-viral software, 418–19
    avoiding root or administrator privileges, 415, 427
    backing up data, 423–25
    digital signatures, 425–27
    encryption, 425–27
    firewalls, 419–20
    googling online, 263
    lifestyle and, 427–30
    overview of, 408–10
    passwords, 416–18
    physical security of system and data, 414
    protection technologies, 410–14
    security patches, 420–22
    strong passwords, 414–16
    technology investment, 412
    Trojan software, 418–19
    while traveling, 430–35
information warfare (IW), 105–06
InfoSec Assessment Methodology (IAM), National Security Agency, 452
infosec, practicing. *See* information security
Infragard, 336
infrastructures, 51–58
    critical information protection, 55–56
    defining, 53–55
    different conceptions of, 55
    overview of, 51–53
    vulnerability of Net, 56–58
insider cybercrime, 48–50
insider trading fraud, 73
in-sourcing vs. outsourcing, 441–42
Instant Messaging (IM), 72, 73–74
integrity, data, 41
intellectual property associations, 492
intellectual property law. *See* IP (intellectual property) law
intelligence
    defining, 34
    gathering and analysis, 255–59
Internal Revenue Service (IRS), 256
international agreements
    defined, 282
    on future cybercrime management, 281–87, 464–66
    U.S. Constitution and, 290–91

International Criminal Police Organization (Interpol), 340
International Intellectual Property Alliance (IIPA), 207
International Security Standard (ISO), 453
Internet
    development of, 54–55
    safety organizations, 491–92
    vulnerability to cybercrime, 56–58
Internet addiction disorder, 151–52, 155
Internet Assigned Numbers Authority (IANA), 55
Internet Content Rating Association (ICRA), 244
Internet Corporation for Assigned Names and Numbers (ICANN), 300
Internet crime, 19
Internet Fraud Crime Report, 202–03
Internet Relay Chat (IRC), 69
Internet Service Providers (ISPs), 99, 188–89, 429
interviewing victims, witnesses, and suspects, 380–84
    legal issues, 380–82
    strategies and practices, 383–84
    technological terms and concepts, important of, 382
inventory of property seized, 357
investigation and prosecution, 331–403.
investigative and arrest powers, defined, 335
investigative hunches, 346
investigative procedures, 342–61
Iowa Ongoing Criminal Conduct Act, 302
IP (intellectual property) law, 295–301
    copyright law, 296–99
    overview of, 295, 301
    patent and trade secrets law, 300–301
    tort law, 301–03
    trademark law, 299–300
IP (Internet Protocol) addresses, 378–79
IRC (Internet Relay Chat), 69
ISO (International Security Standard), 453
ISPs (Internet Service Providers), 99, 188–89, 429
IW (information warfare), 105–06

Joint Functional Component Command for Network Warfare (JFCCNW), 106
judicial system of the United States, 278–79, 306–07
junk science, defined, 376
jurisprudence in cyber law, 279–81
justice
    blogging for, 226–29
    crime definitions and, 19–20
    enforcing laws and regulations, 18–19
    reliance on technology, 31
    restorative, 173
    transferring money between nations, 38
juvenile offenders, 293–94

Kantian theory, 478–81
*Katz v. United States*, 324, 354, 359
key escrow, 426
keylogger software, 82–83, 425–27
knowingly committing cybercrime, 343
laws and regulations, 273–327. *See also* federal regulations and laws
    IP (intellectual property) law, 295–301
    jurisdiction in, 279–81
    legal issues, resolving, 469–70
    legal philosophies and, 276–78

legislative bills and executive approval, 305–06
    overview of, 311–12
    patent and trade secrets law, 300–301
    pornography, protecting children from online, 320–22
    privacy protections, 323–26
    rationale and reach of, 275–76
    regulations, defined, 275
    regulatory law, 295
    summary, 326
    tort law, 301–03

left realism, 172
legal jurisdiction, 279
legal philosophies, 276–78
legal pornography, 243
legislation
    executive approval of, 305–06
    federal, 311–26
    future cybercrime prevention, 463–64
    regulating investigation of cybercrime, 315–20
libel, defined, 301
lifestyle
    of computer abusers/cybercriminals, 131
    and information security, 427–30
Linux operating system, 236–37
logon screen reading, 115–16
long arm jurisdiction, 280
Love Bug, 206

Magna Carta of 1215, 276
males, 149, 172–73
malicious hackers, 127
malware
    anti-malware software, 418–19
    attached to spam, 78
    creating tertiary victimization, 188
    defined, 33
    economic impacts of, 206
    emerging trends in, 99–102
    protecting against, 412–13
    victimless crimes and, 190
    writing and distributing, 64–67, 132
mandatory sentencing, 398
*Manual on the Prevention and Control of Computer-Related Crime* (UN), 283–84
*Mapp v. Ohio*, 352, 353
*The Matrix* (movies), 236
McAfee
    antimalware software, 412, 418
    Oil Change, 422
    PGP (Pretty Good Privacy), 426
MD5 hash value, 378
means, for committing cybercrime, 342–43
media, covering cybercrime, 337–38, 472
medium, for storing information, 32
Melissa, 206
*mens rea*, in evidentiary challenges, 342
MessageLabs, 71–72, 207
metamorphic worms, 101
meta tagging, 300
*MGM v. Grokster and Streamcast Networks*, 87–89, 298
Microsoft
    antitrust suit, 468
    *Halo 2*, 467
    recommended security practices, 438

military
    cyber cases, 279
    recruiting with computer games, 238
    surveillance technologies, 260
Mil Net, 54
Miranda Warnings, 288, 387
misdemeanor crimes, 293, 388
Mitnick, Kevin, 115, 118
modus operandi (M.O.), of cybercriminals,
        118
money
    from online pornography, 243
    as special form of data, 36–38
    from virtual gaming worlds, 239–40
money laundering, 36–37, 48–49
monitoring. *See* surveillance and monitoring
Moonlight Maze, 104
morality, 6
moral nihilism, 480
morphing (child porn), 371–72
Morris, Robert T., 57
motion hearings, 388–90
Motion Picture Association of America
        (MPAA), 207, 462, 467
motives, cybercrime, 118, 120–21, 332,
        342–43
movie files, 87–89
movie pirates, 132
MPAA (Motion Picture Association of
        America), 207, 462, 467
music files, 87–89
music pirates, 132
Mydoom.B., 467

Napster, 87, 207
NAS (National Academy of Science), 262,
        462
National Center for Missing and Exploited
        Children (NCMEC), 244
National Crime Victimization Survey
        (NCVS), 194–95
National Criminal Information Center
        (NCIC), 381, 386
national critical infrastructures (NCI), 55
National Fingerprint File (NFF), 381
National Information Infrastructure (NII), 53
National Infrastructure Advisory Council
        (NIAC), 56
National Security Agency (NSA), 256, 438,
        452, 466, 473
National Security Cyber Partnership
        (NCSP), 464
National Security Presidential Directive 16,
        106
*The National Strategy to Secure Cyberspace*
        (PCIPB), 464
National White Collar Crime Center
        (NW3C), 14, 202–03, 340, 350
natural law, 277, 290
NCIC (National Criminal Information
        Center), 381, 386
negligence, defined under tort law, 301
negligently committing cybercrime, 343
negligent users, 132
netiquette, 10
network-centric warfare, 106–08
N-generation, 221
NIJ (National Institute of Justice)
    cybercrime prevention research of,
        466–67
    electronic crime research of, 212
    on investigation and prosecution, 462–63
    using criminal researchers, 142

nonviolent crimes, defined, 292
normative definitions, 157
Norton, 412, 423, 472
NSA (National Security Agency), 256, 438,
        452, 466, 473

obscene speech, 97
OCTAVE, 453
*Ohio v. Terry*, 347, 355
OJP (Office of Justice Programs), 212
online auction sites
    benefits and risks of, 224
    DoS attacks, 99–100
    fraud, 69, 429
online banking, 222–25
online dating services, 224–25
online gambling, 189
online hoaxes, 73–74
online pornography, 242–47. *See also*
        pornography
    Child Online Privacy Protection Act of
        1998, 247
    controversies over, 245–46
    cyber pornography, 127
    extent of, 246–47
    fraud and, 76
    gender-driven market, 244–45
    illegal, 97–98
    obtained by wardriving, 80–81
    organizations promoting responsible
        practices, 243–44
    toon porn, 244
Open Source Community
    managing cybercrime and, 412, 434, 458
    overview of, 236–38
Open Source Initiative (OSI), 237
open source software, 236–38
operating continuity plans, 447–49
operating system security, 420–22
Operation Buccaneer, 285–86
*Operation Sundevil*, 204
Operation Sundevil, 256–57
Operation Web Snare, 350
ordinary crimes, 177
organizational information security, 435–51
    assessing, 436–37
    change procedures, 440–43
    designing controls for, 437–38
    overview of, 435–36
    risk management, 443–51
    security posture, 440–43
    technology investment and procurement
        decisions, 438–39
organized crimes, 12
organized criminals, 132
original jurisdiction, defined, 280
outsourcing (technical assistance), 441–42
ownership
    establishing virtual property, 240
    vs. possession, 35–36

p2p (peer-to-peer) networks
    circumventing copyrighted works with,
        298
    economic impact of illegal fire sharing,
        208–09
    pirating through, 88–89
packet sniffing, 79–80, 429
passwords
    efficiently, 416–18
    password crackers, 81, 132
    strong, 414–16

patches, 85, 420–22
PCIPB (President's Critical Infrastructure
        Protection Board), 464
PCs (personal computers), 13, 14
PDAs, 416–17
PDAs, information security, 416–17
PDD (Presidential Decision Directive), 464
peacemaking criminology, 173
peace officers, 347
pedophiles, as category of IT abuser, 132
pedophilia
    emotional and psychological harm of,
        190
    evidentiary challenges of child
        pornography, 371–72
    grooming children into posing for
        erotica, 243–44
    overview of, 96–97
penalties
    general deterrence theory based on, 145
    imposing on offenders, 461
people, principle of IA, 43, 47
perception of value, information, 32
peremptory challenges, 392
permissions, authority over, 120
personal computers (PCs), 13, 14
personal information security. *See*
        information security, personal
personality disorders, 152
personal problem solvers, 127
personan jurisdiction, 280
PGP (Pretty Good Privacy), 426
Phillipines telecommunications system, 391
philosophy of computer ethics, 475–77
phishing Web sites
    emerging trends in, 99
    overview of, 71–72
    using spam with, 78
phobia, 123
phone phreaking, 81–82
phone texting crimes, 230
phreakers, 127
physical attacks
    comparing with cyber, 46–47
    cyber case of, 49
    diagnosing and responding to, 50–51
    insider vs. outsider threats to assets,
        47–50
physical evidence, 368
physical monitoring, 350–51
physical security of system and data, 414
Pierson, Christopher, 93
piracy
    of applications software, 87
    creating secondary and tertiary
        victimization, 188
    cybertale about, 90
    differential association theory and, 158
    economic impacts of, 206
    government Websites on ongoing cases
        of, 145
    of music and movies, 87–89
    as victimless crime, 189–90
pirates, 127–28, 132
plain view exceptions, exclusionary rules of
        evidence, 354
plea agreements, 389–90
pluralist view, of social organization, 168
PMS (premenstrual syndrome), 149
Pointsec, 416
poisonous tree exceptions, 354–55

police crime reporting
estimates of crime made from, 193–94
primary victims and, 187
policies, security, 445–48
policy formulating agencies, 494
political activism, IT-enabled, 229–30
political conflict, 168–69
pornography
child. *See* child pornography
history of IT-facilitated, 243
natural interest in sex and, 242–43
online. *See* online pornography
online pornography. *See also* child
pornography
port scanning, 80–81
positive definitions, of behaviors, 158–59
positive law, defined, 278
positivism, defined, 147
possession, vs. ownership, 35–36
Postini, Inc., 207
postmodern criminology, 173
Poulsen, Kevin, 2, 81–82
poverty, 164
pragmatism, 476
pranksters, 127
preliminary hearings, 388–90
premenstrual syndrome (PMS), 149
preponderance of evidence, 302, 349–50
Presidential Decision Directive (PDD), 464
presidential pardons, 170
President's Commission of Critical
Information Infrastructure
Protection (PCCIP), 38, 464
President's Critical Infrastructure Protection
Board (PCIPB), 464
presumptive sentencing, 398
pretrial procedures and hearings, 384–90
arraignment, 387–88
arrest and booking, 386–87
preliminary, grand jury, and motion
hearings, 388–90
Pretty Good Privacy (PGP), 426
primary victimization, 187–88, 214
privacy infringement, 247–64
defined, 248
ethical use of surveillance technologies,
259–64
by firms, employers and schools, 252–55
by governments, 255–59
issues after September 11, 2001, 231–32
key terms and concepts, 265–66
overview, 247–52
references and endnotes, 267–69
snooping and, 249–52
summary, 264–65
privacy organizations, 491–92
privacy protections, federal law, 323–26
Computer Matching and Privacy Act of
1988, 325
Fair and Accurate Credit Transactions
Act of 2003, 325–26
FOIA (Freedom of Information Act) of
1966, 324
Fourth Amendment, 290
Paperwork Reduction Act of 1995, 325
Privacy Act of 1974, 325
Right to Financial Privacy Act of 1976,
325
private keys, 425–27
private search exceptions, 355–56
probable cause, 348–49
procedural law, 287–88

procedures, security, 445–48
professional associations, 474, 492
professional harm, 192, 221–22
professionals, education and training of,
21–22
professional status, 130–31
profiles
categorizing cybercrimes, 125–26
stereotypical adversary, 126–29
programming, 85
programming paragraphs, defined, 33
programming sentences, defined, 33
programming word, defined, 33
program operations audits, 451
proof beyond a reasonable doubt, 349
property
discarded and abandoned exceptions,
356
seized during legal search, 357
virtual, 240
property crime
cybercrime as, 190–91
defined, 292
*The Proposed Council Framework Decision
on Attacks Against Information
Systems*, 285
prosecuting cybercriminals, 384–99. *See
also* investigation and prosecution
arrest and booking, 386–87
law and regulation enforcement. *See*
laws and regulations, enforcing
offender sanctions, purposes of, 396–97
overview of, 384–86
pretrial procedures and hearings, 384–90
proof, challenges in establishing, 377–78
trial procedures and presentation of
evidence, 390–96
trial verdicts, sentencing, and appeals,
396–99
prostitution, 189
protection, of potential victims, 397
protection, technologies for information
security, 410–14
protective sweep exceptions, 355
public keys, in information security, 425–27
public law enforcement *v.* private security,
335–36
public shaming, 147
punishment
Beccaria's writings on, 143
classical/choice crime theory, 143
cruel and unusual, 290
general deterrence theory based on,
144–47
of offenders, 397
pyramid scheme fraud, 75
questioning suspects, 347–48
realism, 476
reasonable suspicion, 347
recklessly committing cybercrime, 343

Recording Industry Association (RIAA),
5–6, 87, 462
recovery planning, 447–49
regulations. *See* laws and regulations
regulatory agencies, 494
regulatory law, 295
reinforcers, punishment theory, 159
remailer systems, 93
rem jurisdiction, defined, 280
research, cybercrime
agencies, 493–94

overview of, 210–13
weak state of, 214
research, defining crime for, 19–20
resources
for committing cybercrimes, 120
of crime perpetrators, in SKRAM, 332
for technical assistance, 460
restorative justice, 173
retribution, on behalf of victims and society,
397
reverse engineering vigilantism, 74–75
RIAA (Recording Industry Association),
5–6, 87, 462
risk and threat analysis, defined, 443
risk management, 443–51
RIT Computer Use and Ethics Survey,
407–09, 415, 472
*Robert T. Morris Jr.v. United States*, 344
*Robert Versaggi vs. State of New York*, 19
Robin Hood Syndrome, 174, 234
root control, defined, 120
root kits, defined, 101
root privileges, 415, 427
rule deontologists, 479
rule of law, 18, 275

SANS (SysAdmin, Audti, Network,
Security) Institute, 340–41
SAN (storage area network) security,
424–25
script kiddies, 102
search warrants, subpoenas and consent to,
356–61
secondary victimization, 188, 214
security. *See* information security
self-esteem, 156–57, 161–62
self-evolving polymorphic tools, 101
self-report offender studies, 195
sentencing policies, 396–99
sex crimes, computer-enabled. *See also*
online pornography
cyber harrassment and threats, 93–94
emotional and psychological harm of,
190
illegal pornography, 97–98
National Youth Internet Safety Study on,
199
online stalking and pedophilia, 95–97
sex games, virtual, 241
sex slavery, child pornography, 98
simulation technology, 238
skills, in cybercrime, 118–19
SKRAM (skills, knowledge, resources,
authority, and motives), 120
slander, defined, 301
smartcards, 417
smart mobs, 229–30
smart weapons, 105
smuggling, in child pornography, 98
snooping, government, 255–59
social construction, of reality, 10–11
social ecology concept, 164
social engineering
cycle, 117
defrauding people with, 43
designing to instill fear, 123–24
as hacking, 84
tactics, 114–17
socialization, 5–6
social norms
normal vs. deviant use of IT, 8–10
standards of, 5–8

social sanctions, 6–7
societal order, prohibiting cybercrime, 272–75
socioeconomic class, causing crime, 164
sociology. *See* cybercrime, as new paradigm
software
    antispyware and anti-adware, 422–23
    defining, 33
    distributing security vulnerabilities, 85
    firewalls, 419–20
    keylogger, 425–27
    open source, 236–38
    password cracking/recovery, 81
    piracy, 87–89, 145
    pirates, 132
    programming, 33
    security patches, 420–22
spam
    defining, 123
    economic impacts of, 207
    emerging trends, 99
spimming, illicit, 72
spoofing, email, 71–72
spying, IT-enabled, 79–86
spyware
    adware bundled with, 411
    defined, 64–65
    and key loggers, 82–83
    protecting against, 422–23
    using spam with, 78
stakeholders, 231–32, 235
stalkers, 95–96, 132
standard setting organizations, 494–95
standards of proof, 345–50
    detaining and questioning suspects, 347–48
    investigative hunches, 346
    preponderance of evidence, 349–50
    probable cause, 348–49
    proof beyond a reasonable doubt, 349
    reasonable suspicion, 347
*State of New York vs. Robert Versaggi*, 19
statistics, cybercrime, 193–203
status offense, defined, 293
stereotypical adversary profiles, 126–29
Steve Jackson Games, Inc., 257
storage, of information, 45–46
strong passwords, 414–16
structured sentencing policies, 397–98
subculture
    computer hacker, 232–36
    cultural deviance theory, 166
    defining, 233
subject matter jurisdiction, defined, 280
subpoenas, 360–61
substantive law, defined, 287
Sullivan, Jerome R., 43–44
summons to appear, 386
Supreme Court. *See* U.S. Supreme Court
surveillance and monitoring, 350–61
    warrants, subpoenas and consent to search, 356–61
surveillance technologies, 259–64
suspects, interviewing, 380–84
swarm crimes, 89, 229–30
system administrators
    information security and, 415, 427
    posting standards and policies, 10
system trespassing, 84
tacit knowledge, 153

target hardening, 407
TCPS (technology-enabled crime, policing and security) theory, 176–79
technical assistance agencies, 339
technical assistance for public and private sectors, 468
technology
    audits, 451
    defining, 30–31
    diffusion, 30–31
    industry organizations, 494–95
    for information security, 410–14
    investment and procurement decisions, 412, 438–39
    R&D, testing, and evaluation, 466–68
telegrams, 256
telegraphers, IT-facilitated sex, 243
telemarketing fraud, disasters, 73
telephone, IT-facilitated sex, 243
telephonic search warrants, 358
teller fraud, 198
terrorism, defined, 103–04
Terrorism Information Awareness Program, 258
terrorist attacks
    criminal laws evolving since, 18
    cyberterrorism as form of, 102–04
    Department of Homeland Security created after, 56
    disaster fraud after, 73
    general deterrence theory and, 148
    government intelligence gathering on, 258–59
    on infrastructure, 53
    privacy issues after 9/11, 231–32
    technological advancements and, 101–02
*Terry v. Ohio*, 347, 355
tertiary victimization, 188–89, 214
testimonial evidence, 372–73
theories. *See* computer abuse and crime theories
threat analysis cube, 50–51
threat fatigue, 443
threats, cyber harassment and, 93–95
toon porn, 244
top sites, defined, 88
Total Information Awareness Program (TIAP), 232, 258
tracking cookies, 78
trade names, defined, 300
trade secrets law, 300–301
traditional criminals, 132
traditional piracy, 207–09
training
    cybercrime requiring, 22–23
    IT-enabling abuse and, 221–22
    need for professional, 21–22
transport value, of information, 32
traveling, and information security, 430–35
Trojans, 64–67, 418–19

UBE (unsolicited bulk email), 77–78
UCBE (unsolicited commercial bulk email), 77–78
UCE (unsolicited commercial email), 77–78
UCR (Uniform Crime Report) system, 193–94
UEMS (unsolicited electronic email solicitations), 77–78

Uniform Crime Report (UCR) system, 193–94
*United States v. Robert T. Morris Jr.*, 344
universal resource locator (URLs), 54–55, 71
UN (United Nations), 282–84
URLs (universal resource locator), 54–55, 71
U.S. Constitution
    constitutional law, 288–91
    freedom of speech, 289–90, 321, 481
    historical influences on, 276–77
    IP (intellectual property) law, 296
    unreasonable search, protections against, 356–57, 359
utilitarianism, 477–78
utopians, 127

victim blaming, 192
victimization, computer-related, 187–93
    among college students, 193
    defined, 186
    harm experienced, 190–92
    interviewing, 380–84
    leading to cybercrime, 189
    primary, 187–88
    secondary, 188
    surveys, 194–95
    tertiary, 188–89
    victimless crimes, 189–90
    of violent vs. property crime, 187
victimless crimes, 189–90, 214
violence, in virtual games, 241–42
violent crimes, defined, 292
virtual gaming worlds, 240
virtual private networks (VPNs), 419
virtual property, 240
viruses
    economic impacts of, 206
    emerging trends in, 100–102
VoIP (voice-over Internet protocol) network telephones, 80
VPNs (virtual private networks), 419

wardriving, 80–81, 434
warez groups, 90
*WarGames* (movie), 234
warrants, 356–61, 386
warwalking, 434
Web spoofing, 71–72
WEP (Wireless Encryption Protocol), 434
white-collar crime
    computerization changing, 12–14, 25–26
    economic impacts of, 204–06
    overview of, 11
white hat hackers, 132
whoral worms, 100
WiFi connections, 420, 433–35
wire fraud, laws governing, 312
Wireless Encryption Protocol (WEP), 434
wireless internet access, 433–35
witnesses
    interviewing, 380–84
    presenting in courtroom procedures, 393
*writ of certiorari*, 288–91

*Zippo Manufacturing Company vs. Zippo Dot Com, Inc., 281*